PERSONALITY THEORIES

ASSUMPTIONS, RESEARCH AND APPLICATIONS

PERSONALITY THEORIES

BASIC ASSUMPTIONS, RESEARCH, AND APPLICATIONS

THIRD EDITION

Larry A. Hjelle
Associate Professor, Psychology
State University of New York
College at Brockport

Daniel J. Ziegler
Dean, Graduate School
and Professor, Psychology
Villanova University

McGRAW-HILL, INC.
New York   St. Louis   San Francisco   Auckland   Bogotá
Caracas   Lisbon   London   Madrid   Mexico   Milan   Montreal
New Delhi   Paris   San Juan   Singapore   Sydney   Tokyo   Toronto

PERSONALITY THEORIES

Basic Assumptions, Research, and Applications

International Edition 1992

5 6 7 8 9 0 KKP   FC 9 6 5 4

This book was set in Times Roman by Better Graphics, Inc.
The editors were Christopher Rogers, Maria E. Chiappetta, and Scott Amerman;

the production supervisor was Kathryn Porzio.

The cover was designed by Fern Logan.

The Photo editor was Barbara Salz.

New drawings were done by J & R Services, Inc.

R. R. Donnelley & Sons company was printer and binder.

Cover painting: ETEREA, original painting by Orlando Augelo-Botero, from the collection of Engman International.

Library of Congress Cataloging-in-Publication Data

Hjelle, Larry A,

    Personality theories; basic assumptions, research, and

applications / Larry A. Hjelle, Daniel J. Ziegler.—3rd ed.
    p.   cm.
    Includes bibliographical references and indexes.
    ISBN 0-07-029079-2
    1. Personality.   I. Ziegler, Daniel J.   II. Title.
BF698. H49   1992
155.2′092′2—dc20

When ordering this title, use ISBN 0-07-112640-6

Printed by Singapore

ABOUT
THE AUTHORS

LARRY A. HJELLE is Associate Professor of Psychology at the State University of New York, College at Brockport. He received his M.S. in experimental psychology from Ohio University (1964), and his Ph.D. in social-personality psychology from the University of Oklahoma at Norman (1967). He has previously taught at Villanova University and the University of Prince Edward Island. Dr. Hjelle has published articles on a wide variety of topics in personality psychology, including locus of control, self-actualization, private self-awareness, and person perception accuracy. Currently he is researching the role of personality variables in mediating the temporal stability of self-report scales. His other research interests include self-monitoring, explanatory style, and personal efficacy. He is a member of the American Psychological Association (APA) and Division 8 (Social-Personality) of the APA.

DANIEL J. ZIEGLER is a Professor of Psychology and Dean of the Graduate School at Villanova University. He received his Ph.D. in psychology from Temple University (1968). A faculty member at Villanova University since 1961, Dr. Ziegler was Chair of the Psychology Department from 1968 to 1987, and Dean of the Graduate School from 1987 to the present. He is the author of many publications in journals and proceedings, most recently in the area of cognitive components in stress. A licensed psychologist for private practice in Pennsylvania, Dr. Ziegler has accumulated much experience in psychological testing and counseling. In addition, he is a nationally known speaker in the corporate world in the area of stress management.

To Our Wives,
Jean and Elizabeth

To Our Children,
Anjanette, Christian,
Daniel, and Mark

CONTENTS

PREFACE

A first course on personality psychology should introduce students to a diversity of theoretical perspectives by which to understand why and how human beings behave as they do in the world. Accordingly, this third edition provides coverage of personality theories representing several different perspectives. In this way, we hope that students will gain an appreciation for the multiplicity of conceptual approaches that can be taken to the study of persons. The study of personality should likewise focus attention on the strategies and results of empirical research. With this in mind, we have updated and broadened our coverage of how researchers validate theoretical propositions through the process of scientific inquiry. Finally, a basic textbook on personality should emphasize the practical applications of theoretical ideas. Toward this end, we have included numerous examples illustrating how major constructs and postulates found in the various approaches can be applied to everyday life. Our overall goal in writing the current edition is to help students achieve a more enlightened awareness of the many rich and fascinating conceptions of personality. The discipline of personology encompasses an array of theories, methods of inquiry, research findings, and personal applications. We trust that this edition of the text provides a well-organized, informative, and accurate account of each of these important elements that comprise the field today. Above all, we hope that the text enables students to appreciate how the insights offered by various theorists may be integrated to better understand the complexity of the human personality and behavior.

As was the case with the second edition of *Personality Theories,* we remain steadfast in our view that personality theories reflect basic assumptions about the nature of humanity. This theme is explicitly stated in the introductory chapter in terms of nine different assumptions underlying personality theories. In developing this innovative approach to the study of personality, a common framework is provided by which to compare and contrast different theoretical viewpoints. Perhaps more important, this approach should stimulate students to see beyond the immediate details of a particular theory toward the basic philosophical views that a theorist assumes in approaching people and their personalities. Feedback from the numerous students and instructors who read our second edition suggests that the basic assumptions framework enhances understanding of differences among theorists in their concept of humanity.

What's New in This Third Edition?

First of all, several chapters have been expanded to include more extensive coverage of personality theories. Specifically, we have added an overview of the perspectives formulated by Carl Jung, Erich Fromm, Karen Horney, Raymond Cattell, Hans Eysenck, and Julian Rotter. Core concepts and principles articulated by each of these theorists has added immeasurably to the understanding of phenomena falling under the personality umbrella. Their respective views of personality are presented in the concluding sections of chapters devoted to a more detailed description of a particular theoretical approach. In Chapter 5, for example, the salient ideas espoused by Erich Fromm and Karen Horney are highlighted after a comprehensive account of the concepts, basic assumptions, empirical findings, and applications associated with Erik Erikson's ego perspective. A brief biographical sketch of each new theorist along with a summary of the contributions and limitations of his or her system of thought is also included.

Second, we have incorporated a new chapter describing the strategies used by researchers to study personality phenomena. We consider how case studies, correlational research, and formal experiments are conducted in order to investigate the validity of theoretical propositions. In addition, we describe various assessment techniques (interviews, self-reports, and projective tests) that are commonly used to gain information about persons. Knowledge of these techniques will enable students to appreciate the important role that assessment plays in the measurement of individual differences. They also will gain an understanding of how assessment strategies are closely related to the way in which researchers approach the study of fundamental questions and issues about personality.

Still other changes have been made in this third edition, while retaining the well-received format and orientation that characterized the previous edition. Most notably, we have included examples of the most recent and up-to-date research findings related to the empirical validation of theoretical concepts. For instance, we discuss current efforts to establish the validity of psychoanalytic hypotheses by means of the method of subliminal psychodynamic activation. A body of recent work on perceived self-efficacy and its role in implementing behavior change is likewise discussed in the context of Bandura's theory. Furthermore, we have sought to make the applications section of each theory chapter as interesting and relevant to the real world as possible. For example, attention is now given to how operant conditioning concepts can be applied to assertiveness training and biofeedback. To further enhance the meaning of the material presented, the text also includes captioned photos and several new figures and tables. Finally, we have added more sample items of self-report scales used by researchers interested in measuring personality traits.

Organization of the Text

The organization of the text is intended to provide a systematic account of the major theories, empirical findings, and applications of personality psychology. The first chapter discusses the issues that characterize personality as a field of study, the functions served by a theory, the components of a theory, and the criteria by which a theory can be evaluated. The chapter also presents the basic assumptions about human nature that serve as a framework for the viewing of differences among theorists in their concept of humanity.

The second chapter provides detailed coverage of the research strategies used to study personality. The strengths and weaknesses of these strategies are stressed in order to give students some proficiency in evaluating the merit of studies cited throughout the remainder of the text. Next, we consider how personality assessment techniques make it possible to obtain useful information about individual differences. The concepts of reliability and validity as they pertain to various self-report and projective measures are also carefully reviewed.

Major theoretical approaches to personality that serve as underpinnings of the field are presented in Chapters 3 through 11. In order of presentation, these include the positions of Sigmund Freud, Alfred Adler, Erik Erikson, Gordon Allport, B. F. Skinner, Albert Bandura, George Kelly, Abraham Maslow, and Carl Rogers. Each theory chapter begins with a brief overview of the major themes and emphases of the perspective under examination. Then comes a biographical sketch of the theorist whose ideas are being featured. These sketches provide vital background information about the life experiences of a theorist and allow students to see why the theorist formulated a particular view of personality. Next comes the most extensive section of each theory chapter, the detailed presentation of the constructs and propostions embedded within the theory itself. Various examples and illustrations are provided in this section so that students can more readily grasp the theoretical concepts described and their practical significance to everyday life. Following this section is a graphic representation and analysis of the theorist's basic assumptions concerning human nature, which links the position of the theorist on our nine assumption dimensions with the theoretical concepts presented in the preceding chapter section. In this fashion, students can see the intimate relationship between concepts of personality and the basic assumptions upon which they were founded. Next we discuss the empirical validation of the theory in question. Our purpose here is to indicate how different personality concepts can and have been empirically tested and to provide a brief glimpse of the amount and kind of research generated by a particular theory. Following this is an application section in each chapter, which directly applies the theory, or an aspect of it, to some relevant facet of human behavior. The goal here is to indicate that, far from being meaningless academic abstractions, personality concepts are vital and relevant and can illuminate a wide range of human behavior and experience.

As noted earlier, this edition has been expanded to include broader coverage of influential personality theories. We believe that students will achieve a more balanced and meaningful understanding of human behavior through learning something about various viewpoints that fall within the framework of a specific perspective. In sequence then, the concluding portion of certain chapters present the basic approaches to personality as proposed by Carl Jung, Erich Fromm, Karen Horney, Raymond Cattell, Hans Eysenck, and Julian Rotter. Altogether, the text provides students with an opportunity to learn about 15 different approaches to explaining personality. We believe that students surveying the field of personality for the first time can readily manage this number of theories in a one semester course.

Each chapter ends with a concise summary of the main points, a bibliography, a list of suggested readings, discussion questions, and a glossary of key terms. These pedagogical aids should make the text quite useful and appealing to students.

The closing chapter of the text reflects on the value of using basic assumptions as a framework from which personality theories can be viewed. We then take a look backward and evaluate the nine major theories featured in the text in terms of the six criteria of a useful theory discussed in Chapter 1. Finally, we make some predictions about the topics and issues that are likely to dominate the field of personality study in the forseeable future.

Acknowledgments

This new edition has profited immensely from the constructive comments and suggestions of a number of individuals. We are especially indebted to a substantial group of reviewers, each of whom carefully read and commented on all or parts of this manuscript. Included among these talented reviewers were: Allen J. Brown, Northeastern University; John S. Duryee, Fairleigh Dickinson University; Robert A. Emmons, University of California at Davis; Randy D. Fisher, University of Central Florida; Jane E. Gordon, State University of New York at Albany; James J. Johnson, Illinois State University at Normal; Chris Langston, Purdue University; Randy J. Larsen, University of Michigan, Ann Arbor; Joseph J. Palladino, University of Southern Indiana; Sharon Presley, California State University at Northridge; Richard N. Williams, Brigham Young University; and Brian T. Yates, American University.

We would also like to thank the Document Preparation Center at SUNY Brockport for providing needed technical assistance during the physical preparation of the manuscript. In particular, we would like to acknowledge Jeanne Kamysz, Lauren Nicholson, and Vicky Willis for their enormous help during the final stages of the project and for making it possible to submit the manuscript in electronic disk form to the publisher.

The professionalism, expertise, and support of the entire McGraw-Hill editorial staff continues to merit our sincere appreciation. Special thanks go to Maria Chiappetta, assistant psychology editor, for her genuinely excellent work in coordinating reviews and helping us bring this project to fruition. Working with her has truly been a pleasure. In addition, our production supervisor, Kathy

Porzio, and senior editing supervisor, Scott Amerman, deserve gratitude for their assistance with respect to crucial aspects of the publication process. Chris Rogers, executive editor, also added immeasurably to the quality of the final work.

Finally, we once again express deep appreciation to our wives, Jean and Elizabeth, for their love and support throughout the process of revising and producing this edition. Jean Hjelle especially deserves heartfelt thanks for her valuable suggestions regarding content and organization of material, reading of galley and page proofs, and for putting up with her husband's grouchiness when work seemed to be going slowly. Her contributions to this edition were truly monumental.

Larry A. Hjelle
Daniel J. Ziegler

CHAPTER 1

PSYCHOLOGY OF PERSONALITY: AN INTRODUCTION TO THE DISCIPLINE

Of all the problems that have faced human beings since the dawn of recorded history, perhaps the most puzzling has been the riddle of our own nature. Many avenues have been explored, utilizing a variety of concepts, yet a satisfactory answer still eludes us. One important reason for the difficulty in getting a clear answer is that there are so many differences among us. Human beings not only come in many shapes and sizes but also behave in exceedingly complex ways. Of the more than five billion people who presently inhabit our planet, no two are exactly alike. The vast differences among us have made it difficult, if not impossible, to identify what we share in common as members of the human race. Consider, for example, the serial killer, the dedicated scientist, the drug addict, the corrupt politician, the nun, and the chief executive officer. Except for the same bodily organs and systems, it is hard to imagine what ''human nature'' these persons have in common. And when we expand our horizons to include people of other cultures, we find even greater diversity in values, aspirations, and lifestyles.

Astrology, theology, philosophy, literature, and the life sciences represent some of the many directions taken to understand the complexity of human behavior and of human nature itself. Some of these avenues have proved to be dead ends, while others are just beginning to flourish. Today the problem is more urgent than ever, since most of the world's ills—zooming population, global warming, ecological pollution, nuclear waste, terrorism, drug addiction, racial prejudice, poverty—are brought about by the behavior of people. Indeed, the quality of human life in the future, probably our very survival, depends upon an increased understanding of the fundamental nature of ourselves and others. Psychology is deeply committed to this undertaking.

The Science of Persons

Psychology's roots can be traced to the ancient Greeks and Romans. Philosophers debated over two thousand years ago about some of the same questions that psychologists grapple with today. But the formal beginning of psychology as a separate discipline is set at 1879 (Fancher, 1990). In that year the first laboratory devoted to the experimental study of psychological phenomena was established by Wilhelm Wundt in Leipzig, Germany. Throughout the ensuing years of its formal existence, psychology has evolved along several lines of inquiry and has produced various conceptual models to guide and interpret the work carried out. One important aspect of the gradual emergence of psychology into a modern-day science is the study of human personality. Today, personality psychology's main objective is to explain why people behave as they do from an empirical, scientific perspective. Scientific psychology prefers to work with relatively simple, straight-forward concepts that are open to empirical test. It also utilizes research methods that are as sound and precise as possible. This orientation necessarily limits the kinds of concepts and methods that can legitimately be used in studying personality. Nevertheless, most psychologists believe that a scientific approach will ultimately be most valuable in unraveling the complex nature of human behavior.

What characterizes modern personality psychology as a science is the process of converting speculations about human nature into concepts that can be empirically studied, as opposed to relying on intuition, folklore, or common sense. For example, rather than guess why teenagers drink and drive, researchers might delve into the nature of adolescence and the personal fable concept. At the same time, the "science of persons" is accompanied by many hazards and is sometimes viewed with ambivalence. While it may seem fascinating to try to gain insight into the causes of our behavior and development, we may actually resist such efforts to see ourselves objectively. There is even a certain amount of resistance to "objectifying" personality within the field of psychology; some psychologists argue that going too far in this direction undermines human uniqueness and complexity. Instead, they urge us to concentrate on the intangible qualities of human beings—their struggles for personal and spiritual enlightenment—as evoked in literary and artistic creations such as a Shakespearean play or a Goya painting. Yet, while literature, art, film, history, and religion may each provide valuable insights into human behavior, it is necessary to distinguish such information from that obtained by scientific scrutiny. Moreover, while science currently does not provide all the answers (and perhaps never will), we must make the most effective use of the empirical information we have while keeping in mind a clear perspective on the limitations inherent in the scientific method as applied to the study of human beings. This study is generally carried out by *personologists*, a term coined by Henry Murray (1938) to designate both personality researchers and theorists.

A second objective of personality psychology is to help people live more satisfying lives. While still pursuing theory and research, many personality psychologists today are concerned with findings ways to promote effective and productive strategies of coping with life events. These efforts include new forms of psychotherapy, various special learning programs, and changes in the psycho-social environment that permit people to become the best they are capable of being. Research on these topics provides one of the sharpest testing grounds for ideas about constructive personality change and is discussed throughout the book.

The Meaning of Personality

The term "personality" has several different meanings. It is a reasonably distinct subfield of academic psychology that encompasses a large number of different and often conflicting theoretical perspectives. Furthermore, it is a discipline that seeks to establish better ways of understanding persons through the use of various research strategies. In later chapters, we will describe many specific examples of how ideas, assumptions, and principles proposed by personologists to explain human behavior have been tested in empirical research. Another distinguishing feature of personality psychology is its emphasis on assessment methods to study, understand, predict, and make valid decisions about individuals. Among these methods are interviewing, administering psychological tests, observing and monitoring behavior, measuring physiological responses, and analyzing biographical and personal documents. Virtually every perspective on personality that will be addressed in this text uses some assessment technique or another. Accordingly, we have devoted a part of the next chapter and portions of the theoretical chapters to personality assessment. Finally, as you will see in the pages to come, personality is a field of inquiry that has provided the groundwork for understanding and treating abnormal behavior. In fact, several personality perspectives (such as psychodynamic, cognitive, and phenomenological) suggest ways to think about and deal with behavioral disorders. Nonetheless, modern personality psychology should not be confused with abnormal or clinical psychology. To oversimplify somewhat, personologists are much more inclined to focus attention on normal rather than abnormal functioning. Beyond this, personality psychology has traditionally distinguished itself from other disciplines within psychology by emphasizing individual differences in persons. Even though personologists recognize that there are similarities in the ways people behave, they are primarily concerned with generating explanations of how and why people differ from one another.

In addition to being a field of study, personality is an abstract concept which integrates the many aspects that characterize what the person is like. Such aspects include emotions, motivations, thoughts, experiences, perceptions, and actions. However, we should not equate personality as a concept with whatever aspect of the individual's functioning it is meant to describe. Instead, the conceptual meaning of personality is multifaceted, encompassing a wide spectrum of internal, mental processes that influence how the person acts across different situations. Given such a complex meaning, no one can expect to find simple definitions of personality as a concept. Even within the field of psychology we will find no generally agreed-upon single definition of the term. There may be as many different definitions of the concept of personality as there are psychologists who have tried to define it.

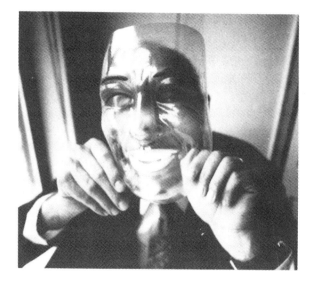

The term "personality" is derived from the Latin word "persona," which referred to a mask worn by an actor in a Greek drama. People tend to equate personality with one's charm, popularity, or public image. (*Arthur Trees/Woodfin Camp & Associates*)

What Is Personality? Alternative Answers

The word "personality" in English is derived from the Latin *persona*. Originally, it denoted the masks worn by theatrical players in ancient Greek dramas; eventually, the term came to encompass the actor's portrayal of a comic or tragic figure as well. Thus, the initial conception of personality was that of a superficial social image that an individual adopts in playing life roles, a "public personality" that people project toward those around them. This view coincides with that of the contemporary layperson who equates personality with charm, social poise, popularity, physical attractiveness, and a host of other socially desirable characteristics. It is this definition that results in such comments as "Mike has personality plus" and "Susan has an obnoxious personality." It is in this sense, too, that charm schools promise to enhance those who enroll with "more personality." Such a conception is generally outside the realm of scientific psychology because it limits the number and kinds of behavior deemed worthy of inclusion in the study of personality.

Personality has also been viewed as the individual's most striking or prominent characteristics. In this sense, a person may be said to have an "outgoing personality" or a "shy personality," meaning that his or her most distinctive attribute appears to be friendliness or shyness. In this instance, personality refers to the overall social impression that an individual conveys in interacting with others (i.e., the few salient characteristics that permeate most or all of the individual's actions in various social settings). Unfortunately, such popular usage of the term neglects the possibility that the individual may be either outgoing or shy depending on the situation. Furthermore, the term "personality" as it is used by all personologists does not imply an evaluation of a person's character or social skills. When we describe Amy as having a "terrific personality," we may be referring to her pleasant disposition, her sincerity, or her willingness to help others. However, this evaluative use of the word (i.e., personalities as good or bad) is not employed by personality psychologists.

An overview of the various meanings of personality in psychology can be gained by considering the views offered by a few recognized theorists in the field. For instance, Carl Rogers described personality in terms of self, an organized, permanent, subjectively perceived entity which is at the very heart of all our experiences. Gordon Allport defined personality as that which an individual really is, an internal ''something'' that determines the nature of the person's interactions with the world. But for Erik Erikson, life proceeds in terms of a series of psychosocial crises, with personality a function of their outcome. George Kelly regarded personality as the individual's unique way of ''making sense'' out of life experiences. Still another conception is that of Raymond Cattell, who described the core structure of personality as comprised of sixteen source traits. Finally, Albert Bandura viewed personality as a complex pattern in which person, behavior, and situation continually influence each other. These divergent conceptions clearly indicate that the meaning of personality in terms of a psychological perspective extends far beyond the original ''superficial social image'' concept. It signifies something much more essential and enduring about a person. Beyond this basic point of agreement, most theoretical definitions of personality have the following features in common.

1 Most definitions emphasize the importance of individuality or distinctiveness. Personality represents those distinct qualities that make one person stand out from all others. Further, it is only through the study of individual differences that the special qualities or combination of qualities that distinguish one person from another can be understood.

2 Most definitions depict personality as some kind of hypothetical structure or organization. Overt behavior, at least in part, is seen as being organized and integrated by personality. In other words, personality is an abstraction based on inferences derived from behavioral observation.

3 Most definitions focus attention on the importance of viewing personality in terms of a life history or developmental perspective. Personality represents an evolving process subject to a variety of internal and external influences, including genetic and biological propensities, social experiences, and changing environmental circumstances.

4 Most definitions construe personality as representing those characteristics of the person that account for consistent patterns of behavior. As such, personality is relatively enduring and stable over time and across situations; it conveys the sense of continuity within the person from time to time or from setting to setting. Aside from these common themes, personality definitions differ substantially from theorist to theorist. To understand what a particular theorist means by the term ''personality,'' the theory must be examined in considerable detail. Close scrutiny of a theory reveals the kinds of behavior on which the theorist focuses and the specific methods that are employed to study this behavior. We should add that definitions of personality are not necessarily true or false, but are more or less useful to psychologists in pursuing research, in explaining regularities in human behavior, and in communicating their conclusions. We shall consider numerous theoretical conceptions of personality in the ensuing chapters of this book. The point to be noted here is that definitions of personality vary with the particular theoretical orientation of a given theorist.

Personality As a Field of Study

As any observant psychology student will note when flipping through a department catalog of course offerings, academic psychologists teach a wide variety of subjects, including social psychology, biopsychology, perception, developmental psychology, and organizational behavior. These areas represent subfields of psychology; personality is one of these. What distinguishes personality from the other psychological domains is its attempt to *synthesize* and *integrate* the principles of these other areas. For example, in the psychology of perception, the basic structures and processes underlying the way people perceive and interpret the world around them are examined. As a field of study, research into perception has uncovered important basic principles; the same is true for other content areas of psychology, such as learning, motivation, and cognitive psychology. But it is personality as a field of study that combines all these principles in an effort to understand the person as an integrated totality.

To understand the complexity of human behavior is a tall order. Often there are different causes for the same behavior shown by two individuals at one time or by the same individual at different times. In the former instance, for example, consider two individuals who bomb an abortion clinic. The first may be motivated by strong religious convictions, whereas the second may be just a thrill seeker. Complexity also exists because behavior arises from two sources: internal causes and the situation in which the behavior occurred. Further, there are times when people cannot explain why they behave in ways contrary to their own expressed intentions. These and many other intricacies of human functioning underscore the fact that personality psychology must strive to be comprehensive in its account of behavioral processes. To be comprehensive, a personologist must incorporate all the principles of general psychology—and the dynamic interrelationships among these principles must be taken into account. We need to know how perception relates to learning, how learning relates to motivation, how motivation relates to development, and so on. Students of personality attempt to formulate theoretical concepts that describe and explain these kinds of complex relationships. All the factors that influence or determine an individual's behavior and experience fall within the domain of the personologist.

With this in mind, it is evident that no other area of psychology attempts to be as comprehensive as the field of personality. Indeed, the study of personality is at the crossroads of most other areas of psychology; it is the converging point of the study of social and intellectual development, of psychopathology and self-actualization, of learning and interpersonal relations, and a host of other important threads that constitute the fabric of modern-day psychology. For many psychologists the breadth of the discipline is not surprising because the focus of study has been nothing less than the "total individual." Given such an ambitious goal, we can rightfully expect the study of personality to be an exciting and challenging undertaking since in many cases we have yet to learn the questions on which to base the answers.

THEORIES OF PERSONALITY

Little agreement presently exists concerning the type of approach that person-ologists should employ to explain basic aspects of human behavior. In fact, at this stage in the development of personology, there are a number of alternative theories to understand the person as an integrated totality as well as to discern the differences between people. For this reason, we should give some attention to what a theory is and what functions it serves in the study and understanding of persons. A theory is a set of interrelated ideas, constructs, and principles proposed to explain certain observations of reality. A theory is always speculative in nature and therefore, strictly speaking, cannot be "right" or "wrong." However, a theory is generally accepted as valid or credible by the scientific community to the extent that factual observations of phenomena (usually based on data derived from formal experiments) are consistent with the explanation of the same phenomena offered by a theory. If human behavior were fully understood in everyday settings, there would be no need for personality theories. Such theories are actually elaborate speculations or hypotheses about what people are like, how they became that way, and why they behave as they do. This book will describe some of these theories, examine their underlying assumptions, report relevant research related to each theory, and provide concrete applications of each to relevant aspects of human behavior. There is much to be gained from the study of personality theories. Our subject matter is human nature; our goal is the understanding of the diversity and complexity of the whole person functioning in the real world.

Theories serve two main functions: they explain and predict behavior. A personality theory is *explanatory* in that it serves to organize human behavior systematically so as to render it intelligible. In other words, a theory provides a meaningful framework or map for simplifying and integrating what we know about a related class of events. For example, without the benefit of a theory, it would be difficult to explain why 5-year-old Raymond has a strong romantic attraction to his mother along with undue resentment toward his father. The problem would be compounded were we to learn that other young boys experience similar feelings. Armed with a theory that posits the universality of these emotions at a certain stage of personality development (along with a rationale for their emergence), we would find it much easier to understand Raymond. We may or may not be correct, but at the very least we would be consistent in making sense of these feelings in children. The explanatory function is especially significant when we consider the enormous range of facts and observations associated with human behavior. A good personality theory provides a meaningful context within which human behavior can be consistently described and interpreted.

A theory should not only explain past and present events but also predict future ones. It should provide a basis for the *prediction* of events and outcomes that have not yet occurred. This purpose clearly implies that a theory's concepts must not only be testable but also capable of being confirmed or disconfirmed. Thus, we should be able to predict specific changes in Raymond's behavior as a function of parental treatment. What will happen if his mother actively encourages Raymond's romantic overtures or if his father rejects him because of these feelings? Not only should such general predictions be possible, but also, ideally, the concepts of a theory should be formulated to permit rigorous and precise empirical testing. A good personality theory directly stimulates psychological research. Conversely, the scientific value of theories that are untestable (i.e., unable to generate predictions for research) is still unknown. Theories must have investigative appeal if they are to help us to understand human nature in all of its individually different manifestations.

Personality theories, then, have distinct scientific functions in psychology. Specifically, theories enable us to explain what people are like (relatively enduring characteristics and how they are organized in relation to one another), how such characteristics are developed over time and influence current behavior, and why people behave the way they do. Theories also allow us to predict new relationships that have never been investigated before. Viewed in this light, theories suggest directions in which planned research may reveal new insights in a variety of areas that are yet unexplored. A crucially important point, however, is that all theories of human behavior are constructed by human beings. Personologists are people, and, like the rest of us, hold divergent views about human nature. Some theorists, for example, believe that human actions have their roots in unconscious motives whose true nature is outside the individual's awareness and whose sources lie deeply buried in the distant past. Others believe that people are reasonably aware of their motives and that their behavior is primarily a result of present conditions. Whatever each theorist's specific beliefs may be, it is evident that personologists have different basic assumptions about human nature, thereby distinguishing themselves from one another. A theorist may recognize and make explicit these basic assumptions, fail to make them explicit, or simply incorporate them so fully that it becomes difficult to recognize them as assumptions.

Basic assumptions profoundly affect a personologist's ideas about the nature of personality. For example, Abraham Maslow believed that most of our actions result from reason and free choice. Thus, his theory focused on what he felt were the "higher" aspects of human nature, on what we could become, and he developed his personality theory accordingly. On the other hand, Sigmund Freud believed that behavior is largely determined by irrational, unconscious factors. His notion that human actions are predetermined resulted in a theory which emphasized the unconscious control of all behavior. Maslow and Freud proposed

drastically different views concerning the fundamental nature of the human organism. This in itself is not the point being emphasized here. Rather, the point is simply that the foundations of a personality theory are deeply rooted in the personologist's basic assumptions about human nature (i.e., about what humans truly are). Indeed, as we shall see, the personality theories discussed in this text deal with issues that go to the very core of what it means to be a human being.

COMPONENTS OF A PERSONALITY THEORY

Thus far, we have noted that the most basic functions of a theory are to explain what is already known and to predict things not yet known to be true. Against the backdrop of the explanatory and predictive purposes of a theory, however, what are the pivotal issues and problems addressed by a personality theory? What does a personality theory actually theorize about? What are the basic components comprising a theory of personality and how are such components assembled in order to create an integrated account of human behavior? These are some of the questions inquisitive students ask when beginning a course of study in personality psychology. Given the significance accorded theories throughout this text, it seems only appropriate to identify at the outset the salient issues that have confronted all theorists. Simply stated, a personality theory is comprised of various "minitheories," each of which is focused on specific issues or questions pertaining to psychological functioning. This section will discuss six issues that a complete theory of personality must seek to resolve. These issues represent the conceptual domain of a personality theory and reveal the nature of its content and the breadth of its coverage.

1 Personality Structure

A major feature of any personality theory, *structural concepts* refer to the relatively enduring characteristics that people exhibit across various circumstances and over time. They represent the basic building blocks of psychological life. In this sense they are analogous to concepts such as atoms and cells in the natural sciences. However, structural concepts are strictly hypothetical in nature. They cannot be microscopically observed like neurons in the brain.

Personologists have proposed a patchwork of concepts by which to explain what people are like. One of the most popular examples of a structural concept is a *trait*. A personality trait refers to a durable quality or disposition to behave in a particular way in a variety of situations. It resembles the kind of concept laypersons use when they make judgments about the stable characteristics of other people. Common examples of traits include impulsivity, honesty, sensitivity, and timidity. Gordon Allport, Raymond Cattell, and Hans Eysenck, three leading traitologists, theorized that personality structure is best conceptualized in terms of hypothetical dispositional qualities that underlie behavior.

On a broader level of analysis, personality structure may also be described in terms of the concept of *type*. A personality type refers to a clustering of several different traits into distinct, discontinuous categories. Compared to trait concepts of structure, typological conceptions imply a greater degree of overall consistency and generality to behavior. Whereas people can have one or another degree of many traits, they are commonly described as being a specific type. For instance, Carl Jung held that people fall into one of two discrete categories: introverts and extroverts. In this view, a person is either one or the other.

Personality theorists differ in both the kinds and number of concepts they employ in characterizing the structure of personality. Some theorists propose a highly complex and elaborate structural system, one in which many component parts are linked to one another in a myriad of ways. Freud's tripartite division of personality into *id, ego,* and *superego* illustrates an extraordinarily complex description of structure and its organization. Other theorists, by contrast, propose a simple structural system, in which a limited number of component parts are identified and have few connections to one another. For example, Kelly, a prominent cognitive theorist, used the singular concept of personal construct to account for the relatively enduring dimensions of personality structure.

In summary, any approach to personality that is to be considered useful must deal in some way with the issue of what are the stable, unchanging aspects of human behavior. The issue of structure and, most importantly, the nature of its organization and influence on the functioning individual, is a key component of all personality theories.

2   Motivation

A unified theory of personality must account for why people do the things they do. Motivational concepts, otherwise known as the *process aspects* of individual functioning, focus on the dynamic, changing features of human behavior. Such questions as "Why do people choose particular goals for which they strive?" and "What specific motives energize and direct behavior?" illustrate the type of issues encountered in this second component of a personality theory.

Efforts to understand the momentary, fluid aspects of behavior have resulted in numerous theoretical insights. Some theories propose that personality processes—ranging from sexual release to the enjoyment of humor—derive from the individual's efforts to reduce tension. The so-called tension reduction model of motivation, originally formulated by Freud, suggests that an individual's physiological (biogenic) needs create tension that compels the individual to seek reduction by satisfying needs. Many kinds of basic needs, such as hunger, thirst, sleepiness, and sex, fit this tension reduction view of human motivation. By contrast, other theories of personality dynamics emphasize the individual's striving toward mastery over the environment and the yearning for new experiences for their own enjoyment. Proponents of this view maintain that as individuals mature, more of their behavior becomes invested in developing skills merely for the sake of competency or for dealing effectively with the environment, and less of their behavior is exclusively in the service of alleviating tension.

Some theorists emphasize that people are motivated to increase tension through new, challenging, and even life-threatening experiences in order to enhance their personal fulfillment. (*Francis de Richemond/The Image Works*)

Of course, we need not be restricted to either a tension reduction or competence motivation model of human motivation. Maslow, a prominent motivational theorist, suggested that at certain times the individual is governed by deficit needs and seeks to reduce tension, whereas at other times, the individual is governed by growth needs and seeks to increase tension as a means of personal fulfillment. Although such an integrated view seems plausible, most theorists have tended to use one or another model to explain what motivates people to behave as they do.

3 Personality Development

If personality refers to stable, enduring characteristics, it becomes more than a matter of idle curiosity to understand how such characteristics develop. *Developmental concepts* focus on the issue of how the structural and motivational aspects of the person's functioning change from infancy to adulthood and old age. An account of such change is a key component of what defines a personality theory.

Personality development occurs throughout life. Accordingly, some theorists have proposed a stage model to account for the patterns of growth and change in a person's life. Freud's theory of how personality is developed in terms of a series of psychosexual stages is one example of this approach. Erikson's formulation of eight stages in the development of the ego illustrates another. Still other theorists, by contrast, emphasize the role of parent-child relationships as a significant factor in understanding the issue of development. Rogers, for instance, placed importance on how the individual's self-concept is molded, both cognitively and emotionally, by parental attitudes and behaviors during the formative years of life.

The growth of personality is influenced by a host of external and internal determinants. On the external or environmental side, such determinants include the individual's membership in a particular culture, social-economic class, and unique family setting. Internal determinants, on the other hand, include genetic, biological, and physiological forces. Further acknowledgment of the many changes that accompany our development—physical, social, intellectual, emotional, and moral, to name but a few—reveals just how complicated the issue of human development truly is.

Membership in a particular culture leads to eventual socialization into normative patterns of thought, feeling, and behavior. Whether we are conscious of it or not, cultural forces shape our self-images, our relationships with others, our needs and styles of satisfying them, and the goals we strive to attain. Likewise, membership in a particular social-economic class significantly influences the values, attitudes, and life-styles we acquire. Indeed, few aspects of our development can be understood without reference to the groups to which we belong. Even in a pluralistic society like ours, social class membership often confers our status as individuals, the roles we enact, and the privileges and opportunities we enjoy. Social class factors also exert considerable influence on our experiences of major forms of stress and conflict and our ways of coping with them. There is even evidence that social class is related to the prevalence of mental illness and to the types of mental disorders found in a population. A recent survey (Myers et al., 1984) in five communities including about 10,000 Americans found that college graduates have far fewer mental health problems than do noncollege graduates. Along these same lines, evidence indicates that the prevalence of mental disorders is highest in poor, black, and urban communities (Gould et al., 1981).

The influence resulting from membership in a specific family setting also has an impact on the personality development of the individual. Of particular importance here is the pattern of parental behavior used to socialize the child with regard to values, beliefs, and goals. Parents serve as role models for identification and through their own actions subtly communicate to their children styles of behavior that will affect the children for the rest of their lives.

Genetic factors are the influences on behavior that are transmitted from parents to children through the mechanisms of heredity. They, too, with the environment, play a key role in determining personality development. For instance, there is solid evidence based on studies of twins that emotional stability, extraversion, altruism, and shyness are strongly heritable (Rose et al., 1988; Rushton et al., 1986). Other personal dispositions that have at least a moderate genetic component include alienation, aggression, desire for achievement, leadership, imagination, and sense of well-being (Tellegen et al., 1988).

The lively debate about the relative importance of environmental and genetic factors (i.e., the nature–nurture controversy) has recently given way to an emphasis on how such factors interact to produce resulting behavioral characteristics. Theorists who take such an interactionist position suggest that no one grows up without being influenced by the environment, nor does anyone develop without being affected by his or her genetic endowment. Stated differently, this view suggests that heredity sets limits on the range of development of characteristics; yet, within the boundaries set by this range, further development of characteristics is determined by environmental factors (Scarr & Carter-Saltzman, 1982; Scarr & McCartney, 1983).

Personality theories differ in the importance given to questions of growth and change occurring throughout life, in delineating the factors responsible for day-to-day development, and in assigning relative weight to genetic and environmental factors through which the person's development is determined. Nonetheless, a complete theory of personality should explain the development of structures and processes underlying human behavior.

4 Psychopathology

Still another issue confronting any personality theory is why some people are unable to adjust to the demands of society and to function effectively. Virtually every personologist gives some consideration to why certain people display pathological or maladaptive styles of behavior in everyday life. *Etiology*, the study and explanation of the causes of abnormal functioning, is the focal issue of this component of personality theory.

Several approaches have been developed to explain the causes of abnormal behavior. Personality theorists who endorse the psychodynamic perspective, for example, believe that unresolved conflicts during childhood eventually bring about abnormal behavior in adulthood. The existence of these conflicts resulting from opposing wishes regarding sex and aggression leads to the development of symptoms. Further, because the conflicts are hidden, the person has no idea what is causing the symptoms, which is all the more distressing. In contrast, the behavioral perspective looks at the behavior itself as the problem. According to theorists taking this approach, it is not necessary to hypothesize elaborate, underlying, unobservable mechanisms to explain abnormal behavior. Instead, one must analyze how an abnormal behavior has been learned through past experience and how such behavior is maintained in the present by circumstances that exist in the person's social environment.

Some theories make the assumption that people's behavior—both normal and abnormal—is shaped by the kind of family group, society, and culture in which they live. We are all part of a social network of family, friends, acquaintances, and even strangers, and the kinds of relationships that evolve with others may promote abnormal behaviors and even cause them to occur. Proponents of the sociocultural model of abnormality maintain that the kinds of stresses and conflicts people experience as part of their daily interactions with those around them can cause and support pathological forms of behavior.

The issue of how to conceptualize the causes of psychopathology has led to a diversity of approaches over the relatively brief history of personality theory. The approaches noted here suggest not only different causes of abnormal behavior but also different treatment approaches. What is important to recognize, however, is that a complete theory of personality must include an informed analysis of why some people find life so distressing and fail to develop effective problem-solving skills.

5 Psychological Health

In attempting to account for the varied aspects of human behavior, a robust theory of personality must provide criteria by which to define the healthy personality. This is the issue of what constitutes the good life and the various perspectives offered by personality theorists represent a vitally important component of their overall conceptual contributions. Duane Schultz addressed the issue when he noted: "Many psychologists believe that research on the healthy personality should be the primary focus of psychology; what other discipline investigates the human condition? What entity has more power to change the world, for good or ill, than the human personality? What has more influence on the substance of our lives than the degree of psychological health we bring to bear on our problems?" (1977, p. 5).

Most theories of personality have dealt with the issue of what constitutes psychological well-being. For example, Freud proposed that mature personality functioning is earmarked by the capacity for productive work and satisfying interpersonal relationships. Although at first glance this criterion for psychological health may seem too global and nonspecific, a more careful consideration of it reveals several important implications. For instance, the capacity for work, according to Freud, involves the ability to establish and pursue long-term goals; to delay gratification of instinctual drives in the pursuit of these goals; and to cope with anxiety in such a way that behavior is not seriously impaired. Likewise, Freud's emphasis on satisfying social relationships involves the ability to experience and enjoy a wide range of emotions without feeling threatened, and to gratify unconscious sexual and aggressive drives creatively.

Psychological health may also be defined in terms of a social learning theory perspective. Bandura (1982), for instance, places particular emphasis on our cognitions about our ability to handle the demands of life. In his terms, *self-efficacy*, or the perception that one is capable of executing those behaviors necessary to reach one's goals, is an essential feature of personal adjustment. Moreover, Bandura claims that people who view themselves as self-efficacious accept greater challenges, expend more effort, and may be more successful in reaching their goals as a result.

Some personologists devote considerable attention to creating a psychological portrait of the good life and what it entails. This is nowhere more evident than in the case of Maslow's theory of self-actualization based on a hierarchy of needs. For Maslow (1987), healthy growth requires a shifting of the relative importance of needs from the most primitive (e.g., physiological and safety) to the most advanced or the most "human" (e.g., truth and beauty). Maslow also conducted a study of actualizers and formalized his observations in terms of a profile of personality attributes which includes such qualities as efficient perception of reality, need for privacy and solitude, and acceptance of self and others.

Without question, the criteria used in assessing mental health is of central importance to any comprehensive theory of personality. A majority of the theories we will discuss provide constructs and propositions pertaining to psychological maturity.

6 Personality Change via Therapeutic Intervention

Since personality theories give some consideration to causes of psychopathology, it naturally follows that they also suggest ways of treating the resulting behavior. Thus, a sixth and final issue of critical relevance to personality theorizing is how to help people acquire new competencies, decrease maladaptive forms of behavior, and achieve positive personality changes.

Many theories of personality have evolved out of a clinical or counseling setting. Therefore, it is hardly surprising that there are almost as many approaches to therapy as there are personality theories. The differences lie not only in methods of treatment but also in the assumptions the theorists hold about personality in general. At one extreme lies psychodynamic theory, which attaches primary importance to unconscious conflicts and early learning experiences as dominant factors controlling behavior. The psychodynamic model of therapeutic intervention is thus focused on helping people gain insight into the unconscious and childhood sources of their conflicts, recognizing how these conflicts interfere with adult life. At the other extreme lies behavioral theory, which holds the view that events in the surrounding environment largely determine behavior. Theorists of this persuasion further assume that people who display maladaptive behavior have either failed to learn the skills needed to cope with the demands of everyday living or they have acquired faulty skills that are being maintained through some form of reinforcement. Accordingly, the behavioral approach to treatment is aimed at helping people learn new behavior to replace the faulty patterns they have developed or unlearn their maladaptive responses.

Change in personality or behavior through therapeutic intervention encompasses many possibilities: change in self-image, interpersonal relationship styles, cognitive processes, emotional reactions, values, life goals, and time management are but a sample of the far more numerous forms of sought-after change by people who undergo therapy. In turn, a thorough account of personality must indicate the means by which undesirable forms of behavior can be modified so that the individual can be reinstated to more effective ways of functioning.

There are several different theoretical approaches to the understanding of personality. In spite of all the diversity, personality theories share a common conceptual framework bounded by six issues concerning human behavior: structure, motivation, development, psychopathology, psychological health, and personality change via therapeutic intervention. Taken collectively, the concepts developed by a theory to explain each of these issues defines what a personality theory is all about. The ways in which theorists deal with these issues serve to define the overall perspectives of each theoretical position.

CRITERIA FOR EVALUATING PERSONALITY THEORIES

Given the vast number of alternative personality theories, how do we evaluate the relative merits of each? That is, above and beyond the explanatory and predictive functions a theory should serve, how are we to decide what makes one theory better than another? Six major criteria have been employed to evaluate personality theories in a systematic fashion. There is consensus in the scientific community that a personality theory should satisfy each of these criteria to some extent in order to receive a favorable overall evaluation. These criteria will be discussed here, and, in the concluding chapter, the comparison of major theories discussed throughout the text will be evaluated in terms of these six criteria.

Verifiability

A theory is positively evaluated to the extent that its concepts lend themselves to verification by independent investigators. This means that a theory must be stated in such a way that its concepts, propositions, and hypotheses are clearly and unambiguously defined and logically related to one another. In this way, the empirical consequences of the theory can be logically deduced and readily tested through formal research. To illustrate, let us imagine that we wish to validate Alfred Adler's claim (Chapter 4) that first-borns tend to be more achievement-oriented as adults than persons of other ordinal positions. Our initial step in validating this hypothesis would be to select an appropriate sample of subjects to study. Next, we would ask each subject to indicate what his or her birth order is. Achievement is a far more difficult variable to measure. We might simply ask subjects to indicate the level of their intellectual achievement in academic settings. Or we might observe subjects' "achievement behavior" in the work setting. Or we might administer a self-report test which purports to assess individual differences in achievement motivation. Although there are many possibilities, the important thing to note here is that a good theory should produce testable hypotheses. A theory articulated in precise language makes that more likely.

Although this requirement is easy to specify, it has proved exceedingly difficult for personality researchers to demonstrate even a moderate amount of empirical support for their preferred theoretical positions. Theories of personality are not necessarily incapable of generating testable propositions, but there has been a paucity of crucial research with respect to most theoretical conceptions. Nonetheless, a good theory should contain testable hypotheses about relationships among phenomena. A theory that is not open to the possibility of being confirmed as well as disconfirmed is a poor theory. It is rendered sterile for all practical purposes.

Heuristic Value

This criterion is of paramount significance to the empirically oriented person-ologist. The issue is the degree to which a theory stimulates investigators to do further research. Personality theories differ immensely in their capacity to fulfill this goal. Some of the most provocative theoretical formulations of personality (e.g., Fromm's humanistic theory and Kelly's personal construct theory) have had only minimal impact on the work of investigators within psychology. This state of affairs usually results from the theorist's failure to define his or her concepts operationally, i.e., in a manner whereby they are linked (at some level) to some sort of measurement operation or some observable quality of behavior. Of course, competent followers of a theorist may enhance the heuristic value of a theory by translating the core concepts into the form which allows for enlightening research activity.

Internal Consistency

This criterion stipulates that a theory should be free of internal contradictions. That is, a good theory should account for varied phenomena in an internally consistent way. Likewise, a worthwhile theory should consist of assumptions and propositions that fit together in a coherent way. On the whole, theories of personality fare reasonably well in meeting this standard, and whenever inconsistent predictions do occur, they can usually be traced to a misunderstanding of the theory's concepts by the investigator. Given a set of assumptions about human nature, it is quite possible to construct a personality theory whose concepts and propositions hang together in a sensible manner.

Parsimony

A theory may also be judged on the basis of the number of concepts required to describe and explain events within its domain. The principle of parsimony states that a simpler and more straightforward explanation is preferred to a more complex one. In other words, the fewer the number of concepts and assumptions required by a theory to account for the phenomena it seeks to explain, the better it is. In contrast, all other things being equal, a theory burdened by excess concepts and assumptions is generally viewed as a poor theory. An example may make the importance of this criterion clearer. Let us assume that countless observations support the conclusions that depressed people (a) typically hold a negative view of themselves, (b) are pessimistic about their future, and (c) have a tendency to interpret ongoing experience in a negative manner. We might therefore theorize that low self-esteem is a prime cause of depression. Our self-esteem principle summarizes an otherwise long list of disparate observations concerning depressed people. It provides a more parsimonious way by which to explain unrelated facts and observations concerning depressed people.

Unfortunately, there are no hard-and-fast rules by which the parsimoniousness of a theory may be assessed. Parsimony is a subjective criterion because current knowledge about the various aspects of personality is far from complete. Moreover, a theory that looks parsimonious today may be unable to account for something that will be discovered tomorrow, whereas a theory that looks too complex today may be the only one that is capable of explaining tomorrow's discovery. Nevertheless, a good theory should not contain too much excess theoretical baggage.

Comprehensiveness

This criterion refers to the breadth and diversity of phenomena encompassed by a theory. The more comprehensive a personality theory is, the more behavioral territory it covers. Thus, a comprehensive theory tends to be favored over a narrow, more circumscribed theory. A further benefit of a comprehensive theory is that it can be used as a logical framework for the incorporation and integration of new discrete facts that have been established by observation or experiment. While some personologists have managed to erect grand-scale theories, other theorists fall short on this score. Relying on a set of assumptions about human nature helps to ensure internal consistency, but it also tends to restrict the theorist's attention to a limited range of behavioral events. In varying degrees, the personologists included in this text emphasize biological, genetic, emotional, cognitive, social, and cultural factors in accounting for human behavior. Each of these approaches to personality inevitably restricts the comprehensive nature of the resulting theory. At the same time, it must be recognized that no current theory can account for all aspects of human functioning. Thus, one must decide whether the phenomena accounted for by one theory are as important or central to human behavior as the phenomena encompassed by another theory. Regrettably, there is no litmus test that allows us to determine the relative importance of each, since it is often unclear just how critical any given phenomenon really is to our understanding of human behavior. Current work on a seemingly trivial problem may yield bold new insights at some point in the future. Accordingly, we must be cautious in making judgments about the worth of personality theories on the basis of comprehensiveness alone.

Functional Significance

A final criterion of a good theory is that it should help people understand everyday human behavior. It should also help people overcome their problems. This is hardly surprising, given the fact that virtually all of us are fascinated by and interested in knowing more about ourselves and other people. Indeed, the ultimate value of a personality theory for the layperson rests in its ability to illumine both the self and interpersonal relationships. Knowledge of the personal and social insights provided by personality theorists can greatly enrich our under-

One criterion of a good theory is that it should help people find solutions to their day-to-day problems. (*Toni Michaels/The Image Works*)

standing and appreciation of the nuances of human affairs. It is hoped that the reader will find something of functional significance in each theoretical perspective presented in this text.

These criteria of verifiability, heuristic value, internal consistency, parsimony, comprehensiveness, and functional significance provide a useful framework for evaluating theories of personality, as well as deciding why one theory might be preferable to another. In comparing the overall worth of theories, however, two questions should be kept in mind. First, do the theories being compared deal with the same phenomena? Two theories that address the same kinds of behavior may each be evaluated in terms of the six criteria noted above. At the same time, we need not choose one theory over another since both may bear fruitful insights in the future. There is also the possibility that both theories may eventually be integrated into a single more all-encompassing theory. The second question pertains to whether the two theories are at the same stage of development. A new and still evolving theory may be unable to explain many phenomena, whereas an old and established theory may enlighten us about many issues and problems accompanying the study of personality. Nevertheless, a new theory may lead to significant contributions in areas formerly left unexplored and show promise of becoming more comprehensive at some later time. In the final analysis, theories of personality should be evaluated on the basis of how well they explain things that are known while allowing us freedom to explore intriguing possibilities that have not yet been examined.

The different basic assumptions that personality theorists make concerning human nature will now be discussed. These assumptions are of paramount significance in understanding and evaluating all personality theories; they will play an important part in the presentation of each theoretical perspective included in this book.

BASIC ASSUMPTIONS CONCERNING HUMAN NATURE

All thinking people entertain certain implicit assumptions about human nature. Personality theorists are no exception to this principle. The suppositions that people make about the nature of human beings are, presumably, rooted in their personal experiences. Such basic assumptions profoundly influence the way that individuals perceive one another, treat one another, and, in the case of personality theorists, construct theories about one another. The assumptions themselves may or may not be fully recognized by the individual, whether a personologist or not.

In this section each of the basic assumptions that one could hold about human nature will be made explicit. We are convinced that *all major theories of personality are built upon different positions on these basic assumptions and that no major personality theory can be fully or properly understood without reference to them.* The differences among theories of personality, to some extent, reflect more fundamental differences among theorists on these assumptions.

The basic assumptions concerning human nature fall within these polarities:

1 Freedom   Determinism
2 Rationality   Irrationality
3 Holism   Elementalism
4 Constitutionalism Environmentalism
5 Changeability   Unchangeability
6 Subjectivity   Objectivity
7 Proactivity   Reactivity
8 Homeostasis   Heterostasis
9 Knowability   Unknowability

The assumptions are portrayed here as relatively continuous, bipolar dimensions along which any personality theorist can place himself or herself or be placed in terms of his or her basic position regarding that assumption. In other words, each assumption is depicted as a continuum with a pole, or extreme position, at its opposite end (e.g., freedom is at one pole of the first continuous dimension, while determinism is at the opposite pole or end). From a philosophical viewpoint, the issues inherent in these assumptions might be considered dichotomous rather than continuous (e.g., people are either free or determined). However, among personologists there are various differences in the extent to which a basic assumption is perceived as characteristic of humanity. For example, theorist A may view persons as less determined than does theorist B. Thus, it is desirable to conceptualize these assumptions as continuous so that important differences among theorists may be more readily apparent. A brief consideration of each assumption follows.

Freedom–Determinism

One of the most basic questions that individuals can ask about themselves is what degree of internal freedom, if any, they actually possess in directing and controlling their thoughts, feelings, and actions. How valid and to what extent is the subjective sense of freedom experienced by people in decision making? To what extent is their behavior actually determined by factors that are partially or totally outside the sphere of their conscious recognition? Philosophers and other thinkers have debated this critical issue for centuries. It is, therefore, not surprising to find that it is by no means a dead issue in modern psychology (Deci & Ryan, 1985).

That major contemporary personality theorists differ sharply from one another on this basic assumption about human nature is quite clear. For instance, Rogers stated that "man does not simply have the characteristics of a machine, he is not simply in the grip of unconscious motives, he is a person in the process of creating himself, a person who creates meaning in his life, a person who embodies a dimension of subjective freedom" (Shlien, 1963, p. 307). By way of direct contrast, Skinner asserted that "autonomous man is a device used to explain what we cannot explain in any other way. He has been constructed from our ignorance, and as our understanding increases, the very stuff of which he is composed vanishes" (1971, p. 200). At this point neither of these positions is established as fact. Rather, they are philosophical assumptions about the nature of humanity.

If a given personality theorist, based on personal experience and a host of other influences impinging upon her intellectual development, assumes that human beings are genuinely capable of free choice, her theory will be profoundly affected. She will likely formulate a theory in which people are seen as primarily responsible for their own actions and, at least to some extent, capable of transcending various environmental influences upon their behavior. She will tend to see free choice as a quintessential part of what it means to be a human being. On the other hand, if a personologist is inclined toward determinism, his theory will depict human behavior as being controlled by definable factors. It then becomes incumbent upon the personologist to specify these factors, and much of his theory will involve this task. In point of fact, deterministically based personality theories differ markedly on the nature of these factors. For example, human behavior could be determined by unconscious motives, external reinforcements, early experiences, physiological processes, genetic factors, cultural influences—each one open to various interpretations. In this context, the major source of agreement among these approaches to personality is that human behavior is determined.

The position, then, that a personologist assumes in the freedom–determinism dimension greatly influences the nature of his or her theory and the implications of the theory as to what humans are. This is equally true for the other basic assumption dimensions as well. *A personality theory reflects the configuration of positions that a theorist takes on the basic assumptions about human nature.*

Rationality–Irrationality

The issue underlying the rationality–irrationality dimension is the degree to which our reasoning powers are capable of influencing our everyday behavior. Are humans primarily rational beings who direct their behavior through reason, or are they principally directed by irrational forces? While no major personality theorist holds that people are "purely" rational or "purely" irrational, there are clear-cut differences among personologists on this basic assumption. For instance, Kelly (1963) stressed the rational processes that people utilize as a model in constructing· his theory of personality. He assumed that every person is a "scientist"—as such, intellectual processes are of paramount significance in understanding human behavior. In direct contrast to this view is Freud's psychodynamic theory, a basic tenet of which is the essential unconsciousness of mental activities. Freud held that "it is our inflated self-esteem which refuses to acknowledge the possibility that we might not be undisputed master in the household of our own minds" (Kohut & Seitz, 1963, p. 118). Are we then the rational masters of our fate, the captains of our behavioral ships, or are we controlled by deep irrational forces whose very existence may be unknown to us?

A personologist's position on this issue powerfully influences the nature of focus of his or her theory. For example, if a theorist assumes that rationality is a particularly potent force in people, her personality theory would depict behavior as being largely governed by cognitive processes. Furthermore, it is quite likely that, at least to some degree, her theory would be concerned with the nature, variety, and development of cognitive processes in personality. If a personologist gravitated toward the opposite position, his theory would tend to portray behavior as motivated primarily by irrational forces of which the person is partially or totally unaware. Depending on the theory's content, the relationship between conscious, rational processes and unconscious, irrational processes might be depicted as analogous to an iceberg, with the conscious, rational processes above the ever slightly fluctuating waterline that separates them from the vast unrecognized depths below. The major focus of this theory would be the content of the "submerged" forces as well as their operation in human behavior. While both "rational-oriented" and "irrational-oriented" theorists may disagree among themselves regarding the nature of "rational" or "irrational" factors in personality, the differences between them on the basic assumption of rationality–irrationality lead to opposing views of humanity.

Holism–Elementalism

The *holistic* assumption maintains that human nature is such that behavior can be explained only by studying persons as integrated totalities. Conversely, the *ele-*

mentalistic position assumes that human nature and its resulting behavior can be explained only by investigating each specific, fundamental aspect of it independently of the rest. The key scientific issue here is the level and unit of analysis to be employed in studying individuals. Are persons best studied as totalities or can they be better understood by examining each of their characteristics separately? Disagreements about this research issue among personologists reflect their more fundamental differences on this assumption.

The holistic view assumes that persons can be understood only as total entities. To explain the elements, it is argued, does not account for the total configuration (or gestalt) which results. Holists maintain that the more one fragments the organism, the more one is dealing with abstractions and not the living human being. As one personologist noted, "Half a piece of chalk is still a piece of chalk, only smaller; half a planarian worm is half of one worm, but still a worm in itself; half a man is not a man at all" (Shlien, 1963, p. 305). Those of a holist persuasion, then, attempt to describe and study personality as a totality.

By way of contrast, advocates of elementalism argue that a systematic understanding of human behavior can be achieved only by means of a detailed analysis of its constituent parts. Elementalists believe that just as one does not question the underlying reality of cellular structures in the study of gross anatomy, one should not deny the critical importance of studying the specific factors underlying the overall behavior of people. In fact, elementalists have long asserted that propositions that are vague and untestable at a general behavioral level are testable at a more elemental level. Thus, it is argued that a true scientific approach to personality must be founded upon specific, precise, and elementalistic concepts that are clearly open to empirical test. Elementalists in personality attempt to devise and research these types of concepts.

Constitutionalism–Environmentalism

Students in personality courses often raise the question: "How much of what is called personality is the result of genetic make-up and how much is the result of the environment?" This "nature–nurture" question has been asked in one form or another since ancient times. The issue is still with us today; it has a surreptitious way of creeping into the thinking of contemporary personality theorists so as to influence their concepts of human nature and, hence, their conceptions of personality structure and development.

Constitutionalism (or inherited traits) has a long history in psychology. Hippocrates and Galen, two ancient Greek physicians, believed that an individual's temperament resulted from his or her unique balance of four bodily humors. Their twentieth-century counterparts have developed sophisticated techniques by which to determine the influence of genetics on general behavioral dispositions or temperaments (Buss & Plomin, 1984). Additionally, the perspectives advanced by Cattell and Eysenck (Chapter 6) emphasize the importance of genetic predisposition and physiological make-up in the development of basic personality traits. An individual's biological substrate is also an important factor in certain major personality theories. For instance, it is central to Freud's concept of the id, the inherited basic component of personality that is fixed in the constitution of the individual.

Environmentalism is also no newcomer to the thinking of psychologists. Watson's emphasis on basic processes of conditioning or learning is based on the underlying premise that environment is of monumental importance in shaping human behavior. In fact, the study of learning is regarded as so important precisely because it is the psychological process through which the environment molds behavior. A long and distinguished list of contributors to psychology preceded that point of view; an equally distinguished group of psychologists followed, and in various ways, developed its implications. These implications for personality are most clearly seen in contemporary behavioristic learning theory, although behaviorism has no monopoly on environmentalism in personality theory. Traces of environmentalism can be found in practically all personality theories.

What are some of the consequences of a personologist leaning toward one or the other side of the constitutionalism–environmentalism dimension? A theorist who is inclined toward constitutionalism will tend to see human nature more as a product of internal physical forces than external environmental agents (e.g., Jane and John are highly aggressive because they have strong ids or because aggression is an inherited trait). While the theorist may acknowledge some environmental influences upon behavior, the concepts she constructs to describe personality will reflect a constitutional presupposition. In contradistinction, the theorist who leans toward environmentalism will view human nature as much more subject to environmental whim (e.g., Jane and John are highly aggressive because of their past conditioning histories—in essence, their environments made them that way). An environmentally inclined personologist will reflect this perspective and, in addition, will focus on the learning processes through which the environment presumably affects personality development.

Finally, it must be recognized that almost all psychologists today adopt an *interactionist* position on this assumption (Blass, 1984; Kihlstrom, 1987; Magnusson, 1981). From this vantage point, human behavior is viewed as always resulting from the interaction of constitution with environment, e.g., a given constitutional factor operates differently under dissimilar environmental circumstances; an environmental influence differs in effect depending upon the constitution of the person on whom it is operating. However, for our purposes, constitution will be conceptually separated from environment so that the precise role of each in a theorist's thinking can be more clearly understood.

Changeability–Unchangeability

The basic issue involved in this assumption is the degree to which the individual is seen as capable of fundamental change throughout life. Simply stated, to what extent can an individual's basic personality make-up over time really change? Furthermore, is basic change a necessary component in the evolution or develop-

Is maternal care a result of biological factors or environmental influences, or both? The position that personality theorists take on this nature–nurture issue shapes their conceptions of humanity. (*Joel Gordon*)

ment of personality? Or are the surface changes that we observe in ourselves and other people merely that—superficial changes in behavior that occur while the basic underlying personality structure remains unalterable and intact? Like the other basic assumptions, differences among personologists on this issue are also reflected in the different emphases of their respective theories.

As noted earlier, most definitions of personality stress a life history, or developmental, perspective. The changeability–unchangeability assumption addresses the question of how much fundamental change in personality can actually take place throughout a lifetime. Even theorists within the same broad tradition in personology can be found to be at odds with one another on this issue. For example, both Freud and Erikson represent the psychodynamic tradition within personality theory, yet they profoundly disagree on this basic assumption.

Erikson (1982) assumes a much greater degree of changeability in personality than did Freud. Emphasizing that life is constant change, he depicts persons as necessarily moving through developmental stages, each of which is earmarked by a particular psychosocial crisis. Depending on the manner in which people resolve these crises, their personality development will proceed in either a favorable or an unfavorable direction. In sharp contrast, Freud (1925) portrayed the basic character structure of individuals as being fixed by the experiences of early childhood. While superficial behavior changes take place throughout life, the underlying character structure remains largely unaltered. For Freud, substantive change in personality can only be achieved with great difficulty at best, and then only through the lengthy and often painful process of psychoanalytic therapy.

Personologists who are committed to changeability may reveal this predilection in a number of ways. For example, their theories could include (1) the concept of developmental stages characterizing the life span, (2) a focus on the forces that produce behavior change, (3) the concepts that explain how people may be discontinuous with their past, or (4) an emphasis upon ongoing personal growth. Regardless of which direction a particular theory takes, it reflects the basic assumption that significant personality changes can and do occur, and that they therefore must be explained in theoretical terms. By contrast, personologists inclined toward the unchangeability assumption are likely to reveal it by positing the existence of enduring core personality structures which underlie the individual's behavior throughout life. Such theorists will stress the relevance of these structures, the constitutional or early environmental factors responsible for their formation, and the way in which these structures essentially characterize the individual's behavior throughout life.

Subjectivity–Objectivity

Do human beings live in a highly personal, subjective world of experience that is the major influence upon their behavior? Or is their behavior influenced primarily, if not exclusively, by external, objective factors? This is the essence of the subjectivity–objectivity issue. Personologists differ markedly on this assumption with such differences clearly reflected in their theories. In fact, a major difference on this assumption, perhaps above all others, seems to be at the philosophic root of the sharp cleavage between behaviorism and phenomenology in contemporary psychology. Some illustrations follow.

Rogers, whose theory represents a phenomenological perspective on personality, has stated: "The inner world of the individual appears to have more significant influence upon his behavior than does the external environmental stimulus" (1964, p. 124). For Rogers (and for phenomenology), the individual's subjective frame of reference is of paramount importance, and his observable behavior is forever unintelligible without reference to it. As is so often the case, Skinner is in direct opposition to Rogers. Skinner (1971), contemporary behaviorism's most influential figure, asserted: "The task of a scientific analysis is to explain how the behavior of a person as a physical system is related to the conditions under which the human species evolved and the conditions under which the individual lives" (p. 14); "We can follow the path taken by physics and biology by turning directly to the relation between behavior and the environment and neglecting supposed mediating state of mind" (p. 15). For Skinner (and for part of contemporary behaviorism), human behavior is largely the result of external, objective factors acting upon us—it is the lawful relationships between these factors and the organism's behavior with which the science of psychology should be exclusively concerned.

A theory constructed by a personologist inclined toward subjectivity would mainly be concerned with the nature of the individual's subjective experience. In fact, this kind of theorist would likely consider the scientific study of *human experience* as the most important part of psychology. Conversely, a personologist tending toward objectivity would likely construct a theory primarily concerned with objective behavioral events and their lawful relationships to measurable factors in the external world. For such a theorist, psychology would truly be the science of *behavior*, and very little emphasis would be placed upon the individual's subjective experience per se.

Proactivity–Reactivity

The proactivity–reactivity issue is directly concerned with the locus of causality in explaining human behavior. That is, where are the real causes of human actions to be found? Do people generate their own behavior internally or is their behavior simply a series of responses to external stimuli? At the heart of the proactive view of human beings is the belief that the sources of all behavior reside within the person. People act rather than react. Personologists adopting a proactive view of human nature firmly believe that the causes of behavior are to be found within; persons determine their behavior internally. Maslow offered the following proactive view of humanity: "Man has his future within him, dynamically active at this present moment" (1961, p. 59). Personologists inclined toward proactivity formulate theoretical concepts that serve to explain how people initiate their own actions.

A reactive position, on the other hand, interprets behavior as fundamentally a reaction to stimuli from the outside world. Persons do not internally cause their actions; they simply react to outside forces. The real causes of behavior are seen as completely external to the person. The reactive position is clearly expressed by Skinner: "No account of what is happening inside the human body, no matter how complete, will explain the origins of human behavior" (1989, p. 18). Reactive-oriented personologists place a premium on concepts reflecting stimulus-response and/or behavior-environment relationships. Such personologists assume that the source of human behavior is the environment in which it occurs.

Homeostasis–Heterostasis

The homeostasis–heterostasis dimension is fundamentally concerned with human motivation. Are individuals motivated primarily or exclusively to reduce tensions and maintain an internal state of equilibrium (*homeostasis*)? Or is their basic motivation directed toward growth, stimulus seeking, and self-actualization (*heterostasis*)? Personologists who take different stands on this issue have diametrically opposed views on the motivational bases of human behavior. As Buhler has stated: "One cannot simultaneously believe in the end goal of homeostasis and the end goal of a fulfilling self-realization" (1971, p. 383).

In the middle of this century, John Dollard and Neal Miller (1950) spoke for the homeostatic position. In their view, personality characteristics are acquired through learning, which always involves a relationship between the factors of drive (e.g., hunger) and reinforcement (e.g., food). Reinforcement, in Dollard and Miller's theory, always reduces the strength of the initial drive stimulus. Thus, people are what they are largely because they have acquired stable characteristics that reduce their various drives and maintain their internal states of equilibrium. Without a homeostatic motivational basis, personality development would be impossible.

At about the same time that Dollard and Miller (1950) were championing homeostasis, Maslow (1987) and Rogers (1951) were launching a far different conception of human motivation. These heterostatic theorists portrayed individuals as basically motivated by a continuing quest for growth and self-actualization. Man does not live by drive reduction alone. Instead of directing their behavior toward tension reduction, human beings, by nature, constantly seek new stimuli and challenging opportunities for self-fulfillment. Personality development occurs because of this basic motivational tendency.

This particular assumption has generated a number of logical derivatives. Personality theories constructed by those of a homeostatic persuasion would be concerned with the nature and variety of people's basic drives or instincts, the various personality mechanisms individuals develop to reduce the tensions generated by these drives, and the processes by which these tension-reducing mechanisms are acquired. Conversely, personality theories developed by those of a heterostatic orientation would emphasize the integration of human motives under self-actualization, future-oriented strivings, and the various means by which persons seek growth and self-fulfillment.

Knowability–Unknowability

William James, the great American psychologist and philosopher, wrote: "Our science is a drop, our ignorance a sea" (1956, p. 54). Herein lies the essence of the knowability–unknowability issue regarding human nature. Ultimately, is human nature fully knowable in scientific terms or is there something in it that transcends the potential of scientific understanding? It is clear that personologists presently do not know all there is to know about human beings—the question posed here is whether they ever will.

Personality theorists differ sharply on this question. To some extent, their differences are related to their positions on the other basic assumptions. For example, a personologist inclined toward determinism and objectivity would view people as scientifically knowable; these two assumptions, in effect, place human behavior potentially within the traditional realm of scientific knowledge.

John B. Watson is a historical personification of the knowability side of this philosophical assumption. According to Lundin (1963), Watson was absolutely convinced that systematic observation and experimentation would reveal the principles underlying human behavior. Using this approach, behavioristic psychologists since Watson's time have developed concepts applicable to personality. Skinner's contemporary behavioristic approach to personality, for example, clearly regarded people as ultimately knowable in scientific terms. On the opposite pole of this dimension is the phenomenological theory of Rogers. In his book *Client-Centered Therapy*, Rogers (1951) argued that each individual lives in a continually changing world of subjective experience of which she or he is the center. He developed this notion by asserting that this personal world of experience is private and can only be known in any genuine or complete sense by the individual alone. Whether we will ever gain complete knowledge about persons, this view necessarily implies that persons are unknowable in scientific terms (given a science of psychology that is concerned with all people).

If a personologist believes that individuals are ultimately knowable in scientific terms, he will proceed to develop and test his theory with methodological rigor, convinced that human nature will eventually be comprehended through this approach. That this may not come to pass in his lifetime does not deter his efforts, since he believes that his work will significantly hasten the progress of psychology toward this ultimate objective. Conversely, should a theorist assume that individuals are unknowable in scientific terms, she would be more inclined to look beyond the ken of science in her quest to understand human beings. In fact, she may be tempted to incorporate traditionally "unscientific" concepts into her theory and/or to argue strongly for a redefinition of the science of psychology so that such concepts might be more acceptable to psychologists. In either case, her theory and methodology reflect the assumption that human nature is unknowable in terms of contemporary psychology.

A Few Words About Basic Assumptions

Close scrutiny of the nine basic assumptions discussed above indicates that there is some conceptual overlap among them. As one example, it is difficult to imagine a theorist who assumes reactivity without a corresponding commitment to objectivity. Part of the belief that human behavior is a reaction to external factors is the conviction that such external, objective factors are important in the first place. However, there is sufficient distinction among the nine assumptions to justify their conceptual separation. The opposite poles of the two overlapping assumptions we have used as examples, proactivity and subjectivity, serve to bear this out. Proactivity relates to a motivational question—do people create their own behavior? Subjectivity refers to an experiential issue—what is the impact of subjective experiences on people's actions?

A major reason for treating these nine assumptions separately is that they permit relevant distinctions to be made among personality theorists. Certain assumptions are more salient than others in a given personality theory; the strength that each assumption carries varies from theory to theory. If, for example, a personologist does not adopt a strong commitment to either pole of the subjectivity–objectivity dimension, this assumption would play a relatively minor role in her theory construction. Another theorist might lean markedly toward one of these two extremes—his thinking would then be dominated by his position on the subjectivity–objectivity issue. Throughout this text the position of major theorists on each basic assumption will be made explicit so that the intimate relationship between assumptions and theory can be fully appreciated.

Finally, it seems worthwhile to consider the source of these basic assumptions: where do they originate? We believe that basic assumptions about human nature are part and parcel of the way that a theorist is; they reflect his or her own personality makeup. Like other deeply held beliefs, values, and attitudes, a theorist's assumptions about human nature contribute to the theorist's complexity as a total person. Thus, basic assumptions are acquired and evolve in the same way as the theorist's other beliefs about the nature of the world.

The implications of this argument are profound. Specifically, conceptions of human behavior reflect to a large extent what personologists think of themselves and those around them. For some theorists, the conclusion is inescapable—by studying their theories, we may learn about them and their viewpoints on personality. Considered in this light, the biographical sketches included in each chapter assume added significance; by studying theorists' lives, we gain additional insights into the personal roots of their theoretical positions.

SUMMARY

Personality theories represent organized attempts to contribute significantly to our understanding of human behavior from within the province of psychology. They are concerned not only with the total functioning of the individual but also with individual differences between people.

There is presently no generally agreed upon single definition of personality. Nonetheless, most theoretical definitions view personality as an individual difference concept, as a hypothetical structure, as a life-long developmental process, and as an entity accounting for consistent patterns of behavior. The field of personality is distinguished within psychology by its attempt to synthesize and integrate relevant principles from all areas of psychology. It is also a subfield of academic psychology that encompasses several theoretical perspectives, an accumulated body of research findings, a variety of assessment techniques, and ways to understand and treat abnormal behavior.

Personality theories have two main functions. The first is to provide a meaningful framework within which to explain things that are known about a related class of events. The second is to predict events and relationships that have not yet been investigated.

Personality theories focus attention on six distinct issues concerning human behavior: structure, motivation, development, psychopathology, psychological health, and behavioral change via therapeutic intervention. The evaluation of such theories is based on six major criteria: verifiability, heuristic value, internal consistency, parsimony, comprehensiveness, and functional significance.

Personality theories are grounded in certain basic assumptions about the nature of human beings. Differences among personality theorists on these assumptions constitute the principal basis for the differences among their respective personality theories. In this chapter, nine basic assumptions concerning human nature were specified and discussed: *freedom–determinism, rationality–irrationality, holism–elementalism, constitutionalism–environmentalism, changeability–unchangeability, subjectivity–objectivity, proactivity–reactivity, homeostasis–heterostasis, and knowability–unknowability.*

BIBLIOGRAPHY

Bandura, A. (1982). Self-efficacy mechanism in human agency. *American Psychologist*, **37**, 122–147.

Blass, T. (1984). Social psychology and personality: Toward a convergence. *Journal of Personality and Social Psychology*, **47**, 1013–1027.

Buhler, C. (1971). Basic theoretical concepts of humanistic psychology. *American Psychologist*, **26**, 378–386.

Buss, A. H., & Plomin, R. (1984). *Temperament: Early developing personality traits.* Hillsdale, NJ: Erlbaum.

Deci, E. L., & Ryan, R. M. (1985). *Intrinsic motivation and self-determination in human behavior.* New York: Plenum.

Dollard, J., & Miller, N. E. (1950). *Personality and psychotherapy.* New York: McGraw-Hill.

Erikson, E. H. (1982). *The life cycle completed.* New York: Norton.

Fancher, R. E. (1990). *Pioneers of psychology* (2nd ed.). New York: Norton.

Freud, S. (1925). Some character types met with in psychoanalysis work. In S. Freud, *Collected papers* (Vol. 4). London: Institute for Psychoanalysis and Hogarth Press.

Gould, M., Wunsch-Hitzig, R., & Dohrenwend, B. S. (1981). Estimating the prevalence of childhood psychopathology. *Journal of the American Academy of Child Psychiatry*, **20**, 462–476.

James, W. (1956). *The will to believe and other essays on popular philosophy.* New York: Dover. (Orig. Publ. 1896).

Kelly, G. (1963). *A theory of personality.* New York: Norton.

Kihlstrom, J. F. (1987). Introduction to the special issue: Integrating personality and social psychology. *Journal of Personality and Social Psychology*, **53**, 989–992.

Kohut, H. & Seitz, P. (1963). Psychoanalytic theory of personality. In J. Wepman & R. Heine (Eds.), *Concepts of personality* (pp. 113–141). Chicago: Aldine.

Lundin, R. (1963). Personality theory in behavioristic psychology. In J. Wepman & R. Heine (Eds.) *Concepts of personality* (pp. 257–290). Chicago: Aldine.

Magnusson, D. (1981). Wanted: A psychology of situations. In D. Magnusson (Ed.), *Toward a psychology of situations: An interactional perspective.* Hillsdale, NJ: Erlbaum.

Maslow, A. H. (1961). Existential psychology—What's in it for us? In R. May (Ed.), *Existential psychology* (pp. 52–60). New York: Random House.

Maslow, A. H. (1987). *Motivation and personality.* (3rd ed.) New York: Harper and Row.

Murray, H. (and collaborators). (1938). *Explorations in personality.* New York: Oxford University Press.

Myers, J. K., Weissman, M. M. Tischler, G. L. Holzer, C. E., Leaf, P. J., Orvaschel, H., Anthony, J. C., Boyd, J. H. Burke, J. D., Kramer, M., & Staltzman, R. (1984). Six-month prevalence of psychiatric disorders in three communities. *Archives of General Psychiatry*, **41**, 959–967.

Rogers, C. R. (1951). *Client-centered therapy: Its current practice, implications, and theory.* Boston: Houghton Mifflin.

Rogers, C. R. (1964). Toward a science of the person. In T. Wann (Ed.), *Behaviorism and phenomenology: Contrasting bases for modern psychology* (pp. 109–140). Chicago: University of Chicago Press.

Rose, R. J., Koskenvuo, M., Kaprio, J., Sarna, S., & Langinvainio, H. (1988). Shared genes, shared experiences, and similarity of personality: Data from 14,288 adult Finnish co-twins. *Journal of Personality and Social Psychology*, **54**, 161–171.

Rushton, J. P., Fulker, D. W., Neale, M. C., Nias, D. K., & Eysenck, H. J. (1986). Altruism and aggression: The heritability of individual differences. *Journal of Personality and Social Psychology*, **50**, 1192–1198.

Scarr, S., & Carter-Saltzman, L. (1982). Genetics and intelligence. In R. J. Sternberg (Ed.), *Handbook of human intelligence*. Cambridge, MA: Cambridge University Press.

Scarr, S., & McCartney, K. (1983). How people make their own environments: A theory of genotype → environment effects. *Child Development*, **54**, 424–435.

Schultz, D. (1977). *Growth psychology: Models of the healthy personality*. New York: D. Van Nostrand.

Shlien, J. (1963). Phenomenology and personality. In J. Wepman & R. Heine (Eds.), *Concepts of personality* (pp. 291–330). Chicago: Aldine.

Skinner, B. F. (1971). *Beyond freedom and dignity*. New York: Knopf.

Skinner, B. F. (1989). The origins of cognitive thought. *American Psychologist*, **44**, 13–18.

Tellegen, A., Lykken, D. T., Bouchard, T. J., Wilcox, K. J., Segal, N. L., & Rich, S. (1988). Personality similarity in twins raised apart and together. *Journal of Personality and Social Psychology*, **54**, 1031–1039.

SUGGESTED READINGS

Buss, D. M., & Cantor, N. (1989) (Eds.). *Personality psychology: Recent trends and emerging directions*. New York: Springer-Verlag.

Carson, R. C. (1989). Personality. *Annual Review of Psychology*, **40**, 227–248.

Mindess, H. (1988). *Makers of psychology: The personal factor*. New York: Human Sciences Press.

Nye, R. (1975). *Three views of man: Perspectives from Sigmund Freud, B. F. Skinner, and Carl Rogers*. Monterey, CA: Brooks/Cole.

Pervin, L. (1990). A brief history of modern personality theory. In L. Pervin (Ed.), *Handbook of personality theory and research* (pp. 3–18). New York: Guilford.

Smith, L. (1985). Problems and progress in the philosophy of science: An essay review. *Journal of the History of the Behavioral Sciences*, **21**, 208–216.

Stevenson, L. (1987). *Seven theories of human nature* (2nd ed.). New York: Oxford University Press.

DISCUSSION QUESTIONS

1 Each of us has a working definition of what we mean by the term "personality." What is your definition? Does it in any way imply acceptance of a particular view of human behavior?

2 What are some of the advantages of studying personality strictly from within the framework of scientific psychology? What are some of the disadvantages or limitations?

3 What is a personality theory, and what are its major functions? What might be the consequences of not having a personality theory?

4 Describe the major issues or questions concerning human behavior that a complete theory of personality must seek to resolve.

5 Briefly discuss the six criteria used by personologists to determine what makes one theory better than another. Which particular criterion do you believe is most relevant for evaluating the overall worth of a theory? Explain.

6 Now that you have studied the nine basic assumptions about human nature, what are your own basic assumptions in this regard? Where do you stand on each of these issues? Can you see any factors in your own life that might have contributed to your stance on these assumptions? Explain.

7 Defend your position on the freedom–determinism assumption. Why do you believe that people are basically free? or determined? Is there any way to resolve this issue within the present framework of science?

8 Do you think that psychology will eventually discover all there is to know about the nature of human beings? If not, what is the current value of studying personality psychology? Explain your views on the matter.

GLOSSARY

Basic assumptions   Philosophical suppositions that people, including personality theorists, make concerning the nature of human beings.

Changeability   Basic assumption that personality is subject to continuous change throughout the individual's lifetime.

Comprehensiveness   Criterion used to evaluate the worth of a theory. An adequate theory must encompass and account for a wide range and diversity of behavioral phenomena.

Constitutionalism   Basic assumption that personality is shaped by genetic and biological factors.

Determinism   Basic assumption that all behavior is caused by the operation of other events and does not occur freely.

Elementalism   Basic assumption that an understanding of human behavior can only be achieved by investigating each specific, fundamental aspect of it independently of the rest.

Environmentalism   Basic assumption that personality is shaped by social and cultural forces.

Etiology   The study and explanation of the causes of abnormal behavior.

Freedom   Basic assumption that people are primarily responsible for their own actions and are capable of transcending environmental influences upon their behavior.

Functional significance   Criterion used to evaluate the worth of a theory. An adequate theory should provide useful approaches to the solution of people's problems.

Heterostasis   Basic assumption that individuals are motivated primarily toward growth, stimulus seeking, and self-actualization.

Heuristic value   Criterion used to evaluate the worth of a theory. An adequate theory should stimulate new ideas for research.

Holism   Basic assumption that behavior can be explained only by studying persons as totalities.

Homeostasis   Basic assumption that individuals are motivated primarily to reduce tensions and maintain an internal state of equilibrium.

Interactionist approach The view within psychology that stresses the importance of both individual differences and situational factors in accounting for behavior.

Internal consistency Criterion used to evaluate the worth of a theory. An adequate theory should account for varied phenomena in an internally consistent way.

Irrationality Basic assumption that human behavior is governed by irrational forces of which the person is partially or totally unaware.

Knowability Basic assumption that principles governing human behavior will eventually be discovered through scientific inquiry.

Objectivity Basic assumption that human behavior is largely the result of external and definable factors acting upon the person.

Parsimony Criterion used to evaluate the worth of a theory. An adequate theory should contain only those concepts and assumptions necessary to account for the phenomena within its domain.

Persona Term used to denote the mask worn by theatrical players in ancient Greek dramas and from which the term ''personality'' is derived.

Personality psychology A distinct subfield of academic psychology that comprises theory, research, and assessment.

Personality structure In personality theory, the concept of structure refers to the more stable and enduring attributes that individuals display over time and across situations.

Personality theories Different systems of internally consistent concepts that are created by investigators to account for the diversity and complexity of the whole person functioning in the real world.

Personologist Murray's term for a personality theorist and/or researcher.

Proactivity Basic assumption that the sources of all behavior reside within the person.

Rationality Basic assumption that human beings are rational organisms capable of directing their behavior through reasoning.

Reactivity Basic assumption that the real causes of human behavior are completely external to the person, that behavior is simply a series of responses to external stimuli.

Self-efficacy Bandura's concept referring to an individual's belief that he or she can execute the behavior required to produce certain response outcomes.

Subjectivity Basic assumption that each person inhabits a highly personal, subjective world of experience that is the major influence upon his or her behavior.

Trait A stable disposition to behave in a particular way as expressed in a person's behavior across a range of social settings (e.g., relaxed and conservative).

Type A category to which people with certain characteristics in common are assigned (e.g., introverts and extroverts).

Unchangeability Basic assumption that personality structure is established in early life and remains intact thereafter.

Unknowability Basic assumption that human behavior transcends the potential of scientific understanding.

Verifiability Criterion used to evaluate the worth of a theory. An adequate theory must contain concepts that are clearly defined, logically related to one another, and amenable to empirical validation.

CHAPTER 2

RESEARCH
AND ASSESSMENT
IN PERSONALITY
PSYCHOLOGY

In the first chapter it was noted that a major criterion for judging the value of a personality theory is the degree to which it stimulates and guides research. In effect, a good theory generates hypotheses that can be readily evaluated through empirical research. The results of such hypothesis-testing research enables us to determine which of a theory's propositions should be accepted or rejected. Ideally, personality psychologists must be able to gather data in the search for facts or principles that can be explained and interpreted in a broader theoretical framework. A theory without supporting research is idle speculation. By the same token, endless fact gathering is meaningless unless it is organized into a more manageable and comprehensible framework. A theory provides this framework for summarizing and representing empirical data in a meaningful way.

Theory-based research (what is known as *pure* or *basic research*) allows us to determine whether the suggested relationships between and among specific phenomena do in fact exist. When two personality theories predict different relationships for a particular class of phenomena, we turn to research to discover which predicted relationship exists. For example, psychodynamic theory predicts that violent entertainment reduces the level of actual violence among viewers by providing an outlet for pent-up aggressive energy (such an outlet is known as "catharsis"). In contrast, social learning theory predicts that aggressive behavior is learned and that the more we observe people resorting to violence, the more we behave violently. The results of studies of the effects of televised and other observed violence cast light on the validity of these competing theories (details of the outcomes of this particular debate can be found in Chapter 8).

Although personality research rarely proceeds without an underlying theoretical rationale, this does not imply that the understanding of personality is never advanced by research activities unrelated to theory or even by "chance" results. Indeed, there is wide latitude with regard to how tight a grip theory holds on personality research. Some personologists conduct studies independently of a theory, hoping to uncover an intriguing finding that might be parlayed into a theory. More commonly, however, personological researchers tend to investigate questions logically derived from a particular theoretical perspective. Most of the research reported in this book began with a theory from which predictions were deduced and tested. Testable predictions, called *hypotheses*, allow us to evaluate the truth and utility of theoretical propositions embedded within a given theory. A personality theory has real value if it suggests specific hypotheses that can be proved correct or incorrect by empirical inquiry. As shown in Figure 2-1, a useful theory generates testable hypotheses which, in turn, reshape and enlarge the theory even more.

The general course of advancement in our understanding of human personality is through a connecting link between theory and research. Theory serves as a kind of running scorecard for hypothesis testing. If the results of hypothesis-testing research are inconsistent with what a theory claims, we are much less inclined to accept the theory. Most likely, we would create a new theory or revise the existing one to better account for the incongruent findings. On the other hand, if results of empirical research are consistent with what a theory says, we are more likely to gain confidence in the theory. It should be noted, however, that whole theories are never tested directly. Rather, specific hypotheses derived from a theory's propositions are tested through research. Accordingly, personality theories are always in various stages of being supported or not supported by research. The more often that empirical data confirm hypotheses drawn from a theory, the more faith we have that the theory is tentatively "correct" in its explanation of certain aspects of human behavior. Confirming data increase the likelihood that a theory is accurate in its account of the nature of things. If, however, research consistently fails to support predictions drawn from a theory, we are much more

FIGURE 2-1 A theory generates testable hypotheses which lead to empirical research and gathering of empirical data. In turn, empirical data confirm, disconfirm, or reshape a theory. A theory also summarizes and organizes empirical data into a more coherent account of the phenomena it seeks to explain.

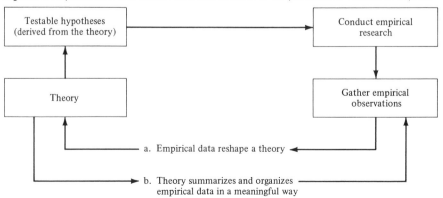

likely to doubt or reject the propositions and the theory from which they were deduced. Disconfirming data decrease the likelihood that a theory is tentatively "correct" in the explanation of phenomena within its domain.

Importance of Personality Research: An Overview

In this chapter we examine the scientific approach to the study of persons and then focus on the research strategies that personologists most frequently use. As we shall see, it is research that allows us to explore the relationships among events and to establish meaningful principles relating to personality. Personality research, whether it involves observation or experimentation, is the means by which we gather information or facts that can provide insights into complex questions about behavior. Ultimately, most personality psychologists hope that the data they gather will be of some value in helping to determine the validity and utility of their theories. There is, then, a continuous interplay between research and theory—or at least there ought to be. Theory serves as both catalyst and guide for the speculation that precedes empirical investigation. It helps bring the data gleaned from research into an overall coherent structure in which each datum is an integral part. But there must be something to bring together: research provides that something.

The cornerstone of the scientific method is its commitment to putting ideas to *empirical test*. This means we determine by careful observation or experimentation the precise facts or relationships between variables. More than that, the methods and procedures used to study variables must be carried out in systematic, reliable ways so that others can verify them. This self-correcting aspect of science constitutes a major strength of the research enterprise because it gradually weeds out erroneous findings so that empirically based information tends to be relatively dependable and accurate. This is not to say that empirical or scientific methods have exclusive ownership of truth. Indeed, there are many different research methods that may be used to study critical issues and the methods sometimes yield conflicting results. Also, no single method is ideal for all purposes and situations. On balance, however, empiricism, through its painstaking process of collecting and analyzing data, is better equipped to grapple successfully with the questions it seeks to answer than is argument, armchair speculation, or good old-fashioned common sense.

Why is it important to put our ideas about human behavior to an empirical test, as opposed to relying on casual observation, reason, or some preconceived notion? Basically, the empirical approach offers two major advantages. The first and perhaps greatest advantage is its intolerance of error. Personality scientists are trained not only to be highly skeptical but also to scrutinize one another's findings with a critical eye. They demand objective data that can be duplicated by others before they accept conclusions as being valid. When two studies yield conflicting findings, personologists seek to learn why the studies reached different conclusions, usually by conducting additional research. This is what makes the "science of persons" different from casual observations or the simple assertion of opinion.

The second advantage offered by the empirical approach is its clarity and precision in developing ideas about how to describe people and why they behave as they do. Commonsense notions about human behavior tend to be vague and ambiguous. For instance, consider the adage "Spare the rod and spoil the child." What precisely does this statement recommend about child rearing? How severely should a child be punished if the rod is not to be spared? What constitutes a spoiled child? A basic problem is that statements like this imply different meanings to different people. When people disagree about this adage, it may be because they are attributing totally different meanings to the statement. Furthermore, commonsense assertions produce little effort to confirm ideas or detect biases, so that many "truisms" about behavior that come to be widely accepted are simply myths. In contrast, the empirical approach requires that we use precise language in describing the events or phenomena of interest to us. Personality researchers, like other scientists, accomplish this goal by stating operational definitions of the particular variables or constructs they study. An *operational definition* describes the exact methods used to create or measure the variables being investigated. For example, a psychologist might operationally define "depression" in terms of subjects' scores on the Beck Depression Inventory, a standard self-report scale of depression (Beck, 1982). Similarly, a psychologist might operationalize the variable of "aggression" by recording the number of aggressive verbal and physical acts that subjects spontaneously display in a given period of time. Many other examples of how personality researchers operationalize in order to evaluate theoretical propositions may be found in specific studies in subsequent chapters.

There are three main types of research strategies that personality psychologists utilize in the study of persons: case studies, correlational studies, and formal experiments. Although different in their specific tactics, these strategies involve someone making careful observations of what someone else is doing or saying. Observation is the fundamental defining characteristic of empirical research in any discipline, including personology. Before proceeding, then, let us briefly consider the nature and importance of observation in the research enterprise.

Observation: A Starting Point

All research, whether it is the study of individual cases, correlational studies, or laboratory experiments, involves observation. Observation is the sine qua non of any approach to personality study. In some cases, hunches for research begin with unsystematic observation. For example, we might casually observe two classmates who, on separate occasions, each blame the instructor for a poor test grade. We might also notice that each classmate has a poor self-image and becomes depressed in response to failure experiences. Could it be that lack of self-esteem is associated with or even causes the tendency to attribute blame to others for failure as well as the tendency to become depressed following failure? Personal observations often pave the way for more refined study of people's behavior.

Another way to learn about behavior is to observe and record it as it naturally occurs (in real-life settings), but in a more systematic and rigorous manner than is

Naturalistic observation allows the psychologist to obtain information about behavior as it occurs in real-life situations. *(Ulrike Welsch)*

evident in unsystematic observation. This is called *naturalistic observation.* In psychology, the play and friendship patterns of children, antisocial behavior in adolescents, eating behaviors of obese and nonobese people, leadership styles of effective business managers, and many clinical phenomena have been investigated through naturalistic observation. Such naturalistic observations do not explain behavior, but they are a rich source of information about what people do in their natural environments.

As straightforward and appealing as naturalistic observation may sound, it also has its limitations. The main problem is that observers are often at the mercy of unpredictable events over which they have little or no control. In addition, there are the problems of observer bias and expectations influencing which aspects of events are attended to and remembered. Third, critics of this approach question the generalization of observations based on a few people or situations. Finally, observers may unwittingly interfere with the actual events they wish to observe or record (Kazdin, 1982). Suppose, for example, that an observer monitors family disputes to study the styles of conflict resolution. How confident can she be that her presence is not a factor that subtly affects the family's approach to resolving conflicts? Despite these problems, the advantage of naturalistic observation is obvious—we get a sample of how people respond to their day-to-day situations amid friends and families without the contrived atmosphere of a laboratory or interview.

Because naturalistic observation prevents researchers from systematically controlling variables in a situation, they must wait until the appropriate conditions occur. To deal with this problem, some investigators conduct controlled field observations. Such a research approach combines features of naturalistic observation and relevant experimental controls. This strategy is illustrated in a study by Regan et al. (1972). These researchers designed a field experiment in order to examine the effect of guilt on helping behavior. A designated confederate approached women shoppers in a mall and asked them to take his picture for a class project, using an expensive camera that had been rigged so that it would not work properly. Half the shoppers were made to feel guilty, being told that they had done something wrong and jammed the camera; the other half were told that the camera "acts up a lot" and it was not their fault. Shortly thereafter, a second female confederate walked by and dropped groceries from her shopping bag. A hidden observer noted that of those who felt guilty, 55 percent stopped and offered help; but of those who did not feel guilty, only 15 percent offered help in picking up the groceries. Clearly, such a study has the marked advantage of investigating behavior in real-life circumstances, giving added confidence that the results can be generalized to other settings.

CASE HISTORY METHOD

The detailed study of a single individual's behavior over an extended period of time is called a *case history* or *case study*. This approach is used frequently in clinical and medical settings in order to diagnose and treat people who have psychological problems. As such, case histories usually deal with abnormal or troubled persons whose lives are studied during psychotherapy or diagnosis (Runyan, 1982). The clinician seeks to achieve an understanding of the person's life experiences and behavior patterns through a variety of procedures, including the person's own recollections, interviews with others who know the person, autobiographical and biographical documents, and any available information from psychological tests. Usually, the clinician is searching for clues in the person's past or present life to determine the causes of the person's difficulties. In turn, case histories provide the primary data enabling clinicians to establish effective strategies to treat emotional disorders.

Case histories made by clinicians working with patients have played an important role in the development of certain personality theories and clinical thinking in general. For instance, Freud's psychodynamic perspective is almost exclusively grounded in the intensive study of single cases. Freud and his fellow psychoanalysts spent years probing deeply into all sorts of behavior: early childhood recollections, dreams, fantasies, physical illnesses, love–hate relationships. In addition to gaining rich insights into the uniqueness of persons, Freud used case studies to support his general theoretical claims. Similarly, Carl Rogers relied heavily on case studies of psychotherapy clients in formulating his phenomenological approach to personality. Though it is largely a detailed description and analysis of a particular individual personality, the case study is an extraordinarily useful research strategy. Periodically, a single case study will suggest a penetrating insight about human behavior, but usually one case does not provide a firm basis for deriving general principles of behavior. However, if a number of case studies are accessible for scrutiny, researchers may be able to identify threads of consistency among them and draw some general conclusions. An example is provided in a recent study by Lewis et al. (1986). This research group compiled case histories on 15 condemned men who were selected as subjects because their execution date was close at hand. Surprisingly, all 15 inmates had histories of severe head injuries, 12 showed signs of brain damage, and many were substantially below average in intellectual functioning. These findings challenge the stereotypic image of criminals sentenced to die as being shrewd and coldly calculating individuals. If anything, the findings suggest a link between neurological impairment and condemnation to death row.

The case study method may also be used to study the lives of normal individuals. A group led by Henry Murray (Murray et al., 1938) at the Harvard Psychological Clinic provides a rare but compelling model for the intensive study of individual lives over a substantial period of time. The Harvard "personologists" (as these researchers called themselves) focused on in-depth assessments of a small group of college males. The objective was to learn about the basic needs, conflicts, values, attitudes, and patterns of social interaction evident among these young men. The assessment techniques included several self-report personality questionnaires and projective tests administered at different times. In addition, assessment of these students involved gathering extensive biographical data and autobiographical sketches, putting them into small-scale experiments, and conducting stress interviews where they were forced to answer embarrassing questions or were challenged to defend some of their most deeply held values. Finally, the students were studied in small group settings so that observers could ascertain their public styles of interpersonal interaction.

The methods used by Murray and his colleagues covered many topics and facets of each student's life and yielded a rich narrative account of each student as a whole in his natural setting. To better assess each student's thoughts, feelings, and actions, Murray assembled a group of experienced psychologists who shared their insights of each student at a staff conference or "diagnostic council." In this council, different researchers from different backgrounds who had studied the same student would offer their respective clinical impressions about the student. Debate would ensue and eventually a conclusion about how best to characterize the student's personality was reached by majority vote.

The eclectic and interdisciplinary nature of the Harvard personologists' approach to the study of personality influenced an entire generation of researchers by directing their attention to the whole person, to the importance of the environment, and to the need for comprehensive assessment. Robert White's *Lives in Progress* (1975), a longitudinal study of three relatively normal individuals, illustrates the importance of the case history as a strategy well-suited for conducting personality research.

Evaluation of the Case History Method

Case history research brings with it its own set of potential strengths and weaknesses, depending on what phenomena is being studied and how the research is conducted. The advantage of such research is that it provides an account of the complexities and idiosyncrasies of an individual's personality conspicuously lacking from other research strategies. If the goal is to study processes going on in one or a few persons and to learn how persons cope with life experiences, then case histories are the strategy of choice. Further, case histories are the only way rare instances of a phenomenon can be investigated. Case study descriptions of multiple personality illustrate this point (Crabtree, 1985). At the same time, we must be mindful of the difficulties and shortcomings encountered in studying only one individual. The chief disadvantage of case studies is that the researcher can never be totally certain about cause-and-effect relationships. Specifically, because researchers cannot control factors that might affect the events or outcomes that they observe, it is always possible that causes other than those they infer may be operating. Second, because a case study examines only one person, its results are of limited generality. Just because one person behaves in a certain way does not mean all people behave that way. Third, the data obtained by the case history method may be retrospective or second-hand in nature and thus distorted by time. Finally, even if the accuracy of such data can be verified, the conclusions drawn about the individual may reflect the personal biases of the investigator. Despite these limitations, case histories can be a rich source of information about particular psychological phenomena. At the very least, it is reasonable to consider the case study as a preliminary research strategy that can offer intriguing hypotheses about human personality. Researchers can then examine these hypotheses with more rigorous experimental procedures.

CORRELATIONAL METHOD

To overcome the limitations of the case history method, personality researchers frequently use an alternative strategy known as the *correlational method*. This approach seeks to determine relationships between and among events (variables) that already exist. A variable is any dimension that can be measured and whose numerical value can vary along some continuum or another. As an example, anxiety is a variable because it can be measured (using a self-report anxiety scale) and because people vary in their level of anxiety. Similarly, accuracy of performance on a task requiring skill is a variable that can be measured. A correlational study could be conducted simply by measuring the anxiety level of several people and by measuring the performance accuracy each attains on a difficult group administered task. If published research findings are replicated, those persons with lower anxiety scores would be found to have higher task performance scores. Because many other factors probably also influence accuracy of task performance (e.g., task familiarity, motivation, intelligence), the relationship with anxiety would not be a perfect one, but it should be noticeable.

Variables in correlational research may include such factors as test scores, demographic characteristics (such as age, birth order, and socioeconomic status), self-report measures of traits, motives, values, and attitudes, physiological responses (such as heart rate, blood pressure, and galvanic skin response), and behavioral styles. Psychologists using the correlational method are interested in discovering answers to specific questions such as: Do college grades relate to occupational success in later life? Is stress related to coronary heart disease? Is there a relationship between self-esteem and loneliness? Is there a relationship between birth order and achievement motivation? A correlational study seeks not only to answer such questions with "yes" or "no," but also to provide a numerical estimate of the degree to which values on one variable are associated with values on the other. In this effort, psychologists compute a descriptive statistical index called the *correlation coefficient* (also known as Pearson's product-moment correlation). The correlation coefficient (symbolized by the lower-case letter *r*) tells us two things: (1) the strength of relationship between two variables and (2) the direction (positive or negative) of the relationship.

The correlation coefficient can range from -1.00 (a perfect negative or inverse relationship) through 0 (no correlation) up to $+1.00$ (a perfect positive relationship). A coefficient near zero indicates that the two variables measured are not related in any useful way. That is, high or low scores on variable X show no consistent relationship to high or low scores on variable Y. An example might be the relationship between the variables of weight and intelligence. In general, heavier people are neither consistently more intelligent nor consistently less intelligent than lighter people. Conversely, a coefficient of $+1.00$ or -1.00 indicates that there is a perfect, one-to-one correspondence between the two variables. Correlations close to perfect almost never occur in personality research, suggesting that although many psychological variables are associated with each other, the degree of association is not very strong. Correlations ranging between $\pm.30$ and $\pm.60$ are fairly common in personality research and are of practical and theoretical value in making predictions. Correlations between 0 and $\pm.30$ must be judged with caution and are only minimally useful in making predictions. Figure 2-2 illustrates the graphic distribution of scores of two variables that would yield different values for correlation coefficients. The horizontal axis represents one variable, and the vertical axis represents the other. Each point indicates the scores of one subject for the two variables.

A *positive correlation* indicates that high scores on one variable tend to be associated with high scores on the other variable or that low scores tend to be associated with low scores. In other words, the two variables increase or decrease together. For example, a positive correlation is regularly found between people's height and weight. In general, taller people tend to weigh more than shorter people. Another example is the positive correlation between the amount of violence children watch on television and their tendency to behave aggressively. On average, the more children watch violence on television the more they tend to be aggressive. A *negative correlation*, on the other hand, indicates that high scores on one variable are accompanied by low scores on the other variable, and

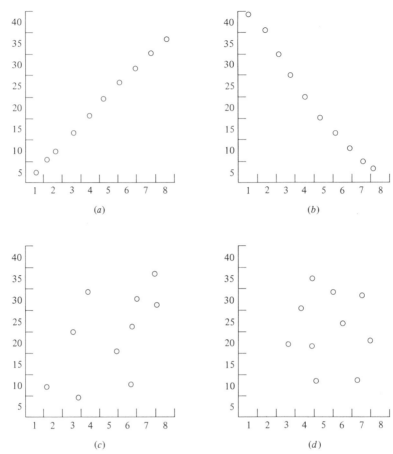

FIGURE 2-2 Scatter diagrams illustrating various degrees of relationship between two variables. Each dot in the diagram represents one person's score on both variables. (a) Perfect positive ($r = +1.00$); (b) Perfect negative ($r = -1.00$); (c) Moderate positive ($r = +.71$); (d) Unrelated ($r = .00$).

vice versa. An example would be the negative correlation between how frequently students are absent from class and how well they perform on exams. In general, students who have a high number of absences tend to earn low exam scores, while students who have a low number of absences tend to earn higher exam scores. Another example is the negative correlation between shyness and assertive behavior. Persons who score high on a measure of shyness tend to be nonassertive, whereas persons who score low on a measure of shyness tend to be assertive. The closer the correlation coefficient is to either $+1.00$ or -1.00, the stronger the relationship is between the two variables being studied. Thus, a correlation of $+.80$ represents a stronger tendency for two variables to be associated than does a correlation of $+.30$. Likewise, a correlation of $-.65$ reflects a stronger relationship than does a correlation of $-.25$. Keep in mind that the magnitude of a correlation depends only on the numerical value of the coefficient, whereas the positive or negative sign placed in front of the coefficient simply indicates whether the correlation is direct or inverse. Thus, an *r* value of + .70 is precisely as strong as an *r* value of − .70. The first one expresses a positive correlation, whereas the second one expresses an inverse or negative correlation. Furthermore, a correlation of − .55 represents a stronger relationship than a correlation of + .35. An understanding of these facets of the correlational statistic will assist you in evaluating the conclusions of such studies.

Evaluation of the Correlational Method

The correlational method offers some unique advantages. The most important one is that it allows researchers to study a broad range of variables that could not be examined with experimental procedures. For instance, after-the-fact (ex post facto) correlational analyses would be the only ethical way to investigate the link between child sexual abuse and emotional problems in later life. Similarly, in order to learn how democratic and authoritarian styles of parenting relate to people's values, correlation is the method of choice since ethical considerations preclude experimental control of how subjects are raised by parents. Accordingly, correlational research widens the scope of psychological phenomenon that personologists are able to investigate.

A second advantage of the correlational method is that it makes it possible to examine many aspects of personality in natural, real-world settings. For example, if we wanted to study the effects of divorce on children's adjustment to and performance in the school setting, we could systematically monitor the social and academic progress of children from divorced families over a period of time. This application of naturalistic observation would require time and effort, but would yield a highly realistic account of complex behavior. For this reason, the correlational method is the preferred research strategy of personologists interested in the study of individual differences and phenomena that do not lend themselves to experimental control. A third advantage of correlational studies is that it is sometimes possible to predict one kind of information by knowing another. For example, research has established a moderately high positive correlation between SAT scores of high-school seniors and their college grades later (Hargadon, 1981). Therefore, by knowing students' SAT scores, college admissions officers can make reasonably accurate predictions regarding applicants' subsequent academic performance. Such predictions are never perfect but are often useful when making admissions decisions. Nevertheless, all personality researchers recognize two serious drawbacks associated with this research strategy. First, use of the correlational method does not allow investigators to control events so as to isolate cause-and-effect relationships. The crux of the problem is that *correlational research cannot demonstrate conclusively that two variables are causally related.* For instance, several correlational studies support a link between the viewing of violent television programs and aggressive behavior on the part of both children and adults (Freedman, 1988; Huston & Wright, 1982). What conclusion might we draw from these studies? One plausible conclusion is that long-term viewing of violence on television leads to an increase in viewers' aggressive urges. Alternatively, it might be concluded that people who are aggressive or have committed aggressive acts prefer to watch television programs with violent content. Unfortunately, the correlational method does not allow us to determine which of these two possibilities is correct. At the same time, correlational studies that do establish a strong association between two variables raise the possibility that the variables are causally related. In reference to the link between viewing violence on television and aggression, for example, experimental research stimulated by correlational findings has led researchers to conclude that exposure to violent programming can contribute causally to aggressive behavior (Eron, 1987).

The second drawback associated with the correlational method is the possible confounding caused by third variables. To illustrate this interpretive problem, consider the relationship between the use of drugs by teenagers and their parents. Does this correlation mean that seeing their parents use drugs causes teenagers to use more drugs? Or does it mean that worrying about their teenagers taking drugs causes parents to use drugs to reduce their worries? Or does some third variable lead to drug use in teenagers and parents alike? Perhaps teenagers and their parents use drugs to cope with the stressful poverty conditions in which their families live! That is, factors relating to a family's socioeconomic status (e.g., poverty) may be the true cause underlying drug use by its members. The possibility that a third (hidden) variable—not measured, and perhaps not even thought of—actually exerts a causal influence over both of the variables that were measured cannot be ruled out when interpreting correlations.

Although correlation does not imply causation, this is not to say that cause-and-effect relationships may not be strongly implicated in certain cases. This is especially true when correlational studies are conducted longitudinally—where, for instance, variables of concern are measured at time one and correlated with measured outcome variables known to follow them at time two. For example, consider the well-established positive correlation between smoking cigarettes and lung cancer. While it is entirely possible that some third unknown variable (such as genetic predisposition) may play a causal role in both smoking and lung cancer, few people would doubt that smoking is the likely cause since it precedes the development of lung cancer in time. Such a strategy (where there is a time lag that separates the measurement of two variables) has also enabled researchers to piece together cause-and-effect relationships in cases where experimentation is not feasible. On the basis of clinical impressions, for example, researchers have long suspected that chronic stress might contribute to many types of physical and psychological problems. Recent advances in the measurement of stress (self-report scales) have allowed researchers to investigate these suspicions using the correlational method. In the domain of physical diseases, for example, accumulating evidence indicates that stress is significantly related to the onset and course of heart disease, diabetes, cancer, and various types of infectious disease (Elliott & Eisdorfer, 1982; Friedman & Booth-Kelley, 1987; Jemmott & Locke, 1984; Smith & Anderson, 1986; Williams & Deffenbacher, 1983). Likewise, correlational research indicates that stress may contribute to drug abuse (Newcomb & Harlow,

1986), sexual difficulties (Malatesta & Adams, 1984), and numerous psychological disorders (Neufeld & Mothersill, 1980). Critics of this research rightfully note that there may be other factors that might artificially inflate the apparent link between stress and illness (Schroeder & Costa, 1984). Thus, one caution remains: although inferences about causality are sometimes strongly implicated by virtue of the strength of the relationship between two variables, it is only by means of experimental methods that real causal relationships can be determined.

EXPERIMENTAL METHOD

The only way that personality researchers can establish cause-and-effect relationships (i.e., whether one variable causes changes in another variable) is by conducting an experiment. This is the fundamental reason why the experimental method is the ideal research strategy in the study of central issues in personality.

The key to the *experimental method*, and the essential difference between it and the case history and correlational methods, is that it permits a researcher to manipulate or alter one variable under carefully controlled conditions while observing its impact on another variable of interest. The variable being manipulated or altered is called the *independent variable*. It is the stimulus condition that the investigator systematically varies in order to assess its impact on another variable. In contrast, the variable that changes, presumably in response to manipulation of the independent variable, is termed the *dependent variable*. It is whatever aspect of a subject's behavior that is observed or measured in response to the independent variable. Thus, the dependent variable is a function of the independent variable; it is "dependent" on changes caused by the experimenter's manipulation of the independent variable.

Although the logic of the experimental method is straightforward, the actual process of conducting an experiment is a fairly complicated undertaking. A well-designed experiment must take into account a number of factors that could affect the clarity and meaning of the results. In practical terms, this means that all variables and conditions (except the independent variable of interest) that could have some bearing on what is being measured must be eliminated or held at a constant level during the experiment. There are several ways to eliminate or control extraneous variables that might influence the dependent variable, but the most common way is to assign subjects randomly to different experimental conditions or groups. *Random assignment* (often done by such means as flipping a coin or using a table of random numbers to determine assignment) ensures that all subjects have an equal chance of being assigned to any condition or group in the experiment. In this way, researchers can be reasonably confident that whatever characteristics subjects may bring to the experiment (such as age, intelligence, ethnic origin, or birth order) have an equal chance of being distributed across the various experimental conditions or groups. As a defining characteristic of the experimental method, randomization rests on the assumption that all subjects at the beginning of an experiment are alike with the exception of one variable: the presence or absence of the independent variable. Therefore, if the subject's behavior changes in response to the manipulation of the independent variable, the researcher can be certain that it and it alone is responsible for the change in behavior. After the researcher has manipulated the independent variable, whatever aspect of a subject's behavior that is observed or measured could not have been caused by any other variable because no other variable was allowed to operate during the experiment.

In its simplest format, the experimental method requires that at least two groups of subjects be compared with each other. Those subjects who receive some special treatment (the manipulation introduced by the experimenter) are said to be *experimental group* subjects. Other subjects who do not receive the special treatment condition are said to be in the *control group*. Subjects in both groups are then compared to see if the treatment manipulation produced any effect in the chosen dependent variable. Table 2-1 provides an overview of the experimental design in which there is just one independent variable and one dependent variable. The control group serves as a baseline against which effect of the treatment condition on the experimental group can be compared. It is crucial that the only difference between the two groups concerns the condition or treatment they receive in regard to the independent variable. This requirement reveals the basic logic of the experimental method. If the two groups are identical in all respects except for the presence or absence of the independent variable, then any difference between the two groups in the dependent variable must be caused by the manipulation of the independent variable. In other words, if the two groups differ in no way other than the variation created by the manipulation of the independent variable, then it is reasonable to infer a causal effect of the independent variable on the dependent variable.

Having identified some of the main features and elements of the experimental approach, let us now consider the method in action, using the procedures and data of one of the most cleverly designed studies in the history of social-personality psychology. Psychologist Stanley Schachter (1959) was intrigued by this proverbial question: Does misery love company? A review of the relevant empirical literature led Schachter to conclude that people who are fearful of something that may happen to them in a novel situation prefer being with someone else, even a total stranger, to being alone. More specifically, he hypothesized that an increase in anxiety would cause a corresponding increase in the preference to be with others (or what psychologists term "the need for affiliation"). To test this hypothesis, Schachter recruited women undergraduates. When subjects arrived for the study, they were greeted by an experimenter in a white laboratory coat who was

TABLE 2-1 DESIGN OF TWO-GROUP EXPERIMENT

Groups	Independent variable	Dependent variable
Experimental	Present	Measured
Control	Absent	Measured

surrounded by a variety of electrical equipment. The experimenter introduced himself as Dr. Zilstein of the Department of Neurology and Psychiatry, and he explained that the purpose of the study was to measure the effects of shock on heart rate and blood pressure. The subjects were then informed (individually) they would receive a series of electric shocks while their pulse and blood pressure were monitored. To manipulate subjects' level of anxiety (the independent variable), Schachter used two different descriptions of the electric shock.

In the ''high-anxiety'' condition, half of the subjects were warned in ominous tones: ''I feel I must be completely honest with you and tell you exactly what you are in for. These shocks will hurt; they will be painful. As you can guess, if, in research of this sort, we're to learn anything at all that will really help humanity, it is necessary that our shocks be intense.'' In the ''low-anxiety'' condition, by contrast, the remaining half of the subjects were told that the shocks would be mild and painless. For example, the subjects were told: ''Do not let the word 'shock' trouble you; I am sure that you will enjoy the experiment. . . . I assure you that what you will feel will not in any way be painful. It will resemble more a tickle or a tingle than anything unpleasant.'' In reality, there was no intention to shock anyone in the study. The instructions given to the subjects were merely intended to create or manipulate different levels of anxiety.

Following the arousal of high and low anxiety, respectively, Dr. Zilstein told the subjects there would be a 10-minute delay while he calibrated the shock apparatus for use. He further explained that subjects might prefer to wait alone or in the company of others in an adjoining room. Each subject was then asked to indicate whether she preferred to wait alone, with others, or had no preference. The subjects' stated preference to be alone or with others, of course, was the dependent variable that interested Schachter, and subjects were not actually shocked in this experiment.

Results of Schachter's study are shown in Table 2-2. As predicted, high-anxiety subjects expressed a much stronger preference for waiting with others than did low-anxiety subjects. The percentage of subjects who preferred to wait with others was nearly twice as high in the high-anxiety condition as in the low-anxiety condition, thus indicating that the manipulation of anxiety level had a pronounced impact on subjects' affiliative behavior.

Schachter (1959) next conducted a follow-up experiment to test the hypothesis

TABLE 2-2   EFFECT OF ANXIETY ON AFFILIATION

| Condition | Waiting preference | | |
	Together	Alone	Don't care
High anxiety	62.5% (N = 20)	9.4% (N = 3)	28.1% (N = 9)
Low anxiety	33.0% (N = 10)	7.0% (N = 2)	60.0% (N = 18)

Source: Adapted from Schachter (1959).

TABLE 2-3 PREFERENCE TO BE WITH OTHERS WHO ARE
CONFRONTED OR NOT CONFRONTED WITH
THE SAME ANXIETY-AROUSING SITUATION

| | Waiting preference | | |
Condition	Together	Alone	Don't care
Could wait with others in the same experiment	60% (N = 6)	0% (N = 0)	40% (N = 4)
Could wait with non-participants	0% (N = 0)	0% (N = 0)	100% (N = 10)

Source: Adapted from Schachter (1959).

that people who feel anxious prefer to affiliate only with others who are going through the same experience. Two groups of women subjects were exposed to the same instructions as the high-anxiety group in the original study. Subjects in one group were given a choice of waiting alone or waiting with other women taking part in the same experiment. Subjects in the other group were given a choice of waiting alone or waiting with women students who were waiting to see their faculty advisors. As displayed in Table 2-3, the results clearly showed that anxious women preferred to wait only with other women subjects in the shock experiment. Schachter summarized his results by concluding that "Misery doesn't love just any company, it loves only miserable company." Subsequent studies have replicated the finding that highly anxious people prefer to affiliate with similar others (Rofe, 1984; Suls & Miller, 1977).

Evaluation of the Experimental Method

Clearly, the experiment is a powerful empirical strategy. Unlike the other strategies we have considered, experimentation allows researchers not only to control and predict phenomena but also to understand them. That, in essence, is what the experimental method is all about. Wherever it can be applied, it provides a certainty of knowledge that cannot be achieved by any other method. Nevertheless, the experimental method does have its limitations, at least for personality psychology. First, it may be unethical to investigate certain questions experimentally, even though it would be simple to do so. For example, psychologists cannot deliberately create conditions that have the potential risk of permanently harming or injuring subjects. Suppose a researcher was interested in studying the effects of chronic loneliness on self-esteem and depression in children. This clearly is a significant empirical issue, but obvious ethical considerations would preclude taking 100 ten-year-olds and randomly assigning 50 of them to an experimental condition in which they are denied the opportunity to establish a network of close relationships!

Another ethical issue centers on deception—that is, misleading or at least not fully informing the subject about the true purpose of an experiment. Recall

Schachter's study of anxiety and affiliation and imagine how you would have felt if you had been one of the participants assigned to the high-anxiety group. An imposing-looking man in a white lab coat announces that, following a short delay, you will be exposed to a series of painful electric shocks. Next you complete a questionnaire inquiring about your affiliative preference and return it to the researcher who, in turn, announces that you won't be shocked after all—it was simply a hoax! No doubt, you might feel foolish even if it was on behalf of science. You may also question whether such deception was actually justified, even if for excellent and scientific reasons. Of course, those who defend the use of deception in research maintain that many aspects of human behavior could not be experimentally investigated if researchers were not permitted to conceal the true purposes of their studies from subjects (Aronson et al., 1985; Christensen, 1988). By the same token, some psychologists (Baumrind, 1985) believe that deception procedures undermine subjects' faith in psychological research and may have lasting negative effects on subjects even when the true nature of a study is disclosed immediately afterward.

Few people now believe that there are simple rules to ensure a balance between the legitimate needs of science and the welfare of human subjects. However, the American Psychological Association (1981) has established a set of ethical principles to guide investigators using human subjects. The essence of these principles includes the following four points: (1) A subject's participation in a study should be voluntary and based on *informed consent*. Subjects should be told in advance about any aspects of the study that might be expected to influence their willingness to participate and should be permitted to withdraw at any time they so desire. (2) Subjects should not be exposed to harmful or dangerous research procedures. If risks of such procedures exist, the investigator should inform the subject of that fact. However, procedures that carry a modest risk of moderate mental discomfort may be acceptable provided that the subject is fully informed and gives his or her voluntary consent. (3) Methodological requirements of a study may necessitate the use of deception regarding matters unrelated to risks. If so, the investigator has a special responsibility to explain and correct any misunderstandings as soon as possible. The deception (cover story) must be disclosed to subjects in a "debriefing" session following the conclusion of the study. (4) Information obtained about a subject during the course of a study must be treated as totally confidential and should never be made available to others without consent of the subject. The subject's right to privacy should never be violated or compromised.

For the personologist, a second major limitation of the experimental research strategy is that too often such research is artificial and limited in relevance to other settings (Carlson, 1984). The criticism is made that experiments carried out in the confines of the laboratory do not depict what a person spontaneously does elsewhere. Furthermore, laboratory experimentation is usually limited to examining phenomena that are of relatively short duration and thus may miss important processes that occur over time. For instance, the results of studies in which college students are crowded into small rooms for 30 minutes may not have much relevance to the long-term effects on behavior of crowded urban living conditions.

For many personologists, then, the only way to really understand personality is to study people's behavior as it occurs in their natural social contexts.

Finally, for all its power, experimental research may be susceptible to certain unintended *artifacts* inherent in the laboratory setting (Rosenthal & Rosnow, 1969). For example, once subjects know they are in an experiment, their behavior may change not because of the manipulation of an independent variable but because they know they are being observed by the experimenter. In addition, subtle cues implicit in the experimental setting may inadvertently communicate that the experimenter has a certain hypothesis and subjects may behave in ways that will confirm it. Such cues are called *demand characteristics* (Orne, 1969) and suggest that the psychological experiment itself is a form of social interaction in which subjects try to guess the purpose and meaning of their involvement and behave accordingly, either to please or frustrate the experimenter. This clearly defeats the power of the experimental method because the subject's observed behavior is influenced by factors not part of the experimental design. Finally, experimenter bias is a possible source of error in research that may lead investigators to unintentionally influence the behavior of their subjects (Rosenthal & Rubin, 1978). Rosenthal (1966) has conducted several studies suggesting that experimenters, without realizing it, send positive nonverbal signals when subjects act in accordance with the experimenters' expectations. To guard against such biasing effects, many studies are now conducted using a double-blind procedure. This strategy requires that neither subjects nor experimenters know to which experimental or control groups the subjects have been assigned.

Critics of the experimental method have not gone unchallenged by defenders of the method. Those who consider the experiment vastly superior to other methods argue that such an approach offers the only legitimate hope for doing hypothesis-testing research. Moreover, it is noted that certain phenomena can be studied in the laboratory that would be quite difficult to study in natural settings (e.g., allowing subjects to be momentarily aggressive in contrast with the commonly held strong inhibitions in real-life situations). Those who defend laboratory experiments also claim there is little empirical support for the assertion that subjects deliberately try to confirm experimental hypotheses—indeed, subjects are more likely to be negativistic than compliant (Berkowitz & Donnerstein, 1982).

What Is the Best Research Strategy?

Our discussion of the three major research strategies used by personality psychologists makes it clear that each has both advantages and disadvantages. The pros and cons associated with each strategy are summarized in Table 2-4. At the same time, it is also evident that there is no one best research strategy in the pursuit of reliable and valid knowledge concerning human personality. Simply stated, no single research method is ideally suited for all purposes and occasions; rather, different questions call for different strategies of study (Duke, 1986). Further, a research method that is appropriate for one question may be entirely inappropriate for another.

TABLE 2-4 SUMMARY OF ADVANTAGES AND DISADVANTAGES ASSOCIATED WITH THREE RESEARCH
METHODS USED BY PERSONALITY PSYCHOLOGISTS

Research method	Advantages	Disadvantages
Case history method	1 Provides an in-depth account of the complexity and uniqueness of the individual.	1 Does not provide a firm basis for deriving general principles of behavior; may lack generalizability.
	2 Avoids artificial and contrived conditions of the laboratory.	2 Data may reflect the interests and personal biases of the investigator.
		3 Cannot disentangle cause-and-effect relationships among variables.
Correlational method	1 Permits study of a broad range of individual difference variables.	1 Cannot demonstrate conclusively that variables are causally related.
	2 Permits study of variables in natural, real-world settings.	2 Possible confounding caused by "third variable" problems.
	3 May determine whether information on one variable can be used to predict a second variable in the future.	3 Reliability and validity of self-report scales may be questionable.
Experimental method	1 Permits isolation and manipulation of specific variables.	1 Ethical issues restrict range of phenomena that can be studied in the laboratory.
	2 Establishes cause-and-effect relationships; statements of causality.	2 Artificial laboratory setting may limit generalizability of findings to other settings.
	3 Collects, records, and analyzes data objectively.	3 Experimental artifacts (e.g., evaluation apprehension, demand characteristics, experimenter bias) may confound variable manipulation.

Much of the ingenuity and creativity in personality research involves selecting
and tailoring the method to the theoretical issue at hand. Beyond this, however, it
should be recognized that personologists do have distinct preferences concerning
how phenomena of interest should be investigated. Preferences regarding how
research should be conducted are due in large part to the fact that different
theoretical perspectives tend to focus attention on phenomena amenable to study
only by using a particular strategy. It is not surprising, for example, that phenomena emphasized by the psychodynamic perspective (such as unconscious
processes and early childhood experiences) have been more extensively studied
by way of the case history approach than by reliance on experimental procedures.
In turn, the link between theoretical focus and preferred method of study suggests
that the research enterprise in personology is a distinct human endeavor. This
point should be kept in mind as we consider empirical evidence in support of
various theoretical propositions in ensuing chapters. Although the goal of all
personality research is to establish facts and principles that can be understood
within a broader framework, perhaps the most that can ever be achieved is partial
understanding. Even so, to replace total ignorance with even partial understanding of the complexities of human behavior appears to be a laudable goal.

PERSONALITY ASSESSMENT

A pervasive theme in the study of personality is individual differences in people's behavior and experience. In pursuing the study of individual differences—how are people different from one another—personologists deal with two related concerns. First, they are interested in describing the host of ways in which people are different. This concern is evidenced by the incredible number of theoretical concepts that personologists have used to describe what is distinctive about an individual. Terms such as *trait, type, motive, value, temperament, schema, belief,* and *factor* represent a mere sampling of the conceptual units that have been used to depict the enduring aspects of human behavior. Second, personologists are interested in developing ways of measuring individual differences (a process called *assessment*). This concern, and the focus of this section, is evidenced by an equally imposing array of psychological tests that personologists have used to determine the individual's distinctive qualities, including thoughts, feelings, and motivations. Individual differences in personality are measured in quantitative terms. Quantification refers to the assessment of personality variables in ways that permit psychologists to express their measurements in numbers (typically based on test scores) rather than in words. As an example, instead of asking, "Is Fred shy?", psychologists ask, "How shy is Fred, relative to others?" In sharp contrast, personality descriptions given by people when engaging in informal observations are rather vague and ambiguous. Consider the description of someone as a "wild and reckless" type. What does this description convey? The problem is that it may convey different meanings to different people. For some, it may mean that this person is quite dangerous and unpredictable. For others, it may simply mean that the person would be the life of the party. Thus, as colorful as they are, informal personality descriptions make it difficult to communicate accurately. To avoid the ambiguity of imprecise descriptions, personality psychologists attempt to provide precise quantitative descriptions of individuals. Formal personality assessment not only makes it possible to obtain information about individual differences in a meaningful and exact manner but also makes it possible to communicate this information to others in a clear and unambiguous fashion.

Testing and Measurement Concepts

There are several important testing concepts that will surface in our subsequent discussion of how personologists assess specific characteristics of people. In particular, assessment techniques must meet four technical criteria before they can be considered scientifically acceptable measures of individual differences in people's enduring qualities. These criteria are standardization, norms, reliability, and validity.

Standardization   A key aspect in the measurement of personality dimensions is that of *standardization*. This concept refers to the uniform procedures that are followed in the administration and scoring of an assessment tool. In the case of a self-report scale, for instance, the examiner must make every effort to ensure that subjects read and understand the printed instructions, respond to the same questions, and stay within any stated time limits. Standardization also involves information (usually contained in an accompanying manual) about the conditions under which the assessment test should or should not be given, who should or should not take the test (sample group), specific procedures for scoring the test, and the interpretive significance of the scores.

Norms The standardization of a personality assessment test includes information concerning whether a particular "raw score" ranks low, high, or average relative to other "raw scores" on the test. Such information, called *test norms*, provides standards with which the scores of various individuals who take the test later can be compared. Usually, the raw scores on a test are converted into percentile scores, which indicate the percentage of people who score at or below a particular score. For example, you might take a 30-item depression scale and obtain a raw score of 18 (that is, you responded in the keyed direction for depression on 18 of the items). The score of 18 has virtually no meaning unless you consult the test norms and learn that it corresponds to the seventy-fifth percentile. This information indicates that you appear to be more depressed than 75 percent of the sample of pretested people that provided the comparative basis for the test norms. Thus, test norms permit the comparison of individual scores to a representative group so as to quantify the individual's relative rank standing to others.

Reliability Another requirement of all personality assessment techniques is that they must have demonstrated *reliability*. This means that repeated administrations of the same test or another form of the test should yield reasonably similar results or scores. Thus, reliability refers to the consistency or stability of an assessment technique when given to the same group of people on two different occasions. This kind of reliability is termed *test–retest reliability* (Anastasi, 1988). To determine test–retest reliability, the scores from the first administration are correlated with those of the second by a simple correlation procedure. The magnitude of the resulting correlation coefficient gives us an estimate of the test's consistency over time. Although there are no fixed guidelines about acceptable levels of reliability, the reliability coefficients for most standardized psychological tests are above $+.70$. The closer this statistic approaches $+1.00$, the more reliable the test is (i.e., when retested, people's scores tend to match their first scores quite closely). A second kind of reliability is determined by splitting the test into two sets (e.g., odd-numbered items versus even-numbered items), summing people's scores for each set, and correlating the two sets of summed scores with each other. The correlation between these sets is termed *split-half reliability* and reflects the test's internal consistency. If the composite set of test items is consistently measuring the same underlying personality dimension, then people who score high on odd items should also score high on even items, and people who score low on odd items should also score low on even items (again reflected in a high positive correlation).

A third type of reliability is based on the correlation of two versions of the same test (made up of similar items) administered to the same group of individuals. If the scores on these different forms are about the same, the test yields *reliability of parallel forms*. In such a case, the correlation of two parallel forms would indicate that the items on both tests measure the same thing.

Finally, reliability also applies to the degree of agreement between two or more judges in scoring the same assessment test. This is called *interscorer reliability* and must be demonstrated whenever scoring involves subjective interpretations, such as those made by personologists examining projective data. Interscorer reliability tends to be especially low with qualitative data in general, such as interview conversations, dream reports, and other open-ended response formats that are not objectively quantified. However, agreement is increased when judges use manuals with explicit scoring rules and instructions for analyzing such data (Yin, 1984).

Validity   Although quite important, reliability is not the only crucial concept in personality assessment. Of perhaps even greater importance is the question of whether or not a test measures what it is intended to measure or predicts what it is supposed to predict. This issue has to do with a cardinal criterion of an assessment technique's worth—the concept of *validity*. Psychologists frequently distinguish among three kinds of validity: (1) content validity, (2) criterion-related validity, and construct validity.

Content Validity   To be considered valid, an assessment device must include items whose contents are representative of the entire domain or dimension it purports to measure. For instance, suppose you were to take a personality test measuring shyness. If content-valid, such a test should include items that actually reflect the personal (e.g., "Is your shyness a major source of personal discomfort?"), social (e.g., "Do you get embarrassed when speaking in front of a large group?"), and cognitive (e.g., "Do you believe that others are always judging you?") aspects of shyness. A content-valid test of shyness would assess each of these components defining the construct of shyness. Content validity is almost entirely determined by agreement among experts that each item does in fact represent aspects of the variable or attribute being measured.

Criterion-Related Validity   Personality assessment is commonly undertaken for the purpose of making predictions about specific aspects of an individual's behavior. The behavioral criterion being predicted may include academic performance in graduate school, suitability for a therapy program, and occupational success, to cite a few examples. The extent to which a test accurately forecasts some agreed-upon criterion measure is determined by correlating subjects' scores on the test with their scores on the independently measured criterion. For example, suppose the criterion is success in law school as measured by law school grade point average (GPA). The Law School Aptitude Test would be validated if it accurately predicted the criterion (i.e., law school GPA).

There are two subtypes of criterion-related validity. The first is called *predictive validity* and involves determining the capacity of a test to predict some criterion behavior in the future. An intelligence test has predictive validity if it accurately predicts subsequent grades in school. The second is called *concurrent validity* and involves determining the extent to which a test correlates significantly with another currently existing criterion measure. For example, if patients' scores on a test that measures paranoid tendencies are positively correlated with the ratings of paranoid tendencies made by clinical psychologists, concurrent validity exists. Of course, the clinicians must not have prior knowledge of the patients' paranoid test scores. Otherwise, their ratings may be biased by their knowledge, a situation called *criterion contamination.*

Construct Validity   The third type of measurement validation, and the one most crucial to personality assessment as a whole, is called *construct validity.* The concept of construct validity addresses the question of how well a test measures something that, in reality, is but a useful abstract invention (Cronbach & Meehl, 1955). The abstract nature of many psychological constructs—such as self-actualization, ego identity, social interest, and repression—makes this approach complicated and the results uncertain. Simply stated, there are no firmly established criterion measures for these and other abstract concepts of personality functioning (or what are otherwise called *hypothetical constructs*). Although it may be possible to observe instances of repression, for example, repression per se cannot be directly observed. It has no physical reality. Furthermore, a hypothetical construct whose presence cannot be inferred by some behavior criterion is useless in personality psychology, which takes an empirical approach to knowledge. It is at this point that concern for construct validity comes into play.

Construct validation is the process whereby evidence is gathered to demonstrate that a test measures a particular hypothetical construct derived from a theory. It is an elaborate and laborious process requiring several studies that examine the correlations between test scores and whatever measures assumed to be related to the construct in question. One way to do this involves correlating test scores of the construct in question with scores from another test that purportedly measures the same construct. This procedure is technically known as *convergent validation* (Campbell & Fiske, 1959). Suppose we have a new test that we think measures the construct of self-esteem. If our new test does, in fact, measure self-esteem, it should correlate positively with another established and validated measure of self-esteem. Further, if several different self-esteem measures agree with each other and with our new test, we have some evidence for the construct validity of our new test of self-esteem.

Another way to demonstrate construct validity is to show that an assessment device does not correlate with measures of qualities that it was not intended to measure—notably qualities unrelated to the conceptual definition that the theorist formulated. This aspect of the validation process is technically termed *divergent validity* (Campbell & Fiske, 1959). For example, if our new self-esteem test does not correlate with measures of other, conceptually distinct qualities, we have evidence of discriminant validity (since our self-esteem measure is discriminated from non-self-esteem measures, as it should be). This is an important step in establishing the construct validity of an assessment technique.

The complexities involved in demonstrating the construct validity of a personality assessment technique extend well beyond the scope of this text. However, as we now shift attention to different kinds of approaches to the assessment of personality, we should keep in mind that the value of any assessment device is ultimately determined by evidence supporting its construct validity. If an assessment technique shows signs of poor construct validity, then using the technique could result in findings that have nothing to do with the concept the personologist wants to examine.

TYPES OF ASSESSMENT TECHNIQUES

A variety of assessment techniques are available to personologists in gathering information about people. They include questionnaires, inkblots, personal documents, behavioral assessment procedures, peer judgments, and what people reveal when asked questions about themselves. Each has specific strengths and weaknesses regarding the kinds of responses obtained, scoring, interpretation, reliability, and validity. In this section, we will consider three ways to measure or assess an individual's personality: interviews, self-report personality tests, and projective techniques.

Interview Assessment Techniques

The interview is one of the oldest and most widely used methods of collecting information about persons (Aiken, 1984). In the interview, the personologist obtains information from the person being evaluated by asking relevant questions and listening to answers. The interviewer and respondent engage in a face-to-face dialogue for the purpose of achieving a specific goal. In fact, the way in which an interview is conducted depends on the particular objective or goal in question. An employment interview, for instance, seeks to assess the personality characteristics of a job applicant. A research interview aims to gather information about a person concerning a specific research topic under investigation. A clinical interview has as its goal the diagnosis of a patient's problems and the type of therapy technique that may be most appropriate for a given diagnosis. There is considerable variety in the degree to which interviews may be *structured* or *unstructured*. In the former type of interview, questions are carefully worded and skillfully presented in a prescribed order. The structured format is illustrated by the following sequence of predesigned questions: "How long have you been

A competent interviewer can obtain valuable information about the individual's personality, social and family relationships, and plans for the future. *(Christopher Morrow/Stock, Boston)*

married?'' ''How many children do you and your spouse have?'' ''Do you believe that children should be allowed to do whatever they want?'' ''If you had a teenager would you allow him or her to quit school and take a part-time job?'' As can be seen, the most personal and potentially threatening questions appeared last. The strategy behind asking general and innocuous questions first is that they should be least threatening for respondents and pave the way for divulging more intimate information once they have developed a sense of trust toward the interviewer (White & Spiesman, 1982).

In the unstructured interview, by contrast, questions are phrased in such a way as to allow the person considerable latitude in responding. The interviewer may comment, ''You feel that your spouse really lets you down,'' or ''That must have been a very stressful experience.'' The respondent is free to reveal whatever information he or she desires to such questions. In turn, the interviewer may abandon a certain line of questioning if it seems to be generating no useful information and pursue some other area of questioning. Compared to a structured interview, an unstructured one allows the personologist more flexibility to probe the respondent's thoughts and feelings in the context of give-and-take exchange.

Strengths and Weaknesses of Interview Techniques   Interview asssessment, when used by a highly skilled interviewer, can produce extremely valuable information about the individual's personality and life situation. The ability to communicate effectively with others, perceptions of self and significant others, level of anxiety, plans for the future, and job satisfaction are a few examples of data that can be obtained from a well-conducted interview. A well-planned interview can also be profitably used in hypothesis-testing research. At the same time, issues of reliability and validity may arise in the event that respondents are free to ramble about their past and present life experiences. Indeed, there is scant evidence that unstructured interviews have much reliability or validity. Structuring the kinds of questions asked of the person is one way to make interview information more reliable and valid. This is why the structured format tends to be favored in the research setting, whereas the unstructured format tends to be favored by clinical psychologists in the therapeutic setting.

As just noted, the interview technique provides a rich source of personality data. Nevertheless, the interpretation of such data is highly subjective and may reflect the theoretical biases of the interviewer. Further, the impact of the interviewer's own personality can subtly influence how truthful and disclosing the person will be in an assessment setting. This can result in the withholding or distorting of information vital to the purpose of an interview. Still, an assessment interview, especially when supplemented by more objective sources of data, is one of the most basic and indispensable of all assessment techniques.

Self-Report Assessment Techniques

No account of the assessment of individual differences would be complete without a discussion of *self-report inventories*. In fact, self-report inventories are more widely used than any form of personality assessment. These are paper-and-pencil tests that ask people to respond to questions concerning their traits, values, attitudes, motives, feelings, interests, and abilities. Numerous examples of these tests appear throughout this book. The term "self-report" as used here refers to any information the person reveals directly about him- or herself by responding to specific questions or items with a limited number of prescribed choices (e.g., "yes," "no," "always," "don't know"). Figure 2-3 illustrates different types of response formats commonly used in self-report personality measures.

A general feature of self-report tests is standardization of response alternatives (see Figure 2-3). That is, people taking the tests have to select either true or false, agree or disagree, an alternative that varies from 1 (very characteristic of me) to 6, and so on. In this way, objectivity is achieved by restricting the degree of freedom people have in responding to test items. Similarly, standardization of scoring procedures minimizes the risk of personal bias of the person scoring the test.

Self-report inventories differ in regard to the number of personality dimensions they measure at one time. *Single-trait tests* usually are developed and used by academic researchers to measure some specific aspect of personality. The researchers then examine whether people who score at the upper and lower ends on the trait measure perform differently on a behavioral measure or differ on other

FIGURE 2-3 EXAMPLES OF DIFFERENT RESPONSE FORMATS USED IN SELF-REPORT PERSONALITY SCALES

I feel angry when others criticize me. Yes No Uncertain (Circle your answer)	

| I worry a lot about people like me. | 1. Very characteristic of me
2. Moderately characteristic of me
3. Characteristic of me
4. Uncharacteristic of me
5. Moderately uncharacteristic of me
6. Very uncharacteristic of me | (Circle the number that best describes you) |

I do my best to keep my emotions under control.   (Circle the point that best fits your feelings)

Never   Rarely   Sometimes   Often   Always

friendly ____	cautious ____	(Check those adjectives that are characteristic of you)
depressed ____	dominant ____	
reliable ____	secure ____	

I feel pretty bad when I tell a lie.

  -3 -2 -1 0   1   2   3   (Circle the number that indicates your degree of agreement or disagreement)

Strongly   Strongly
disagree   agree

self-report measures. An implicit assumption of this methodology is that the trait dimension being measured applies equally well to all individuals. In other words, any person participating in the study may receive a high score (or may receive a medium or low score), but every person's score is equally meaningful as a representation of that person's personality. Some single-dimension tests also provide separate measures of two or three traits. Examples of single-trait tests include the State-Trait Anxiety Inventory (Spielberger et al., 1970), the Locus of Control Scale (Rotter, 1966), the Sensation Seeking Scale (Zuckerman, 1978), and the Self-Monitoring Scale (Snyder, 1974). The scores obtained from these tests are assumed to reflect relatively stable individual differences along specific trait dimensions. In addition to single-trait scales, there are many self-report inventories that measure several personality dimensions simultaneously. These *multidimensional tests* have the advantage of providing a more comprehensive overview of the person being assessed and are used extensively in clinical, counseling, and personnel settings. For instance, the Sixteen Personality Factor Questionnaire (16-PF) is a 187-item test which measures 16 source traits of the normal personality identified by Raymond Cattell (1965). Scores derived from each of the source trait measures (e.g., submissive–dominant, trusting–suspicious, and practical–imaginative) are plotted on a graph to provide a personality profile. This profile may be used by psychologists who work in applied settings and are called upon to

Psychologists rely heavily on self-report inventories to assess what an individual's personality is like. Some of these inventories are designed to measure several different trait dimensions; others assess only a particular personality trait. *(Hazel Hankin)*

make important employment and promotion decisions about people. Many multidimensional tests have evolved through decades of research. We will examine a representative example in a moment. First, however, let us consider a single-trait test of personality.

Single-Trait Tests   There are literally hundreds of single-trait tests available to researchers and new tests are being developed all the time as needed for investigative purposes. Space permits the description of only one such test here.

The Self-Consciousness Scale   This scale was developed by Fenigstein et al. (1975) to measure two distinct dimensions of self-consciousness. The first subscale assesses private self-consciousness, defined as the extent to which test takers are aware of their own moods, attitudes, thoughts, and bodily states. Sample items include:

1 I'm always trying to figure myself out.
2 I'm quick to notice changes in my mood.
3 I think about myself a lot.

The second subscale measures public self-consciousness, or the extent to which people are aware of and concerned about themselves in social situations. Sample items include:

1 I'm concerned about the way I present myself.
2 I usually worry about making a good impression.
3 I'm self-conscious about the way I look.

Like other well-constructed trait measures, test–retest correlations indicate that both of these self-conscious subscales have reasonably good reliability. In addition, normative data show an absence of gender differences. The validity of the test has been established by comparing the social behavior of people who score high and low, respectively, on each subscale. Many studies indicate that people who score high in private self-consciousness behave in ways that are more consistent with their inner traits, values, and attitudes (Fenigstein, 1987; Carver & Scheier, 1987). In addition, these high scorers are better able to predict how they will act in a variety of circumstances and are more acutely aware of their emotional reactions to events (Scheier et al., 1978; Scheier & Carver, 1977). Not surprisingly, people who score high in public self-consciousness are more sensitive to what others think of them and conform more to social norms to avoid negative evaluations than do those who score low on this trait. People who score high on this subscale are also more concerned with their physical appearance than those who score low.

Multidimensional Tests   As noted previously, these tests typically are used by psychologists to evaluate the diagnostic status of clients or to make personnel decisions about people. Next we will examine the most extensively used and researched multidimensional personality test.

The Minnesota Multiphasic Personality Inventory   The most widely used multi-trait self-report test is the MMPI (Lubin et al., 1985). It was originally devised by Hathaway and McKinley (1943) to aid clinical psychologists in the diagnosis of psychological disorders. The developers also believed that this test would be useful in evaluating the effectiveness of psychotherapy. Hathaway and McKinley used an empirical strategy to construct the MMPI. Specifically, they administered hundreds of true–false items to several groups of people in mental institutions who had been diagnosed as having certain psychological disorders. These diagnoses had been determined through psychiatric interviews with the patients. The control group consisted of relatives and friends of the patients, who were tested when they came to visit them. The responses were then analyzed empirically, and those items that a diagnostic group answered differently than the control group were retained for the test. For instance, if people who had been diagnosed as depressed were more likely to answer false to "I usually feel that life is interesting and worthwhile," this item became part of the depression scale. By systematically carrying out this procedure on patient groups with different psychiatric diagnoses, the test developers established 10 separate "clinical scales" (see Table 2-5). The test also has 4 "validity scales" that assess whether the person was careless, deceptive, or misunderstood the instructions in taking the test (see Table 2-5). The "lie scale," for instance, indicates the extent to which a person responds in a socially desirable but untruthful way to statements in order to be viewed in a favorable manner ("I can't remember ever having a bad night's sleep").

An updated and restandardized version of the MMPI was published in 1989. Known as the MMPI-2, this test is approximately the same length (567 items) as the original inventory, but is different in a number of ways. Items with sexist wording and outmoded content have been modified, items with objectionable content have been eliminated, and national norms that are more representative of the present population have been calculated. These and other significant revisions should enhance the value of the MMPI-2 and make it preferable over the original version of the test.

Two general approaches are used when interpreting MMPI data: clinical and actuarial. In *clinical interpretation* an expert inspects each of the scale scores, notes the features of the profiles (such as clustering of certain high scale scores), and adds a mix of personal experience about individuals of each profile type to make inferences regarding the pathological problems and traits of the person. By contrast, when an *actuarial interpretation* is made, the psychologist (or computer) merely checks MMPI atlases that provide empirically established characteristics which describe each profile class or code type. The process of comparing the profile of a person with a large number of previous profiles leads to an interpretation based on statistical baserates and norms (without any subjective evaluation by the psychologist). Matching the person's profile with previous MMPI test takers also enables the clinician to determine the appropriate diagnostic category and course of therapy to be undertaken.

Though the MMPI has proved to be a valuable diagnostic tool, it is by no means limited in usage to the clinical setting (Kunce & Anderson, 1984). It is also used to determine whether individuals have personality attributes that are either compatible or incompatible with the demands of a job being sought (Dahlstrom et al., 1975). However, use of the test as a screening device for job applicants has become quite controversial. In fact, lawsuits have been filed concerning the question of whether the test constitutes an invasion of privacy (Dahlstrom, 1980).

The MMPI has also been used extensively in studies concerning family dynamics, eating disorders, substance abuse, suicide, and readiness for treatment or rehabilitation (Butcher & Keller, 1984). In addition, it has been the chief source of items for a number of other personality tests, including the Taylor Manifest Anxiety Scale (Taylor, 1953), the Jackson Personality Inventory (Jackson, 1974), and the California Psychological Inventory (Gough, 1987). Finally, the fact that the MMPI has been translated into nearly 125 foreign languages is a testimonial to its popularity and value as a clinical assessment technique (Butcher, 1984).

TABLE 2-5 SUBSCALES OF THE MMPI, INCLUDING SAMPLE ITEMS SIMILAR IN CONTENT TO ILLUSTRATE THOSE ON THE MMPI, AND CHARACTERISTIC DESCRIPTIONS ASSOCIATED WITH HIGH SCORES

Clinical scales	Sample item (with keyed response)	Characteristics associated with high scores
Hypochon-driasis (Hs)	At times I get strong cramps in my intes-tines (True)	Indicates person is cynical, hostile, and complaining and has abnormal concern with bodily functions
Depression (D)	I am often very tense on the job (True)	Indicates person is distressed, pessimistic, and shy
Hysteria (Hy)	Sometimes there is a feeling like some-thing is pressing in on my head (True)	Indicates person is repressed and depen-dent and has multiple but unfounded physical complaints
Psychopathic deviate (Pd)	My activities and interests are often criti-cized by others (True)	May indicate antisocial and impulsive be-havior leading to trouble with legal or authority figures
Cannot say (?)	Number of items left unanswered or marked "cannot say"	High scores may indicate evasiveness
Lie scale (L)	I smile at everyone I meet (True)	Indicates a tendency to portray oneself in an overly favorable light
Frequency scale (F)	There is an international plot against me (True)	Suggest carelessness, confusion, or faking bad in responding to it
Correction scale (K)	I feel bad when others criticize me (False)	Measures defensiveness or denial of symptoms
Masculinity–femininity (MF)	I like to arrange flowers (False)	Indicates females are aggressive and re-bellious and males are passive and esthetic
Paranoia (P)	There are evil people trying to influence my mind (True)	Often indicates abnormal suspiciousness, delusions of persecution or grandeur, and guardedness
Psychas-thenia (Pt)	The things that run through my head sometimes are horrible (True)	Indicates person is anxious and rigid and feels inadequate
Schizo-phrenia (Sc)	Things around me do not seem real (True)	Indicates person is withdrawn and has pe-culiar ideas and perhaps hallucinations and delusions
Hypomania (Ma)	Sometimes I think so fast I can't keep up (True)	Indicates person is hyperactive, impulsive, optimistic, and in some instances confused or disoriented
Social intro-version (Si)	I have the time of my life at parties (False)	Often indicates person is shy, disinterested in others, and uninvolved in social rela-tionships

Strengths and Weaknesses of Self-Report Techniques   Assessment of individual differences is a vital aspect of personology. Given the empirical nature of this issue, you may wonder why so much emphasis has been placed on self-reports as the basis for measuring those differences. Perhaps the major reason is that self-report tests provide more thorough, precise, and systematic information about an individual's personality than does casual information. The objectivity of scoring minimizes any personal or theoretical bias on the part of the person scoring a self-report test. In addition, self-report measures can be administered easily by someone with relatively little formal training. Self-report tests usually have greater reliability than do other assessment techniques—a definite advantage. Finally, multidimensional inventories allow for measurement of several different personality traits at once.

Despite their popularity among professional psychologists, self-report tests do have problems that need to be considered. The major limitations of self-report tests are that they are susceptible to deliberate deception, the influence of social desirability, and response sets (Kleinmuntz, 1982).

Personologists who use self-report techniques must depend on the willingness of respondents to give accurate information about themselves. This poses no problem provided that test takers are honest in their responses. However, some self-report scales are dominated by transparent items, making it relatively easy for people to give misleading information about themselves. Deliberate deception is most likely to occur when the person believes there is something to be gained from fraudulent responding (Furnham, 1990). A job applicant might "fake good" by intentionally agreeing with those items he or she believes will create a favorable impression in an employment situation. Alternatively, a person might also "fake bad" by intentionally endorsing items that he or she believes will create the impression of being more psychologically disturbed than is actually true. This might occur in a situation where a person is being assessed to determine competency to face charges for a criminal offense.

The best defense against this problem is to build safeguards into tests to detect deliberate deception. The MMPI, for example, includes validity scales designed to indicate whether respondents are lying, defensive, or evasive when answering the test items. Another option is to include filler items that can make the purpose of a test less obvious to a person. Nevertheless, these efforts may be only partially successful in detecting the extent to which a respondent is engaging in conscious deception. If possible, important decisions about a person should not be based on self-report data alone.

Another shortcoming of self-report scales is the tendency among some people to respond to items in ways that make them "look good." This tendency is called *social desirability* and is a problem that can occur in all assessment techniques, not just self-reports. Unlike deliberate deception, people who display social desirability bias may be unaware of their tendency to slant answers in a favorable direction as opposed to giving candid answers. They unintentionally present themselves in a favorable light that probably does not correspond to reality.

Several strategies may be used to detect or reduce the problem of social desirability response bias. Some self-report tests (such as the MMPI) include questions intended to assess the likelihood that a respondent is giving socially desirable answers. Other tests are constructed to directly measure the extent to which people give self-flattering responses. For example, the Marlowe-Crowne Social Desirability Scale (Crowne & Marlowe, 1964) is designed to measure the tendency of people to present themselves in a favorable light. Another way to deal with the problem is to carefully evaluate the social desirability of each item before it is included in a test. In any event, it is clear that assessment psychologists must be cognizant of the potential contaminating bias of social desirability when interpreting test scores.

A final problem associated with self-report measures is the tendency of some people to respond in a particular way regardless of the content of the items. For instance, some people are more likely than others to agree with virtually every question on a test. This *acquiescence response set* is a major problem on self-report scales that require a true–false or a yes–no answer (like the MMPI). Furthermore, if this response set is not counteracted in some way, the scores of highly acquiescent people will be distorted and not accurately reflect their personality traits. Fortunately, the acquiescence response tendency is a relatively easy problem to counter. Many test makers phrase the items so that true or false or yes or no responses are equally likely to be indicative of the trait being measured. Thus, any bias coming from the tendency to respond "true" or "yes" is balanced when the test is scored.

Projective Assessment Techniques

Projective tests of personality are primarily designed to assist the clinical psychologist in diagnosing the nature and severity of a particular person's emotional disturbance. The rationale for these tests is based on Freud's theory that unconscious processes are important for understanding psychopathology. Accordingly, the purpose of projective personality assessment is to uncover the person's unconscious conflicts, fears, and concerns. Frank (1939) coined the term *projective technique* to describe assessment methods that present people with ambiguous stimuli for which there is no obvious culturally defined meaning. Such techniques, which share a rather indirect approach to personality assessment, allow people to "project" upon ambiguous material their feelings, needs, attitudes, and ways of viewing life. The responses elicited by the test stimuli (such as inkblots or vague pictures) presumably reveal signs of pent-up impulses, ego defenses, and other "interior" aspects of personality. All projective techniques share a set of important features. They all use ambiguous or unstructured test stimuli. The test taker is never told the purpose of the test or how responses will be scored or interpreted. Instructions emphasize that there are no correct or incorrect answers and that the test taker is free to respond in any manner he or she sees fit. Finally, scoring and interpretation relies heavily on subjective clinical judgments.

There are a number of different types of projective techniques. Lindzey (1959) has sorted these techniques into five different categories. They are:

1 Associative techniques require people to respond to a stimulus with the first word, thought, or feeling that comes to mind. Examples include the Menninger Word Association Test (Rapaport et al., 1968) and the Rorschach Inkblot Test (Rorschach, 1942).

2 Constructive techniques require people to create or construct something. In the Thematic Apperception Test (Morgan & Murray, 1935), for example, a series of pictures of simple scenes are presented to people who are asked to tell stories about what is happening in the scenes and what the characters are feeling.

3 Completion techniques direct people to complete the thought begun in an incomplete stimulus such as a sentence (e.g., "What annoys me . . ."). Two examples are the Picture-Frustration Study (Rosenzwerg, 1945) and the Rotter Incomplete Sentences Test (Rotter & Rafferty, 1950).

4 Expressive techniques ask people to express themselves through such activities as drawing a picture or acting out their feelings in a psychodrama. The Draw-A-Person Test (Machover, 1949), for example, requires individuals to draw a picture of a person and then to draw one of the opposite sex.

5 Choice or ordering techniques require people to select from or arrange in

The Draw-A-Person Test is a projective technique commonly used by psychologists to assess children's inner thoughts and feelings. *(Peter Vandermark/ Stock, Boston)*

some preferred order a set of test stimuli. For example, the Szondi Test (Szondi, 1944) instructs people to choose from a set of pictures of individuals those they like best and those they like least. These techniques are now seldom used.

It should be added that these five categories of projective techniques are not mutually exclusive. Many projective tests use two or more techniques.

To give you a better understanding of the administration, scoring, and interpretation of projective tests, we will focus on one that is frequently used to assess unconscious processes—the Rorschach Inkblot Test.

The Rorschach Inkblot Test   Hermann Rorschach, a Swiss psychiatrist, developed the Rorschach Inkblot Test in 1921. In the ensuing years it has become the most popular and widely used projective technique (Sweeney et al., 1987). The test consists of a series of ten cards. Each card contains bilaterally symmetrical inkblots that Rorschach produced by spilling ink on a piece of paper and then folding the paper in half (see Figure 2-4). Five of the cards are black and white (with shades of gray) and the remaining five are colored. Each blot is printed at the center of a white cardboard card with an approximate size of 7 by 10 inches. The Rorschach usually is administered by a single examiner to a single person in a two-stage procedure. The first stage begins with the examiner encouraging the person to relax and to respond to the test stimuli in a spontaneous fashion. Next, the examiner says: "I am going to show you a series of inkblots, and I want you to tell me what you see in each of them." The person then takes each card (in predetermined order), looks at it, and describes what he or she sees in the inkblot, or what the inkblot suggests or resembles. Meanwhile, the examiner records exactly what the person says about each blot (e.g., "That reminds me of two bears dancing around a campfire"). This verbatim record or protocol is then analyzed. The examiner also monitors the person's behavior during the test, especially noting specific gestures and how long it takes the person to respond to each blot.

After responding to all ten inkblots, the person is shown the inkblots in the same order once again. During this stage, called "the inquiry," the examiner attempts to establish what characteristics of the inkblot determined the person's earlier response. If, for example, the person said the first card reminded him or her of an elephant, then the examiner would ask: "What was it about the blot that caused you to see an elephant?" Basically, the examiner is concerned with two questions during this second phase of the procedure. First, relative to each of the person's responses, what portion of the card does the response represent? Second, what features or qualities of the blot led to the response (e.g., shape, color, human or animal characteristics)? These questions must be asked about each response given by the person.

Several systems have been devised for scoring and interpreting the Rorschach (Beck, 1945; Klopfer & Davidson, 1962; Piotrowski, 1957). Each system is complicated and requires extensive training in clinical assessment as well as knowledge of personality theory, psychopathology, and development psychology. Regardless of the system used, virtually all of them evaluate the person's responses on the basis of four scoring factors (Klopfer & Davidson, 1962):

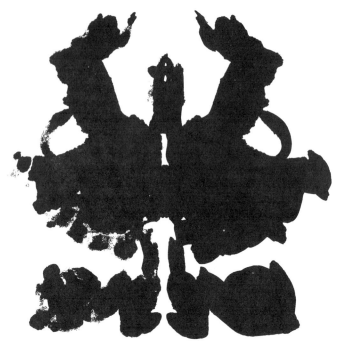

FIGURE 2-4   An inkblot similar to those used in the Rorschach Test. The person is asked to explain what he or she sees in the inkblot. (*Lisa Brusso*)

1 *Location* refers to which part or area of the blot prompted the response. The examiner is especially interested in determining if the person's response related to the entire blot, the space surrounding the blot, or a minor or unusual detail of the blot.

2 *Determinants* represent the features of the blot (e.g., form, color, shading, apparent movement) that were important in determining the person's response. For instance, a color determinant is scored if a person reports seeing blood stains in the blot because parts of the blot are red.

3 *Content* reflects the subject matter of the person's response—whether it is human, animal, plant, object, and so on. Most systems for scoring content specify several categories for classifying responses, such as human figures, animal figures, sexual objects, clothing, and geography.

4 *Popular/original* focus on how typical or atypical a given response is in relation to normative data for a particular Rorschach card. This is usually a category scored in terms of degree since the large number of responses recorded for the Rorschach make it rather unlikely that a totally unique response will be given.

Further analysis is based on the frequency of responses that fall into each of the above-mentioned categories. Ratios of one category to others may also be computed to provide additional personality information. Such scoring schemes represent a quantitative approach to the test because a variety of numerical scores on several different dimensions are generated. Of equal significance, however, is an analysis of the actual content of a person's responses, which constitutes a qualitative approach to the test. Content of responses (whether, for instance, the person sees mostly humans or animals) makes a great deal of difference in the interpretation of the person's personality characteristics.

How useful is the Rorschach in assessing personality? From an empirical perspective, researchers are quite skeptical about the psychometric properties of the test (Anastasi, 1988; Gamble, 1972; Kendall & Norton-Ford, 1982). Specifically, its internal reliability is low, its test–retest reliability is low, and both its concurrent and predictive validity are questionable in the majority of cases (Peterson, 1978). Further complicating the picture is the fact that the Rorschach lacks acceptable interjudge reliability. Studies generally find disappointingly low agreement rates between two or more judges scoring the same test responses. In short, without adequate reliability and validity data, skeptics challenge the usefulness of the Rorschach as an assessment strategy.

To overcome these and other problems, researchers have sought to develop scoring schemes with better psychometric properties. Noteworthy for its effort to standardize the Rorschach by developing objective criteria and norms for children and adults is a system devised by Exner (1978; 1986). Called the Comprehensive System, this attempt at standardization suggests that the Rorschach can be a good assessment tool. Efforts have also been made to interpret Rorschach responses by computer and to create an inkblot system with parallel forms that can be group-administered (Holtzman, 1988). Despite these advances, the Rorschach is still not widely accepted for assessment purposes outside the clinical setting.

The controversy surrounding the Rorschach is not likely to subside in the near future. Despite efforts to establish reliable and valid scoring systems of the type being developed by Exner (1986), empirically minded psychologists will continue to criticize the soundness and validity of the test as an adequate measure of personality functioning. Likewise, many psychologists will continue to use the test in clinical practice regardless of what research says about the instrument. Even if the Rorschach is regarded only as a supplemental diagnostic tool, however, it is not likely that its popularity will decline in the foreseeable future (Lubin et al., 1985).

Strengths and Weaknesses of Projective Techniques   Proponents of projective tests claim that they possess two unique strengths. First, the testing stimuli are relatively ambiguous to people. As such, the person does not know how the test provides information to the examiner. It is this rather indirect method that makes it possible to help disguise the real purpose of the test and it reduces the possibility that people will engage in intentional deception. Second, the indirect method used in projective tests allows them to circumvent conscious defenses, thus making them sensitive to aspects of personality that are usually hidden.

Critics of projective tests point out that they are poorly standardized, in large part because there are no established methods of administration, scoring, and interpretation. In particular, the scoring of these tests often relies on the skill and clinical intuition of the examiner, thus making their reliability distressingly low. In fairness to projective tests, however, evidence suggests that extensive training in a specific scoring system leads to satisfactory levels of inter-judge agreement (Goldfried et al., 1971; Exner, 1986).

A more serious problem concerns the interpretation of a person's scored responses to a projective test. Although clinical psychologists usually rely on their interpretive skills in analyzing the data generated by projective techniques, the techniques should be able to rise and fall on the basis of their own merits. Unfortunately, interpretation of such tests depends all too often on the personal insights and intuition of the clinician. The scientific status of projective tests is certainly not enhanced by this approach.

Finally, critics maintain that there is little convincing evidence to support the validity of projective tests (Aiken, 1984; Peterson, 1978). Accordingly, psychologists are well-advised not to base an entire diagnosis solely on projective tests. Instead, projective tests should be considered in the context of other information obtained through interviews, case histories, and self-report tests.

In summary, despite the problems that plague projective tests, many clinical psychologists continue to be drawn toward them as a means of exploring the person's unconscious conflicts, fantasies, and motives (Singer & Kolligian, 1987). Nonetheless, the use of these tests should not be accepted as a substitute for convincing evidence of reliability and validity.

SUMMARY

A theory serves as a catalyst for empirical study of important personality phenomena and provides a meaningful framework for interpretation of established facts and principles. Unlike casual observations or commonsense notions about human behavior, personality researchers demand objective and replicable data before they accept conclusions as valid. A research orientation to the study of persons likewise demands clear and precise definition of procedures that will be used to measure the variables being investigated.

Observation underlies all research approaches in personality psychology. Unsystematic observation, naturalistic observation, and controlled field observation were each discussed as avenues for more rigorous study of people's behavior. Chief advantages and disadvantages of each were presented as well.

Three research strategies in the study of personality are the case history method, the correlational method, and the experimental method. Each strategy involves someone making objective observations of what someone else is doing or saying.

The case history or case study method seeks to provide an in-depth account of a particular individual's personality. Its primary focus is diagnosis and treatment of persons suffering from emotional problems. Additionally, case histories have played a role in the development of certain personality theories and the study of normal persons over many years. Several assessment techniques may be used in conducting a case history, including biographical and autobiographical sketches, personality and projective tests, interviews, and information provided by others who know the person reasonably well. Although case histories are a valuable source of insights about people, several shortcomings encountered in studying one person at a time were noted. Specifically, case histories do not identify factors that might cause the events observed, the results obtained are of limited generality, and the data collected may be subject to personal bias and/or difficult to verify in terms of accuracy.

The correlational method is used to determine the relationships between and among variables that already exist. Researchers who employ the correlation method are generally interested in finding answers to specific questions, such as Do college grades predict occupational success in later life? The correlation coefficient, the primary statistical measure, indicates the direction and strength of the relationship. This coefficient can vary from -1.00 (a perfect negative relationship) to $+1.00$ (a perfect positive relationship). As a personality research strategy, the correlational method allows study of many aspects of human behavior in natural settings. Further, it permits study of many variables that ethical issues would otherwise not allow to be studied. Nonetheless, the correlational approach does not conclusively demonstrate that one variable caused the other, even if the two variables are highly correlated. Correlation does not imply causation. It was also noted that third variable problems may confound the interpretation of correlational findings.

The experimental method permits researchers to establish cause-and-effect relationships via the process of manipulating a given variable under carefully controlled conditions while observing changes in a second variable as a result. The manipulated variable (stimulus condition controlled by the investigator) is the independent variable. The person's observed response or behavior (outcome of an experiment) is the dependent variable. In its simplest form, an experiment requires two groups of subjects. The experimental group is exposed to the independent variable whereas the control group is not. Assignment of subjects to either group, based on randomization, ensures that both groups are the same except for the presence or absence of the independent variable. An example of the experimental method was cited in connection with the question, "Does misery love company?" Results indicated that women subjects preferred the presence of others only when made to feel highly anxious by the anticipation of painful shock. A follow-up experiment indicated that high-anxiety subjects only prefer the presence of others who are confronted with the same situation.

Although a powerful research strategy, experimentation does have limitations when applied to the study of human behavior. Ethical considerations may preclude its use. Another limitation is that experiments carried out in a laboratory setting are often artificial and thus, results are of limited generality. Artifacts inherent in the laboratory (e.g., demand characteristics, evaluation apprehension) may unintentionally influence the results of a study. Finally, it was noted that the principle of informed consent governs the conduct of experimental research. Subjects are told in advance of any potential risks and are allowed to withdraw from an experiment at any time without repercussions.

Each research strategy used to study personality has distinct advantages and disadvantages. Moreover, no single research method is ideally suited for generating answers to all questions.

The measurement of individual differences, otherwise called *assessment,* is an integral facet of personality psychology. Techniques for the assessment of personality should be evaluated in terms of standardization, norms, reliability, and validity. Reliability refers to the consistency of test responses and is determined in either of two ways: test–retest and split-half. Validity reflects whether a test measures what it purports to measure. Several forms of validity were discussed, including content validity, criterion validity, and construct validity.

Being able to measure aspects of an individual's personality is central to the process of scientific inquiry. The major approaches to personality assessment are interview techniques, self-report personality tests, and projective techniques.

Principal features of unstructured and structured interviews as assessment devices were discussed and illustrated. The structured format is favored in the research setting, whereas the unstructured format is favored in the therapeutic setting.

Self-report assessment techniques are of two general types: single-trait tests and multidimensional tests. The former measure a particular aspect of personality such as was illustrated by the self-consciousness scale. The latter measure several aspects of personality at once and thus provide a more comprehensive assessment of the respondent's make-up. The Minnesota Multiphasic Personality Inventory, the most commonly used multitrait scale, was discussed in terms of its value as a diagnostic tool. Self-report measures are objective in that people have minimal freedom in responding to test items and scoring procedures are not influenced by personal or theoretical bias. Potential problems inherent in self-report tests include deliberate deception (i.e., faking good or bad), social desirability bias, and response sets (acquiescence).

Projective techniques attempt to probe unconscious or subtle aspects of personality by having people project their feelings, needs, and values into their interpretation of ambiguous stimuli. Several different categories of these techniques were noted and the Rorschach Inkblot Test was described as a representative example. Proponents of projective tests assert that such tests reduce the likelihood of respondent deception and are sensitive to unconscious features of personality dynamics. Critics maintain that projective tests are poorly standardized, weak in reliability and validity, and susceptible to subjective interpretation.

BIBLIOGRAPHY

Aiken, L. R. (1984). *Psychological testing and assessment* (4th ed.). Boston: Allyn & Bacon.

American Psychological Association (1981). Ethical principles of psychologists. *American Psychologist,* **36**, 633–638.

Anastasi, A. (1988). *Psychological testing* (6th ed.). New York: Macmillan.

Aronson, E., Brewer, M., & Carlsmith, J. M. (1985). Experimentation in social psychology. In G. Lindzey & E. Aronson (Eds.), *Handbook of social psychology* (3rd ed., Vol. 1). New York: Random House.

Baumrind, D. (1985). Research using intentional deception: Ethical issues revisited. *American Psychologist, 40,* 165–174.

Beck, A. T. (1982). *Depression: Clinical, experimental, and theoretical aspects.* New York: Harper and Row.

Beck, S. J. (1945). *Rorschach's test: Basic processes* (Vol. 1). New York: Grune & Stratton.

Berkowitz, L., & Donnerstein, E. (1982). External validity is more than skin deep. *American Psychologist, 37,* 245–257.

Butcher, J. N. (1984). Current developments in MMPI use: An international perspective. In J. N. Butcher & C. D. Spielberger (Eds.), *Advances in personality assessment* (Vol. 4). Hillsdale, NJ: Erlbaum.

Butcher, J. N., & Keller, L. S. (1984). Objective personality assessment. In G. Goldstein & M. Hersen (Eds.), *Handbook of psychological assessment.* New York: Pergamon Press.

Campbell, D. T., & Fiske, D. W. (1959). Convergent and discriminant validation by the multitrait–multimethod matrix. *Psychological Bulletin, 56,* 81–105.

Carlson, R. (1984). What's social about social psychology? Where's the person in personality research? *Journal of Personality and Social Psychology, 47,* 1304–1309.

Carver, C. S., & Scheier, M. F. (1987). The blind men and the elephant: Selective examination of the public–private literature gives rise to a faulty perception. *Journal of Personality, 55,* 524–541.

Cattell, R. B. (1965). *The scientific analysis of personality.* Baltimore: Penguin.

Christensen, L. (1988). Deception in psychological research: When is its use justified? *Personality and Social Psychology Bulletin, 14,* 664–675.

Crabtree, A. (1985). *Multiple man: Explorations in possession and multiple personality.* New York: Praeger.

Cronbach, L. J., & Meehl, P. E. (1955). Construct validity in psychological tests. *Psychological Bulletin, 52,* 281–302.

Crowne, D. P., & Marlowe, D. (1964). *The approval motive: Studies in evaluative dependence.* New York: Wiley.

Dahlstrom, W. G. (1980). Screening for emotional fitness: The Jersey City case. In W. G. Dahlstrom & L. E. Dahlstrom (Eds.), *Basic readings on the MMPI: A new selection on personality measurement.* Minneapolis: University of Minnesota Press.

Dahlstrom, W. G., Welsh, G. S., & Dahlstrom, L. E. (1975). *An MMPI handbook* (Vol. 2). *Research applications.* Minneapolis: University of Minnesota Press.

Duke, M. P. (1986). Personality science: A proposal. *Journal of Personality and Social Psychology, 50,* 382–385.

Elliott, G. R., & Eisdorfer, C. (Eds.) (1982). *Stress and human health: Analysis and implications of research.* New York: Springer.

Eron, L. D. (1987). The development of aggressive behavior from the perspective of a developing behaviorism. *American Psychologist, 42,* 435–442.

Exner, J. E. (1978). *The Rorschach: A comprehensive system* (Vol. 2). *Current research and advanced interpretation.* New York: Wiley.

Exner, J. E. (1986). *The Rorschach: A comprehensive system* (Vol. 1). *Basic foundations* (2nd ed.). New York: Wiley.

Fenigstein, A. (1987). On the nature of public and private self-consciousness. *Journal of Personality, 55,* 543–553.

Fenigstein, A., Scheier, M. F., & Buss, A. H. (1975). Public and private self-consciousness: Assessment and theory. *Journal of Consulting and Clinical Psychology, 43,* 522–527.

Frank, L. K. (1939). Projective methods for the study of personality. *Journal of Personality,* **8,** 389–413.

Freedman, J. L. (1988). Television violence and aggression: What the evidence shows. In S. Oskamp (Ed.), *Applied social psychology annual* (Vol. 8, pp. 144–162). Newbury Park, CA: Sage.

Friedman, H. S., & Booth-Kelley, S. (1987). The "disease-prone personality": A meta-analytic view of the construct. *American Psychologist,* **42,** 539–555.

Furnham, A. (1990). Faking personality questionnaires: Fabricating different profiles for different purposes. *Current Psychology: Research and Reviews,* **9,** 46–55.

Gamble, K. R. (1972). The HIT: A review. *Psychological Bulletin,* **77,** 172–194.

Goldfried, M. R., Stricker, G., & Weiner, I. B. (1971). *Rorschach handbook of clinical and research applications.* Englewood Cliffs, NJ: Prentice-Hall.

Gough, H. G. (1987). *The California Psychological Inventory administrator's guide.* Palo Alto, CA: Consulting Psychologists Press.

Hargadon, F. (1981). Tests and college admissions. *American Psychologist,* **36,** 1112–1119.

Hathaway, S. R., & McKinley, J. C. (1943). *Manual for the Minnesota Multiphasic Personality Inventory.* New York: The Psychological Corporation.

Holtzman, W. H. (1988). Beyond the Rorschach. *Journal of Personality Assessment,* **52,** 578–609.

Huston, A. C., & Wright, J. C. (1982). Effects of communication media on children. In C. B. Kopp & J. B. Krakow (Eds.), *The child: Development in a social context.* Reading, MA: Addison-Wesley.

Jackson, D. N. (1974). *Jackson Personality Inventory Manual.* Port Huron, MI: Research Psychologists Press.

Jemmott, J. B., & Locke, S. E. (1984). Psychosocial factors, immunologic mediation, and human susceptibility to infectious diseases: How much do we know? *Psychological Bulletin,* **95,** 78–100.

Kazdin, A. E. (1982). The token economy: A decade later. *Journal of Applied Behavior Analysis,* **15,** 431–445.

Kendall, P. C., & Norton-Ford, J. (1982). *Clinical psychology.* New York: Wiley.

Kleinmuntz, B. (1982). *Personality and psychological assessment.* New York: St. Martin's Press.

Klopfer, B., & Davidson, H. H. (1962). *The Rorschach technique: An introductory manual.* New York: Harcourt, Brace & World.

Kunce, J. T., & Anderson, W. P. (1984). Perspectives on uses of the MMPI in non-psychiatric settings. In P. McReynolds & G. J. Chelune (Eds.), *Advances in psychological assessment* (Vol. 6, pp. 41–76). San Francisco: Jossey-Bass.

Lewis, D. O., Pincus, J. H., Feldman, M., Jackson, L., & Bard, B. (1986). Psychiatric, neurological, and psychoeducational characteristics of fifteen death-row inmates in the United States. *American Journal of Psychiatry,* **143,** 838–845.

Lindzey, G. (1959). On the classification of projective techniques. *Psychological Bulletin,* **56,** 158–168.

London, M., & Bray, D. W. (1980). Ethical issues in testing and evaluation for personnel decisions. *American Psychologist,* **35,** 890–901.

Lubin, B., Larsen, R. M., Matarazzo, J. D., & Seever, M. (1985). Psychological test usage patterns in five professional settings. *American Psychologist,* **40,** 857–861.

Machover, K. (1949). *Personality projection in the drawing of the human figure.* Springfield, IL: Charles C Thomas.

Malatesta, V. J., & Adams, H. E. (1984). The sexual dysfunctions. In H. E. Adams & P. B. Sutker (Eds.), *Comprehensive handbook of psychopathology.* New York: Plenum.

Morgan, C. D., & Murray, H. A. (1935). A method for investigating fantasies: The Thematic Apperception Test. *Archives of Neurology and Psychiatry, 34*, 289–306.

Murray, H. A., Barrett, W. G., & Homburger, E. (1938). *Explorations in personality.* New York: Oxford University Press.

Neufeld, R. W., & Mothersill, K. J. (1980). Stress as an irritant of psychopathology. In I. G. Sarason & C. D. Spielberger (Eds.), *Stress and anxiety* (Vol. 7). New York: Hemisphere.

Newcomb, M. D., & Harlow, L. L. (1986). Life events and substance use among adolescents: Mediating effects of perceived loss of control and meaninglessness in life. *Journal of Personality and Social Psychology, 51*, 564–577.

Orne, M. (1969). Demand characteristics and the concept of quasi-experimental control. In R. Rosenthal & R. Rosnow (Eds.), *Artifact in behavioral research* (pp. 143–179). New York: Academic Press.

Peterson, R. A. (1978). Review of the Rorschach. In O. K. Buros (Ed.), *Eighth mental measurements yearbook* (pp. 1042–1045). Highland Park, NJ: Gryphon.

Piotrowski, Z. A. (1957). *Perceptanalysis.* New York: Macmillan.

Rapaport, D., Gill, M. M., & Schafer, R. (1968). *Diagnostic psychological testing.* New York: International Universities Press.

Regan, D. T., Williams, M., & Sparling, S. (1972). Voluntary expiation of guilt: A field experiment. *Journal of Personality and Social Psychology, 24*, 42–45.

Rofe, Y. (1984). Stress and affiliation: A utility theory. *Psychological Review, 91*, 235–250.

Rorschach, H. (1942). *Psychodiagnostics.* Berne, Switzerland: Huber.

Rosenthal, R. (1966). *Experimenter effects in behavioral research.* New York: Appleton-Century-Crofts.

Rosenthal, R., & Rosnow, R. L. (Eds.) (1969). *Artifact in behavioral research.* New York: Academic Press.

Rosenthal, R., & Rubin, D. (1978). Interpersonal expectancy effects: The first 345 studies. *Behavioral and Brain Sciences, 1*, 377–415.

Rosenzwerg, S. (1945). The picture-association method and its application in a study of reactions to frustration. *Journal of Personality, 14*, 3–23.

Rotter, J. B. (1966). Generalized expectancies for internal versus external control of reinforcement. *Psychological Monographs, 80* (1, Whole No. 609).

Rotter, J. B., & Rafferty, J. E. (1950). *Manual for the Rotter incomplete sentences blanks.* New York: Psychological Association.

Runyan, W. M. (1982). *Life histories and psychobiography: Explorations in theory and method.* New York: Oxford University Press.

Schachter, S. (1959). *The psychology of affiliation.* Palo Alto, CA: Stanford University Press.

Scheier, M. F., Buss, A. H., & Buss, D. M. (1978). Self-consciousness, self-report of aggressiveness, and aggression. *Journal of Research in Personality, 12*, 133–140.

Scheier, M. F., & Carver, C. S. (1977). Self-focused attention and the experience of emotion: Attraction, repulsion, elation, and depression. *Journal of Personality and Social Psychology, 35*, 625–636.

Schroeder, D. H., & Costa, P. T. (1984). Influence of life events stress on physical illness: Substantive effects or methodological flaws? *Journal of Personality and Social Psychology, 46*, 853–863.

Singer, J. L., & Kolligian, J., Jr. (1987). Personality: Developments in the study of private experience. *Annual Review of Psychology, 38*, 533–574.

Smith, T. W., & Anderson, N. B. (1986). Models of personality and disease: An interactional approach to Type A behavior and cardiovascular disease. *Journal of Personality and Social Psychology, 50*, 1166–1173.

Snyder, M. (1974). Self-monitoring of expressive behavior. *Journal of Personality and Social Psychology,* **30**, 526–537.

Spielberger, C. D., Gorsuch, R. L., & Lushene, R. E. (1970). *Manual for the State-Trait Anxiety Inventory.* Palo Alto, CA: Consulting Psychologists Press.

Suls, J. M., & Miller, R. L. (Eds.) (1977). *Social comparison processes: Theoretical and empirical perspectives.* Washington, DC: Hemisphere.

Sweeney, J. A., Clarkin, J. F., & Fitzgibbon, M. L. (1987). Current practice of psychological assessment. *Professional Psychology: Research and Practice,* **18**, 377–380.

Szondi, L. (1944). *Schicksalsanalyse.* Basel, Switzerland: Benno, Schwabe.

Taylor, J. A. (1953). A personality scale of manifest anxiety. *Journal of Abnormal and Social Psychology,* **48**, 285–290.

White, K. M., & Spiesman, J. C. (1982). *Research approaches to personality.* Monterey, CA: Brooks/Cole.

White, R. W. (1975). *Lives in progress: A study of the natural growth of personality* (3rd ed.). New York: Holt, Rinehart and Winston.

Williams, N. A., & Deffenbacher, J. L. (1983). Life stress and chronic yeast infections. *Journal of Human Stress,* **9**, 6–31.

Yin, R. K. (1984). *Case study research: Design and methods.* Beverly Hills, CA: Sage.

Zuckerman, M. (1978). Sensation seeking. In H. London & J. E. Exner (Eds.), *Dimensions of personality.* New York: Wiley.

SUGGESTED READINGS

Angleitner, A., & Wiggins, J. S. (Eds.). (1985). *Personality assessment via questionnaire: Current issues in theory and measurement.* Berlin: Springer-Verlag.

Bromley, D. B. (1986). *The case-study method in psychology and related disciplines.* New York: Wiley.

Craik, K. H. (1986). Personality research methods: An historical perspective. *Journal of Personality,* **54**, 19–51.

Lamiell, J. T. (1987). *The psychology of personality: An epistemological inquiry.* New York: Columbia University Press.

Neale, J. M., & Liebert, R. M. (1986). *Science and behavior: An introduction to methods of research* (3rd ed.). Englewood Cliffs, NJ: Prentice-Hall.

Shaughnessy, J. J., & Zechmeister, E. B. (1985). *Research methods in psychology.* New York: Knopf.

DISCUSSION QUESTIONS

1 What are some of the advantages offered by the empirical approach to the study of personality as opposed to the commonsense or the intuitive approach?

2 Describe the case history method as a research strategy for the study of personality. What are some of the strengths and limitations of a case history method?

3 Discuss some of the circumstances in which an investigator would prefer to use the correlational method in connection with the study of personality issues.

4 Why is it that personality researchers prefer using the experimental method to investigate various issues or questions of interest? What factors, besides the independent variable, does an investigator need to consider when interpreting the results of an experiment?

5 Discuss some of the ethical principles governing the conduct of an experimental study. Who is responsible for ensuring that such principles are enforced?

6 Explain the difference between predictive validity and concurrent validity.

7 Explain the difference between reliability and validity in reference to a self-report personality test. Which do you think might be more important? Why?

8 Self-report personality tests are commonly used in personality assessment. Discuss some of the strengths and weaknesses accompanying self-report measures. Is it possible to overcome or negate the weaknesses?

9 How do projective techniques differ from self-report tests in the assessment of personality? Do projectives have any particular advantages or disadvantages in comparison to self-report measures?

GLOSSARY

Acquiescence   A response set of tending to say "yes" or "true" to test items regardless of their content.

Artifact   Unintended factors in a laboratory experiment that may influence the manipulation of the independent variable (e.g., subject's awareness of being observed by an experimenter).

Assessment   The measurement of individual differences having to do with various personality traits.

Basic research   Research designed to examine general relationships among phenomena rather than specific questions about applied issues.

Case study method   Research strategy whereby a particular person is studied in great detail.

Concurrent validity   Degree to which a test correlates with an independent measure of the same characteristic or variable obtained at the same time.

Construct validity   Extent to which there is evidence that a test measures a particular hypothetical construct; involves validation of both the test and the theoretically related characteristic that underlies it.

Content validity   Degree to which a test includes items that are relevant to the variable being measured.

Control group   In an experiment, a group of subjects who do not receive the experimental treatment but are otherwise comparable to the experimental group. Responses of this group can be compared with those of the experimental group to determine any differences.

Convergent validity   Degree to which a test correlates with another test that supposedly measures the same characteristic or construct in question.

Correlation coefficient   A numerical index indicating the strength and direction of the relationship between two variables. Positive correlation indicates that high values on one variable go together with high values on the other variable; negative correlation indicates that high values of one variable go together with low values of the other.

Correlational method   Research strategy used to determine the extent to which two or more variables are associated or covary with one another.

Demand characteristics   Subtle clues in the experimental setting that convey to subjects the behavior the experimenter wants to observe. Such clues may result in confirmation of the experimental hypothesis.

Dependent variable   In an experiment, the variable that is measured after the independent variable has been manipulated; variable that is measured as the outcome of an experiment.

Divergent validity   The degree to which a test does not measure qualities it was not intended to measure.

Empirical test   Method in which systematic observations of the events or variables are obtained in order to achieve verifiable information. The premise of the scientific method that knowledge should be acquired through observation.

Experimental group   In an experiment, the subjects who receive some special treatment in regard to the independent variable.

Experimental method   Research strategy in which the experimenter manipulates one or more (independent) variables under carefully controlled conditions and observes whether there are changes in another (dependent) variable as a result.

Hypothesis   A specific prediction about the relationship between two or more variables that is logically derived from a theory.

Independent variable   In an experiment, the variable that is manipulated by the experimenter in order to determine its impact or influence on another (dependent) variable. It is the variable hypothesized to be the ''cause'' in a cause-and-effect relationship.

Informed consent   The ethical principle that stipulates research subjects must freely choose to participate, after being informed about the study, the procedures that will be used, and any potential risks involved in the study.

Multidimensional tests   Self-report personality inventories that provide measures of several aspects of the respondent's personality at once (e.g., MMPI).

Naturalistic observation   Careful observation of behavior as it occurs in real-life settings without direct intervention by an investigator.

Operational definition   A definition that specifies the procedures and conditions that will be used to measure a variable; defining a concept in terms of the operations through which it is measured.

Predictive validity   Degree to which a test can accurately predict some criterion-related measure in the future.

Projective techniques   A class of psychological tests that ask people to respond to ambiguous stimuli in ways that may reveal their needs, feelings, and conflicts; a familiar example is the Rorschach Inkblot Test.

Random assignment   The assignment of research subjects to different groups or conditions in an experiment on the basis of chance; randomization eliminates all factors from an experiment except for the presence or absence of the independent variable.

Reliability   The measurement of consistency or stability of a test (or other kind of measurement technique). The consistency of scores when a test is administered repeatedly to the same group of people is called test–retest reliability. The consistency of scores across items within a test is called split-half or internal reliability.

Self-report techniques   Self-report tests in which the response format, administration, and scoring features are standardized.

Single-trait tests   Self-report tests that measure a specific trait of the respondent's personality (e.g., sensation seeking).

Social desirability   A tendency seen in some people to give socially acceptable answers to test items.

Standardization   The use of uniform procedures in the administration and scoring of a psychological test.

Structured interview   An interview that follows a set format (i.e., questions), thus allowing the person little or no freedom to digress from the information sought by the interviewer. An unstructured interview, by contrast, allows the person maximum freedom to divulge information in a more spontaneous manner.

Test norms   Established standards of performance for a test (e.g., mean, median, and percentile).

Validity   Degree to which a test measures what it purports to measure.

CHAPTER 3

THE PSYCHODYNAMIC PERSPECTIVE IN PERSONALITY THEORY: SIGMUND FREUD

When psychology gained its independence from philosophy and became a science in the second half of the nineteenth century, its goal was to use laboratory-based introspection to discover the basic elements of mental life in the human adult. Known as the *structural school* and developed primarily by Wilhelm Wundt (who, as noted in Chapter 1, founded the first psychological laboratory in Leipzig, Germany, in 1879), this approach emphasized the analysis of conscious processes into their fundamental elements, together with the discovery of the laws that govern connections among these elements. Thus, even psychologists of that era were taken aback by the thoroughly different and radical approach to the study of human beings which was developed almost single-handedly by Sigmund Freud, then a young Viennese physician. Rather than treating consciousness as the center of mental life, Freud likened the mind to an iceberg, only a small segment of which protruded above the surface of the water. In contrast to the then-prevailing image of humans as rational and conscious beings, he theorized that individuals are in a perpetual state of conflict motivated by a second, more comprehensive realm of mental functioning—*unconscious* sexual and aggressive urges.

Freud was the first to portray the mind as a battleground for the warring factions of instinct, reason, and conscience. The term "psychodynamic" refers to this incessant struggle among the various aspects of personality. As such, psychoanalytic theory exemplifies a psychodynamic perspective in that it gives a prominent role to the complex interplay among processes of personality (e.g., instincts, motives, drives) that compete or wrestle with each other for control over the person's behavior. The theme that personality is a dynamic set of processes—

of the psychodynamic perspective, particularly Freud's version of it. A secondary implication of this dynamic quality in personality is that behavior is determined, rather than capricious or haphazard. The determinism assumed by the psychodynamic perspective applies to everything we do, think, or feel—even including events that many people would regard as accidents and slips of the tongue. This notion brings us to a final major theme of the psychodynamic perspective. Specifically, this viewpoint stresses the importance of unconscious mental processes in determining people's behavior. For Freud, not only is what we do often irrational, but also the meanings and causes of our behavior are seldom available to our conscious mental processes.

It would be impossible to provide an adequate account of contemporary personality theory without acknowledging Freud's system. Whether one accepts or rejects any or all of his ideas, no one can reasonably deny that Freud has had a profound and lasting intellectual impact on Western civilization in the twentieth century. Indeed, it can be argued that few ideas in the entire history of civilization have had such a broad and enormous influence. This is a sweeping statement, but it is difficult to think of many close competitors for such a distinction. His view of the human condition, striking violently against the prevailing assumptions of Victorian society, offers a complex and compelling way to understand those aspects of mental life that are obscure and apparently unreachable.

In nearly 45 years of active writing and clinical practice, Freud developed (1) the first comprehensive personality theory; (2) an extensive body of clinical observations based on his therapeutic experience and self-analysis; (3) a compelling method for treating neurotic disorders; and (4) a procedure for the investigation of mental processes which are almost inaccessible in any other way. In this chapter, Freud's personality theory and its underlying assumptions will be examined. Selected research stimulated by the theory as well as illustrative applications to everyday human behavior will also be discussed.

SIGMUND FREUD: A Psychodynamic Theory of Personality

BIOGRAPHICAL SKETCH

Sigmund Freud was born May 6, 1856, at Freiberg, Moravia, a small Austrian town now part of central Czechoslovakia. He was the oldest of seven children, although his father, a wool merchant, had two sons by a former marriage and was a grandfather when Sigmund was born. When he was 4 years old, his family suffered financial setbacks and moved to Vienna. He remained a resident of that city until he emigrated to England in 1938, the year before he died.

From an early age, Freud excelled as a student. Despite the limited financial position of his family which forced all members to live in a crowded apartment, Freud had his own room and even an oil lamp by which to study. The rest of the family made do with candles. Like other young people of his time, he had a classical education, studying Greek and Latin and reading the classics of great poets, playwrights, and philosophers—Shakespeare, Kant, Hegel, Schopen-

Sigmund Freud *(The Bettmann Archive)*

hauer, and Nietzsche. In fact, his intense love of books led him to run up a debt at a bookstore which he had no means to settle, and for which his father, hard-pressed for money, could offer no sympathy (Puner, 1947, p. 47). Freud had a superb command of the German language and at one time earned a prize for his literary skills, but he also had considerable fluency in French, English, Spanish, and Italian.

Freud recalled that he often had childhood dreams of becoming a general or minister of state. However, since he was Jewish, all professional careers except medicine and law were closed to him—such was the prevailing anti-Semitic climate of the times. He reluctantly decided upon a medical career and entered the Faculty of Medicine of the University of Vienna in 1873. During his medical school days, Freud came under the influence of the eminent physiologist Ernst Brucke. Brucke promoted the idea that living organisms were dynamic energy systems obeying the laws of the physical universe. Freud took these ideas seriously and later applied them to his dynamic view of psychological functioning (Sulloway, 1979).

Freud's ambition during medical school was to make a name for himself by discovering something important. His research contributions included identifying new characteristics of nerve cells in goldfish and verifying the existence of testes in male eels. However, his most important discovery was that cocaine could be used to cure many ills. He took the drug himself without any harmful effects and praised it as a near panacea as well as an effective anesthetic (Byck, 1974). His enthusiasm for cocaine later subsided when the drug's addictive properties became known (Ellenberger, 1970).

After receiving his medical degree in 1881, Freud accepted a position at the Institute of Cerebral Anatomy and did research comparing adult and fetal brains; he never intended to practice medicine. However, he soon resigned his post and entered private practice as a neurologist primarily because scientific work offered minimal monetary rewards and anti-Semitism within academe curtailed promotions. In addition, Freud had fallen in love and realized that if he ever were to marry, he would need a better-paying position.

The year 1885 marked a crucial turning point in Freud's career. He received a research grant to travel to Paris and study for 4 months with Jean Charcot, one of the most prominent neurologists of the time. Charcot was investigating the causes and treatment of hysteria, a psychological disorder which manifested itself in a variety of physical problems. Hysterical patients displayed such bodily symptoms as paralysis of the limbs, blindness, and deafness. Through hypnotic suggestion, Charcot was able to induce or eliminate many of these hysterical symptoms. Although Freud later rejected hypnosis as a therapeutic technique, he was excited by Charcot's lectures and clinical demonstrations. During his brief stay at the famed Salpêtrière hospital in Paris, Freud was transformed from a neurologist to a psychopathologist (Steele, 1982).

In 1886 Freud married Martha Bernays, a marriage that lasted more than half a century and produced three daughters and three sons. The youngest child, Anna, followed in her father's professional footsteps, eventually taking over a leadership role in the psychoanalytic movement and becoming a renowned child analyst. It was also during this time that Freud began to collaborate with Josef Breuer, one of Vienna's most distinguished physicians. Breuer had previously achieved some success with hysterical patients by encouraging them to talk freely about their symptoms. Together, Breuer and Freud launched an investigation of the psychological underpinnings of hysteria, along with therapeutic considerations of the illness. Their work culminated in the publication of *Studies in Hysteria* (1895), a book in which the two men theorized that hysterical symptoms resulted from repressed memories of traumatic events. The beginnings of psychoanalysis are sometimes traced to the date of this landmark publication, but the most creative period in Freud's life lay just ahead.

The personal and professional relationship between Freud and Breuer ended abruptly at about the time *Studies in Hysteria* (1895) was published. The reasons why the two colleagues parted as embittered enemies are not altogether clear. Freud's biographer, Ernest Jones (1953), contends that Breuer's strong disagreement with Freud about the role of sexuality in the etiology of hysteria precipitated the break. Another scholar (Steele, 1982) speculates that Breuer was like a "father figure" to the younger Freud and was therefore destined to be eliminated because of Freud's strong Oedipal strivings. For whatever reasons, the two men never again met as friends.

Freud's insistence that the basis of hysteria and other mental disturbances was sexual in nature led to his resignation from the Vienna Medical Society in 1896. At this point, Freud had developed little, if any, of what was later to become known as psychoanalytic theory. Moreover, his evaluation of himself and of his work parallel the observation made by Jones. "I have restricted capacities or talents. None at all from the natural sciences; nothing for mathematics; nothing for anything quantitative. But what I have, of a very restricted nature, is probably very intense" (1953, p. 119).

The years between 1896 and 1900 were lonely yet productive ones for Freud.

During this period he began to analyze his own dreams and, after the death of his father in 1896, he initiated the practice of analyzing himself the last half-hour of each day. His most outstanding work, *The Interpretation of Dreams* (1900), was based on analyses of his own dreams. However, fame and recognition were far from instant. At first, this masterpiece was all but ignored by the psychiatric community and Freud received only $209 in royalties for his labors. Incredible as it may seem, it took 8 years to sell the 600 original printings of the book.

In the 5-year period following the publication of *The Interpretation of Dreams*, Freud's prestige grew to include the general populace as well as medical practitioners throughout the world. In 1902 The Psychological Wednesday Society was formed, open to only a select group of his intellectual followers. The name of the organization was changed to the Vienna Psychoanalytic Society in 1908. Many of Freud's colleagues subsequently became famous psychoanalysts in their own right (including Ernest Jones, Sandor Ferenczi, Carl Jung, Alfred Adler, Hans Sachs, and Otto Rank). Later, Adler, Jung, and Rank were to defect from Freud's ranks and develop their own rival schools of thought.

The period of 1901–1905 was an especially productive one in Freud's life. He published several books, including *The Psychopathology of Everyday Life* (1901), *Three Essays on Sexuality* (1905a), and *Jokes and Their Relation to the Unconscious* (1905b). In *Three Essays* Freud proposed that children are born with sexual urges and that their parents are selected as their initial sexual objects. Public outrage was immediate and widespread. Freud was branded as a pervert, an obscene and wicked man. For good measure, medical institutions were boycotted for tolerating Freud's emphasis on the sexual life of children.

In 1909 a single incident propelled the psychoanalytic movement from relative isolation to international recognition. G. Stanley Hall invited Freud to Clark University in Worcester, Massachusetts, to give a series of lectures. The lectures were well-received, and he was awarded an honorary doctoral degree. Freud's future at this time appeared quite promising. He had achieved considerable fame and acceptance to have an international waiting list of patients. But he had problems, too. For one, he had lost practically all his life savings in 1919 due to the war. A 26-year-old daughter died in 1920. Perhaps his greatest hardship was his fear for the lives of two sons who were in the war. It was out of the historical context of World War I, especially the rising tide of anti-Semitism, that Freud, at age 64, developed his theory of a universal human death instinct—a wish to die. Despite his pessimism about the future of humankind, however, he continued to articulate his ideas in a long series of books. The more important ones include *Introductory Lectures on Psycho-Analysis* (1920a), *Beyond the Pleasure Principle* (1920b), *The Ego and the Id* (1923), *The Future of an Illusion* (1927), *Civilization and Its Discontents* (1930), *New Introductory Lectures on Psychoanalysis* (1933), and *An Outline of Psychoanalysis* published posthumously in 1940. Freud was an exceptionally gifted writer as evidenced by his winning the coveted Goethe Prize for literature in 1930.

World War I had a profound impact on Freud's life and theory. His clinical work with German soldiers broadened his understanding of the variety and subtlety of psychopathology. The rise of anti-Semitism during the 1930s also strongly affected his conception of the social nature of man. In 1932, for example, he was a persistent target of Hitler's policies (the Nazis in Berlin held numerous book burnings of his publications). Freud commented on the event: "What progress we are making. In the Middle Ages they would have burnt me, nowadays they are content with burning my books" (Jones, 1957, p. 182). It was only through the diplomatic efforts of influential citizens that he and certain members of his family were allowed to leave Vienna shortly after the Nazi invasion in 1938.

Freud's final years were difficult ones. From 1923 on he suffered from an advancing cancer of the throat and jaw (he smoked 20 Cuban cigars every day), but he obstinately refused all forms of drug therapy with the exception of a few aspirin. He persisted in his work, despite the ordeal of a total of 33 operations to halt the spreading cancer (which forced him to wear an awkward prosthesis to fill the resulting gap between what had been the nasal and oral cavities, and prevented him at times from speaking). Still one more test of his stoic courage was in store: the Nazi invasion of Austria in 1938, during which his daughter Anna was detained by the Gestapo. She was eventually released and allowed to rejoin her family in England.

Freud died on September 23, 1939, in London, England, a displaced Jewish expatriate. A three-volume biography written by his friend and colleague Ernest Jones, entitled *The Life and Work of Sigmund Freud* (1953, 1955, 1957), is recommended as a perceptive assessment of Freud's life. Subsequently, a 24-volume edition has been published in England and sold to a worldwide audience. For additional insight into Freud's personal life the reader is directed to Clark (1980), Isbister (1985), and Vitz (1988).

PSYCHOANALYSIS: BASIC CONCEPTS AND PRINCIPLES

The term "psychoanalysis" has three meanings: (1) a theory of personality and psychopathology, (2) a method of therapy for personality disturbances, and (3) a technique for investigating an individual's unconscious thoughts and feelings. This entanglement of theory with therapy, and with the assessment of persons, permeates nearly every aspect of Freud's ideas concerning human behavior. Underlying this web of entanglement and complexity, however, are a relatively small number of basic concepts and principles reflecting Freud's psychodynamic approach to personality. We begin with his view of how the mind is organized, a view that is often termed Freud's "topographical model."

Levels of Consciousness: The Topographical Model

For a long time in the theoretical development of psychoanalysis, Freud employed a *topographical model* of personality organization. According to this model, psychic life can be represented by three levels of consciousness—the conscious, the preconscious, and the unconscious. Taken together, Freud used this mental "map" of the mind to describe the degree to which mental events such as thoughts and fantasies vary in accessibility to awareness.

The *conscious* level consists of whatever sensations and experiences you are aware of at a given moment in time. For example, at this moment your conscious may include the present train of thought in this text and a dim awareness that you are beginning to get hungry. Freud insisted that only a small part of mental life (thoughts, perceptions, feelings, memories) is contained in the realm of consciousness. Whatever the content of conscious experience may be for a given person at a given time, it is the result of a selective screening process largely regulated by external cues. Furthermore, it is actually conscious only for a brief time and can be quickly submerged into preconscious or unconscious levels as the person's attention shifts to different cues. As such, the conscious represents only a small percent of all the bits of information stored in the mind.

The *preconscious* domain, sometimes called "available memory," encompasses all experiences that are not conscious at the moment but which can easily be retrieved into awareness either spontaneously or with a minimum of effort. Examples might include memories of everything you did last Saturday night, all the towns you ever lived in, your favorite foods, or an argument you had with a friend yesterday. In Freud's view, the preconscious bridges the conscious and unconscious regions of the mind. For instance, under the influence of certain therapeutic techniques, unconscious material may emerge into the preconscious and from there become conscious.

The deepest and major stratum of the human mind is the *unconscious*. It is the storehouse for primitive instinctual drives plus emotions and memories that are so threatening to the conscious mind that they have been repressed, or unconsciously pushed into the unconscious mind. Examples of material that might be found in your unconscious include a forgotten trauma in childhood, hidden feelings of hostility toward a parent, and repressed sexual desires of which you are unaware. For Freud, such unconscious material is responsible for much of your everyday behavior.

Freud was not the first to focus attention on the importance of unconscious processes in understanding human functioning. Several eighteenth- and nineteenth-century philosophers had suggested the general idea of an inner world unknowable to the conscious self (Ellenberger, 1970). Unlike his philosophical predecessors, however, Freud, gave the concept of an unconscious life an empirical status. Specifically, he stressed that the unconscious must not be conceived as a hypothetical abstraction but rather as a reality which can be demonstrated and thus proved. Freud firmly believed that the really significant aspects of human behavior are shaped and directed by impulses and drives totally outside the realm of awareness. Not only are these forces unconscious, but also there is great resistance within the individual to them ever becoming conscious or expressed directly in behavior. In contrast to preconscious modes of thought, unconscious ones are completely inadmissible to awareness, yet they largely determine the actions of people. However, unconscious material may be expressed in disguised or symbolized form, as when unconscious instinctual urges are indirectly satisfied in dreams, play, and work. This insight was utilized by Freud in his work with disturbed persons.

The Anatomy of Personality Structure

The concept of unconscious mental processes was central to Freud's early description of personality organization. However, during the early 1920s he revised his conceptual model of mental life and introduced three basic structures in the anatomy of personality: *id, ego,* and *superego.* This tripartite division of personality is known as the *structural model* of mental life, although Freud felt the divisions should be understood as hypothetical processes rather than as specific "structures" of personality. Freud insisted that these structures be considered hypothetical constructs because the field of neuroanatomy was not sufficiently advanced to locate them within the central nervous system. The interrelationships between these personality structures and the levels of consciousness (i.e., topographical model) are diagrammed in Figure 3-1. The figure shows that all of the id is unconscious, while both ego and superego operate at all three levels of awareness. The conscious encompasses all three personality structures, although the major portion of it is made up of id impulses.

The Id   The word "id" comes from the Latin word for "it" and refers exclusively to the primitive, instinctive, and inherited aspects of personality. The id functions entirely in the unconscious and is closely tied to instinctual biological urges (to eat, sleep, defecate, copulate) that energize our behavior. Indeed, Freud believed that it is raw, animalistic, and chaotic, knows no laws, obeys no rules, and remains basic to the individual throughout life. Operating on a primitive basis, it is free from all inhibitions. The id, as the oldest and original structure of the mind, expresses the primary principle of all human life—the immediate discharge of psychic energy produced by biologically rooted drives (especially sex and

FIGURE 3-1   The relationship of the structural model to levels of awareness.

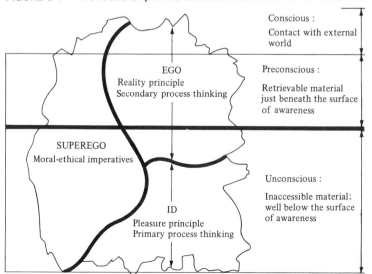

aggression) which, when pent up, create tension throughout the personality system. Immediate tension reduction is called the *pleasure principle*, and the id obeys it, manifesting itself in an impulsive, irrational, and narcissistic (exaggeratedly self-loving) manner, regardless of the consequences of its actions for others or its own self-preservation. Furthermore, since the id does not recognize fear or anxiety, it takes no precautions in expressing its purpose—a fact which Freud felt may result in danger for the individual and/or society. Expressed differently, the id may be likened to a blind king whose brute power and authority are compelling but who must rely on others to properly distribute and use his power.

Freud considered the id as a mediator between the organism's somatic and mental processes. He described it as being "somewhere in direct contact with somatic processes, and takes over from them instinctual needs and gives them mental expression, but we cannot say in what substratum this contact is made" (1915–1917, p. 104). As such, it acts as a reservoir for all the primitive instinctual urges and derives its energy directly from bodily processes.

Freud identified two mechanisms the id employs to rid the personality of tension: *reflex actions* and *primary process*. In the former, the id responds automatically to sources of irritation, thereby promptly removing the tension which the irritant elicits. Examples of such inborn reflex mechanisms are coughing in response to a tickling throat and tearing in response to dirt in the eye. It should be recognized, however, that reflex actions are not always successful in reducing the source of irritation or tension. For instance, no reflex action will allow a hungry baby to acquire food. When reflex action cannot alleviate the tension, a second id function, called the primary process, takes over. The id forms a mental image of an object previously associated with satisfaction of a basic need. In the case of the hungry baby, the primary process might conjure up an image of the mother's breast or a bottle of milk. Other examples of primary process thinking are found in nocturnal dreams, the hallucinations of psychotics, and the mental functioning of newborn infants.

Primary process is an illogical, irrational, and fantasy-oriented form of human thought characterized by the inability to inhibit impulses and to discriminate between the real and the unreal, between the me and non-me. The tragedy of behaving in accord with primary process is that the individual cannot differentiate between the actual object that will gratify a need and a mental image of the object (e.g., between water and a mirage of water for a person stranded in the desert). Confusion of the two would eventually lead to death unless some external source of satisfaction were present. Thus, Freud believed that the most compelling task confronting the infant is to learn to delay gratification of primary needs. The capacity to postpone such gratification first emerges when infants learn that there is an external world apart from their own needs and desires. As this realization develops, the second structure of personality, ego, appears.

The Ego The ego (the Latin word for "I") is the decision-making component of the psychic apparatus that seeks to express and gratify the desires of the id in accordance with the constraints imposed by the outside world. The ego acquires its structure and functions from the id, having evolved from it, and proceeds to borrow some of id's energy for its own use in response to the demands of social reality. The ego thus helps ensure the safety and self-preservation of the organism. In its battles for survival against both the external social world and the instinctual demands of id, the ego must continuously differentiate between things in the mind and things in the outer world of reality. The hungry person in search of food, for example, must distinguish between a mental image of food and an actual perception of food if tension reduction is to occur. That is, he or she must learn to acquire and consume food before the tension can be reduced. This goal is accomplished through establishing suitable courses of action that enable the id to express its instinctual needs in accordance with the norms and ethics of the social world, a feat not always achieved. Such a goal requires the person to learn, think, reason, perceive, decide, memorize, and so on. Accordingly, the ego uses cognitive and perceptual strategies in its endeavor to satisfy the wishes and demands of the id.

In contrast to the id's pleasure-seeking nature, the ego obeys the *reality principle,* the aim of which is to preserve the organism's integrity by suspending instinctual gratification until either an appropriate outlet and/or environmental condition that will satisfy the need can be found. The reality principle enables the individual to inhibit, redirect, or gradually release the id's raw energy within the bounds of social restrictions and the individual's conscience. For instance, expression of the sexual drive is delayed until an appropriate "object" and environmental circumstances are available. Thus, when the object and conditions are ideal, the pleasure principle is satisfied. The reality principle introduces a measure of rationality into our behavior.

Unlike the id, the ego distinguishes between reality and fantasy, tolerates moderate amounts of tension, changes as a function of new experience, and engages in rational cognitive activity. By relying on the power of rational thought, or what Freud termed *secondary process*, the ego is able to establish appropriate courses of action to satisfy instinctual needs without endangering the safety of the individual and/or others. The ego, then, is the "executive" of personality and the seat of intellectual processes and problem solving. As we will discuss later, one of the main goals of psychoanalytic therapy is to free some of the ego's energy so that it can generate higher levels of problem solving.

The Superego   In order for a person to function effectively in society, he or she must acquire a system of values, norms, and ethics that are reasonably compatible with that society. These are acquired through the process of "socialization," and in terms of the structural model of psychoanalysis, are developed through the formation of a superego (combining two Latin words meaning "over-I").

The superego is the last component of personality to be developed and represents an internalized version of society's norms and standards of behavior. In Freud's view, the human organism is not born with a superego; rather, children must acquire it through interactions with parents, teachers, and other "formative" figures. As the moral-ethical arm of personality, the superego results from the child's prolonged dependence upon parents. It makes its formal appearance when the child is said to know right from wrong, good from bad, moral from immoral (at around 3 to 5 years of age). Initially, the superego reflects only parental expectations of what constitutes good and bad behavior. The child's every effort is expended to live up to these expectations so as to avoid conflict and punishment. However, as the child's social world begins to broaden (via school, religious, and peer groups), his or her superego expands to incorporate whatever behavior these groups also deem appropriate. The superego may be considered an individualized reflection of society's "collective conscience," although the child's perceptions of the real values of society may be distorted.

Freud divided the superego into two subsystems—the *conscience* and the *ego-ideal*. Conscience is acquired through the use of punishment by the parents. It is concerned with things that parents say are "naughty" behavior and for which the child is reprimanded. It includes the capacity for punitive self-evaluation, moral prohibitions, and guilt feelings when the child fails to achieve what he or she should be doing. The rewarding aspect of the superego is the ego-ideal. It is derived from whatever the parents approve or value and leads the individual to pursue standards of excellence which, if achieved, generate a sense of self-esteem and pride. For example, the child who is rewarded for scholarly efforts will feel proud whenever he or she shows academic accomplishment.

The superego is said to be fully developed when self-control replaces parental control. However, this principle of self-control is not served by the reality principle. The superego, while attempting to inhibit completely any id impulse that would be condemned by society, also tries to guide the person toward absolute perfection in thought, word, and deed. In short, it tries to persuade the ego that the pursuit of perfectionistic goals is better than the pursuit of realistic ones.

INSTINCTS: THE ENERGIZING FORCE OF BEHAVIOR

Psychoanalytic theory is based on the notion that human beings are complex energy systems. Limited by nineteenth-century conceptions of physics and physiology, Freud was taught that human behavior is activated by a unitary kind of energy in accordance with the *law of conservation of energy* (i.e., energy may be converted from one state to another, but it is all the same energy). Freud accepted this principle of nature, translated it into psychological terms, and theorized that the source of psychic energy derives from neurophysiological states of excitation. He further postulated that each person has a fixed amount of such energy available for mental activity, and that the goal of all human behavior was the reduction of tension created by the unpleasant accumulation of energy over time. For example, if most of your energy is presently being expended to recognize the words on this page, then little is left for other types of mental activity, like daydreaming or viewing a TV program. Similarly, the reason you are reading these words may be to reduce tension associated with an exam scheduled for next week.

Freud thus depicted human motivation as based entirely upon energy aroused by the body's tissue needs. He believed that the total amount of psychic energy derived from tissue needs is invested in mental activities designed to reduce the excitation created by the need. In Freudian theory, mental representations of these bodily excitations reflected in the form of wishes are termed *instincts*. Instincts, therefore, represent innate bodily states of excitation that seek expression and tension release. Freud maintained that all human activity (thinking, perceiving, remembering, and dreaming) is determined by the instincts; their influence on behavior can be devious and disguised as well as direct. People behave because instinctual tension impels them to, their actions serving to reduce this tension. As such, instincts are "the ultimate cause of all activity" (Freud, 1940, p. 5).

A Matter of Life and Death

Although there may be an indeterminate number of instincts, Freud recognized the existence of two basic groups of them—*life* and *death* instincts. The former group (collectively termed *Eros*) includes all the forces that serve to maintain vital life processes and ensure the propagation of the species. Because of the significance attributed to them in the psychic organization of individuals, the sex instincts were singled out by Freud as the most salient of the life instincts for the development of personality. The energy force underlying the sexual instincts is called *libido* (from the Latin word for "wish" or "desire") or *libidinal energy*, a term that came to refer to the energy of the life instincts in general. Libido is that portion of psychic energy that seeks its gratification from purely sexual activities.

Freud theorized that there is not one sexual instinct, but many. Each is associated with a different bodily source or region called an *erogenous zone*. In a sense, the entire body is one large erogenous zone—but the three emphasized by psychoanalytic theory are the mouth, the anus, and the genitals. Freud believed that erogenous zones were potential sources of tension and that manipulating these areas relieved the tension and produced pleasurable sensations. Thus, biting or sucking produces oral pleasure, emptying of the bowels creates anal pleasure, and masturbating produces genital pleasure.

A second category, the death instincts (also termed *Thanatos*), underlies all the manifestations of cruelty, aggression, suicide, and murder. Unlike the libidinal energy of the life instincts, no specific name was assigned to the energy system of the death instincts. However, Freud considered them to be biologically rooted and equally as important as the life instincts in determining the individual's behavior. Furthermore, he saw an empirical basis for the death instinct in the principle of *entropy* (i.e., a thermodynamic law which states that any energy system seeks a state of balance or equilibrium). Quoting Schopenhauer, Freud boldly claimed that "The goal of all life is death" (1920b, p. 38). What he intended to convey is that there exists in all living organisms a compulsion to reestablish the inanimate state out of which they were formed. That is, Freud believed that human beings have an unconscious wish to die. This view should be tempered, however, by the fact that modern psychoanalysts pay scant attention to the death instinct. It is probably the most controversial and least-accepted concept in Freud's theory.

What Instincts Are Really Like

All instincts have four features: a source, an aim, an object, and an impetus. The *source* of the instinct is the bodily condition or need from which it arises. The sources of life instincts are clearly embedded in neurophysiology (e.g., hunger or thirst). In the case of death instincts, the sources were not as clearly defined by Freud in physiological terms. The *aim* of an instinct is always to abolish or reduce the excitation deriving from its need. If the aim is achieved, the person then experiences a momentary state of blissfulness. Although there are numerous ways of attaining the aim of an instinct, there is a consistent tendency to maintain the state of excitation at a minimal level (in accord with the pleasure principle).

The *object* refers to any person or thing in the environment or within the individual's own body that provides for the satisfaction (i.e., the aim) of an instinct. The activities leading to instinctual pleasure are not necessarily fixed. In fact, the object may be susceptible to change throughout the course of the individual's life. In addition to flexibility in the choice of objects, individuals are capable of delaying expression of instinctual energy for prolonged periods of time.

Practically every behavioral process in psychoanalytic theory can be described in terms of (1) the attachment or investment of energy in an object (*cathexis*) or (2) an obstacle preventing gratification of an instinct (*anticathexis*). Object cathexis is illustrated by emotional attachments (i.e., energy being invested) to other people, one's word, and one's ideals, whereas anticathexis is represented by external or internal barriers preventing immediate reduction of instinctual drives. Thus, the interplay between instinct expression and its inhibition, between cathexis and anticathexis, forms the bulwark of the psychoanalytic motivational system.

Finally, the *impetus* refers to the magnitude of energy, force, or pressure that is used to satisfy or gratify the instinct. It may be estimated indirectly by observing the number and kinds of obstacles the individual will overcome in seeking a specific goal.

The key to understanding the dynamics of instinctual energy and its expression via object-choices is the concept of *displacement*. This concept represents the shift in behavioral activity by which energy is discharged and tension reduction attained. Displacement occurs when, for some reason, the original object-choice of an instinct cannot be reached. In such instances, the instinct can displace and thus express its energy by focusing upon some object-choice other than the original one. Consider the following not too uncommon situation: Your boss intimidates you into working and you come home and slam the door, kick the dog, and lash out at your roommate. What's happening? You are displacing your anger onto irrelevant targets which allow for the indirect expression of the emotion.

Freud suggested that a wide range of social-psychological phenomena could be understood in terms of displacement of the two primary instincts, sex and aggression. For instance, the socialization of the child may be explained, in part, as a result of the sequential displacement of the sexual drive from one object to another in relation to the demands imposed by parents and society. Similarly, racial prejudice and wars can be attributed to the displacement of the aggression drive. Freud even suggested that the entire fabric of modern civilization (art, music, literature) is a product of displaced sexual and aggressive energy. Unable to obtain direct and immediate gratification, human beings have learned to displace their instinctual energy onto persons, things, and activities other than those permitting direct tension release. Thus, elaborate religious, political, economic, and other institutional structures result.

PERSONALITY DEVELOPMENT: THE PSYCHOSEXUAL STAGES

The psychoanalytic theory of development is based on two premises. The first, the *genetic* approach, emphasizes that early childhood experiences play a critical role in shaping adult personality. In fact, Freud believed that the basic foundation of an individual's personality was laid down by the tender age of 5! The second premise is that a certain amount of sexual energy (libido) is present at birth and thereafter progresses through a series of *psychosexual* stages that are rooted in the instinctual processes of the organism.

Freud hypothesized a series of four sequential stages of personality development: *oral*, *anal*, *phallic*, and *genital*. A period of *latency*, normally occurring between the ages of 6 or 7 and the onset of puberty, was included by Freud in the overall scheme of development, but, technically speaking, it is not a stage. The first three stages of development extend from birth to 5 years of age and are called *pregenital* stages, since the genital zones of the body have not yet attained a dominant role in personality formation. The fourth stage coincides with the onset of puberty. The names of these stages are based on the region of the body whose stimulation allows for the discharge of libidinal energy in a rich assortment of ways. Table 3-1 summarizes the stages of psychosexual development identified by Freud.

Consistent with Freud's emphasis on biology, all of the stages are closely associated with erogenous zones, sensitive areas of the body surface that function as sites for the expression of libidinal urges. These erogenous zones include the ears, eyes, mouth (lips), breasts, anus, and genitals.

The term "psychosexual" emphasizes that the major factor underlying human development is the *sexual instinct* as it progresses from one erogenous zone to another over the course of a person's life. According to the theory, at any particular point in the developmental sequence some region of the body seeks objects or activities to produce pleasurable tension. Psychosexual development is a biologically determined sequence, invariant in its order of unfolding and characteristic of all persons regardless of their cultural heritage. The individual's social experiences at each stage presumably leave some permanent residue in the form of attitudes, traits, and values acquired at that stage.

The logic of this formulation was explained by Freud in terms of two factors—

TABLE 3-1   SUMMARY OF FREUD'S STAGES OF PSYCHOSEXUAL DEVELOPMENT

Stage	Age range	Libidinal focus	Developmental tasks and experiences
Oral	0–18 months	Mouth (sucking, biting, chewing)	Weaning (from breast or bottle). Separation from mothering one
Anal	1½–3 years	Anus (retaining or expelling feces)	Toilet training (self-control)
Phallic	3–6 years	Genitals (masturbating)	Identifying with same-sex adult role model
Latency	6–12 years	None (sexually dormant)	Expanding social/peer contacts
Genital	Puberty onward	Genitals (becoming heterosexually intimate)	Establishing intimate/caring relationships; contributing to society through work

frustration and *overindulgence*. In the case of frustration, the child's psychosexual needs (e.g., sucking, biting, or chewing) are thwarted by the mothering one and thus fail to be optimally gratified. In overindulgence, the parents provide little or no incentive for the child to master internal functions (e.g., control over elimination activity) and thus instill feelings of dependence and incompetence. In either case, Freud felt that the outcome would be an overinvestment of libido which, depending upon its intensity, would then become manifest in adulthood in the form of residual behaviors (traits, values, attitudes) associated with the psychosexual stage at which these experiences occurred.

A related concept in psychoanalytic theory is that of *regression* (reverting to an earlier stage of psychosexual development and displaying the childish behavior appropriate to that period). For example, an adult faced with a highly stressful situation may regress and deal with it by bursting into tears, sucking the thumb, or wanting a good "stiff" drink. Regression is actually a special case of what Freud called *fixation* (being developmentally arrested or stopped at a particular psychosexual stage). Regression and fixation are seen as complementary by Freudians; the probability of regression depends mainly upon the strength of fixation (Fenichel, 1945). Fixation represents a failure to move forward from one stage to another as expected and leads to an overemphasis on the psychosexual needs that were prominent during the fixated stage. For example, a 10-year-old boy who persists in sucking his thumb is exhibiting an oral fixation; energy is invested in an activity appropriate to an earlier stage of development. The weaker the resolution of developmental challenges or tasks, the more vulnerable the individual is to the forces of regression under conditions of emotional or physical stress later in life. Each individual's personality structure is thus characterized in terms of the stage of psychosexuality he or she has reached or at which he or she has become fixated. A variety of adult *character types*, soon to be discussed, are connected with each of the psychosexual stages of development. Let us now examine some of the highlights in this odyssey of personality development.

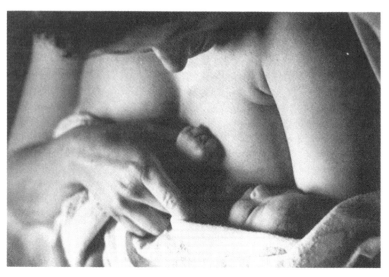

During the oral stage of psychosexual development, the major source of pleasure is derived from sucking, biting, and swallowing. These actions (via breast
feeding) reduce tension in the infant. (*Joel Gordon*)

The Oral Stage

The *oral* stage extends from birth to approximately 18 months of age. Infants are
totally reliant upon caregivers for survival; dependency is their only way of
obtaining instinctual gratification. The mouth is obviously the body structure most
frequently associated at this time with both reduction of biological drives and
pleasurable sensations. Infants obtain nourishment from sucking at the breast or
bottle; at the same time, sucking movements are pleasurable. Therefore, the oral
cavity—including the lips, tongue, and associated structures—becomes their
basic focus of activity and interest. In fact, Freud believed that the mouth remains
an important erogenous zone throughout life. Even in adulthood there are vestiges
of oral behavior in the forms of gum chewing, nail biting, smoking, kissing, and
overeating—all of which Freudians cite as evidence of the attachment of libido to
the oral zone.

Pleasure and sexuality are intertwined in Freud's account of development. In
this context, sexuality refers to a stage of excitation which, for the infant, is
connected with the intake of food. Accordingly, the first pleasure-producing
objects are the mother's breast or the bottle, and the first region of the body that
experiences the pleasure of tension reduction is the mouth. Sucking and swallowing thus become the prototype of every later sexual gratification. A central task of
the infant during this oral-dependent period is to establish general attitudes
(rudimentary ones, to be sure) of dependence, independence, trust, and reliance
in regard to other people. Since the infant is initially unable to distinguish between
its own body and the mother's breast, the gratification of hunger and the expression of affection are confused during sucking. This confusion accounts for the

infant's egocentrism. In time, the mother's breast loses value as a love object and is replaced by a part of the infant's own body. The infant sucks its thumb or tongue in order to lessen the tension created by a lack of continuous maternal care.

The oral stage ends when the infant is weaned. A central premise of psychoanalytic theory is that all infants experience some difficulty in giving up the mother's breast or bottle and its accompanying pleasure. The greater such difficulty becomes, that is, the greater the amount of libido concentrated at the oral stage, the less will be available for dealing with conflicts at subsequent stages.

Freud postulated that the infant who is given either excessive or insufficient amounts of stimulation is likely to become an *oral-passive* personality type in adulthood. The oral-passive type is cheerful and optimistic, expects the world to "mother" him or her, and continually seeks approval at the expense of everything else. His or her psychological adjustment is characterized by gullibility, passivity, immaturity, and excessive dependency.

During the latter half of the first year of life, a second phase of orality commences—the *oral-aggressive* or *oral-sadistic* phase. By now the infant has acquired teeth, thus making biting and chewing important means of expressing frustration caused by the mother's absence or by delay of gratification. The infant comes to seek oral satisfaction in aggressive acts, such as spitting. Fixation at the oral-sadistic stage is reflected in adults who are argumentative, pessimistic, "bitingly" sarcastic, and often cynical about everything around them. Persons of this character type also tend to exploit and dominate others as long as their own needs exist.

The Anal Stage

The *anal* stage begins at about 18 months and continues into the third year of life. During this time, young children derive considerable pleasure from both the retention and expulsion of feces and gradually learn to enhance this pleasure by delaying bowel movements (i.e., allowing minor pressure to be exerted against the lower intestine and anal sphincter). Although bowel and bladder control are fundamentally the consequence of neuromuscular maturation, Freud was convinced that the way in which toilet training is approached by parents and caretakers has specific effects on later personality development. With the onset of toilet training the child must learn to distinguish between the demands of the id (pleasure from immediate defecation) and the social constraints imposed by parents (self-control over excretory needs). In fact, Freud claimed that all later forms of self-control and mastery have their origin in the anal stage.

Freud identified two general orientations that parents often take in dealing with the inevitable frustrations of toilet training. Some parents are rigid and demanding about toilet training, insisting that their child "go potty right now." In response, the child may refuse to perform for Mommy and Daddy and become constipated. If this tendency to "hold back" becomes excessive and generalizes to other modes of behavior, the child may become an *anal-retentive* personality type. The

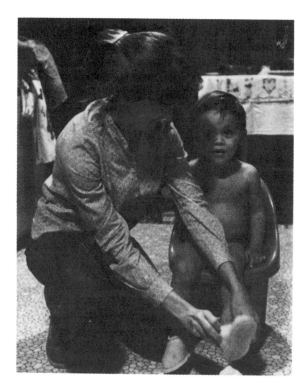

During the anal stage of psychosexual development, the major source of pleasure is derived from defacation. In Freud's view, toilet training represents the child's first attempt to control instinctual impulses. (*Jock Pottle/ Design Conceptions*)

anal-retentive adult is extremely obstinate, stingy, orderly, and punctual. This person also lacks the ability to make fine distinctions or to tolerate confusion and ambiguity. In contrast, a second outcome of anal fixation due to parental strictness about toilet training is the *anal-expulsive* type. Traits associated with this type of personality include destructiveness, disorderliness, impulsiveness, and even sadistic cruelty. With respect to adult love relationships, such a person tends to perceive others primarily as objects to be possessed.

Alternatively, some parents encourage their child to have regular bowel movements and praise the child lavishly for so doing. In Freud's view, this more permissive approach to the child's efforts at self-control fosters positive self-esteem and may even lead the child to develop creative tendencies.

The Phallic Stage

Between the ages of 3 through 6, the child's libidinal interests once again shift to a new erogenous zone of the body, the genitals. During this *phallic* stage of psychosexual development, children can be observed examining their sex organs, masturbating, and expressing interest in matters pertaining to birth and sex. Although their notions of adult sexuality are usually inaccurate, vague, and poorly formulated, Freud believed that most children understand sexual relations more clearly than their parents may suspect. They might have witnessed their parents having

intercourse, or perhaps they have fantasized the "primal scene" based on parental remarks or the comments of other children. Freud also felt that most children
view sexual intercourse as the father's aggressive act against the mother. It should
be emphasized that Freud's description of this stage has proved to be the basis for
considerable controversy and misunderstanding of his work. Furthermore, many
parents cannot accept the idea that their 4-year-old has sexual desires.

The dominant conflict of the phallic stage is what Freud termed the *Oedipus
complex* (called the *Electra complex* in girls). Freud modeled his description of
this complex after *Oedipus Rex*, the Greek tragedy by Sophocles, in which
Oedipus, king of Thebes, unwittingly murdered his father and committed incest
with his mother. When Oedipus realized his enormous sin, he punished himself by
tearing out his eyes. Although Freud recognized that the story of *Oedipus Rex* was
a Greek myth, he also saw this tragedy as a symbolic description of one of man's
greatest psychological conflicts. In effect, the myth symbolizes every child's
unconscious desire to possess the opposite-sexed parent and simultaneously
dispose of the same-sexed parent. The typical male child does not, of course,
actually kill his father nor does he have sexual intercourse with his mother, but
Freudians believe that he does have the unconscious wish to do both. Moreover,
Freud saw support for the Oedipus complex in the kinship ties and practices
within clans in various primitive societies.

The normal development and resolution of the Oedipus complex is somewhat
different for boys and girls. Let us consider first what happens to boys. The boy's
initial love object is the mother or surrogate mother. She has been a prominent
source of gratification for him since birth. He wants to possess his mother—to
express his erotically tinged feelings toward her just as older people that he has
observed express such feelings. He may, for example, try to seduce his mother by
proudly showing her his penis. This act shows the young boy aspiring to his
father's role, since the father is perceived as a competitor who prevents him from
fulfilling his wish for genital gratification. Hence, the father becomes the chief
rival or enemy of his son. At the same time, the boy is dimly aware of his
inferiority in comparison to his father (whose penis is larger); he realizes that the
father is not likely to tolerate or accept his son's romantic affections for the
mother. The ensuing rivalry results in the boy's fear that his father will hurt him—
more specifically, he may come to fear that his father will cut off his penis! The
boy's imagined threat of retaliation from his father, what Freud termed *castration
anxiety,* forces the boy to renounce his wish to have incestuous relations with his
mother.

Somewhere between 5 and 7 years of age, the Oedipus complex is normally
resolved as the boy *represses* (puts out of awareness) his sexual desires for the
mother and begins to *identify* with his father (incorporates his father's characteristics). The process of father identification, called *identification with the ag-
gressor,* serves several functions. First, it provides the boy with a conglomerate
set of values, morals, attitudes, and gender-related behaviors, all of which delineate for him what it means to be a male. Second, by identifying with the father, the
boy can vicariously retain the mother as a love object, since he now possesses the

attributes valued by the mother vis-à-vis the father. But even more important than these aspects of oedipal resolution is the fact that the boy internalizes his parents' prohibitions and standards of basic moral conduct. It is this specific quality of identification that Freud felt paved the way for the child's development of a superego or conscience. Thus, the superego is heir to the resolution of the Oedipus complex.

The feminine verson of the boy's Oedipus complex in Freudian theory is the Electra complex. Freud based his description of this complex after the Greek character Electra, who persuades her brother, Orestes, to kill their mother and their mother's lover in revenge for the death of their father. Like the boy, the girl's first love object is the mother. However, as she moves into the phallic stage she realizes that, unlike her father or brother, she lacks a penis (which may symbolize a lack of power). As soon as the girl makes this anatomical discovery, she wishes she had one. In the language of Freud, the girl develops *penis envy* which, in a certain sense, is the psychologial counterpart of castration anxiety in the boy. (Little wonder why Freud is anathema to advocates of the feminist movement!) Thereafter the girl becomes openly hostile toward her mother, blaming the mother for depriving her of a penis, or holding the mother responsible for taking the penis away from her as punishment for some misdeed. In some instances, Freud suggested that the girl may also devalue her own femininity because of her "defective" condition. At the same time, the girl wishes to possess her father because he has the enviable organ. Believing that she is unable to acquire a penis, the girl seeks other sources of sexual pleasure as penis substitutes. Sexual gratification is focused in the clitoris and, for girls ages 5 to 7, clitoral masturbation is sometimes accompanied by masculine fantasies in which the girl's clitoris becomes a penis.

Most experts agree that Freud's explanation of the Electra conflict resolution is obscure (Lerman, 1986). One reason suggested is that mothers do not have the same apparent power in the family as fathers and therefore are not as threatening. Another is that since she originally does not have a penis, the girl cannot develop the same intensity of fear as the boy regarding mutilation as retribution for an incestuous desire. For the latter reason, Freud theorized that girls develop a less compulsive sense of morality in adulthood. No matter how this issue is interpreted, Freud suggested that the girl eventually resolves her Electra complex by repressing her attraction to the father and identifying with the mother. In other words, by becoming more like her mother, the girl gains symbolic access to her father and increases the chances that she will marry someone like him. Later, some women desire to have as their first-born a baby boy, a phenomenon which orthodox Freudians interpret as an expression of penis substitution (Hammer, 1970). Needless to say, advocates of the feminist movement regard the Freudian outlook toward women as not only demeaning, but absurd (Gilligan, 1982).

Adult males fixated at the phallic stage behave in a brash, boastful, and reckless manner. Phallic types strive to be successful (success symbolizes winning out over the opposite-sexed parent) and attempt at all times to assert their masculinity and virility. Such males have to convince others that they are "real men.'' One way of proving it is by unrelenting conquests of women—i.e., by being Don Juans. In the case of women, Freud noted that phallic fixation results in traits of flirtatiousness, seductiveness, and promiscuity, although the individual may appear naive and innocent in sexual relationships. Alternatively, some women may strive to be superior to men by becoming, in the Freudian view, markedly assertive. Such women are depicted as ''castrating females.'' Unresolved Oedipal problems were also considered by Freud as the primary source of subsequent neurotic patterns, especially those pertaining to impotence and frigidity.

The Latency Period

Between the ages of 6 and 7 and the onset of the early teens, the child passes through a period of comparative sexual quiescence termed the *latency* period. Now the child's libido is channeled through sublimation into nonsexual activities such as intellectual pursuits, athletics, and peer relations. Latency can be viewed as a period of preparation for the important growth that will take place in the final psychosexual stage. The decline in the sexual drive was regarded by Freud as partly due to the physiological changes in the child's body and partly due to the emergence of ego and superego structures in the child's personality. Consequently, latency does not qualify as a stage of psychosexual development since no new erogenous zone emerges and the sexual instinct is presumed dormant.

Freud devoted only minor attention to the developmental processes occurring during latency, a strange fact when one considers that it occupies a chronological span of the child's life equally as long as that of the combined preceding stages. It seems to be an intermission for the theorist as much as it is for the child.

The Genital Stage

With the onset of puberty comes a resurgence of sexual and aggressive drives coupled with an increased awareness of and interest in the opposite sex. The initial phase of the *genital stage* (a period extending from adolescence until death) is brought about by biochemical and physiological changes in the organism. The reproductive organs mature, and the endocrine system secretes hormones that result in secondary sex characteristics (e.g., beards in males, breast development in females). These changes have the combined effect of increasing the adolescent's state of excitability and sexual activity. In other words, entry into the genital stage marks the most complete satisfaction of the sexual instinct.

From a Freudian perspective, all individuals go through a ''homosexual'' period in early adolescence. The new outburst of sexual energy is directed toward a person of the same sex (e.g., teachers, neighbors, peers) in much the same way that characterized the resolution of the Oedipal conflict. Although overt homosexual behavior is by no means a universal experience of this period, Freud believed that young adolescents prefer the company of their same-sex peers. Gradually, however, the object of libidinal energy shifts to a member of the opposite sex, and courting begins. The "crushes" of early adolescence normally lead to the selection of a marriage partner and the raising of a family.

The *genital character* epitomizes the ideal type of personality in psychoanalytic theory. This is the person who, having developed mature and responsible social-sexual relationships, experiences satisfaction through heterosexual love. While Freud opposed sexual license, he did condone greater sexual freedom than Viennese bourgeois society permitted. To discharge libido through sexual intercourse makes the physiological control of genital impulses possible; it stems the damming up of instinctual energies and thus culminates in a genuine concern for one's partner, free from any residue of guilt or conflict.

Freud believed that in order for people to attain the ideal genital character, they must relinquish the passivity of early childhood days when love, security, physical comfort—indeed, all gratifications—were freely given and nothing was expected in return. They must learn to work, postpone gratification, share with others in a warm and caring way, and above all, assume a more active role in dealing with life's problems. By contrast, if there have been severe traumatic experiences in early childhood with corresponding libido fixations, adequate adjustment during this stage becomes difficult if not impossible. Freud, in fact, maintained that significant conflicts in later years are replays of sexual conflicts rooted in childhood experiences.

NATURE OF ANXIETY

Freud's early experiences in treating disorders that were psychological rather than physical in origin first unlocked his curiosity about the nature of anxiety. This interest at first (in the 1890s) led him to propose that the anxiety experienced by many of his neurotic patients was a consequence of inadequately discharged libidinal energy. He further theorized that the state of increased tension resulting from blocked libido and undischarged excitation was converted into and manifested by anxiety neuroses. However, as he acquired additional insight while treating neurotics, Freud discovered the inadequacy of this interpretation of anxiety. Accordingly, some 30 years later he revised his theory to state that anxiety is an ego function which alerts the person to sources of impending danger that must be counteracted or avoided. As such, anxiety enables the person to react to threatening situations in an adaptive way (Freud, 1926).

Where Anxiety Originates

According to this later view, the first source of human anxiety lies in the neonate's inability to master internal and external excitations. Since infants cannot control their new world, a diffuse sense of impending peril overwhelms them. This situation creates a traumatic condition known as *primary anxiety*, the essence of which is exemplified by the birth process. Thus, in Freud's view, the experience of biological separation from the mother acquires a traumatic quality so that later separations (e.g., being left alone, being left in the dark, or discovering a stranger in the place of one's mother) produce strong anxiety reactions. Such a feeling of distress and helplessness is apparent in the birth trauma, in weaning, and later on in castration anxiety; all of these experiences lead to increased tension and apprehension.

Types of Anxiety: In What Ways Do People Feel Anxious?

Based on the sources of threat to the ego (the outside environment, the id, and the superego), psychoanalytic theory identifies three types of anxiety.

Realistic Anxiety   The emotional response to threat and/or perception of real dangers in the external world (e.g., dangerous animals or final examinations) is called *realistic anxiety*. It is essentially synonymous with fear and may have a debilitating effect on the person's ability to cope effectively with the source of danger. Realistic anxiety abates as the source of threat subsides. In general, it helps to ensure self-preservation.

Neurotic Anxiety   An emotional response to the threat that unacceptable id impulses will become conscious is called *neurotic anxiety*. It is caused by the fear that the ego will be unable to control raging instinctual urges, particularly those of a sexual or aggressive nature. The anxiety derives from a fear of the severe negative consequences that may result from doing something terrible. For instance, the small child quickly learns that active discharge of his or her libidinal or destructive urges will be met by threats of retaliation from parents or other social agents. Neurotic anxiety is initially experienced as realistic anxiety, because punishment originally derived from an external source. *Ego defenses* (to be explained shortly) are thus deployed to hold down the child's id impulses, and they surface only in the form of general apprehension. It is only when the instinctual impulses of the id threaten to break through the ego controls that neurotic anxiety occurs.

Moral Anxiety   When the ego is threatened by punishment from the superego, the ensuing emotional response is called *moral anxiety*. It occurs whenever the id strives toward active expression of immoral thoughts or acts, and the superego responds with feelings of shame, guilt, or self-condemnation. Moral anxiety derives from an objective fear of parental punishment for doing or thinking something (e.g., cursing or shoplifting) that violates the perfectionistic dictates of the superego. Hence, it directs behavior into activities that are acceptable to the person's moral code. The subsequent development of the superego leads to *social anxiety,* which is evident in concerns over exclusion from peer-group membership because of unacceptable attitudes or actions. Freud further believed that anxiety originating from within the superego ultimately extended to fear of death and to the anticipation of an afterlife of punishment for past or present transgressions.

Ego Defense Mechanisms

The major psychodynamic functions of anxiety are to help the person avoid conscious recognition of unacceptable instinctual impulses and to allow impulse gratification in appropriate ways at appropriate times. *Ego defense mechanisms* help to carry out these functions as well as to protect the person from overwhelming anxiety. Freud defined an ego defense mechanism as a mental strategy used by the individual to defend against open expression of id impulses and opposing superego pressures. He suggested that the ego reacts to the threatened breakthrough of id impulses in either of two ways: (1) by blocking the impulse from expression in conscious behavior, or (2) by distorting it to such a degree that the original intensity is markedly reduced or deflected.

All defense mechanisms share two common characteristics: (1) they operate at an unconscious level and are therefore self-deceptive and (2) they distort, deny, or falsify perception of reality, so as to make anxiety less threatening to the individual. It should also be noted that people rarely rely upon a single defense mechanism to defend themselves against anxiety; typically, people employ several defense mechanisms to resolve conflict and thereby relieve anxiety (Cramer, 1987). Some principal defensive strategies are reviewed below.

Repression Freud regarded *repression* as the primary ego defense, not only because it serves as a basis for more elaborate mechanisms of defense but also because it involves the most direct approach in avoiding anxiety. Sometimes described as "motivated forgetting," repression is the process of excluding distressing thoughts and feelings from consciousness. As a result of repression, individuals are neither aware of their own anxiety-provoking conflicts nor do they remember emotionally traumatic past events. For example, a person who has suffered a terrifying personal failure through repression may become unable to recount the experience.

The relief from anxiety provided by repression is not without cost. Freud theorized that repressed thoughts and impulses remain active in the unconscious and require continuous expenditure of psychic energy to prevent their emergence into conscious awareness. This persistent drain on the ego's resources may seriously limit the amount of energy available for more adaptive, self-enhancing, and creative behavior. However, the constant striving of repressed material for overt expression may find momentary gratification through dreams, jokes, slips of the tongue, and other manifestations of what Freud called the "psychopathology of everyday life." Moreover, from the Freudian perspective, repression is centrally involved in all neurotic behavior, psychosomatic ailments (e.g., ulcers), and psychosexual disorders (e.g., impotence, frigidity). It is the most basic and widely used defense mechanism.

Projection As a defense mechanism, *projection* ranks next to repression in terms of theoretical importance. It involves the process by which the person attributes unacceptable internal thoughts, feelings, and behaviors to other people or to the environment. Projection thus enables a person to blame someone or something else for his or her own shortcomings. The golf player who muffs a shot and looks critically at his club is engaging in a primitive projection. On a different level, the young woman who is unaware of her own lustful strivings but sees everyone she dates as attempting to seduce her is also projecting. Finally, there is the classic example of the student who inadequately prepares for an exam and then attributes his or her failing grade to an unfair test, the cheating of others, or a professor who neglected to explain the points at issue. Projection has also been used as an explanation of social prejudice and scapegoating, since ethnic and racial stereotypes provide a convenient target for the attribution of one's own negative personal characteristics (Adorno et al., 1950).

Displacement   In the defense mechanism called *displacement*, the expression of an instinctual impulse is redirected from a more threatening person or object to a less threatening one. A common example is the child who is scolded by her parents and proceeds to hit her little sister, kick her dog, or smash her toys. Displacement is also observed in an adult's hypersensitivity to minor annoyance. Consider, for instance, the wife who is criticized by an overdemanding employer and reacts with violent rage to the slightest provocation by her husband or children. She fails to recognize that, as objects of her hostility, they are simply substitute targets for the boss. In each of these instances, the original object of the impulse has been replaced by one that is far less threatening to the individual. A less common form of displacement is turning against the self, whereby hostile impulses toward others are redirected to oneself, producing feelings of depression and self-deprecation.

Rationalization   Another important way in which the ego attempts to cope with frustration and anxiety is to distort reality and thus protect self-esteem. *Rationalization* refers to "fallacious reasoning" in that it misrepresents irrational behavior in order to make it appear rational and thus justifiable to oneself and others. Silly mistakes, poor judgments, and failures can be explained away by people through the magic of rationalization. One frequently employed type, known as "sour grapes," is based on one of Aesop's fables about a fox who could not reach the grapes he desired and thus concluded that they were sour anyway. People rationalize in the same way, as in the example of a man who is snubbed when asking for a date and consoles himself by concluding that the woman really was not all that attractive anyway. Similarly, a student who is denied admission to dental school may convince herself that she really did not want to be a dentist anyway.

Reaction Formation   Sometimes the ego can guard against a forbidden impulse by expressing its opposite in both thought and behavior. This is known as *reaction formation*. As a defensive process it operates in two steps: first, the unacceptable impulse is repressed; next, the exact opposite is expressed on a conscious level. Reaction formation is especially evident in socially acceptable behavior that is compulsive, exaggerated, and rigid. For instance, a woman threatened by her own conscious sexual desires may become a staunch crusader to ban pornographic movies in her community. She may also actively picket particular movie houses or write to production companies about the degrading state of films today. Freud theorized that many males who ridicule homosexuals are defending against their own latent homosexual feelings.

Regression   Still another prominent defense mechanism that people use to defend themselves against anxiety is *regression*. This involves reverting to immature and childlike patterns of behavior. It is a way of alleviating anxiety by retreating to an earlier period of life that was more secure and pleasant. Readily observed forms of regression displayed by adults include losing their temper, pouting, giving people "the silent treatment," using baby talk, destroying property, rebelling against authority, and driving fast and recklessly.

Sublimation   According to Freud, *sublimation* is an ego defense that enables the person adaptively to divert impulses so that they may be expressed via socially approved thoughts or actions. Sublimation is considered the only healthy, constructive strategy against objectionable impulses because it allows the ego to change the aim or object (or both) of impulses without inhibiting their expression. The instinctual energy is diverted into other channels of expression—ones that

Freud believed that strong unconscious, aggressive urges can be redirected or sublimated into socially acceptable outlets. Thus, surgeons might be engaging in sublimation with each cut. (*N. R. Rowan/The Image Works*)

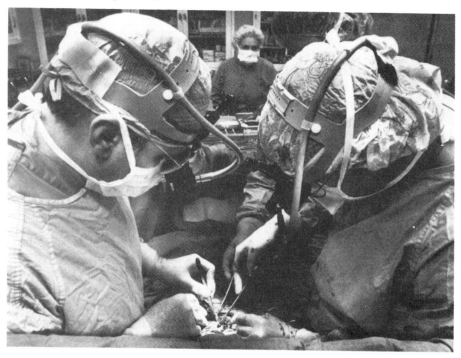

society considers acceptable (Golden, 1987). For example, if during development, masturbation becomes too anxiety-provoking to a young boy, he may sublimate his impulses into a socially approved substitute activity, such as football, hockey, or other sporting endeavors. In like manner, a woman with strong, unconscious aggressive and sadistic drives may become a surgeon or first-rate novelist. By doing so, she may demonstrate her superiority over others, but in a way that contributes to society.

Freud claimed that the sublimation of sexual instincts served as the prime instigator for great advances in Western culture and knowledge. As he said, "The sublimation of the sexual motive is an especially conspicuous feature of cultural evolution; sublimation alone makes it possible for the zealous scientific, artistic, and ideological activities which play so important a part in our civilized lives" (Cohen, 1969, p. 34).

Denial When someone refuses to acknowledge that an unpleasant event has occurred, he or she is engaging in *denial*. Consider the father who refuses to believe that his daughter has been brutally raped and murdered and acts as though she is still alive. As another illustration, consider the child who denies the death of a pet and persists in believing that it is still alive. Denial of reality is also evident when people say, or insist, "It can't happen to me," in spite of overwhelming evidence to the contrary (such as when a physician informs a patient of a terminal disease diagnosis). According to Freud, denial is most typical of young children or immature older individuals (though persons who usually function in a mature manner may occasionally use denial when faced with extremely traumatic situations).

Denial and the other defense mechanisms described here represent ways in which the psyche protects itself from internal and external threat. In every case psychological energy is expended to maintain the defense, thereby limiting the flexibility and strength of the ego. Moreover, to the extent they are working effectively, defenses create a distorted picture of our needs, fears, and aspirations. Freud noted that we all use defense mechanisms to some extent. They become problematic only when we rely on them excessively. The seeds for serious psychological problems are sown only when our defenses, with the exception of sublimation, lead to major distortions of reality (Vaillant, 1986).

Having concluded our discussion of Freud's key psychodynamic concepts, let us turn our attention to the basic assumptions that underlie this profound theory of humanity.

FREUD'S BASIC ASSUMPTIONS CONCERNING HUMAN NATURE

The unifying theme of this book is that all personality theorists hold certain assumptions about human nature. Furthermore, such assumptions, while neither directly verifiable nor unverifiable, help delineate the essential differences and similarities among the various theoretical perspectives. Now that the core concepts of psychoanalytic theory have been discussed, Freud's position on the nine

	Strong	Moderate	Slight	Midrange	Slight	Moderate	Strong	
Freedom							■	Determinism
Rationality							■	Irrationality
Holism	■							Elementalism
Constitutionalism	■							Environmentalism
Changeability							■	Unchangeability
Subjectivity				■				Objectivity
Proactivity		■						Reactivity
Homeostasis	■							Heterostasis
Knowability	■							Unknowability

FIGURE 3-2 Freud's position on the nine basic assumptions concerning human nature. (The shaded areas indicate the degree to which the theorist favors one of the two bipolar extremes.)

assumptions presented in Chapter 1 can be examined. His position on the respective dimensions (depicted in Figure 3-2) is as follows.

Freedom–Determinism Freud was a strict biological determinist (Kline, 1984). He assumed that all human events (actions, thoughts, feelings, aspirations) are governed by laws and determined by powerful instinctual forces, notably sex and aggression. Thus, human beings are seen as essentially mechanistic; they are governed by the same natural laws that apply to the behavior of other organisms. If this were not so, a rigorous psychological science could not exist.

In such a theoretical system, there is no room for concepts such as free will, choice, personal responsibility, volition, spontaneity, and self-determination. Freud clearly recognized the individual's overpowering illusion of freedom, yet he insisted that persons are incapable of actually "choosing" between alternative courses of action, and that their behavior is determined by unconscious forces of which they can never be fully aware. The clearest examples of determinism noted by Freud include misplacing personal possessions, forgetting familiar names and addresses, and so-called "slips" of the tongue and pen (termed "parapraxes"). He interpreted such occurrences as revealing something of the person's unconscious motives.

Rationality–Irrationality In Freud's view, people are motivated by irrational, almost uncontrollable, instincts which are largely outside the sphere of conscious awareness. While a degree of rationality exists within the ego, this component of personality structure is ultimately subservient to the demands of the id. The only real glimmer of rationality that Freud detected in humanity resided in his conception of psychoanalytic therapy as a vehicle for systematic personality change. Insight into unconscious motivation via psychoanalysis would pave the road for mastery and control over oneself. His credo—*where id was, there shall ego be*—

reflects his optimism that the forces of reason can tame the person's primitive and irrational drives. In spite of his conviction that a higher degree of rationality could be attained through psychoanalysis, Freud's theory of personality is firmly anchored to the importance of irrational elements in human behavior. The idea of a rational person in control of his or her destiny is nothing but a myth in this view.

Holism–Elementalism   Freud leaned toward a holistic view of persons, believing that they must be studied as totalities in order to be understood. Central to his theory is the portrayal of the individual in terms of id-ego-superego interactions and interdependencies. The person's behavior cannot be fully grasped without reference to the dynamic interplay of these three structures of mental life. Although Freud believed that these structures might ultimately be reduced to a more elementalistic level of analysis (probably biological or neurological), he never attempted this task himself. Finally, Freud relied almost exclusively upon the clinical method in developing his theory, a method that stresses the unity of personality.

Constitutionalism–Environmentalism   Several of Freud's early concepts (e.g., psychic energy, instincts, pleasure principle) were derived from neuroanatomy and neurophysiology (Weinstein, 1968). Psychoanalytic theory never substantially altered its course from this beginning and, on balance, Freud must be regarded as having adopted a constitutional position concerning human nature. As indicated earlier, the all-powerful id is the inherited, constitutional basis of personality structure and development. In addition, Freud viewed psychosexual development as a biologically determined sequence characteristic of all persons regardless of their cultural heritage. What human beings are, then, is very much a result of innate biological hereditary factors.

Conversely, Freud emphasized the importance of the person's early environmental history for understanding behavior. He stressed that parental influence during early childhood years had profound, irreversible effects upon subsequent personality growth. Further, the ego evolves only to meet environmental demands with which the id cannot deal, while the superego is exclusively a product of the social world. The net importance of environmental factors, however, is secondary to biologically rooted instincts in psychoanalytic theory.

Changeability–Unchangeability   Perhaps more than any other personologist presented in this text, Freud was strongly committed to the unchangeability assumption. Indeed, his entire theory of human development is based on the assumption that adult personality is shaped by early childhood experiences. As you will recall, Freud depicted the individual as progressing through a series of distinct psychosexual stages; adult personality structure can be described in terms of the psychosexual stage that the person has reached or became fixated upon. Thus, each individual's basic character structure is formed early in life and persists unaltered into the adult years.

Although Freud believed that a person's character type is formed in early childhood, he did consider psychoanalytic therapy to be beneficial for those persons seeking to gain insight into the sources of their current problems. By "getting in touch" and learning something new about past experiences in their lives, such persons can learn to cope more adaptively with present and future problems. At the same time, Freud recognized that analytical therapists are dealing with personality and behavior patterns that have been repeated and reinforced throughout their patients' lives. Not only must such patients unlearn faulty styles of behavior, but also they must acquire new ones, which may be likened to the acquisition of a new skill such as tennis or a foreign language. These goals, while not impossible, are extremely difficult and painful to attain, particularly if the patients, for reasons they only dimly recognize, fight every step of the way. The weapons they use are the same ones they used in childhood to fight their parents' efforts to socialize them (e.g., negativism, domination, helplessness, hostility, and despair). Therefore, even in analytical therapy, there is very little optimism about the possibility of real and sustained personality change in adulthood. For Freud, observed changes in people's behavior are more often than not merely that—superficial modifications that leave the core structure intact.

Subjectivity–Objectivity Freud saw persons as living in a subjective world of feelings, emotions, perceptions, and meanings. While he recognized the "private world" of an individual as an important part of personality, Freud also considered it to be a guide to something else—objective conditions like traumas, repressions, and universal human drives. Thus, psychoanalytic theory claims that a person's uniqueness is partly determined by external realities (e.g., parental attitudes and behavior, sibling relationships, social norms). Once the person is exposed to these objective conditions, however, they persist experientially to form the permanent world of unique, subjective meanings within which he or she resides. In conclusion, while Freud leans somewhat toward subjectivity, this assumption does not play a pivotal role in his theory.

Proactivity–Reactivity Concerning the question of the locus of causality in explaining human behavior, B. F. Skinner (1954) noted some time ago that Freud's account of human actions followed a traditional pattern of looking *inside* the person for the causes of behavior. Consequently, in this sense only, Freud must be construed as assuming a proactive view of human nature. As will become evident in subsequent chapters, however, Freud's proactivity takes a form markedly different from that assumed by humanistic or phenomenological points of view.

The essense of Freud's proactive position is clearly reflected in his concept of motivation: the locus of causality for all human behavior is found in the energy flowing from the id and its instincts. People do not consciously generate their own behavior; rather, the sexual and aggressive instincts generate the psychic energy which underlies the multiplicity of human actions. Individuals, then, are not proactive in the full sense of the term. They are reactive to the extent that their instincts have external objects that operate as environmental stimuli to elicit their behavior. For example, sex "objects" in the environment initiate expression of the sexual instinct, thus suggesting shades of reactivity within the theory. Weighing all factors, Freud's position on this assumption seems best described as a moderate inclination toward proactivity.

Homeostasis–Heterostasis   Freud believed that all human behavior was regulated by the tendency to reduce excitations created by unpleasant bodily tensions. The id instincts constantly clamor for expression, and people behave to reduce the tensions generated by this instinctual energy source. Thus, instead of seeking tension or excitement, individuals are actually driven to seek a tensionless state of nirvana, a view of motivation clearly reflecting a homeostatic position. From a psychodynamic perspective, the person is basically an id-driven "instinct satisfier" who never quests for conditions that would upset homeostatic balance.

Knowability–Unknowability   There are many indications that Freud was committed to the belief that human nature is ultimately knowable in scientific terms. For instance, he insisted that people obey the same laws of nature as any other living organism. Likewise, he viewed human beings as biologically determined organisms whose deepest motivations can be uncovered by the scientifically based techniques of psychoanalysis. To be sure, Freud never considered psychoanalysis as a complete theory of personality (Nuttin, 1956). Nevertheless, he viewed psychoanalysis as a part of the science of psychology and, as such, a system of thought that would shed substantial light upon the true nature of humans. It is likely that Freud's training in natural science, coupled with his personal rejection of the validity of mysticism, religion, and other nonscientific belief systems, fostered his conviction that science holds the key to the enigma of human nature.

Thus we conclude our assessment of Freud's position on the nine basic assumptions regarding human nature. Let us now consider some illustrative empirical studies stimulated by the theory.

EMPIRICAL VALIDATION OF PSYCHODYNAMIC CONCEPTS

Having studied Freud, students inevitably ask, "What scientific evidence is there to support psychodynamic concepts?" Insofar as a theory's concepts are regarded as empirically valid conceptualizations of the phenomena they purport to explain, it is only natural to expect the scientific testing of hypotheses derived from those concepts. In the years that followed his death, personologists all but totally ignored the objective and systematic verification of Freud's central concepts. A quick overview of the history of psychoanalysis as a method of therapy explains in good part why this was so. In Freud's time analysts generally were not interested in the use of research methods for investigating the theory. Freud himself did not stress empirical validation based on controlled, systematic study of phenomena in the laboratory as do most psychologists today. When Rosenzweig (1941), an American psychologist, wrote to Freud to tell him of his laboratory studies of repression, Freud wrote back that psychoanalytic concepts were based on a wealth of clinical observations and thus were not in need of independent experimental verification. This entire antiresearch attitude was further fostered by the fact that experimental psychology, still in its infancy, had little to offer. Even today, despite their formal training in the biological sciences, some practicing analysts oppose the use of research techniques (Kernberg, 1986). Many believe that the only method appropriate to verify psychodynamic hypotheses is the clinical interview, that is, the verbalizations of patients undergoing intensive, long-term therapy. Until recently, the primary source of evidence for determining the "truthfulness" of Freudian concepts has been the systematic accumulation of patients' reconstructed life histories. Most analysts consider the clinical assessment of patients' reported experiences as highly relevant confirmations of the theory.

Although clinical study of the individual case has served as the main method for developing and testing psychodynamic formulations, there are several deficiencies associated with its use. Foremost is the fact that despite all efforts to remain objective in the therapeutic setting, the analyst is not a truly impartial observer. Moreover, clinical observations of patients in the therapeutic setting cannot be duplicated and verified in controlled experiments. Freud's own investigations and those of other analysts hardly allow for replication because they were carried out under conditions of privacy and confidentiality.

Another methodological shortcoming derives from the professional training of most analysts. Such training, which necessarily includes a self-analysis plus intensive supervision by a seasoned training analyst during the initial stages of practice, commonly results in an unusually strong philosophical and personal commitment to the assumptions of Freudian theory. This commitment predisposes analysts to bias their interpretations of the patient's disturbance and its causation. Complicating the validity of clinical observations even further is the patient's own bias. Patients often know what is proper and improper to report during therapy sessions—hence, they may unwittingly seek approval by presenting experiential material that conforms to the analyst's expectations (Erdelyi, 1985). Collectively, these deficiencies are potent sources for the "self-fulfilling prophecy" concerning the validity of Freud's observations. Given such limitations, it is understandable why most psychologists refuse to consider individual case reports of therapeutic effectiveness as sufficient evidence for Freud's conceptions of personality (Shevrin, 1986).

The major pitfall confronting the personologist interested in testing Freudian theory is that there is no known way of replicating clinical observations and conclusions in a controlled experiment. A second related problem in determining the validity of psychoanalysis centers on the lack of operational definitions of theoretical concepts (i.e., the concepts are often defined in a way that prevents the clear derivation and testing of hypotheses). Also, when results based on such imprecise or ambiguous theorizing are obtained, it is virtually impossible to know whether they are supportive of the theory. This does not mean that psycho-analysis is an invalid theory. Rather, it means that, at present, there are no commonly agreed upon methods and procedures by which the theory's concepts can be objectively evaluated. Finally, psychoanalytic theory has a "postdictive" character. In other words, it more adequately explains past behavior than predicts future behavior.

Where, then, can one look for valid evidence pertaining to various aspects of Freudian theorizing? With some justification, personologists debunk most animal studies on the grounds of artificiality and oversimplification of conceptually complicated processes. Basically, the search for adequate evidence has taken the direction of developing experimental analogs (i.e., simulating theoretical concepts in a laboratory setting) of psychoanalytic constructs. No attempt is made here to cover exhaustively the literally thousands of investigations concerning Freudian theory (see Fisher & Greenberg, 1985, and Masling, 1983, 1986, for reviews of psychoanalytic studies). Instead, the focus is on illustrative and representative research. In the next few pages, we shall briefly sample selective studies drawn from two key investigative areas: (1) repression, and (2) unconscious conflict.

The Experimental Study of Repression

Repression is a key concept for most psychoanalysts (Cramer, 1988; Erdelyi, 1985; Grunbaum, 1984), and there has been more experimental research focused on it than any other single concept in Freudian theory (Westen, 1990). Early research on repression examined the differential recall of materials with neutral or positive associations versus materials with threatening or unpleasant associations (e.g., Jersild, 1931; Meltzer, 1930; Rosenzweig, 1933). In general, the results of these studies indicated that unpleasant or negative experiences are recalled less often than positive or neutral ones. Soon it was recognized, however, that the Freudian concept of repression does not imply that experiences associated with unpleasant affective meaning are repressed (Sears, 1936). The essence of repression, instead, was believed to depend on the presence of an "ego threat" (a basic threat to self-esteem) and not on mere unpleasantness or threat. Later it was also observed that when the cause of repression (the ego threat) was removed, the repressed material is restored to consciousness, a finding interpreted as indicating the "return of the repressed" (e.g., Flavell, 1955; Zeller, 1950). In other words, if the threat is eliminated it becomes safe for the repressed material to reenter awareness. Freud no doubt would have considered such research as silly demonstrations of what is already known from clinical observations.

The results of much of the experimental research on repression are clear, but their interpretation is very much a matter of debate. A case in point is a widely cited study by D'Zurilla (1965). In this experiment, college students first were shown 20 words and tested for recall in order to establish that there were no initial group differences in performance (there were none). Next, all subjects were exposed to a series of 10 slides. Each slide contained an inkblot and two of the words that had been previously presented. For each slide the subjects had to report which of the two words best described the inkblot. Following these initial procedures, D'Zurilla divided his subjects into two groups and introduced his experimental manipulation. The experimental group was told that the inkblot test was designed to detect latent homosexual tendencies. They were told that one of the two words on each slide was the choice homosexuals tend to make, while the other word was usually chosen by heterosexuals. Subjects in the control group were told only that they were taking part in the development of a new psychological inkblot test. After responding to all of the slides, subjects in both groups were given another recall test; again, no group differences were found.

Subjects in the experimental group were then ego-threatened by being told that they had chosen 9 out of 10 "homosexual" words. Subjects in the control group, by contrast, were informed that they had "done very well" on the test. After 5 minutes, subjects in both groups were given another recall test. This time, as expected, ego-threatened subjects did less well than they had before, while control group subjects actually improved from their prior recall performance. D'Zurilla then tried to eliminate the repression effect by revealing the deception to his subjects, explaining that the inkblot test did not actually measure homosexual tendencies. Following this revelation, the recall test was administered once more. As predicted, the groups recalled equally well, indicating that the threat had been removed.

Although these results seem to support the concept of repression, some doubt is cast on this conclusion by findings from interviews conducted after the experiment. Specifically, D'Zurilla asked his subjects to describe what they had thought about during the 5-minute interval following the ego-threat induction. Repression theory would predict that subjects would have avoided thinking about things related to the threatening task. Contrary to this prediction, most of the experimental subjects (ego-threatened) reported that they had thought a great deal about the inkblots and their own "homosexual tendencies." In contrast, only a few control subjects indicated that they had thought about the task at all.

According to a different interpretation of D'Zurilla's findings, ego-threatened subjects may have spent the post-threat interval ruminating about their anxiety-related thoughts and these competing cognitions could have interfered with their ability to recall the words. In a study similar to D'Zurilla's, Holmes and Schallow (1969) sought to obtain evidence that a response interference interpretation is at least as plausible as that involving repression. In addition to an ego-threatened group and a control group, these investigators added a group that was not ego-threatened but that was distracted during the 5-minute retention interval by exposure (at 30-second intervals) to irrelevant portions of a movie. Again, the data clearly indicated that following the threat the ego-threatened group recalled less well than the control group, replicating the repression effect previously reported by D'Zurilla. However, recall in the distracted group was significantly lower than that of the control group and almost equal to that of the ego-threatened group. Following debriefing, there were no recall differences among the three groups. Holmes and Schallow therefore concluded that *response interference*, rather than repression, mediates the effects of threat on recall. Indeed, after an extensive review of the experimental literature on repression, Holmes (1974) concluded that there is no evidence that repression exists. He comments that "in view of the amount and consistency of the data accumulated to this point, and pending new data supporting the concept of repression, the continued use of repression as an explanation for behavior does not seem justifiable" (p. 651).

Despite past difficulties in demonstrating clear-cut empirical evidence in support of the phenomenon of repression, efforts to investigate this basic psychodynamic concept continue unabated (Geisler, 1985; Lewicki & Hill, 1987). Noteworthy of this continued interest in repression is a recent study by Davis and Schwartz (1987). These investigators reasoned that repression as a defensive strategy should be associated with a diminished ability to recall unpleasant or negative memories. Female college students were asked to think back to their own childhood (until the time they were 14 years of age) and recall in a sentence or two any experience, situation, or event that came to mind. They were also asked to recall childhood experiences associated with each of five specific emotions (happiness, sadness, anger, fear, and wonder) and to indicate the earliest experience recalled for each emotion and the age at which it occurred. Prior to providing recollections of their childhood experiences, all subjects completed the Taylor Manifest Anxiety Scale (a measure of anxiety) and the Marlowe-Crowne Social Desirability Scale (a measure of defensiveness). They were then divided into repressors (low anxiety–high defensiveness) and nonrepressors (high anxious and low anxious nonrepressors) on the basis of their responses to these two questionnaires. The results of this study are depicted in Figure 3-3. As predicted by

FIGURE 3-3   Mean number of memories in each recall condition for low-anxious subjects, high-anxious subjects, and repressors. (*Source: Davis and Schwartz, 1987, p. 158. Copyright 1987 by the American Psychological Association. Reprinted by permission.*)

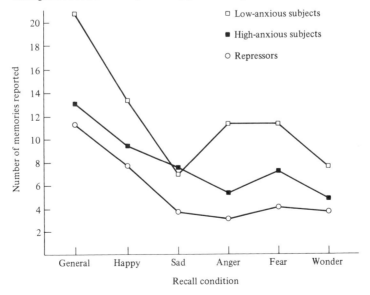

repression theory, repressors recalled appreciably fewer negative emotions than did low-anxious and high-anxious subjects. Additionally, repressors were significantly older than low-anxious and high-anxious subjects at the time of the earliest negative memory recalled. Davis and Schwartz viewed their pattern of results as "consistent with the hypothesis that repression involves an inaccessibility to negative emotional memories and indicates further that repression is associated in some way with the suppression or inhibition of emotional experiences in general. The concept of repression as a process involving limited access to negative affective memories appears to be valid" (1987, p. 155).

What is the scientific status of repression as a defense mechanism? Taken as a whole, research findings appear to indicate only marginal support for the existence of repression. Erdelyi and Goldberg (1979) have presented a succinct exposition of the current status of the psychological literature on repression. They maintain that clinical observations and studies provide a wealth of data consistent with the phenomenon of repression, but that the lack of rigor in the clinical approach poses serious difficulties. Experimental studies, on the other hand, have rigor, but the rigor is achieved at a serious cost; namely, at a substantial reduction in the complexity of the processes investigated. Faced with this impasse, we can either conclude that the phenomenon of repression does not exist (Holmes, 1974), or we can conclude as Erdelyi and Goldberg (1979) did, that the lack of compelling evidence reflects instead the inadequacies of the experimental methodologies used. One promising new direction is suggested by reformulating the issue of repression in terms of how people selectively process and retain the flow of information that enters their sensory-perceptual system. Reflective of this information-processing approach is Bower's (1981) work on mood- or state-dependent memory. His research shows that the individual's mood state leads to the recall of more mood-congruent information or experiences. For instance, people who feel happy are more likely to recall more happy childhood events than do people who feel sad. Conversely, people who feel sad are more likely to recall unpleasant childhood memories than do people who feel happy. Although Bower does not claim to be studying repression directly, it is hoped that this important ego defense can be investigated more fruitfully when placed in an information-processing or cognitive framework (Edelson, 1986; Erdelyi, 1985). Nevertheless, at this time, there is no solid empirical support for the claim that people use repression to deal with threatening or unpleasant experiences as hypothesized by Freud.

Unconscious Conflict: The Subliminal Psychodynamic Activation Method

According to Freud, conflict over unconscious, unacceptable libidinal and aggressive impulses is an intrinsic part of everyone's life. Freud further theorized that such conflict first develops in childhood and continues into adult life, where its influence on overt behavior includes the development of symptoms. In the past, analytically oriented researchers investigated the hypothesis that psychopathology (i.e., symptoms) expresses unconscious conflict almost exclusively through the use of interviews and case studies. To avoid some of the problems associated with these methods, Silverman (1976, 1983) developed a laboratory method for testing psychoanalytic predictions about unconscious conflict and its role in the development of manifest psychopathology. His method is called *subliminal psychodynamic activation.*

The technique of subliminal psychodynamic activation requires the use of a tachistoscope (a device that exposes verbal or pictorial material on a screen for only fractions of a second and thus well below the threshold for conscious recognition). In general, the experimental procedure involves tachistoscopic exposures of either conflict-intensifying or conflict-alleviating stimuli and then observing whether the predicted behavioral effects do occur. In the first instance, the stimuli being presented subliminally are expected to arouse unconscious conflict and thus increase psychopathological reactions or otherwise interfere with adaptive behavior. In the latter instance, the stimuli being presented subliminally are expected to alleviate unconscious conflict and thus decrease pathological disturbance or to enhance adaptive behavior. For example, the subliminal stimulus "Mommy and I Are One" might be comforting to some subjects, whereas the subliminal stimulus "I Am Losing Mommy" might be upsetting.

Silverman and his colleagues have conducted numerous studies to demonstrate that subliminal presentation of conflict-intensifying stimuli does affect the level of manifest psychopathology to a significant degree (summarized by Silverman, 1983). The first of these studies investigated the effects on stuttering of stimulating conflict over oral aggressive and anal wishes, the conflicts that psychoanalytic theory most consistently has linked with this disturbance (Silverman et al., 1972). The subliminal stimuli were a picture of a lion charging with its teeth bared (oral aggressive condition), a picture of a dog defecating (anal condition), and a picture of a butterfly (control condition). Stuttering was assessed by having individuals with this speech disturbance paraphrase two short passages they had just read and telling stories in response to two Thematic Apperception Tests (TAT) cards. As expected, subjects showed a significant increase in stuttering during the paraphrase task in both the oral aggressive and the anal conditions compared to the control condition. However, there was no speech disturbance effect as assessed by the TAT-story-telling task.

Silverman (1976) has also used the subliminal psychodynamic activation method to test a cardinal feature of the Freudian theory of depression—namely, that such a symptom involves a turning of unconscious aggressive wishes against the self. The results of several studies (involving depression-prone patients) showed that the subliminal presentation of content designed to arouse aggressive wishes (e.g., the words "Cannibal Eats Person" or a picture of one person stabbing another) led to an intensification of depressive feelings. No such increase in depressive feelings (as assessed by self-ratings on mood rating scales), however, was evidenced after the subliminal presentation of a neutral stimulus (picture of a bird flying).

Another type of subliminal psychodynamic activation study has focused on psychoanalytic hypotheses about the importance of oedipal conflicts in competitive behavior. Here is a representative experiment conducted by Silverman et al. (1978). Male college students first participated in a competitive dart-throwing tournament. Afterward, they were exposed to one of three different subliminal messages: Beating Dad Is Wrong, Beating Dad Is Okay, and People Are Walking. The first message was intended to increase oedipal conflict, the second to decrease it, and the third to neutralize it. Following the subliminal activation procedure, subjects were again tested for dart-throwing accuracy. As predicted by psychoanalytic theory, the subjects seeing the message Beating Dad Is Wrong had significantly lower dart scores than subjects seeing the neutral message, whereas the subjects seeing the message Beating Dad Is Okay had significantly higher dart scores than subjects seeing the neutral message (see Figure 3-4).

Other studies using the subliminal psychodynamic method have confirmed psychoanalytic hypotheses about (1) schizophrenia as it relates to oral-receptive conflicts (Silverman et al., 1982), (2) female sexual guilt as it relates to unresolved Electra issues (Geisler, 1986), and (3) male homosexuality as it relates to unresolved oedipal issues (Silverman & Fishel, 1981).

Silverman's research program is extensive and thought-provoking. As this brief overview suggests, the subliminal psychodynamic activation method has proven capable of demonstrating a number of psychological effects consistent with psychoanalytic theories about the influence of unconscious conflicts on behavior. Nevertheless, close scrutiny of portions of this research also reveals problems (Balay & Shevrin, 1988). Critics point out that efforts to replicate subliminal psychodynamic activation effects have consistently failed to find any effects at all. Haspel and Harris (1982) and Heilbrun (1980), for example, failed repeatedly to replicate the results of the Silverman et al. dart-throwing experiment. Furthermore, psychodynamic activation effects appear to occur only when the stimuli are presented below the threshold of consciousness (Hardaway, 1990). In other words, if conflict-related stimuli are presented above threshold for awareness, they fail to intensify psychopathology. Finally, a word needs to be said about the ethics of exposing subjects (especially psychiatric patients) to subliminal activation designed to affect their behavior. Silverman comments that "the intensification of psychopathology that our experimental method brings about lasts but for a brief period of time, with the degree of pathology then receding to its baseline

FIGURE 3-4 Effects of oedipal conflict on competitive performance in a dart-throwing tournament. (*Source: Silverman, Ross, Adler, and Lustig, 1978, p. 346. Copyright 1978 by the American Psychological Association. Adapted by permission.*)

	Subliminal presentation of three stimuli		
	"Beating dad is wrong"	"Beating dad is okay"	"People are walking"
Dart score			
Prestimulus mean	443.7	443.3	439.0
Poststimulus mean	349.0	533.3	442.3
Difference	−94.7	+99.0	+3.3

level. This becomes understandable when it is borne in mind that this method does no more than many real-life everyday events with which people are constantly confronted'' (Silverman, 1976, p. 626). He also informs his subjects prior to an experiment that they will be exposed to subliminal stimulation and offers them the option of learning either at the outset or at the end of the study the content of their particular subliminal stimulus.

It is unclear why several other researchers have not been able to replicate Silverman's findings (Fisher et al., 1986; Oliver & Burkham, 1982). The need for replication is especially mandatory when dealing with key hypotheses as controversial as those based on Freudian theory. Silverman is to be commended for his efforts to document the power of unconscious conflicts on behavior through the subliminal psychodynamic activation method. However, failure to replicate his results (with few exceptions) suggests that empirical support for Freud's theory of psychopathology is far from convincing.

A Word of Caution   Taken collectively, the two research areas reviewed here illustrate how psychoanalytic hypotheses might be subjected to empirical test. They also reveal the breadth of interest in determining the scientific validity of psychoanalytic propositions. However, careful analysis of these kinds of investigations indicates that many do not provide direct, unequivocal support for the validity of Freud's discoveries about human behavior and experience. For this reason, it is probably wise to conclude that the scientific credibility of major Freudian insights has not been convincingly established.

Freud's theory is extremely difficult to verify because many psychoanalytic concepts are difficult to define operationally and to measure empirically. Some personologists, in fact, argue that psychoanalytic hypotheses are inherently untestable, that Freud's concepts are too vague, complex, and imprecise to be put to empirical test (Holt, 1985). In their view, any attempt to assess the validity of psychoanalytic claims is doomed to failure and should, therefore, be abandoned. As we see it, efforts to evaluate the scientific status of psychoanalytic ideas have yielded some impressive achievements. Yet, overall progress has been modest at best. The major challenge facing psychoanalytic theory today is whether its concepts can be translated into operational procedures which allow for unequivocal test or whether it will eventually yield to another theory that is equally comprehensive and functionally significant but more amenable to systematic investigation and verification. Put differently, psychoanalytic theory, like any complex theory that claims to be scientific, must constantly seek new data using a variety of research methods, and then evolve accordingly.

APPLICATION: PSYCHOANALYTIC THERAPY— PROBING THE UNCONSCIOUS

Psychoanalytic theory has been applied to the understanding of virtually every area of human behavior. Such diverse fields as anthropology, art, criminology, history, economics, education, philosophy, sociology, and religion have felt its impact. Without exaggeration, there is no other theory in modern-day psychology that is as extensive in its range of concrete applications as psychoanalysis. To be sure, psychoanalysis has not escaped bitter criticism from contemporary person-ologists. For example, many believe that in Freud's theory there is an over-emphasis upon the negative, pathological side of human life accompanied by a deemphasis upon the positive, healthy, self-actualizing aspects of human exis-tence. However, even those who reject Freud's theory acknowledge his many seminal contributions to the solution of human problems. It is to one of these, perhaps the most significant and far-reaching application of psychoanalytic theory to date, that we now turn.

Assessment Techniques: What Happens in Psychoanalysis

Consideration of the therapeutic methods of psychoanalysis seems appropriate since Freud's clinical experience with neurotic patients was the basis for his theory of humanity. Today there are several psychoanalysts who practice therapy strictly in accordance with Freud's theoretical views and methods of treatment. In addition, there are many other mental health workers who are distinctly psycho-analytically oriented in their professional activities. To see what a Freudian therapist actually does, consider the following brief case history:

> Robert, 18 years of age, is referred to the psychoanalyst by his family physician. For the past year he has experienced a variety of symptoms such as headaches, dizziness, heart palpitations, waking up in the middle of the night with extreme anxiety—all of these pervaded by a constant, periodically overwhelming fear of death. Basically, Robert thinks that he has a brain tumor and is going to die. Yet, in spite of numerous medical tests and examinations, no physical basis for his symptoms can be found. The physician finally concludes that Robert's "symptoms" are probably psychologically based.
>
> Robert arrives at the analyst's office accompanied by his parents. He describes his problems and depicts his relationships with his parents as "rosy," although he feels that his father is "a little on the strict side." He does not allow Robert to go out on week nights, makes him come in by 11 P.M. on weekends, and successfully broke off Robert's relationship with a girl one year ago because he thought Robert was getting "too close" to her. But Robert shows no conscious resentment about any of this, instead describing the events in an unemotional, matter-of-fact fashion.

In the eyes of a psychodynamic therapist, Robert's symptoms are seen as determined, rooted in early childhood experiences, and motivated by unconscious factors. Collectively, these facts prevent Robert from using his own resources to change his feelings and behavior. However, Dr. F. (as we shall call our therapist) believes that through psychoanalysis Robert can be led to understand the cause of his intense fear of death and related symptoms, thereby making it possible for him to overcome them. Essentially, Dr. F's task in psychoanalysis is to get Robert to face his problems, master them, and then conduct his life with greater conscious awareness of his real motives (i.e., strengthen his ego). Freud believed that psychoanalysis was unrivaled as the vehicle for constructive personality change.

Toward this end, Robert would be expected to see Dr. F. almost daily for a period of several years. Successful analysis requires a great deal of time, effort (usually painful), and expense. Briefly, in Freudian theory, it takes a long time for the patient to become the way that he is; consequently, it will take a long time for him to change. Nonetheless, Freud believed that patients, especially those who were bright and well-educated, could benefit substantially from the insights they gained from analysis. Discussed below are illustrative assessment techniques used in psychoanalysis, applicable to Robert's problem or any other problem area faced by orthodox practicing analysts.

Free Association The therapeutic situation is arranged in order to maximize free association. In this procedure, Robert would be instructed to relax, either in a chair or on the classic couch, and verbalize whatever thoughts and memories that come to mind, no matter how trivial, absurd, embarrassing, or illogical they may seem. Dr. F. would stay out of view during this procedure to minimize Robert's inhibitions. As the basic rule agreed upon by those undergoing psychoanalysis, *free association* is based on the premise that one association leads to another that is deeper in the unconscious. Associations verbalized by the patient are interpreted as symbolic expressions of repressed thoughts and feelings.

In line with Freud's deterministic position, then, the patient's "free associations" are not really free at all. Like his other behavior, Robert's cognitive and affective associations are determined by unconscious processes. Because of repression and unconscious motivation, Robert is unaware of the underlying (i.e., symbolic) meaning of what he is saying aloud. By employing free association, Dr. F. believes that Robert's relaxed state will permit repressed material to emerge

A patient undergoing psychoanalysis typically lies on a couch while the therapist sits behind her, out of sight. The patient is encouraged to say whatever comes into her mind, no matter how trivial or embarrassing her thoughts seem. (*Judith D. Sedwick/The Picture Cube*)

gradually, thus releasing more psychic energy for adaptive use. Dr. F. should also be in a better position to understand the nature of Robert's unconscious conflicts and their presumed cause. Perhaps, for example, Robert's free associations will lead him to disclose his earlier feelings of intense resentment toward his father (the oedipal theme) and corresponding childhood wishes that his father would die.

Interpretation of Resistance During the initial stage of psychoanalysis Freud discovered that the patient is usually unable or quite reluctant to recall repressed conflicts and impulses. The patient resists. Thus, despite the fact that Robert consciously desires to change his feelings and end his suffering, he unconsciously resists Dr. F.'s efforts to help him eliminate his old, unsatisfactory behavior patterns. It is Dr. F.'s task to make Robert aware of his resistance maneuvers; it is necessary to deal with them successfully if therapeutic progress is to occur.

Resistance is a means of keeping the unconscious conflict intact, thereby impeding any attempts to probe into the real sources of personality problems. Resistance reveals itself in many ways and provides a graphic illustration of how emotionally threatening the therapy process can be. It may cause the patient to be late for therapy sessions, "forget" them, or simply find excuses for not coming. It is also evidenced when the patient is temporarily unable to free-associate, e.g., "I remember one day when I was a little kid and my mother and I were planning to go out shopping together. My father came home, and, instead, the two of them went out, leaving me behind with a neighbor. I felt . . . (pause) . . . For some reason, my mind is suddenly a complete blank right now." The ultimate form of resistance, of course, is for the patient to terminate therapy prematurely. Skillful interpretation of the reasons for resistance is one method Dr. F. would employ to help Robert bring repressed conflicts into the open and rid himself of unconscious defenses.

Dream Analysis Another prominent technique for uncovering the secrets of the patient's unconscious is that of *dream analysis*. Freud considered dreams as a direct avenue to the unconscious, since he viewed their contents as determined by repressed wishes. Indeed, he referred to dreams as "the royal road to the unconscious." As a result of his extensive clinical experiences, Freud believed that dreams were to be understood and interpreted as essentially symbolic wish fulfillments whose contents partially reflect early childhood experiences. By means of rather elaborate techniques of dream interpretation involving analysis of the disguised meaning of dream symbols, psychoanalysts believe that they can enhance the patient's understanding of the causes of both symptoms and motivational conflicts.

For example, Robert may report a dream in which his father is departing (death symbol) on a train while Robert remains on the platform holding hands with his mother and former girlfriend, while feeling at once pleased and intensely guilty. If the therapeutic moment is right, Dr. F. might help Robert to see that this dream reflects his long-repressed, oedipal-related wish for his father's death, rekindled last year by the father's severing of Robert's love relationship with his girlfriend. Thus, through dream analysis and interpretation, Robert may begin to gain greater insight into the real conflict underlying his present symptoms.

Analysis of Transference   Earlier in the chapter, displacement was identified as a defense mechanism in which an unconscious impulse is discharged upon some person or object other than the one toward which it was initially directed. When it occurs in therapy, this phenomenon is termed *transference*. More precisely, transference occurs whenever patients displace onto the analyst feelings of love or hatred which they had previously attached to a significant other (often a parent). Freud believed that transference reflected the patient's need to find a love object in order that repressed love feelings might be expressed. The analyst serves as a substitute love object in such a setting. Transference may reveal itself in direct verbal communication, free association, or the content of dreams. As an example, Robert might be showing signs of transference if he said something like the following: ''Dr. F., why the hell did you decide to take a two-week vacation with your damned beloved wife when we were just starting to get somewhere in analysis?'' On a deeper level, Robert is emotionally reacting to Dr. F. as he formerly felt toward his father in childhood (the oedipal theme again).

Insofar as the phenomenon of transference operates unconsciously, the patient is totally unaware of its functional importance. Not interpreting the transference immediately, the therapist encourages its development until the patient has established what Freud called a *transference neurosis*. In essence, this is a ''miniature neurosis'' that enhances insight into the patient's deeply ingrained ways of perceiving, feeling, and reacting to significant figures from early life. According to Freud, as patients become gradually aware of the true meaning of their transference relationship with the analyst, they gain insight into their past experiences and feelings, relating these more fully to their ongoing difficulties. Orthodox psychoanalysts regard analysis of transference as absolutely vital to the therapeutic process—successful outcomes depend utterly upon it.

In Robert's case, Dr. F.'s interpretation of the transference relationship may reveal that Robert both loved and hated his father a great deal. Deeply resenting his father's relationship with his mother, Robert strongly wished his father dead. But also loving his father, Robert felt extremely guilty and thus deeply repressed this wish. However, revitalized by his father's severing of the relationship between Robert and his new ''love object'' (former girlfriend), this buried feeling charged into consciousness in the distorted form of a fear of his own death. Thus, Robert's own overwhelming death fear (his central symptom) may be interpreted psychoanalytically as a symbolic wish for his father's death (an unconscious dread that he will kill his father) accompanied by an overriding guilt resulting in unconscious self-punishment for this wish. Robert's intense death fear and accompanying symptoms nicely accomplish this self-punishment objective. Other elements, such as a possible relationship between castration anxiety and fear of death, could also be worked into this kind of interpretation of Robert's symptoms. And the therapist, of course, employs all the previous techniques (not only analysis of transference) in arriving at the final interpretation.

Emotional Reeducation Encouraging patients to convert their newly discovered intellectual insights into everyday living is called *emotional reeducation.* In different ways, each of the previous therapeutic techniques is designed to help patients achieve greater insight into the causes of their behavior. However, the goal of insight alone, while necessary in psychoanalytic therapy, is not a sufficient condition for behavioral change. Urged by the analyst, patients must eventually apply their self-understanding to their day-to-day existence; they must learn to think, perceive, feel, and behave differently. Otherwise, psychoanalysis is nothing more than an emotionally draining exercise of excessive duration and expense.

Emotional reeducation is primarily employed during the final phases of therapy since the insights upon which it depends must necessarily be acquired first. Thus, Dr. F., having led Robert progressively toward a deeper understanding of the origins of his fear of death and accompanying symptoms, would help him to explore concrete ways of restructuring his feelings and behavior. Based on his newly acquired self-understanding, Robert would be encouraged to get rid of his childhood "hangups," begin to relate to his father as he is now, function more autonomously in relation to his parents, and develop more mature love relationships. In time, Robert should be able to accomplish these objectives with Dr. F.'s support. A good deal of this emotional reeducation would stem from therapeutic discussions of Robert's present life situation in light of his now well-understood past emotional history. When Robert makes substantial progress in these realms on his own, therapy is terminated by mutual agreement.

Each of the assessment techniques discussed above is illustrative of "classical" psychoanalysis as it is practiced today, variations of which are dealt with in detail elsewhere (Kernberg, 1976; Greenly et al., 1981). Robert's case exemplifies the emphasis on the Oedipus complex and the importance Freud placed upon early experience in subsequent neurotic behavior. Psychoanalytic therapy can be an extremely lengthy process, often involving 1 hour per day, 5 days per week, and extending over a period of 1 to 5 years and even longer! Thus, it is a very expensive form of therapy, often limited to the affluent. However, the major goal of analysis is nothing less than to produce basic changes in an individual's personality structure. Increased insight, personal integration, social effectiveness, and psychological maturity are the objectives. Obviously, such goals cannot be accomplished quickly or easily. Regardless of the ultimate judgment that history will pass on its actual therapeutic benefits (Wolpe, 1981; Kline, 1984), psychoanalysis stands as a significant pioneering effort in the continuing attempt to alleviate human misery.

Recent Developments in Psychoanalytic Therapy Psychoanalysts and other contemporary therapists have introduced many treatment variations and innovations, not the least of which is the practical matter of how long therapy should continue. As noted, traditional analysis is open-ended and may continue for years. Luborsky (1984) describes three contemporary changes in psychoanalytic therapy, the first of which sets a time limit (usually 25 sessions) on the duration of therapy. As such, analysis is now more structured and focused than traditional analysis. A second variant described by Luborsky is group or family therapy conducted from an analytical perspective. Here the therapist is afforded the opportunity to gather information about how patients deal with each other. Finally, some analysts prescribe medication in conjunction with traditional assessment techniques. Luborsky cautions against the overreliance on medication, which, he believes, may counteract insight, mask symptoms, and substitute for the therapeutic relationship.

SUMMARY

Freud's psychoanalytic theory of personality was presented as an example of a psychodynamic approach to the study of human behavior. The psychodynamic orientation holds that unconscious mental conflicts control the person's behavior. Sigmund Freud, the founder of psychoanalysis, based his psychodynamic concepts almost entirely on extensive clinical observation of neurotic patients as well as self-analysis.

Freud proposed three levels of consciousness—the conscious, preconscious, and unconscious—to describe the degree to which mental processes vary in accessibility to awareness. The most significant mental events take place in the unconscious (which is instinctual and separate from reality).

In Freudian theory, human personality is comprised of three structural components—id, ego, and superego. The id, representing the instinctual core of the person, is primitive, impulsive, and obedient to the pleasure principle. Reflex actions and primary process thinking are used by the id in obtaining immediate gratification of instinctual urges. The ego represents the rational part of personality and is governed by the reality principle. Its task, through secondary process thinking, is to provide the individual with an appropriate plan of action in order to satisfy the demands of the id within the constraints of the social world and the individual's conscience. The superego, the final structure developed, represents the moral branch of personality. It has two subsystems, the conscience and the ego-ideal.

Freud's motivational theory is based on the concept of instinct, defined as an innate state of excitation which seeks tension release. Two categories of instinct are recognized in psychoanalytic theory: life (Eros) and death (Thanatos) instincts. An instinct has four essential properties: (1) source, (2) aim, (3) object, and (4) impetus.

Freud's account of psychosexual development is based on the premise that sexuality begins at birth and progresses thereafter through a biologically defined set of erogenous zones until adulthood is reached. Freud conceived of personality development as proceeding through the following stages: oral, anal, phallic, and genital. The latency period is not a psychosexual stage of development. Freud theorized that during psychosexual development, unresolved conflicts lead to fixation and character types. Thus, adults fixated at the anal-retentive stage tend to be stingy, rigid, and compulsively neat.

Freud recognized three types of anxiety: reality, neurotic, and moral. He proposed that anxiety serves as a warning signal to the ego of impending danger from instinctual impulses. In response, the ego employs a number of defense mechanisms, including repression, projection, displacement, rationalization, reaction formation, regression, sublimation, and denial. Defense mechanisms operate unconsciously and distort the person's perception of reality.

Freud's theory is founded upon certain basic assumptions concerning human nature. Psychoanalytic theory reflects (1) a strong commitment to the assumptions of determinism, irrationality, unchangeability, homeostasis, and knowability; (2) a moderate commitment to the assumptions of holism, constitutionalism, and proactivity; and (3) a slight commitment to the assumption of subjectivity.

A number of psychoanalytic concepts have yet to be submitted to rigorous empirical investigation. Freud claimed empirical validity for his theory on the basis of clinical observations of patients in therapy and was opposed to experimental/laboratory-based approaches. Nonetheless, efforts to establish the validity of certain psychoanalytic concepts have been made. Illustrative studies focused on the experimental assessment of repression and subliminal psychodynamic activation of unconscious conflict and its impact on pathological behavior. These studies provide empirical support for certain key psychoanalytic hypotheses. Caution should be exercised in accepting the results of such studies at face value.

Applications of psychoanalytic concepts to everyday life are numerous. One of the most significant of these, psychoanalytic therapy, uses well-developed methods such as free association, interpretation of resistance, dream analysis, and analysis of transference to probe the unconscious with the aim of making possible a deeper understanding of the self. These newly acquired self-insights are then converted into a person's everyday life through the method of emotional reeducation. Recent changes in the practice of psychoanalysis include setting time limits on therapy, focusing on group or family dynamics, and prescribing medication in conjunction with traditional assessment techniques.

BIBLIOGRAPHY

Adorno, I., Frenkel-Brunswick, E., Levinson, D., & Sanford, R. (1950). *The authoritarian personality.* New York: Harper and Row.

Balay, J., & Shevrin, H. (1988). The subliminal psychodynamic activation method: A critical review. *American Psychologist, 43,* 161–174.

Bower, G. H. (1981). Mood and memory. *American Psychologist, 36,* 129–148.

Breuer, J., & Freud, S. (1895). Studies in hysteria (Trans. A. Brill). In J. Strachey (Ed.), *The standard edition of the complete psychological works of Sigmund Freud* (Vol. 2). London: Hogarth.

Byck, R. (Ed.). (1974). *Cocaine papers by Sigmund Freud.* New York: Meridian.

Clark, R. W. (1980). *Freud: The man and the cause*. New York: Random House.

Cohen, J. (1969). *Personality dynamics: Eyewitness series in psychology*. Chicago: Rand McNally.

Cramer, P. (1987). The development of defense mechanisms. *Journal of Personality*, **55**, 597–614.

Cramer, P. (1988). The Defense Mechanism Inventory: A review of research and discussion of the scales. *Journal of Personality Assessment*, **52**, 142–164.

Davis, P. J., & Schwartz, G. E. (1987). Repression and the inaccessibility of affective memories. *Journal of Personality and Social Psychology*, **52**, 155–162.

D'Zurilla, T. (1965). Recall efficiency and mediating cognitive events in "experimental repression." *Journal of Personality and Social Psychology*, **1**, 253–257.

Edelson, M. (1986). The convergence of psychoanalysis and neuroscience: Illusion and reality. *Contemporary Psychoanalysis*, **22**, 479–519.

Ellenberger, H. F. (1970). *The discovery of the unconscious*. New York: Basic Books.

Erdelyi, M. H. (1985). *Psychoanalysis: Freud's cognitive psychology*. New York: Freeman.

Erdelyi, M. H., & Goldberg, B. (1979). Let's not sweep repression under the rug: Toward a cognitive psychology of repression. In J. F. Kihlstrom & F. J. Evans (Eds.), *Functional disorders of memory*. Hillsdale, NJ: Erlbaum.

Fenichel, O. (1945). *The psychoanalytic theory of neurosis*. New York: Norton.

Fisher, C. B., Glenwick, D.S., & Blumenthal, R. S. (1986). Subliminal oedipal stimuli and competitive performance: An investigation of between-groups effects and mediating subject variables. *Journal of Abnormal Psychology*, **95**, 292–294.

Fisher, S., & Greenberg, R. P. (1985). *The scientific credibility of Freud's theories and therapy*. New York: Columbia University Press.

Flavell, J. (1955). Repression and the "return of the repressed." *Journal of Consulting Psychology*, **19**, 441–443.

Freud, S. (1900/1953). The interpretation of dreams. In J. Strachey (Ed. & Trans.), *The standard edition of the complete psychological works of Sigmund Freud* (Vols. 4 and 5). London: Hogarth.

Freud, S. (1901/1960). The psychopathology of everyday life. In *Standard edition* (Vol. 6). London: Hogarth.

Freud, S. (1905a/1953). Three essays on sexuality. In *Standard edition* (Vol. 7). London: Hogarth.

Freud, S. (1905b/1960). Jokes and their relation to the unconscious. In *Standard edition* (Vol. 8). London: Hogarth.

Freud, S. (1915–1917/1943). *A general introduction to psychoanalysis*. New York: Doubleday.

Freud, S. (1920a/1955). Introductory lectures on psycho-analysis. In *Standard edition* (Vol. 18). London: Hogarth.

Freud, S. (1920b/1955). Beyond the pleasure principle. In *Standard edition* (Vol. 18). London: Hogarth.

Freud, S. (1923/1961). The ego and the id. In *Standard edition* (Vol. 19). London: Hogarth.

Freud, S. (1926/1959). Inhibitions, symptoms, and anxiety. In *Standard edition* (Vol. 20). London: Hogarth.

Freud, S. (1927/1961). The future of an illusion. In *Standard edition* (Vol. 22). London: Hogarth.

Freud, S. (1930/1961). Civilization and its discontents. In *Standard edition* (Vol. 21). London: Hogarth.

Freud, S. (1933/1964). New introductory lectures on psychoanalysis. In *Standard edition* (Vol. 21). London: Hogarth.

Freud, S. (1940/1964). An outline of psychoanalysis. In *Standard edition* (Vol. 23). London: Hogarth.

Geisler, C. (1985). Repression: A psychoanalytic perspective revisited. *Psychoanalysis and Contemporary Thought*, **8**, 253–298.

Geisler, C. (1986). The use of subliminal psychodynamic activation in the study of repression. *Journal of Personality and Social Psychology*, **51**, 844–851.

Gilligan, C. A. (1982). *In a different voice: Psychological theory and women's development*. Cambridge, MA: Harvard University Press.

Golden, G. K. (1987). Creativity: An object relations perspective. *Clinical Social Work Journal*, **15**, 214–222.

Greenley, J. R., Kepecs, J. G., & Henry, W. E. (1981). Trends in urban American psychiatry: Practice in Chicago in 1962 and 1973. *Social Psychiatry*, **16**, 123–128.

Grunbaum, A. (1984). *Foundations of psychoanalysis: A philosophical critique*. Berkeley: University of California Press.

Hammer, J. (1970). Preference for gender of child as a function of sex of adult respondents. *Journal of Individual Psychology*, **31**, 54–56.

Hardaway, R. A. (1990). Subliminally activated symbiotic fantasies: Facts and artifacts. *Psychological Bulletin*, **107**, 177–195.

Haspel, K. C., & Harris, R. S. (1982). Effect of tachistoscopic stimulation of subconscious oedipal wishes on competitive performance: A failure to replicate. *Journal of Abnormal Psychology*, **91**, 437–443.

Heilbrun, K. S. (1980). Silverman's psychodynamic activation: A failure to replicate. *Journal of Abnormal Psychology*, **89**, 560–566.

Holmes, D. S. (1974). Investigations of repression: Differential recall of material experimentally or naturally associated with ego threat. *Psychological Bulletin*, **81**, 632–653.

Holmes, D. S., & Schallow, J. (1969). Reduced recall after ego threat: Repression or response competition? *Journal of Personality and Social Psychology*, **13**, 145–152.

Holt, R. R. (1985). The current status of psychoanalytic theory. *Psychoanalytic Psychology*, **2**, 289–315.

Isbister, J. N. (1985). *Freud: An introduction to his life and work*. Cambridge, Eng: Polity Press.

Jersild, A. (1931). Memory for the pleasant as compared with the unpleasant. *Journal of Experimental Psychology*, **14**, 284–288.

Jones, E. (1953). *The life and work of Sigmund Freud*. (Vol. 1, 1856–1900). *The formative years and the great discoveries*. New York: Basic Books.

Jones, E. (1955). *Years of maturity* (Vol. II, 1901–1919). New York: Basic Books.

Jones, E. (1957). *The last phase* (Vol. III, 1919–1939). New York: Basic Books.

Kernberg, O. F. (1976). *Object relations theory and classical psychoanalysis*. New York: Jason Aronson.

Kernberg, O. F. (1986). Institutional problems of psychoanalytic education. *Journal of the American Psychoanalytic Association*, **34**, 799–834.

Kline, P. (1984). *Psychology and Freudian theory*. London: Methuen.

Lerman, H. (1986). *A mote in Freud's eye: From psychoanalysis to the psychology of women*. New York: Springer.

Lewicki, P., & Hill, T. (1987). Unconscious processes as explanations of behavior in cognitive, personality, and social psychology. *Personality and Social Psychology Bulletin*, **13**, 355–362.

Luborsky, L. (1984). *Principles of psychoanalytic psychotherapy.* New York: Basic Books.

Masling, J. (1983). *Empirical studies of psychoanalytic theories* (Vol. 1). Hillsdale, NJ: Erlbaum.

Masling, J. (1986). *Empirical studies of psychoanalytic theories* (Vol. 2). Hillsdale, NJ: Erlbaum.

Meltzer, H. (1930). The present status of experimental studies of the relation of feeling to memory. *Psychological Review*, 37, 124–139.

Nuttin, J. (1956). Human motivation and Freud's theory of energy discharge. *Canadian Journal of Psychology*, **10**, 167–178.

Oliver, J. M., & Burkham, R. (1982). Subliminal psychodynamic activation in depression: A failure to replicate. *Journal of Abnormal Psychology*, **91**, 337–342.

Puner, H. W. (1947). *Freud: His life and his mind.* New York: Dell.

Rosenzweig, S. (1933). The recall of finished and unfinished tasks as affected by the purpose with which they were performed. *Psychological Bulletin*, **30**, 698.

Rosenzweig, S. (1941). Need-persistive and ego-defensive reactions to frustration as demonstrated by an experiment on repression. *Psychological Review*, **48**, 347–349.

Sears, R. R. (1936). Experimental studies of projection: I. Attribution of traits. *Journal of Social Psychology*, **7**, 151–163.

Shevrin, H. (1986). An argument for the evidential standing of psychoanalytic data. *Behavioral and Brain Sciences*, **9**, 257–259.

Silverman, L. H. (1976). Psychoanalytic theory: "The reports of my death are greatly exaggerated." *American Psychologist*, **31**, 621–637.

Silverman, L. H. (1983). The subliminal psychodynamic activation method: Overview and comprehensive listing of studies. In J. Masling (Ed.), *Empirical studies of psychoanalytic theories* (Vol. 1, pp. 69–100). Hillsdale, NJ: Erlbaum.

Silverman, L. H., & Fishel, A. K. (1981). The Oedipus complex: Studies in adult male behavior. In L. Wheeler (Ed.), *Review of personality and social psychology* (Vol. 2, pp. 43–67). Beverly Hills, CA: Sage.

Silverman, L. H., Klinger, H., Lustbader, L., Farrell, J., & Martin, A. D. (1972). The effects of subliminal drive stimulation on the speech of stutterers. *Journal of Nervous and Mental Disease*, **155**, 14–21.

Silverman, L. H., Lachmann, F. M., & Milich, R. H. (1982). *The search for oneness.* New York: International Universities Press.

Silverman, L. H., Ross, D.L., Adler, J. M., & Lustig, D. A. (1978). Simple research paradigm for demonstrating subliminal psychodynamic activation: Effects of oedipal stimuli on dart throwing accuracy in college males. *Journal of Abnormal Psychology*, **87**, 341–357.

Skinner, B. F. (1954). Critique of psychoanalytic concepts and theories. *The Scientific Monthly*, **79**, 300–305.

Steele, R. S. (1982). *Freud and Jung: Conflicts of interpretation.* London: Routledge & Kegan Paul.

Sulloway, F. J. (1979). *Freud: Biologist of the mind.* New York: Basic Books.

Vaillant, G. E. (Ed.) (1986). *Empirical studies of ego mechanisms of defense.* Washington, DC: American Psychiatric Press.

Vitz, P. C. (1988). *Sigmund Freud's Christian unconscious.* New York: Guilford Press.

Weinstein, E. (1968). Symbolic neurology and psychoanalysis. In J. Marmor (Ed.), *Modern psychoanalysis: New directions and perspectives* (pp. 225–250). New York: Basic Books.

Westen, D. (1990). Psychoanalytic approaches to personality. In L. A. Pervin (Ed.), *Handbook of personality theory and research* (pp. 21–65). New York: Guilford Press.

Wolpe, J. (1981). Behavior therapy versus psychoanalysis: Therapeutic and social implications. *American Psychologists,* **36**, 159–164.

Zeller, A. (1950). An experimental analogue of repression. I. Historical summary. *Psychological Bulletin,* **47**, 39–51.

SUGGESTED READINGS

Bettelheim, B. (1982). *Freud and man's soul.* New York: Knopf.

Bowers, K., & Meichenbaum, D. (Eds.) (1984). *The unconscious reconsidered.* New York: Wiley.

Breger, L. (1981). *Freud's unfinished journey: Conventional and critical perspectives in psychoanalytic theory.* London: Routledge & Kegan Paul.

Freeman, L., & Stream, H. S. (1988). *Freud and women.* New York: Continuum.

Gay, P. (1988). *Freud: A life for our time.* New York: Norton.

Masson, J. M. (Ed.). (1985). *The complete letters of Sigmund Freud to Wilhelm Fliess, 1887–1904.* Cambridge, MA: Belknap Press of Harvard University Press.

McGuire, W. (Ed.). (1974). *The Freud/Jung letters.* Princeton, NJ: Princeton University Press.

Mitchell, J. (1974). *Psychoanalysis and feminism: Freud, Reich, Laing, and women.* New York: Pantheon.

Roazen, P. (1975). *Freud and his followers.* New York: Knopf.

DISCUSSION QUESTIONS

1 Do you agree or disagree with Freud that the two major motives underlying human behavior are sex and aggression? State your reasons.

2 Describe the nature and function of the id, ego, and superego, the three basic structures of personality. In what ways do the interactions among these structures create conflict within the individual?

3 Which of the defense mechanisms described in this chapter do you think you rely upon most? How do they help you feel better?

4 Using Freud's model of psychosexual development, how would you explain the behavior of a person who is excessively neat and tidy?

5 How does Freud explain the development of sex roles in boys and girls during the phallic stage? Do you agree with Freud's explanation?

6 Do you agree with Freud that it is impossible to live a normal, healthy existence without direct gratification of the sex instinct?

7 Does empirical evidence support the psychoanalytic claim that unconscious conflicts are the cause of pathological behavior? Is there any evidence to support the claim that people repress unpleasant or threatening experiences?

8 What is Freud's position on the free-will vs. determinism issue? What is his position regarding the constitutionalism vs. environmentalism issue?

9 What are some of the problems encountered in testing the validity of Freudian concepts based on the clinical or case study method?

10 Imagine yourself lying on a couch talking to a psychoanalyst. Which areas of your life would you be most willing to discuss? most reluctant? Do you think that you could

understand yourself better as a result of this process? What would you expect to gain? How do you think such insight might come about?

GLOSSARY

Anal character   Freud's concept for a personality type that expresses fixation at the anal stage of development. As an adult, this person is characterized by stinginess, stubbornness, and hoarding of possessions (anal-retentive) or by hostility, disorderliness, and cruelty (anal-aggressive).

Anal stage   The second stage of psychosexual development, during which bowel control is achieved and pleasure is focused on the retention or expulsion of feces.

Anticathexis   An obstacle preventing the gratification of an instinct.

Castration anxiety   Fear by young boys that their father will castrate them because of their sexual rivalry for the mother.

Cathexis   The investment of psychic energy in an object, idea, or behavior.

Character type   Freud's classification of people into categories based on fixation at a particular stage of psychosexual development.

Conscience   A subsystem of the superego that refers to the individual's capacity for punitive self-evaluation, moral prohibitions, and guilt feelings when he or she fails to live up to internalized standards of perfection.

Conscious   Those thoughts and feelings a person is aware of at any given moment.

Death instinct   Freud's idea that people are driven toward self-destruction and death (often turned outward as aggression).

Defense mechanisms   Unconscious reactions that protect a person from unpleasant emotions such as anxiety and guilt; ego-protective tendencies that distort or hide threatening impulses from oneself.

Denial   Defense mechanism that protects a person against threatening experiences from the environment by blocking out their existence.

Displacement   Defense mechanism that involves redirection of feelings or impulses to someone to whom they do not apply because of possible retaliation from the appropriate object. For example, a student who is criticized by an instructor and becomes irritated with his or her roommate.

Dream analysis   Psychoanalytic technique in which the symbolism of dreams is interpreted in order to help patients understand the causes of their symptoms and motivational conflicts.

Ego   The reality-oriented aspect of personality structure in psychoanalytic theory; it involves perception, reasoning, learning, and all other mental activities necessary to interact effectively with the social world.

Ego-ideal   That aspect of the superego involving standards of perfection taught to the child by the parents. It leads the individual to establish goals which, if achieved, generate a sense of self-esteem and pride.

Electra complex   The feminine version of the boy's Oedipus complex in Freudian theory.

Emotional reeducation   A psychoanalytic technique employed during the final phase of treatment whereby the patient is encouraged to convert insights into changes in everyday living.

Entropy   A thermodynamic law which states that any energy system seeks a state of balance. In psychoanalytic theory, entropy means that there exists in all living organisms a compulsion to reestablish the inanimate state out of which they were formed.

Erogenous zones   Those parts of the body where the inner and outer skin join and are sources of tension or excitation.

Fixation   The arrested development of an individual at one of the early psychosexual stages, caused by an excess of frustration or overindulgence.

Free association   Psychoanalytic procedure for probing the unconscious whereby the individual speaks freely about everything that comes to mind, regardless of how trivial, absurd, or obscene it may seem.

Frustration   Thwarting of a need or desire by a mothering one. Also, being blocked in the achievement of personal goals.

Genital character   Freud's term for ideal mental health. This is a person who is sexually potent, capable of intimate relationships with others, and contributes to society via productive work.

Genital stage   Fourth and final stage of psychosexual development in which mature heterosexual relationships are developed (extending from adolescence until death).

Id   That aspect of personality structure that contains everything inherited, present at birth, and fixed in the individual's constitution. It is animalistic, irrational, and free from all inhibitions.

Identification   The process whereby a child takes on the characteristics of another, usually a parent, in order to relieve his or her own anxieties and reduce internal conflicts.

Instinct   An innate bodily state of excitation that seeks expression and tension release. For Freud, mental representations of innate bodily excitations are reflected in the form of wishes.

Latency period   Period during which libidinal energy lies dormant and attention is focused on the development of interests and skills through contact with same-sexed peers.

Libido   That portion of psychic energy that seeks its gratification from purely sexual activities (sexual energy).

Life instinct (Eros)   Freud's idea that people are driven toward self-preservation.

Moral anxiety   Feelings of shame and guilt experienced by the person when the ego is threatened by punishment from the superego.

Neurotic anxiety   An emotional response of fear experienced when the ego is threatened by uncontrollable instinctual desires (fear that id impulses will get one into trouble).

Oedipus or **Electra complex**   The process during the phallic stage in which the child desires sexual union with the opposite-sexed parent, feels threatened by the same-sexed parent, and eventually resolves the conflict by identifying with the same-sexed parent. The child experiences erotic feelings toward the parent of the opposite sex and has feelings of hatred and jealousy toward the parent of the same sex.

Oral character   Freud's concept for a personality type that expresses fixation at the oral stage of development. As an adult, this person is characterized by passivity, dependency, and gullibility (oral passive) or by pessimism, exploitativeness, and sarcasm (oral sadistic).

Oral stage   The first stage of psychosexual development in which the mouth is the primary source of interest and pleasure.

Overindulgence   A term used to describe parents who provide little or no incentive for a child to gain self-control.

Penis envy   In psychoanalytic theory, the young girl's desire to possess a penis and her anatomical discovery that she lacks one.

Phallic character   Freud's concept for a personality type that expresses fixation at the phallic stage of development. As an adult, this person is characterized by brashness, exhibitionism, excessive pride, and competitiveness.

Phallic stage   The third stage of psychosexual development in which the sex organs become the primary focus of pleasure or gratification.

Pleasure principle   An orientation that calls for the immediate gratification of all wants and needs, regardless of reality demands or constraints.

Preconscious   Those thoughts and feelings of which a person is not aware at any given moment, but which can be summoned to awareness with little or no difficulty (e.g., what is your birth date?)

Primary process   Gratification of an instinctual need by fantasy. Psychological phenomenon whereby the individual reduces tension by forming a mental image of an object previously associated with satisfaction of a basic drive.

Projection   Defense mechanism in which a person attributes his or her own unacceptable desires to others.

Psychoanalysis   Theory of personality structure, development, dynamics, and change created by Freud. It places heavy emphasis on the role of biological and unconscious factors in the determination of behavior. It also maintains that human behavior is basically irrational and results from the interaction of the id, ego, and superego.

Psychodynamic theory   Theory or viewpoint that stresses unconscious mental or emotional motives as the basis of human behavior.

Psychosexual development   Theory formulated by Freud to account for personality development in terms of changes in the biological functioning of the individual. Social experiences at each stage presumedly leave some permanent residue in the form of attitudes, traits, and values acquired at that stage.

Rationalization   Defense mechanism in which the individual provides plausible but inaccurate justifications for his or her failures.

Reaction formation   Defense mechanism in which anxiety is reduced by repressing one set of impulses or feelings and overemphasizing an opposite set of impulses or feelings.

Realistic anxiety   An emotional response triggered by threat or perception of real dangers in the external environment.

Reality principle   An orientation that calls for the postponement of instinctual gratification until either an appropriate object and/or condition that will satisfy the urge can be found.

Reflex action   Process by which the id rids itself of tension by automatically responding to sources of irritation.

Regression   Defense mechanism in which the individual retreats to an earlier developmental stage that was more secure and pleasant and/or the use of less mature responses in attempting to cope with stress.

Repression   Defense mechanism in which unwanted thoughts or impulses are prevented from entering one's conscious awareness.

Resistance   Tendency to resist uncovering of repressed material in therapy; also tendency to maintain self-defeating behavior patterns by discontinuing therapy prematurely.

Secondary process   In psychoanalytic theory, cognitive-perceptual skills that enable the individual to satisfy instinctual needs without endangering his or her own safety or that of others.

Sexual instinct   Freud's idea that people are driven toward sexual gratification or pleasure.

Structural model   The tripartite division of personality structure postulated by Freud, consisting of id, ego, and superego.

Sublimation Form of displacement in which an id impulse is channeled into a socially acceptable activity.

Superego The ethical or moral dimension of personality structure in psychoanalytic theory; it represents the individual's internalized version of society's norms and standards of behavior as learned from the parents via reward and punishment.

Topographical model Freud's model of three regions of the mind (conscious, preconscious, and unconscious).

Transference An important phenomenon in psychoanalytic therapy whereby the patient transfers feelings toward significant others from the past (usually one of the parents) onto the therapist.

Unconscious That aspect of the psyche that contains one's unacceptable conflicts and desires. These can be brought to the conscious mind through techniques such as free association and dream interpretation.

CHAPTER 4

THE PSYCHODYNAMIC PERSPECTIVE REVISED: ALFRED ADLER AND CARL JUNG

An important aspect of the history of psychodynamic theory has been the emergence of several loosely related theories serving to either extend or revise Freud's approach to personality. Freud attracted and inspired many people of considerable intellectual power who followed in his footsteps (Gay, 1989). Some of these scholars remained faithful to the integrity of psychoanalysis and simply refined and updated certain key concepts. Others veered off in new directions and developed different, often antagonistic, points of view.

Two of the most prominent figures who broke with Freud and went on to establish their own original systems of thought were Alfred Adler and Carl Jung. Both were early members of the psychoanalytic movement and ardent supporters of Freud's sweeping and novel theoretical system. Eventually, however, both voiced their *opposition* to what they felt was the master's excessive emphasis on sexuality and aggression as the centers of human life. Other theorists also took issue with Freud on many fronts and proceeded to create rival schools of thought. However, with the exception of Adler and Jung, none of these revisionists produced full-fledged theories that could compete with Freud's by encompassing major aspects of human behavior.

Space does not permit detailed coverage of both Adler's and Jung's theoretical approaches to personality. Accordingly, we will focus attention on Adler and, following a discussion of his major concepts, take a less detailed look at the core ideas found in Jung's theory. To be sure, both theorists have made substantial contributions to our understanding of personality, and some of their ideas have been incorporated into the mainstream of contemporary personology. The cornerstone of Adler's system is the view that the person cannot be separated from the social community. Like the social cognitive approaches that we will review in Chapter 8, Adler stressed the *social determinants* of personality. Other significant themes espoused by this Viennese psychiatrist focus on the ability of people to (1) shape their own destinies, (2) overcome primitive drives and an uncontrollable environment in striving for more fulfilling lives, and (3) improve themselves and the world around them through self-understanding.

Like Adler, Jung deplored the immense importance that Freud placed on instinctual sexual urges. A central theme espoused by Jung is that people are influenced by their future aspirations as well as by their past experiences. Jung was also the first personality theorist to argue that opposing forces of personality must be integrated into a coherent whole in order for psychological health to be achieved. The emphasis on *personal growth* as well as other highlights of Jung's revised version of classical psychoanalysis will be discussed at the end of the chapter.

ALFRED ADLER: An Individual Theory of Personality

BIOGRAPHICAL SKETCH

Alfred Adler, the third of six children, was born in Vienna on February 7, 1870. Like Freud, he was the son of a middle-class Jewish merchant; but, while Freud was raised in a ghettolike district and remained forever conscious of his membership in a persecuted minority, Adler took his ethnic background lightly. There were few other Jewish children in the locale where he matured so that his accent and general outlook remained more Viennese than Jewish. Unlike Freud, who referred to the topic frequently, Adler made no pronouncements on the subject of anti-Semitism and converted to Protestantism in his adult years.

Adler described his childhood as a difficult and unhappy time. He enjoyed a warm relationship with his mother during his first 2 years of life, but he lost that pampered position when his younger brother was born. He then acquired a preference for his father, whose favorite he remained throughout his childhood. Death and illness were Adler's constant companions throughout his early years. When he was 3 years old his younger brother died in a bed next to him. In addition, he twice narrowly escaped being killed in street accidents. At the age of 5 Adler contracted a severe case of pneumonia and came very close to death. Later, he attributed his interest in becoming a doctor to that near-fatal illness.

Adler was a mediocre student during his early school years. In fact, in secondary school he did so poorly in mathematics that he had to repeat the course. His teacher advised his father to take him out of school and apprentice him to a shoemaker because he was unfit for anything else. However, his father encouraged him to continue in school and, through persistence and hard work, he subsequently became the best mathematics student in the class.

When at 18 Adler entered the University of Vienna, it was one of the leading European medical centers. Around it surged the life of the theater, music, and the socialist political philosophy which earned the city her nickname, Red Vienna.

Alfred Adler. *(Courtesy The Bettmann Archive)*

Throughout his student years, Adler exuberantly joined in. He became particularly intrigued by socialism and attended a number of political meetings. It was at one of these meetings that he met his future wife, Raissa Epstein, a Russian student who was also attending the University of Vienna. They were married in 1897.

Adler received his medical degree in 1895. For a time after receiving his degree Adler specialized in ophthalmology (eye diseases) in a run-down part of the city. Then, after a period of practice in general medicine, he became a psychiatrist. From 1902 to 1911, he was an active member of the inner circle that evolved around Sigmund Freud. But Adler soon began to develop ideas which were at odds with those of Freud and others sympathetic to psychoanalytic theory, ideas which became increasingly irreconcilable with those of Freud. Thus Adler resigned as president of the Vienna Psychoanalytic Society in 1911, left the society along with 9 of the other 23 members, and formed the Society for Free Psychoanalysis—much to the annoyance of Freud and some of his loyal associates. The following year, 1912, the name was changed to the Society for Individual Psychology.

From the mid-1920s onward, Adler devoted increasing portions of his time to giving lecture tours throughout Europe and the United States. With the rise of Hitler and the totalitarian wave that was sweeping Europe, he foresaw a catastrophe and believed that if his psychology were to survive anywhere it would be in America. Accordingly, in 1935, he and his wife took up residence in New York City, shortly thereafter accepting a visiting professorship in medical psychology at the Long Island College of Medicine (now Downstate Medical Center, State University of New York) and continuing his private psychiatric practice. Two of Adler's four children, Alexandra and Kurt, became psychiatrists in their father's tradition.

Adler was an indefatigable lecturer of great spontaneity and popularity. He was on a lecture tour when he suddenly died in Aberdeen, Scotland, on May 28, 1937.

When Freud learned of Adler's death, he wrote to a friend who had indicated that he was very much moved by the news: "I don't understand your sympathy for Adler. For a Jew boy out of a Viennese suburb a death in Aberdeen is an unheard-of career in itself and a proof of how far he had got on. The world really rewarded him richly for his service in having contradicted psychoanalysis" (Jones, 1957, p. 208).

A prolific and forceful writer, Adler published some 300 books and articles during his lifetime. *The Practice and Theory of Individual Psychology* (1927a) is perhaps the best introduction to his theory of personality. Among his many other important books now available in English translation are *The Neurotic Constitution* (1917a); *Study of Organ Inferiority and Its Psychical Compensation* (1917b); *Understanding Human Nature* (1927b); *The Science of Living* (1929); *The Pattern of Life* (1930); *What Life Should Mean to You* (1931); and *Social Interest: A Challenge to Mankind* (1939). Several professional journals have also been founded by Adler's followers. Devoted primarily to disseminating theoretical and research papers on individual psychology, they include: *Journal of Individual Psychology; American Journal of Individual Psychology;* and *International Journal of Individual Psychology.*

Adler's ideas have had a profound impact on contemporary developments in clinical and personality psychology. In particular, Adler's emphasis on social interest as a salient criterion of mental health has inspired a value orientation to psychotherapy. In addition, his concern with conscious, rational processes encouraged the beginnings of ego psychology (Ansbacher, 1977). His stress on social forces in personality development is evident in the later work of Erich Fromm, Karen Horney, and Harry Stack Sullivan, all of whom saw Freud as lacking a sociological orientation. Relatedly, his focus on the volitional and creative aspects of personality has influenced either directly or indirectly such prominent psychologists and psychiatrists as Gordon Allport, Abraham Maslow, Rollo May, Viktor Frankl, and Albert Ellis. Indeed, this chapter is replete with indicators of the contemporary nature of Adler's concepts: the need for a theory of relevance; the sense of inferiority and compensatory strivings; organ inferiority and psychosomatics; the "inferiority complex" (so much a lay term now)—the forerunner of a psychology of physical handicap; the role of neglect in the development of the antisocial personality; competence as the signpost of maturity; self-esteem and lust for power; the concept of life-style; stress and adaptation; birth order; self-actualization and service to others; psychological health; and creativity—to mention but a few. An excellent introductory presentation of Adlerian concepts has been written by Manaster and Carsini (1982).

BASIC TENETS OF INDIVIDUAL PSYCHOLOGY

Adler is often portrayed as a disciple of Freud who eventually rebelled against the teachings of his master and then proceeded to develop his own ideas. However, close scrutiny of Adler's life and work reveals that he was actually a colleague of Freud and should in no way be considered a "neo-Freudian." The seeds of

Adler's later theories are, in fact, evident in the writings that predate the period of his association with Freud (Ellenberger, 1970). Moreover, Adler never studied under Freud, nor did he ever undergo psychoanalysis, as required for becoming a practicing psychoanalyst (Orgler, 1972). Unfortunately, the two never reconciled after their break in 1911, and Freud remained hostile and bitter toward Adler for the rest of his life. As our discussion of basic concepts will reveal, much of Adler's individual psychology developed as an antithesis to Freudian theory.

1 The Individual as a Unified and Self-Consistent Entity

The notion that a human being is a unified and self-consistent organism constitutes the foremost assumption of Adlerian psychology (Adler, 1927a). In fact, when Adler christened his theory "individual psychology," it was because the term "individual" in its original Latin sense meant indivisible, that which cannot be divided. More specifically, Adler held that no life expression can be viewed in isolation, but must always be regarded in relation to the total personality. The person is an indivisible unity in regard both to the mind–body relationship and to the various activities and functions of the mind. Adler believed that the foremost challenge confronting individual psychology is to prove this unity in each individual: in the thinking, feeling, acting, the so-called conscious and unconscious, in every expression of personality. This self-consistent and unified personality structure Adler designated as the individual's *style of life,* a concept which more than any other epitomizes his effort to deal with the human being as a totality.

2 Human Life as a Dynamic Striving for Perfection

To regard the human being as an organic unity requires a unitary psychodynamic principle. This Adler derived directly from life itself, namely, that life cannot be conceived without on-going movement, movement in the direction of growth and expansion. Indeed, only in the movement toward identifiable goals can the individual be perceived as a unified and self-consistent entity.

In proposing this striving for perfection, Adler reasoned that people are not just pushed from behind by internal or external causes but rather are pulled from the front: they are always moving toward personally significant life goals. The goals people envision for themselves and the unique ways they struggle to reach them provide the key to an understanding of the meaning they give to their lives. In Adler's system these life goals are largely self-selected, suggesting that people are capable of determining their own actions and destinies in the constant quest for perfection. With the attainment of these goals, people not only will enhance their personal self-esteem but also will provide themselves with niches in the world.

3 The Individual as a Creative and Self-Determined Entity

While acknowledging the importance of heredity and environment in forming personality, Adler (1964) insisted that the individual is distinctly more than a mere product of these two forces. Specifically, he viewed people as possessing a *creative power* which places them in control of their lives; free, conscious activity is the defining character of human beings. This creative power affects virtually every facet of the person's existence—perception, memory, imagination, fantasy, and dreams. It makes each person a self-determined individual, the architect of his or her own life.

It is this belief in human creativity and freedom, more than any other, which prompts many psychologists to recognize Adler as a forerunner of modern humanistic psychology.

4 The Social Embeddedness of the Individual

Adler's holistic vision of human nature was comprehensive; he saw the person not only as a unified relational system but also as an integral part of larger systems—the family, community, indeed humanity itself: "Individual Psychology regards and examines the individual as socially embedded. We refuse to recognize and examine an isolated human being" (Adler, 1956, p. 2). Paramount to Adlerian theory, then, is the conviction that all behavior occurs in a *social context* and that the essence of human nature can be grasped only through the understanding of social relationships. Furthermore, every person has a natural aptitude for *community feeling* or *social interest,* the innate ability to engage in cooperative reciprocal social relations. Individual psychology thus assumes an essential cooperative harmony between individual and society, with conflict as an unnatural condition. The emphasis on the social determinants of behavior is, in fact, so central to Adler's conception of persons that it has earned him the reputation of being the first social psychologist in the modern history of personology.

5 Individual Subjectivity

Firmly anchored in the phenomenological tradition, Adler theorized that behavior is always dependent on people's opinions of themselves and the environments with which they must cope. Individuals live in a world of their own making, in accordance with their own "schema of apperception." Adler further argued that people are motivated by *fictional goals*—privately held beliefs about present and future events—that regulate behavior. For example, an individual might live by the credo "honesty is the best policy" or "every man for himself" or by a belief in an afterlife that will reward the virtuous and punish the wicked. Persons are portrayed as behaving in accordance with these private beliefs, whether they are objectively real or not: "It has the same effect on me whether a poisonous snake is actually approaching my foot or whether I merely believe that it is a poisonous snake" (quoted in Ansbacher, 1971, p. 58). In Adler's scheme of things, then, behavior is clearly a reflection of the individual's subjective perception of reality. Following are the central theoretical concepts grounded in these basic tenets of individual psychology.

INDIVIDUAL PSYCHOLOGY: BASIC CONCEPTS AND PRINCIPLES

Adler (1964) believed that the major purpose of a personality theory should be to serve as an economical and fruitful guide for therapists, and ultimately for everyone, in effecting change toward more psychologically healthy behavior. Thus, unlike Freud, he formulated a very parsimonious theory of the person in the sense that a limited number of core concepts and principles support the entire theoretical edifice. It can be presented under seven general headings: (1) inferiority feelings and compensation, (2) striving for superiority, (3) style of life, (4) social interest, (5) creative self, (6) birth order, and (7) fictional finalism.

Inferiority Feelings and Compensation

Very early in his career, while he was still associated with Freud, Adler (1907/1917b) published a monograph entitled *Study of Organ Inferiority and Its Psychical Compensation*. In this work he developed a theory as to why a person becomes afflicted with one illness rather than another and why a specific area of the body is affected rather than another. He proposed that in each individual, certain organs are somewhat weaker than others, making the person more susceptible to illnesses and diseases involving these organs. More to the point, Adler theorized that every person succumbs to disease in that region of the body which has been less well-developed, less successfully functioning, and generally "inferior" from birth. Thus, for example, some people are born with severe allergies which may affect the lungs in particular. These people would often suffer from bronchitis or upper respiratory infections. Adler further observed that people with

People with physical disabilities often strive to compensate for their weakness or defects. *(Ken Robert Buck/The Picture Cube)*

severe organic weaknesses or defects will often try to *compensate* for them by training and exercise, which often results in the development of the individual's greatest skill or strength: "In almost all outstanding people we find some organ imperfection; and we gather the impression that they were sorely confronted at the beginning of life but struggled and overcame their difficulties" (Adler, 1931, p. 248).

History and literature provide many examples of exceptional achievements that can be traced to the effort taken to overcome organ inferiorities. Demosthenes, a childhood stutterer, became one of the world's greatest orators. Wilma Rudolph, physically handicapped as a child, went on to win three Olympic gold medals in track. Theodore Roosevelt, a weak and sickly child, became a specimen of physical fitness as an adult as well as President of the United States. Thus, *organ inferiority*—that is, congenitally weak or poorly functioning organs—can lead to striking accomplishments in a person's life. But it can also lead to excessive feelings of inferiority if the person's attempts at compensation are unsuccessful.

There was, of course, nothing novel in the idea that the organism tries to repair its own weaknesses; physicians had long been aware that where one kidney functioned poorly, for example, the other would become overdeveloped and attempt to do the work of two. But Adler suggested that this process of compensation also occurs in the *psychological* sphere; that people often strive to compensate not only for organ inferiorities but also for *subjective feelings of inferiority,* those that arise from uniquely felt psychological or social disabilities.

Inferiority Complexes and Their Origins Adler believed in the thesis that feelings of inferiority begin in infancy. Specifically, he reasoned that the human infant experiences a prolonged period of dependency during which it is quite helpless and must rely upon adults to survive. This experience causes the infant to develop feelings of inferiority in comparison to larger, stronger, and more powerful people in the family. Furthermore, these early inferiority feelings mark the beginning of a lifelong struggle to achieve superiority over the environment as well as perfection and completion. In essence, Adler maintained that striving for superiority was the prime motivating force in life.

Thus, for Adler, virtually everything people do is designed to overcome their feelings of inferiority and thereby establish a sense of superiority. However, inferiority feelings, for whatever reason, can become excessive in some people. The result is an inferiority complex—exaggerated feelings of weakness and inadequacy. Adler identified three childhood handicaps as contributing to an inferiority complex: *inferior organs, overindulgence,* and *neglect.*

First, children born with inferior physical organs may develop feelings of psychological inferiority. Overindulged children, on the other hand, grow up lacking confidence in their abilities because others have always done things for them; they are plagued by deep-seated inferiority feelings for they believe it impossible to tackle life's obstacles on their own. Finally, parental neglect can cause an inferiority complex because neglected children basically feel unwanted;

they go through life lacking confidence in their ability to be useful and to gain affection and esteem from others. As will be seen later in this chapter, each of these three childhood handicaps can play a crucial role in the emergence of neurosis in adulthood.

Regardless of the circumstances that give rise to inferiority feelings, however, a person may react by overcompensating and thus develop what Adler called a *superiority complex*. This involves a tendency to exaggerate one's physical, intellectual, or social skills. A person, for instance, may believe she is smarter than others but not feel she must show her intelligence by reciting what she knows about movie stars. Another person may feel he must demonstrate all he knows about movie stars on every occasion to everyone who will listen to him. This person may even neglect everything else just to prove he knows more than anyone else about movie stars. In any event, the technique of *overcompensation* is an exaggeration of a healthy striving to overcome persistent feelings of inferiority. Accordingly, the person possessing a superiority complex tends to be boastful, arrogant, egocentric, and sarcastic. One gets the impression that this individual has so little self-acceptance (i.e., such a low opinion of himself or herself) that only by "putting down" others can he or she feel important.

Striving for Superiority

As just noted, Adler held that inferiority feelings are the source of all human striving toward self-expansion, growth, and competence. But what is the ultimate goal for which we strive and which gives a measure of consistency and unity to our lives? Are we simply urged on by the need to be rid of our inferiority feelings? Or are we motivated by the drive to ruthlessly dominate others? Or perhaps we seek high status? In searching for answers to these questions, Adler's thinking changed markedly over the years. In his earliest theorizing, Adler believed that the great dynamic force governing human behavior was a striving to be aggressive. Later he abandoned the idea of an aggressive impulse in favor of the "will to power." In this concept, weakness was equated with femininity and power with masculinity. It was at this stage that Adler proposed the idea of "masculine protest," a form of overcompensation that both genders employ in an effort to supplant feelings of inadequacy and inferiority. However, Adler eventually rejected the concept of masculine protest as a satisfactory explanation for the motivation of normal people. Instead, he developed a more general viewpoint in which people are seen to be striving for superiority, a condition quite different from the superiority complex. Thus, there were three distinct stages in his theorizing on the ultimate goal of human life: to be aggressive, to be powerful, and to be superior.

In his later years, Adler concluded that the *striving for superiority* is the fundamental law of human life, "a something without which life would be unthinkable" (Adler, 1956, p. 104). All people share this "great upward drive" from minus to plus, from below to above, from incompletion to perfection, and from inability to capability in facing the problems of life. It is difficult to overstate the importance Adler attributed to this general life force: he regarded the striving for superiority—to be our best possible self—as the master motive in his theory.

Adler believed that the striving for superiority is innate and that we are never free of it because it is life itself. Nevertheless, it must be nurtured and cultivated if we are to actualize our human potentialities. At birth, it exists as potentiality, not actuality. It remains for each of us to actualize this potential in our own way. Adler suggested that this process begins during the fifth year when we develop a life goal that serves as a focus for our superiority strivings. Although somewhat obscure and generally unconscious when first formed in childhood, the life goal eventually provides guidelines for motivation, organizing our lives and giving it direction.

Adler (1964) offered several additional ideas about the nature and operation of the striving for superiority. First, he saw it as one fundamental motive, rather than a combination of separate urges, with its roots in the infant's awareness that it is impotent and inferior to those in its surroundings. Second, this great upward drive is universal in nature; it is common to all, the normal and the abnormal alike. Third, the goal of superiority can take either a negative (destructive) or a positive (constructive) direction. A negative direction is evident in the case of poorly adjusted people who strive for superiority through selfishness and concern for personal glory at the expense of others. In contrast, well-adjusted people express their striving in a positive direction; their efforts for a superior way of life are intimately bound up with concern for the welfare of others. Fourth, Adler argued that the striving for superiority calls for a considerable expenditure of energy and effort; a person's level of tension is increased rather than decreased as a consequence of this energizing force in life. And fifth, the striving for superiority occurs at both the individual and the societal levels; we strive for perfection not only as individuals; as members of society, we strive to perfect our culture. Unlike Freud, then, Adler viewed the individual and society as essentially in harmony with one another.

In summary, Adler portrayed human beings as living in concert with their social world but perpetually striving to create a better world. Nonetheless, to theorize that humankind has only one ultimate goal—to improve its culture—tells us nothing about how we, as individuals, try to attain this goal. This issue Adler dealt with in his concept of style of life.

Style of Life

Style of life, originally called the "life plan" or "guiding image," represents the most distinctive feature of Adler's dynamic theory of personality. It is this concept, idiographic in nature, that identifies the person's unique mode of adaptation to life, most notably including the person's self-created goals and means of achieving them. According to Adler, the *style of life* encompasses the unique pattern of traits, behaviors, and habits which, when taken together, defines the flavor of a person's existence.

How does the person's style of life come into being? To answer this we must briefly return to the concepts of inferiority and compensation, for they determine the basis of our life-style. Adler theorized that in infancy we all experience inferiorities, either imaginary or real, that motivate us to compensate in some way. To illustrate, a child who is poorly coordinated might concentrate his compensatory strivings on developing superior athletic ability. His behavior, shaped by the awareness of his physical limitations, in turn becomes his style of life—a set of behaviors designed to compensate for an inferiority. Our life-style, then, is based on our efforts to overcome our inferiorities and thereby establish a sense of superiority.

In Adler's view, the style of life is so firmly ingrained by the age of 4 or 5 that it is almost totally resistant to change thereafter. Of course, people continue to learn new ways of expressing their unique life-style, but these are merely elaborations and extensions of the basic structure that was laid down at an early age. The life-style so formed persists and becomes the guiding framework for later behavior. In other words, everything we do is shaped and directed by our unique life-style; it determines which aspects of our environment we will attend to and which aspects we will ignore. All of our psychological processes (e.g., perceiving, thinking, feeling) are organized into a unified whole and gain their meaning from the context of our life-style. Consider, for example, the person who strives to become superior by developing her intellectual competence. From Adler's perspective, her life-style would predictably involve sedentary activities—intensive reading, studying, thinking—anything that serves to increase the level of her intellectual competence. She would arrange even the minute details of her daily routine—recreations and hobbies, relations to family, friends, and acquaintances, and social activities—in accordance with the goal of intellectual superiority. By contrast, another person working toward physical perfection would structure his life in such a way that this goal might be attained. Everything he does is done with an eye to athletic superiority. Clearly, then, in Adlerian theory all aspects of a person's behavior issue from his or her style of life. The intellectual remembers, reasons, judges, feels, and acts quite differently from the athlete, since the two are psychological poles apart in terms of their respective styles of life.

Personality Types: Life-Style Attitudes   Adler maintained that our style of life accounts for the consistency of our personality throughout life as well as our general orientation to the outside world. In this vein, he noted that the true form of our life-style can be discerned only from the manner in which we approach and solve certain problems in life. Work, friendship, and love are the three unavoidable tasks that each person must face in life. Adler also stressed that none of these life tasks stands alone—they are always interrelated—and that their solution depends on our life-style: "A solution of one helps toward the solution of the others, and indeed we can say that they are all aspects of the same situation and the same problem—the necessity for a human being to preserve life and to further life in the environment in which he finds himself" (Adler, 1956, p. 133).

Because each life-style is unique to the person who created it, only gross generalizations about personality types are possible. With this understanding in mind, Adler (Dreikurs, 1950) reluctantly proposed a typology of life-style attitudes which classifies people in terms of their solution of the three major life tasks. The classification itself is generated by a two-dimensional scheme, with "social interest" constituting one dimension and "degree of activity" the other. *Social interest* represents a feeling of empathy for all of humanity and manifests itself through cooperation with others for social advancement rather than personal gain. It constitutes the major criterion of psychological maturity in Adlerian theory and is the opposite of selfish interest. *Degree of activity* refers to the person's movement toward the solution of life's great problems and would coincide with what today might be called "arousal" or "energy level." All persons, as Adler viewed it, have their own level of energy by which they attack the problems of life. This level of energy or activity, usually established during childhood, may vary from the very lethargic, hesitant person to the one who is constantly in a frenzy of activity. It is only when combined with social interest, however, that degree of activity becomes constructive or destructive.

Adler's first three types of life-style attitudes—the ruling, the getting, and the avoiding—all lack social interest but differ in their degree of activity. The fourth type, the socially useful person, has both high social interest and high degree of activity. Adler reminds us that no typology, regardless of how sophisticated it may seem, can accurately describe the person's strivings for superiority, completeness, and wholeness. Nonetheless, a description of these life-style attitudes can, to some extent, facilitate the understanding of human behavior from Adler's perspective.

The Ruling Type   People who are assertive, aggressive, and active with little, if any, social awareness or interest are of the ruling type. Such people are active but in an unsocial way, and hence behave without concern for others' welfare. They possess a dominating attitude toward the outside world and confront the major life tasks in a hostile, antisocial manner. Juvenile delinquents and drug addicts are two examples of what Adler considered to be the ruling type of person.

The Getting Type   As the name suggests, people with this life-style attitude relate to the outside world in a parasitic manner, "leaning" on others to satisfy most of their needs. Such people lack social interest. Their main concern in life is getting as much as possible from others. Because they possess a low degree of activity, however, they are not likely to hurt others.

The Avoiding Type   People with this predisposition have neither sufficient social interest nor activity to solve their own problems. Fearing failure more than desiring success, their lives are marked by the socially useless behavior of running away from the tasks of life. In other words, their goal is to sidestep all problems in life, thereby avoiding any possiblity of failure.

The Socially Useful Type   This type of person is the epitome of maturity in Adler's system. Such a person embodies both a high degree of social interest and a high level of activity. Socially oriented, this person expresses a genuine concern for and communion with other people. He or she regards the three major tasks of

Freely giving of one's time to help serve food to the less fortunate expresses one of the real meanings of social interest. *(Emilio A. Mercado/Jeroboam)*

work, friendship, and love as social problems. Further, the person realizes that solving these life tasks requires cooperation, personal courage, and a willingness to contribute to the welfare of others.

Adler's two-dimensional theory of life-style attitudes is missing one possible combination: high social interest–low activity. It is not possible to have high social interest without also possessing a high degree of activity. In other words, people with social interest are compelled to do something that will benefit other people.

Social Interest

Still another crucial concept in Adler's individual psychology is that of social interest. The concept of *social interest* reflects Adler's strong belief that we humans are social creatures—that we must consider our relationship to others and to the larger sociocultural context in which we live if we are to fully understand ourselves. But more than this, it reflects the decisive although gradual change that occurred in Adler's thinking as to what constitutes the great driving force underlying all human striving.

Very early in his career, Adler theorized that people are driven by an insatiable lust for personal power and need to dominate. In particular, he held that people are pushed by the need to overcome their deep-seated feelings of inferiority and pulled by their desire to be superior. These views met widespread protest. Indeed,

Adler was severely criticized for emphasizing selfish motives while ignoring social ones. Many critics considered Adler's view of motivation as nothing more than a dressed-up version of Darwin's doctrine of the survival of the fittest. Later on, however, as his system matured, Adler came to feel that persons are strongly motivated by positive social urges. Specifically, he saw human beings as motivated by an innate social instinct which causes them to relinquish selfish gain for community gain. The essence of this view, captured in the social interest concept, is that people subordinate their own needs in favor of the greater social good.

Social interest derives from the German neologism *Gemeinschafttsgefuhl*, a term which cannot be fully expressed by an English word or phrase. It means something on the order of "social feeling," "community feeling," or "sense of solidarity." It also implies membership in the human community, i.e., a feeling of identification with humanity and kinship for each member of the human race.

Adler considered the potential for social interest to be innate. Since every human being has some amount of it, every person is a social creature by nature, not by habit. However, like any other innate predisposition, social interest does not emerge automatically but needs to be consciously developed. It has to be nourished to fruition through proper guidance and training.

Development of social interest takes place in a social environment. Other people, initially the mother, then other family members, and finally those beyond the home, contribute to this developmental process. However, it is the mother, the child's first and most influential contact with another person, who exerts the greatest impact on the development of social interest. Essentially, Adler viewed her job as twofold: to encourage mature social interest and to help direct it beyond her scope. Both functions are difficult to perform and are always influenced to some extent by how the child interprets the mother's behavior.

Since social interest arises in the mother–child relationship, the mother's task is to foster in her child a sense of cooperation, relatedness, and comradeship, qualities Adler considered to be closely intertwined. Ideally, the mother should display a genuine love for her child—a love centered on the well-being of the child, not the vanity of the mother. This healthy love relationship develops from a true caring about people and enables the mother to nurture her child's social interest. Her affection for her husband, her other children, and for people in general, provides a role model for the child, who learns from this demonstration of broad social interest that there are other important people in the world.

Many life-style attitudes associated with mothering may also stifle the child's sense of social interest. If, for instance, the mother concentrates solely on her children, she will not be able to teach them to transfer social interest to other people. Likewise, if she favors her husband and shuns her children and society, her children will feel unwanted and cheated, and their potential for social interest will remain dormant. Any behavior that intensifies the children's feelings of being neglected and unloved brings about a lack of autonomy and an inability to cooperate.

Adler viewed the father as the second most important source of influence in fostering a child's social interest. First, he must have a positive attitude toward his wife, his occupation, and society. In addition, his developed social interest must manifest itself in his relationship with his children. For Adler, the ideal father is one who treats his children as fellow human beings and who cooperates on an equal footing with his wife in caring for them. The father must also avoid the dual errors of emotional detachment and paternal authoritarianism, which, surprisingly, have similar effects. Children who experience paternal detachment tend to pursue a goal of personal superiority rather than one based on social interest. Similarly, paternal authoritarianism leads to a faulty style of life. Children whose father is tyrannical learn to strive for power and personal, rather than social, superiority.

Finally, Adler considered the relationship between wife and husband to have an enormous impact on the children's development of social feeling. If, for instance, the marriage is unhappy, children have little chance of acquiring social interest. If the wife turns her emotional support away from her husband and toward the children, the children are harmed since overprotection smothers social interest. If the husband openly criticizes his wife, the children lose respect for both parents. If there is dissension between husband and wife, the children learn to play one parent against the other. The eventual losers in this game are the children; they inevitably lose when their parents demonstrate no love for one another.

Social Interest as a Barometer of Psychological Health   According to Adler, the degree of social interest represents a useful yardstick for measuring the person's psychological health. He referred to it as the "barometer of normality," the criterion to be used in judging the worth of a person's life. Thus, in Adler's view our own lives have value only to the extent that we add value to the lives of others. Normal or healthy persons are genuinely concerned about others and their goal of superiority is social, encompassing the well-being of all people. Although they realize that all is not right with the world, they are committed to the task of improving the lot of humankind. In short, they know that their own lives have no ultimate value unless they contribute to the lives of their fellow human beings and even to the lives of those yet unborn.

Maladjusted people, by contrast, are those who lack social interest. As we will see later, they are self-centered, strive for personal superiority and superiority over others, and lack social goals; each lives a life that has only private meaning (preoccupied with self-interest and self-protection).

Creative Self

Earlier we noted that the foundations of the life-style are laid down in the early years of life. Adler argued that the life-style becomes so firmly crystallized by the time children are 5 years old that they proceed in the same direction for the rest of their days. Interpreted one way, this account of how the life-style is formed would seem to indicate that Adler is just as deterministic in his thinking as Freud. Both theorists, in fact, stressed the importance of early experiences in the development of the adult personality. But, unlike Freud, Adler held that behavior in later years is not simply a reliving of early experiences, but rather a characteristic expression of the person's personality that was formed during the initial years of life. More to the point, the notion of the life-style is not as mechanistic as it may seem, especially when we consider the concept in Adler's system called the *creative self*.

The creative self is the superordinate construct in Adler's theory, his ultimate achievement as a personologist. Once he discovered and blended it into his system, all other concepts were subordinated to it. Here at last was the active principle of human life—that which imparts meaning to life—that Adler had been seeking. Succinctly stated, Adler maintained that the *style of life is shaped by the person's creative power*. In other words, each person is empowered with the freedom to create his or her own life-style. Ultimately, people are solely responsible for who they are and how they behave. This creative power is responsible for the person's life goal, determines the method of striving for the goal, and contributes to the development of social interest. This same creative force also dominates the person's perceptions, memories, fantasies, and dreams. It makes each person a free (self-determined) individual.

In assuming the existence of a creative force, Adler did not deny heredity and environment as determining forces in shaping personality. Every child is born with a unique genetic endowment, and he or she soon comes to have social experiences different from those of any other person. People, however, are much more than products of heredity and environment. They are creative beings who not only react to their environment but also act on it and make it react to them. A person uses heredity and environment as the bricks and mortar of personality, but the architectural design reflects the person's own style. Thus, in the end, only the person can assume responsibility for his or her style of life and attitude toward the world.

What is the origin of human creative power? What causes it to develop? These questions were not completely answered by Adler. The best answer to the first question seems to be that human creative power is the outcome of a long evolutionary history. Humans possess a creative force because they are human. We know that the creative force blossoms during early childhood and that it accompanies the development of social interest, but exactly why and how it develops remains unexplained. Nonetheless, its presence enables each of us to create our own unique life-style out of the abilities and opportunities given us by heredity and environment. Adler's concept of the creative self underscored his belief that human beings are the masters of their own fate.

Order of Birth

In accordance with his emphasis on the social context of personality development, Adler focused attention on birth order as a major determinant of life-style attitudes. Specifically, he reasoned that even though children have the same parents and grow up in nearly the same family setting, they do not have identical social environments. The experiences of being older or younger than one's siblings and of being exposed to parental attitudes and values that vary as a result of the arrival of more children create unique conditions in childhood that profoundly influence the formation of the life-style.

For Adler, the child's numerical rank in the family constellation is of considerable importance. Particularly important are the perceptions of the situation that are likely to accompany the position occupied. Thus, it is the meaning that children attribute to the situation that actually determines in what way their particular ordinal positions will influence their life-style. Moreover, because perceptions are inevitably subjective, children born in any position may create for themselves any life-style. In general, though, certain personality characteristics are commonly found in children born at a specific position. Adler focused on four such birth-order positions: the first-born, the only-born, the second-born, and last-born child.

The First-Born (Oldest) Child   According to Adler, the first-born child is in the enviable position for a time of being an "only child." Usually the parents are thrilled if not somewhat anxious about the arrival of their first-born and are thus totally devoted to doing all the "right things" for their new baby. The first-born thus receives the parents' undivided love and care. In turn, she or he often enjoys a secure and serene existence—until another child is born to remove the favored status. This event dramatically changes the child's situation and view of the world.

Adler often referred to the first-born as a "dethroned monarch," and noted that this might be a very traumatic experience. Seeing that a younger sibling is winning the contest for parental attention and affection, the oldest child's natural inclination is to fight back in order to regain his or her former supremacy in the family. However, the battle to recapture the original position of being the center of attention in the family is doomed from the beginning; things will never be quite the same as they were, no matter how hard the first-born tries. Eventually the child learns that the parents are too busy, too harassed, or too unconcerned to tolerate infantile demands. Then, too, the parents exercise far more power than the child and are likely to counter troublesome (attention-getting) behavior with punishment. The final outcome of this family struggle is that the first-born child "trains himself for isolation" and masters the strategy of surviving alone and independently of the need for anyone's affection or approval. Adler further suggested that the oldest child is likely to be conservative, power-oriented, and predisposed toward leadership. Therefore, he or she often becomes the upholder of family attitudes and moral standards.

The Only-Born Child   Adler argued that the only child is in the unique position of not having other siblings with whom to compete. This fact, coupled with a vulnerability to being pampered by the mother, often leads an only child into an intense rivalry with the father. She or he thus becomes "tied to the mother's apron strings" and expects pampering and protection from all others too. Dependency and self-centeredness are the leading qualities of this life-style.

Such a child continues to be the focus of family attention throughout childhood.

In later life, however, a rude awakening occurs—the discovery that he or she is no longer the center of attention. The only child never had to share the center stage nor to compete with other siblings for it. The result, in Adler's view, is that the only child often has difficulty interacting with peers.

The Second-Born (Middle) Child   The second child has, from the very beginning, a pacesetter in the form of an older brother or sister and is thus stimulated, or perhaps challenged, to outdo the older child's exploits. This spurs the second-born, often generating a faster rate of development than the first-born exhibited. For example, the second child may begin talking and walking at an earlier age than did the first child. "He behaves as if he were in a race, as if someone were a step or two in front and he had to hurry to get ahead of him. He is under full steam all the time" (Adler, 1931, p. 148).

As a result of all this, the second-born is characterized by being highly competitive and ambitious. Her life-style is one of constantly trying to prove that she is better than her older sibling. Thus, the middle child is characterized by being achievement-oriented, using both direct and devious means to surpass the older sibling. Adler also felt that the middle child may set unrealistically high goals, thereby virtually ensuring the likelihood of eventual failure. It is of some interest to note that Adler himself was a middle child.

The Last-Born (Youngest) Child   The situation of the last-born child is unique in several ways. First, this child never experiences the shock of dethronement by another sibling and, as the "baby" or "pet" of the family, may be pampered not only by the parents but, particularly in large families, by older siblings as well. Second, if the parents are economically strapped, this child may be relegated to the role of "tag-along kid" who has nothing of his own and must get by on hand-me-downs from other family members. Third, with older role models that set the pace, all of whom are bigger and more privileged than he is, he is likely to experience strong feelings of inferiority along with a lack of independence.

Nevertheless, the last-born possesses one advantage: a high motivation to surpass older siblings. As a result, this child often becomes the fastest swimmer, the best musician, the most talented artist, or the most ambitious student in the family. Adler sometimes spoke of the "fighting youngest child" as the child most likely to become a revolutionary.

Each of the above examples represents a stereotypic description of the "typical" oldest, only, middle, and youngest child. And, as previously noted, not every child in each of these categories will fit the general life-style descriptions proposed by Adler. What he was suggesting is that each child's original position in the family is likely to present certain kinds of problems (e.g., having to give up being the center of attention after having held the limelight for some time, having to compete with others who have more expertise, and so on). Thus, Adler's interest in birth order relationships was nothing more than an attempt to discover the kinds of problems faced by children and the kinds of solutions they might develop in trying to cope with these problems.

According to Adler, last-born children who are pampered by other members of the family become quite vulnerable to feelings of inferiority. *(Erika Stone/Photo Researchers)*

Fictional Finalism

As already stated, Adler believed that everything we do in life is marked by our striving for superiority. The striving aims to bring about perfection, completion, and wholeness in our lives. Further, Adler felt that this universal motivational tendency takes concrete form as a striving toward a subjectively experienced superordinate goal. To appreciate his reasoning here, we need to examine Adler's concept of *fictional finalism,* the idea that human behavior is directed toward a future goal of its own making.

Soon after Adler broke away from the group that surrounded Freud, he came under the influence of Hans Vaihinger, a prominent European philosopher. Vaihinger, in a book entitled *The Philosophy of "As If"* (1911), advanced the notion that people are more affected by their expectations of the future than by their actual past experiences. He further argued that many people proceed through life acting "as if" certain ideas were objectively true. For Vaihinger, then, people are motivated not by what is true, but by what they *believe* to be true. Vaihinger's book so impressed Adler that he adopted several of its concepts for his theory.

Adler theorized that our ultimate goals (those goals which give our lives direction and purpose) are *fictional goals* that can neither be tested nor confirmed against reality. Some persons may, for instance, conduct their lives in the belief that with hard work and a little luck, they can accomplish almost anything. To Adler, this belief constitutes a *fiction* simply because there are many people who work hard and yet never accomplish anything of real merit. Another example of a fiction that exerts a powerful influence on the lives of countless people is the belief that God will reward them in heaven for living a virtuous life on earth. Belief in God and heaven can be considered fictional in nature because there is no empirical or logical way of proving their existence. Nevertheless, such beliefs are real to persons who embrace a religious system of faith. Other examples of fictional beliefs which may affect the course of our lives include "honesty is the best policy," "all people are created equal," "all people are basically selfish," and "men are superior to women."

According to Adler, each person's quest for superiority is guided by the fictional goal that he or she has adopted. He also believed that the person's fictional goal of superiority is self-determined; it is formed by the person's own creative power, therefore making it individually unique. Thus, as a subjectively held ideal, the fictional goal of superiority has great significance. When a person's fictional goal is known, all subsequent actions make sense and his or her "life story" takes on added meaning.

Although fictional goals have no counterpart in reality, they often help us to deal with reality more effectively. In fact, Adler insisted that if such goals do not serve us well in coping with daily life, they should be modified or discarded. It may seem strange to say that a fiction may be useful, but an example will clear up this point. A physician may strive to be excellent in her field of specialization. But excellence has no final limits. She can always learn more about her specialty. Certainly, she could devote more time to reading medical journals than she presently does. She might also enhance her knowledge by attending professional conventions and medical seminars. Yet the physician's ultimate goal, by its very nature, will never be completely attained. Her striving to attain excellence is, however, a useful and healthy striving. Both she and her patients are likely to benefit from her fictional goal.

Fictional goals may also be dangerous and harmful to the person. Consider, for instance, the hypochondriac who acts as if she were sick. Or the paranoid who acts as if he were being persecuted. Perhaps the most devastating instance of a destructive fiction was the Nazi-induced belief that Aryans constitute a super race. The belief obviously has no basis in reality, yet Adolf Hitler convinced many Germans to act *as if* Aryans were a super race.

In summary, Adler's concept of fictional finalism reveals the extent to which he emphasized a teleological, or goal-directed, view of human motivation. Personality, as he saw it, is influenced more by subjective expectations about what might happen in the future than by experiences of the past. Our behavior is guided by our perception of our fictional goal in life. This goal does not exist in the future but in our present perception of the future. Although our fictional goals have no objective existence, they nonetheless exert an enormous influence on our strivings for superiority, perfection, and unity.

We have now completed coverage of Adler's core theoretical concepts of personality. The next section will focus attention on the basic assumptions about human nature which underlie his system.

ADLER'S BASIC ASSUMPTIONS CONCERNING HUMAN NATURE

Adler is regarded by many as a "neo-Freudian," and he undoubtedly did much to revise the psychoanalytic movement as a whole. But while he was admittedly an early associate of Freud's, many of Adler's ideas depart more radically from traditional psychodynamic theory than may generally be recognized. Indeed, careful consideration of Adler's theoretical concepts strongly suggests that, far from being a "neo-Freudian," he may actually be more accurately understood as a precursor of contemporary humanistic and phenomenological psychology. Nowhere is this interpretation of Adlerian theory more compelling than in his basic assumptions concerning human nature (see Figure 4-1).

Freedom–Determinism   Adler's strong commitment to the freedom assumption is revealed in the following quotation: "We regard man as if nothing in his life were causally determined and as if every phenomenon could have been different . . . in psychology we cannot speak of causality or determinism" (Adler, 1956, p. 91). Rejecting the concept of psychic determinism, Adler (1927a) instead argued that each individual's personality is largely his or her own creation. And the embodiment of the freedom assumption in Adler's system is the concept of creative self. Ultimately, the person's creative powers play a vital part in the construction of a superordinate fictional goal and consequent style of life.

However, there is some limitation on the idea of total freedom in individual psychology in that life-style is at least somewhat influenced by the fictional life goal that originates in early childhood experiences (e.g., birth order). Even this fictional goal, however, is not a product of objective factors; it stems instead from the budding person's creative powers (e.g., the subjective meaning that a person attaches to his or her ordinal position within the family). It seems that, as Adler worked toward his crowning theoretical achievement of the creative self, a strong underlying assumption of freedom became more and more evident.

FIGURE 4-1   Adler's position on the nine basic assumptions concerning human nature.

	Strong	Moderate	Slight	Midrange	Slight	Moderate	Strong	
Freedom	■							Determinism
Rationality		■						Irrationality
Holism	■							Elementalism
Constitutionalism				■				Environmentalism
Changeability							■	Unchangeability
Subjectivity	■							Objectivity
Proactivity	■							Reactivity
Homeostasis							■	Heterostasis
Knowability							■	Unknowability

Figure 3-1 Adler's position on the nine basic assumptions concerning human nature.

Rationality–Irrationality On balance, Adler definitely inclines toward rationality, an inclination most evident in his concept of the creative self. Recall that in Adlerian theory the creative power of human beings enables them to envisage goals, make decisions, and select various life plans consistent with their purposes and values. The notion of such creative power requires a commitment to rationality for its base.

But strains of irrationality can be detected in Adler's system, most notably in his concept of the overriding fictional goal that guides the person's life. Blurred by an overlay of childhood experiences, this goal is largely unconscious, i.e., people are largely unaware of the fictional goal or at least its true significance in their lives (Adler, 1956). Thus, a significant part of what people strive for in life, however rationally they may do it, remains largely unknown to them. Nevertheless, the sheer weight that Adler assigns to the creative self in his theory clearly tilts this parameter in the direction of rationality.

Holism–Elementalism Adler's complete commitment to the holism assumption is evident in almost every facet of his work. As previously indicated, Adler even named his position "Individual Psychology" in order to stress his holistic view of the person as a single, indivisible, self-consistent, and unified entity. And, as discussed earlier, the foremost tenet of individual psychology is that of "the individual as a unified and self-consistent entity."

On a more specific level, Adler depicted the creative self in childhood as fashioning a fictional final goal toward which people strive all their lives; indeed, the entire style of life is largely predicated on this final goal. Adler (1956) argued that the ultimate unity of the personality is found in this individually unique final goal, the governing principle of a person's life-style and direction. In short, the person's behavior can be understood only in the context of this finalistic or teleological conception of human striving. Adler's commitment to the holism assumption could not be more explicit or complete.

Constitutionalism–Environmentalism "Do not forget the most important fact that neither heredity nor environment are determining factors. Both are giving only the frame and the influences which are answered by the individual in regard to his styled creative power" (Adler, 1956, p. xxiv). In this assertion, Adler clearly establishes his position on the constitutionalism–environmentalism dimension: while both constitution and environment must be acknowledged as factors in personality make-up, each is utterly dwarfed by the significance of the creative self. In individual psychology, it is not what you have (constitution) or what you experience in life (environment) but what you do with each that counts.

To be sure, Adler recognized the role of hereditary factors in human nature (e.g., social interest and striving for superiority are innate, and organ inferiority influences personality development). But by the same token, recall that social interest develops in a family setting, striving for superiority is actualized by each person in his or her own way, and the effects of organ inferiorities (positive or negative) upon personality development depend on how people react to these constitutional shortcomings. Likewise, while Adler recognized the importance of environmental influences (e.g., birth order) on personality makeup, the crucial point is how the person chooses to perceive and react to such influences. So Adler's position on this assumption might best be understood as "middle of the road"; because of the overriding power of the creative self in fashioning personality, neither constitution nor environment seems invested with very much force in Adlerian theory.

Changeability–Unchangeability   While Freud and Adler differed dramatically on many of the basic assumptions about human nature, they appeared to see eye-to-eye on the issue of unchangeability. Like Freud, Adler insisted that the first 5 years of life are absolutely formative in personality makeup and that personality *fundamentally* changes little or not at all after those formative years. But the unchangeability assumption manifests itself differently in Adler's theory than it does in Freud's.

The key reflection of unchangeability in Adler's system is found in his concept of style of life. Rooted in early inferiority feelings and compensation, style of life crystallizes at around age 5 and thereafter influences all aspects of the person's behavior. Indeed, via life-style, people live out the rest of their days striving for superiority and forever seeking to attain the fictional final goals created during their early childhood years. And while style of life may manifest itself in different ways at different periods, it basically does not change throughout life. Adler's commitment to the unchangeability assumption seems quite strong indeed.

Subjectivity–Objectivity   Adler was totally committed to the subjectivity assumption. Starting with the basic tenet of "individual subjectivity" underlying Adlerian theory as discussed earlier, subjectivity is evident in virtually every major concept of individual psychology. Consider, for example, that the child's objective order of birth is not as important in personality formation as the subjective *meaning* that the child attaches to the position and its accompanying situation. Similarly, social interest initially develops as a function of how the child *interprets* the mother's behavior, rather than in response to the objective content of that behavior. Subjectivity is also preeminently manifest in Adler's concept of fictional finalism. For Adler, the entire style of life is based on the person's pursuit of a *subjective* fictional goal *experienced in the present.*

Adler (1956) used the term "schema of apperception" to describe the process by which each of us interprets the facts of our existence. He believed that all objective events must first be processed through and transformed by the intermediary psychological metabolism of this subjective schema before they have any impact on personality or behavior: "The conceptual world, is, as we both assumed and found to be the case, subjective in its form. . . . The whole framework in which we place what is perceived is only subjective" (Adler, 1956, p. 83). Thus, interpretation is fundamental to a person's view of the world. Adler's commitment to the subjectivity assumption is clearly evident.

Proactivity–Reactivity   As noted earlier, a basic tenet of individual psychology regards "human life as a dynamic striving for perfection." Herein lies support for Adler's total commitment to the proactivity assumption. In Adlerian theory, the locus of behavioral causality is always found *within* the person—specifically in the persistent, future-oriented, and all-consuming striving for superiority or perfection. Indeed, Adler postulates only one proactive and dynamic force underlying all human activity: the quest for superiority in life. Anchored in the subjectively experienced inferiority feelings of infancy and childhood, this ever-present desire is aimed at the person's self-created fictional final goal; all life activity is organized around this goal. Far from merely reacting to external environmental stimuli, then, the person in Adlerian psychology is depicted solely in terms of self-generated, future-oriented striving.

Homeostasis–Heterostasis   To appreciate Adler's position on this assumption, it is worth repeating a brief quote from his writings: "The impetus from minus to plus never ends. The urge from below to above never ceases" (Adler, 1930, p. 398). This is most definitely not the language of a homeostatically inclined theorist who sees people as motivated to reduce tensions and maintain an internal state of equilibrium. Rather, such language clearly implies *tension increase* in the constant impulse from "minus to plus," from "below to above."

Adler's strong commitment to heterostasis is evident in his concept of life's fundamental motive—the striving for superiority. People do not reduce tensions in this lifelong striving; they generate tensions in the ongoing struggle to achieve their fictional goals. However, Adler's version of heterostasis is of a somewhat different nature than that commonly encountered in the humanistic and phenomenological psychologies of today. In the latter versions of heterostasis, people are portrayed as self-actualizing (i.e., constantly moving in the direction of actualizing their full potentialities in life). Typically, these potentialities are seen as innate, and the person simply follows the natural growth inclination to fulfill them. In the Adlerian view of heterostasis, people are portrayed as constantly striving for superiority and the final fictional goal. This conveys a sense of people completing their subjective life mission rather than simply fulfilling all of their potentialities. So in Adlerian psychology it could be argued that people are actually growing in directions against their original inclinations and potentialities, insofar as the striving for superiority, life-style, and fictional goals are rooted in earlier inferiority feelings. Nonetheless, in individual psychology people are growing, moving forward, and generating tension increase—all of which reveal Adler's strong commitment to the heterostasis assumption.

Knowability–Unknowability   We noted earlier that Adler was influenced by Vaihinger's (1911) *The Philosophy of "As If."* This philosophy, which quickly became Adler's, is called *idealistic positivism*. This term, for our purposes, might best be understood to mean that ideational constructs (e.g., "fictions"), even when they may contradict reality, have great practical value and are indispensable for human life (Adler, 1956). Phrased differently, what is important in life is *not* what is or may be absolutely true (for who can know this?) but what *we believe* to be absolutely true. Regarding the knowability–unknowability issue in person-ology, this philosophical doctrine would seem to apply to psychological science as much as it does to people. That is, rather than fruitlessly searching for the "absolute truth" of human nature, psychological science is better off developing theoretical concepts (personological "fictions") that are practical and useful for people attempting to understand themselves and their life circumstances.

This is precisely what Adler did in constructing his theory. Viewed in this light, it may be no accident that the first book in which Adler fully addressed the general issue of human nature, *Understanding Human Nature* (1927b), was also his first written for the general public. Thus, the apparent simplicity and pragmatic nature of many of Adler's concepts, far from suggesting an essential lack of mystery in human nature, may actually reflect his conviction that this is the best that psychological science can do to depict human nature. And Adler realized that his science did not, could not, have all the answers: "I must admit that those who find a piece of metaphysics in Individual Psychology are right. . . . Whether you call it speculation or transcendentalism, there is no science which does not have to enter the realm of metaphysics" (Adler, 1956, p. 142). Given his underlying philosophical position, then, Adler clearly must be placed on the unknowability side of this basic assumption.

We turn now to the question of how the concepts of individual psychology have been empirically tested.

EMPIRICAL VALIDATION OF INDIVIDUAL PSYCHOLOGY CONCEPTS

Virtually no effort has been made to test the empirical validity of Adlerian concepts in a systematic or programmatic way. The scarcity of experimental literature can be traced to two key factors.

First, many of Adler's concepts are global in nature, lacking the kind of clear-cut operational definitions that are necessary for rendering a theory testable. This is especially true for concepts like *social interest, fictional finalism, creative self,* and *striving for superiority*. To illustrate, does social interest refer to underlying attitudes, to observable behavior, to good intentions toward others, or to all three? How would a researcher determine whether or not a given type of behavior reflects social interest? People whose stated goal is to improve the quality of life for everyone might take hostages and make bombs to radically alter governmental policies; their destructive behavior may be motivated by good intentions and commendable goals, but their means are highly questionable. Other people might donate generously to worthwhile causes, but do so primarily in order to enhance their public image or to lower their taxes. Here, the behavior is admirable, but the motivation underlying the behavior is selfish. Clearly, then, the concept of social interest is open to several alternative interpretations and is quite dependent upon the values held by the observer. As a consequence, it is often unclear to the experimentalist what logical operations should be used in order to measure such a construct.

Second, Adler's theory is not fully systematized, particularly with regard to overlapping terms (e.g., ''neurotic style of life,'' ''mistaken style of life,'' ''pampered style of life''). As a result, the relational statements of the theory are rather vaguely stated. For example, are the struggles for personal superiority and masculine protest the same, or merely overlapping constructs? If different, are they totally separate entities, or related to one another? These problems should be regarded not as criticisms, but as challenges to those who are interested in expanding Adlerian theory in the direction of increased possibilities for rigorous experimental or objective verification. Regrettably, few personologists have thus far heeded this challenge.

Thus, while individual psychology may be of high practical relevance, direct empirical tests of its concepts are sparse in number. This makes it impossible to render a definitive assessment about the theory's current empirical validity. However, Adlerian psychology has played a significant role in drawing attention to birth order and its effect on personality development. A few select studies consistent with the gist of Adler's theoretical insights follow. In addition, we shall consider recent efforts to construct a reliable and valid measure of social interest.

Empirical Evidence for Birth Order Effects

As mentioned earlier, Adler emphasized the person's ordinal position within the family constellation as an important factor in life-style development. This emphasis paved the way for a vibrant research literature dealing with the effects of ordinal position on the development of a host of behavioral characteristics. It should be noted, however, that much of this research does not directly test Adler's ideas. Moreover, not all of the findings are supportive of Adler's birth order predictions. Ernst and Angst (1983) and Falbo and Polit (1986) provide excellent reviews of the relevant research literature on birth order effects.

Achievement   Adler maintained that first-borns are concerned with power and authority. He attributed such concern to the fact that first-borns have had to undergo ''dethronement'' with the arrival of the second child. One way for them to regain power and authority as adults is through outstanding achievement. Thus, first-borns would be expected to attain high levels of accomplishment and eminence, to excel in intellectual pursuits, and to be outstanding. These predictions have received much empirical support. Belmont and Marolla (1973), in a massive investigation of nearly 400,000 young adult males from the Netherlands, found a strong, positive correlation between birth order and a nonverbal test of intellectual aptitude. First-borns surpassed later-borns in intellectual achievement in families where the number of children ranged between two and nine. In a similar study of how American students performed on the National Merit Test, Breland (1974) demonstrated that this positive relationship between birth order and intellectual attainment held true even when level of schooling achieved by their parents, the family's income, and the mother's age were controlled. Additional studies on this topic report that first-borns tend to have higher IQs than second-borns, who tend to have higher IQs than third-borns, and so on (Zajonc &

Markus, 1975). The differences are not large—only a few IQ points at most—but they do seem to be real. Why do such differences exist? One possibility is suggested by the *confluence model* proposed by Zajonc (1986). According to this theory—certainly different than what Adler proposed but still in the spirit of his theorizing—each person's intellectual growth depends upon the amount of intellectual stimulation he or she receives within the family. A first-born child benefits from the fact that for some period of time (until the birth of another child), he or she lives with two adults who provide a relatively "enriched" intellectual environment. A second-born child, in contrast, lives with two adults who divide their attention with another child; thus the average level of his or her intellectual stimulation is somewhat lower. Such effects become even stronger for third-borns, and continue to grow as the number of children in a family increases. Particularly at a disadvantage, according to Zajonc's interpretation, should be the youngest child. And this is exactly what the data show.

Other studies have found that first-borns are overrepresented relative to their proportion in the population in virtually every field of academic endeavor. For instance, Wagner and Schubert (1977) found that oldest sons were overrepresented among United States presidents, whereas defeated candidates for the presidency did not show such an overrepresentation. Zweigenhaft (1975) likewise found that members of the U.S. Congress were overrepresented by first-borns. Finally, Melillo (1983) found that first-borns were overrepresented among women earning doctorates (M.D., Ph.D., Ed.D., and D.S.W.).

Psychopathology   Another line of research has investigated the relation of ordinal position to different psychological disorders, again supporting some of Adler's hypotheses. As you will recall, Adler maintained that the last-born child was likely to be the most pampered member of the family. This pampering, he believed, would lead to conflict between seeking independence from others and dependence on them as a means of coping with life's problems. Furthermore, Adler thought that last-borns' proclivity toward excessive dependence on others as an easy and immediate solution to problems would be evidenced in a high incidence of alcoholism. In support of this prediction, Barry and Blane (1977) reviewed several studies examining the ordinal position of alcoholics and found that last-borns were overrepresented among alcoholics in the majority of cases.

Adler further theorized that only-born children are highly selfish and overly concerned with being the center of attention. Most research has failed to confirm this prediction. Indeed, one study showed that only-born college students displayed more cooperative behavior than did first- or last-born students (Falbo, 1978). Falbo and Polit (1986) also conducted a thorough review of the research literature and concluded that only-borns were as psychologically stable as were children from multiple-sibling families.

The fact that research on birth order effects continues at a brisk pace demonstrates the considerable heuristic value of Adler's ideas. Nevertheless, numerous contradictions and ambiguities do plague this area of research, often resulting from disregard of such factors as family size, spacing between siblings, and social class.

Assessment of Social Interest

Earlier we noted that Adler's concept of social interest has been given various interpretations by different individuals. In fact, the concept is quite ambiguous, with so many ramifications that it does not yield readily to operational definition. Further, Adler himself was quite opposed to the use of psychological tests to assess his personality constructs (Rattner, 1983). Nevertheless, efforts to devise reliable and valid self-report measures of social interest have appeared in the psychological literature (Crandall, 1975; Greever et al., 1973; Mozdzierz et al., 1986).

The Social Interest Scale (SIS) developed by Crandall (1975; 1984) is a 15-item test consisting of trait adjectives arranged in pairs (see Table 4-1). The respondent is instructed to select which trait from each pair (e.g., considerate vs. wise) he or she would rather possess. Choices of such adjectives as "sympathetic," "helpful," and "cooperative" are assumed to be indicative of social interest.

The psychometric properties of the SIS appear adequate for a research instrument. Test–retest reliability over a 5-week interval was .82 and over a 14-month interval was .65. Internal reliability falls within the range of .71 to .76 (Crandall, 1980). Studies in which scores on the SIS are correlated with a variety of other personality traits and social behaviors also confirm the value of the scale in assessing Adler's conceptualization of social interest (Zarski et al., 1986). For example, SIS scores are positively correlated with measures of helping, empathy, responsibility, liking of others, and being liked by others. Conversely, SIS scores are negatively correlated with measures of self-centeredness and hostility (Crandall, 1980; 1981). Crandall (1975) also reported that SIS scores correlate positively with a personal value system emphasizing the importance of equality, peace, and family security. This scale seems worthy of additional empirical study.

Greever et al. (1973) have also developed a self-report test for determining the person's degree of social interest. Called the Social Interest Index (SII), items for the test were selected on the basis of Adler's writings and consensus among three prominent Adlerians. Sample items are presented below:

1 I don't mind helping out friends.
2 I feel jobs are important because they make you take an active part in the community.
3 I feel I have a place in the world.
4 As far as I am concerned, marriage is for life.

Instructions require the test taker to indicate, using a 5-point scale of personal relevance, the extent to which each item applies to him or her ("not at all like me" or "very much like me"). The items are scored to measure the level of social interest the person has attained in each of four areas: work, friendship, love, and self-significance. The scoring system is such that high SII scores are indicative of high social interest, while low SII scores reflect low social interest. In a more global sense, SII scores reflect a varying relationship to democratic cooperation, accepting self and others, having a place in the world, and feeling that one is part

TABLE 4-1   SAMPLE ITEMS ILLUSTRATING THE SOCIAL INTEREST SCALE

Subject indicates which adjective trait he or she would rather possess by placing an X on the line next to each pair. Choice of first trait for items on the left and second trait for items on the right are scored as reflecting high social interest.

_____ **1** forgiving		_____ **1** alert	
_____ **2** gentle		_____ **2** cooperative	
_____ **1** generous		_____ **1** ambitious	
_____ **2** individualistic		_____ **2** patient	
_____ **1** respectful		_____ **1** realistic	
_____ **2** original		_____ **2** moral	
_____ **1** considerate		_____ **1** neat	
_____ **2** wise		_____ **2** sympathetic	
_____ **1** trustworthy		_____ **1** imaginative	
_____ **2** wise		_____ **2** helpful	

Source: Crandall, 1975, p. 483.

of the continuity of that world. Greever et al. (1973) demonstrated that SII scores did not correlate with a measure of socially desirable responding. Internal reliability was .81, and consistency over a 2-week period was .79. It should be stressed, however, that most studies using the SII are limited to college-age subjects and that any generalizations to other segments of the population still await further research (Leak et al., 1985).

We now turn our attention to how Adler's ideas can be applied to an understanding of neurotic behavior and its therapeutic treatment.

APPLICATION: NEUROSIS AND ITS TREATMENT

Above all else, Adler wanted to create a practical psychology that would be relevant to the everyday world of human affairs. In particular, he sought to develop a system that would account for the causes of neuroses as well as furnish a basis for the psychological treatment of such disorders. In this section, Adler's theoretical concepts will be applied to the understanding of neuroses and their mitigation via Adlerian therapy.

The Nature of Neurosis

From Adler's perspective, *neurosis* was a broad-based diagnostic term intended to encompass a variety of behavioral disorders for which persons often sought treatment from the psychiatrists of the day. These disorders manifested themselves in an equally rich variety of symptoms (e.g., anxiety, morbid doubts or fears, obsessions, compulsions). Relatedly, Adler (1956) observed how neurotic persons used their past and present experiences to avoid responsibility and to maintain self-esteem. In opposition to Freud's notion that symptoms function as a means of controlling and satisfying instinctual impulses, Adler construed symptomatic behavior as a safe-guarding mechanism: a protective strategy in the service of the self. The symptom provides "the excuse," "the alibi," or "the extenuating circumstance" protecting the prestige of the person.

What Is Neurosis?   While Adler wrote volumes on neurotic behavior, perhaps his best definition of *neurosis* for our purposes is the following: "Neurosis is the natural, logical development of an individual who is comparatively inactive, filled with a personal, egocentric striving for superiority, and is therefore retarded in the development of his social interest, as we find regularly among the more passive pampered styles of life" (Adler, 1956, p. 241).

Once this definition is separated into its component parts, a number of Adler's insights regarding the neurotic personality become evident. "Comparatively inactive" refers to the "degree of activity" dimension found in Adler's typology of life-style attitudes. For Adler, neurotics are characterized by a lack of activity necessary for the correct solutions to their life problems. Perhaps this is just as well, since Adler believed that if they did have a higher degree of activity, such people would tend to become criminals!

A second key phrase in Adler's definition, "a personal, egocentric striving for superiority," suggests that neurotics typically strive toward selfish life goals. In other words, neurotic persons strive unduly hard toward exaggerated goals of self-enhancement at the expense of genuine concern for their fellow human beings—the essential meaning of the "retarded in the development of his social interest" phrase in the foregoing definition. Moreover, Adler (1956) believed that neurotic individuals set their superiority goals higher than normal people and then proceed to strive for these goals with more rigidity. Adler saw both tendencies as compensations for the deep-seated inferiority feelings of neurotics.

The final phrase in Adler's definition of neurosis, "passive pampered styles of life," reflects his conviction that neurotics basically *want to be pampered by others*. Lacking social interest and the degree of activity required to meet life tasks, neurotics want to depend exclusively on others to cope with life's daily problems.

To better appreciate the nature of neurosis from an Adlerian perspective, consider the following brief case illustration:

Gwen, an 18-year-old mathematics major completing her freshman year, came to the college counseling center with complaints of anxiety, bodily signs of stress (e.g., muscular tension in the shoulders and neck region before exams), occasional depression, and great dissatisfaction with her academic performance. She could give no clear reasons for the anxiety and also felt that her somatic tensions were much greater than normal. Further, while her grades ranged from average to above-average (i.e., "C" to "B"), Gwen was intensely dissatisfied and occasionally distraught about this performance, feeling instead that she should be earning "As," particularly in her math courses. As counseling progressed, it became evident that Gwen had always experienced extreme difficulty making friends and relating to peers. She tended to be haughty and aloof in interpersonal relationships, believing most people to be frivolous and intellectually inferior to her. This interpersonal difficulty was most striking in the recitation groups associated with her math courses (a source of great worry and discomfort to her), in which students were expected to work together with the recitation instructor in unraveling the complexities of the math lectures and textbooks.

Gwen was an only child. Her father was a successful physician and her mother a respected high-school mathematics teacher. She grew up with material goods in abundance (including free access to credit cards) and parents who catered to her every whim. She attended small private schools, received a great deal of tutorial attention, and excelled academically in these circumstances. Matriculating at a large prestigious university away from home represented a dramatic change in Gwen's life, and constituted much more of an adjustment problem for her than it does for most college students. Gwen's neurotic difficulties came to the fore during this period.

Within the framework of Adlerian theory, Gwen basically lacks the degree of activity required to solve her present life problems. She is striving toward an egocentric goal of superiority, and, lacking in social interest, wants to go through life being pampered by others. Her neurotic symptoms are the result.

What Causes Neurosis?   Gwen's unfortunate psychological condition, like that of other neurotics, is by no means exclusively her own doing. While Adler insisted that people are responsible for their own behavior and life direction (i.e., freedom assumption), he also felt that the neurotic life-style results from the person being "overburdened" during childhood. Specifically, the same three conditions described earlier in this chapter as leading to inferiority complexes were also seen by Adler as likely to overburden the child: (1) organ inferiorities, (2) pampering, and (3) neglect. Each of these overburdening childhood experiences fosters a self-centered, noncooperative, and unrealistic life-style characteristic of neurotics.

Of the three overburdening childhood situations, pampering appears best to fit Gwen's case, since it encompasses all those family environments in which children are raised to receive without giving. Having been pampered and given excessive attention throughout her childhood years, Gwen lacked social feeling and failed to learn the give-and-take inherent in adult cooperative relationships. Support for her having been a pampered child is indicated by the fact that she could not function in the math recitation classes since total attention could not be focused on her.

In summary, neurotics are people who have acquired faulty life-styles, usually because they experienced either physical afflictions, pampering, or rejection during early childhood. Under such conditions, Adler believed, these children became highly anxious, felt insecure, and began to develop protective strategies to cope with feelings of inferiority. Adler would thus argue that underneath her other behavior, Gwen always felt anxious and insecure, and probably developed at least some self-serving strategies to cope with her inferiority feelings. Her haughty and aloof approach to interpersonal relationships and her view of others as intellectually inferior is consistent with this interpretation.

The Onset of Neurosis   Faced with an overburdening childhood situation, the creative self fashions what Adler termed a "mistaken" or neurotic style of life. Essentially, the neurotically predisposed person, deficient in social interest, creates a selfish fictional goal, thereby missing out on the fundamental value which Adler (1939) attributed to human life. Such a person regrettably but necessarily goes through life with great underlying insecurity, constantly threatened self-esteem, and oversensitivity (Adler believed that neurotics behave as if they were living in a land of enemies). Almost inevitably, then, this mistaken style of life will clash with human interrelatedness; plainly, as is illustrated in Gwen's case, the neurotic life-style is incompatible with the demand of cooperative social living.

Adler viewed this fundamental conflict as occurring in relation to any one or all of the three major life tasks mentioned earlier in this chapter—work, friendship, and love. Confronting these tasks, which demand fellowship and cooperation, the neurotic's entire life-style and fictional goals are under constant siege. Thus, what Adler termed an *exogenous factor* always precipitates the outbreak of actual symptoms in a neurotically predisposed person: "We must remember that it is the exogenous situation which sets the match to the fire" (Adler, 1944, p. 4). Under such circumstances, the creative self reaches frantically for means to protect its threatened self-esteem as well as for plausible excuses for its personal weaknesses. The person may begin to believe in an arrogant way that he or she is superior to others and act in ways consistent with this belief. Similarly, the person may strive to be perfect and belittle others.

In Gwen's case, the exogenous factor seemed to be her matriculation at a university away from home and the accompanying demands to function autonomously (in an unpampered fashion) in pursuing her occupational goals. Uprooted from her pampered circumstances, Gwen's self-centered life-style was severely threatened; she was being forced to give of herself due to the social demands of the educational setting. This was particularly evident in the math recitation class, a situation that caused her considerable worry and discomfort.

The Treatment of Neurosis

Adler's approach to treating neurosis logically follows from his clinical conception of the nature of neurosis. If neurotic symptoms are products of the patient's mistaken style of life and underdeveloped social interest, then the goal of therapy should be to correct such mistakes while encouraging the development of social interest. Succinctly stated, the goals of therapy for Adler are threefold: (1) to recognize mistaken beliefs about ourselves and others; (2) to eliminate faulty goals; and (3) to implement new life goals that will enable us to realize our full human potential. In turn, Adler maintained that these therapeutic goals could best be accomplished through understanding the patient, enhancing the patient's self-understanding, and strengthening the patient's social interest.

Understanding the Patient   For Adler, if the therapist is to help the patient achieve greater self-understanding, she or he must first attain a workable understanding of the patient's fictional goals and life-style. For example, what is it that Gwen is striving for? What are her egocentric fictional goals and how do these relate to her current unhappy life-style? According to Adler, such understanding can best be realized by addressing such patient factors as earliest childhood recollections, birth order position, childhood disorders, dreams, and the exogenous factor precipitating the onset of neurosis. In the case of earliest childhood recollections, for instance, Adler would ask Gwen to report her earliest memories. He would then compare these recollections with related facts that Gwen had already given him about her more recent life experiences to understand the common themes or goals that, often unconsciously, guide her behavior. To illustrate, suppose Gwen's earliest recollection was as follows:

> At one of my birthday parties I remember that my mother gave me a kind of jigsaw puzzle for a present. Try as I could during the party, I couldn't put it together, even though some of the other children at the party could. When my mother left the room, the other children laughed at me and made fun of me because I couldn't do it. When my mother returned, she did it for me. My mother could always do things like that—she is a mathematics teacher.

This memory, irrespective of its accuracy, would be considered a valuable clue as to the nature of Gwen's life-style and her associated goals of personal superiority.

In attempting to understand the patient's personality, Adler (1956) also employed such procedures as empathy, intuition, and guessing. Through empathy, or putting himself in the place of the patient, Adler believed that he could achieve a workable intuition about the patient's mistaken life plan. When uncertain, Adler resorted to guessing, generating hypotheses about the causes of patient behavior that would constantly be tested and revised against the backdrop of subsequent patient behavior. Intimately associated with these procedures was Adler's careful attention to patient expressive behavior (e.g., body language, facial expressions, gait, posture, gestures) and symptoms. Like Freud, Adler observed every facet of patient behavior, leaving little unnoticed.

Through such means an Adlerian therapist should be able to achieve insight into Gwen's mistaken style of life. It may be, for example, that Gwen is striving for the fictional goal of total intellectual superiority over all others in a given field (e.g., mathematics). She will symbolically solve those jigsaw puzzles and nobody will ever laugh at her again! She may even wind up superior to her mother in this respect. A "mistaken" life-style such as Gwen's could easily be unconsciously constructed around such fictional goals.

Enhancing Patient Self-Understanding   For treatment to progress successfully, it is not enough that the therapist understand the patient's mistaken life plan. The patient must also come to understand it, and to accept such understanding. In other words, the patient must gain *insight* into the nature of his or her faulty goals, style of life, and consequent neurotic symptoms. Thus, Gwen needs to understand her fictional goal of total intellectual superiority, the neurotic life-style she has constructed around it, and the self-destructive price that she is currently paying for it. Eventually, she must come to realize that psychological health requires a cooperative attitude toward others and a willingness to contribute to the enhancement of society.

Adler was quite clear about what he actually did to enhance such patient self-understanding: "I have found it best merely to search for the patient's neurotic line of operation in all his expressions and thoughts and to unmask it, and at the same time train the patient unobtrusively to do the same" (Adler, 1956, p. 334). Without ever pushing or offending patients, Adlerian therapists gradually bring them to the point where they want to listen and to understand their basic mistaken or faulty life-styles. As the prominent Adlerian therapist Rudolf Dreikurs (1973) notes, tact and the avoidance of dogmatic assertions are critical throughout this process. Thus, interpretations offered by the therapist might include phrases such as "Would you like me to tell you . . .?" or "Could it be . . .?" The therapist would also provide clear explanations so that "the patient knows and feels his own experience instantly" (Adler, 1956, p. 335). Once she is stripped of her mistaken goals of *egocentric superiority* and possessed of a clear understanding of the symptomatic consequences of her neurotic life-style, Gwen will presumably reorient herself to life in a more socially constructive fashion. In turn, she should gradually move toward reorganization of her perceptions and begin to behave differently toward others (e.g., perceive others in terms other than intellectual inferiority) and discard her haughty and aloof interpersonal style. It should be noted that throughout this process Adler constantly stressed that the patient, not the therapist, bears primary responsibility for a successful outcome.

Strengthening Social Interest   The centrality of social interest as a therapeutic objective is paramount for Adler: "All my efforts are devoted towards increasing the social interest of the patient. I know that the real reason for his malady is his lack of cooperation, and I want him to see it too. As soon as he can connect himself with his fellow men on an equal and cooperative footing, he is cured" (Adler, 1956, p. 347). This quotation reveals that Adlerian therapy is an exercise in cooperation. The therapist's task is to give the patient the kind of interpersonal contact with a fellow human being that can enable the patient to transfer this awakened social feeling to others. This the therapist does by unconditionally encouraging social interest in the patient, decreasing his or her feelings of inferiority while simultaneously activating the seeds of social interest. In a sense, the Adlerian therapist belatedly assumes the functional role of mother in developing social feeling. And as social interest gradually develops in the therapeutic context, the patient substitutes useful life goals for selfish ones, gains courage, and learns to live without defensive excuses (neurotic symptoms) for a mistaken life-style.

Strengthening social interest represents a kind of reorientation and reeducation of the patient, processes viewed by Adlerians as the most important phase in therapy (Ansbacher, 1977). It is not enough that Gwen simply understand her neurotic life-style: she must take action to change it. She must come to see that there is more to life than attaining total intellectual superiority for herself. She must appreciate her place in society, recognize and adopt socially useful goals, and learn to pursue these goals with vigor. A more healthy life-style and the elimination of neurotic symptoms should follow.

It is now time to consider another follower of Freud whose disenchantment with several aspects of orthodox psychodynamic theory led to a remarkably different approach to personality. We continue our discussion of the revision of psychoanalysis by exploring the concepts of Carl Jung, considered by many to be one of the great thinkers of this century.

CARL JUNG: An Analytical Theory of Personality

Although controversial, Freud's writings soon attracted a group of leading thinkers of the day to study with him in Vienna. Some of these scholars eventually left the psychoanalytic fold to establish their own approaches to the understanding of the person. Foremost among these defectors from the Freudian camp was Carl Jung.

Like Freud, Jung devoted himself to the study of dynamic, unconscious influences on human behavior and experience. However, unlike Freud, Jung contended that the unconscious contains more than a person's repressed sexual and aggressive urges. According to Jung's system of personality, known as *analytical psychology,* human beings are motivated by intrapsychic forces and images derived from their shared evolutionary history. This inherited unconscious includes deep-rooted spiritual concerns and explains the universal human striving for creative expression and psychic completion.

Another source of disagreement between Freud and Jung concerned the role of sexuality as a predominant motive force of personality. Whereas Freud saw libido mainly as sexual energy, Jung viewed libido as a diffuse and creative life force that manifested itself in numerous ways, such as religion and power. Thus, for Jung, libidinal energy is concentrated on various needs as they arise, be they biologic or spiritual. Like Adler, he rejected Freud's contention that the brain "is an appendage to the genital glands."

Jung's view of human personality is perhaps the most complex, unorthodox, and controversial in the personological tradition. He fashioned a unique and thought-provoking theory that clearly stands apart from all other approaches to the study of the person.

BIOGRAPHICAL SKETCH

Carl Gustav Jung was born in Kesswyl, Switzerland, in 1875. He grew up in the Swiss city of Basel. The son of a pastor in the Swiss Reformed Church, he was a deeply introverted, lonely child, but an excellent student. He was an avid reader, particularly on religious and philosophical topics, and enjoyed the solitude of long

Carl G. Jung. *(Courtesy The Bettmann Archive)*

walks during which he marveled at the mysteries of nature. During his childhood years, Jung (1961) recalled he was preoccupied with dreams, supernatural visions, and fantasies. He believed he possessed secret information about the future and also had a fantasy he was two different people.

Jung studied medicine at the University of Basel and received his medical degree with a specialty in psychiatry in 1900. The same year he accepted a position as an assistant in a Zurich mental hospital where he worked under the supervision of Eugen Bleuler, who coined the term "schizophrenia." Jung's (1906/1960) curiosity about the complex life of schizophrenic patients soon brought him into contact with Freud's work. After reading Freud's *Interpretation of Dreams,* Jung began a regular correspondence with Freud. The two finally met in Freud's home in Vienna in 1907. The visit marked the beginning of both an intense personal and a professional relationship. Freud was deeply impressed by Jung's intellectualism and believed that Jung might be the ideal spokesman for psychoanalysis because he was not Jewish. Jung was adopted as an "eldest son," dubbed as Freud's "successor and crown prince," and elected as first president of the International Psychoanalytic Association in 1910. By 1913, however, the two men severed their relationship in classic oedipal fashion (Alexander, 1982). The following year, Jung resigned as president of the psychoanalytic group and also withdrew as a member. Both personal and theoretical reasons precipitated the break, and Freud and Jung never saw each other again.

For the next 4 years, Jung went through a severe mental crisis and became so debilitated that he resigned his lectureship at the University of Zurich. He was obsessed with exploring his own dreams and fantasies, which, according to some scholars, brought him to the edge of madness (Stern, 1976). It was only toward the end of World War I that he emerged from his journey of self-exploration to create an approach to personality emphasizing human aspirations and spiritual needs. Jung credited all later writings and creative activity to this period of agonizing introspection into the depths of his own unconscious. His autobiography, *Memories, Dreams, and Reflections* (1961), begins with the statement: "My life is a story of the self-realization of the unconscious" (p. 3).

A tragic episode in Jung's life involved accusations of his being a Nazi sympathizer during World War II. Jung vehemently denied the charges of harboring pro-Nazi sentiments and was eventually exonerated. The rest of his life was devoted to traveling and lecturing throughout the world. He broadened his understanding of human nature by exploring diverse cultures in America, Africa, and Asia. Jung's *analytical psychology* eventually attracted a worldwide audience, and his numerous books remain influential even today.

Jung died in 1961 at the age of 86 in Kusnacht, Switzerland.

ANALYTICAL PSYCHOLOGY: BASIC CONCEPTS AND PRINCIPLES

Jung's revision of psychoanalysis involves a spectacular array of complex ideas drawn from such diverse fields as psychology, philosophy, astrology, archeology, mythology, theology, and literature. This breadth of intellectual study coupled with Jung's arcane writing style makes his theory one of the most difficult to understand in the entire discipline of personology. With these difficulties clearly in mind, we hope the following succinct presentation will serve as a starting point for future reading and thought.

The Structure of Personality

Jung (1931/1969) theorized that the *psyche* (his term for personality) is composed of three separate but interacting structures: the ego, the personal unconscious, and the collective unconscious.

The *ego* is the center of the conscious mind. It represents that component of the psyche consisting of all those thoughts, feelings, memories, and perceptions that give us a sense of temporal continuity and identify us as human beings. It constitutes our awareness of ourselves and is responsible for seeing that the ordinary activities of our waking life are carried out.

The *personal unconscious* houses conflicts and memories that once were conscious but have since been repressed or forgotten. It also consists of sense impressions that were not vivid enough to have been consciously registered at first. Thus, Jung's concept of the personal unconscious is somewhat similar to Freud's concept of the unconscious. Jung (1913/1973) went beyond Freud, however, by emphasizing that the personal unconscious contains *complexes* or clusters of emotionally charged ideas, feelings, and memories acquired from a person's developmental past or ancestral experiences. He believed that such complexes, organized around common themes, may become strong enough to dominate the person's behavior. A person with a power complex, for example, may expend considerable psychic energy on activities that are either directly or symbolically related to the theme of power. The same would be true of someone whose personality is dominated by a mother, father, money, sex, or any other kind of complex. For Jung, once a complex is formed, it seizes control of the person's behavior and determines how he or she perceives the world. Furthermore, Jung noted that the material of the personal unconscious, unique to the person, is usually accessible to consciousness. As a result, components of a complex, or even an entire complex, may become conscious and have a disproportionate influence on the person's life.

Finally, Jung (1936/1969) proposed the existence of a deeper structure within the psyche he called the *collective unconscious*. The collective unconscious is a storehouse of latent memory traces of our human and even prehuman ancestors. It reflects the thoughts and feelings that each of us shares with our fellow human beings as a result of our common evolutionary past. As Jung himself put it, "the collective unconscious contains the whole spiritual heritage of mankind's evolution, born anew in the brain structure of every individual" (Campbell, 1971, p. 45). Thus, the contents of the collective unconscious are due to heredity and are the same for all of humankind. It is important to note that the concept of a collective unconscious was a key source of disagreement between Jung and Freud.

Archetypes   Jung (1968) hypothesized that the contents of the collective unconscious consist of powerful, primordial images called *archetypes* (literally "original models"). Archetypes are innate ideas or memories that predispose people to perceive, experience, and react to their world in certain ways. They are not actual memories or images as such, but rather are predispositions that lead people to enact universal patterns of feeling, thought, and action in response to an object or experience. What is inherited is the tendency to respond emotionally, cognitively, and behaviorally to particular experiences—for example, when a parent, a lover, a stranger, a snake, a flood, or a death is encountered.

Among the many archetypes described by Jung are the mother, the child, the hero, the wise old man, the sun god, the trickster, God, and death (see Table 4-2).

TABLE 4-2   EXAMPLES OF JUNGIAN ARCHETYPES

Archetypes	Definitions	Symbols
Anima	The feminine qualities present in all men	Woman, Virgin Mary, Mona Lisa
Animus	The masculine qualities present in all women	Man, Christ, Don Juan
Persona	The artificial social roles we enact in public	Mask
Shadow	The repressed animalistic urges that we would prefer not to recognize in ourselves	Satan, Hitler, Hussein
Self	The embodiment of unity, harmony, and wholeness within the personality	Mandala or "magic circle"
Wise Old Man	The personification of wisdom and maturity in life	Prophet
God	The final realization of psychic reality projected onto the external world	Eye of the sun

Each of these, Jung argued, is associated with a tendency to express a particular kind of feeling or thought toward a corresponding object or situation. For example, an infant's perception of its mother will consist of aspects of her actual characteristics infused with unconscious conceptions of such archetypal maternal qualities as nurturance, fertility, and dependency. Jung further proposed that archetypal images and ideas are frequently reflected in dreams and are often manifested in a culture's use of symbols in art, literature, and religion. Specifically, he maintained that symbols from very different cultures often show striking similarities because they emerge from archetypes that are shared by the entire human race. For instance, Jung found numerous cultures in which *mandalas* or "magic circles" served as symbolic representations of the unified wholeness of the self. Jung felt that an understanding of archetypal symbols enabled him to make sense of his patient's dreams.

Some Prominent Archetypes

The number of archetypes in the collective unconscious may be limitless. However, those that are given prominent attention in Jung's system include the persona, the anima and animus, the shadow, and the self.

Persona, derived from the Latin word meaning "mask," is the public face we reveal in our relationships with other people. It represents the various roles we play in response to social demands and, according to Jung, serves to impress others or to conceal ourselves from them. In a sense, the persona archetype is necessary if we are to get along with other people in everyday life. However, Jung warned that if this archetype is valued too highly, then we become shallow, locked into a particular role, and detached from genuine emotional experience.

In contrast to the persona's role in our adjustment to the social world, the *shadow* archetype represents the dark, sinister, and animalistic side of our psyche. It contains our socially unacceptable sexual and aggressive impulses and immoral thoughts and passions. But the shadow also has positive features. Jung viewed it as the source of vitality, spontaneity, and creativity evident in a person's life. Indeed, Jung believed that it is the function of the ego to channel the forces of the shadow, to curb the evil side of our nature enough so that we can live in harmony with others, while allowing enough expression of our impulses to enjoy a robust and creative existence.

The anima and animus archetypes reflect Jung's recognition of the inherent androgynous (bisexual) nature of human beings. *Anima* represents the feminine, passive side of men, while *animus* represents the masculine, assertive side of women. These archetypes are based, at least partially, on the biological fact that both men and women secrete varying amounts of male and female hormones. Jung further theorized that these archetypes evolved over eons of time in the collective unconscious as a result of experiences with the opposite sex. Men have become, at least to some extent, "feminized" through cohabitation with women over the ages, and the reverse holds true for women. Like all archetypes, Jung insisted that anima and animus must be expressed in proper balance in order for progress toward self-realization to come about. In other words, a man must express his feminine qualities as well as his masculine qualities, and a woman must exhibit her masculine qualities along with her feminine ones. Otherwise, these necessary attributes will remain undeveloped, leading to a one-sidedness in personality growth and functioning.

The *self* is the most salient archetype in Jung's theory. It is the core of personality around which all other elements are organized and unified. When this integration of all aspects of the psyche has been achieved, the person has a sense of unity, harmony, and wholeness. Thus, for Jung, the development of the self is the ultimate goal of human life. More will be said about this process of self-realization when we consider Jung's concept of individuation.

The primary symbol of the self archetype is the mandala, or magic circle. In Jung's view, the unity and oneness of the self as symbolized by the completeness of mandalalike figures is revealed in dreams, fantasies, myths, and various religious and transcendental experiences. Jung further believed that religion was a great facilitator of the person's striving toward wholeness and completeness. At the same time, balancing all parts of the psyche is a difficult process, one Jung insisted could not be fully achieved until at least middle age. Furthermore, the self archetype cannot be realized until integration and harmony among all the other systems of the psyche, both conscious and unconscious, comes about. Thus, the mature self requires persistence, perceptiveness, and great wisdom.

Ego Orientations

One of Jung's (1921/1971) best-known contributions to personology is his description of two general orientations or attitudes toward life: *extraversion* and *introversion*. Both orientations are viewed as existing simultaneously in each person, although one usually becomes dominant. Extraversion refers to an attitude of interest in the outer world of people and things. The extravert is likely to be outgoing, talkative, friendly, and focused on things outside of the self. Introversion, in contrast, signifies a preoccupation with the internal world of one's own thoughts, feelings, and experiences. The introvert is more likely to be contemplative, aloof, reserved, and focused on self. For Jung, a person is not exclusively an extravert or introvert; instead, these orientations exist simultaneously and in opposition, even though one tends to be dominant and conscious while the other is nondominant and unconscious. The combination of these dominant and nondominant ego orientations, Jung believed, creates personalities that display distinctive and predictable patterns of behavior.

Psychological Functions

Soon after he formulated his ideas about extraversion and introversion, Jung began to realize that this pair of opposites did not fully explain all the differences in how people relate to the world. Accordingly, he extended his typology to include what he called the *psychological functions*. The four basic functions of the psyche posited by Jung (1921/1971) are thinking, feeling, sensing, and intuiting.

Jung grouped thinking and feeling together as *rational* functions since they involve making judgments about life experiences. *Thinking* is characterized by an intellectual style of relating to the world. A thinking-oriented person seeks to understand the meaning of daily experiences through the use of logic and reason. Its opposite function, *feeling,* is the appraisal of reality in terms of the experience of positive or negative emotions. A feeling-oriented person focuses attention on the emotional aspects of an experience in terms of good or bad, pleasant or unpleasant, stimulating or dull. According to Jung, when the thinking function is dominant, the person is oriented toward making a conscious judgment of whether an experience is true or false. By contrast, when the feeling function is dominant, the person is oriented toward making a conscious judgment of whether an experience is inherently pleasant or unpleasant.

Jung called the second pair of opposing functions—sensing and intuiting—the *irrational* functions because they involve passive recording of life experiences without evaluating or interpreting them. *Sensing* is the direct, realistic perception of the external world without judgment. A sensation-oriented person is acutely aware of the taste, smell, and feel of stimuli in the surrounding world. *Intuiting,* by contrast, is characterized by the subliminal, unconscious perception of daily experiences. An intuition-oriented person relies on hunches and guesses to grasp the meaning of events in life. Jung suggested that when the sensing function is dominant, the person deals with reality in terms of appearance as if he or she were a photographer. On the other hand, when the intuitive function is predominant, the person is responsive to unconscious images, symbols, and the hidden meaning of experiences.

Jung felt that everyone has the capacity for each of these four psychological functions. However, just as one ego orientation (extraversion or introversion) is usually dominant and conscious, so too is only one function of the rational or irrational pair usually dominant and conscious. The members of the remaining pair are submerged in the unconscious and take on an auxiliary (inferior) role in influencing the person's behavior. Of course, any one of the psychological functions can be manifested in the dominant mode; that is, there are thinking, feeling, sensing, and intuiting types of individuals. As Jung envisioned it, the integrated or "individuated" person would utilize all the opposing functions in dealing with life circumstances.

Jung also theorized that the two ego orientations and four psychological functions can interact to yield eight different personality types. For instance, the *extravert-thinking type* of person is focused on learning practical facts about the objective world. This type tends to be cold and dogmatic and to live his or her life in accordance with fixed rules. Hogan (1976) suggests that Freud was Jung's prototype for this type of person. In contrast, the *introvert-intuitive type* is preoccupied with the meaning of his or her own inner world of reality. This type tends to be eccentric, aloof, and indifferent to other people. Hogan (1976) notes that Jung may have been thinking of himself here.

From Jung's perspective, the later years of life are when people become focused on self-realization through pursuing creative activities. *(David Grossman/Photo Researchers)*

Personality Development

Unlike Freud, who concentrated on the earliest years of life as decisive in the formation of fixed personality growth patterns, Jung viewed personality development as a dynamic and evolving process that continues throughout a person's life. He had little to say about socialization processes in childhood and did not accept Freud's view that only past events (notably psychosexual conflicts) determine the person's behavior. For Jung, the person is continually learning new skills, reaching out for new goals, and progressing toward self-realization. He placed great emphasis on the person's life goal of "coming to selfhood" through the striving for unity among the different components of personality. This striving toward integration, harmony, and wholeness is a theme also echoed in existential and humanistic theories of personality.

For Jung, life's ultimate goal is the realization of a *whole self*—that is, becoming a single, separate, and indivisible being. Progress in this direction is unique to each person, covers the entire life span, and involves a process Jung termed *individuation*. Oversimplified, individuation is a dynamic and evolving process whereby the person seeks to integrate the many opposing forces in the psyche. In its ultimate form, then, individuation involves the full development and expression of all elements of the psyche. In turn, the self archetype becomes the center of personality and reconciles the many polarities that make up the psyche within a grand unity, thereby releasing energy for continued personal development. Fulfillment of individuation, which is no easy task, results in what Jung called *self-actualization*. For Jung, only bright and well-educated persons who have considerable leisure time are eligible for the attainment of this final stage of personality development. These restrictions necessarily exclude the vast majority of humanity.

Concluding Comments

In deviating from Freud's theory, Jung has enriched our conception of the contents and structure of the human psyche. His concepts of the collective unconscious and archetypes, while difficult if not impossible to test empirically, continue to fascinate many people. Jung's emphasis on the unconscious as a rich, vital source of wisdom has renewed interest in his theory among the current generation of students and professional psychologists (Dry, 1981; Stevens, 1983). In the same direction, Jung was one of the first to recognize the positive implications of religious, spiritual, and even transcendental experiences for personal growth. He thus merits the distinction of being a key forerunner of the humanistic movement in personology. We should hasten to add that analytical psychology has enjoyed an upsurge of popularity and acceptance in the U.S. intellectual community in recent years (Mattoon, 1981). Theologians, philosophers, historians, and members of many other disciplines have found Jung's creative insights quite useful in their own work.

Nonetheless, most of Jung's theory remains at a level of conjecture. His major concepts have yielded little in the way of serious attempts at hypothesis testing. This is partly due to the fact that many Jungian concepts are not defined precisely enough to validate. Jung's own skepticism about the value of the scientific method in validating his ideas should also be acknowledged (Hillman, 1979). Except for his studies of complexes using the word-association test (Jung, 1909/1973), Jung sought confirmation for his theory in myths, legends, folklore, and dreams and fantasies of his patients.

Research designed to test Jung's theory, sparse as it is, has focused almost exclusively on his psychological types. The *Myers-Briggs Type Indicator* (Myers & McCaulley, 1985), a self-report questionnaire designed to measure individual differences in Jung's typology, is widely used in such research. Studies based on this instrument (e.g., Cann & Donderi, 1986; Carlson, 1980; Fling et al., 1981) support certain Jungian predictions about how various personality types should differ in terms of personal memories and the content of dreams. However, such studies may be confounded by the fact that the Myers-Briggs departs from Jung's eight basic types by identifying sixteen different personality types, some of which are not independent of one another. Like so many other theories covered in this text, far more research is needed if Jung's theory is to have a lasting impact in the field of personality.

SUMMARY

Alfred Adler and Carl Jung, two early members of the psychoanalytic movement, eventually disagreed with Freud on key theoretical issues and proceeded to revise psychodynamic theory in markedly different directions. Adler's individual psychology depicts the human being as single, indivisible, self-consistent, and unified. Jung's analytical psychology portrays personality as shaped by future aspirations as well as by inherited predispositions and draws attention to the integration of opposing psychic forces for the achievement of psychological health.

Adler developed a parsimonious and pragmatic theory designed to be helpful to people in understanding themselves and others. The basic tenets of this personological system include the individual as a unified and self-consistent entity, human life as a dynamic striving for perfection, the individual as a creative and self-determined entity, and the social embeddedness and subjectivity of the individual.

Adler viewed people as experiencing inferiority feelings during childhood for which they attempt to compensate. Rooted in these inferiority feelings of childhood, people spend their lives striving for superiority. Indeed, each person develops a unique style of life in which he or she strives for fictional final goals involving superiority or perfection. Furthermore, Adler believed that a person's style of life is most evident in his or her attitude and behavior toward the three major life tasks—work, friendship, and love. Based upon the dimensions of social interest and the degree of activity in relation to these three life tasks, Adler distinguished four basic types of life-style attitudes: the ruling, getting, avoiding, and socially useful types.

Adler theorized that style of life is developed by the individual's creative power. Also, of some influence on personality development is ordinal position within the family. Adler stressed four such birth order positions: the first-born, only-born, second-born, and last-born child. A final construct emphasized in individual psychology is social interest, a person's innate tendency and striving to help society attain the goals of an ideal community. For Adler, degree of social interest provides a barometer of psychological health.

Adler's basic assumptions about human nature strongly suggest that, far from being the "neo-Freudian" that he is often considered, he may actually be more accurately understood as a precursor of contemporary humanistic and phenomenological psychology. Individual psychology reflects (1) a strong commitment to the assumptions of freedom, holism, unchangeability, subjectivity, proactivity, heterostasis, and unknowability; (2) a moderate commitment to the rationality assumption; and (3) a "middle of the road" position on the constitutionalism–environmentalism dimension.

While Adler's theoretical concepts are acknowledged to have high practical relevance, empirical tests of these concepts have been meager in number. Difficulties in empirically validating the constructs of individual psychology stem mainly from their global nature and the less than fully systematized status of this theoretical system. Nonetheless, in this chapter empirical studies concerned with birth order effects were summarized. Findings indicate that first-borns are high in intellectual achievement and that last-borns are overrepresented among alcoholics. The Social Interest Scale and the Social Interest Index, two self-report tests used to assess Adler's concept of social interest, were also discussed in terms of their psychometric properties and relationship to other self-report measures.

Adler's concepts were applied to the understanding of neurosis and its treatment. His ideas about the nature, causes, and onset of neurosis were described in reference to a young woman experiencing social problems in adjusting to college life. Adler's approach to therapy emphasizes the importance of understanding the patient's life-style, enhancing self-insight, and strengthening social interest.

Another striking revision of Freud's psychodynamic theory is Jung's analytical psychology. A major disagreement between the two concerned the nature of the libido. Freud saw it as mainly sexual energy, whereas Jung saw it as a creative life energy that could be applied to the person's continuous growth.

Jung viewed the psyche as comprised of three separate but interacting structures: ego, personal unconscious, and collective unconscious. Ego represents everything of which the person is conscious. The personal unconscious is a reservoir of repressed memories and clusters of interrelated thoughts and feelings called complexes. The collective unconscious is comprised of primordial elements called archetypes. Archetypes represent universal experiences of our ancient human ancestors that predispose us to react in certain ways to current experiences. The most significant archetypes noted in Jungian theory are the persona, the shadow, the anima, the animus, and the self. The self archetype is symbolized by a mandala or magic circle.

Two ego orientations or attitudes toward life posited by Jung are extraversion and introversion. Extraverts tend to be outgoing, sociable, and focused on the outside world, whereas introverts tend to be reflective, aloof, and focused on the self. Jung also proposed the existence of four psychological functions: thinking, feeling, sensing, and intuiting. Thinking and feeling are rational functions and sensing and intuiting are irrational functions. By combining the two ego orientations and the four psychological functions, eight different personality types are identified in Jung's theory (e.g., an extrovert-thinking type).

Jung's account of personality development emphasizes movement toward self-realization through balancing and integrating the various elements of the psyche. He used the term "individuation" to describe the lifelong process by which all aspects of the personality become organized around the self. The individuation process allows the self to become the center of personality and, in turn, enables the person to attain self-actualization. For Jung, few people ever achieve this highest level of personal development.

Analytical psychology has exerted widespread influence on the intellectual community in recent years. Nonetheless, most of Jung's major concepts have not been empirically tested. A small body of research using a questionnaire called the *Myers-Briggs Type Indicator* has sought to validate Jungian predictions concerning relationships between psychological types and memories and dreams. Far more research is needed, however, if Jung's theory is to have a lasting influence within psychology.

BIBLIOGRAPHY

Adler, A. (1917a). *The neurotic constitution.* New York: Moffat.
Adler, A. (1917b). *Study of organ inferiority and its psychical compensation: A contribu-*

tion to clinical medicine. S. E. Jellife, Trans. New York: Nervous and Mental Disease Publication. (Original work published 1907.)

Adler, A. (1927a). *The practice and theory of individual psychology*. New York: Harcourt, Brace.

Adler, A. (1927b). *Understanding human nature*. Garden City, NY: Garden City Publishing.

Adler, A. (1929). *The science of living*. New York: Greenberg.

Adler, A. (1930). *The pattern of life*. New York: Holt, Rinehart and Winston.

Adler, A. (1931). *What life should mean to you*. Boston: Little, Brown.

Adler, A. (1939). *Social interest: A challenge to mankind*. New York: Putnam.

Adler, A. (1944). Physical manifestations of psychic disturbances. *Individual Psychology Bulletin*, **4**, 3–8.

Adler, A. (1956). *The individual psychology of Alfred Adler: A systematic presentation of selections from his writings*. H. L. & R. R. Ansbacher (Eds.). New York: Basic Books.

Adler, A. (1964). *Superiority and social interest: A collection of later writings*. H. L. & R. R. Ansbacher (Eds.). Evanston, IL: Northwestern University Press.

Alexander, I. E. (1982). The Freud-Jung relationship—The other side of Oedipus and countertransference: Some implications for psychoanalytic theory and psychotherapy. *American Psychologist*, **37**, 1009–1018.

Ansbacher, H. L. (1971). Alfred Adler and humanistic psychology. *Journal of Humanistic Psychology*, **11**, 23–63.

Ansbacher, H. L. (1977). Individual psychology. In R. J. Corsini (Ed.), *Current personality theories* (pp. 45–82). Itasca, IL: Peacock.

Barry, H., III, & Blane, H. T. (1977). Birth order of alcoholics. *Journal of Individual Psychology*, **62**, 62–79.

Belmont, L., & Marolla, F. A. (1973). Birth order, family size, and intelligence. *Science*, **182**, 1096–1101.

Breland, H. M. (1974). Birth order, family configuration, and verbal achievement. *Child Development*, **45**, 1011–1019.

Campbell, J. (1971). *Hero with a thousand faces*. New York: Harcourt Brace Jovanovich.

Cann, D. R., & Donderi, D. C. (1986). Jungian personality typology and the recall of everyday and archetypal dreams. *Journal of Personality and Social Psychology*, **50**, 1021–1030.

Carlson, R. (1980). Studies of Jungian typology: II. Representations of the personal world. *Journal of Personality and Social Psychology*, **38**, 801–810.

Crandall, J. E. (1975). A scale of social interest. *Journal of Individual Psychology*, **31**, 187–195.

Crandall, J. E. (1980). Adler's concept of social interest: Theory, measurement, and implications for adjustment. *Journal of Personality and Social Psychology*, **39**, 481–495.

Crandall, J. E. (1981). *Theory and measurement of social interest: Empirical tests of Alfred Adler's concept*. New York: Columbia University Press.

Crandall, J. E. (1984). Social interest as a moderator of life stress. *Journal of Personality and Social Psychology*, **47**, 164–174.

Dreikurs, R. (1950). *Fundamentals of Adlerian psychology*. New York: Greenberg.

Dreikurs, R. (1973). *Psychodynamics, psychotherapy, and counseling*. Chicago: Alfred Adler Institute.

Dry, A. M. (1981). *The psychology of Jung*. New York: Wiley.

Ellenberger, H. (1970). Alfred Adler and individual psychology. In *The discovery of the unconscious: The history and evolution of dynamic psychiatry*. New York: Basic Books.

Ernst, C., & Angst, J. (1983). *Birth order: Its influence on personality*. Berlin: Springer-Verlag.

Falbo, T. (1978). Only children and interpersonal behavior: An experimental and survey study. *Journal of Applied Social Psychology, 8,* 244–253.

Falbo, T., & Polit, D. F. (1986). Quantitative review of the only child literature: Research evidence and theory development. *Psychological Bulletin, 100,* 176–189.

Fling, S., Thomas, H., & Gallaher, M. (1981). Participant characteristics and the effects of two types of meditation vs. quiet sitting. *Journal of Clinical Psychology, 37,* 784–790.

Gay, P. (1989). *The Freud reader*. New York: Norton.

Greever, K., Tseng, M., & Friedland, B. (1973). Development of the social interest index. *Journal of Consulting and Clinical Psychology, 41,* 454–458.

Hillman, J. (1979). *The dream and the underworld*. New York: Harper and Row.

Hogan, R. (1976). *Personality theory: The personological tradition*. Englewood Cliffs, NJ: Prentice-Hall.

Jones, E. (1957). *The life and work of Sigmund Freud*. New York: Basic Books.

Jung, C. G. (1906/1960). The psychology of dementia praecox. In *The collected works of C. G. Jung* (Vol. 3). Princeton, NJ: Princeton University Press.

Jung, C. G. (1909/1973). The psychological diagnosis of evidence. In *The collected works of C. G. Jung* (Vol. 2). Princeton, NJ: Princeton University Press.

Jung, C. G. (1913/1973). On the doctrine of complexes. In *The collected works of C. G. Jung* (Vol. 2). Princeton, NJ: Princeton University Press.

Jung, C. G. (1921/1971). Psychological types. In *The collected works of C. G. Jung* (Vol. 6). Princeton, NJ: Princeton University Press.

Jung, C. G. (1931/1969). The structure of the psyche. In *The collected works of C. G. Jung* (Vol. 8). Princeton, NJ: Princeton University Press.

Jung, C. G. (1936/1969). The archetypes and the collective unconscious. In *The collected works of C. G. Jung* (Vol. 9). Princeton, NJ: Princeton University Press.

Jung, C. G. (1961). *Memories, dreams, and reflections*. New York: Random House.

Jung, C. G. (1968). *Analytical psychology: Its theory and practice* (The Tavistock Lectures). New York: Pantheon.

Leak, G. K., Millard, R. J., Perry, N. W., & Williams, D. E. (1985). An investigation of the nomological network of social interest. *Journal of Research in Personality, 19,* 197–207.

Manaster, G. J., & Corsini, R. J. (1982). *Individual psychology*. Itasca, IL: Peacock.

Mattoon, M. A. (1981). *Jungian psychology in perspective*. New York: Free Press.

Melillo, D. (1983). Birth order, perceived birth order, and family position of academic women. *Individual Psychology, 39,* 57–62.

Mozdzierz, G. J., Greenblatt, R. L., & Murphy, T. J. (1986). Social interest: The validity of two scales. *Individual Psychology, 42* 35–43.

Myers, M. B., & McCaulley, M. H. (1985). *Manual: A guide to the development and use of the Myers-Briggs Type Indicator*. Palo Alto, CA: Consulting Psychologists Press.

Orgler, H. (1972). *Alfred Adler: The man and his work*. New York: New American Library.

Rattner, J. (1983). *Alfred Adler*. New York: Ungar.

Stern, P. J. (1976). *C. G. Jung: The haunted prophet*. New York: Dell.

Stevens, A. (1983). *Archetypes*. New York: Quill.

Vaihinger, H. (1911). *The philosophy of "as if."* New York: Harcourt, Brace.

Wagner, M. E., & Schubert, H. J. (1977). Sibship variables and United States presidents. *Journal of Individual Psychology, 62,* 78–85.

Zarski, J. J., Bubenzer, D. L., & West, J. D. (1986). Social interest, stress, and the prediction of health status. *Journal of Counseling and Development, 64,* 386–389.

Zajonc, R. B. (1986). Mining new gold from old research. *Psychology Today,* February, 46–51.

Zajonc, R. B., & Markus, G. B. (1975). Birth order and intellectual development. *Psychological Review,* **82,** 74–88.

Zweigenhaft, R. L. (1975). Birth order, approval seeking, and membership in Congress. *Journal of Individual Psychology,* **31,** 205–210.

SUGGESTED READINGS

Ansbacher, H. L. (1984). *Alfred Adler revisited.* New York: Praeger.

Brome, V. (1978). *Jung: Man and myth.* New York: Atheneum.

Hannah, B. (1976). *Jung: His life and work.* New York: Putnam.

McGuire, W. (Ed.), (1974). *The Freud/Jung letters.* Princeton, NJ: Princeton University Press.

Mosak, H. (Ed.). (1973). *Alfred Adler: His influence on psychology today.* Park Ridge, NH: Noyes.

Stepansky, P. E. (1983). *In Freud's Shadow: Adler in context.* Hillsdale, NJ: Analytic Press.

DISCUSSION QUESTIONS

1 Compare Adler's basic assumptions about human nature to those of Freud. On this basis, can you see why your authors do not regard Adler as truly a neo-Freudian? Do you agree?

2 Do you agree with Adler that childhood feelings of inferiority play an important part in people's lives? To illustrate, can you see any present areas of strength or accomplishment in your own life that seem to have their roots in earlier inferiority feelings?

3 What do you think of Adler's concept of striving for superiority? How do you strive for superiority in your life? Can you see how your own direction and goals in this regard differ from those of your friends?

4 Do you agree with Adler that social interest is the barometer of psychological health? If so, why? If not, why not?

5 Now that you have studied Adler's theory, think about your ordinal position in your family. Can you see how being the first-born, second-born, youngest, or only child has affected your overall personality development?

6 Describe Adler's approach to the explanation of the neurotic life-style. In what ways does Adler differ from Freud in the treatment of neurotic patients? Are the goals of therapy different for Adler as opposed to Freud?

7 How does Jung distinguish between the personal unconscious and the collective unconscious? Do you agree with Jung that the collective unconscious exists? If yes, what evidence would you cite to support your agreement?

8 Describe Jung's concept of archetypes. Which archetype did Jung associate with the attainment of self-realization in adulthood?

9 What are the four psychological functions of the psyche postulated by Jung? Which function dominates your conscious life? Which function best describes the person you are emotionally closest to?

10 Compare and contrast Adler and Jung on each of the following: the ultimate goal of life, the causes of psychopathology, and the nature of human motivation.

GLOSSARY

Analytical psychology   Jung's theory of personality that emphasizes opposing forces within the psyche and the striving toward selfhood through the process of individuation.

Anima   The feminine qualities of the male; an archetype in Jung's theory.

Animus   The masculine qualities of the female; an archetype in Jung's theory.

Archetype   Universal images or symbols contained in the collective unconscious that predispose one to have a certain feeling or thought toward a current object or situation (e.g., the hero or wise man).

Birth order   The individual's ordinal position (e.g., first-born) within the family, which, in turn, plays an important role in shaping his or her life-style.

Collective unconscious   The deepest level of the psyche containing memories and images inherited from our human and prehuman ancestors.

Compensation   Attempt by a person to replace feelings of inadequacy with feelings of adequacy through development of physical or mental skills.

Creative self   Concept used by Adler to reflect his belief that each person is empowered with the freedom to actively create his or her own personality.

Ego   Term used by Jung to represent everything of which we are conscious.

Extraversion   Basic ego orientation postulated by Jung to account for the person's style of relating to the outside world. Extraversion is characterized by interest and involvement in the world of people and things external to the self.

Fictional finalism   Term used by Adler to convey the notion that human behavior is guided by imagined or fictional goals that can be neither tested nor confirmed against reality.

Individuation   Term used by Jung to describe the process of integrating the opposing elements of personality in order to become whole.

Individual psychology   Adler's theory of personality that emphasizes the uniqueness of each individual and the processes by which people overcome their limitations and struggle to reach their life goals.

Inferiority complex   Deep pervasive feeling that one is inferior to other people. It is often associated with faulty attitudes and behaviors.

Inferiority feelings   Feelings of inadequacy, ineptness, and incompetence which emerge during infancy and thus serve as the basis for strivings for superiority.

Introversion   Basic ego orientation postulated by Jung to account for the person's style of relating to the world. Introversion is characterized by a contemplative and aloof approach to life.

Mandala   Symbolic representation of the unified wholeness of self; also called ''magic circles'' in Jung's theory.

Organ inferiority   Congenitally weak or poorly functioning organ in the body (e.g., a visual defect) that gives rise to feelings of inferiority on the part of the individual. For Adler, an organ inferiority often leads an individual to striking accomplishments in life.

Overcompensation   A form of compensation that does more than rid the person of feelings of inadequacy—it leads to superiority or outstanding achievement. A person who overcompensates may act as though he or she feels superior to others (i.e., evidence a superiority complex).

Persona   An archetype in Jung's theory consisting of the roles people enact in response to the social demands of others; the public face revealed to others.

Personal unconscious   A structure of the psyche in Jung's theory containing repressed memories and forgotten experiences or material that was not vivid enough to make a conscious impression at first.

Psyche   Jung's term for personality structure (including ego, personal unconscious, and collective unconscious).

Psychological functions   A group of four functions of the psyche proposed by Jung to explain differences in how people relate to the world. Thinking and feeling were grouped together as rational functions since they involve making judgments about life experiences. Sensing and intuiting were grouped together as irrational functions since they involve passive recording of life experiences.

Self   An archetype in Jung's theory that becomes the center of the psyche if all the opposing forces of personality are integrated through the process of individuation.

Shadow   An archetype in Jung's theory representing the evil and animalistic side of human personality.

Social interest   The feeling of empathy for the rest of humanity which manifests itself as cooperation with others for social advancement rather than for personal gain. For Adler, social interest is a useful yardstick of psychological health.

Striving for superiority   The striving to achieve mastery over one's limitations and to develop to one's fullest potential. Adler viewed this striving as the great dynamic force underlying human behavior.

Style of life   The unique configuration of traits, motives, cognitive styles, and coping techniques that characterizes the behavior of an individual and gives it consistency.

Superiority complex   In Adler's theory, a tendency to exaggerate one's importance in order to overcome persistent feelings of inferiority.

CHAPTER 5

THE EGO PSYCHOLOGY AND RELATED PERSPECTIVES IN PERSONALITY THEORY: ERIK ERIKSON, ERICH FROMM, AND KAREN HORNEY

Many theorists who came after Freud sought to revise psychoanalytic thought in such a way as to grant a greater role to ego processes and the development of these processes. Foremost among these revisionists commonly identified as *ego psychologists* was Erik Erikson. Like other post-Freudian theorists to whom this label has been applied, Erikson focuses major attention on the ego and its adaptive capacities in relation to individual development. It does not follow, however, that he neglects either biological or social factors in his theory. In fact, he stresses the idea that any psychological phenomenon must be understood in terms of the reciprocal interplay of biological, behavioral, experiential, and social factors. Other features that distinguish Erikson's theoretical orientation include (1) an emphasis on developmental change throughout the entire life cycle; (2) a focus on the "normal" or "healthy" rather than on the pathological; (3) a special emphasis on the importance of achieving a sense of identity; and (4) an effort to combine clinical insight with cultural and historical forces in explaining personality organization. However, Erikson's discussion of the "Eight Ages of Man" represents his most original and important contribution to personality theory. His attempt to show how culture can influence personality development has provided students of human behavior with fresh and genuine advances in understanding the major psychological problems that confront humanity today. Accordingly, his ideas are the primary focus of this chapter.

The emergence of ego psychology was preceded by a group of related theories concerned primarily with how aspects of the social and cultural environment influence personality development. Similar to the perspectives presented by Adler and Erikson, these theories offered new ways of thinking about parent–child relationships, motivational processes, and human personality in general. In so doing, they deemphasized Freud's doctrine of instinctual, sexual motives in human nature. While there are many prominent members of this revisionist group, we have limited our coverage to two who most energetically questioned and even abandoned some of the tenets of classical psychoanalysis in their theories: Erich Fromm and Karen Horney. The theoretical perspectives created by these two noteworthy personologists will be briefly considered later in this chapter.

ERIK ERIKSON: AN EGO THEORY OF PERSONALITY

BIOGRAPHICAL SKETCH

The son of a Danish father and a Jewish mother, Erik Erikson was born in 1902 near Frankfurt, Germany. His parents separated before his birth, and his mother subsequently married Dr. Theodor Homburger. Young Erik was not told for some years that Dr. Homburger was, in fact, his stepfather. Later, in signing his first psychoanalytic articles, Erikson used his stepfather's surname as his own, although he chose to be known by his original name when he became a naturalized American citizen in 1939.

Unlike any other personologist discussed in this text, Erikson did not pursue formal education beyond high school. He attended a "humanistic gymnasium" in Germany, and although he was a mediocre student, he did excel in the subjects of history and art. Shortly after graduation, spurning his adoptive father's urgings that he become a physician, Erikson left home to travel across central Europe. A year later, he enrolled in an art school. However, he soon became restless again and set out for Munich to study at the famous art school there, the Dunst-Akademie. Two years later, Erikson moved to Florence, Italy, although for a period he wandered aimlessly throughout Italy, soaking up sun and visiting art galleries.

In 1927 Erikson ended his occupational "moratorium" when he accepted an invitation from Peter Blos, a high-school classmate, to teach at a small, experimental American nursery school in Vienna. The school had been established by Anna Freud for children whose parents were learning to become psychoanalysts. Some of Erikson's young students were in analysis themselves, and eventually their teacher—Herr Erik, as he was affectionately called—joined them.

Erikson's introduction to the study of psychoanalysis began at a mountain spa near Vienna. There, as a tutor, he first came to know the Freud family and was subsequently selected as an acceptable candidate for training at the Vienna Psychoanalytic Institute. From 1927 to 1933 Erikson continued his training in psychoanalysis under the guidance of Anna Freud. This constituted his only formal academic training aside from a certificate he acquired from the Maria Montessori Teachers Association in Vienna.

During his years in Vienna, Erikson married Joan Serson, a Canadian who was also a member of the experimental school led by Anna Freud. In 1933 the Erikson

Erik H. Erickson. *(Courtesy of Erik H. Erickson)*

family (including two sons) went to Copenhagen, where Erikson attempted to regain his Danish citizenship and to help establish a psychoanalytic training center in that country. When this proved impractical, the family emigrated to the United States and settled in Boston, where a psychoanalytic society had been founded the year before. For the next 2 years he practiced in Boston, specializing in the treatment of children. He also served on the staff of Henry Murray's clinic at Harvard and held a clinical and academic appointment as Research Fellow in psychology in the Department of Neuropsychiatry of the Harvard Medical School. Erikson even enrolled as a candidate for the Ph.D. degree in psychology at Harvard, but withdrew from the program after he failed his first course.

In 1936 Erikson accepted a teaching position at the Yale University School of medicine. In 1938 he undertook a field trip to the Pine Ridge Reservation in South Dakota to observe how members of the Sioux Indians raised their children. This study marked Erikson's initial focus on the influence of culture on childhood development, a concern that was to be evident in much of his later professional work.

In 1939 Erikson moved to California, where he resumed his analytic work with children and furthered his interest in anthropology and history. By 1942 he was a professor of psychology at the University of California at Berkeley. What followed was an intense period of close clinical observation and reflection as Erikson established himself as a key figure in psychoanalysis. His professorship at Berkeley tragically ended, however, when he refused to sign a loyalty oath. He was later reinstated as politically reliable but chose to resign because others were fired for the same "crime." He published his first book, *Childhood and Society,* in 1950 (revised and reissued in 1963). This work soon won him international recognition as a leading spokesman of ego psychology.

In 1951 Erikson joined the Austen Riggs Center in Stockbridge, Massachusetts, a private residential treatment center for disturbed adolescents. He also maintained part-time teaching appointments at several universities throughout the United States. For the next decade his writings and research extended the theory of psychosocial development originally proposed in *Childhood and Society*.

In 1960, following a year at the Center for Advanced Studies of the Behavioral Sciences at Palo Alto, California, Erikson rejoined Harvard University as lecturer and professor of human development. He remained at Harvard until his retirement in 1970.

In the years following his retirement, Erikson has continued to devote much time to the application of his scheme of the human life cycle to the study of historical persons and American children, predominantly minority groups. His brilliant psychobiographical study of the origins of militant nonviolence, *Gandhi's Truth* (1969), won him a Pulitzer Prize and the National Book Award in philosophy and religion. Moreover, he has published three other important books— *Young Man Luther: A Study in Psychoanalysis and History* (1958); *Insight and Responsibility* (1964a); and *Identity: Youth and Crisis* (1968a)—as well as editing another, *Youth: Change and Challenge* (1963b). Robert Coles, a Harvard psychiatrist and student of Erikson, acknowledged his mentor's accomplishments as a theoretician and practitioner of psychoanalysis in a volume entitled *Erik H. Erikson: The Growth of His Work* (1970). Despite advancing age, Erikson continues to be active in the Erikson center in Cambridge, Massachusetts. His most recent publications include *In Search of Common Ground* (1973); *Life History and the Historical Moment* (1975); *Toys and Reasons: Stages in the Ritualization of Experience* (1977); *Identity and the Life Cycle: A Reissue* (1979); *Adulthood* (1978); *The Life Cycle Completed* (1982); and *Vital Involvement in Old Age* (1986). At this writing Erikson and his wife reside in Cambridge, Massachusetts.

EGO PSYCHOLOGY: PSYCHOANALYSIS COMES OF AGE

Erikson's theoretical formulations are exclusively concerned with ego development. Although he has steadfastly insisted that his own ideas are nothing more than a systematic extension of Freud's conceptions of psychosexual development in light of new discoveries in the social and biological sciences, Erikson does represent a decisive departure from classical psychoanalysis in four essential ways. First, his work marks a sweeping shift in emphasis from the id to the ego, one which Freud only partially acknowledged during the final years of his work. From Erikson's vantage point, the ego rather than the id is the basis of human behavior and functioning. He regards the ego as an autonomous structure of personality that follows a course of social-adaptive development which parallels the development of the id and the instincts. This view of human nature, called *ego psychology,* constitutes a radical change from earlier psychodynamic thought in that it depicts persons as much more rational, and, therefore, conscious in making decisions and solving problems. Whereas Freud believed that the ego struggles to resolve conflict between instinctual urges and moral constraints, Erikson argues that the ego is an autonomous system that deals with reality through perception, thinking, attention, and memory. As a result of his emphasis on the adaptive functions of the ego, Erikson views the person as becoming more competent in dealing with the environment over the course of development.

Second, Erikson introduces a new perspective concerning the person's relationship to parents and the cultural context in which the family is located. Whereas Freud concerned himself with the influence of parents on the child's emerging personality, Erikson stresses the historical setting in which the child's ego is molded. He relies on case studies of people living in different cultures to show how the ego's development is inextricably bound up with the changing nature of social institutions and value systems.

Third, Erikson's theory of ego development encompasses the entire life span of the individual (i.e., from infancy to adolescence and eventually maturity and old age). In contrast, Freud limited himself to the effects of early childhood experiences and devoted no attention to developmental issues beyond the genital stage. Closer inspection makes it evident, however, that some degree of correspondence does exist between the two theorists with respect to the first five stages of life.

Finally, Freud and Erikson differ on the nature and resolution of psychosexual conflicts. Freud's objective was to unravel the existence and operation of unconscious mental life and explain how early trauma may bring about psychopathology in adulthood. Conversely, Erikson's mission is to draw attention to the human capacity to triumph over the psychosocial hazards of living. Thus, his theory focuses on *ego qualities* (i.e., virtues) that emerge at various developmental periods. Perhaps this distinction is the key to understanding Erikson's own conception of personality organization and development. Freud's fatalistic warning that human beings are doomed to social extinction if left to their instinctual strivings is countered by Erikson's optimistic premise that every personal and social crisis furnishes challenges that are conducive to growth and mastery over the world. To know how a person has mastered each of a series of significant life problems and how the inadequate mastery of early problems incapacitates him or her in dealing with later problems is, for Erikson, the only avenue to understanding a person's life.

Insofar as major theoretical differences between Erikson and Freud have been stressed, it would be only reasonable to note that there are also substantive areas of similarity. For example, both theorists consider the stages of personality as being predetermined and invariant in order of appearance. Erikson also acknowledges the biological and sexual foundations of all later motivational and personal dispositions and is committed to Freud's structural model (id, ego, superego) of personality. Despite these overlapping areas of agreement, many personologists see Erikson's theoretical framework as radically different from the one offered by classical psychoanalysis.

THE EPIGENETIC PRINCIPLE

Central to Erikson's theory of ego development is the assumption that human development is characterized by a series of stages that are universal to humankind. The process whereby these stages unfold is governed by the *epigenetic principle* of maturation. By this Erikson means:

(1) that the human personality in principle develops according to steps predetermined in the growing person's readiness to be driven toward, to be aware of, and to interact with, a widening social radius; and (2) that society, in principle, tends to be so constituted as to meet and invite this succession of potentialities for interaction and attempts to safeguard and to encourage the proper rate and the proper sequence of their enfolding. (1963a, p. 270)

In *Childhood and Society* (1963a), Erikson partitioned the life span into eight separate stages of psychosocial ego development, colloquially "the eight stages of man." He postulates that these stages are the result of the epigenetic unfolding of a "ground plan" of personality that is genetically transmitted. An epigenetic conception of development (*epi* means "upon" and *genetic* means "emergence") reflects the notion that each stage in the life cycle has an optimal time (i.e., critical period) in which it is dominant and hence emerges, and that when all of the stages have unfolded according to plan, a fully functioning personality comes into existence. Furthermore, Erikson hypothesizes that each psychosocial stage is accompanied by a *crisis,* that is, a turning point in the individual's life that arises from physiological maturation and social demands made upon the person at that stage. In other words, each of the eight phases in the human life cycle is marked by a "phase specific" developmental task, a problem in social development that must be addressed, though not necessarily resolved, at that particular time. The characteristic behavior patterns exhibited by the person are determined by the manner in which each of these tasks or crises is eventually resolved. Conflict is a vital and integral part of Erikson's theory, because growth and an expanding interpersonal radius are associated with increased vulnerability of the ego functions at each stage. At the same time, he notes that crisis connotes "not a threat of catastrophe but a turning point and, therefore, the ontogenetic source of generational strength and maladjustment" (1968b, p. 286).

Each psychosocial crisis, when viewed as a dimensional attribute, includes both a positive and a negative component. If the conflict is resolved satisfactorily (i.e., the person has a history of ego achievements), the positive component (e.g., basic trust, autonomy) is to a large degree absorbed into the emerging ego and further healthy development is assured. Conversely, if the conflict persists or is resolved unsatisfactorily, the developing ego is damaged and the negative component (e.g., mistrust, shame, and doubt) is to a large degree incorporated into the ego. While the various theoretically defined conflicts emerge in developmental sequence, this does not mean that earlier achievements and failures are necessarily permanent. Ego qualities attained at each stage are not impervious to new inner conflicts or to changing conditions (Erikson, 1964a). The major point, however, is that the person must adequately resolve each crisis in order to progress to the next stage of development in an adaptive and mature fashion.

All eight stages in Erikson's psychosocial theory are charted in Table 5–1. The far left column indicates each stage, the second column the approximate age range in which it occurs, the third column the contrasting positive and negative components of each stage, and the far right column the ego strength or virtue associated with successful resolution of each crisis. Consistent with the principle of epi-

TABLE 5-1   THE EIGHT STAGES OF PSYCHOSOCIAL DEVELOPMENT

Stage		Approximate age	Psychosocial crisis	Virtue
1	Oral–sensory	Birth–1 year	Basic trust vs. mistrust	Hope
2	Muscular–anal	1–3 years	Autonomy vs. shame and doubt	Will power
3	Locomotor–genital	3–6 years	Initiative vs. guilt	Purpose
4	Latency	6–12 years	Industry vs. inferiority	Compe-tence
5	Adolescence	12–19 years	Ego identity vs. role confusion	Fidelity
6	Early adulthood	20–25 years	Intimacy vs. isolation	Love
7	Middle adulthood	26–64 years	Generativity vs. stagnation	Care
8	Late adulthood	65–death	Ego integrity vs. despair	Wisdom

Adapted from *Childhood and Society*, by Erik H. Erikson, 1963a, p. 273.

genesis, each stage builds upon the resolution and integration of previous psycho-social conflicts. Nevertheless, Erikson proposes that all the crises are present in some form from the beginning of postnatal life, each one having its special time of priority in the genetically determined sequence of development.

Although Erikson assumes that the eight stages are a universal feature of human development, he also believes that there is some cultural variation in the way that people deal with the problems of each stage and in the possible solutions to these problems. For example, puberty rites exist in all cultures, yet vary widely from one culture to another in their form of expression and their impact on the person. Moreover, Erikson feels that in every culture there is a "crucial coordina-tion" between the developing individual and the social environment. This coordi-nation is evidenced by what he calls "a cogwheeling of the life cycles," a law of reciprocal development that ensures that society's caretakers are most fit to provide care and support at the time when developing persons need it most. Thus, in Erikson's view, the needs and capacities of the generations intertwine. This complex pattern of interdependence between the generations is reflected in Erik-son's concept of *mutuality*.

PERSONALITY DEVELOPMENT: THE PSYCHOSOCIAL STAGES

As noted earlier, Erikson proposes that personality development occurs over the entire life span. His analysis of socialization can best be presented by describing the distinctive features of the eight stages of psychosocial development.

1 Infancy: Basic Trust versus Mistrust

The first psychosocial stage corresponds to Freud's oral stage and encompasses the first year of life. For Erikson, a general sense of *trust* is the cornerstone of a healthy personality, while others regard this same characteristic as "confidence."

An infant with a basic sense of "inner certainty" experiences the social world as a safe, stable place and people as nurturant and reliable. This sense of certainty is only partially conscious during infancy.

Erikson believes that the degree to which infants are able to acquire a sense of trust in other people and in the world depends upon the quality of maternal care that they receive.

> Mothers, I think, create a sense of trust in their children by that kind of administration which in its quality combines sensitive care of the baby's individual needs and a firm sense of personal trustworthiness within the trusted framework of their culture's life style. This forms the basis in the child for a sense of being "all right," of being oneself, and of becoming what other people trust one will become. (Erikson, 1963a, p. 249)

Thus, a sense of trust does not depend on the amount of food or the expressions of affection the infant receives; rather, it is related to the mother's ability to give her baby a sense of familiarity, consistency, and sameness of experience. In addition, Erikson stresses the fact that infants must trust not only the external world but the internal world as well; they must learn to trust themselves and, in particular, the capacity of their organs to cope effectively with biological urges. Such behavior is shown when the infant can tolerate the mother's absence without suffering undue "separation" anxiety.

The question of what evokes life's first major psychological crisis has been carefully considered by Erikson. He attributes the crisis to a quality of maternal care which is unreliable, inadequate, and rejecting. This fosters in the infant a psychosocial attitude of fear, suspicion, and apprehension toward the world in general and people in particular that will manifest its ill effects in later stages of personality development. Erikson also feels that a sense of *mistrust* may be augmented when the mother turns from the baby as the primary focus of her attention to other pursuits that she had given up during and following pregnancy (e.g., resuming a career or becoming pregnant again). Finally, parents who display divergent patterns of child care, who lack self-confidence in their role as parents, and who have value systems conflicting with the culture's dominant life-style may create an atmosphere of ambiguity for the child, resulting in feelings of distrust. The behavioral consequences of a seriously defective development of basic trust, according to Erikson, are acute depression in infants and paranoia in adults.

A basic premise of psychosocial theory is that the crisis of trust versus mistrust (or any other subsequent crisis) is not permanently resolved during the first year or two of life. Consistent with the epigenetic principle, trust versus mistrust will reappear at each successive stage of development, although it is focal during infancy. However, adequate resolution of the crisis of trust does yield major consequences for the future development of the infant's personality. The establishment of self-trust and trust in mother enables infants to tolerate the frustrations that they will inevitably experience during subsequent stages of development.

Erikson notes that the emergence of healthy growth in the infant does not result exclusively from a sense of trust but rather from a favorable ratio of trust over mistrust. It is as important to learn what *not* to trust as to learn what *to* trust. The ability to anticipate danger and discomfort are also essential for mastery of the environment and effective living; thus, basic trust should not be viewed in terms of an achievement scale. In animals, Erikson contends, there is almost an instinctive readiness to acquire this psychosocial ability, but in humans it must be learned. Further, he suggests that mothers in different cultures and social classes will teach trust and mistrust in different ways. Yet the attainment of basic trust is universal in substance, namely, that one can trust the social world in the form of one's mother, that she will come back and feed one the right thing at the right time.

The psychosocial strength, or virtue, gained from successful resolution of the trust versus mistrust conflict is termed *hope* by Erikson. Trust, in other words, becomes the infant's capacity for hope, which, in turn, is the foundation of the adult's faith in some form of institutionalized religion. Hope as the first ego strength also serves to maintain the person's belief in the meaning and trustworthiness of a common cultural world. Conversely, Erikson emphasizes that when religious institutions fail to provide tangible significance for the person, these institutions may become irrelevant, outmoded, and possibly even be replaced by other more significant sources of faith and conviction in the future (e.g., commitment to scientific and artistic endeavors and social action programs).

2 Early Childhood: Autonomy versus Shame and Doubt

Acquisition of a sense of basic trust sets the stage for the struggle to attain a certain degree of *autonomy* and self-control and to avoid shame, doubt, and humiliation. This period parallels Freud's anal stage and unfolds during the second and third years of life. For Erikson, through interaction with parents during toilet training, the child discovers the difference between holding as a form of caring and holding as a destructive form of restraint. The child also learns to distinguish between letting go in the sense of a relaxed "letting it be," and letting go as a type of destructive release. This stage, therefore, becomes decisive for the ratio of goodwill and willfulness. A sense of self-control without loss of self-esteem is the ontogenetic source of confidence in free will; a sense of overcontrol and loss of self-control can give rise to a lasting propensity for doubt and shame (Erikson, 1968b).

Prior to this stage, children are almost completely dependent on others for their care. However, as they rapidly gain neuromuscular maturation, language, and social discrimination, they begin to explore and interact with their environment more independently. In particular, they feel pride in their newly discovered locomotor skills and want to do everything themselves (e.g., bathing, dressing, and feeding themselves). There is a tremendous desire to explore, choose, and manipulate coupled with an attitude toward parents of "let me do it" and "I am what I will."

In Erikson's view, satisfactorily meeting the psychosocial crisis of this stage depends primarily on the parents' willingness to gradually allow children freedom to control those activities that affect their lives. At the same time, Erikson stresses that parents must maintain reasonable but firm limits in those areas of children's lives that are either potentially or actually harmful to themselves or destructive to others. Autonomy does not mean giving the child unrestricted freedom; rather, it means that parents must maintain "degrees of freedom" over the child's growing capacity to exercise choice.

Erikson regards the child's experience of *shame* as something akin to rage turned inward because the child has not been allowed to exercise autonomy and self-control. Shame may come about if the parents are impatient and insist on doing for children what they are capable of doing themselves or, conversely, if parents expect of children what they are not capable of doing themselves. To be sure, every parent has occasionally pushed his or her child beyond the limits of appropriate expectation. It is only when parents are persistently overprotective or insensitive that children acquire a dominant sense of shame with respect to others and a dominant sense of doubt about their own effectiveness in controlling the world and themselves. Rather than feeling self-confident about their ability to cope effectively with the environment, such children are conscious of being scrutinized (disapprovingly) or of being considered essentially helpless. They are uncertain of their "willpower" and of those who would dominate or exploit it. The result is a psychosocial attitude of self-doubt, humiliation, and power-lessness.

Erikson believes that the attainment of a stable sense of autonomy adds substantially to the child's sense of trust. This interdependence of trust and autonomy may sometimes impair future psychological growth. For example, children who have acquired a "shaky" sense of trust may, during the autonomy stage, become hesitant, fearful, and insecure about asserting themselves; hence, they continue to seek help and encourage others to do things for them. As adults, Erikson finds that such people are likely to manifest obsessive-compulsive behavior (to ensure control) or paranoid apprehension of secret persecutors.

The societal counterpart of autonomy is the institution of law and order. Despite the possible emotional connotation of this term, Erikson believes that parents must convey a deep and abiding commitment to justice and a respect for the rights and privileges of others if their children are to be prepared to accept a limited autonomy in adulthood.

> Willpower is the unbroken determination to exercise free choice as well as self-restraint in spite of the unavoidable experience of shame, doubt, and a certain rage over being controlled by others. Good will is rooted in the judiciousness of parents guided by their respect for the spirit of the law. (Erikson, 1968b, p. 288)

3 Play Age: Initiative versus Guilt

Initiative versus guilt is the final psychosocial conflict experienced by the preschool child during what Erikson calls the "play age." It corresponds to the developmental period Freud designated as the phallic stage and extends roughly from about age 4 to entry into formal school. This is when the child's social world challenges him or her to be active, to master new tasks and skills, and to win approval by being productive. Children also begin to assume additional responsibility for themselves and for that which defines their world (toys, pets, and, occasionally, younger siblings). They become interested in the work of others, in trying out new things, and in assuming the responsibilities available in the society around them. The facility for language and motor skills makes possible associations with peers and older children beyond their immediate home environments, thus allowing participation in a variety of social games. This is the age when children begin to feel that they count as persons and that life has a purpose for them. "I am what I will be" becomes the child's dominant sense of identity during the play age. To quote Erikson: "Initiative adds to autonomy the quality of undertaking, planning, and attacking a task for the sake of being on the move, where before self-will, more often than not, inspired acts of defiance or, at any rate, protested independence" (Erikson 1963a, p. 155).

Whether children will leave this stage with their sense of *initiative* favorably outbalancing their sense of *guilt* depends largely upon how parents react to their self-initiated activities. Children who are encouraged to undertake their own activities have their sense of initiative reinforced. Initiative is further facilitated when parents acknowledge their children's curiosity and do not ridicule or inhibit fantasy activity. Erikson indicates that children become increasingly goal oriented in this stage as they begin to identify with people whose work and personalities they can understand and admire. Their learning is vigorous and they begin making projects.

In psychosocial theory, the sense of guilt in children is caused by parents who are unwilling to allow them the opportunity of completing tasks on their own. A sense of guilt is also fostered by parents who employ excessive amounts of punishment in response to the child's urge to love and be loved by the opposite-sexed parent. Erikson shares Freud's view of the sexual nature of the developmental crisis involved (i.e., sex-role identification and the Oedipus and Electra complexes), but his own view is decidedly more social in scope. In any event, the child who is immobilized by guilt experiences feelings of resignation and unworthiness. Such children are fearful of asserting themselves, hang on the fringes of groups, and rely unduly on adults. They lack the *purpose* or courage to establish and pursue tangible goals. Erikson also suggests that a persistent sense of guilt may evolve into a variety of adult forms of psychopathology including generalized passivity, sexual impotence or frigidity, and psychopathic acting out.

Finally, the degree of initiative acquired in this phase of the child's life is related by Erikson to the economic system of the community. He states that the child's future potential to work productively and achieve self-sufficiency within the context of his or her society's economic system depends markedly upon the ability to master this psychosocial crisis.

4   School Age: Industry versus Inferiority

The fourth psychosocial period occurs from about 6 to 12 years of age ("school age"), and corresponds to the latency period in Freudian theory. Here for the first

Children acquire a sense of industry as they learn the skills that will be needed in society. (*Karen R. Preuss*/*Jeroboam*)

time the child is expected to learn the rudimentary skills of the culture via formal education. This period of life is associated with the child's increased powers of deductive reasoning and self-discipline as well as the ability to relate to peers according to prescribed rules. For example, it is not until this age that children can participate in "take-turn" games that demand compliance with elaborately structured rules (Piaget, 1983). The child's love for the parent of the opposite sex and rivalry with the same-sexed parent are typically sublimated and expressed by an inner desire to learn and to be productive.

Erikson notes that in primitive cultures the education of children is uncomplicated and socially pragmatic. Facility with utensils, tools, weapons, and other objects is directly related to the child's future role as an adult. Conversely, in cultures where there is a written language, children are first educated in the tools of literacy which, in time, enable them to master the complex skills demanded by various occupations and activities. In effect, although the kind of instruction offered children will vary with the culture, children do become sensitized to the *technological ethos* of their culture and their identity with it.

According to Erikson, children develop a sense of *industry* when they begin to comprehend the technology of their culture through attending school. The term "industriousness" captures the major developmental theme of this period because children are now preoccupied with the manner in which things are made and operate. Such interest is reinforced and facilitated by people in their neighborhoods and schools who introduce them to the "technological elements" of the social world by teaching and working with them. The child's ego identity is now "I am what I learn."

The danger of this stage lies in the potential development of a sense of *inferiority* or incompetence. For instance, if children doubt their skill or status among their peers, they may be discouraged from pursuing further learning (attitudes toward teachers and learning are instilled during this period). A sense of inferiority may also develop if children discover that their gender, race, religion, or socioeconomic status—rather than their own skill and motivation—is what determines their worth as persons. The result is that children may lose confidence in their ability to function effectively in the working world.

As noted above, the child's feeling of competence and industry is, at least in literate cultures, largely affected by her or his educational achievement. Erikson perceives a possible negative effect from this limited definition of success. To be specific, if children accept scholastic accomplishment or work as the only standard by which to judge their self-worth, they may become mere slaves to their culture's work force and its established role hierarchy (Karl Marx described such persons as submitting to "craft-idiocy"). Therefore, a genuine sense of industry involves more than simply how to be a good worker. For Erikson, industry includes a feeling of being interpersonally competent—the confidence that one can exert positive influence on the social world in quest of meaningful individual and social goals. The psychosocial strength of *competency* thus underlies the basis for effective participation in the social-economic-political order.

5   Adolescence: Ego Identity versus Role Confusion

Adolescence, the focus of the fifth stage in Erikson's chart of the life cycle, is regarded as highly significant in the person's psychosocial development. No longer a child but not yet an adult (roughly from the ages of 12 to 13 to about 19 to 20 in American society), the adolescent is confronted with various social demands and role changes that are essential for meeting the challenges of adulthood. In fact, Erikson's theoretical interest in adolescence and the problems accompanying it have led him to present a more elaborate analysis of this phase than of any other stage of ego development.

The new psychosocial dimension that appears during adolescence has *ego identity* at the positive end and *role confusion* at the negative end. The task confronting adolescents is to consolidate all the knowledge they have gained about themselves (as sons or daughters, students, athletes, musicians, Girl Scouts, choirboys, etc.) and integrate these various self-images into a personal identity that shows awareness of both a past and a future that follows logically from it. Erikson (1982) stresses the psychosocial nature of ego identity, with the focus not on conflicts between psychic structures but rather on a conflict with the ego itself, namely, of identity versus role confusion. Emphasis is placed on the ego and the way it is affected by society, particularly peer groups. Ego identity can therefore be defined as follows:

> The growing and developing youths, faced with this physiological revolution within them, are now primarily concerned with attempts at consolidating their social roles. They are sometimes morbidly, often curiously, preoccupied with what they appear to be

in the eyes of others as compared with what they feel they are and with the question of how to connect the earlier cultivated roles and skills with the ideal prototypes of the day. . . . The integration now taking place in the form of ego identity is more than the sum of the childhood identifications. It is the inner capital accrued from all those experiences of each successive stage, when successful identifications led to a successful alignment of the individual's basic drives with his endowment and his opportunities. The sense of ego identity, then, is the accrued confidence that one's ability to maintain inner sameness and continuity (one's ego in the psychological sense) is matched by the sameness and continuity of one's meaning for others. (Erikson, 1963a, p. 261)

Erikson's definition reveals three elements involved in the formation of an identity. First, young people must perceive themselves as having "inner sameness and continuity" over time. In this case, the person must form a self-image that is fused with the past and linked with the future. Second, significant others must also perceive a "sameness and continuity" in the person. This means that adolescents need confidence that the inner unity that they have developed earlier will be recognized in others' perceptions of them. Insofar as adolescents may be uncertain about both their self-concepts and their social images, then feelings of doubt, confusion, and apathy may counteract their emerging sense of selfhood. Finally, young people must have "accrued confidence" in the correspondence between the internal and external lines of continuity. Their self-perceptions must be validated by appropriate feedback from their interpersonal experiences.

Socially and emotionally, the maturation of adolescents encompasses new ways of appraising and evaluating the world and their relationship to it. They can conceive of ideal families, religions, philosophies, and societies which, in turn, they can compare and contrast with the imperfect persons and institutions of their own limited experience. To quote Erikson: "The adolescent mind becomes an ideological mind in search of an inspiring unification of ideals" (1968b, p. 290). Thus, a "diffusion of ideals" results from the person's failure to accept the values and ideologies offered by parents, churches, and other sources of authority. The person who suffers from identity diffusion has neither reevaluated past beliefs about the self and the world nor achieved a resolution that leads to an overall approach to life that seems to "fit." A "crisis of identity" thus becomes a pressing psychosocial concern.

In Erikson's judgment, the foundation for a successful adolescence and the attainment of an integrated identity originate in early childhood. Above and beyond what adolescents bring with them from childhood, however, the development of personal identity is significantly affected by the social groups with which they identify. Erikson has stressed, for example, how overidentification with popular heroes (movie stars, superathletes, rock musicians) or counterculture groups (revolutionary leaders, "skinheads," delinquents) cuts off a "budding identity" from its milieu, thus stifling the ego and restricting emergent identity. Likewise, the search for identity may be harder for certain groups of people than for others. For instance, it may be difficult for a young woman to achieve a firm sense of identity in a society where she is accorded second-class status. In Erikson's view, the feminist movement has attracted many supporters for the very reason that society, until recently, has frustrated women's effort to attain a positive identity (i.e., society has been reluctant to assimilate women into new social and occupational roles). Minority group members are also beset by difficulties in establishing a firm and coherent sense of identity (Erikson, 1964b).

Erikson also considers the adolescent's vulnerability to the stresses of rapid, social, political, and technological change to be a factor which may jeopardize the development of identity. Such change, exacerbated by the information explosion, contributes to a nebulous sense of uncertainty, anxiety, and discontinuity. It also threatens to break down many traditional and cherished values which young people have learned and experienced as children. The gap between generations reflects at least some of this generalized dissatisfaction with the established values of society, perhaps best illustrated by the unscrupulous behavior of prominent political and corporate figures during the past decade. The corrupt ways of national leaders has turned the truths of one generation into the myths of the next. Accordingly, Erikson interprets much of the social protest in young people as an attempt to restructure their own value system so as to commit themselves to goals and principles that give meaning and direction to their lives.

The failure of the young person to develop a personal identity results in what Erikson has called the *identity crisis*. The crisis of identity, or role confusion, is most often characterized by an inability to select a career or pursue further education. Many adolescents in the throes of this age-specific conflict experience a profound sense of futility, personal disorganization, and aimlessness. They feel inadequate, depersonalized, and alienated and sometimes even seek a ''negative identity,'' an identity which is opposite to the one prescribed for them by their parents and peers. Some delinquent behavior is interpreted by Erikson in this way. However, the failure to establish adequate personal identity does not necessarily doom the adolescent to a life of perpetual defeat. Perhaps more than any other personologist discussed in this text, Erikson has emphasized that life is constant change. Resolving problems at one stage of life is no guarantee against their reappearance at later stages—or against discovery of new solutions to them. Ego identity is a lifelong struggle.

In most and perhaps all societies, special delays in the assumption of adult roles and commitments are granted to certain segments of the adolescent population. Erikson coined the term *psychosocial moratorium* to denote these intervals between adolescence and adulthood. In the United States and other technologically advanced countries, the psychosocial moratorium has been institutionalized in the form of a system of higher education that enables young people to explore a number of different social and occupational roles before deciding what to do with their lives. In other instances, young people in large numbers have taken to wandering, joining religious cults, or exploring alternatives to traditional marriage and family life before settling down in a community.

The virtue associated with successful resolution of the crisis of adolescence is *fidelity*. As used by Erikson, fidelity refers to the adolescent's ''ability to sustain loyalties freely pledged in spite of the inevitable contradictions of value systems'' (1968b, p. 290). As the cornerstone of identity, fidelity represents the young person's capacity to perceive and abide by the social mores, ethics, and ideologies of society. The meaning of the term "ideology" as used in this context should be clarified. According to Erikson, an *ideology* is an unconscious set of values and assumptions reflecting the religious, scientific, and political thought of a culture; the purpose of an ideology is "to create a world image convincing enough to support the collective and the individual sense of identity" (Erikson, 1958, p. 22). Ideologies provide young people with oversimplified but definite answers to the basic questions associated with identity conflict, i.e., "Who am I?" "Where am I going?" "Who will I become?" Inspired by ideology, young people also become drawn to activities that challenge the established ways of a culture—rebellions, riots, and revolutions. On a broader scale, Erikson contends that a lack of faith in an ideological system may result in widespread confusion and disrespect for those who govern the systems of social rule.

6   Early Adulthood: Intimacy versus Isolation

The sixth psychosocial stage marks the formal beginning of adult life. This is generally a period in the life cycle when a person becomes involved in courtship, marriage, and early family life; it extends from late adolescence until early adulthood (ages 20 to 25). During this time, young adults usually orient themselves toward enriching vocations and "settling down." Erikson maintains, as did Freud, that it is only now that a person is genuinely ready for social as well as sexual intimacy with another person. Prior to this time, much of the person's sexual behavior was motivated by the search for ego identity. In contrast, the earlier attainment of personal identity and the involvement in productive work that mark this period give rise to a new interpersonal dimension with *intimacy* at one extreme and *isolation* at the other.

Erikson's use of the term "intimacy" is multidimensional in meaning and scope. He has in mind the sense of intimacy most of us share with a spouse, friends, siblings, and parents or other relatives. However, he also speaks of intimacy with oneself, that is, the ability to "fuse your identity with somebody else's without fear that you're going to lose something yourself" (Evans, 1967, p. 48). It is this aspect of intimacy (i.e., merging our own identity with that of another person) that Erikson considers essential for the establishment of a truly meaningful marriage. Likewise, he contends that a true sense of intimacy cannot be attained unless the young person has already achieved a stable identity. In other words, to be really intimate with another person or oneself, a person must have already developed a firm sense of who and what she or he is. By contrast, adolescent "falling in love" may be nothing more than an attempt to explore our own identity through the use of another person. This is corroborated by the fact that marriages of the young (aged 16 to 19) are not as enduring (in terms of divorce statistics) as marriages of those in their twenties. Erikson sees this as a result of the fact that many people, especially women, marry someone in order to find their own identity in and through that person. In his view, it is not possible to attain healthy intimate relationships by seeking identity in this fashion.

Erikson's description of one who is capable of intimacy closely resembles Freud's definition of the healthy person, namely, one who has the ability to love and to work. Although Erikson does not feel that this formula can be improved, it is intriguing to consider the question of whether (in Erikson's scheme) a celibate (e.g., priest) is capable of establishing a sense of intimacy. The answer is a resounding "yes," since Erikson believes that intimacy involves something more than just sexual closeness; it may also embrace empathy and openness between friends or, in the broader sense, a commitment to one's fellow human beings.

The chief danger of this psychosocial stage is self-absorption or the avoidance of interpersonal relationships. The inability to enter into comfortable and intimate personal relationships leads to feelings of loneliness, social emptiness, and isolation (Peplau & Perlman, 1982). Self-absorbed people may seek interpersonal encounters which are purely formal (employer–employee) and superficial (weekend health clubs). They insulate themselves against any type of real involvement because they are threatened by the demands and risks of intimacy. Self-absorbed people are also likely to have attitudes of futility and alienation about their vocations. Finally, Erikson believes that social conditions (e.g., the difficulty of achieving intimacy in an urbanized, mobile, impersonal, technological society) may hinder the establishment of a sense of intimacy. In cases of extreme isolation, he cites examples of antisocial or psychopathic personality types (i.e., people who lack an ethical sense) who manipulate and exploit others without feeling remorse. These are the young adults whose inability to share their identities with others makes it impossible for them to enter into deep and committed relationships.

Healthy resolution of the intimacy-versus-isolation crisis promotes the psychosocial strength of *love*. In addition to its romantic and erotic qualities, Erikson regards love as the ability to commit oneself to others and abide by such commitments, even though they may require self-denial and compromise. This type of love is expressed when a person shows an attitude of care, respect, and responsibility toward another.

The social institution linked with this stage of the life cycle is *ethics*. For Erikson, an ethical sense emerges as we recognize the value of committing ourselves to lasting friendships and social obligations—as well as the importance of honoring such commitments even if they require personal sacrifice. People who lack such an ethical sense are ill-equipped to face the next stage in psychosocial development.

7 Middle Adulthood: Generativity versus Stagnation

Erikson's seventh stage of development corresponds to the middle years of life (ages 26 to 64) and focuses on the issue of *generativity* versus *stagnation*. Generativity occurs when a person begins to show concern not only for the welfare of the next generation but also for the nature of the society in which that generation will live and work. He contends that each adult must either accept or reject the challenge of assuming responsibility for the continuation and betterment of whatever is instrumental to the maintenance and enhancement of the culture. This

A person displays generativity by showing concern for the welfare of ensuing generations. *(Joel Gordon)*

conviction is based on Erikson's belief that evolutionary development has "made man the teaching and instituting as well as the learning animal" (1968b, p. 291). Generativity, then, represents the older generation's concern to establish and guide those who will replace them. It is best exemplified by the sense of personal fulfillment associated with the production, rearing, and subsequent achievement of one's offspring. However, the expression of generativity is evidenced not only in parents but also in those who contribute to the guidance and betterment of young people. Adults who invest their time and energy in youth organizations such as Little League, the Boy and Girl Scouts, and the like may be generative. Beyond this, the creative and productive elements of generativity are personified in everything that is passed from one generation to the next (e.g., technological products, ideas, and works of art). An ultimate concern for the future welfare of humanity embodies the developmental theme of this second phase of adulthood.

If the capacity of adults for generativity surpasses their sense of stagnation, the virtue that emerges is *care*. Care stems from the feeling that something or someone matters; it is the psychological opposite of apathy. For Erikson, care represents "a widening commitment to take care of the persons, the products, and the ideas one has learned to care for" (1982, p. 67). As the basic virtue of adulthood, care is not merely a duty or obligation, but a natural desire to make a contribution to ensuing generations.

Adults who fail to establish a sense of generativity slip into a state of self-absorption in which their personal needs and comforts are of dominant concern. These are persons who care for no one and nothing except that which nourishes their self-indulgence. Lacking generativity, such persons cease to function as productive members of society, live only to gratify their needs, and are interpersonally impoverished. This is commonly known as the "crisis of middle age"—a sense of hopelessness and feeling that life is meaningless. According to Erikson, the unwillingness to take care of certain persons, things, or ideas is the core pathology of adulthood. It is responsible for much of human prejudice, destruction, and atrocities, and "has far-reaching implications for the survival of the species as well as for every individual's psychosocial development" (1982, p. 70).

8 Late Adulthood: Ego Integrity versus Despair

The final psychosocial stage (65 to death) marks the closing of people's lives. It is a time when people look back and review the choices they made and reflect on the previous achievements and failures of their lives. In practically all cultures this period signals the onset of old age, a time often beset with numerous demands: adjustments to deterioration of physical strength and health, to retirement and reduced income, to the death of spouse and close friends, and to the need to establish new affiliations with one's age group (Erikson et al., 1986). There is also a definite shift in a person's attention from future concerns to past experiences during the aging years.

Erikson believes that this final phase of adulthood is not so much marked by the appearance of a new psychosocial crisis but rather by the summation, integration, and evaluation of all the preceding stages of ego development:

> Only in him who in some way has taken care of things and peple and who has adapted himself to the triumphs and disappointments adherent to being, the originator of others or the generator of products and ideas—only in him may gradually ripen the fruit of these seven stages—I know no better word for it than ego integrity. (Erikson, 1963a, p. 268)

The sense of *ego integrity* thus arises from the person's ability to glance back on his or her life in full perspective (including marriage, children or grandchildren, career, accomplishments, social relationships) and humbly but assuredly affirm, "I am satisfied." The impending reality of death is no longer feared, since such persons see their own existence continuing through either offspring or creative accomplishments. Erikson also believes that only in old age does true maturity and a practical sense of the "wisdom of ages" come into being, provided that the person is so "gifted." At the same time, he notes that "the wisdom of old age remains aware of the relativity of all knowledge acquired in one lifetime in one historical period. Wisdom is an informed and detached concern with life itself in the face of death itself" (1982, p. 61).

At the other extreme are people who regard their lives as a series of unfulfilled opportunities and missed directions. Now, in the sunset years, they realize that it is far too late to start over again or to seek out new paths to integrity. The lack or loss of ego integration in such persons is marked by a hidden dread of death, a feeling of irrevocable failure, and an incessant preoccupation with what "might have been." Erikson observes that there are two prevailing moods in the embittered and disgusted old person—regret that life cannot be lived over again and rejection of one's shortcomings and deficiencies by projecting them onto the outside world. At times, Erikson is poetic in his description of *despair* in the old person: "Fate is not accepted as the frame of life, death not as its finite boundary. Despair indicates that time is too short for alternate roads to integrity; this is why the old try to 'doctor' their memories" (1968b, p. 291). In cases of severe psychopathology, Erikson suggests that bitterness and remorse may lead the old person to become senile, depressed, hypochondriacal, and intensely spiteful and paranoid. Fear of being placed in an institution is common among such individuals.

Recently, Erikson co-authored a book entitled *Vital Involvement in Old Age* (1986) in which he discusses ways of helping senior citizens attain a sense of ego integrity. The book itself is based on studies of several people in their eighties on whom life-history data had been collected since 1928. Erikson traced their life histories and examined how they dealt with previous psychosexual stages. He concludes that old people must become involved in such activities as grandparenting, politics, and fitness programs if they are to maintain vitality in the face of declining physical and mental abilities. In short, Erikson insists that old people must do more than ruminate about their past life if they are to maintain ego integrity.

Now that we have concluded a description of Erikson's epigenetic developmental theory, reflection is in order upon what new perspectives it offers. First, Erikson has formulated a theory in which the roles of society and of persons themselves are accorded equal emphasis with respect to the development of personality throughout life. This perspective, in turn, has enabled those in the helping professions to appraise the problems of adults as—at least to some extent—failures to resolve genuine adult personality crises, rather than see them merely as residual effects of early childhood conflicts and frustrations. Second, Erikson has been keenly sensitive to the teenage years, regarding this period as pivotal in the formation of a person's psychological and social well-being. Finally, Erikson has stimulated a sense of optimism by demonstrating that each stage of psychosocial growth has the potential for both strength and weakness, so that failure at one stage of development does not necessarily indicate doom at a later stage. Let us now consider Erikson's position on the nine basic assumptions about human nature.

ERIKSON'S BASIC ASSUMPTIONS CONCERNING HUMAN NATURE

Robert Coles, in a biographical account of Erikson's work, observed that "When a man builds on another man's work, as Erikson has on Freud's, he does not always have to repeat his predecessor's every single tenet or assumption" (1970,

	Strong	Moderate	Slight	Midrange	Slight	Moderate	Strong	
Freedom						■		Determinism
Rationality		■						Irrationality
Holism	■							Elementalism
Constitutionalism							■	Environmentalism
Changeability	■							Unchangeability
Subjectivity						■		Objectivity
Proactivity		■						Reactivity
Homeostasis						■		Heterostasis
Knowability		■						Unknowability

FIGURE 5-1   Erikson's position on the nine basic assumptions concerning human nature.

p. xx). Erikson's assumptions about humans do in fact differ from those of Freud. His positions on the basic assumptions about human nature, discussed below, are depicted in Figure 5-1.

Freedom–Determinism   In Erikson's view, human behavior is primarily determined. Biological maturation interacting with the individual's expanding social radius produces a rich complexity of behavioral determinants. Parental treatment, school experiences, peer groups, and cultural opportunities all play a powerful role in charting the course of a person's life. In fact, the outcomes of the first four stages of psychosocial development are practically fixed by these types of environmental forces, whereas resolutions of the crises associated with the remaining four stages are less dependent upon such external factors. Erikson firmly believes that each person, especially during the latter four developmental stages, has some capacity to resolve earlier and present crises. Thus, there is some acknowledgment of freedom in Erikson's theory; individuals, to this extent, are responsible for their successes and failures.

Although Erikson accepts the id as the biological foundation of personality, he is less than totally committed to determinism, as is reflected in his theoretical preoccupation with ego development. He regards the ego as an autonomous personality structure that is particularly prone to alteration from adolescence onward. Unlike Freud, he does not believe that personality is utterly fixed by experiences in childhood. Nevertheless, the choices of adults are always restricted by the ever-present effects of childhood experiences. For example, it is difficult to achieve intimacy in young adulthood without a previously developed sense of basic trust. When Erikson's total theory is placed on the freedom–determinism scale, determinism is accorded more weight.

Rationality–Irrationality   Erikson's primary theoretical concern, the psychosocial development of the autonomous ego, reveals his abiding commitment to the importance of rationality, since reasoning processes are such an integral part of ego functioning. Such processes are most evident in the person's attempt to resolve the final four psychosocial crises of the life cycle.

Similar to other ego psychologists in the psychoanalytic movement, Erikson feels that an emphasis on rationality was lacking in Freud's account of human behavior. However, he has often stated that he is supportive of the psychoanalytic tradition and, as such, accepts Freud's basic theoretical concepts, e.g., the biological and sexual foundations of personality, and the structural model (id, ego, superego). Within the psychoanalytic framework, Erikson helped to move the emphasis toward ego, consciousness, and rationality. He invests people with a much larger measure of rationality than did Freud.

Holism–Elementalism   Erikson's strong commitment to a holistic image of persons is clearly evident in his epigenetic account of development. People are portrayed as moving through eight broad stages of psychosocial experience. While doing so, they are attempting to resolve crises of the most profound nature—e.g., ego identity, ego integrity—and always within the matrix of highly complex personal, cultural, and historical forces.

Consider, for example, the holistic theme underlying the two concepts of ego identity (adolescence) and ego integrity (maturity and old age). In the former, persons are seen as expending many years discovering who they are and developing a stable sense of continuity between past and future. Specific elements of adolescent behavior can only be fully understood when interpreted within the total gestalt of the ego-identity versus role-confusion crisis. During the period of maturity and old age, the person attempts to grasp his or her life as a totality, to see meaning in it, and to view it in perspective. Old-age-related behaviors are understood within the holistic framework of the ego-integrity versus despair crisis. In Erikson's epigenetic conception, then, an individual's personality can be understood only with reference to her or his entire life cycle as it is lived within the context of complex and dynamic environmental forces.'

Constitutionalism–Environmentalism   Erikson's tendency toward environmentalism is evidenced by his strong emphasis on parental, cultural, and historical factors in personality development. The individual's life course must be understood in the context of these external influences. The degree to which persons resolve their early psychosocial crises is largely determined by parental treatment; child-rearing practices, in turn, are significantly influenced by cultural and historical factors. Resolution of subsequent psychosocial crises is a function of the individual's interaction with cultural opportunities. Erikson's environmentalism, then, is broad in scope. However, his environmentalist commitment, while strong, is somewhat less than total, since he endorses Freud's belief in the biological, instinctual basis of personality.

Changeability–Unchangeability   Erikson's theory reflects an undeniably strong commitment to the changeability assumption. He has carefully delineated the way in which the ego progresses through a series of psychosocial stages, beginning at birth and continuing until old age and death. Each psychosocial stage, as you will recall, is characterized by a "phase-specific" developmental crisis; depending on how each crisis is resolved, the individual's personality growth progresses in one direction or another. In short, Erikson depicts people as constantly evolving and attempting to meet the challenges posed by each developmental stage that they encounter.

For Erikson, human life is marked by inevitable change. Viewed in a rich psychohistorical context, persons are forever grappling with new developmental tasks, facing turning points in their lives, acquiring new ego qualities, and changing. Perhaps more than any other point of divergence between Erikson and Freud, their disagreement on the changeability–unchangeability assumption captures the essential difference in their respective theoretical positions. For Freud, adult personality is fully determined by interactions that take place during the first years of life. Erikson, by contrast, maintains that there is no end to human development—that it continues throughout the life cycle.

Subjectivity–Objectivity   The major concepts employed by Erikson in describing psychosocial growth (e.g., trust, mistrust, hope) refer to significant subjective experiential states. Furthermore, each person's capacity to deal with a given psychosocial crisis depends upon his or her unique resolutions of former crises. However, the crises themselves are catalyzed by biological maturation interacting with an expanding social world. Biological maturation is not unique to an individual, and such maturation is seen by Erikson as constantly interacting with objective, external factors (e.g., family and society). In this sense, psychosocial stages and crises are objectively determined, strongly suggesting that Erikson leans somewhat toward the assumption of objectivity.

Proactivity–Reactivity   From largely reactive developmental beginnings, the person in Erikson's system becomes progressively more proactive over time, with the unfolding of each successive psychosocial stage. In fact, successful resolution of the first four crises (hope, will power, purpose, competence) is a prelude to proactive functioning in subsequent life stages. During these earlier periods, however, the biological maturation level of persons limits the part that they can play in generating their own behavior.

By way of contrast, Erikson's descriptions of the stages from adolescence to old age clearly convey the idea that people are capable of internally generating their behavior. Concepts such as the search for an adequate sense of ego identity, intimacy, generativity, and ego integrity are best understood from a proactive frame of reference. In Erikson's scheme, then, people are essentially proactive for most of their lives. Throughout the life stages, however, human development results from reactions to biological, social, and historical realities; in this broad sense, there is some acknowledgement of reactivity in Erikson's view of human nature.

Homeostasis–Heterostasis   In Erikson's view, people are constantly being challenged by psychosocial crises, each of which is potentially conducive to growth and mastery over the world. As persons successfully resolve one crisis, they move on to the next. There is an unmistakable sense of forward movement in Erikson's portrayal of human development that clearly suggests a heterostatic view of motivation as its base. It is the nature of people to grow and confront the different challenges of each developmental stage.

A further indication of Erikson's heterostatic commitment is the fact that successful resolution of each psychosocial crisis allows a person more opportunity for growth and self-fulfillment. Consider, for example, that the entire adult stage (approximately 45 years of life) is described in terms of generativity versus stagnation. The use of such concepts reflects the intimate relationship between personal growth and healthy development in Erikson's system. However, Erikson's tendency toward heterostasis is tempered by his acceptance of the biological-instinctual basis of personality proposed by Freud. People strive to grow, but only within the constraints mandated by their instinctual endowment. Thus, Erikson's commitment to the heterostasis assumption is best construed as moderate.

Knowability–Unknowability   While Erikson has adopted several traditional psychoanalytic concepts of personality, he has also formulated new ones by resorting to various clinical, anthropological, and psychohistorical research strategies. Some commitment to the ultimate knowability of human nature is suggested by his development of a comprehensive account of the human life cycle. Nevertheless, Erikson's reliance upon multidisciplinary approaches outside "hardcore" science coupled with his lack of a single, rigorous scientific means of researching personality suggests a less-than-complete commitment to man's knowability through science. When compared with Freud, Erikson seems less convinced of the indispensability of science for understanding human behavior.

We now turn our attention to the empirical status of Erikson's theory and some of the research it has inspired.

EMPIRICAL VALIDATION OF PSYCHOSOCIAL CONCEPTS

Erikson's theory has had a major impact on the growing field of life-span developmental psychology (Papalia & Olds, 1986; Santrock, 1985). His ideas have also been applied to the fields of early childhood education, vocational counseling, social work, and business. It should further be noted that Erikson has undertaken extensive psychohistorical studies of such noteworthy persons as Martin Luther, Adolf Hitler, Mahatma Gandhi, and George Bernard Shaw. *Psychohistory* is a form of inquiry that attempts to relate the major themes of a person's life to historical events and circumstances (Crosby & Crosby, 1981; Runyan, 1982). The recent upsurge of interest among personologists in exploring biographical and autobiographical approaches to the study of persons owes much of its impetus to Erikson's work in psychohistory (Moraitis & Pollack, 1987).

Despite its popularity, Erikson's theory has not generated an impressive amount of empirical research. In part, the lack of systematic research bearing on Erikson's position may reflect the fact that his ideas are complex and abstract. More to the point, concepts such as mutuality, fidelity, and psychosocial moratorium are not defined with the precision needed to establish their empirical adequacy. Another difficulty stems from the fact that validation of Erikson's theory requires extensive longitudinal studies in order to assess developmental changes as people proceed through the life cycle. The collection of longitudinal data is costly and time-consuming. As a result, efforts to document Erikson's explanations of the ways in which psychosocial stages influence one another have been relatively sparse to date. Finally, it should be noted that Erikson has not shown any real interest in empirically testing his own concepts and what research he has reported is based on informal case studies.

In a more positive vein, certain concepts of psychosocial theory are quite amenable to rigorous investigation. For instance, Erikson has established the criteria for psychosocial health and ill health for each crisis period in terms of well-defined behavioral characteristics. Such well-formulated descriptions allow for the direct study of the resolution of earlier crises in currently manifested behaviors and attitudes. The theory also seems to lend itself to empirical test inasmuch as it deals with the social dimensions of development as opposed to theories which focus on the intrapsychic nature of personality. Finally, Erikson has achieved an orderly sequential account of the relevant psychosocial phenomena of personal development, whereas other theorists often lack this longitudinal synthesis of developmental problems. Until carefully planned studies are brought to fruition, however, the empirical status and developmental implications of Erikson's theory remain obscure.

Although Erikson feels no need to validate his theory empirically, others have made attempts to do so. Accordingly, let us now consider some instances where research conducted to test the richness of Erikson's theorizing has occurred.

Research on Ego Identity Statuses

As has been noted, Erikson (1968a) devotes more theoretical attention to the period of adolescence than to any other psychosocial stage of the life cycle. Our review of empirical findings reported below indicates that the majority of studies published to date deal almost exclusively with this phase of Erikson's comprehensive account of human development.

Marcia (1966, 1967, 1980) has conducted several studies of the antecedents and consequences of identity formation during adolescence. Based on Erikson's writings, Marcia claims that it is possible to distinguish four distinct orientations or *ego identity statuses:* (1) identity diffusion, (2) foreclosure, (3) moratorium, and (4) identity achievement. These statuses (displayed in Table 5-2) are defined in terms of the two separate dimensions of crisis and commitment as they apply to two general areas of functioning: the person's occupation and ideology (i.e., religion and politics). The term *crisis* refers to a time of struggle in a person's life

TABLE 5-2 THE FOUR EGO IDENTITY STATUSES DESCRIBED BY
MARCIA (1966)
Each quadrant of the matrix is derived by probing the subject's
crisis and commitment via semistructured interview questions in
reference to occupational and ideological choices.

Has a crisis been experienced?

		Yes	No
Has a commitment been made?	**Yes**	Identity achievement	Foreclosure
	No	Moratorium	Identity diffusion

as he or she explores alternative career choices and gives intense thought to what type of beliefs and values to follow. *Commitment* involves making firm occupational and ideological decisions and establishing goal strategies by which to realize the decisions. Determination of the person's ego identity status is made by rating his or her responses to a standardized interview technique developed by Marcia (1966).

Identity diffusion is characterized by a "commitment to a lack of commitment." Such a person may or may not have experienced a period of crisis, but in either case there is little, if any, commitment to visions, values, and roles. *Foreclosure* is the status of a young person who has firm commitments but whose life reveals little or no evidence that there ever was a crisis. An example of someone who has "foreclosed" on an identity is the college student who is committed to becoming a dentist because his father and grandfather were dentists. The identity status of *moratorium* applies to persons who are currently in a state of crisis (exploring alternatives) but whose commitments are vague and general. The college student who can readily imagine herself becoming a chemist, a minister, or a journalist illustrates the sense of ongoing struggle coupled with vague commitments so characteristic of this status. Finally, the *identity achievement* status pertains to people who have experienced a period of crisis and have made firm commitments to occupational and ideological goals and positions.

The existence of these four ego identity statuses is now well-documented (Bourne, 1978; Marcia, 1980). Additionally, several investigations have examined the relationship of the identity statuses described above to differences in family interaction patterns. This line of research, summarized by Marcia (1980) and Waterman (1982), indicates that foreclosures have more affectionate relationships with their parents than do persons of any other status. Foreclosed men also are more likely than men of other statuses to turn to their families for advice and support in making decisions about important life events. As a result, the person avoids much of the "struggle" for identity commitments, without critically considering their far-reaching implications. In contrast, people occupying the moratorium and achievement statuses tend not to turn to their parents when important life decisions need to be made. They also tend to be more critical of their parents and to experience a higher level of family conflict. Individuals with a diffused sense of identity report the most distance between themselves and their parents. These adolescents perceive their parents as indifferent and rejecting and thus lack the role models that foreclosed persons have.

Research exploring the relationship between identity status and the academic motivation and achievements of college students has also been of particular interest to investigators. This research shows that identity achievers more often decide to major in mathematics, biology, chemistry, and engineering, whereas identity diffuse students are more attracted to sociology, education, and physical education (Adams & Fitch, 1983; Marcia & Friedman, 1970). In a similar vein, a study by Waterman and Waterman (1970) found that students with firm commitments to occupational goals had more positive evaluations of their educational experiences than students who were uncertain about their occupational goals upon graduation. Identity achieved students also have higher grades than students who occupy the other statuses (Cross & Allen, 1970). Finally, in a particularly interesting study, Marcia (1967) found that students with strong identities were less adversely affected (as assessed by lowered self-esteem scores) by failure on tasks viewed by them to be associated with academic success.

Other recent research has established associations between ego identity status and social influence processes. For example, identity diffuse students are the most likely to conform in response to peer group pressures (Adams et al., 1985). Identity achievers also show a willingness to conform to peer group members, but only when such conformity leads to the attainment of achievement goals. This kind of openness to the opinions of others is something you would expect of a person who has a secure sense of ego identity.

Research on Identity Achievement and Later Capacity for Intimacy

According to Erikson's epigenetic theory of psychosocial development, successful management of each conflict helps the person to confront the next stage (and the next conflict) with a more positive orientation. Thus, having a strong sense of identity makes it easier for the maturing person to develop a capacity for intimacy. A study conducted by Kahn et al. (1985) sought to document the idea that developing a firm identity during young adulthood makes one more likely to achieve intimacy during middle age. To do so, these investigators (in 1963) obtained a self-report measure of identity strength among a group of sophomore and junior art students. In 1981, 18 years later, 60 percent of the original sample of students completed a follow-up questionnaire regarding their personal, family, and professional lives since leaving art school. The measure of intimacy gathered at this time was marital status; specifically, students were asked to check one of the following categories: never married, living together, married, separated, divorced, or widowed. A second question elicited the number of divorces, if any.

In line with Erikson's theory, the results revealed a strong relationship between achievement of ego identity and capacity for intimacy in midlife. However, the overall pattern was overshadowed by sex differences. Identity formation predicted whether or not men had married—those who had a strong sense of identity in 1963 were far more likely to have established enduring marital relationships during the 18-year follow-up. Put differently, only 1 of the 35 men with high identity was unmarried in 1981! In contrast, women were just as likely to get married as not, regardless of identity achievement. Among those women who had married, however, there was a strong relationship between identity achievement and marital stability. In fact, more than two-thirds of the low identity women experienced marital disruption during the 18-year follow-up. Men with stable and unstable marriages did not differ in terms of identity formation. Kahn et al. (1985) interpreted these patterns as suggesting that the paths for achieving intimacy may be different for the sexes.

> For men the attainment of intimacy centers around the decision whether or not to get married. It is at this point that identity achievement based on the traditional male roles of instrumentality, effectance, and competence becomes crucial. Women, on the other hand, may be bound by the social prescription of marriage, so that identity achievement has little to do with whether they get married. However, the attainment of intimacy for these women seems to hinge on the ongoing stability of the relationship. It is here that an identity based on anxiety management and a facility with more emotional, expressive tasks comes to fruition in the establishment of stable marriage. (p. 1321)

Collectively, the findings reported by Kahn et al. (1985) suggests the existence of different patterns of identity development in men and women. In turn, these differences indicate the importance of creating new models that focus specifically on women's development (Gilligan, 1982).

APPLICATION: ADOLESCENCE IN AMERICA OR "WHO AM I?"

Erikson has applied his theoretical views to such fascinating and diverse topics as children's play behaviors (1937), childhood in American Indian tribes (1945), juvenile delinquency (1968a), identity problems of black youth (1964b), and dissent in youth (1970). In particular, he has stressed how various social-emotional experiences influence the formation of identity in the adolescent and early adult years. More than any other personologist, Erikson is credited for having emphasized ego identity as the central psychosocial issue facing the adolescent in contemporary American society.

From Erikson's viewpoint, the two fundamental questions confronting young people today are "Who am I?" and "How will I fit into the adult world?" In a rigidly patterned culture (e.g., Islamic countries) where many prescribed social and gender roles exist, such identity issues are minimized since there are relatively few options available. In such a context, identity is conferred upon the young person and commitment to the status quo is taken for granted. By comparison, American society offers a much wider scope of potential occupational, ideological, and interpersonal opportunities to its young people. As a result, American adolescents are more vulnerable to identity problems precisely because they have more options. Erikson suggests that it is the democratic system in America that poses special problems in this regard since democracy requires ''self-made identities.'' In American society, then, young people bear considerable responsibility for defining who they are and how they will carve out their own niche in the adult world.

When democracy is coupled with the technological sophistication of our social world, identity crises are further intensified. Our technology demands an extended period of formal education. Such prolonged education, often involving financial dependence upon parents during the college years, markedly extends the young person's exploration of what his or her life as an adult will be like. Further, considering the exceedingly rapid social change in which basic values and norms are continually questioned, the young person's identity problems become immeasurably more complicated. American adolescents have not only more time to search for their identities but also more alternatives from which to select.

Three major areas of current-day adolescent behavior that can be interpreted, at least in part, as manifestations of the identity crisis are discussed below. They are (1) the problem of career choice, (2) peer-group membership, and (3) alcohol and drug use.

The Problem of Career Choice   Erikson believes that the inability to settle on an occupational identity is a source of great concern to many young people. Simply stated, the adolescent must define who she or he is before a decision on what she or he wishes to become is possible. Since different life-styles accompany different occupations in our society, selecting a career is, in reality, selecting a whole way of life. To make a wise choice, young people must have an accurate view of themselves as well as a reasonably good estimate of where they might best ''fit'' in the working world. In the final analysis, a person's career choice may well represent a definition and expression of the kind of person that she or he intends to become.

Adolescent vocational indecision, then, often reflects a more fundamental indecisiveness about personal identity. This is especially true for young women who, because of their biological potential for bearing children, are faced with the choice of wife and mother roles versus other career goals or some combination of the two. Some women who opt for the former may eventually believe they have no ego identity apart from their marital role. Because traditional society has often dictated passive acceptance of ''feminine'' values and aspirations, contemporary adolescent women experience significant vocational conflict in the struggle for identity achievement (Goldberg, 1983). By the same token, young men are subjected to intense pressure to pursue a career and are more susceptible than women to the potentially disruptive effects of competing for lucrative jobs: a sense of integrity and personal worth often hang in the balance.

Peer-Group Membership   Even in the best of circumstances adolescents have a difficult time establishing a clear and positive ego identity. Rejecting parents as models in establishing their identity, adolescents often seek in their peers an alternative source of support as they reorganize their conceptions of themselves. In our culture, peer-group bonds are particularly strong during this period; they often affect the adolescent's values and attitudes more than parents, schools, religious institutions, or any other source of social influence (Maccoby, 1990). Such groups help to reassure young people at a time when they are undergoing dramatic physiological and cognitive changes. By communicating their own feelings as well as sharing vicariously in the experiences of peers, adolescents are able to cope with otherwise confusing and sometimes frightening situations.

Erikson (1968a) noted that the cliquishness and uniformity of dress and gesture so often observed in adolescent groups are really defenses against identity confusion. If young people are uncertain about who they are, dressing and acting like their friends provides some sense of internal stability and security. Moreover, wearing apparel, hairstyles, and music serve to symbolize their separateness from parents and the associated adult world. Membership in a peer group also provides exposure to new and different ideologies—political, social, economic, and religious. Erikson believes that the appeal of various ideologies and alternative lifestyles for adolescent groups is largely based on the identity search. In part, they are searching for new personal values to replace childhood rules. Furthermore, learning to believe in and act upon a new set of social values while experimenting with and possibly rejecting an old ideology can strengthen the adolescent's emerging sense of identity.

Alcohol and Drug Use   The extraordinary range of recreational drugs known to be currently available, the most widely used of which is alcohol, makes it clear that there are no simple explanations of the factors that lead to their use or abuse by adolescents. The immediate and long-term effects of any drug depends in part on the user's personality, mood, motivation, previous experience with the drug, body weight and physiology, dose and potency of the drug, the method of administration, and the setting in which the drug is taken (Leavitt, 1982). The effects of drugs vary not only for different people but also for the same person in different situations.

After increasing dramatically in the 1960s and early 1970s, adolescent use and abuse of alcohol and other drugs appears to have leveled off in the 1980s. Results of a large national survey on drug use among high-school seniors in the United States (Johnston et al., 1988) indicates that recreational drug use has largely remained stable in the 1980s, and that the use of two drugs—marijuana and sedatives—even declined somewhat. These declines are encouraging, yet there is little doubt that widespread alcohol and drug use are here to stay for the foreseeable future.

Depending on the person and the drug, the motive that initiates and sustains drug use among young people may range from curiosity, thrill-seeking, peer pressure and acceptance, escape from stress, and rebellion against authority to more philosophical rationales such as desire for self-knowledge, self-improvement, creativity, spiritual enlightenment, or expansion of consciousness. When these motives are considered in terms of Erikson's theory, a case can be made for their relation to an underlying sense of identity confusion. Young people who do not know who they are might find alcohol- and drug-related experiences attractive in exploring the outer boundaries of selfhood; they may think that they can find a dimension of themselves that evades them in the sober, "straight" world.

Using alcohol and drugs may also temporarily relieve the emotional stresses accompanying the identity crisis. Beset by career indecision, parental conflict, and fragile peer relationships, young persons may see such drugs as a vehicle for momentarily stepping outside themselves. Moreover, when adolescents are surrounded by a drug-using peer group, so crucial to their identity search, it is easy to understand how they could be "pressured" toward drugs, especially if their group status is contingent upon drug use. A person with an established sense of ego identity could resist such pressure; adolescents with identity diffusion would probably find it difficult not to conform.

It would be erroneous to assume that all facets of adolescent behavior can be explained in terms of Erikson's identity concept. Nonetheless, the concept of identity crisis furnishes an excellent theoretical perspective from which to view the diversity of psychological problems displayed during this period of life. By attempting to elucidate the mainstreams of psychosocial development, Erikson has made a rich and lasting contribution to personological theory.

OTHER REVISIONS OF PSYCHODYNAMIC THEORY: A CULTURAL AND AN INTERPERSONAL EMPHASIS

Like Erikson, many other post-Freudian psychodynamic theorists emphasized the role of cultural and interpersonal factors in shaping personality. Although these theories acknowledged their indebtedness to Freud and accepted the importance of early childhood experiences and the dynamics of anxiety and the defense mechanisms, they all departed from Freud's theory. More precisely, these theorists rejected the idea that human behavior can be explained in terms of biological forces of an instinctive nature. They argued that Freud failed to recognize the impact of environmental factors in the development of personality and psychopathology. Correspondingly, many of these theorists challenged Freud's view that "anatomy is destiny." For them, personality differences between the sexes can be understood only in the context of sociocultural influences. We will briefly discuss two key figures whose theories differed significantly from traditional psychoanalysis, Erich Fromm and Karen Horney. Both of these revisionists proposed ideas that clearly reflect the themes that are most salient in post-Freudian psychodynamic thinking.

Erich Fromm. *(Courtesy of the Bettmann Archive)*

ERICH FROMM: A Humanistic Theory of Personality

No theorist has more emphatically stressed the social determinants of personality than Erich Fromm. As a humanistic personologist, Fromm argued that a person's behavior can be understood only in the light of cultural forces existing at a particular moment in history. He believed that needs unique to the human being evolved through the history of humankind and that different social systems have, in turn, influenced their expression. In Fromm's view, personality is the product of the dynamic interaction between needs inherent in human nature and the forces exerted by social norms and institutions. He was the first to formalize a theory of character types based on a sociological analysis of how people in a society actively shape the social process and the culture itself.

BIOGRAPHICAL SKETCH

Erich Fromm was born in 1900 in Frankfurt, Germany, the only child of Jewish parents. He grew up in two very different worlds, one the orthodox Jewish world, and the other the Christian world where he experienced occasional episodes of anti-Semitism. Fromm's family life was less than ideal. He described his parents as ''highly neurotic'' and himself as an ''unbearable, neurotic child'' (Funk, 1982).

Fromm was 14 when World War I broke out in Europe. Although he was too young to fight, he was overwhelmed by the human destructiveness and irrationality that surrounded him. He later wrote: ''I was a deeply troubled young man who was obsessed by the question of how war was possible, by the wish to understand the irrationality of human mass behavior, by a passionate desire for peace and international understanding'' (Fromm, 1962, p. 9). The answers Fromm sought to his questions were powerfully shaped by his study of Freud and Karl Marx. Freud's writings helped him understand that human beings are not aware of the significant determinants of their behavior. From Marx he learned that sociopolitical forces exert considerable power over the lives of people.

Unlike Freud, Jung, and Adler, Fromm had no medical training. Instead, he studied psychology, sociology, and philosophy and received a Ph.D. from the University of Heidelberg in 1922. Fromm then pursued psychoanalytic training at the Berlin Psychoanalytic Institute. He emigrated to the United States in 1934 to escape the Nazi menace, first lectured at the Chicago Psychoanalytic Institute, and subsequently entered private practice in New York City. He published his first book, *Escape from Freedom,* in 1941. In it, Fromm stressed the ways in which societal forces and ideologies mold the character structure of the individual. This perspective, further elaborated in numerous books that followed thereafter, led to Fromm being dropped as a member of the International Psychoanalytic Association (Roazen, 1973).

In 1945, Fromm joined the William Alanson White Institute of Psychiatry. He subsequently lectured at several universities in the United States and served as professor of psychiatry at the National University in Mexico City from 1949 until his retirement in 1965. He and his wife moved to Switzerland in 1976, where he died of a heart attack in 1980.

HUMANISTIC THEORY: BASIC CONCEPTS AND PRINCIPLES

Fromm sought to broaden the scope of classical psychoanalytic theory by emphasizing the role that sociological, political, economic, religious, and anthropological factors play in molding personality. His approach to personality begins with an analysis of the human condition and how it has changed since the end of the Middle Ages (at the close of the fifteenth century) to the present day. As an outgrowth of his historical analyses, Fromm (1941/1956) concluded that the essence of human existence today is marked by loneliness, isolation, and alienation. At the same time, he believed that each period of history has been characterized by increasing individuality as people have struggled toward ever-greater personal freedom to develop all of their potentialities. However, the large measure of autonomy and choice enjoyed by people living in contemporary Western societies has been achieved at the expense of insecurity and feelings of personal insignificance. In Fromm's view, men and women today are caught in a painful dilemma. The unparalleled freedom from rigid social, political, economic, and religious constraints (as we know it in American culture today) has been offset by a decline in security and a sense of belonging. Fromm suggested that this basic *split between freedom and security* has caused a unique predicament in the human condition. Human beings strive for freedom and autonomy, but this very struggle has produced feelings of alienation from nature and society. People need to have power and choice over their lives, but they also need to feel connected and related to other human beings. The intensity of this conflict and the different ways in which it is resolved, according to Fromm, are dependent on the political and economic systems of the society.

Mechanisms of Escape

How do people cope with feelings of loneliness, insignificance, and alienation that accompany freedom? One way is to renounce freedom and surrender individuality and choice. Fromm described a number of strategies that are used by people to "escape freedom." The first of these mechanisms, *authoritarianism,* is defined as the "tendency to fuse one's self with somebody or something outside of oneself in order to acquire the strength which the individual self is lacking" (Fromm, 1941/1956, p. 163). Authoritarianism is manifested in either masochistic or sadistic tendencies. In its masochistic form, individuals behave in an excessively dependent, submissive, and helpless manner toward other people. In its sadistic form, by contrast, individuals strive to exploit, dominate, and control other people. Fromm theorized that both tendencies are typically found in the same person. For example, in a highly authoritarian military structure the same individual may willingly submit to the commands of superior officers but humiliate or ruthlessly exploit soldiers of lower rank. A second escape mechanism described by Fromm is *destructiveness*. Here the person attempts to overcome feelings of inferiority and aloneness by destroying or subduing others. From Fromm's perspective, duty, patriotism, and love are common rationalizations for destructive acts.

Finally, Fromm believed that people can escape from their feelings of loneliness and alienation through unconditional conformity to social norms that govern behavior. Termed *automaton conformity,* the person who uses this strategy seeks to become just like everyone else by behaving in a completely conventional manner. "The individual ceases to be himself; he adopts entirely the kind of personality offered to him by cultural patterns; and he therefore becomes exactly as all others are and as they expect him to be" (Fromm, 1941/1956, p. 208). Fromm suggested that the lack of such individuality is deeply ingrained in the social character of most people today. Like certain animals with protective coloring, persons who are conforming automatons become indistinguishable from their surroundings. They adopt the same values, pursue the same career goals, purchase the same products, and share the same thoughts and feelings as almost everyone else within the culture.

In contrast to the three mechanisms of escape from freedom described above, Fromm suggested that people can escape their sense of loneliness and alienation through the experience of positive freedom.

Positive Freedom

Fromm felt that people can be separate and unique beings without, at the same time, losing their sense of unity with others and social reality. He called this kind of freedom of being part of the world and yet independent from it *positive freedom*. The achievement of positive freedom demands that people be spontaneously active in their lives. For Fromm, spontaneous activity is commonly seen in young children who tend to act according to their inner natures and not according to social conventions and prohibitions. In *The Art of Loving* (1956/1974), one of his best-known books, Fromm emphasized that love and work are the key components to developing positive freedom through the process of spontaneous activity. Through love and work people reunite with others but without sacrificing their sense of individuality or integrity.

Human Existential Needs

Thus far we have described Fromm's view of the human condition in terms of separation from nature and isolation from others. In addition, he believed that human nature is uniquely characterized by five existential needs. These needs have nothing to do with sexual and aggressive instincts. Instead, Fromm (1973) theorized that the conflict between striving for freedom and striving for security is the most powerful motivating force in people's lives. The freedom–security dichotomy, a universal and inescapable fact of human nature, has created these existential needs. The five human existential needs identified by Fromm are:

1 *The need for relatedness.* To overcome their feelings of isolation from nature and themselves, all persons need to care for, share with, and be responsible for others. The ideal way of relating to the world is through what Fromm called "productive love," which enables people to work together and at the same time maintain their individuality. If the need for relatedness is not satisfied, people become narcissistic; they respond only to their own selfish concerns and are unable to commit themselves to others.

2 *The need for transcendence.* All persons need to surpass or transcend their passive animal nature, to become active and creative shapers of their own lives. The optimal resolution of this need is creativeness; the act of creating (children, ideas, art, or material goods) allows people to rise above the accidental and passive nature of their existence, thereby achieving a sense of freedom and significance. Failure to satisfy this vital need causes people to become destructive.

3 *The need for rootedness.* Human beings need to be an integral part of the world, to feel that they belong. According to Fromm (1973), this need arises at birth when the person is severed from his or her biological ties within the mother's womb. In late childhood, each person is torn from the safety of parental care. In late adulthood, each person confronts the reality of being torn from life itself as death approaches. Thus, throughout life, people have needs for roots, for a sense of stability and permanency similar to the security of their early maternal ties. By contrast, those who maintain symbiotic ties with parents, home, or community as a way of fulfilling the need for rootedness are unable to experience personal integrity and freedom.

4 *The need for identity.* Fromm insisted that all persons need to have an inner sense of oneness with self, an identity that sets them apart from others in terms of

Fromm believed that organized religion often provides people with a frame of orientation by which to confer meaning on their lives. *(Jack Spratt/The Image Works)*

their awareness of who and what they truly are. In short, each person must be able to say "I am I." Persons with clear and distinct feelings of individuality perceive themselves as being in control of their lives as opposed to having their lives governed by others. Acting as everyone else acts, even to the point of blind conformity, prevents the person from achieving an authentic sense of identity.

5 *The need for a frame of orientation and devotion.* Finally, Fromm theorized that humans need a stable and consistent way of interpreting the complexities of the world. A frame of orientation is a set of beliefs that allows people to organize and comprehend their perceptions of reality, without which they would be puzzled and unable to act purposefully. Fromm (1981) stressed the importance of developing an objective and rational view of the natural and social world. A rational perspective, he argued, is an absolute necessity for the maintenance of sanity.

People also need an object of devotion, an overall goal or God to whom they can attribute the meaning of life. The object of devotion provides a sense of direction in people's search for a purposeful existence. Such an "ultimate concern" enables people to transcend their isolated existence and confers meaning on their lives.

In keeping with Fromm's economic-political focus, he suggested that the way in which these needs are expressed or satisfied depends on the type of social conditions that engulf the person. In effect, the opportunities that a particular society offers people to satisfy their existential needs mold their personality structure—what Fromm called "basic character orientations." Moreover, in Fromm's theory, as in Freud's, the person's character orientation is viewed as stable and consistent over time.

Social Character Types

Fromm (1947) identified five social character types that are prevalent in contemporary societies. These social character types, or forms of relatedness to others, represent the interaction of existential needs and the social context in which people live. Fromm grouped them into two general classes: *nonproductive* (unhealthy) and *productive* (healthy) types. The nonproductive category includes the receptive, exploitative, hoarding, and marketing character orientations, whereas the productive category represents Fromm's caricature of ideal psychological health. Fromm is careful to note that none of these character types exists in pure form because nonproductive and productive qualities blend together in differing proportions in particular persons. Consequently, the mental health or illness implications of a given social character type depends upon the ratio of positive to negative traits manifested by the individual.

1 *Receptive* types believe that the source of everything that is good in life lies outside of themselves. They are overly dependent and passive, incapable of doing anything without outside help, and feel that their main task in life is to be loved rather than to love. Receptive persons may be described as submissive, gullible, and sentimental. In its less extreme version, though, persons with receptive orientations may be optimistic and idealistic.

2 *Exploitative* types take whatever they need or desire from others through force or cunning. They, too, are incapable of producing things by their own efforts and so they acquire love, possessions, thoughts, and emotions by appropriating them from others. Negative descriptive traits for exploitative characters include aggressive, arrogant, egocentric, and seducing. Their positive qualities include self-confidence, pride, and impulsiveness.

3 *Hoarding* types strive to accumulate material possessions, power, and love, and they struggle to avoid sharing any of their hoard. Different from the preceding two, hoarding characters tend to live in the past and are repelled by anything new. Reminiscent of Freud's anal-retentive personality, they are rigid, suspicious, and stubborn. Some of the positive attributes Fromm used to describe the hoarding personality include cautious, loyal, and reserved.

4 *Marketing* types operate from a frame of reference that states that personality or self is valued only as a commodity to be sold or exchanged for success. They are interested in maintaining appearances and in knowing the right people, and are willing to show any personality trait that will increase their success in selling themselves to potential customers. They relate to others through superficial roles and are guided by the motto "I am as you desire me" (Fromm, 1947, p. 73).

In addition to representing the ultimate in alienation, the marketing orientation can be described by the following key trait labels: opportunistic, aimless, tactless, indiscriminate, and wasteful. On the more positive side, marketing types may be open-minded, curious, and generous. Fromm viewed the marketing personality as a product of modern capitalistic societies such as the United States and western European countries.

5 In contrast to the nonproductive orientations, the *productive* character type represents Fromm's view of the ultimate goal in human development. This type is independent, integrated, spontaneous, loving, creative, and committed to the social good. It is clear from Fromm's writing (1955, 1968) that he regarded this orientation as the answer to the inherent contradictions of human existence. It encompasses the human capacity for productive reasoning, loving, and working. Through productive reasoning, people can know themselves for who they are and thereby avoid self-delusion. The power of productive love enables people to passionately love all that is alive (biophilia). Fromm characterized it in terms of the qualities of care, responsibility, respect, and knowledge. Finally, productive work provides people with a means of producing the basic necessities of life through creative self-expression. The ultimate product of realizing these powers inherent in all persons is a mature and integrated character structure.

In essence, the productive orientation is the ideal condition for people in Fromm's humanistic theory. Nonetheless, it is unlikely that anyone has yet achieved all of the characteristics of the prototypical productive person. At the same time, Fromm beleived that through drastic social reform the productive orientation could become the dominant type in any culture. Fromm (1968) envisioned the perfect society as one in which the basic needs of human existence are satisfied. He called this society *humanistic communitarian socialism*.

Concluding Comments

Fromm's theory attempts to show how broad sociocultural forces interact with unique human needs in shaping personality. His principal thesis is that character structures (personality types) are linked with particular social structures. In the tradition of humanistic reform, he also argued that through radical change in social and economic conditions it is possible to create a society where both the individual's and society's needs can be met.

Unfortunately, most of Fromm's theoretical claims, notably his theory of character development, were stated so globally that they cannot be studied in their present form. In fact, very few attempts have been made to empirically investigate Fromm's theory (Maccoby, 1981, 1988). Case studies and informal cultural observations provide the only substantive source of support for his concepts. Nevertheless, his books remain quite popular, reaching professional and lay audiences all over the world. Countless people have found his cogent and thought-provoking commentary on a broad spectrum of social issues to be relevant to our times.

KAREN HORNEY: A Sociocultural Theory of Personality

Like Adler, Jung, Erikson, and Fromm, Karen Horney also took issue with key tenets of Freudian theory. Most important, she insisted that Freud erred in making physical anatomy the basis of psychological differences between women and men. Horney argued that Freud's assertions about feminine psychology, especially his contention that women are motivated by the driving force of ''penis envy,'' were illogical and based on nineteenth-century Viennese culture. Horney also objected to Freud's theory of instincts and felt that psychoanalysis should adopt a more sociocultural orientation.

Horney stressed the importance of cultural and social influences on personality throughout her work. Although her theory deals far more with neurotic than normal personalities, many of her ideas offer provocative insights into the understanding of individual differences and interpersonal relationships.

BIOGRAPHICAL SKETCH

Karen Horney (nee Danielson) was born near Hamburg, Germany, in 1885. Her father was a devoutly religious sea captain who believed that women were inferior to men. Her Dutch mother was an attractive and freethinking woman some 18 years younger than her husband. Most of Horney's childhood and adolescent years were consumed by doubts about her self-worth, heightened by feelings of unattractiveness. She compensated by becoming an excellent student. Years later she confided, ''If I couldn't be beautiful, I decided I would be smart'' (Rubins, 1978, p. 14).

At age 14 Horney decided that she would become a physician. This goal was undertaken in 1906 when she entered the University of Freiburg, becoming one of the first women in Germany permitted to study medicine. There she met and married Oskar Horney, a political science student, in 1910. Horney received her medical degree from the University of Berlin in 1915. For the next 5 years she underwent training in psychoanalysis at the Berlin Psychoanalytic Institute. Throughout much of this period, Horney suffered severe bouts of depression and was reported to have been rescued by her husband from a suicide attempt (Rubins, 1978).

By 1926 Horney's marriage began to dissolve as she found herself overwhelmed by a number of personal problems. The premature death of her brother, the separation and death of her parents within a year, and the ever-increasing doubts about the value of psychoanalysis left her feeling quite despondent. Nonetheless, after she and her husband separated in 1927, Horney's psychiatric career blossomed. She worked at the Berlin Psychoanalytic Institute and became increasingly involved with teaching, writing, and traveling.

In 1932, during the Depression, Horney came to the United States and assumed the position of Associate Director of the Chicago Psychoanalytic Institute. Two years later she moved to New York, where she lectured at the New York Psychoanalytic Institute. Ensuing differences with Freud's doctrines led other

Karen Horney. *(Courtesy of the Association for the Advancement of Psychoanalysis, Inc., of the Karen Horney Psychoanalytic Institute and Center).*

members of the institute to disqualify her as an instructor and training analyst in 1941. Shortly afterward she founded the American Institute of Psychoanalysis. Horney was dean of this institute until she died of cancer in 1952.

SOCIOCULTURAL THEORY: BASIC CONCEPTS AND PRINCIPLES

Horney's (1937, 1939) *sociocultural* view of personality was prompted by three major considerations. First, she rejected Freud's pronouncements regarding women, in particular his notion that penis envy is preordained by their biological nature. In fact, that was her initial point of departure from the orthodox Freudian point of view. Second, while living in Chicago and New York, Horney exchanged ideas with such prominent figures as Erich Fromm, Margaret Mead, and Harry Stack Sullivan. They reinforced her conviction that sociocultural conditions exert a profound impact on the individual's development and functioning. Third, Horney's clinical observations of striking differences in personality dynamics between patients seen in Europe and the United States confirmed the powerful influence of cultural forces. More specifically, these observations led her to conclude that unique interpersonal conditions of a person's life are at the core of disturbed personality functioning.

Personality Development

Horney (1950) agreed with Freud on the importance of childhood experiences in shaping adult personality structure and functioning. Despite this common ground, the two differed on the specifics of how personality is formed. Horney dismissed Freud's claim that there are universal psychosexual stages and that the child's sexual anatomy dictates the course of personality development. Instead, she

According to Horney, basic anxiety results from feeling lonely, helpless, and deserted in a hostile environment. *(E. Budd Gray/Jeroboam)*

argued that the social relationship between the child and the parents is the decisive factor in determining personality growth.

According to Horney (1939), childhood is characterized by two needs: the need for *satisfaction* and the need for *safety*. Satisfaction encompasses all of the basic physiological needs—food, water, sleep, and so on. Although Horney recognized the importance of satisfying needs ensuring physical survival, she did not regard them as having key significance in shaping personality. What is essential in the child's development is the need for safety. The child's fundamental motive in this case is to feel wanted, loved, and protected from a dangerous or hostile world. Horney felt that the child was completely dependent upon the parents in having its safety need met. If the parents demonstrate genuine affection and warmth toward the child, thereby satisfying the need for safety, healthy personality development will likely ensue. Conversely, if the parents act in ways that obstruct the child's need for safety, abnormal personality development is likely to ensue. A wide range of parental behaviors may frustrate a child's need for security: indifference, unfair punishment, erratic behavior, ridicule, unkept promises, overprotection, and obvious preference for a sibling (Horney, 1945). However, the main result of such parental mistreatment is the creation within the child of an attitude of *basic hostility*. The child is now caught between dependence on the parents and resentment toward them, a conflict which Horney believed summons the defense of repression into operation. In effect, the insecure child is motivated by feelings of helplessness, fear, love, and guilt to repress his or her hostile feelings toward the parents in order to survive (Horney, 1945).

Unfortunately, the repressed feelings of resentment and hostility caused by the parents do not remain isolated; instead, they manifest themselves in all the relationships the child has or will have with other people. At this point, the child is said to be experiencing *basic anxiety,* "a feeling of being isolated and helpless toward a world potentially hostile" (Horney, 1950, p. 18). Basic anxiety is an intense and pervasive feeling of insecurity and represents one of Horney's most primary concepts.

Basic Anxiety: The Etiology of Neurosis

Unlike Freud, Horney did not believe that anxiety is an inevitable part of the human condition. Instead, she maintained anxiety results from feelings of insecurity in interpersonal relations. More generally, Horney suggested that anything that disrupts a child's feeling of security in relation to his or her parents causes basic anxiety. Accordingly, the etiology of neurotic behavior is found in disturbed parent–child relationships. As you will recall, if the child experiences love and acceptance, he or she will feel secure and likely develop normally. If, on the other hand, the child does not feel secure, there will be hostility toward the parents, and this hostility will eventually be generalized to everyone and become basic anxiety. In Horney's view, a child with excessive basic anxiety is headed toward becoming a neurotic adult.

Neurotic Needs: Strategies for Coping with Basic Anxiety

To cope with the feelings of insecurity, helplessness, and hostility that accompany basic anxiety, the child often resorts to the use of certain defensive strategies. Horney (1942) identified 10 such strategies for coping with basic anxiety, which she called *neurotic needs* or *neurotic trends.* These 10 neurotic needs are presented in Table 5-3, along with their corresponding behaviors.

Horney maintained that all people depend on these needs to cope with the inevitable experiences of rejection, hostility, and helplessness in life. However, the neurotic person is inflexible in his or her use of these needs in reacting to different situations. The neurotic person tends to rely compulsively on only one of these needs to the exclusion of all the others. In contrast, the healthy person shifts easily from one need to another as circumstances change. For example, when the need for affection arises, the healthy person attempts to satisfy it. When the need for power arises, he or she attempts to satisfy that need, and so forth. Horney explained that the neurotic person, unlike the healthy person, makes one of these needs the indiscriminate strategy of all social interactions. "If it is affection that a person must have, he must receive it from friend and enemy, from employer and bootblack" (Horney, 1942, p. 39). In short, needs are considered neurotic when a person makes one of them an insatiable way of life.

TABLE 5-3   TEN NEUROTIC NEEDS IDENTIFIED BY HORNEY (1942)

Excessive needs for	Behavioral definitions
1 Affection and approval	Indiscriminate striving to be loved and admired by others; overly sensitive to criticism, rejection, or unfriendliness.
2 Having a partner to take control	Excessive dependence on others and fearful of being abandoned or left alone; overvaluing love because love can solve everything.
3 Restricting life within narrow limits	Preference for a life-style in which routine and orderliness are paramount; being undemanding, content with little, and submitting to the will of others.
4 Power	Domination and control of others for its own sake; having contempt for weakness.
5 Exploiting others	Dread of being exploited or made to look "stupid" by others but thinking nothing of taking advantage of them.
6 Social recognition	Wish to be admired and respected by others; basing self-image on public status.
7 Personal admiration	Drive to create an inflated self-image devoid of flaws and limitations; living to be flattered and complimented by others.
8 Personal ambition	Intense striving to be the very best regardless of the consequences; dreading failure.
9 Self-sufficiency and independence	Avoidance of any relationship that involves commitment or obligation; distancing self from anything or anyone.
10 Perfection and unassailability	Attempt to be completely moral and flawless in every respect; maintaining an appearance of perfection and virtue.

Moving Toward, Away from, and Against Other People

In her book *Our Inner Conflicts* (1945) Horney clustered her list of 10 neurotic needs into 3 general categories. Each of the three categories represents an interpersonal coping strategy aimed at making the person feel safe and secure in the world. In other words, they function to reduce anxiety and to make life more bearable. In addition, Horney felt that each strategy reveals the general orientation the person is likely to take in relating to other people.

Moving Toward People: The Compliant Type   *Moving toward people* involves a style of interaction characterized by dependence, unassertiveness, and helplessness. This person, whom Horney called the *compliant type,* is guided by the irrational belief that "If I give in I shall not be hurt" (Horney, 1937, p. 97).

Compliant types need to be wanted, loved, protected, and guided by others. They enter into relationships only to avoid feeling lonely, helpless, or unwanted. However, compliance may mask a repressed need to be aggressive. Thus, although the person tends to be self-effacing toward others, below the surface there often exists rage, anger, and hostility.

Moving Away from People: The Detached Type   *Moving away from people* as an interpersonal coping strategy is evidenced by those individuals who adopt a protective ''I don't care about anything'' attitude. Such people, whom Horney called *detached types,* are guided by the erroneous belief that ''If I withdraw, nothing can hurt me'' (Horney, 1937, p. 99).

Detached types are determined not to get emotionally involved with others in any way, whether in romance, work, or recreation. As a result, they lack genuine concern for others, settle for superficial enjoyments, and simply go through the motions of life. This strategy is characterized by the desire for privacy, independence, and self-sufficiency.

Moving Against People: The Hostile Type   *Moving against people* is a coping style characterized by dominance, hostility, and exploitation. This person, whom Horney called the *hostile type,* operates from the self-delusional belief that if ''I have power, no one can hurt me'' (Horney, 1937, p. 98).

The hostile type assumes that others are aggressive and that life is a struggle against all. Thus, any situation or relationship is looked at from the perspective of ''What can I get out of it?''—whether it has to do with money, prestige, contacts, or ideas. Horney noted that the hostile type is capable of acting politely and friendly, but the person's behavior is always a means to the end of attaining control and power over others. All functioning, in fact, is directed toward enhancing the person's prestige, position, or personal ambition. Thus, this strategy coincides with the need to exploit others, to receive social recognition, and to be admired.

As with the 10 neurotic needs, each of the 3 interpersonal coping strategies is designed to minimize feelings of anxiety created by social forces in childhood. In Horney's view, the fundamental coping strategies are used by everyone at some time or another. Furthermore, she believed that the three coping strategies are in conflict with each other for both the healthy and the neurotic person. For the healthy person, however, the conflict is not as emotionally charged as it is for the neurotic. Therefore, the healthy person has much greater flexibility, being able to pass from one strategy to another as circumstances warrant. The neurotic person, on the other hand, experiences considerable conflict among the three strategies in an effort to deal with life and its necessarily people-oriented contacts. He or she utilizes only one of the three coping strategies whether that strategy is appropriate or not. It follows that the neurotic person is both less flexible and less effective in solving problems than the healthy person is.

Feminine Psychology

As noted earlier, Horney (1926/1967) disagreed with almost every assumption that Freud made about women. She totally rejected Freud's view that women literally envy the male penis and blame their mothers for their not having a penis. She also believed that Freud was wrong in concluding that women unconsciously desire to have a male baby as a way of symbolically obtaining a penis. Horney countered these degrading views of women with the concept of *womb envy,* suggesting that men may unconsciously be jealous of women's ability to bear and nurse children. Finally, Horney pointed out that psychoanalysis was created by a "male genius, and almost all those who have developed his ideas have been men" (Horney, 1926/1967, p. 54). It must be realized that Horney's opposition to Freud's assumptions about women created considerable controversy at the time. In fact, she was disqualified as a training analyst and was eventually expelled from the male-dominated psychoanalytic school of thought. As an early feminist, however, Horney did much more than criticize Freud. She set forth her own theory of feminine psychology, one that recast the differences between men and women in terms of sociocultural influences.

Horney insisted that women often feel inferior to men because their lives are based on economic, political, and psychological dependency on men. Historically, women have been treated as second-class citizens, denied equal rights, and socialized to overvalue their perceptions of "superior" men. Likewise, they have been enmeshed in male-dominated social systems that constantly make them feel dependent and inadequate. Horney argued that many women do aspire to be more masculine, but not because they lack penises. Rather, she saw women's "overvaluation" of masculinity as motivated by a desire for power and privilege. "The wish to be a man . . . may be an expression or a wish for all those qualities or privileges which in our culture are regarded as masculine, such as strength, courage, independence, success, sexual freedom, right to choose a partner" (Horney, 1939, p. 108).

Horney (1926/1967) also emphasized the role conflicts that many women experience in their relationships with men. In particular, she contrasted the traditional feminine role of marriage and motherhood with a more liberated role of pursuing careers and other goals. She suggested that these contrasting roles accounted for the neurotic needs that some women displayed in their love relationships with men.

In drawing attention to the importance of culture and gender roles, Horney's ideas fit in quite well with the feminist *zeitgeist* of our times (Westkott, 1986). The rapid changes in the roles and relationships of the two sexes that are occurring in modern societies would certainly have been welcomed by Horney. Her numerous articles on feminine psychology continue to be cited by investigators today.

Concluding Comments

Horney's theory was based almost entirely on her clinical observations of neurotic patients. Her detailed account of neuroses as expressions of disturbed human relationships, frequently illustrated by interesting case studies, may constitute the most influential of her contributions to modern personality theory. Nevertheless, her nearly exclusive concern with disturbed people imposes serious limitations on the comprehensiveness of her theory. To her credit, Horney attempted to be as precise and consistent as possible in theorizing about the origins and development of neurosis. In this theorizing we also see an optimistic view of humanity based on the belief that all people have the capacity for positive growth.

Unfortunately, the empirical literature offers virtually no direct evidence to support or reject Horney's concepts. Despite the absence of research evidence, however, Horney's theoretical and clinical ideas have had a vast appeal. She wrote expressly for people without professional training, and her books are still popular today. Thus, Horney's approach to personality is of far more than historical interest.

SUMMARY

Various post-Freudian theorists revised psychodynamic theory by granting a greater role to the ego and its functions. Erik Erikson, one of the most prominent ego psychologists, emphasizes developmental change throughout the life cycle and the understanding of personality against the background of social and historical forces. Unlike Freud, Erikson regards the ego as an autonomous personality structure; his theory focuses on ego qualities that emerge at predictable times throughout life. The significance of social and cultural sources of influence in shaping personality is also evident in the theories formulated by Erich Fromm and Karen Horney.

Erikson asserts that ego development proceeds through a series of universal stages. In his epigenetic conception of human development, each stage in the life cycle has an optimal time to emerge. The sequential unfolding of these life stages is a function of the individual's biological maturation interacting with his or her expanding social radius.

In Erikson's view, eight psychosocial stages characterize the human life cycle. Each is marked by a particular kind of crisis or turning point in the person's life. The eight stages, depicted in terms of the essential psychosocial conflicts associated with each, are as follows: (1) basic trust versus mistrust, (2) autonomy versus shame and doubt, (3) initiative versus guilt, (4) industry versus inferiority, (5) ego identity versus role confusion, (6) intimacy versus isolation, (7) generativity versus stagnation, and (8) ego integrity versus despair. The individual's personality is determined by the resolutions of these conflicts.

Erikson's theory is rooted in his basic assumptions about human nature. His psychosocial theory reflects (1) a strong commitment to the assumptions of holism, environmentalism, and changeability, and (2) a moderate commitment to the assumptions of determinism, rationality, objectivity, proactivity, heterostasis, and knowability.

Illustrative research bearing upon the empirical validity of Erikson's theory was discussed in terms of ego identity statuses, and identity achievement and later capacity for intimacy. It was noted, however, that Erikson's theory has thus far generated only minimal research.

The application of Erikson's theory was focused on the understanding of adolescence in American society. Diverse areas of contemporary adolescent behavior—the problem of career choice, peer-group membership, and alcohol and drug use—were interpreted as partial reflections of the identity crisis.

Erich Fromm continued the post-Freudian trend in emphasizing the impact of social and cultural influences on personality. He argued that the gap between freedom and security has increased to the point where loneliness, insignificance, and alienation capture the essence of the human condition today. Some are motivated to escape from freedom through the mechanisms of authoritarianism, destructiveness, and automaton conformity. The healthy way to escape is through achieving positive freedom by means of spontaneous activity.

Fromm identified six existential needs unique to human beings. Based on the conflicting drives for freedom and security, they include the needs for relatedness, transcendence, rootedness, identity, a frame of orientation and devotion, and excitation and stimulation.

Fromm proposed that the way in which existential needs are satisfied by prevailing social, economic, and political conditions produce basic character orientations. Nonproductive character types include the receptive, exploitative, hoarding, and marketing. The productive type represents the goal of human development in Fromm's theory and is based on reason, love, and work.

Karen Horney rejected Freud's emphasis on physical anatomy as the basis of personality differences between men and women. She argued that the social relationship between child and parents is the decisive factor in shaping personality development. For Horney, childhood is dominated by the needs for satisfaction and security; parental behavior frustrating the child's need for security creates basic hostility which, in turn, leads to basic anxiety. Basic anxiety is a feeling of being helpless in a hostile world and is the foundation for neuroses.

Horney identified 10 neurotic needs used by persons to cope with feelings of insecurity and helplessness engendered by basic anxiety. Unlike healthy persons, neurotic persons focus on one of these needs in reacting to different situations. Horney later grouped neurotic needs into three general interpersonal coping strategies: moving away from people, moving against people, and moving toward people. In neurotic persons, one of these strategies is usually dominant.

Horney disagreed with Freud that women possess penis envy and suggested instead that men were envious of women's ability to bear and nurse children. She also believed that women may feel inferior because of their economic, political, and psychological dependency on men. Horney emphasized sociocultural influences, notably male domination and discrimination, as the basis for explaining female development.

BIBLIOGRAPHY

Adams, G. R., & Fitch, S. A. (1983). Psychological environments of university departments: Effects of college students' identity status and ego stage development. *Journal of Personality and Social Psychology, 44,* 1266–1275.

Adams, G. R., Ryan, J. H., Hoffman, J. J., Dobson, W. R., & Nielsen, E. C. (1985). Ego identity status, conformity behavior, and personality in late adolescence. *Journal of Personality and Social Psychology, 47,* 1091–1104.

Bourne, E. (1978). The state of research on ego identity: A review and appraisal. I. *Journal of Youth and Adolescence, 7,* 223–251.

Coles, R. (1970). *Erik H. Erikson: The growth of his work.* Boston: Little, Brown.

Crosby, F., & Crosby, T. L. (1981). Psychobiography and psychohistory. In S. Long (Ed.), *Handbook of political behavior* (Vol. 1). New York: Plenum.

Cross, H. J., & Allen, J. G. (1970). Ego identity status, adjustment, and academic achievement. *Journal of Consulting and Clinical Psychology, 34,* 288.

Erikson, E. H. (1937). Configurations in play—Clinical notes. *Psychoanalytic Quarterly, 6,* 139–214.

Erikson, E. H. (1945). Childhood and tradition in two American Indian tribes. In *The Psychoanalytic study of the child* (Vol. 1, pp. 319–350). New York: International Universities Press.

Erikson, E. H. (1958). *Young man Luther: A study in psychoanalysis and history.* New York: Norton.

Erikson, E. H. (1963a). *Childhood and society* (2nd ed.). New York: Norton.

Erikson, E. H. (1963b). *Youth: Change and challenge.* New York: Norton.

Erikson, E. H. (1964a). *Insight and responsibility.* New York: Norton.

Erikson, E. H. (1964b). Memorandum on identity and Negro youth. *Journal of Social Issues, 20,* 29–42.

Erikson, E. H. (1968a). *Identity: Youth and crisis.* New York: Norton.

Erikson, E. H. (1968b). Life cycle. In *International Encyclopedia of the Social Sciences* (Vol. 9, pp. 286–292). New York: Crowell Collier & Macmillan.

Erikson, E. H. (1969). *Gandhi's truth.* New York: Norton.

Erikson, E. H. (1970). Reflections on the dissent of contemporary youth. *Daedalus, 99,* 154–176.

Erikson, E. H. (1973). *In search of common ground.* New York: Norton.

Erikson, E. H. (1975). *Life history and the historical moment.* New York: Norton.

Erikson, E. H. (1977). *Toys and reasons: Stages in the ritualization of experience.* New York: Norton.

Erikson, E. H. (1978). *Adulthood.* New York: Norton.

Erikson, E. H. (1979). *Identity and the life cycle: A reissue.* New York: Norton.

Erikson, E. H. (1982). *The life cycle completed.* New York: Norton.

Erikson, E. H., Erikson, J. M., & Kivnick, H. Q. (1986). *Vital involvement in old age.* New York: Norton.

Evans, R. I. (1967). *Dialogue with Erik Erikson.* New York: Harper and Row.

Fromm, E. (1941/1956). *Escape from freedom.* New York: Avon.

Fromm, E. (1947). *Man for himself: An inquiry into the psychology of ethics.* New York: Holt, Rinehart and Winston.

Fromm, E. (1955). *The sane society.* New York: Holt, Rinehart and Winston.

Fromm, E. (1956/1974) *The art of loving.* New York: Harper and Row.

Fromm, E. (1962). *Beyond the chains of illusion: My encounter with Marx and Freud.* New York: Touchstone.

Fromm, E. (1968). *The revolution of hope.* New York: Harper and Row.

Fromm, E. (1973). *The anatomy of human destructiveness.* New York: Holt, Rinehart and Winston.

Fromm, E. (1981). *On Disobedience and other essays.* New York: Seabury Press.

Funk, R. (1982). *Erich Fromm: The courage to be human.* New York: Continuum.

Gilligan, C. (1982). *In a different voice: Psychological theory and women's development.* Cambridge, MA: Harvard University Press.

Goldberg, H. (1983). *The new male–female relationship.* New York: Morrow.

Horney, K. (1926/1967). *Feminine psychology.* New York: Norton.

Horney, K. (1937). *The neurotic personality of our time.* New York: Norton.

Horney, K. (1939). *New ways in psychoanalysis.* New York: Norton.

Horney, K. (1942). *Self-analysis.* New York: Norton.

Horney, K. (1945). *Our inner conflicts.* New York: Norton.

Horney, K. (1950) *Neurosis and human growth: The struggle toward self- realization.* New York: Norton.

Johnston, L. D., O'Malley, P. M., & Bachman, J. G. (1988). *Illicit drug use, smoking, and drinking by America's high-school students, college students, and young adults, 1975-1987.* Washington, DC: National Institute on Drug Abuse.

Kahn, S., Zimmerman, G., Csikszentmihalyi, M., & Getzels, J. W. (1985). Relations between identity in young adulthood and intimacy at midlife. *Journal of Personality and Social Psychology, **49,** 1316-1322.

Leavitt, F. (1982). *Drugs and behavior.* New York: Wiley.

Maccoby, E. E. (1990). Gender and relationships: A developmental account. *American Psychologist, **45,** 513-520.

Maccoby, M. (1981). *The leader.* New York: Simon and Schuster.

Maccoby, M. (1988). *Why work: Leading the new generation.* New York: Simon and Schuster.

Marcia J. E. (1966). Development and validation of ego-identity status. *Journal of Personality and Social Psychology, **3,** 551-558.

Marcia, J. E. (1967). Ego identity status: Relationship to change in self-esteem, ''general adjustment,'' and authoritarianism. *Journal of Personality, **35,** 118-133.

Marcia, J. E. (1980). Identity in adolescence. In J. Adelson (Ed.), *Handbook of adolescent psychology.* New York: Wiley.

Marcia, J. E., & Friedman, M. L. (1970). Ego identity status in college women. *Journal of Personality, **44,** 675-688.

Moraitis, G., & Pollack, G. H. (Eds.) (1987). *Psychoanalytic studies of biography.* Madison, CT: International Universities Press.

Papalia, D., & Olds, S. (1986). *Human development* (3rd ed.). New York: McGraw-Hill.

Peplau, L. A., & Perlman, D. (1982). Perspectives on loneliness. In L. A. Peplau & D. Perlman (Eds.), *Loneliness: A sourcebook of current theory, research, and therapy.* New York: Wiley.

Piaget, J. (1983). Piaget's theory. In P. H. Mussen (Ed.), *Handbook of child psychology* (Vol. 1). New York: Wiley.

Roazen, P. (1973). *Sigmund Freud.* Englewood Cliffs, NJ: Prentice-Hall.

Rubins, J. L. (1978). *Karen Horney: Gentle rebel of psychoanalysis.* New York: Dial Press.

Runyan, W. M. (1982). *Life histories and psychobiography: Explorations in theory and method.* New York: Oxford University Press.

Santrock, J. W. (1985). *Adult development and aging.* Dubuque, IA: W. C. Brown.

Waterman, A. S. (1982). Identity development from adolescence to adulthood: An extension of theory and a review of research. *Developmental Psychology, **18,** 341-358.

Waterman, A. S., & Waterman, C. (1970). The relationship between ego identity status and satisfaction with college. *The Journal of Education Research, **64,** 165-168.

Westkott, M. (1986). *The feminist legacy of Karen Horney*. New Haven, CT: Yale University Press.

SUGGESTED READINGS

Baumeister, R. F. (1986). *Identity: Cultural change and the struggle for self.* New York: Oxford University Press.

Domino, G., & Affonso, D. D. (1990), A personality measure of Erikson's life stages: The inventory of psychosocial balance. *Journal of Personality Assessment, 54,* 576–588.

Fromm E. (1976). *To have or to be?* New York: Harper and Row.

Quinn, S. (1987). *A mind of her own: The life of Karen Horney.* New York: Summit Books.

Roazen, P. (1976). *Erik H. Erikson: The power and limits of his vision.* New York: Free Press.

Slugoski, B. R., Marcia, J. E., & Koopman, R. F. (1984). Cognitive and social interactional characteristics of ego identity statuses in college. *Journal of Personality and Social Psychology, 47,* 646–661.

Stevens, R. (1983). *Erik Erikson: An introduction.* New York: St. Martin's Press.

DISCUSSION QUESTIONS

1 In what ways does Erikson's theory modify and/or extend Freud's psychodynamic view of personality? Are the two theorists compatible in their ideas concerning psychological health and psychopathology?

2 Do you agree with Erikson that ego identity versus role confusion is the central crisis of adolescence? Do you believe that you have experienced this crisis to any degree? If so, can you see how it may have affected other areas of your life, e.g., career choice, relationships with parents, love relationships?

3 Erikson maintains that ego identity is a lifelong struggle. Do you agree? If so, what are some of the identity problems that might be faced by a person as he or she enters young adulthood, middle adulthood, and old age?

4 Explain Marcia's four ego identity statuses. Which status best characterizes you and your friends?

5 Do you agree with Fromm that most people today enjoy considerable freedom and autonomy but at the expense of feeling lonely, insecure, and alienated from others?

6 Do you believe that the marketing character orientation, as envisioned by Fromm, is the dominant personality type in capitalistic societies such as our own? If not, what character orientation(s) do you believe is (are) more prevalent today? Explain your position.

7 How does Horney explain the difference between normal and neurotic persons in terms of neurotic needs or trends?

8 According to Horney, what type of parental attitudes and behaviors tend to threaten or undermine the child's need for security? Do you think that most modern-day American parents are sensitive to their children's needs for security?

9 Now that you have studied Erikson, Fromm, and Horney, can you discern any basic similarities in their respective theories concerning the issue of personality dynamics? Cite specific concepts to support your answer.

10 Compare and contrast the views of Erikson, Fromm, and Horney concerning the influence of early childhood events on the development of adult personality structure.

GLOSSARY

Autonomy The inner sense that one is a self-governing person, able to exert some influence over those events that affect one's life.

Basic anxiety For Horney, the person's pervasive feeling of being lonely and isolated in a hostile world.

Basic hostility For Horney, the child's feeling of anger toward those (i.e., parents) who have rejected or mistreated him or her.

Basic trust The inner feeling that one's social world is a safe and stable place and that caring others are nurturant and reliable.

Care The psychosocial virtue accruing from generativity that enables a person to feel that someone or something matters.

Competency The psychosocial strength stemming from a sense of industry which enables a person to feel that she or he is able to deal effectively with the environment.

Despair The feeling evident among old people that life has been a series of unfulfilled opportunities and missed directions.

Ego identity The totality of self-perceptions that confer upon one a sense of uniqueness and continuity over time.

Ego integrity The feeling of fulfillment at the culmination of the life cycle as one takes stock of one's life, including job, accomplishments, and children.

Ego psychology A theoretical view of personality that has its origins in psychoanalytic theory, but has evolved new perspectives and ways of understanding human behavior that are significant departures from Freud's original theory. Emphasizes the ego (rationality) rather than the id as the basis of human behavior and functioning.

Epigenetic principle The assumption that human development proceeds in terms of a series of invariant stages that are universal to humanity and that each stage is accompanied by a crisis that arises from biological maturation and social demands made upon a person at that stage.

Exploitative character type In Frommian theory, an individual who takes what he or she wants from others by force or guile.

Fidelity The psychosocial virtue issuing from a sense of ego identity that enables a young person to perceive and act in terms of an ideology despite its contradictions and limitations.

Foreclosure Ego identity status in which the young person has never experienced a crisis concerning career choice or ideological beliefs but has nevertheless made firm commitments regarding them.

Generativity Accompanying middle age, it reflects a concern for the welfare of the next generation and the type of society in which that generation will live and work.

Guilt Feelings of unworthiness and self-doubt experienced by children whose parents are unwilling to allow them the opportunity of completing tasks on their own.

Hoarding character type In Frommian theory, an individual who is stingy, stubborn, and oriented toward the past.

Hope The psychosocial virtue accompanying a sense of basic trust which serves as the foundation for perceiving meaning in one's existence.

Humanistic communitarian socialism Fromm's utopian society in which basic human needs would be satisfied and individuals would develop their potential to the fullest extent.

Humanistic psychoanalysis Personality theory formulated by Fromm that emphasizes the role exerted by sociological, political, economic, religious, and anthropoligical factors in molding the individual's character development.

Identity achievement   Ego identity status in which the young person has experienced a crisis concerning career choice and ideological beliefs and has attained firm commitment regarding them.

Identity crisis   In Erikson's theory, a period of time during which a young person struggles with such questions as "Who am I?" and "Where am I going?" The young person plagued by an identity crisis often lacks a clear idea of his or her social role and assumes whatever role seems appropriate to a given situation.

Identity diffusion   Ego identity status in which the young person may or may not have experienced a crisis concerning career choice and ideological beliefs, but nonetheless shows little or no commitment to them.

Industry   Corresponding to the school age, it reflects a concern with being on the move, learning new skills, and completing tasks on one's own.

Inferiority   Feelings of self-doubt and incompetence resulting from a lack of industry; a low sense of self-worth.

Initiative   Associated with the play age, it reflects an active interest in the work of others, trying out new things, and the inner sense that one is able to undertake activities.

Intimacy   Associated with young adulthood, it includes sexuality, deep relationships with others, and a commitment to one's fellow beings.

Isolation   Feelings of social emptiness and futility resulting from the failure to attain intimacy.

Life cycle   The sequence of psychosocial stages from birth to death.

Love   The psychosocial virtue issuing from a sense of intimacy which enables the young person to commit himself or herself to others and to abide by such commitments, even though they may require self-denial and compromise.

Marketing character type   In Frommian theory, an individual who is keenly interested in maintaining appearances and who values self as a commodity to be exchanged or sold for success; represents the ultimate in alienation.

Mistrust   A sense of fear, suspicion, and apprehension in the infant toward the world in general and people in particular due to a style of maternal care which is inadequate or rejecting.

Moratorium   Ego identity status in which the young person is currently experiencing a crisis concerning career choice and ideological beliefs and whose commitments are vague and general.

Moving against people   An interpersonal coping strategy in Horney's theory that aims at the control of basic anxiety through the domination and exploitation of others; also called the *hostile type*.

Moving away from people   An interpersonal coping strategy in Horney's theory that aims at the control of basic anxiety through emotional detachment from others; also called the *detached type*.

Moving toward people   An interpersonal coping strategy in Horney's theory that aims at the control of basic anxiety through excessive dependence on others; also called the *compliant type*.

Mutuality   A term used by Erikson to represent the notion that the needs and capacities of different generations are interdependent.

Need for excitement and stimulation   For Fromm, innate human need to experience a constantly stimulating environment in order to maintain high levels of alertness and to function well.

Need for a frame of orientation and devotion   For Fromm, need of an individual to develop a consistent and meaningful belief system by which to interpret the complexities of the social and physical world.

Need for identity   For Fromm, unique human need to see oneself as distinctly different from others.

Need for relatedness   For Fromm, basic human need to care for and share with others.

Need for rootedness   For Fromm, basic human need to be an integral part of the social world; to feel that one belongs.

Need for transcendence   For Fromm, need of an individual to surpass his or her animal-like existence and to become an active shaper over the course of direction of his or her life.

Productive character type   In Frommian theory, an individual who is integrated, loving, and creative. Represents the ultimate goal in human development.

Psychohistory   A type of inquiry that attempts to relate a person's major life themes to particular historical events and circumstances.

Psychosocial crisis   A critical period in an individual's life, engendered by physiological maturation and social demands, which has the potential for either a positive or negative outcome.

Psychosocial moratorium   A period during late adolescence when a person is allowed some delay in assuming adult roles and responsibilities.

Purpose   The psychosocial virtue issuing from a sense of initiative that enables a child to become increasingly goal-oriented.

Receptive character type   In Frommian theory, an individual who is passive, gullible, and highly dependent on others.

Shame   The child's sense of rage turned inward upon the self because he or she has not been allowed to exercise autonomy by the parents.

Stagnation   A state of self-absorption in which only the individual's personal needs are of central concern.

Willpower   The psychosocial virtue accompanying autonomy which enables a child to exercise free choice as well as self-restraint.

Wisdom   The psychosocial virtue accompanying a sense of ego integrity that enables the person to appreciate the relativity of knowledge acquired in one lifetime.

CHAPTER 6

THE DISPOSITIONAL PERSPECTIVE IN PERSONALITY THEORY: GORDON ALLPORT, RAYMOND CATTELL, AND HANS EYSENCK

Two major themes underlie the *dispositional perspective* on personality. The first is the idea that people possess broad predispositions (i.e., traits) to respond in certain ways in diverse situations. What this suggests is that people display consistency in their actions, thoughts, and emotions across time, events, and experiences. In effect, the essence of personality is defined by those dispositional qualities that people carry around with them, that belong to them, that somehow are an enduring part of them.

A second major theme of the dispositional perspective bears on the fact that no two people are exactly alike. This was discussed in Chapter 1, in which the concept of personality was defined in part by an emphasis on the characteristic ways individuals differ from one another. This theme is perhaps the most compelling and salient idea characterizing the dispositional approach to personality theory and research. Indeed, every personological perspective, in one way or another, must deal with the issue of individual differences if it is to remain viable in the marketplace of psychological science.

Many personologists have emphasized the understanding of personality in terms of the dispositional qualities or tendencies that reside within the individual. Gordon Allport, one of the most influential advocates of the dispositional perspective, believed that each person is unique and that the person's uniqueness can best be captured by specifying his or her particular personality traits. Allport's emphasis on the uniqueness of the person is, however, only one of the features of his theoretical position. In addition, there is a strong focus on the ways in which cognitive and motivational processes influence behavior. Furthermore, Allport's theory represents a blend of humanistic and personalistic approaches to the study

238

of human behavior. It is humanistic in its attempt to recognize all aspects of the human being, including the potential for growth, transcendence, and self-realization. It is personalistic in that it seeks to understand and predict the development of the real individual person (Allport, 1968b). As a theoretician, Allport may also be broadly described as an eclectic because he incorporates insights from philosophy, religion, literature, and sociology, blending such ideas into an understanding of the richness and complexity of personality. In fact, Allport's belief that each person's behavior derives from a particular configuration of personal *traits* is the trademark of his orientation to personology. His trait theory of personality will be discussed at some length in this chapter.

A number of other personologists have also taken on the challenge of building comprehensive schemes for the identification and measurement of the basic traits that form the core of personality. Nowhere is this more evident than in the conceptual and empirical contributions of Hans Eysenck and Raymond Cattell. Using a complex psychometric technique known as *factor analysis,* these theorists have tried to show how the underlying organization of trait dimensions influences the individual's observed behavioral qualities. Eysenck sees two major type dimensions as critically important in personality: introversion–extraversion and stability–neuroticism. A third type dimension, called psychoticism–superego strength, is also seen by Eysenck as underlying the structure of personality. Cattell, in contrast, views personality as consisting of at least 16 major trait dimensions. He also believes that equations can be used for predicting behavior based on precise measures of traits weighted according to their relevance to the situation. Cattell and Eysenck share a common commitment to a scientific model of human behavior. The salient features of their respective theories will be highlighted later in this chapter. Finally, there are psychologists who oppose the dispositional point of view on the grounds that people's behavior shows little traitlike consistency across time and circumstances. We will address this issue in the empirical validation section of the chapter. Let us now consider the biographical sketch of Allport.

GORDON ALLPORT: A Dispositional Theory of Personality

BIOGRAPHICAL SKETCH

Gordon Willard Allport, the youngest of four brothers, was born in Montezuma, Indiana, in 1897. His father, a country doctor, moved the family to Ohio shortly after Gordon's birth, and the youngest Allport received his early education in the Cleveland public schools. He characterized his family life as marked by trust and affection, along with a strong emphasis on the Protestant work ethic.

Allport was scholarly from an early age; he described himself as a social isolate who was skilled with words but poor at sports. After he graduated from high school, he enrolled at Harvard University at the urging of his older brother Floyd, who was then a graduate student in psychology at the same university.

Gordon Allport.

Although he took several psychology courses at Harvard, Allport majored in economics and philosophy. He also participated in a number of volunteer service projects during his undergraduate years. After graduating in 1919, Allport accepted an offer to teach sociology and English at Robert College in Constantinople, Turkey. The following year he won a fellowship for graduate study in psychology at Harvard.

Allport received his Ph.D. in psychology in 1922. His dissertation focused on traits of personality and was the first such study done anywhere in the United States. During the next two years, Allport studied at the universities of Berlin and Hamburg in Germany and Cambridge in England. Returning from Europe, he served as an instructor for two years in Harvard's Department of Social Ethics. There he taught a course entitled "Personality: Its Psychological and Social Aspects." It was the first course on personality ever offered in the United States.

In 1926 Allport accepted the position of assistant professor of psychology at Dartmouth College, where he stayed until 1930. In that year, he was invited by Harvard to return at the same rank in the Department of Social Relations. He was promoted to Professor of Psychology in 1942 and held this position until his death in 1967. During his long and distinguished career at Harvard, Allport influenced several generations of students through his popular undergraduate course. He also came to be considered the "dean of American personality study."

Allport was a prolific author. Among his widely known publications are *Personality: A Psychological Interpretation* (1937); *The Individual and His Religion* (1950); *Becoming: Basic Considerations for a Psychology of Personality* (1955); *Personality and Social Encounter* (1960); *Pattern and Growth in Personality* (1961); and *Letters from Jenny* (1965). He also coauthored two widely used personality tests: *The A-S Reaction Study* (with F. H. Allport, 1928) and *A Study of Values* (with P. E. Vernon, 1931; revised with G. Lindzey in 1951 and again in 1960). A complete list of his writings may be found in *The Person in Psychology*

(Allport, 1968a). His autobiography is presented in Volume 5 of *A History of Psychology in Autobiography* (1967, pp. 3–25).

WHAT IS PERSONALITY?

In his first book, *Personality: A Psychological Interpretation,* Allport described and classified over 50 different definitions of personality. He concluded that an adequate synthesis of existing definitions might be expressed in the phrase "what a man really is" (1937, p. 48). What this definition possesses in the way of comprehensiveness it certainly lacks in precision. Recognizing this, Allport went a step further and asserted that "personality is something and does something. . . . It is what lies behind specific acts and within the individual" (1937, p. 48). Eschewing the notion of personality as merely a hypothetical entity, then, Allport argued that it is a real entity within the person.

The question remains, however, "What is the nature of this *something?*" Allport (1937) answered by proposing a precise definition of personality which he subsequently revised to read as follows: "Personality is the dynamic organization within the individual of those psychophysical systems that determine his characteristic behavior and thought" (1961, p. 28). What does all this mean? First, the phrase "dynamic organization" suggests that human behavior is constantly evolving and changing; a person is not a static entity in Allport's theory, although there is an underlying structure that integrates and organizes the various elements of personality. The reference to "psychophysical systems" reminds us that both "mind" and "body" elements must be considered when describing and studying personality. The inclusion of the term "determine" is a logical consequence of Allport's psychophysical orientation. Basically, the implication is that personality is comprised of "determining tendencies" which, when aroused by appropriate stimuli, give rise to actions through which the individual's true nature is revealed. The word "characteristic" in Allport's definition simply highlights the paramount importance that he attached to the uniqueness of the single person. No two people are alike in this personological system. Finally, the phrase "behavior and thought" is a blanket designed to cover everything the person does. Allport believed that personality expresses itself in some way in virtually all observable human actions.

In arriving at his conceptual definition, Allport noted that the terms *character* and *temperament* have often been used as synonyms for personality. Allport explained how each may be readily distinguished from the concept of personality. The word "character" traditionally connotes a moral standard or value system against which the person's actions are evaluated. For example, whenever another person is considered of "good character," a personal judgment as to the social and/or ethical desirability of his or her personal qualities is really the topic. Character thus is actually an ethical concept. Or, as Allport (1961) put it, character is personality *evaluated;* personality is character *devaluated.* Character, then, should not be considered as some special region contained within personality.

Temperament, by contrast, is the "raw material"—along with intelligence and physique—out of which personality is fashioned. Allport (1961) considered the term particularly useful in referring to the hereditary aspects of a person's emotional nature (such as susceptibility to emotional arousal, prevailing mood state, and fluctuation and intensity of moods). Representing one aspect of a person's genetic endowment, temperament limits the development of personality. Temperamentally speaking, you certainly "can't make a silk purse out of a sow's ear" in Allport's system. Like any good definition of personality, then, Allport's concept states clearly both what it is and what it is not.

CONCEPT OF TRAIT

As noted at the outset of this chapter, the dispositional approach to personality asserts that no two people are completely alike. Any one person behaves in a consistent and different fashion from all others. Allport's explanation for this is found in his concept of *trait,* which he regarded as the most valid "unit of analysis" for representing what people are like and how they differ from one another behaviorally.

What is a trait of personality? Allport defined a trait as a "neuro-psychic structure having the capacity to render many stimuli functionally equivalent, and to initiate and guide equivalent (meaningfully consistent) forms of adaptive and expressive behavior" (1961, p. 347). In simpler terms, *a trait is a predisposition to act in the same way in a wide range of situations.* For instance, if a person is basically shy, he or she will tend to be quiet and reserved in many different situations—sitting in class, eating at the cafeteria, studying in the dorm, shopping with friends. If, on the other hand, a person is basically friendly, he or she will tend to be talkative and outgoing in these same situations. Allport's theory predicts that a person's behavior is relatively stable over time and across situations.

Traits are psychological entities that render many stimuli as well as many responses equivalent. Many stimuli may evoke the same response, or many responses (feelings, perceptions, interpretations, actions) have the same functional meaning in terms of the trait. To illustrate this idea, Allport (1961) cited the case of a fictitious Mr. McCarley whose leading trait is a "fear of communism." For him, this trait renders equivalent the social stimuli of Russians, African-American and Jewish neighbors, liberals, most college professors, peace organizations, the United Nations, and so forth. All are perceived and labeled as "communists." In addition, such a trait triggers hostile response sequences which are equivalent in their capacity to reduce the perceived threat of communism. Mr. McCarley might support nuclear war against Russians, write hostile letters to the local newspaper about blacks, vote for extreme right-wing political candidates and policies, join the Ku Klux Klan or John Birch Society, criticize the UN, and/or participate in any one of a number of other equivalent hostile responses. Figure 6-1 shows schematically the range of possibilities.

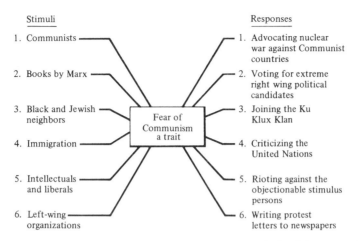

FIGURE 6-1   The generality of a trait as determined by equivalence of stimuli that arouse it and by equivalence of responses that it produces. (*Source: Adapted from Allport, 1961, p. 322.*)

Needless to say, a person may engage in a number of these activities without necessarily possessing undue hostility or fear of communism. Additionally, everyone who votes for right-wing candidates or opposes the UN does not necessarily fall in the same personological category. However, this example shows that a person's traits are organized and expressed on the basis of perceived similarities. That is, many situations, because of their perceived equivalence, arouse a certain trait which then initiates and guides a variety of behaviors that are equivalent in giving expression to the trait. It is this conception of equivalence of stimuli and responses, united and mediated by a trait, that constitutes Allport's trait theory of personality.

For Allport, traits are not linked to a small number of specific stimuli or responses; rather, they are relatively generalized and enduring. By uniting responses to numerous stimuli, traits produce fairly broad consistencies in behavior. A trait is what accounts for the more permanent, enduring, trans-situational features of our behavior. It is a vital ingredient of our "personality structure." At the same time, traits may also be focal in nature. For example, the trait of dominance may be aroused only when the person is in the presence of specific others, his or her children, spouse, or intimate acquaintances. In each case he or she immediately becomes ascendant. However, the trait of dominance is not activated in the event that the person discovers a $10 bill on the floor of a friend's home. Such a stimulus would arouse the trait of honesty (or dishonesty as the case may be). It would not arouse dominance. Allport thus admits that personality traits are embedded within social situations, adding, "any theory that regards personality as stable, fixed, invariable is wrong" (1961, p. 175). As an analogy, water can have the shape and texture of a liquid, a solid (ice), or some substance along the continuum (snow, hail, sleet). It is the degree of environmental warmth that determines its physical form.

It should be emphasized, however, that traits do not lie dormant waiting to be aroused by external stimuli. In fact, people actively seek out social situations that encourage the expression of their traits. A person possessing a strong disposition of sociability not only responds in a charming manner when in a group of people but also initiates contacts with others when she is alone. In other words, the person is not a passive "reactor" to the situation, as B. F. Skinner might suggest; rather, the situations in which she is likely to find herself are often those in which she has actively placed herself. From Allport's perspective, traits and situations interact to determine which behaviors actually occur. The two components are functionally interdependent. By emphasizing the interactions between personal dispositions and situational variables, Allport's theory has much in common with the social learning theories of Albert Bandura and Julian Rotter (Chapter 8).

The "Traits" of Traits

In Allport's system, traits themselves may be said to have "traits" or defining characteristics. Shortly before his death, Allport (1966) published an article entitled "Traits Revisited" in which he summarized all that he had learned in response to the question, "What is a trait of personality?" In this article, he proposed that eight basic criteria define a personality trait:

1 *A trait has more than nominal existence.* Personality traits are not fictions; they are a very real and vital part of everyone's existence. Every person possesses inside his or her skin these "generalized action tendencies." Aside from "fear of communism," other readily recognized traits include "fear of capitalism," "aggressiveness," "meekness," "honesty," "dishonesty," "introversion," and "extraversion." Allport's main point here is that these personal characteristics are *real*—they actually exist inside people and are not simply theoretical make-believe.

2 *A trait is more generalized than a habit.* Traits account for the relatively permanent and general features of our behavior. Habits, while enduring, refer to more specific tendencies and are thus less generalized in terms of the situations which may arouse them or the responses which they evoke. For example, a child may brush her teeth twice a day and continue to do so because she is encouraged by her parents. This is a habit. However, with the passing of years, the child may also learn to brush her hair, wash and iron her clothes, and clean her room. All of these habits woven together may form the trait of personal cleanliness.

3 *A trait is dynamic or at least determinative in behavior.* As already noted, traits do not lie dormant waiting to be aroused by external stimuli. Rather, they motivate people to engage in behaviors that are conducive to expressing their traits. For example, a college student with a strong "sociability" trait does not just sit around and wait to attend parties to be sociable. She actively seeks out parties so that she can express her sociability trait. Traits, then, guide and direct a person's actions.

4 *A trait's existence may be established empirically.* While traits cannot be observed directly, Allport argued that it is possible to verify their existence. Evidence for the existence of traits may be derived from observations of a person's behavior over time, case histories or biographies, and statistical techniques that determine the degree of coherence among separate responses to the same or similar stimuli.

5 *A trait is only relatively independent of other traits.* To paraphrase a well-known saying, "No trait is an island." There is no rigid boundary separating one trait from another. Rather, the personality is comprised of a network of overlapping traits only *relatively* independent of one another. To illustrate, Allport (1960) cited a study in which the traits of insight and humor were found to be highly correlated with one another. Clearly, these are separate traits, but they nevertheless are somehow related. While it is impossible to draw causal conclusions from such correlational data, we might speculate that if a person possessed a high degree of insight, he or she would likely perceive the ludicrous aspects of the human condition and be led to develop a well-rounded sense of humor. Much more likely from Allport's viewpoint, however, is that traits overlap primarily because of the person's tendency to react to events in an integrated fashion.

6 *A trait is not synonymous with moral or social judgment.* Despite the fact that many traits (e.g., sincerity, loyalty, greed) are subject to conventional social judgment, they still represent true traits of personality. Ideally, an investigator would first discover traits as they exist in a given person and then seek neutral, devaluated words to identify them. In Allport's opinion, personologists should be studying *personality*, not *character*.

7 *A trait may be viewed in light of either the personality that contains it or its distribution in the population at large.* Take shyness as an illustration. Like any other trait, it has both unique and universal aspects. When viewed uniquely, shyness could be studied in terms of the influence it exerts in a given person's life. Conversely, this trait could be studied "universally" by constructing a reliable and valid "shyness scale" and determining how people differ on it.

8 *Acts or even habits that are inconsistent with a trait are not proof of the nonexistence of the trait.* As an illustration, consider Nancy Smith, who is always neat in her personal appearance; with never a hair out of place and her attire impeccable, she indubitably possesses the trait of neatness. But this trait would never be inferred if we observed her office desk, apartment, or car. Her personal belongings in each case are carelessly arranged, cluttered, and downright sloppy. Why the apparent contradiction? For Allport, there are three possible explanations. First, not everyone shows the same degree of integration with respect to a given trait. What is a major trait for one person may either be a minor or nonexistent trait for another person. In Nancy's case, neatness may be restricted to her person. Second, the same person may possess contradictory traits. The fact that Nancy is meticulous with respect to her personal appearance and yet slovenly with regard to her belongings further suggests the limited scope of neatness in her life. Third, there are instances where social situations, rather than personality traits, are the prime movers of behavior. If Nancy is running to catch a plane, for example, she may not care whether her hair blows all over the place or her clothing becomes disheveled in the process. Therefore, to observe that not all Nancy's actions are consistent with an underlying disposition of neatness is no proof that the disposition does not exist within her.

Common Traits versus Individual Traits

In his early writings, Allport (1937) distinguished between *common* traits and *individual* traits. The former (also called *dimensional* or *nomothetic traits*) includes any characteristic shared by several people within a given culture. We might say, for example, that some people are more assertive than others or that some people are more polite than others. The logic for assuming the existence of common traits is that members of a culture are subject to similar evolutionary and social influences; therefore, they develop roughly comparable modes of adjustment. Examples include proficiency in the use of language, political and/or social attitudes, value orientations, anxiety, and conformity. The majority of people within our culture could be measurably compared with one another on these common dimensions.

According to Allport, what usually (but not invariably) results from such trait comparisons among individuals is a normal distribution curve. That is, when common trait test scores are plotted on a graph, they approximate a bell-shaped curve, with the bulk of cases piling up as average scores in the middle and the rest tapering off toward the extremes. Figure 6-2 illustrates this situation for the common trait "dominance–submission." The dimensionality of common traits thus allows the personologist to compare one person with another along meaningful psychological dimensions (as might be done for common physical characteristics such as height and weight).

While regarding such cross-comparisons as legitimate and useful, Allport (1968a) also believed that traits are never expressed by any two people in exactly the same way. The psychological pervasiveness and expression of dominance for Linda is unique to her. To this extent, Linda's dominance cannot really be

FIGURE 6-2   The distribution of scores based on a test measuring the dominance–submission trait continuum.

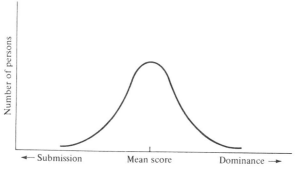

compared with Susan's. *Individual* traits (also called *morphological traits*) designate those characteristics peculiar to the person that do not permit comparisons among people. It is these "genuine and neuropsychic units that guide, direct, and motivate specific acts of adjustment" (1968a, p. 3). Always operating in unique ways within each person, this category of traits most accurately reflects the personality structure of any given person. For Allport, then, the true personality surfaces only when individual traits are examined, using such resources as a person's case history, diary, letters, and other such personal documents. Consequently, the common trait of dominance can be profitably studied by comparing Linda, Susan, and everybody else on some meaningful yardstick (e.g., a dominance test or scale). But dominance as an individual trait can only be understood by studying its unique functioning in Linda, in Susan, and in everybody else considered one at a time. In the final analysis, Allport believed that the only way to understand uniqueness is to focus on individual traits.

Types of Personal Dispositions

Later in his career, Allport came to realize that using the term "trait" to describe both common and individual characteristics was quite confusing. He therefore revised his terminology and called individual traits *personal dispositions*. Common traits were simply renamed *traits*. The definition of personal disposition now included the phrase "peculiar to the individual," but otherwise remained the same as his earlier definition of trait.

Allport was deeply committed to the study of personal dispositions. However, it became evident to him that not all personal dispositions are equally pervasive and dominant in a person's life. He therefore proposed three types: cardinal, central, and secondary dispositions.

Cardinal Dispositions   A *cardinal disposition* is one that is so pervasive that almost everything a person does can be traced to its influence. This highly generalized disposition cannot remain hidden unless, of course, it is a trait such as seclusiveness, where its possessor might become a hermit whose dispositions would be known to no one. In other instances, however, this kind of master sentiment or ruling passion makes its possessor famous or infamous. Allport insisted that very few people possess a cardinal disposition.

Allport pointed to historical and fictional characters as examples of cardinal dispositions. Thus, we refer to people as being chauvinists, Scrooges, Machiavellians, Don Juans, or Joans of Arc. Or consider that Albert Schweitzer was said to have had one cardinal disposition in his life, "reverence for every living organism." Finally, Florence Nightingale was said to be "driven by compassion" for her fellow human beings. The theme of the lives of these individuals reveals the all-pervasive quality of cardinal dispositions.

Central Dispositions   Less pervasive but still quite generalized characteristics of the person are called *central dispositions*—the so-called building blocks of personality. Central dispositions might best be regarded as those attributes mentioned in an honest letter of recommendation (e.g., punctual, attentive, and responsible). As such, they represent those tendencies in the person's behavior that others can readily discern.

"How many central dispositions does the average person possess?" Allport approached this question by asking students "to think of some one individual of your own sex whom you know well" and "to describe him or her by writing words, phrases, or sentences that express fairly well what seem to you to be the essential characteristics of this person" (1961, p. 366). Ninety percent of the students listed between 3 and 10 essential characteristics: the average number listed was 7.2. Allport thus concluded that the number of central dispositions by which a person can be described is surprisingly small, perhaps no more than between 5 and 10. From the person's own vantage point, the number of central dispositions may be few indeed. H. G. Wells once commented that there were only two dominant themes in his life: interest in an ordered world society and sex.

Secondary Dispositions   Traits that are less conspicuous, less generalized, less consistent, and thus less relevant to the definition of a personality are called *secondary dispositions*. Food and clothing preferences, specific attitudes, and situationally determined characteristics of the person would be classified under this rubric. Consider, for instance, a person who never acts submissively except when a police officer gives him a speeding ticket. Allport noted that a person must be known quite intimately in order to discern his or her secondary dispositions.

THE PROPRIUM: DEVELOPMENT OF SELFHOOD

No personologist, least of all Allport, believes that personality is a mere bundle of unrelated dispositions. Personality embodies a unity, pattern, and integration of all those aspects of a person that make him or her distinctive. It is therefore reasonable to assume that there is an overall principle that organizes attitudes, values, motives, perceptions, and dispositions into a unified whole. For Allport, the problem of identifying and describing the nature of personality integration required an all-inclusive construct such as the self, ego, or style of life. But all these terms had accumulated too many ambiguous connotations and semantic ambiguities for Allport's taste. So he coined a new term—the *proprium*.

For Allport, the proprium represents the positive, creative, growth-seeking, and forward-moving quality of human nature. It is "the self-as-known—that which is experienced as warm and central, as of importance" (1968a, p. 4). It's the "me" part of subjective experience. In short, it's selfhood.

Allport (1955) viewed the proprium as including all aspects of personality that contribute to a sense of inward unity. He also saw it as marking the consistency associated with the person's dispositions, intentions, and long-range goals. At the same time, he did not regard it as a homunculus or "little person dwelling within the person." The proprium is not a thing separate from the person as a whole.

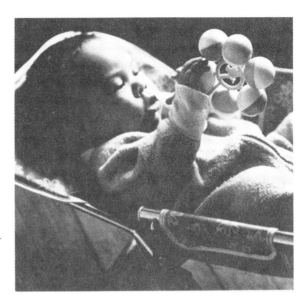

As the sense of bodily self develops, infants begin to distinguish themselves from objects they may be manipulating. *(Joel Gordon)*

Rather, it is an organizing and unifying agent that functions to make for the uniqueness of a person's life.

Allport (1961) identified seven different aspects of "selfhood" which are involved in the development of the proprium from infancy to adulthood. These so-called *propriate functions* evolve slowly over time and their ultimate consolidation constitutes the "self" as an object of subjective knowledge and feeling. The following propriate functions of personality are presented in order of their sequential appearance in the developing individual (see Table 6-1).

Sense of Bodily Self   The first aspect of the proprium to evolve is the sense of a bodily self. During the first year of life, infants become aware of many sensations that emanate from the muscles, tendons, joints, internal organs, and so on. These recurrent sensations constitute the bodily self. In turn, infants begin to distinguish themselves from other objects. Allport believed that the bodily self remains an anchor for self-awareness throughout life. However, most adults are unaware of it unless pain or illness strike (e.g., we are usually unaware of our little finger until it is smashed in a door).

Sense of Self-Identity   The second aspect of the proprium to unfold, self-identity, is most evident when, through language, the child recognizes himself or herself as a distinct and constant point of reference. Unquestionably, the most important anchorage for the feeling of self-continuity as time passes is the child's own name. By learning his or her name, the child begins to realize that he or she is the same person in spite of the great changes in growth and interaction with the world that are taking place. Clothing, toys, and other precious possessions also

TABLE 6-1   DEVELOPMENTAL STAGES OF THE PROPRIUM AS PROPOSED BY ALLPORT

Stage	Aspect of proprium	Definition
1	Bodily self	Awareness of bodily sensations
2	Self-identity	Continuity of self despite changes taking place
3	Self-esteem	Pride in one's accomplishments
4	Self-extension	Self comes to include relevant aspects of the social and physical environment
5	Self-image	Goals and aspirations begin to reflect the expectations of significant others
6	Self as rational coper	Abstract reasoning and logic applied to solving everyday problems
7	Propriate striving	Unified sense of self and planning for long-range goals

strengthen this sense of identity. But self-identity is not firmly established all at once. For instance, a 2-year-old may be unaware that he or she is cold, feels tired, or needs to eliminate. Like Erikson, Allport felt that self-identity continually changes until it becomes consolidated in adulthood.

Sense of Self-Esteem   During the third year of life, the next form of the proprium—self-esteem—starts to emerge. For Allport, self-esteem is the feeling of pride that results when the child accomplishes things on his or her own. Self-esteem thus depends on the child's success in mastering tasks in the world. Parents frequently consider this the age of negativism since the child resists almost any adult proposal as a threat to integrity and autonomy. Allport argued that if parents frustrate the child's urge to explore and manipulate the environment, the sense of self-esteem can be outweighed by feelings of shame and anger.

Later, by the age of 4 or 5, self-esteem acquires a competitive flavor, reflected by the child's delighted ''I beat you!'' when she or he wins a game. Peer approval likewise becomes an important source of affirmed self-esteem as the childhood period continues to unfold.

Sense of Self-Extension   From approximately 4 to 6 years of age, the proprium is elaborated through self-extension. According to Allport, children experience self-extension as they come to realize that not only do their physical bodies belong to them but also do certain significant aspects of their environment, including people. During this period children learn the meaning of ''mine.'' With it comes jealous possessiveness, e.g., ''This is *my* ball,'' ''I *own* the doll house.'' *My* mommy, *my* sister, *my* dog, *my* house are regarded as integral parts of the self and are to be guarded against loss, especially against takeover by another child.

Self-Image   The fifth form of the proprium begins to develop around the age of 5 or 6. Now is the time when the child comes to know what parents, relatives, teachers, and others expect him or her to be. It is also during this period that the child begins to distinguish between the "good me" and the "bad me." As yet, however, the child has no clearly developed conscience, nor an image of how she or he would like to be as an adult. As Allport stated: "In childhood the capacity to think of oneself as one is, as one wants to be, and as one ought to be is merely germinal" (1961, p. 123).

Sense of Self as Rational Coper   Between 6 and 12 years of age, the child begins to realize that he or she has the rational capacity to find solutions to life's problems and thereby cope effectively with reality demands. Reflective and formal thought appear, and the child begins to think about thinking. But the child does not yet trust himself or herself to be an independent moral agent, but rather dogmatically believes that his or her family, religion, and peer group are right; this stage of propriate development reflects intense moral and social conformity.

Propriate Striving   Allport (1961) believed that the core problem for the adolescent is the selection of a career and other life goals. The adolescent knows that the future must follow a plan and, in this sense, her or his selfhood assumes a dimension entirely lacking in childhood. Pursuing long-range goals, having a sense of directedness and intentionality in striving for defined objectives, imparting to life a sense of purpose—this is the essence of propriate striving. In adolescence and young adulthood, however, propriate striving is not fully developed because the renewed search for self-identity comes into play. Much like Erikson's concept of ego-identity, Allport viewed the realization of propriate strivings as requiring a unified sense of selfhood. Only in adulthood, when all aspects of self are consolidated, does this occur.

In addition to the first seven aspects of the proprium just described, Allport (1961) suggested there is a *self-as-knower* that transcends and synthesizes all the other propriate functions. In his view, the self-as-knower represents the subjective self or the "I" which is aware of the objective "me." As the final stage in the development of the proprium, it refers to the unique human capacity for self-recognition and self-consciousness.

FUNCTIONAL AUTONOMY: THE PAST IS PAST

Basic to Allport's theory is the idea that personality is a dynamic (motivated) growing system. In fact, he held that "any theory of personality pivots upon its analysis of the nature of motivation" (1961, p. 196). Allport offered his own analysis of motivation by listing four requirements that an adequate theory of motivation must meet.

1 *It must recognize the contemporaneity of motives.* According to Allport, while knowledge about our past helps to reveal the present course of our lives, such historical facts are useless unless they can be shown to be dynamically active in the present. In his words, "Past motives explain nothing unless they are also present motives" (1961, p. 220). Thus, Allport disagreed with Freud's contention that the child is the father of the man.

2 *It must recognize the existence of many kinds of motives.* Many theorists have suggested that human motives can be reduced to one type, such as drive reduction, striving for superiority, or the need for security. Being a true eclectic, Allport felt that there is some truth in all these formulations of motivation, adding, "Motives are so diverse in type that we find it difficult to discover the common denominator" (1961, p. 221). Thus, many motivational concepts must be used if we are to understand the complex nature of human motivation. It is not possible, however, to reduce this complexity to one master motive.

3 *It must recognize the dynamic force of cognitive processes.* Not surprisingly, Allport insisted that an adequate theory of motivation must consider the person's long-range goals, values, and intentions. He believed that the key to understanding a person's present behavior is to ask, "What do you want to be doing five years from now?" or "What are you trying to do with your life?" Few other theorists covered in this text placed as much importance on the person's cognitive processes, especially future plans and intentions, as Allport did.

4 *It must recognize the concrete uniqueness of motives.* In contrast to theorists who assume a schedule of motives common to all people, Allport believed that the study of motivation must focus on how motives function in unique ways in each person's life. In addition, he argued that each person's motives must be defined concretely rather than abstractly. The distinction between a concrete and abstract description of a motive is illustrated by the following example.

Concrete: Susan intends to become a dentist.
Abstract: Susan is sublimating an aggressive drive.

The concept of *functional autonomy* of motives provides, in Allport's view, the necessary foundations for a theory of motivation which satisfies the four criteria specified above. In many ways it constitutes the core of his trait theory.

The concept of functional autonomy simply means that adult motives are not related to past motives. The past is past—no strings. In other words, the reasons why an adult now engages in some behavior are independent of whatever reasons that might have originally caused him or her to engage in that behavior. Put another way, the personality is liberated from its past; the bonds to the past are historical, not functional. Obviously, such a view of motivation angered psychoanalysts and behaviorists alike, with their respective strong emphases upon early childhood developmental stages and conditioning experiences as crucial to contemporary adult personality functioning.

Allport offered many examples to support his idea that much of adult behavior is caused by functionally autonomous motives. For instance, he pointed to the case of a young student

> who first undertakes a field of study in college because it is required, because it pleases his parents, or because it comes at a convenient hour may end by finding himself absorbed in the topic, perhaps for life. The original motives may be entirely lost. What was a means to an end becomes an end in itself. (1961, p. 235)

Other examples of behavior under the control of functionally autonomous motives includes (a) the skilled craftsman who perfects his product even though his income no longer depends on the extra effort; (b) the miser who continues to amass money while living in poverty; and (c) the businesswoman who continues to work hard even after attaining a comfortable salary. In each case the behavior that was once motivated by a need for money persists in the absence of that motivation. In other words, the original reason for the behavior is missing, yet the behavior persists. This is the essence of Allport's concept of functional autonomy.

Two Kinds of Functional Autonomy

Allport (1961) distinguished between two levels or types of functional autonomy. The first, *perseverative functional autonomy,* refers to feedback mechanisms in the nervous system that are governed by simple neurological principles. These mechanisms become neurologically self-maintaining over time and help to keep the organism on track. The marked inclination of people to satisfy their drives in familiar and routine ways (e.g., eating and going to bed at the same times each day) is an example of this type of functional autonomy.

In contrast to the repetitious activities that characterize perseverative auton-omy, *propriate functional autonomy* refers to the person's acquired interests, values, attitudes, and intentions. It is the master system of motivation that imparts consistency to the person's striving for a congruent self-image and a higher level of maturity and growth. Propriate autonomy further suggests that people need not be constantly rewarded to sustain their efforts:

> How hollow to think of Pasteur's concern for reward, or for health, food, sleep, or family, as the root of his devotion to his work. For long periods of time he was oblivious of them all, losing himself in the white heat of research. And the same passion is seen in the histories of geniuses who in their lifetime received little or no reward for their work. (Allport, 1961, p. 236)

Propriate functional autonomy, then, is a distinct step above merely "keeping the person going." It represents the striving for values and goals, the perception of the world in terms of those values and goals, and the sense of responsibility that people take for their lives.

Allport's concept of functional autonomy has been the target of considerable controversy and attack. Not only are those of psychoanalytic and behavioristic persuasion ruffled by it, but personologists of other theoretical persuasions would simply like to see some of the issues that this concept raises adequately ad-dressed. For instance, how does functional autonomy evolve? Precisely how does a motive divest itself of its childhood origin and still continue as a motive? And how does a motive evolve? Allport responded to such questions by noting that the phenomenon of functional autonomy would never be understood until the neu-rophysiological processes involved are elucidated. However, he did suggest that the process of propriate autonomy is governed by three psychological principles.

1 *The principle of organizing the energy level.* This principle states that propri-ate autonomy is possible because the energy level possessed by the person is in excess of that required to satisfy survival needs and demands for immediate adjustment. An example would be a retired person who channels his or her energies into new interests and activities.

2 *The principle of mastery and competence.* For Allport, mature adults are intrinsically motivated to master and extract meaning from the environment and to pursue future goals. Hence, whatever behavior enhances their competence will become incorporated into propriate striving.

3 *The principle of propriate patterning.* This principle asserts that all propriate motives are firmly rooted within the person's self-structure (proprium). As a result, the person structures his or her life around the proprium, pursuing that which enhances the self and rejecting the rest. Propriate patterning is a unifying tendency in personality and reveals Allport's view of the person as a process that is continually changing and becoming.

THE MATURE PERSONALITY

Unlike many personologists whose theories grew out of their work with unhealthy or immature personalities, Allport never practiced psychotherapy, nor did he consider clinical observations to be relevant to personality theorizing. He simply refused to believe that mature and immature people really had much in common. In fact, he felt that most other personologists of his day could not even identify a healthy personality, and, worse still, that there was little concerted effort to define or describe one. So Allport began a long search to establish an adequate description of the healthy personality, or what he termed the "mature personality."

Allport (1961) believed that the emergence of personal maturity is a continuous and lifelong process of *becoming*. He also saw a qualitative difference between the mature and the immature or neurotic personality. The behavior of mature persons is functionally autonomous and is motivated by conscious processes. In contrast, the behavior of immature persons is dominated by unconscious motives stemming from childhood experiences. Allport concluded that the psychologically mature adult is characterized by six attributes.

1 *The mature person has a widely extended sense of self.* Truly mature persons can get "outside" of themselves. They actively participate in work, family and social relationships, hobbies, political and religious issues, or whatever else they experience as valuable. Each activity requires authentic ego involvement and commitment resulting in some direction to life. For Allport, self-love is a prominent factor in everyone's life, but it need not dominate the person's life-style.

2 *The mature person has a capacity for warm social interactions.* There are two kinds of interpersonal warmth subsumed under this criterion—*intimacy* and *compassion*. The intimate aspect of warmth is seen in a person's capacity to show deep love for family and close friends unencumbered by possessive and jealous feelings. Compassion is reflected in a person's ability to tolerate differences (concerning values or attitudes) between the self and others, which allows the person to show profound respect and appreciation for the human condition and a sense of kinship with all people.

Mature persons are able to laugh at themselves and recognize the absurdities in life they share with the rest of humanity. *(Jim Harrison/Stock, Boston)*

3 *The mature person demonstrates emotional security and self-acceptance.* Mature adults have a positive image of themselves and are thus able to tolerate frustrating or irritating events as well as their own shortcomings without becoming inwardly bitter or hostile. They also deal with their emotional states (e.g., depression, anger, guilt) in such a way that they do not interfere with the well-being of others. For example, if they are having a bad day, they do not fly off the handle at the first person they see. Furthermore, they express their beliefs and feelings with consideration for those of others.

4 *The mature person demonstrates realistic perception, skills, and assignments.* Healthy people see things as they are, not as they wish them to be. They are in direct contact with reality; they do not continually distort it perceptually to fit their needs and fantasies. Moreover, healthy people possess appropriate skills for their work, provisionally setting aside personal desires and impulses while a task takes precedence. Allport quotes Harvey Cushing, the famous brain surgeon, to convey this aspect of maturity: "The only way to endure life is to have a task to complete" (1961, p. 290). Mature people, then, perceive other persons, objects, and situations for what they are; they possess sufficient skills to deal with reality; and they strive for personally relevant and realistic goals.

5 *The mature person demonstrates self-insight and humor.* Socrates observed that there is one paramount rule for achieving the good life: "Know thyself." Allport called this "self-objectification." By it, he meant that mature adults have an accurate picture of their own strengths and weaknesses. Humor is an important ingredient in self-insight because it prevents pompous self-glorification and just plain phoniness. It allows people to see and appreciate the utterly ludicrous aspects of their own or anyone else's life situation. Humor, as Allport saw it, is the ability to laugh at the things one cherishes (including oneself) and still cherish them.

6 *The mature person has a unifying philosophy of life.* Mature adults can "put it all together" with a clear, consistent, and systematic way of seeing meaning in their lives. Allport noted that people do not have to be an Aristotle in order to comprehend life's purpose in terms of an intelligible theory. Instead, they simply need a value system that will present them with a dominant goal or theme that makes their lives meaningful. Different people may develop different central values around which their lives will purposefully revolve. They may choose the pursuit of truth, social welfare, religion, or whatever—there is no one best value or philosophy in Allport's opinion. Allport's point is that a mature person has a set of deeply held values which serve as a unifying foundation for his or her life. A unifying philosophy of life therefore provides a kind of overriding value orientation that gives meaning and significance to practically everything the person does.

Attention is now shifted to the basic assumptions underlying Allport's dispositional theory of personality.

ALLPORT'S BASIC ASSUMPTIONS CONCERNING HUMAN NATURE

Allport waged a lifelong battle against those who insisted that their own systems offered the only legitimate way to understand human behavior. He especially took issue with psychoanalysis and behaviorism for failing to recognize the unique, conscious, and dynamic aspects of personality. Indeed, it was Allport, more than anyone else, who championed an eclectic approach to the study of personality. In his view, nearly all theories contribute important insights, principles, and perspectives to our understanding of human experience and behavior. At the same time, he believed that other theories grossly ignored the healthy, mature person.

> Some theories of becoming are based largely upon the behavior of sick and anxious people or upon the antics of captive and desperate rats. Fewer theories have derived from the study of healthy human beings, those who strive not so much to preserve life as to make it worth living. (Allport, 1955, p. 18)

The reasons underlying Allport's opposition to psychoanalysis and behaviorism are even more apparent when considering his basic assumptions about human nature (see Figure 6-3).

Freedom–Determinism With the exception of Alfred Adler, Allport supported the concept of human freedom more than any other personologist covered thus far in this text. This position is illustrated in a published conversation between Allport and Richard Evans: "I would say that we have more freedom than most of today's psychology admits. I would not, however, argue for the absolute, untrammeled freedom espoused by some of the existentialists. The answer lies somewhere in the middle course" (Evans, 1971, p. 59).

	Strong	Moderate	Slight	Midrange	Slight	Moderate	Strong	
Freedom			■					Determinism
Rationality	■							Irrationality
Holism		■						Elementalism
Constitutionalism				■				Environmentalism
Changeability				■				Unchangeability
Subjectivity			■					Objectivity
Proactivity	■							Reactivity
Homeostasis							■	Heterostasis
Knowability		■						Unknowability

FIGURE 6-3   Allport's position on the nine basic assumptions concerning human nature.

Allport's emphasis on freedom is most clearly revealed in his account of personality development. He viewed human growth as an active process of "becoming" in which the individual takes some responsibility for charting the course of his or her life. At least part of the "dynamic organization" so essential to Allport's definition of personality is thus self-determined.

However, Allport's trait concept puts serious limits on the absolute degree of freedom in human behavior. That is, once traits are formed in a person, they largely determine his or her perceptions and actions. As explained earlier, traits are potent governors of both selection of and responses to various stimuli. Human actions are thus initiated and guided by specific traits. Allport further believed that situational determinants play a central role in influencing a person's behavior. Thus, while granting significantly more free choice to people than is characteristically encountered in either psychoanalysis or behaviorism, Allport's overall commitment to human freedom is best judged as slight.

Rationality–Irrationality   Allport was extremely committed to the belief that human beings function in rational ways. In fact, he emphatically opposed Freud's emphasis on unconscious, irrational elements in human behavior (Allport, 1961). He agreed with Freud that such forces do dominate the lives of the emotionally disturbed—this, indeed, is what distinguishes neurotic from healthy individuals. But Allport argued that Freud erred in assuming that unconscious processes dominate the functioning of sound and healthy persons. Mature persons are fully capable of conscious, rationally based actions; they conduct their lives in terms of goals, long-range plans, and an overall philosophy—all of which are founded upon rationality.

The belief in human rationality underscores practically all of Allport's theoretical formulations. For example, he insisted that one important criterion of an adequate theory of motivation is that it attribute dynamic force to the person's cognitive processes, such as thinking, planning, and intending (Allport, 1961). He also considered the self as a rational coper to be an integral part of proprium development. Finally, it will be recalled that Allport described mature persons as possessing realistic perceptions, skills, and assignments. This clearly implies that such persons know where they are going and how to get there. In short, the Allportian person is exquisitely rational.

Holism–Elementalism   Allport's theory reflects an intricate interweaving of the holism and elementalism assumptions, although the former is considerably stronger in his system. To appreciate this counterbalance of forces, recall that Allport's unit of analysis is the "trait." People are studied largely in terms of their exhibited traits, which seems to suggest a straightforward, elementalist approach to personological research. Yet, Allport argued that personality will never be fully understood by examining each trait separately. While he believed that some system of "dimensions or conceptual schemata" (traits) was essential to personality study, Allport maintained that a trait must be related to the total pattern of personality of which it is a part (Evans, 1971).

Underlying the trait elements, then, is a unifying, holistic entity—the proprium—which includes all aspects of personality that contribute to inward unity (Allport, 1955). Moreover, the most essential ingredient in this totality of personality is propriate striving (Allport, 1961). Rather than being merely a static unity at any given time, the person is depicted as continually seeking inward unity by striving for distant goals, objectives, and ideals. While he recognized the empirical necessity of studying "elements" in personology, Allport believed that such elements can never be properly understood apart from the more holistic frame of reference of propriate striving.

Constitutionalism–Environmentalism   Allport strikes a near-perfect balance between constitution and environment in his conception of human nature. He believed that genetic and environmental factors are equally influential in determining human behavior.

For Allport, neither heredity alone nor environment alone determines the way personality is fashioned. Instead, it is through the reciprocal influence of heredity and environment that intelligence, interests, aptitudes, values, and any other personality characteristics emerge. Although he conceded that psychology still has much to learn about the precise operations of genetic and environmental influences (Evans, 1971), Allport regarded both as of equal importance in human functioning.

Changeability–Unchangeability   Allport's theory reflects an equal mixture of the changeability and unchangeability assumptions. A clue to the former is found in the phrase "dynamic organization" so central to his definition of personality. This phrase reveals that whatever personality is, there is at least some room for it to grow and evolve during the course of a lifetime. But, the real key to changeability in trait theory is found in Allport's conception of motivation. In his system, people are depicted as forward-moving, future-oriented, and growing.

And, as we noted in Chapter 1, one important reflection of the changeability assumption in any theory is a major concept that explains how people may be discontinuous with their past. Allport found such a concept in the functional autonomy of motives. According to this view of motivation, a person's motives can change during his or her life and, in this sense, so can the person.

The unchangeability assumption is equally evident in Allport's theory. The reader need consider only its title—a *trait* theory of personality—to grasp the idea. Traits are what account for the enduring aspects of a person's behavior over time and across situations. Such a perspective suggests that there are at least some important things about people that remain fairly stable over time. Further, as was also noted in Chapter 1, the unchangeability assumption is likely to reveal itself in concepts of core personality structures that underlie the individual's behavior throughout life. Allport's trait concept fits this description. His construct of the proprium as the subjective center of personality likewise suggests an underlying stream of stability. Thus, along the continuum of changeability-unchangeability, Allport's overall position is best judged as midrange.

Subjectivity–Objectivity   Despite Allport's interest in the uniqueness of the individual personality, he did not regard subjective experience (subjectivity) as particularly critical in understanding the person. Specifically, in his approach to personality study he considered uniqueness to be of paramount importance. However, in his system it is to be found in the dynamic organization of personal dispositions rather than in the quality of the person's subjective experience. There is, then, a difference between the concepts of *uniqueness* and *subjectivity*. Allport strongly emphasized the former in his theory while manifesting at best only a slight commitment to the latter.

The subjectivity assumption surfaces when Allport's concept of the proprium is examined. The proprium encompasses all those aspects of personality that are distinctive and relevant to the person's life. It aids the person in drawing distinctions between matters of subjective importance and matters of fact. Yet, while Allport's proprium contains within it the seeds of subjectivity, he did not regard subjectivity per se as the key to understanding a person. For him, the world of subjective experience is only one component of many that constitute the complexity of personality. Psychology, in his view, will become truly scientific only when it can deal with the issue of individual uniqueness.

Proactivity–Reactivity   In describing the concept of propriate striving, Allport noted that directedness, or intentionality, is the cement that holds a person's life together. That is, in order to function well, a person needs a defining objective toward which he or she strives. The assumption of proactivity evident in this description is even more unmistakable in Allport's caricature of propriate patterning: "The essential nature of man is such that it presses toward a relative unification of life (never fully achieved). . . . As a consequence of this quest—which is the very essence of human nature—we note that man's conduct is to a large degree proactive . . . " (Allport, 1961, p. 252).

For Allport, people live in a world of future goals, life ambitions, and strivings which are generated from within. Functional autonomy serves to sever reactive ties to the past; propriate striving negates any account of behavior merely in terms of reactions to present stimuli. Allport's commitment to the proactivity assumption is strong and explicit.

Homeostasis–Heterostasis Allport recognized the validity of homeostatic drives as the primitive and animal-like part of human motivation. But he also insisted that tension reduction does not account for all human conduct. Basically, Allport felt that growth and change are the most conspicuous features of the human personality. "The healthy child and adult are continually building up tensions . . . and are going way beyond the basic, safety level of homeostasis. New experiences, which most of us crave, cannot be put in terms of tension-reduction, nor can our desire to acquire knowledge for its own sake, to create works of beauty and usefulness, nor to give and receive love. . . ." (Allport, 1961, p. 90). Thus, there is a strong commitment to heterostasis throughout Allport's theory.

Knowability–Unknowability Like most other humanistically minded person-ologists, Allport was less than optimistic about the ultimate power of scientific methodology to unravel the mystery of human behavior. More to the point, he believed that although it is possible to study specific aspects of the individual, science alone could not provide total understanding of human nature. As an illustration, Allport (1966) advocated what he termed "heuristic realism" as the basic empirical approach to personality study. This doctrine holds that inasmuch as within every individual there exist generalized action tendencies or traits, it is psychology's task to discover what they are. Because traits are never directly observed but only inferred, however, there are major scientific obstacles to uncovering their true nature. Yet the persistent "heuristic realist" presses onward. While he knows that his efforts probably will not wholly succeed, because of both the complexity of personality and the inadequacy of present methods for its study, he prefers to believe that the future of personality is partly or approximately knowable (Allport, 1966).

In effect, Allport maintained that personality can be studied empirically—but one defined "limb" at a time. The degree to which science can eventually put these appendages together to form the complete person, however, remains a largely unanswered question. Furthermore, Allport's idiographic approach to personality research, emphasizing as it does, normal individual development, renders it difficult to grasp human nature as a whole because it studies people one at a time. Perhaps Allport said it best in concluding his discussion of the "heuristic realism" approach to the study of the person: "Along the way we regard him as an objectively real being whose tendencies we can succeed in knowing—at least in part . . ." (Allport, 1966, pp. 8–9). Allport's commitment to the knowability assumption is therefore less than complete.

EMPIRICAL VALIDATION OF TRAIT THEORY CONCEPTS

To what extent have psychologists demonstrated the empirical validity of All-port's theoretical conceptions of personality? An exhaustive search of the relevant literature indicates that Allport has stimulated almost no research designed to validate his theory of traits to date. Several renowned writers in personology agree (Maddi, 1989; Pervin, 1989; Ryckman, 1989). Although Allport certainly has a creative personological system, it seems that almost no one has taken the time or trouble to test the empirical validity of its concepts and relational statements. In an empirical discipline like psychology, no theory will endure unless it generates testable predictions based on its major constructs. Allport's theory is no exception.

Two factors account for the paucity of research bearing on Allport's theory. First, the theory is populated with rather vague and ill-defined concepts. Concepts such as propriate striving, self as rational coper, and personal disposition do not readily lend themselves to operational definition. Second, Allport neglected to specify the ways in which his trait concepts are related to his formulations about the development of the proprium. In fact, the various developmental stages of the proprium are described in general terms, and there is little attempt to specify the variables that control the emergence, maintenance, and modification of the phenomena of the self. Given these obstacles, it remains very difficult to design adequate empirical tests of Allport's theory.

Although trait theory has failed in the heuristic sense, it has had some influence on those presently studying and writing about personality (Maddi, 1989). Allport's impact can be largely attributed to his strong advocacy for the *idiographic* study of individuals. This approach seeks to understand a particular person's characteristic pattern of behaving. Within personology, researchers using the idiographic approach have typically gathered information through autobiographical histories, personal diaries and letters, dream reports, open-ended questionnaires, and verbatim recordings of interviews. These techniques can reveal a wealth of information about individual uniqueness (Carlson, 1988; Lamiell, 1987). However, Allport cautioned that such procedures should not be used to the exclusion of formal methods associated with the *nomothetic* approach. This approach seeks to establish lawful principles of personality functioning that apply to people in general. As Allport viewed it, the individual person should be studied on his or her own terms—that is, idiographically. At the same time, he also argued that personologists should be open to alternative methods of study if they are to understand the relationship between traits and behavior.

Letters from Jenny: An Idiographic Trait Study

The value of idiographic methods as a means of revealing an individual's personal dispositions is best illustrated in Allport's *Letters from Jenny* (1965). This case study was based on the personal correspondence of a middle-aged woman named Jenny Grove Masterson who wrote, during the last years of her life, some 300 letters to a young married couple living and teaching in an Eastern college town. Allport acquired Jenny's letters in the 1940s, and he subsequently used them as pedagogical material in his personality course at Harvard. The following are excerpts from those letters (Allport, 1965):

> Ross called to see me last week—he is still in the Dr.'s hands. He looks very poorly. I invited him to . . . have luncheon with me, and he did. . . . It was a swell luncheon, and he seemed to enjoy it. You know . . . the way to bring Ross to his senses is to give him what he wants and then leave him alone. (p. 70)

> I did not intend to say so much, but I'm heartsore, and sick, and truly discouraged. Ross cares absolutely nothing at all for me—I am a great drawback and burden to him. (p. 53)

Allport (1942) asked 39 judges to read Jenny's letters in sequence and then to characterize her central dispositions. Labeled *content analysis,* this procedure resembles a commonsense, or impressionistic, approach to personality study. The judges listed 198 trait names to describe Jenny, several of which proved to be synonyms, so Allport reduced the list to eight central traits which he felt were highly descriptive of Jenny's personality. Baldwin (1942), one of Allport's students, subsequently extended the content analysis of Jenny's letters to include a more elaborate and statistical treatment of the data. Using a method called *personal structure analysis,* he instructed raters to count the number of times particular topics and themes (e.g., money, art, women, nature) occurred in each of the letters and to correlate such categories of thought that clustered together. Baldwin's study confirmed that Jenny's personality was described quite accurately in terms of the eight central traits which had emerged from Allport's prior analysis.

Paige (1966), yet another of Allport's protégés, conducted a still more qualified analysis of Jenny's letters. He used a computer program specifically designed to recognize and "tag" certain designated adjectives in the letters that were used in conjunction with each other. For example, any terms Jenny used to express aggression, hostility, and opposition were coded together under the tag category "Attack." The program also yielded the frequency with which various tag words in a given letter were associated with all others in the same letter. Paige then subjected these tag categories to a factor analysis. Based on this computerized evaluation of the document, eight highly stable trait factors were identified as descriptive of Jenny. These factorially derived traits turned out to be quite similar to Allport's list. Table 6-2 lists in parallel fashion the clusters obtained by content analysis based on a careful reading of the series, along with the factors obtained by Paige in his factorial study. Allport interpreted the similarity of the two lists (derived from two divergent types of analysis) as indicative of the validity of his subjective impressions about Jenny's personality-trait structure.

Is Behavior Traitlike?

Over the past two decades the trait approach to personality has been the subject of a particularly interesting and important controversy. This controversy concerns

TABLE 6-2   CENTRAL TRAITS IN JENNY'S PERSONALITY AS DETERMINED BY
IMPRESSIONISTIC AND FACTOR-ANALYTIC METHODS OF ASSESSMENT

Commonsense traits	Factorial traits
1 Quarrelsome–suspicious, aggressive	**1** Aggression
2 Self-centered (possessive)	**2** Possessiveness
3 Sentimental	**3** Need for affiliation, need for family acceptance
4 Independent–autonomous	**4** Need for autonomy
5 Esthetic–artistic	**5** Sentience
6 Self-centered (self-pitying)	**6** Martyrdom
7 (No parallel)	**7** Sexuality
8 Cynical–morbid	**8** (No parallel)
9 Dramatic–intense	**9** ("Overstate")

Source: Adapted from Allport, 1966, p. 7.

the degree to which people's behavior actually does show traitlike consistency across time and circumstances. To a large extent, this question is not asked within the dispositional perspective, since trait theorists assume that people's behavioral tendencies are stable over time and across situations. It follows from this assumption that measures of a trait (usually a self-report questionnaire) should accurately predict other behaviors that are conceptually related to the trait. That is, if people are stable in their personality traits, then the thoughts, feelings, and actions that reflect a given trait should be highly correlated across different situations.

Critics of trait theory have focused on two key points. First, they argue that people often behave differently in different situations. It was a 1968 book, *Personality and Assessment,* by Walter Mischel, that claimed that people exhibit far less consistency across situations than is assumed by trait theorists. Mischel reviewed decades of research and concluded that "with the possible exception of intelligence, highly generalized behavioral consistencies have not been demonstrated, and the concept of personality traits as broad predispositions is thus untenable" (1968, p. 146). In light of these realities, Mischel maintains that behavior is characterized by more situational specificity than consistency. Second, the critics of trait theory suggest that traits reflect nothing more than labels for behaviors we believe go together (Schweder, 1982). In other words, traits represent our stereotypes or conceptions of personality characteristics that we assume go together rather than actual consistencies in behavior. Needless to say, these two criticisms of trait theory have generated lively debate because they strike at the very heart of the concept of personality itself. Why, indeed, should the concept of personality be considered important in predicting behavior if people are not consistent in their actions?

Evidence in support of Mischel's (1968, 1973) contention that situational factors exert more influence than personality traits in determining how people act is quite impressive. Specifically, he showed that the correlation is weak between behavior performed in one situation and behavior along the same dimension performed in a different situation. In fact, the average cross-situational correlation coefficient that he estimated was only +.30 (1.00 is perfect). Such a small coefficient means that behavior as assessed in one situation accounts for only 9 percent (.30 × .30 = .09 = 9 percent) of the behavior being measured in another situation, with the remaining 91 percent left unaccounted for. In practical terms, this implies that someone who is very shy in one situation might be very outgoing in another.

Aggregating Behaviors   Mischel's views have attracted many critics who have sought to defend the value of the trait position. For instance, Epstein (1983, 1986) argues that the data used in much of the research reviewed by Mischel involved single acts or measures of behavior on single occasions and thus led to an underestimate of cross-situational consistency. According to Epstein, researchers typically use a personality trait measure to predict a single measure of behavior, such as the amount of time spent working on a challenging laboratory task or the likelihood of donating blood, as indicated on a 10-point scale. While the trait measure itself may be a good predictor of the behavior under study, Epstein argues that this would never be known because the single measure of behavior is likely to be highly unreliable. It is no wonder, states Epstein, that correlations between personality trait scores and behavior often fail to break the +.30 barrier. The problem is simply that researchers do not measure behavior correctly. The solution is aggregation.

As a research procedure, *aggregation* involves gathering single measures of the same behavior on numerous occasions. For instance, if the amount of time students watch television is a topic of interest, the researcher would observe their behavior each night over the course of several weeks. This would enable the researcher to obtain a far more reliable and representative estimate of how much time students spend in front of the "boob tube" than by observing them just one night. By aggregating data, Epstein and other dispositional personologists contend that consistency between trait measures and behavior should be found. Epstein (1979) has demonstrated this point in four separate studies. He found that there was a large increase in the stability coefficients for several kinds of measures (e.g., physiological measures, headaches, positive and negative emotions, social behavior) when the number of occasions upon which the measures were based increased. A number of other studies also support the usefulness of aggregation in establishing links between personality traits and behavior (for a review of this literature, see Rushton et al., 1983).

Identifying Consistent Traits   Other researchers have argued that Mischel neglected to consider that some people are more consistent than others in behavior and that a particular person will be more consistent on some traits than on other traits (Bem & Allen, 1974; Kenrick & Stringfield, 1980). The heart of this argument is that traits are only likely to predict behavior among people for whom the trait is especially relevant. In reference to Allport, these would be either cardinal or central dispositions.

Kenrick and Stringfield (1980) explored this line of reasoning by having subjects complete a self-report measure of 16 traits and then go back and indicate how much their behaviors varied from situation to situation for each of the traits. Subjects also placed marks next to the single traits among the 16 on which they felt they were most and least consistent from one situation to another. Finally, Kenrick and Stringfield had parents and friends of the subjects complete the same 16-trait rating scale as they applied to the subject. The average correlation between subject's self-reports and report of the raters was $r = +.25$. However, when guided by the notion that some people may be more consistent than others, a different pattern of results emerged. Specifically, when Kenrick and Stringfield considered only the trait that each subject marked as "most consistent," the self/parent, self/friend, and parent/friend ratings correlated $r = +.62$, $r = +.61$, and $r = +.61$, respectively. On the other hand, when they considered only the trait that each subject marked as "least consistent," the three kinds of ratings correlated $r = +.16$, $r = +.12$, and $r = +.39$, respectively. These results suggest a picture of traitlike stability if one studies people who view themselves as consistent on that trait. It should be noted, however, that Kenrick and Stringfield did not obtain ratings of actual behavior. Mischel and Peake (1982, 1983) have shown that studies using the method employed by Kenrick and Stringfield yield high levels of prediction only when global personality trait ratings are used, not when actual behavior is considered. Nonetheless, recent studies have confirmed Kenrick and Stringfield's findings, and a growing number of personologists see the method as potentially useful in predicting behavior among people for whom the trait is relevant (Baumeister & Tice, 1988).

Interactionism   The traitism–situationism debate has subsided in recent years. Many personologists now recognize that both personality traits and situational variables are important determinants of behavior. This approach, termed *interactionism*, represents the idea that we should pay more attention to how personality traits and situations interact with each other to influence behavior. This is an idea with a long history. In fact, Allport wrote as early as 1937 (p. 331) that "traits are often aroused in one situation and not in another." He is to be credited for recognizing more than 50 years ago an ascending theme in personality psychology today. We will say more about the importance of interactionism when we review Bandura's social cognitive theory in Chapter 8.

Let us now consider an application of Allport's theory.

APPLICATION: THE STUDY OF VALUES

We noted earlier in this chapter that Allport stressed the importance of a unifying philosophy of life in his description of the mature person. He also maintained that such a philosophy is founded upon *values*—basic convictions about what is and is not of real importance in life. Believing that a person's efforts to find order and meaning in life are governed by values, Allport proceeded to identify and measure basic value dimensions. The success of his effort is evident in the well-known personality test that he helped to develop—the *Study of Values*. This test was originally published in 1931 and is currently in its third edition (Allport et al., 1960). Within the framework of trait theory, this test illustrates Allport's attempt to dissect an enormously complex component of personality (values) into empirically measurable terms.

To accomplish this difficult task, Allport needed a conceptual model that could account for value differences among persons. He found the required model in the work of Eduard Spranger, a European psychologist. In his book *Types of Men,* Spranger (1922) outlined six major value types. Conceived as the basic alternative value directions evidenced in human life, not as six main types of people, these values are found in varying degrees in all people; people construct the unity of their lives around them (Allport, 1961). Thus, no one person falls exclusively under any one value category; rather, different value combinations are more or less salient in the lives of different people. For Allport, these values are best described as deep-level traits. They are described as follows:

1 *The Theoretical.* The person emphasizing this value is primarily concerned with the discovery of *truth.* Such a person is characterized by a rational, critical, and empirical approach to life. The theoretical person is highly intellectual and tends to pursue a career in science or philosophy.

2 *The Economic.* The economic person places highest value on whatever is *useful* or *pragmatic.* He or she is thoroughly "practical" and conforms closely to the stereotype of the successful American businessperson. Such a person is keenly interested in making money and regards unapplied knowledge as wasteful. Many great feats of engineering and technology have resulted from the demands that economic persons have made upon science.

3 *The Aesthetic.* This person places highest value on *form* and *harmony.* Judging each single experience from the standpoint of grace, symmetry, or fitness, such a person perceives life as a procession of events, with each individual impression enjoyed for its own sake. The person need not be a creative artist but is aesthetic to the degree that his or her chief interest is in the artistic episodes of life.

4 *The Social.* The highest value of the social type is *love of people.* Such a person is likely to view the theoretical, economic, and aesthetic attitudes as cold and inhuman, regarding love as the only suitable form of human relationship. In its purest form, the social attitude is altruistic and closely related to the religious value.

5 *The Political.* The dominant interest of the political person is *power.* Vocational activities of this type of person are not necessarily confined to the realm of politics, since leaders in any field generally place a high value on power and influence. Thus, clear individual differences in the power value do exist. At the

Industrial and technological development often results from the demands that economic persons make upon science. *(Joseph Schuyler/Stock, Boston)*

same time, direct expression of this motive overrides all others in that political types yearn for personal power, influence, and renown above all else.

6 *The Religious.* This person is mainly concerned with understanding the world as a *unified whole.* There are, however, different modes of expressing this desire to understand. For instance, some religious persons are "immanent mystics" who find meaning in the affirmation and active participation in life, while others are "transcendental mystics," striving to unite themselves with a higher reality by withdrawing from life (e.g., monks). Regardless of the particular type of expression, the religious person seeks unity and higher meaning in the cosmos.

Allport assessed individual differences in the relative strength of these six values by means of the *Study of Values* test. Developed and standardized with college students, the test consists of 45 questions and requires about 20 minutes to complete. Like other multidimensional personality tests, the *Study of Values* yields scores on each value dimension which are then combined to form an overall profile of the test taker. These profiles are particularly helpful for classroom demonstration and can be of value when helping clients select occupations. On the whole, the reliability and validity data support the utility of the test. Also, average scores on the six values differ in expected directions for different occupational groups. Business students score highest on the economic value, art and design students on the aesthetic value, and theology students on the religious value (Allport et al., 1960). Although no longer as popular as it once was, the test accurately reflects Allport's belief that values are an essential ingredient of an individual's personality.

FACTOR ANALYTIC APPROACHES TO PERSONALITY

In contrast to Allport's idiographic study of traits, a dramatically different perspective on trait psychology is provided by a statistical technique known as *factor analysis*. Theorists who utilize factor analysis assume that the fundamental dimensions of personality are common to everyone; that is, the core elements out of which personality structure is formed are universal. Factor analytic trait theorists further assume that people have enduring predispositions to respond in consistent ways and that there is a hierarchical organization to basic personality dimensions. Finally, such theorists believe that we can quantitatively measure the degree to which various traits reside in different people. The emphasis placed on the quantitative measurement of traits is a key feature of factor analytic approaches to personality study. Two notable figures illustrating this rigorously quantitative science of traits are Raymond Cattell and Hans Eysenck. Their respective contributions to personology are the focus of this chapter section. First, however, we need to take a brief detour and consider the procedural steps involved in conducting a factor analysis of the unitary structures of personality.

The Method of Factor Analysis

Factor analysis is a highly complicated mathematical procedure and well beyond the scope of this book, but its underlying logic is relatively simple to grasp. In effect, it is a method that attempts to determine the degree of covariation among a large set of psychological variables as they are measured across a large group of subjects. The basic assumption is that certain characteristics correlate, or covary, in such a way as to define a separate psychological dimension or factor. By examining patterns of covariation ("what goes with what"), factor analysis allows us to take large masses of data based upon different measures and reduce them into a smaller, more manageable set of clusters or factors. Suppose, for example, that an investigator wants to determine the interrelationships among 50 different personality variables, each represented by a score on a test or an item in a test. Rather than attempting to study all the interrelationships among these variables (over 12,000 correlations), the investigator can search for a smaller number of variables that characterize the overall set of 50. The variables forming the smaller set are called *factors*.

The initial step in performing a factor analysis is to obtain measures of several variables from a large sample of subjects. The measures may take many forms, including self-reports, observer ratings, and objective behavioral assessments. The type or source of data is not important provided that the same kinds of measures are used for all subjects. It should be obvious that exactly what data are collected and analyzed has a profound impact on what personality dimensions emerge from a factor analytic study. What comes out of factor analysis depends on what the psychologist puts into it!

The second step in the procedure is to determine the degree of relationship of every variable with every other variable in the total set. Thus, in a 50-variable study, the relationship between variable one and variable two, and that between one and three, two and four, and so on, must be determined as well as the relationship between variables two and three, two and four, and so on. The measure of degree of relationship is the correlation coefficient, and the total array of correlations among all variables is the *correlation matrix*. The following step is to determine whether or not there are clusters of variables within the total correlation matrix that go together to form dimensions or functional unities of the total set. In this procedure, called *factor extraction,* the multiple intercorrelations among all variables are reduced to a relatively small number of factors. Variables that are strongly intercorrelated are considered to be measuring, to a great extent, the same factor. At bottom, factors "are simply structures or patterns produced by covariances of measures" (Kerlinger, 1973, p. 671).

Once the common factors have been extracted from the correlation matrix, the next step in the analysis is to determine the factor loadings of the individual measures on the factors. *Factor loadings* are correlations between the factor as a whole and the specific item measures that comprise the factor. This is an indication of the degree to which an item measure goes along with the underlying dimension that constitutes the factor. Item measures that correlate relatively strongly with the factor (usually required to be higher than .40) are said to "load on" that factor. By contrast, item measures that do not correlate strongly with the factor are not considered to contribute to the factor. In short, the nature of the factor is defined by the item measures that load on it.

The final step in factor analysis is to name or label the factors. The labeling process is intended to reflect, as closely as possible, the content of the item measures that load on the factor—particularly the item measures with the highest loadings. The label chosen for a given factor suggests something about what it is that a group of related cluster of item measures or variables may be measuring. It should be noted that the label assigned to a given factor is highly subjective and may lead to problems and disagreements. For instance, two psychologists studying the same set of factors may choose different names for each one and thus arrive at different conclusions about the nature of the dimensions underlying the set of variables being investigated. Therefore, extreme care must be exercised in selecting factor or trait names.

In summary, factor analysis is a statistical tool for summarizing and simplifying sets of variables, reducing a relatively large set of variables to a relatively small set of personality trait dimensions or factors. The procedural steps in carrying out a typical factor analysis are these: (1) collecting measures from a large number of subjects on each of a number of variables; (2) intercorrelating all variables; (3) extracting factors from the correlation matrix; (4) determining the factor loadings of the item measures on the factors; (5) interpreting and naming the factors. With this preliminary information about the mechanics of factor analysis in hand, let us now examine how Cattell and Eysenck have used the procedure to identify the basic dimensions of human personality.

RAYMOND CATTELL: A Trait Theory of Personality

Unlike many other theorists, Cattell did not begin with clinical impressions or intuitive notions about human nature. Rather, his approach to personality is based firmly on using rigorous empirical methods of research. Cattell's commitment to constructing a scientific model of behavior is guided by one central goal: to discover (by the method of factor analysis) the basic traits of personality. He believes, as did Allport, that traits constitute the core structure of personality and are ultimately responsible for what a person will do in a given situation. Also like Allport, Cattell distinguishes between common and unique traits. However, he disagrees with Allport's view that traits actually exist within the person. For Cattell, traits do not have any real physical or neural status, and, as such, can be inferred only from precise measurement of overt behavior.

Cattell's effort to develop a trait theory of personality based on sophisticated statistical analyses of objective behavioral data is to be applauded. This effort has also resulted in perhaps the most complex system of thought in personology today. Despite the complexity of his theory, Cattell's concepts demand serious consideration by the student of personality.

BIOGRAPHICAL SKETCH

Raymond B. Cattell was born in 1905 in Staffordshire, England. He recalls in his autobiography (Cattell, 1974) that his childhood years were happy and filled with such activities as sailing, exploring caves, and swimming. However, the relative tranquility of his childhood was interrupted when England entered World War I. Barely 9 years old, Cattell saw hundreds of wounded soldiers returning from France being treated in a converted hospital near his home. He later realized how these experiences shaped his own life: "Silently there came an abiding sense of seriousness into my life, compounded of a feeling that one could not be less dedicated than these [wounded soldiers], and of a new sense, for a boy, of the brevity of life and the need to accomplish while one might" (Cattell, 1974, p. 63).

At 16 Cattell entered King's College of the University of London, where he majored in physics and chemistry. A few months before graduating with high honors, he realized that his training in the physical sciences did not prepare him for an already strong interest in social problems. Disregarding the advice of classmates and friends, Cattell decided to pursue a graduate degree and career in psychology. He received his Ph.D in 1929 from the University of London. During his years of graduate study, Cattell served as research assistant to Charles Spearman, the famous British psychologist who developed the method of factor analysis.

Raymond B. Cattell. *(Courtesy of Raymond B. Cattell)*

After receiving his doctorate in psychology, Cattell worked for 5 years (1932–1937) as a director of a psychology clinic in England before going to New York to spend a year as a research associate of the learning theorist E. L. Thorndike at Columbia University. He has remained in the United States ever since. In 1938 he joined the faculty of Clark University as G. Stanley Hall Professor of Psychology and then subsequently accepted a position as lecturer in psychology at Harvard in 1941. In 1945, Cattell moved to the University of Illinois, where he was to remain for nearly 30 years as Director of the Laboratory of Personality and Group Analysis. Cattell retired from the University of Illinois in 1973 and moved to Boulder, Colorado, where he founded the Institute for Research on Morality and Self-Realization. Since 1977 he has been a visiting professor at the University of Hawaii, as well as Professor Emeritus at Illinois. As of this writing, he is still actively involved in research and writing.

One of the most prolific of all personality theorists, Cattell has published some 35 books and 400 research articles in the course of his career. His more notable books include *Description and Measurement of Personality* (1946); *Personality: A Systematic, Theoretical, and Factual Study* (1950); *The Scientific Analysis of Personality* (1965); *The Inheritance of Personality and Ability* (1982); and *Beyondism: Religion from Science* (1987).

TRAIT THEORY: BASIC CONCEPTS AND PRINCIPLES

Cattell's theory seeks to explain the complicated transactions between the personality system and the more inclusive sociocultural matrix of the functioning organism. He is convinced that an adequate theory of personality must take into account the multiple traits that comprise the personality, the extent to which these traits are genetically and environmentally determined, and the ways in which genetic and environmental factors interact to influence behavior. He also contends that an adequate theory of personality functioning and growth must be firmly grounded in systematic research methods and precise measurements. Multivariate statistics and factor analysis are his preferred methods for personality study.

According to Cattell (1965), personality is that which permits us to predict what a person will do in a given situation. In line with his mathematical analysis of personality, he maintains that the prediction of behavior can be achieved by means of a *specification equation*. The general formula used by Cattell to predict behavior with any degree of accuracy is stated in the following form:

$$R = f(S, P)$$

What this formula signifies is that the nature of a person's specific response (R), meaning what he or she does or thinks or verbalizes, is some unspecified function (f) of the stimulus situation (S) at a given moment in time, and of the existing personality structure (P). The specification equation indicates that the person's specific response to any given situation is a function of all the combined traits relevant to that situation, each trait interacting with situational factors that may affect it.

Cattell recognizes how difficult it is to predict a person's behavior in a given situation. To increase predictive accuracy, the personologist must consider not only what traits a person possesses but also such nontrait variables as the person's temporary moods and particular social roles called for in the situation. Furthermore, it is necessary to weigh each trait according to its relevance to the situation in question. For example, if the person were in an emotionally arousing situation, the trait of anxiety would be assigned a high weight in predicting his or her response. Therefore, the equation $R = f(S, P)$ is an oversimplification of Cattell's trait theory. However, for learning purposes, this general formula conveys Cattell's strong belief that human behavior is determined and can be predicted.

Structural Principles: Categories of Traits

Although Cattell acknowledges that behavior is determined by the interaction of traits and situational variables, his major organizing concept of personality resides in his descriptions of the various kinds of traits he has identified. For Cattell, traits are relatively permanent and pervasive tendencies to respond with consistency from one situation to another and from one time to another. To put it another way, traits are hypothetical mental structures inferred from behavior which predispose the person to behave uniformly across various circumstances and across time. Traits reflect the person's stable and predictable characteristics and are by far the most important of Cattell's concepts.

As noted previously, Cattell (1965, 1978) relies heavily on factor analysis to investigate the structural elements of personality. As a result of conducting many different factor analyses of data collected on thousands of subjects, he concludes that traits can be classified or categorized in several ways. Let us consider the ways in which traits (Cattell also uses the term *factors*) can be distinguished.

Surface Traits versus Source Traits   A *surface trait* is represented by a set of behavioral characteristics that all seem to "hang" together. For instance, the observed characteristics of inability to concentrate, indecision, and restlessness may cluster together to form the surface trait of neuroticism. Here, the trait of neuroticism is evidenced by a cluster of overt elements that seem to go together; it does not derive from any single one. Because surface traits do not have a unitary basis and are not consistent over time, Cattell does not regard them as having explanatory value in accounting for behavior.

Source traits, in contrast, are the basic, underlying structures which Cattell views as constituting the building blocks of personality. They represent the unitary dimensions or factors that ultimately determine the consistencies in each person's observed behavior. In effect, source traits exist at a "deeper" level of the personality and are the causes of behavior in diverse domains over an extended period of time.

After extensive factor analytic research, Cattell (1979) concluded that approximately 16 source traits constitute the underlying structure of personality (see Table 6-3). These personality trait factors are perhaps best known in connection with a scale that now measures them: the *16 PF* (Sixteen Personality Factor Questionnaire). This self-report scale, along with several others that Cattell designed, has proved to be quite useful and popular in both applied and research settings. Further discussion of source traits as assessed by the 16 PF will follow shortly.

Constitutional versus Environmental-Mold Traits   Cattell maintains that source traits can be divided into two subtypes—depending on their origins. *Constitutional traits* derive from the biological and physiological conditions of the person. For example, recovery from cocaine addiction may cause a person to be momentarily irritable, depressed, and anxious. Cattell would contend that these behaviors result from changes in the person's physiology and thus reflect constitutional source traits.

Environmental-mold traits, on the other hand, are determined by influences in the social and physical environment. These traits reflect learned characteristics and styles of behaving and form a pattern that is imprinted on the personality by the individual's environment. Thus, a person who is raised on a Midwest farm behaves differently than a person who grows up in an inner-city ghetto.

Ability, Temperament, and Dynamic Traits   Source traits can be further classified in terms of the modality through which they are expressed. *Ability traits* determine the person's skill and effectiveness in pursuing a desired goal. Intelligence, musical aptitude, and hand–eye coordination are a few examples. *Temperament traits* relate to other emotional and stylistic qualities of behavior. For example, people may either work quickly or slowly on a task or respond calmly or hysterically to a crisis. Cattell considers temperament traits to be constitutional source traits that determine a person's emotionality. Finally, *dynamic traits* reflect the motivational elements of human behavior. These are traits that activate and direct the person toward particular goals. Thus, a person may be charac-

TABLE 6-3   MAJOR SOURCE TRAITS AS REPRESENTED ON THE SIXTEEN PERSONALITY FACTOR INVENTORY (16 PF)

Factor label	Cattell's label for the factor	High score description	Low score description
A	Outgoing–Reserved	easygoing adventurous warmhearted	cynical stiff detached
B	Intelligence	bright abstract-thinking	stupid concrete-thinking
C	Stable-Emotional	mature realistic calm	changeable unrealistic uncontrolled
E	Dominant–Submissive	self-assertive competitive stubborn	humble retiring meek
F	Sober– Happy-go-lucky	serious taciturn	enthusiastic light-hearted
G	Conscientious–Expedient	responsible moralistic stoic	disregards rules neglectful fickle
H	Venturesome–Shy	adventurous uninhibited	timid aloof
I	Tough-minded– Tender-minded	self-reliant independent	clinging dependent
L	Trusting–Suspicious	accepting of conditions	hard to fool
M	Imaginative–Practical	creative artistic	conventional down-to-earth concerns
N	Shrewd–Forthright	socially skilled astute	socially clumsy unpretentious
O	Apprehensive–Placid	worrying troubled	secure complacent
Q1	Radical–Conservative	freethinking liberal	respecting traditional ideas
Q2	Self-sufficient– Group-dependent	prefers own decisions	sound follower
Q3	Undisciplined–Controlled	follows own urges	exacting
Q4	Relaxed–Tense	composed tranquil	driven overwrought

Source: Adapted from *The Scientific Analysis of Personality* by R. B. Cattell, 1965.

terized as ambitious, power-oriented, or interested in acquiring material possessions.

Common versus Unique Traits   Like Allport, Cattell (1965) also believes that classifying traits as either common or unique makes sense. A *common trait* is one that is shared in varying degrees by all members of the same culture. Examples include self-esteem, intelligence, and introversion. *Unique traits,* in contrast, are those shared by few or perhaps no other people. Cattell suggests that unique traits are especially evident in the areas of interests and attitudes. For example, Sally is the only person with a consuming interest in collecting 1930 infant mortality records for the countries of Sweden and Canada. Very few people, if any, would share this interest.

Practically all of Cattell's research focuses on common traits, but the acknowledgement of unique traits in his theory provides a means for him to emphasize the uniqueness of our personalities. He further suggests that the organization of common traits within our personalities is always unique. However, we should not be misled by Cattell's recognition of the unique combination of traits within a single person. In reality, he is far more concerned with discovering general principles of behavior than in understanding the personality of a single individual.

Sources of Data for Factor Analysis

We have already noted that Cattell places heavy emphasis on the use of factor analysis to identify the major traits of personality. However, before the factor analytic procedure can be applied, masses of data must first be collected from large numbers of people. Cattell draws his data from three basic sources: life record data (L-data), self-rating questionnaire data (Q-data), and objective test data (OT-data).

The first, *L-data,* involves the measurement of behavior in actual, everyday situations such as school performance or interactions with peers. Such data may also include trait ratings provided by people who know the person well in real-life settings (e.g., co-workers). *Q-data,* by contrast, refers to the person's self-ratings about his or her behavior, feelings, or thoughts. Such information reflects the person's introspections and self-observations. Cattell has developed numerous specific self-report tests to obtain Q-data, the most notable being the Sixteen Personality Factor Questionnaire (Cattell et al., 1970). At the same time, he has expressed concern about this type of data when subjects may not know themselves very well or may deliberately bias or falsify their answers. Thus, he warns investigators that these data must be interpreted with caution. Finally, *OT-data* are derived from the creation of special situations in which the person's performance on certain tasks may be objectively scored. The defining characteristic here, according to Cattell, is that the person is placed in contrived "miniature situations" and responds without being aware of the dimensions on which he or she is being evaluated. For example, a person may be asked to respond to a Rorschach test in which the inkblots do not provide him or her with unambiguous information he or she can fake. Therefore, OT-data are resistant to faking.

Empirical Derivation of Source Traits   Cattell refers to his reliance on multiple data sources in order to capture the complexity of personality as a *multivariate research strategy.* This approach takes into account many different manifestations of personality simultaneously but involves no experimental manipulation of variables. Cattell argues that if multivariate, factor analytic research is indeed able to determine the true functional unities of personality, then the same factors or source traits should be obtained from the three different kinds of data. This is a logical assertion assuming that each data source is in fact measuring common underlying trait dimensions in the personality.

Initially, Cattell conducted factor analytic studies using only L-data and found 15 factors that appeared to account for most of personality. He and his associates then sought to determine whether similar factors would emerge from Q-data. Literally thousands of questionnaire items were constructed and administered to large numbers of people and factor analyses were conducted to see which items went together. The result of this massive research effort is the 16 PF. A list of source traits derived from the 16 PF is presented in Table 6-3. In general, the factors found with Q-data match those found with L-data, but some were unique to each kind of data. Specifically, the first 12 factors listed in Table 6-3 were found in both Q-data and L-data, whereas the last 4 factors were derived from Q-data that could not be matched to L-data.

Concerning the strength of source traits, Cattell (1965) proposes that one trait is stronger than another if it has high loadings in more samples of the *personality sphere* (i.e., the total domain of traits that can be used to describe people). Thus, factor A (outgoing–reserved) is the strongest trait listed in Table 6-3 since it exerts more influence on behavior in various situations than any other trait. Whether the situation is performance in the college classroom, efficiency of the office secretary, battle record of the field soldier, or success in marriage, factor A makes a significant contribution to performance. There are fewer situations in which factor B (more intelligent–less intelligent) makes an important contribution, still fewer in which factor C (stable–emotional) plays a significant role, and so on down the list. The strength of a trait, then, is determined by its importance in controlling variation in behavior across settings.

Role of Heredity and Environment   Cattell is virtually unique among major personologists in that he has tried to determine the relative contributions of heredity and environment to the development of traits. He devised a statistical procedure for this purpose—*multiple abstract variance analysis (MAVA)*—that estimates not only the presence or absence of genetic influence but also the degree to which traits are due to genetic or to environmental influences (Cattell, 1960). MAVA involves gathering data on the resemblances between identical twins raised in the same family, non-twin siblings raised in the same family, identical twins raised apart, and non-twin siblings raised apart. Results from the MAVA technique (based on personality tests administered to assess a particular trait) suggest that the importance of genetic and environmental influences varies widely from trait to trait. For example, his data indicate that about 65 to 70 percent of the variation in scores on measures of intelligence and assertiveness can be accounted for by genetic factors, whereas the genetic influence on traits such as conscientiousness and neuroticism is perhaps half that. In general, Cattell estimates that about two-thirds of personality is determined by environmental influences and one-third by heredity.

In addition to the influence exerted by immediate situational factors, Cattell believes that much of people's behavior is determined by the groups to which they belong (such as families, churches, peer groups, schools, and nations). Just as people can be described in terms of their traits, so can traits be used to describe social groups with which people are affiliated. The trait dimensions along which groups can be objectively described are called their *syntality*. Using factor analysis, Cattell (1949) studied the syntality of various religious, school, and peer groups. He also investigated several traits that compose the syntality of entire nations (Cattell et al., 1952). The major traits found to identify the syntality of countries included size, morale, affluence, and industriousness. No other personologist has done more than Cattell to provide a detailed description of the traits characterizing an entire society and their impact on people's behavior.

Concluding Comments

If prominence in the field of personality were measured by the sheer volume of research, then Cattell would be considered as the foremost personologist of our time. His research has touched almost every issue we have deemed relevant to personality theory—structure, development, motivation, psychopathology, psychological health, and change. Furthermore, we cannot help but be impressed by his efforts to construct a theory based on precise measurement techniques. As one supporter notes, there is a great deal to admire about Cattell: "It seems fair to say that Cattell's original blueprint for personality study has resulted in an extraordinarily rich theoretical structure that has generated more empirical research than any other theory of personality" (Wiggins, 1984, p. 190). Unfortunately, however, Cattell's theory has been overlooked by many personality psychologists and is virtually unknown among the general public. Critics point out that Cattell's work is couched in technical language and thus difficult to understand. There have also been specific criticisms directed at his heavy reliance on factor analysis and the subjectivity involved in naming or interpreting the source traits derived from this statistical method. Despite the lack of attention and acclaim he rightly deserves, Cattell remains convinced that his approach will eventually enable us to understand the structure and function of personality. We hope that this brief review will encourage students to read more about Cattell's trait theory of personality. His undergraduate text, *The Scientific Analysis of Personality* (1965), is highly recommended.

Cattell is by no means the only personologist concerned with discovering the basic structure of personality traits. Hans J. Eysenck has also employed factor analysis to identify the number of dimensions needed to explain human behavior. Eysenck's trait-type theory is discussed next and completes our coverage of the dispositional perspective on personality.

HANS EYSENCK: A Trait-Type Theory of Personality

Eysenck agrees with Cattell that the goal of psychology is to predict behavior. He also shares Cattell's commitment to factor analysis as the way to piece together the personality puzzle. However, Eysenck's use of factor analysis differs some-what from Cattell's. Eysenck's research strategy is to begin with a well-developed hypothesis about some basic trait one wants to measure, followed by precise measurement that pertains to this trait. In contrast, Cattell contends that by administering batteries of tests and then subjecting the resulting data to factor analysis, the natural elements of personality will emerge. Thus, Eysenck's ap-proach is far more theoretically anchored than is Cattell's. Also unlike Cattell, Eysenck is convinced that no more than three *supertraits* (which he calls *types*) are needed to account for most of human behavior. As you will recall, Cattell points to at least 16 traits or factors of personality structure. Finally, Eysenck places far more emphasis on the importance of genetic factors in personality development than does Cattell. This is not to say that Eysenck ignores environ-mental or situational influences on personality, but he argues that traits and types are determined primarily by heredity. Although the exact influence of genetics on behavior is still uncertain, a growing number of psychologists believe that Ey-senck might be right (Loehlin et al., 1988).

BIOGRAPHICAL SKETCH

Hans Jurgen Eysenck was born in Berlin, Germany, in 1916. Both his parents were in the entertainment field. His father was an acclaimed actor and singer, and his mother was a silent film star. They planned a career in show business for their son, and at the age of 8 Eysenck had a minor role in a movie. However, his parents divorced when he was 2 years old, so he was raised by his maternal grandmother.

Upon graduation from high school, Eysenck decided to pursue his education abroad, in part because he wanted to escape the rise of Nazi persecution. Years later he wrote, "I knew that there was no future for me in my unhappy homeland" (Eysenck, 1982, p. 289). After a year in France, he settled in England, where he studied psychology at the University of London. In 1940 he completed his Ph.D. During World War II, Eysenck worked as a psychologist at a psychiatric hospital where military patients suffering from stress reactions were treated. Following this, in 1946, he became a lecturer in psychology at the University of London and, simultaneously, director of the Institute of Psychiatry at Maudsley Hospital in London. He also served as a visiting professor in various universities in the United States. He retired from the Psychology Department at the University of London in 1983. He is presently writing his autobiography as well as enjoying his favorite hobby, tennis.

Eysenck has been an extremely prolific author, publishing approximately 45 books and 600 research articles. His major theoretical works include *Dimensions of Personality* (1947); *The Scientific Study of Personality* (1952); *The Structure of Human Personality* (1970); and *Personality and Individual Differences* (coauthored with his son, Michael Eysenck, 1985). Eysenck is also a highly controversial figure in psychology. This is due in part to his central role in two of psychology's most heated debates—the heritability of intelligence and the effec-

Hans J. Eysenck. *(Courtesy of Hans J. Eysenck)*

tiveness of psychotherapy. He has argued that intelligence is mostly determined by heredity, and that traditional, verbal therapies (notably psychoanalysis) have little or no value in the treatment of mental disorders. Both of these positions have been less than wholeheartedly accepted in the field, as Eysenck has acknowledged. "I have usually been against the establishment and in favor of the rebels. But I prefer to think that on these issues the majority were wrong, and I was right" (Eysenck, 1982, p. 298).

BASIC CONCEPTS AND PRINCIPLES OF TRAIT-TYPE THEORY

The essence of Eysenck's theory is that the elements of personality can be arranged hierarchically. In this scheme (indicated in Figure 6-4), certain supertraits or *types*, such as extraversion, exert a powerful influence over behavior. In turn, he sees each of these supertraits as being comprised of several component *traits*. The component traits either are more superficial reflections of the underlying type dimension, or are specific qualities that contribute to that dimension. Finally, traits are composed of numerous *habitual responses,* which, in turn, are derived from a multitude of *specific responses*. Consider, for example, a person who is observed to make the specific responses of smiling and holding out his hand upon meeting someone. If we observe him to do it every time he meets someone, we can assume that this behavior is his habitual response for greeting another person. This habitual response may correlate with other habitual responses, such as liking to talk to other people, going to parties, and so forth. This cluster of habitual responses forms the trait of sociability. As illustrated in Figure 6-4 on the trait level, sociability correlates with such response dispositions as activity, liveliness, and assertiveness. Taken together, these traits define a supertrait or type that Eysenck calls *extraversion*.

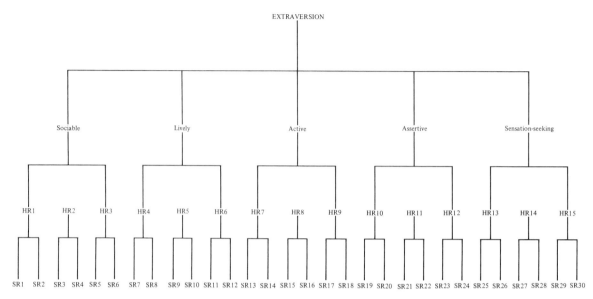

FIGURE 6-4   Eysenck's hierarchical model of personality structure. (*Source: Adapted from* The Biological Basis of Personality *by H. J. Eysenck, 1967, p. 36)*

In considering Eysenck's *hierarchical model* of personality structure, it should be noted that the word "type" refers to dimensions of personality that he regards as normally distributed along a continuum. Thus, for example, the type concept of extraversion is a dimension with a low end and a high end along which people may fall at various points between the two extremes. It is not a dimension on which people can be classified as either low or high; Eysenck does not imply discontinuity when he uses the word "type."

Basic Personality Types

Eysenck has used a variety of procedures for gathering data about people: self-reports, observer ratings, biographical information, assessments of physique and physiology, and objective psychological tests. These data are factor analyzed to determine the structure of personality. In his early research, Eysenck (1947, 1952) found two basic type dimensions that he labeled as *introversion–extraversion* and *neuroticism–stability* (a factor sometimes called *instability–stability*). These two personality dimensions are orthogonal, that is, they are statistically independent of each other. Accordingly, it is possible to separate people into four groups, each being a combination of low or high on one type dimension, together with low or high on the other type dimension. As shown in Table 6-4, a series of traitlike adjectives define the characteristics associated with each categorical type. Two points should be kept in mind when considering the nature of these four groups.

TABLE 6-4 FOUR SEPARATE CATEGORIES OF PEOPLE BASED ON THE TWO MAJOR DIMENSIONS OF PERSONALITY PROPOSED BY EYSENCK Each category, including the traits that are embedded in it, results from the combination of a high or low level of introversion or extraversion with either a high or low level of stability or neuroticism.

	Stable	Neurotic
Introvert	Calm Even-tempered Reliable Controlled Peaceful Thoughtful Careful Passive	Moody Anxious Rigid Sober Pessimistic Reserved Unsociable Quiet
Extravert	Leadership Carefree Lively Easygoing Responsive Talkative Outgoing Sociable	Touchy Restless Aggressive Excitable Changeable Impulsive Optimistic Active

Source: Adapted from *The Inequality of Man* by H. J. Eysenck, 1975.

First, both type dimensions are normally distributed and continuous and thus allow for a wide range of individual differences. Second, the trait descriptions associated with each type category are of relatively extreme individuals. Most people tend to be closer to the midpoint between high and low endpoints on both type dimensions and therefore have less extreme characteristics than are listed in Table 6-4.

As revealed in Table 6-4, people who are both introverted and stable tend to be controlled, careful, and thoughtful in their actions. Conversely, the combination of introversion and neuroticism tends to create a more anxious, pessimistic, and reserved quality in behavior. The combined qualities of extraversion and stability introduce a carefree, easygoing, and sociable quality into behavior. Finally, people who are high in both extraversion and neuroticism tend to be aggressive, impulsive, and excitable. We should add that, for Eysenck, individual differences are to be valued. Thus, no single combination of these personality types is more desirable than another. Behaving in carefree and outgoing ways has its good and bad points, as does behaving in quiet and reserved ways. The ways are simply different.

More recently, Eysenck (1976) has added a third type dimension of personality, which he calls *psychoticism-superego strength*. People high on this supertrait dimension tend to be egocentric, impulsive, insensitive to others, and opposed to social customs. They are often seen as troublesome, as not fitting in well with others, and as intentionally upsetting other people. Eysenck has suggested that psychoticism is a genetic predisposition toward becoming either psychotic or psychopathic. He further regards it as a personality continuum along which all people can be located and as being more common in men than in women.

Neurophysiological Bases of Traits and Types   An intriguing aspect of Eysenck's theory is his attempt to specify a neurophysiological basis for each of his three personality supertraits or types. Introversion–extraversion is closely linked to levels of *cortical arousal* as indicated by electroencephalographic recordings. Eysenck (1982) uses the term "arousal" to denote a continuum of excitation, ranging from a lower extreme (e.g., sleep) to an upper extreme (e.g., state of panic). He believes that introverts are overaroused and thus are highly sensitive to incoming stimulation; for this reason, they avoid situations that are apt to overwhelm them. In contrast, Eysenck suggests that extraverts are underaroused and thus are highly insensitive to incoming stimulation; accordingly, they constantly seek out situations that are apt to excite them.

Eysenck hypothesizes that individual differences in stability–neuroticism reflect the degree to which the *autonomic nervous system* reacts to stimuli. Specifically, he links this dimension with the limbic system, the brain's visceral or feeling system, which influences motivation and emotional behavior. Persons high on neuroticism tend to react more quickly to painful, novel, disturbing, or other stimuli than do more stable persons. Such persons also exhibit a more persistent reaction (even after the stimulus has disappeared) than do highly stable persons.

Eysenck's work on specifying the basis for the psychoticism dimension is in an exploratory stage. However, he tentatively links this dimension with the *androgen hormone system,* in which chemicals from the body's endocrine glands are released into the blood and, in turn, regulate the development and maintenance of masculine characteristics. There is very little research to support Eysenck's speculations about the association between sex hormones and psychoticism.

Eysenck's neurophysiological interpretation of the dimensions of personality is closely tied to his theory of psychopathology. In particular, the kind of symptoms or disorders that befall a person are related to the combined impact of personality traits and nervous system functioning. For instance, the person who is high on the dimensions of introversion and neuroticism is a prime candidate for anxiety disorders: phobias, obsessions, and compulsions. In contrast, the person who is high on the extraversion and neuroticism dimensions is at risk for psychopathic (antisocial) disorders. However, Eysenck hastens to add that psychological disorders do not automatically occur as a result of genetic predisposition. "What is genetically inherited are predispositions for a person to act and behave in a certain manner, when put in certain situations" (Eysenck, 1982, p. 29). Accordingly, Eysenck's belief in the genetic foundations of various disorders is tempered by his equally strong belief that environmental factors can alter to some extent the development and maintenance of such disorders.

Measurement of Personality Traits   Like Cattell, Eysenck has constructed a number of self-report questionnaires to assess individual differences associated with his three supertrait dimensions of personality. The most recently developed of these inventories is the *Eysenck Personality Questionnaire (EPQ)* (Eysenck & Eysenck, 1975). Sample items from the EPQ are presented in Table 6-5. It should be noted that the EPQ includes items relevant to the measurement of each of the trait factors that comprise Eysenck's model of personality structure. Additionally, the EPQ includes a lie scale aimed at detecting a person's tendency to fake responses to look good. A Junior EPQ has been constructed for use with children between the ages of 7 and 15 (Eysenck & Eysenck, 1973).

The fact that Eysenck and Cattell use different personality questionnaires to obtain data for their factor analytic studies may partially explain why they differ in their estimates of the number of traits needed to account for personality. This is because the results of factor analysis are very dependent on the source or type of data obtained. In any case, Eysenck is convinced that his two major type dimensions, introversion–extraversion and stability–neuroticism, have been empirically validated by several researchers using many different types of personality tests.

TABLE 6-5   SAMPLE ITEMS FROM THE EYSENCK PERSONALITY QUESTIONNAIRE

Extraversion–introversion		
1 Do you like going out a lot?	Yes	No
2 Do you like mixing with people?	Yes	No
3 Would you call yourself happy-go-lucky?	Yes	No
Stability–instability		
1 Does your mood often go up and down?	Yes	No
2 Are you an irritable person?	Yes	No
3 Do you often feel "fed-up"?	Yes	No
Psychoticism		
1 Do good manners and cleanliness matter to you?	Yes	No
2 Do you try not to be rude to people?	Yes	No
3 Do you enjoy cooperating with others?	Yes	No
Lie scale		
1 Do you sometimes laugh at a dirty joke?	Yes	No
2 As a child did you always do as you were told immediately and without grumbling?	Yes	No

Source: Adapted from the adult EPQ by Eysenck and Eysenck, 1975; published by EdITS (Educational and Industrial Testing Service), San Diego, Calif.

Most of this supporting evidence comes from studies focused on behavioral differences between introverts and extraverts.

Differences Between Introverts and Extraverts

Eysenck places great emphasis on the conceptual clarity and precise measurement of his theoretical concepts. To date, most of his efforts have been aimed at determining whether there are significant differences in behavior associated with individual differences along the *introversion–extraversion* continuum. Eysenck argues that individual differences in behavioral functioning can be discovered through factor analysis and measured through the use of questionnaires as well as in laboratory procedures. Our brief review reflects this overall methodology.

A review of studies (Wilson, 1978) based on testing predictions derived from Eysenck's theory presents an impressive array of findings. For instance, extraverts have greater tolerance for pain than do introverts; they engage in more talk and coffee breaks at work than do introverts; and excitement enhances their performance whereas it interferes with the performance of introverts. Some additional empirically established ways in which introverts and extraverts have been found to differ include:

Research suggests that extraverts participate in exciting activities in order to increase their level of cortical arousal. *(Bill Ross/Woodfin Camp & Associates)*

1 Introverts prefer theoretical and scientific vocations (e.g., engineering and chemistry), whereas extraverts tend to prefer people-oriented jobs (e.g., sales and social work).

2 Introverts report more frequent masturbation than do extraverts, but extraverts engage in sexual intercourse earlier in life, more often, and with more partners than do introverts.

3 Introverts attain higher grades in college than do extraverts. Also, students who withdraw from college for psychiatric reasons tend to be introverts, whereas those who withdraw for academic reasons tend to be extraverts.

4 Introverts show higher arousal levels in the mornings, whereas extraverts show higher arousal levels in the evening. Furthermore, introverts work better in the morning, and extraverts work better in the afternoon.

One of the most striking differences between introverts and extraverts is in their sensitivity to stimulation. This difference can be easily demonstrated by the "lemon drop test" (Corcoran, 1964). When four drops of lemon juice are placed on a person's tongue, it turns out that introverts secrete almost twice the amount of saliva as do extraverts. The basis of this interesting finding is related to different patterns of physiological functioning in introverts and extraverts. Specifically, Eysenck proposes that the ascending reticular activating system in the brain stem is responsible for controlling the differences in response to stimulation between introverted and extraverted subjects.

Concluding Comments

There is much to be admired in Eysenck's diligent efforts to piece together the personality puzzle. He is regarded by many psychologists as a first-rate scholar who is highly creative in his attempts to establish a scientific model of personality structure and functioning. Throughout his writings, Eysenck has consistently emphasized the role of neurophysiological and genetic factors in explaining individual differences in behavior. In addition, he has stressed the need for rigorous measurement as the cornerstone for constructing a sound theory of personality. Also noteworthy are his contributions to the study of criminology, education, psychopathology, and behavior change. In general, it seems reasonable to conclude that Eysenck's theory will increase in popularity as efforts continue to refine and extend his trait position at both theoretical and empirical levels.

SUMMARY

The dispositional view assumes that people possess stable inner qualities that endure over time and across situations. In addition, emphasis is placed on the traitlike ways in which individuals differ from each other. As an early proponent of trait theory, Gordon Allport regarded the explanation of an individual's uniqueness as the paramount goal of psychology. He viewed personality as the dynamic organization of those internal psychophysical systems that determine a person's characteristic behavior and thought.

Allport considered the trait as the most valid unit of analysis for understanding and studying personality. In his system, traits are predispositions to respond in an equivalent manner to various kinds of stimuli. In short, traits account for a person's behavioral consistency over time and across situations. They may be classified under one of three headings—cardinal, central, or secondary—according to their degree of pervasiveness within a personality. Allport also distinguished between common and personal dispositions. The former are generalized traits to which most people within a given culture can be compared, whereas the latter refer to characteristics peculiar to a person which do not permit comparisons with others.

The overall construct that unifies traits and provides direction for the person's life is termed the proprium. This concept designates the "self-as-known," including all aspects of personality that contribute to an inward sense of unity. Another key concept in Allport's theory is that of functional autonomy. This principle asserts that adult motives are not related to the earlier experiences in which they originally appeared. Allport further distinguished between perseverative functional autonomy (feedback mechanisms in the nervous system) and propriate functional autonomy (the person's acquired interests, values, attitudes, and intentions). The latter allows for the development of the truly mature person, the salient characteristics of which Allport carefully delineated.

Allport's opposition to psychoanalytic and behavioristic conceptions of personality are clearly evident in his basic assumptions concerning human nature. His trait theory reflects (1) a strong commitment to the assumptions of rationality, proactivity, and heterostasis; (2) a moderate commitment to the holism and knowability assumptions; (3) a slight commitment to the assumptions of freedom and subjectivity; and (4) a midrange position on the constitutionalism–environmentalism and changeability–unchangeability dimensions.

While trait theory has stimulated almost no research to date in direct support of its core concepts, Allport has made some interesting empirical contributions to the personological literature. He advocated the idiographic approach to personality study, which is directed toward uncovering the uniqueness of each person. One such study, *Letters from Jenny,* was described to illustrate the potential value of personal documents in identifying a person's unique pattern of traits.

Trait theories of personality have been the target of criticism in recent years. Mischel argues that people show far less consistency across situations and over time than is claimed by trait psychologists. He also maintains that behavior is determined primarily by situational factors. Supporters of the trait position have counterargued that evidence for cross-situational consistency does exist when behavior is measured correctly. Epstein reports that when single measures of behavior are aggregated over several occasions, traits do predict consistent trends in behavior. Some personologists have argued that significant correlations between traits and behavior are likely only among people for whom a trait is relevant. A study supporting that prediction based on self-report measures of friendliness and conscientiousness was described. Finally, it was noted that the interaction between traits and situational factors is becoming a dominant view in personology.

The application of Allport's theory was discussed in reference to the Study of Values. Based on Spranger's value types, this self-report personality test assesses the relative strength of six different value orientations Allport believed to be essential to a unifying philosophy of life. Brief descriptions of people whose lives are dominated by either theoretical, economic, aesthetic, social, political, or religious values were presented.

Factor analytic theorists like Raymond Cattell and Hans Eysenck have used sophisticated assessment and statistical techniques to discover the basic traits that underlie personality structure. Factor analysis is a tool for determining the degree of covariation among a large set of variables as they are measured across a large group of people. The procedure was described in terms of collecting multiple measures from a large number of people, generating a table of intercorrelations among the measured variables (the correlation matrix), determining the factor loadings, and naming the factors that emerged.

Cattell's trait theory views personality as that which permits us to predict what a person will do in a given situation, as expressed in the equation $R = f(S, P)$. For Cattell, traits are hypothetical constructs which predispose the person to behave consistently across circumstances and time. He sees the essence of personality structure as consisting of approximately 16 source trait factors. In turn, source traits can be divided into constitutional or environmental-mold traits. Ability, temperament, and dynamic traits represent additional categories of trait classifications in Cattell's system. Cattell also makes a distinction between common and unique traits.

Cattell uses three types of data to identify source traits: life records (L-data), self-rating questionnaires (Q-data), and objective tests (OT-data). The Sixteen Personality Factor Questionnaire (16 PF) was devised by Cattell to measure source traits using self-report data. Cattell also developed a statistical tool called multiple abstract variance analysis to estimate the relative contributions of heredity and environment to a given trait. He estimates that one-third of personality is determined by genetics and two-thirds by environmental influences. Finally, he has studied how the syntality or defining characteristics of groups influence personality.

The trait-type theory of Eysenck is also based on factor analysis. His hierarchical model of personality structure includes the dimensions of types, traits, habitual responses, and specific responses. Types represent supertrait dimensions along which people may be located at various points between two extremes. Eysenck emphasizes that personality types are dimensional and that most people do not fall into separate categories.

Unlike Cattell, Eysenck sees only two major types or traits as underlying personality structure: introversion–extraversion and stability–neuroticism. Overt behaviors resulting from the combinations of these two type dimensions were discussed. For instance, people who are both introverted and stable tend to be controlled in their actions, whereas people who are extraverted and stable tend to be carefree. Eysenck argues that individual differences in these two supertraits, as well as a third factor called psychoticism–superego strength, are closely linked to differences in neurophysiological functioning. Eysenck places far more emphasis on the genetic foundations of traits than does Cattell.

Eysenck has developed several questionnaires to assess the three major supertraits underlying his hierarchical model of personality. The Eysenck Personality Questionnaire was illustrated and research showing behavioral differences between introverts and extraverts was cited.

BIBLIOGRAPHY

Allport, G. W. (1937). *Personality: A psychological interpretation*. New York: Holt, Rinehart and Winston.

Allport, G. W. (1942). *The use of personal documents in psychological science*. New York: Social Science Research Council. Bulletin 49.

Allport, G. W. (1950). *The individual and his religion*. New York: Macmillan.

Allport, G. W. (1955). *Becoming: Basic considerations for a psychology of personality*. New Haven, CT: Yale University Press.

Allport, G. W. (1960). *Personality and social encounter: Selected essays*. Boston: Beacon Press.

Allport, G. W. (1961). *Pattern and growth in personality*. New York: Holt, Rinehart and Winston.

Allport, G. W. (Ed.) (1965). *Letters from Jenny*. New York: Harcourt, Brace & World.

Allport, G. W. (1966). Traits revisited. *American Psychologist,* **21,** 1–10.

Allport, G. W. (1967). Autobiography. In E. Boring & G. Lindzey (Eds.), *A history of psychology in autobiography* (Vol. 5, pp. 1–25). New York: Appleton-Century-Crofts.

Allport, G. W. (1968a). *The person in psychology: Selected essays*. Boston: Beacon Press.

Allport, G. W. (1968b). Personality: Contemporary viewpoints (1). In D. Sills (Ed.), *International encyclopedia of the social sciences*. New York: Macmillan and Free Press.

Allport, G. W., & Allport, F. H. (1928). *A-S reaction study*. Boston: Houghton Mifflin.

Allport, G. W., Vernon, P. E., & Lindzey, G. (1960). *A study of values* (3rd ed.). Boston: Houghton Mifflin.

Baldwin, A. (1942). Personal structure analysis: A statistical method for investigating the single personality. *Journal of Abnormal and Social Psychology,* **37,** 163–183.

Baumeister, R. F., & Tice, D. M. (1988). Meta-traits. *Journal of Personality,* **56,** 571–598.

Bem, D. J., & Allen, A. (1974). On predicting some of the people some of the time: The search for cross-situational consistencies in behavior. *Psychological Review,* **81,** 506–520.

Carlson, R. (1988). Exemplary lives: The use of psychobiography for theory development. *Journal of Personality,* **56,** 105–138.

Cattell, R. B. (1946). *Description and measurement of personality*. New York: World Book.

Cattell, R. B. (1949). The dimensions of culture patterns by factorization of national character. *Journal of Abnormal and Social Psychology,* **44,** 443–469.

Cattell, R. B. (1950). *Personality: A systematic, theoretical, and factual study*. New York: McGraw-Hill.

Cattell, R. B. (1960). The multiple abstract variance analysis equations and solutions: for nature-nurture research on continuous variables. *Psychological Review, 67,* 353–372.

Cattell, R. B. (1965). *The scientific analysis of personality.* Baltimore: Penguin Books.

Cattell, R. B. (1974). Autobiography. In G. Lindzey (Ed.), *A history of psychology in autobiography* (Vol. 6, pp. 59–100). Englewood Cliffs, NJ: Prentice-Hall.

Cattell, R. B. (1978). *The scientific use of factor analysis.* New York: Plenum.

Cattell, R. B. (1979). *Personality and learning theory: The structure of personality in its environment* (Vol. 1). New York: Springer.

Cattell, R. B. (1982). *The inheritance of personality and ability.* New York: Academic Press.

Cattell, R. B. (1987). *Beyondism: Religion from science.* New York: Praeger.

Cattell, R. B., Bruel, H., & Hartman, H. P. (1952). An attempt at a more refined definition of the cultural dimensions of syntality in modern nations. *American Sociological Review, 17,* 408–421.

Cattell, R. B., Eber, H. W., & Tatsuoka, M. M. (1970). *Handbook for the 16 personality factor questionnaire.* Champaign, IL: IPAT.

Corcoran, D. W. (1964). The relation between introversion and salivation. *American Journal of Psychology, 77,* 298–300.

Epstein, S. (1979). The stability of behavior. I. On predicting most of the people most of the time. *Journal of Personality and Social Psychology, 37,* 1097–1126.

Epstein, S. (1983). A research paradigm for the study of personality and emotions. In M. M. Page (Ed.), *Personality: Current theory and research.* Lincoln: University of Nebraska Press.

Epstein, S. (1986). Does aggregation produce spuriously high estimates of behavioral stability? *Journal of Personality and Social Psychology, 50,* 1199–1210.

Evans, R. (1971). Gordon Allport: A conversation. *Psychology Today,* April, 62–65.

Eysenck, H. J. (1947). *Dimensions of personality.* London: Routledge & Kegan Paul.

Eysenck, H. J. (1952). *The scientific study of personality.* London: Routledge & Kegan Paul.

Eysenck, H. J. (1967). *The biological basis of personality.* Springfield, IL: Charles C. Thomas.

Eysenck, H. J. (1970). *The structure of human personality* (3rd ed.). London: Methuen.

Eysenck, H. J. (1975). *The inequality of man.* London: Temple Smith.

Eysenck, H. J. (1976). *Sex and personality.* Austin: University of Texas Press.

Eysenck, H. J. (1982). *Personality, genetics, and behavior.* New York: Praeger.

Eysenck, S. B., & Eysenck, H. J. (1973). Test-retest reliabilities of a new personality questionnaire for children. *British Journal of Educational Psychology, 43,* 26–130.

Eysenck, H. J., & Eysenck, M. W. (1985). *Personality and individual differences.* New York: Plenum.

Eysenck, H. J., & Eysenck, S. B. (1975). *Manual of the Eysenck Personality Questionnaire.* San Diego, CA: EdITS.

Kenrick, D. T., & Stringfield, D. O. (1980). Personality traits and the eye of the beholder: Crossing some traditional philosophical boundaries in the search for consistency in all of the people. *Psychological Review, 87,* 88–104.

Kerlinger, F. N. (1973). *Foundations of behavioral research* (2nd ed.). New York: Holt, Rinehart and Winston.

Lamiell, J. T. (1987). *The psychology of personality: An epistemological inquiry.* New York: Columbia University Press.

Loehlin, J. C., Willerman, L., & Horn, J. M. (1988). Human behavior genetics. *Annual Review of Psychology, 39,* 101–133.

Maddi, S. R. (1989). *Personality theories: A comparative analysis* (5th ed.). Homewood, IL: Dorsey Press.

Mischel, W. (1968). *Personality and assessment.* New York: Wiley.

Mischel, W. (1973). Toward a cognitive social learning reconceptualization of personality. *Psychological Review, 80,* 252–283.

Mischel, W., & Peake, P. K. (1982). Beyond déjà vu in the search for cross-situational consistency. *Psychological Review, 89,* 730–755.

Mischel, W., & Peake, P. K. (1983). Analyzing the construction of consistency in personality. In M. M. Page (Ed.), *Personality: Current theory and research.* Lincoln: University of Nebraska Press.

Paige, J. (1966). Letters from Jenny: An approach to the clinical analysis of personality structure by computer. In P. Stone (Ed.), *The general inquirer: A computer approach to content analysis.* Cambridge, MA: MIT Press.

Pervin, L. A. (1989). *Personality: Theory and research* (5th ed.). New York: Wiley.

Rushton, J. P., Brainerd, C. J., & Pressley, M. (1983). Behavioral development and construct validity: The principle of aggregation. *Psychological Bulletin, 94,* 18–38.

Ryckman, R. M. (1989). *Theories of personality* (4th ed.). Pacific Grove, CA: Brooks/Cole.

Schweder, R. A. (1982). Fact and artifact in trait perception: The systematic distortion hypothesis. In B. A. Maher & W. B. Maher (Eds.), *Progress in experimental personality research* (Vol. 11). New York: Academic Press.

Spranger, E. (1922). *Lebensformen* (3rd ed.). Halle, Germany: Niemeyer. (Trans: P. Pigors, *Types of men.* Halle: Niemeyer, 1928.)

Wiggins, J. S. (1984). Cattell's system from the perspective of mainstream personality theory. *Multivariate Behavioral Research, 19,* 176–190.

Wilson, G. (1978). Introversion/extroversion. In H. London & J. E. Exner (Eds.), *Dimensions of personality* (pp. 217–261). New York: Wiley.

SUGGESTED READINGS

Cattell, R. B. (1985). *Human motivation and the dynamic calculus.* New York: Praeger.

Evans, R. I. (1970). *Gordon Allport: The man and his ideas.* New York: Dutton.

Eysenck, H. J. (1978). *Crime and personality* (3rd ed.). London: Paladin.

Eysenck, H. J. (Ed.) (1981). *A model for personality.* New York: Springer-Verlag.

Gray, J. A. (1981). A critique of Eysenck's theory of personality. In H. J. Eysenck (Ed.), *A model for personality.* Berlin: Springer-Verlag.

Howarth, E., & Zumbo, B. D. (1989). An empirical investigation of Eysenck's typology. *Journal of Research in Personality, 23,* 343–353.

Maddi, S. R., and Costa, P. T. (1972). *Humanism in personology: Allport, Maslow, and Murray.* Chicago: Aldine-Atherton.

DISCUSSION QUESTIONS

1 Select any person that you know well and list his or her essential personality characteristics. Do these characteristics appear to be what Allport means by "central traits"? How useful is the concept of "central traits" for describing a person in everyday terms?

2 List what you believe to be your own essential personality traits. Does this list fully capture your own intuitive sense of self (i.e., your subjective sense of who you are as a total person)? Or do you also find Allport's concept of "proprium" necessary to describe

your total personality? What precisely does the concept of proprium add to your personality description that was missing from your list of central traits?

3 What do you think of Allport's concept of "functional autonomy?" Can people really sever their motivational ties to the past, or is this concept a theoretical illusion? Bolster your argument with examples that you have observed.

4 How well do Allport's six characteristics of a "mature personality" fit your own idea of what constitutes a healthy personality? Can you think of any features a healthy personality might possess that are not in any way related to Allport's six characteristics?

5 What are the main steps involved in using factor analysis to identify the underlying traits of personality structure? Why do you think that Cattell and Eysenck disagree as to the number of major traits comprising personality as determined by the factor analytic technique?

6 How do Allport, Cattell, and Eysenck differ in their approaches to classifying personality traits? Give examples to illustrate how each theorist conceptualizes the term "trait." To what extent, if any, do these three theorists agree that traits interact with situations to determine behavior?

7 Do you agree with Eysenck that three major trait dimensions of personality are largely responsible for a significant portion of human behavior? Do you also agree with Eysenck that individual variations along each trait dimension reflect differences in neurophysiological functioning?

8 Based on cited research findings, what are some major behavioral differences separating introverts from extraverts? How is introversion–extraversion as an individual difference continuum measured in such research?

9 Do you agree with Mischel that people display far less consistency across situations than is claimed by trait theorists? What are some of the rebuttals to Mischel's position cited by those who are supportive of the trait position?

GLOSSARY

Ability trait   For Cattell, a trait that determines the person's effectiveness and skill in the pursuit of goals.

Bodily self   That aspect of the proprium based on the person's perception of his or her body. Allport considered it to be a lifelong anchor for self-awareness.

Cardinal disposition   For Allport, a characteristic so pervasive that virtually all of a person's activities can be traced to its influence.

Central disposition   For Allport, a characteristic that influences the person's behavior in a variety of settings; central traits are the "building blocks" of personality structure.

Character   Term used by Allport to refer to a moral standard or value system against which a person's actions are evaluated.

Common trait   For Allport, any generalized disposition against which most people within a given culture can reasonably be compared (also called *nomothetic trait*).

Constitutional trait   For Cattell, a source trait that is rooted in the biological and physiological condition of the person and very resistant to change.

Correlation matrix   The total array of correlations among all variables in a factor analytic study.

Dispositional perspective   An approach to personality emphasizing the enduring qualities or traits that reside within the person and that render the person's behavior consistent over time and across situations.

Dynamic trait   For Cattell, a trait that activates and directs the person toward particular goals in a given situation.

Environmental-mold trait   For Cattell, a source trait learned through experience with the environment.

Extraversion   In Eysenck's theory, one end of the introversion–extraversion type dimension of personality characterized by a tendency to be sociable, impulsive, and excitable.

Factor analysis   Statistical procedure used to determine those psychological variables or test responses that cluster together within a matrix of intercorrelations. Used by Cattell and Eysenck to identify the underlying traits of personality structure.

Factor loading   Correlation between a single item and the factor to which it is being related.

Factors   Basic dimensions that emerge when data are reduced by means of factor analysis.

Functional autonomy   For Allport, process whereby a given form of behavior becomes an end or goal in itself despite the fact that it may originally have been adopted for another reason. What was formerly a means to an end becomes an end in itself.

Idiographic view   Approach to personality study whereby the uniqueness of each person is the primary goal of investigation. Allport championed the idiographic approach.

Individual trait   For Allport, a trait unique to the individual (also called *personal disposition*).

Introversion   In Eysenck's theory, one end of the introversion–extraversion type dimension of personality characterized by a tendency to be reserved, controlled, and introspective.

L-data   In Cattell's theory, measures of behavior in everyday life situations or ratings of such behavior (e.g., interactions with peers).

Neuroticism   In Eysenck's theory, one end of the neuroticism–stability type dimension of personality characterized by a tendency to be anxious, moody, and depressed.

Nomothetic view   Empirical approach to the study of personality that seeks to establish general laws of human functioning.

OT-data   In Cattell's theory, measures of a person's performance on tasks that may be objectively scored (e.g., responses to an inkblot).

Propriate striving   For Allport, the person's motivation to enhance self through the pursuit of important, long-range goals. Such motivation involves an increase, not a decrease, in level of tension.

Proprium   According to Allport, all aspects of a person that make him or her unique. It also represents the positive, creative, and forward-moving quality of human nature.

Psychophysical system   An integral part of Allport's definition of personality which suggests that both mental and physical factors must be considered when we seek to understand human functioning.

Psychoticism   In Eysenck's theory, one end of the psychoticism–superego strength type dimension of personality characterized by a tendency to be solitary and insensitive to others.

Q-data   In Cattell's theory, personality data obtained from self-report questionnaires (e.g., the 16 PF).

Secondary disposition   For Allport, a trait that has little or no influence on behavior, such as a specific food preference.

Self as rational coper   Term used by Allport to describe a person's realization that he or she can cope effectively with reality demands and achieve personal goals.

Self-esteem   The favorableness of a person's self-image in Allport's theory.

Self-extension The person's feelings about his or her material possessions. For Allport, such feelings are an integral part of the person's self-image.

Self-identity In Allport's theory, the person's recognition of self as a distinct and constant point of reference relative to others.

Self-image In Allport's theory, the diversity of roles a person plays in order to gain the approval of others and to manage their impressions of who and what the person is.

Self-objectification Term used by Allport to refer to the ability to know oneself objectively and to recognize one's strengths and weaknesses.

Sixteen Personality Factor Inventory (16 PF) Self-report test developed by Cattell to measure the 16 source traits of personality.

Source trait For Cattell, underlying structures that constitute the core or basic building blocks of personality; source traits are revealed through factor analysis in Cattell's system.

Specification equation Formula proposed by Cattell to indicate that a person's response is a consequence of the stimulus situation at a given moment and all the traits relevant to that situation.

Stability In Eysenck's theory, one end of the neuroticism–stability type dimension of personality characterized by a tendency to be calm, controlled, and unemotional.

Study of Values Self-report personality test developed by Allport to measure six basic value dimensions or types.

Superego strength In Eysenck's theory, one end of the psychoticism–superego strength type dimension characterized by a tendency to be empathic, sensitive, and cooperative.

Supertrait In Eysenck's theory, general and continuous trait dimensions, such as introversion–extraversion, that exert a powerful influence on behavior.

Surface trait For Cattell, observable behaviors that appear to be clustered together but are in fact controlled by an underlying source trait.

Temperament According to Allport, the raw materials (intelligence and physique) of which personality is molded.

Temperament trait For Cattell, a constitutional source trait influencing the person's emotional or stylistic quality of behaving.

Trait theory Theoretical conception of personality that postulates the existence of underlying dispositions or characteristics that initiate and direct behavior. Traits are typically inferred from overt behavior or self-report measures.

CHAPTER 7

THE LEARNING-BEHAVIORAL PERSPECTIVE IN PERSONALITY THEORY: B. F. SKINNER

The theorists reviewed so far have all concerned themselves with what goes on inside the person, with the internal structures and dynamics underlying observable behavior patterns. Whether it be the unconscious mental processes and conflicts described by Freud, the archetypes posited by Jung, or the supertraits identified by Eysenck, attention has centered on a "within the person" look. Of course, theorists like Adler, Erikson, Fromm, and Horney recognized the crucial role of cultural, social, family, and interpersonal influences on human behavior. Even Cattell noted that behavior is the result of a complex interplay between traits and situations. Yet, one can hardly escape the conclusion that for all of these theorists, the real action was taking place beneath the skin. Equally impressive is the fact that *learning* accounts for much of our behavior. Through learning we acquire knowledge, language, attitudes, values, fears, personality traits, and insights into ourselves. If personality is the residue of learning, it would seem important to know what learning is and how it occurs. Accordingly, this chapter is concerned with the learning approach to personality.

Personality from the learning perspective consists of all the tendencies a person has acquired over the course of a lifetime. It is an accumulated set of learned behavior patterns. The *learning-behavioral* approach thus concerns itself with the person's overt actions as determined by his or her life experiences. Unlike Freud and many other personologists, behavioristic-learning theorists see no need to speculate about mental structures and processes buried away in the "mind." Instead, they emphasize the external environment as the key determinant of the person's behavior. It is the environment, rather than internal mental events, that shapes the person.

The belief that environmental forces determine how we behave is best seen in the work of B. F. Skinner. More than any other psychologist, Skinner argued that nearly all behavior is directly governed by environmental contingencies of reinforcement. In his view, to explain behavior (and thus, implicitly, to understand personality) we need only analyze the functional relations between observable action and observable consequences. Skinner's efforts have provided the foundation for a science of behavior unparalleled in human history. In the eyes of many, he is one of the most influential psychologists of our time (Davis et al., 1982). This chapter is devoted to his *operant conditioning* point of view.

As we shall see in the following chapter, Skinner's radical behaviorism differs markedly from social learning theories of personality. While the approaches of Albert Bandura and Julian Rotter reflect some of the emphases of the learning-behavioristic perspective, they offer an expanded view of behavior that stresses the interplay of factors inside and outside of people. Before we get ahead of ourselves, however, let us direct attention to B. F. Skinner the person.

B. F. Skinner: An Operant Conditioning Theory of Personality

BIOGRAPHICAL SKETCH

Burrhus Frederic Skinner was born in 1904 in Susquehanna, Pennsylvania. He was reared in a warm and stable home where learning was esteemed, discipline was apparent, and rewards were given when deserved. Throughout his childhood, Skinner spent many hours designing and building things—roller-skate scooters, steerable wagons, merry-go-rounds, blow guns, and similar gadgets. This boyhood fascination with mechanical inventions foreshadowed his later concern with modifying observable behavior. He also enjoyed school and recalled that he acquired a sound education from a fine few teachers.

Skinner received his B.A. degree in English literature in 1926 from Hamilton College, a small liberal arts school in upstate New York. He remembered, however, that he never really adjusted to student life. In addition to being disappointed by the lack of intellectual interest shown by his fellow students, he was quite disillusioned by some of the curriculum requirements (such as daily chapel). His participation in several escapades designed to embarrass those faculty members the students found to be arrogant led to threats of expulsion by the college president, but he was permitted to graduate. Ironically, Skinner did not take any psychology courses as an undergraduate. Following college, Skinner returned to his parents' home and attempted to become a writer. Although encouraged by a letter from the poet Robert Frost, the desire to be a writer met with disastrous results: "I read aimlessly, built model ships, played the piano, listened to the newly-invented radio, contributed to the humorous column of a local paper but wrote nothing else, and thought about seeing a psychiatrist" (Skinner, 1967, p. 394).

Eventually Skinner gave up writing as a career and entered the psychology

B. F. Skinner. (*Photo by Jill Krementz*)

graduate program at Harvard University. Vividly aware that he was far behind in a new field, he set up a rigorous study schedule and adhered to it for almost two years. He was awarded a Ph.D. degree in 1931.

From 1931 to 1936, Skinner worked as a Harvard postdoctoral fellow. His research endeavors focused on the nervous system of animals. In 1936 he accepted a teaching position at the University of Minnesota, remaining there until 1945. This was a period of remarkable productivity and established Skinner as one of the leading behaviorists in the United States. In the fall of 1945 he became chairman of the psychology department at Indiana University, a position he held until 1947, when he rejoined Harvard as William James Lecturer. He remained at Harvard until he retired in 1974.

Skinner was accorded many honors throughout his career. He received the President's Medal of Science and was a 1971 recipient of the American Psychological Association's Gold Medal Award with the following citation: "To B. F. Skinner—pioneer in psychological research, leader in theory, master in technology, who has revolutionized the study of behavior in our time" (American Psychologist, 1972, p. 72). Skinner also received the APA's Presidential Citation for Lifetime Contributions to Psychology in 1990.

Skinner was a voluminous writer. His books include *The Behavior of Organisms* (1938); *Walden Two* (1948); *Science and Human Behavior* (1953); *Verbal Behavior* (1957); *Schedules of Reinforcement* (1957, with C. B. Ferster); *Cumulative Record* (1961); *The Technology of Teaching* (1968); *Contingencies of Reinforcement* (1969); *Beyond Freedom and Dignity* (1971); *About Behaviorism* (1974); *Particulars of My Life* (1976); *Reflections on Behaviorism and Society* (1978); *The Shaping of a Behaviorist* (1979); *A Matter of Consequences* (1983); *Enjoy Old Age* (1983, with M. E. Vaughan); and *Upon Further Reflection* (1987). Perhaps best known among college students is Skinner's *Walden Two,* a novel depicting a utopian community based on the control of behavior through psychological principles of reinforcement. In addition, *Festschrift for B. F. Skinner,* edited by P. Dews (1970)—a collection of edited papers—was presented to Skinner on his sixty-fifth birthday. His autobiography appears in Volume 5 of the *History of Psychology in Autobiography* (Skinner, 1967, pp. 385–413). Skinner died in 1990 after a year-long battle with leukemia.

SKINNER'S APPROACH TO PSYCHOLOGY

Most personological theorists share two perspectives: (1) a commitment to the study of persistent differences among people and (2) a reliance on hypothetical constructs to account for the variety and complexity of human behavior. These perspectives constitute the mainstream, if not the essence, of most theorizing about personality to date. Skinner believed that abstract theories were unnecessary and should be abandoned in favor of an approach based solely on how the environment affects the individual's behavior (1983). He insisted that psychology, especially the field of learning, was not sufficiently advanced to justify efforts devoted to grand-scale, formalized theory building. In addition, he contended that there was no need for theory-directed research since it provides ''explanations of observed facts which appeal to events taking place in different terms and measured, if at all, in different dimensions'' (Skinner, 1961, p. 39). Finally, Skinner argued that theories of human behavior often given psychologists a false sense of security about their state of knowledge, when in fact they do not comprehend the relationships between ongoing behavior and its environmental antecedents.

In light of Skinner's apparent *antitheoretical* position, it is questionable whether he should be included in a volume concerned with personality theories. We will not address that philosophical issue, except to note that Skinner admitted to being a theorist, thus justifying our presentation of his approach to the study of personality. In one interview he stated:

> I defined theory as an effort to explain behavior in terms of something going on in another universe, such as the mind or the nervous system. Theories of that sort I do not believe are essential or helpful. Besides, they are dangerous; they cause all kinds of trouble. But I look forward to an overall theory of human behavior which will bring together a lot of facts and express them in a more general way. That kind of theory I would be very much interested in promoting, and I consider myself to be a theoretician. (Evans, 1968, p. 88)

Thus, while Skinner's view of a theory is far different from that of most personologists, he was nonetheless committed to the task of constructing a theory of human behavior.

Out with the Autonomous Person

As a radical behaviorist, Skinner rejected all notions that humans are autonomous beings whose behavior is determined by the presumed existence of internal factors (e.g., unconscious impulses, archetypes, traits). Such mentalistic concepts, he noted, originated in primitive animism and have persisted because there is ignorance of the environmental conditions governing behavior.

> Autonomous man serves to explain only the things we are not able to explain in other ways. His existence depends upon our ignorance, and he naturally loses status as we come to know more about behavior. . . . We do not need to try to discover what personalities, states of mind, feelings, traits of character, plans, purposes, intentions, or the other prerequisites of autonomous man really are in order to get on with a scientific analysis of behavior. (Skinner, 1971, pp. 12–13)

Skinner's objection to intrapsychic causes is not that they are inappropriate phenomena to study but rather that they are shrouded in terminology that makes operational definitions and empirical tests impossible. In the history of science, he observed, it has usually been necessary to completely abandon mentalistic conceptions rather than modify them into a form that permits empirical study. To explain why a competent student flunks out of college, we might easily say "because he had a strong fear of failure," "because he lacked motivation," or "because he cut classes as a result of an unconscious fear of success." Such hypotheses about the student's dismissal from college may sound like explanations, but Skinner warned that they explain nothing unless the motives involved are explicitly defined and unless the antecedents of flunking out are established.

Thus, if a mentalistic concept is invoked to explain behavior, it must be translatable into terms relevant to the experimental operations involved in investigation and measurement. To settle for less would be to resort to the very armchair philosophizing that Skinner so vehemently deplored. We could start with what can be observed (i.e., the incident of flunking out) and then determine whether additional explanations augment the understanding of the behavior in question. If a competent student flunks out of college, is it not more illuminating to examine what environmental conditions preceded that behavior than to propose as its cause some mental entity that cannot be objectively identified? For instance, did dormitory noise disrupt her sleep so that she could not study effectively? Did financial hardship cause her to work 40 hours per week and thus limit her time to study? Or did she play on the varsity basketball team whose schedule forced her to miss numerous classes and exams? These questions clearly reveal that Skinner placed responsibility for the person's actions on environmental circumstances rather than on the autonomous person within. For Skinner, the environment is everything and explains everything.

In Skinner's system, then, no attempt is made to ask questions or to infer processes about the person's inner state. It is considered irrelevant for a scientific explanation of behavior. To avoid the notion that describing is explaining, Skinner argued that the human organism is a "black box" whose contents (motives, drives, conflicts, emotions, etc.) should be discarded from the domain of empirical inquiry. Organismic variables add nothing to our understanding of human activity and only serve to delay the development of a scientific analysis of behavior. According to Skinner, adequate explanations can be accomplished without recourse to any constructs other than those accounting for the functional relationships between various stimulus conditions and behavioral responses overtly emitted by the person. However, Skinner did not categorically reject the study of inner events or what is sometimes called "higher mental processes." Indeed, he believed that psychologists must provide adequate explanations of private events, but the events studied must be capable of being reliably and objectively measured. It is this emphasis on objectivity that characterized Skinner's attempt to recognize the legitimacy of internal states and events.

Down with Physiological-Genetic Explanations

Unlike a growing number of psychologists, Skinner did not emphasize the importance of neurophysiological or genetic factors in accounting for human behavior. This disregard for physiological-genetic conceptions of behavior was based on his conviction that they do not facilitate behavioral control. Skinner explained his aversion to "physiologizing" by noting: "Even when it can be shown that some aspect of behavior is due to season of birth, gross body type, or genetic constitution, the fact is of limited use. It may help us in predicting behavior, but is of little value in an experimental analysis or in practical control because such a condition cannot be manipulated after the individual has been conceived" (1974, p. 371). Thus, Skinner did not deny the validity of biological-genetic elements of behavior, but rather ignored them because they are not (at least currently) amenable to modification through manipulation. Moreover, he insisted that even if brain scientists eventually discover the biological-genetic variables affecting behavior, only a behavioral analysis will provide the clearest account of the effects of these variables.

What Behavioral Science Should Be

Skinner assumed that all behavior is lawfully determined, predictable, and able to be brought under environmental control. To understand behavior is to control it, and vice versa. He was unalterably opposed to any admission of free will or any other "volitional," uncaused event. Human beings in his system are machines—highly complicated ones, but machines nonetheless. While he was by no means the first psychologist to propose a *mechanistic approach* to the study of behavior (Watson advocated throwing out mentalistic concepts in the 1920s), his formulation was exceptional in that he carried the idea to its logical conclusion. To Skinner, the science of human behavior is basically no different from any other data-oriented natural science; thus, its goals are the same—prediction and control of the phenomena studied (overt behavior in this case).

Skinner further argued that since all science advances from the simple to the complex, it is logical to study infrahumans prior to studying humans. The former enables the psychologist to discover more easily the basic processes and principles of behavior. Among other advantages, the researcher is able to exert more precise control over the conditions influencing an animal's environment and to collect data over longer periods of time. There is, of course, a serious question as to how much of the findings uncovered by studying one species (e.g., rats) are truly applicable to another species (e.g., humans). Skinner, however, advocated the use of lower species as experimental subjects because he believed there was ample evidence showing a definite relationship between principles of behavior established at that level and their application to human functioning. To illustrate, the development of teaching machines and programmed textbooks are direct products of Skinner's work in the animal laboratory.

Skinner also differed from other researchers in that he stressed the analysis of a *single organism's behavior*. He believed that the study of a single organism was appropriate because the factors governing such organisms are identical to the laws that govern all organisms. Thus, while the behavior of individual rats, pigeons, or people may vary, the underlying principles controlling that behavior do not. By studying one rat, one pigeon, or one person, Skinner believed that such basic principles can be discovered and generalized to other organisms.

This orientation, referred to as the *single-subject experimental design*, does not require the traditional statistical techniques that most students learn in their psychological training. Instead of seeking to make predictions about the behavior of the nonexistent average individual, Skinner maintained that psychologists should attempt to predict the influence of one or more controlled variables upon a specified component of an individual organism's behavior in a controlled environment. This approach requires a nonstatistical strategy which yields laws relevant to real individual behavior. This, said Skinner, is what psychology as a behavioral science should have as its aim. Skinnerian psychology might be summarized by a statement Skinner (1956) quoted from Pavlov: "Control your conditions and you will see order."

In keeping with his behavioristic approach, Skinner advocated a *functional analysis* of the behaving organism. Such an analysis seeks to establish exact, real, and specifiable relationships between the organism's overt behavior (responses) and the environmental conditions (stimuli) that control it. The variables employed must be external, visible, and defined in quantitative terms. It is the cause-and-effect relationships emerging from a functional analysis that become the universal laws of behavioral science. The practical goal is to be able to manipulate the environmental (independent) variables from which predictions are made and then to measure the resulting changes in behavior (dependent variables). Thus, psychologists can work within the boundaries of a natural science and yet discover laws relevant to the behavior of individual organisms.

Personality Viewed from a Behavioristic Perspective

We have now considered some of the reasons why Skinner adopted an experimental approach to the study of behavior. But what about the study of personality? Is it completely lost in Skinner's uncompromising emphasis on a functional, cause-and-effect analysis of behavior? Simply stated, the answer to the latter question is "No," provided that established scientific criteria are met. As we have seen, for instance, Skinner did not accept the idea of a personality or self that instigates and directs behavior. He considered such an approach a vestige of primitive animism, a doctrine that presupposed the existence of something akin to spirits within the body which moved it (Skinner, 1989). Nor would he have accepted explanations of behavior such as this: "The Rev. Jones and some 980 members of the People's Temple Church killed themselves in the jungle of Guyana because they were emotionally disturbed."

Skinner's *radical behaviorism* emphasized the intensive analysis of the person's idiosyncratic learning history and unique genetic endowment:

> In a behavioral analysis, a person is an organism . . . which has acquired a repertoire of behavior. . . . [He] is not an originating agent; he is a locus, a point at which many genetic and environmental conditions come together in a joint effect. As such, he remains unquestionably unique. No one else (unless he has an identical twin) has his genetic endowment, and without exception no one else has his personal history. Hence no one else will behave in precisely the same way. (Skinner, 1974, pp. 167–168)

For Skinner, then, the study of personality involves the discovery of the unique pattern of relationships between the behavior of an organism and its reinforcing consequences. According to this point of view, individual differences in personality are to be understood in terms of behavior-environment interactions over time. To study the presumed properties and influences of some hypothetical construct within the person is just a waste of time.

RESPONDENT AND OPERANT BEHAVIOR

In considering Skinner's approach to personality, two kinds of behavior need to be distinguished: respondent and operant. We will discuss respondent behavior first because it provides the backdrop for understanding Skinner's operant conditioning principles of learning.

Respondent behavior refers to a specific response that is elicited by a known stimulus, the latter always preceding the former in time. Familiar respondents include pupillary constriction or dilation to changes in light stimulation, knee jerk to a hammer tapped on the patellar tendon, and shivering to cold. In each of these examples, the relationship between the stimulus (e.g., decrease in light stimulation) and response (e.g., pupillary dilation) is involuntary and spontaneous—it always occurs. Thus, respondent behavior usually entails reflexes involving the autonomic nervous system. However, respondent behavior may also be learned. For instance, the actress who perspires profusely and has "butterflies in her stomach" prior to performing in front of a live audience is probably displaying respondent behavior. To understand how this and other respondent behaviors can be learned, it is helpful to consider the contributions of Ivan Pavlov, the first person to be identified with behaviorism.

Pavlov, a Russian physiologist, first discovered, while studying the physiology of digestion, that respondent behavior can be classically conditioned. He observed that food placed in the mouth of a hungry dog automatically evokes salivation. In this case, salivation is an unlearned response or, as Pavlov called it, an *unconditioned response* (UCR). It is elicited by the food, which is termed the *unconditioned stimulus* (UCS). Pavlov's great discovery was that if a previously neutral stimulus is repeatedly paired with the UCS, eventually the neutral stimulus acquires the capacity to elicit the UCR when it is presented alone without the UCS. For example, if a bell is sounded each time immediately before the food reaches its mouth, gradually a dog will begin to salivate to the sound of the bell, even if the food is no longer presented. The new response, salivation to the bell sound, is termed a *conditioned response* (CR), while the previously neutral eliciting stimulus, the bell, is known as the *conditioned stimulus* (CS). Figure 7-1 illustrates the process of *classical conditioning*.

In later studies Pavlov noticed that if he ceased to provide food after the bell was sounded, the dog would eventually stop salivating to the bell altogether. This process is called *extinction* and demonstrates that *reinforcement* (food) is essential for both the acquisition and the maintenance of respondent learning. Pavlov also found that if a dog is given a prolonged rest period during extinction, it will once again salivate when the bell is sounded. This phenomenon is appropriately called *spontaneous recovery*.

While Pavlov's initial experiments were carried out with animals, other researchers began to examine basic processes of classical conditioning in humans. An experiment conducted by Watson and Rayner (1920) illustrates how classical conditioning plays a key role in shaping emotional responses such as fear and anxiety. These investigators conditioned an emotional fear response in an 11-month-old boy known in the annals of psychology as "Little Albert." Like many infants, Albert was initially unafraid of a live white rat. Furthermore, he had never been seen in a state of fear or rage. Watson and Rayner's procedure was to present a tame white rat (CS) together with a loud noise (UCS) produced by striking the gong of a steel bar with a claw hammer just behind Albert's back. After the rat and the frightening sound were paired seven times, a strong fear response (CR)—crying and falling over—was elicited when the rodent alone was presented. Five days later, Watson and Rayner exposed Albert to other stimuli that resembled the rat in that they were white and furry. They found that Albert's fear response was generalized to a variety of stimuli, including a rabbit, a sealskin coat, a Santa Claus mask, and even Watson's hair. Most of these conditioned fears were still evident a month after the original conditioning. Unfortunately,

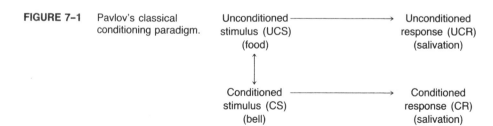

FIGURE 7-1 Pavlov's classical conditioning paradigm.

Many childhood fears are learned through classical conditioning. (*David H. Krathwohl/Stock, Boston*)

Albert was released from the hospital (where the study was conducted) before Watson and Rayner got around to extinguishing the fears they had conditioned. Little Albert was never heard of again. Watson and Rayner were roundly criticized in later years for failing to ensure that Albert experienced no lasting ill effects. Cruel though this case may seem in retrospect, it does reveal how similar fears (of strangers, dentists, and doctors) may be acquired through the process of classical conditioning.

Respondent behavior is Skinner's version of Pavlovian or classical conditioning. He also called it *type S conditioning* to stress the significance of the stimulus that comes before and elicits the response. However, Skinner believed that most animal and human behavior cannot be accounted for in terms of classical conditioning. Rather, he emphasized behavior that is not linked to any known stimulus. Consider the behavior you are engaging in right now—reading. It is definitely not a reflex, and the stimuli that govern it (exams and grades) do not precede it. Instead, your reading behavior is primarily influenced by stimulus events that follow it—specifically, its consequences. Because this type of behavior implies an active organism that "operates" on the environment so as to change it in some way, Skinner labeled it *operant behavior*. He also called it *type R conditioning* to emphasize the effect of the response on future behavior.

Operant behavior (produced by operant conditioning) is determined by the events that follow the response. That is, a behavior is followed by a consequence, and the nature of the consequence modifies the organism's tendency to repeat the behavior in the future. For example, riding a skateboard, playing the piano, throwing a Frisbee, and writing our name are considered operant response patterns, or operants, since they are controlled by the consequences that follow their respective performances. They are voluntary, learned responses for which an identifiable stimulus does not exist. Skinner felt that it was pointless to speculate about the origins of operant behaviors since no known stimulus or internal cause is responsible for their occurrence. They occur spontaneously.

If the consequences of the response are favorable to the organism, then the likelihood of the operant being emitted again in the future is thereby increased. When this happens, the consequence is said to be *reinforcing* and the operant response which has been affected by the reinforcement (in the sense that it is more likely to occur) has been conditioned. The strength of a positive reinforcing stimulus is thus defined in terms of its effects on the subsequent frequency of the response that immediately preceded it.

Alternatively, if response outcomes are unfavorable or nonreinforcing, then the likelihood of the operant occurring again is decreased. For example, you will soon stop smiling at a person whose consistent response to your smile is a scowl or no smile at all. Skinner thus suggested that operant behavior is controlled by *negative consequences*. By definition, negative or aversive consequences weaken the behavior that produces them and strengthen the behavior that removes them. If a person consistently scowls, you will eventually try to avoid him or her altogether. Likewise, if you park your car in a space marked "For the President Only" and your car is ticketed every day as a consequence, you will undoubtedly soon stop parking there.

In order to study operant behavior in the laboratory, Skinner devised a deceptively simple type of procedure called the *free operant method*. In this procedure, a semistarved rat is placed in a "free-operant chamber" (commonly known as a "Skinner box") which is empty except for a lever and a food dish at one end of it. At first, the rat will normally exhibit a variety of operants: walking, sniffing, scratching, grooming, and urinating. Such responses are not elicited by any recognizable stimulus; they are spontaneously emitted. Eventually, in the course of its exploratory activity, the rat will press the lever, causing a pellet of food to be automatically delivered to the dish under the lever. Because the response of lever pressing has an initially low probability of occurrence, it must be considered purely accidental with regard to feeding; i.e., we cannot predict when the rat will press the lever, nor can we make the rat do it. However, by depriving it of food in advance, say for 24 hours, we can ensure that the lever-pressing response will eventually have a high probability of occurrence in this particular situation. This is done through a method called *magazine training*, whereby the experimenter delivers a food pellet each time the rat presses the lever. It can then be observed that the rat spends more time in the vicinity of the lever and the feeding dish until, in due course, it is pressing the lever at an ever-increasing rate. Lever pressing thus gradually becomes the rat's most frequent response under conditions of food deprivation. In the operant conditioning situation, then, the rat's behavior is instrumental (i.e., operates on the environment) in producing the reinforcement (food). If nonreinforced trials now occur, that is, if food fails to appear consistently following the lever-pressing response, the rat eventually stops pressing and undergoes *experimental extinction*.

Now that we have reviewed the nature of operant conditioning, it may be helpful to consider an example of it encountered in almost any family with young children—the operant conditioning of crying behavior. Whenever young children are in obvious pain, they cry, and the parents' immediate reaction is to express attention and other positive reinforcements. Since attention is reinforcing for the child, the crying response naturally becomes conditioned. However, crying may occur even when pain is absent. Most parents insist that they can discriminate between crying due to distress and crying evoked by the desire for attention, yet many parents persist in reinforcing the latter.

Is it possible for parents to eliminate conditioned crying behavior or is the child destined to be a "crybaby" the rest of his or her life? A case study reported by Williams (1959) illustrates how conditioned crying was extinguished in a 21-month-old child. Due to serious illness during the first 18 months of life, the child had received considerable attention from his concerned parents. In fact, because of his screaming and crying when put to bed, the parents or an aunt, who lived with the family, stayed in his bedroom until he fell asleep. These bedside vigils usually took from 2 to 3 hours. By remaining in the room until he went to sleep, the parents were undoubtedly providing positive reinforcement for the maintenance of the child's crying behavior. He had his parents under perfect control. To extinguish this objectionable behavior, the parents were instructed to leave the child awake in the bedroom by himself and to ignore any subsequent crying. Within a period of 7 nights, the crying behavior had virtually disappeared. By the tenth night, the child even smiled as his parents left the room and could be heard making happy sounds as he fell asleep. A week later, however, the child immediately began screaming when his aunt put him to bed and left the room. She returned to the room and remained there until the child went to sleep. This one instance of positive reinforcement was sufficient to necessitate going through the entire extinction process a second time. By the ninth night the child's crying was finally extinguished, and Williams reported that no remission occurred within a 2-year follow-up period.

Schedules of Reinforcement

The essence of operant conditioning relies on the fact that reinforced behavior tends to be repeated, whereas behavior that is nonreinforced or punished tends not to be repeated or is extinguished. Hence, the concept of reinforcement occupies a key role in Skinner's theory.

The rate at which operant behavior is acquired and maintained is a function of the schedule of reinforcement employed. A *schedule of reinforcement* is a rule stating the contingencies under which reinforcements will be presented. The simplest contingency rule would be to reinforce the organism every time it emits the desired response. This is termed a *continuous reinforcement* schedule and is commonly used at the outset of all operant conditioning when the organism is learning to acquire the correct response. In most everyday life situations, however, this is neither a feasible nor an economical way to maintain the desired response, since reinforcement of behavior does not usually occur on a uniform or regular basis. Most human social behavior is reinforced only some of the time. A baby cries many times before he or she elicits the mother's attention. A scientist tries many approaches before arriving at a correct solution to a difficult problem. In both these instances, a number of unreinforced responses occur before one of them is reinforced.

Skinner carefully studied how *intermittent* or *partial reinforcement* schedules influence operant behavior. Although many different reinforcement schedules are possible, they can all be categorized according to two basic dimensions: (1) the individual is reinforced only after a fixed or irregular *time interval* has elapsed since the previous reinforcement (called *interval reinforcement* schedules) and (2) the individual is reinforced only after a fixed or irregular *number of responses* have been made since the previous reinforcement (called *ratio reinforcement* schedules). In terms of these two dimensions, the following four basic schedules of reinforcement have attracted the most attention.

1 *Fixed-ratio reinforcement schedule (FR).* In a fixed-ratio schedule, the organism is reinforced following a predetermined or "fixed" number of appropriate responses. This schedule is common in everyday life and exercises considerable control over behavior. For many jobs, employees are paid partly or even exclusively according to the number of units they produce or sell. In industry, this system is known as piecework pay. A FR schedule usually generates extremely high operant levels, since the more the organism responds, the more reinforcement it receives.

2 *Fixed-interval reinforcement schedule (FI).* In a fixed-interval schedule, the organism is reinforced after a set or "fixed" time interval has elapsed since the previous reinforcement. On the human level, FI schedules are operative in paying salaries for work done by the hour, week, or month. Similarly, giving a child a weekly allowance constitutes a FI form of reinforcement. Universities typically operate in terms of a FI time schedule. Examinations are administered on a regular basis and reports of academic progress are issued at designated time intervals. Interestingly, FI schedules yield low rates of responding immediately after the reinforcement has been obtained, a phenomenon called *postreinforcement pause*. This is evidenced by students who experience difficulty in studying after a midterm exam (assuming that they have done well) since a long interval will elapse before the next exam occurs. They literally pause in their studies.

3 *Variable-ratio reinforcement schedule (VR).* On this schedule, the organism is reinforced on the basis of some predetermined average number of responses. Perhaps the most dramatic illustration of human behavior under the control of a VR schedule is compulsive gambling. Consider the actions of a person operating a slot machine, or one-armed bandit. These devices are programmed so that reinforcement (i.e., money) is distributed according to the number of times a person pays to pull the handle. However, the payoffs are unpredictable, irregular, and rarely yield returns surpassing what the gambler invests. This explains why owners of gambling casinos receive far more reinforcement than do their patrons. Furthermore, extinction of behavior acquired on a VR schedule is extremely slow, since the organism does not know precisely when the next reinforcement will be forthcoming. Thus, a gambler compulsively feeds coins into a machine, even though the returns are slim, in the conviction that next time she or he will "hit the jackpot." Such persistence is typical of the behavior generated by VR reinforcement schedules.

Slot machines are on a variable-ratio reinforcement schedule. (*Frank Siteman/Stock, Boston*)

4 *Variable-interval reinforcement schedule (VI).* The organism is reinforced on this schedule after a variable time interval has elapsed. Like the FI schedule, reinforcement in this condition is time-contingent. However, the time between reinforcements on a VI schedule varies around some average value rather than being fixed. As a general rule, rates of responding under VI schedules are a direct function of the interval length employed, with short intervals generating high rates and long intervals generating low rates. Also, VI schedules tend to establish steady response rates and are slow to extinguish. After all, the organism cannot precisely anticipate when the next reinforcement is going to be delivered.

Illustrations of true VI schedules are not common in everyday life, although several variations can be observed. A parent, for example, may praise a child's behavior on a rather random basis, thus assuring that the child will continue to behave appropriately during nonreinforced intervals. Similarly, professors who give ''pop quizzes'' that vary from 1 every 3 days to 1 every 3 weeks, averaging 1 every 2 weeks, is using a VI schedule. Students can be expected to maintain a relatively stable rate of studying under these conditions since they would never know when the next pop quiz would be coming. As a rule, VI schedules generate higher rates of responding and greater resistance to extinction than do FI schedules.

Conditioned Reinforcement

Learning theorists recognize two types of reinforcement—primary and secondary. A *primary* reinforcement is any event or object that possesses inherent reinforcing properties. Thus, it does not require prior association with other reinforcement in order to satisfy biological needs and drives. Primary reinforcers for humans include food, water, physical comfort, and sex. Their reward value to the organism is independent of learning. A *secondary* or *conditioned* reinforcement, on the other hand, is any event or object that acquires its reinforcing qualities through close association with a primary reinforcement in the past conditioning history of the organism. Examples of common secondary reinforcers in humans are money, attention, affection, and good grades.

A slight alteration in the standard operant conditioning procedure demonstrates how a neutral stimulus can acquire reinforcing powers for other behavior. When a rat is trained to bar-press in a Skinner box, a tone comes on momentarily (as the animal makes the response), followed by a pellet of food. In this case, the tone acts as a *discriminative stimulus* (i.e., the animal learns to respond only in the presence of the tone since the tone signals the arrival of the food reward). After the animal has acquired this specific operant response, extinction is begun: when it bar-presses neither the food nor the tone appears. In time the rat ceases to bar-press altogether. Next, the tone is presented whenever the animal engages in bar pressing, but the food pellet is withheld. Despite the absence of the primary reinforcer, the animal learns that bar pressing elicits the tone so it continues to respond persistently, thereby overcoming the extinction phase of the experiment. In other words, the stabilized rate of bar pressing reflects the fact that the tone is now functioning as a conditioned reinforcing agent. The exact rate of responding depends on the strength of the tone as a conditioned reinforcer (i.e., the number of times the tone was associated with the primary reinforcer, food, during the acquisition phase of conditioning). Skinner demonstrated that virtually any neutral stimulus may become reinforcing in its own right if it is associated with other stimuli that have primary reinforcing properties. Thus, the phenomenon of conditioned reinforcement greatly increases the range of possible operant conditioning, particularly in reference to human social behavior. Stated in another way, if everything we learned had to be contingent upon primary reinforcement, the occasions for learning would be very restricted and the complex variety of human activity would not exist.

A significant feature of conditioned reinforcement is its propensity to become generalized when paired with more than one primary reinforcement. Money is an especially conspicuous example. It is obvious that money cannot nourish any of our primary drives. Yet, through the establishment of a cultural exchange system, money is a powerful and robust agent for obtaining a host of basic gratifications. For example, money enables us to obtain stylish clothes, flashy cars, medical aid, and education. Other kinds of generalized conditioned reinforcers include flattery, praise, affection, and submission of others. These so-called *social reinforcers* (because they involve the behavior of other people) often act in subtle and intricate ways but are essential to the maintenance of our behavior in a variety of situations. Attention is a simple case. The case of a child who gains attention by feigning illness or misbehaving is familiar. Children often are noisy, ask ridiculous questions, interrupt adult conversations, show off, tease younger siblings, and wet their beds as a means of attracting attention. The attention of a significant other—parent, teacher, loved one—is an especially effective generalized reinforcer which may promote strong attention-getting behavior.

A still stronger generalized reinforcer is social approval. For example, many people spend a great deal of time preening themselves before a mirror, hoping to elicit an approving glance from their spouses or dates. Both women's and men's fashions are subject to approval and remain in vogue only as long as social approval is forthcoming. High school students compete for the varsity team in athletics or participate in extracurricular events (drama, debate, school yearbook) in order to procure approval from parents, peers, teachers, and neighbors. Good grades in college are *positively reinforcing* because they have been followed in the past by parental praise and approval. As powerful conditioned reinforcers, satisfactory grades also foster studying behavior and the pursuit of higher academic goals.

Skinner (1971) believed that conditioned reinforcers are extremely potent in the control of human behavior. He also noted that since each person is subjected to a unique history of conditioning, it is improbable that all people will be governed by the same reinforcers. For instance, some people are strongly reinforced by entrepreneur success; others are more readily rewarded by affectionate responses; and still others derive reinforcement from athletic, academic, or musical accomplishments. The possible variations in behavior maintained by conditioned reinforcers are endless. Accordingly, the understanding of human conditioned reinforcers is far more complex than the understanding of a food-deprived rat bar pressing for the reinforcing properties of a tone.

Controlling Behavior Through Aversive Stimuli

In Skinner's view, a great deal of human behavior is controlled by the use of *aversive* (unpleasant or painful) stimuli. Two commonly employed methods of aversive control are *punishment* and *negative reinforcement*. These terms are often used synonymously to describe the conceptual properties and behavioral effects of aversive control. Skinner offered the following distinction: "You can distinguish between punishment, which is making an aversive event contingent upon a response, and negative reinforcement, in which the elimination or removal of an aversive stimulus, conditioned or unconditioned, is reinforcing" (Evans, 1968, p. 33).

Punishment   *Punishment* refers to any aversive stimulus or event whose presentation follows and depends on the occurrence of some operant response. Instead of strengthening the response it follows, punishment decreases, at least temporarily, the probability that the response will recur. The intended purpose of punishment is to induce people not to behave in given ways. Skinner (1983) observed that it is the most common technique of behavioral control in modern life.

According to Skinner, punishment can occur in two very different ways, which he calls *positive punishment* and *negative punishment* (see Figure 7-2). Positive punishment occurs whenever a behavior leads to an aversive outcome. Some examples are these: if children misbehave, they are spanked or scolded; if students cheat on an exam, they are dismissed from the course or school; if adults are caught stealing, they are fined or imprisoned. Negative punishment, by contrast, occurs whenever a behavior is followed by the removal of a (presumably) positive reinforcer. For instance, a child's TV watching privileges are denied as a result of misbehavior. A widely used approach to negative punishment is the time-out procedure. In this procedure, a person is momentarily removed from a situation in which certain reinforcers are available. Thus, for example, an unruly fourth-grader thriving on attention might be removed from the classroom setting.

Negative Reinforcement   Unlike punishment, *negative reinforcement* is the process whereby the organism terminates, escapes, or avoids an aversive stimulus. Any behavior that prevents an aversive state of affairs thereby tends to increase in frequency and is said to be negatively reinforced (see Figure 7-2). Escape behavior is such a case. Thus, a person who escapes from the hot sun by moving indoors is more likely to move indoors when the sun is again hot. It should be noted that escaping from an aversive stimulus is not the same as avoiding it, since the aversive stimulus which is avoided is not physically present. Consequently, another way of dealing with unpleasant conditions is to behave in ways

	Positive	**Negative**
Reinforcement	Presentation of pleasant stimuli	Removal of unpleasant stimuli
Punishment	Presentation of unpleasant stimuli	Removal of pleasant stimuli

FIGURE 7-2   Positive and negative reinforcement and punishment. Both reinforcement and punishment can be accomplished in two ways, depending on whether a response is followed by the presentation or removal of a pleasant or unpleasant stimulus. Notice that reinforcement strengthens a response; punishment weakens it.

that prevent their occurrence—to learn to avoid them. This strategy is referred to as *avoidance* learning. For example, if studying allows a child to avoid housework, negative reinforcement is being used to increase studying. Avoidance behavior is also evidenced when drug addicts develop clever and adroit schemes to maintain their habits and thereby shun the aversive consequences of being incarcerated.

Skinner (1971, 1983) opposed the use of all forms of behavioral control based on aversive stimuli. He especially singled out punishment as being ineffective in the control of behavior. For one thing, because of its threatening nature, the tactic of punishing unwanted behavior may generate undesirable emotional and social side effects. Anxiety, fear, antisocial actions, and loss of self-esteem and confidence are just a few of the possible negative by-products associated with the use of punishment. The threat imposed by aversive controls may also encourage people to develop patterns of behavior that are even more objectionable than the ones for which they were initially punished. Consider, for instance, the parent who tries to improve a child's mediocre performance in school by physically punishing her or him. Later, in the parent's absence, the child may adopt other behaviors that are more maladaptive—playing hookey, becoming a dropout, vandalizing school property. Regardless of the outcome, it is clear that punishment has failed to instill desirable behavior in the child. While punishment may temporarily suppress unwanted or maladaptive behavior, Skinner's main objection was that the punished behavior is likely to reappear in settings where the agent of punishment is not present. "A child who has been severely punished for sex play is not necessarily less inclined to continue; and a man who has been imprisoned for violent assault is not necessarily less inclined toward violence. Punished behavior is likely to reappear after the punitive contingencies are withdrawn" (Skinner, 1971, p. 62). It is easy to recognize everyday examples of this point. The child who learns through spanking not to swear around the house may do so freely elsewhere. The motorist who receives a few speeding tickets may buy a fuzz buster and continue to speed freely when no radar patrol is in the area.

In place of aversive types of behavioral control, Skinner (1978) recommended *positive reinforcement* as the most effective method to eliminate undesired behav-

Physical restraint is one punishment used to prevent people from acting in an unlawful manner.
(*Susan S. Perry/Woodfin Camp & Associates*)

ior. He argued that positive reinforcers do not generate the negative by-products associated with aversive stimuli; hence, they are more suitable in shaping the person's behavior. For example, convicted felons are subjected to intolerable conditions in many penal institutions (witnessed by numerous prison riots in the United States over the past several years). It is obvious that most attempts to rehabilitate the criminal have failed miserably, a conclusion supported by the high rate of recidivism or recurring offenses. Skinner's approach would be to arrange environmental conditions within prisons so that behavior resembling that of law-abiding citizens is positively reinforced (e.g., reinforcing the criminal for learning socially adaptive skills, values, and attitudes). This type of penal reform would require a team of behavioral experts knowledgeable in the principles of learning, personality, and psychopathology. In Skinner's view, such reform could be effectively implemented with the currently existing resources available to psychologists trained in the methods of behavioral psychology.

Skinner's demonstration of the power of positive reinforcement has influenced the behavioral strategies used in child care, education, business, and industry. In all these areas, there has been a trend toward increased emphasis on rewarding desirable behavior rather than punishing undesirable behavior.

Stimulus Generalization and Discrimination

A logical extension of the principle of reinforcement is that behavior strengthened in one situation is likely to recur when the organism encounters other situations that resemble the original one. If this were not so, our behavioral repertoires would be so severely limited and chaotic that we would probably spend most of our waking moments relearning how to respond appropriately to each new situation. In Skinner's system, the tendency of reinforced behavior to extend to a variety of related settings is called *stimulus generalization*. This phenomenon can be readily observed in everyday life. For example, a child rewarded for learning the subtleties of good manners at home will usually generalize this behavior to appropriate situations outside the home setting; such a child does not need to learn how to behave politely in each new social situation. Stimulus generalization may also result from unpleasant experiences. A young woman who has been sexually assaulted by a stranger may generalize her shame and hostility to all persons of the opposite sex because they remind her of the physical and emotional trauma imposed by the stranger. Similarly, a single frightening or aversive experience with a person belonging to an identifiable ethnic group (whites, blacks, Hispanics, Orientals) may be sufficient grounds for a person to stereotype and thus avoid future social contacts with all such group members.

Although the capacity to generalize responses is an important aspect of much of our everyday social interaction, it is equally apparent that adaptive behavior requires the ability to make discriminations in different situations. *Stimulus discrimination*, the obverse of generalization, is the process of learning how to respond appropriately in various environmental settings. Examples are legion. A motorist survives the rush hour by discriminating between red and green traffic lights. A child learns to discriminate between the family pet and a vicious dog. An adolescent learns to discriminate between behavior that results in peer approval and behavior that irritates or alienates others. A diabetic readily learns to discriminate between foods containing high and low amounts of sugar. Indeed, practically all intelligent human behavior depends on the ability to make discriminations.

Discrimination is acquired through reinforcement of responses in the presence of some stimuli and nonreinforcement of them in the presence of other stimuli. Discriminative stimuli thus enable us to anticipate the probable outcomes associated with emitting a particular operant response in different social situations. Accordingly, individual differences in discriminative ability are dependent upon unique histories of differential reinforcement. Skinner suggested that healthy personality development results from a blend of generalization and discrimination capacities; we regulate our behavior so as to maximize positive reinforcement and minimize punishment.

Successive Approximations: How to Get the Mountain to Come to Mohammed

Skinner's first attempts at operant conditioning were focused on responses normally emitted at moderate or high frequency (e.g., pigeons' key pecking or rats' bar pressing). However, it soon became evident that the standard procedure for operant conditioning was ill-suited for vast numbers of complex operant responses whose probability of spontaneous occurrence was near zero. In the realm of human behavior, for instance, it is doubtful that the general strategy of operant conditioning would be successful in helping patients on a psychiatric ward to acquire appropriate interpersonal skills. In order to alleviate this problem, Skinner (1953) devised a procedure by which psychologists could efficiently and rapidly accelerate the time required to condition almost any behavior within the repertoire and capabilities of the person. This procedure, called the *method of successive approximation* or *shaping*, consists of reinforcing closer and closer approximations of the desired operant behavior. It is a step-by-step process whereby one response is reinforced and then replaced by another which more closely resembles the desired outcome.

Skinner maintained that the process of shaping governs the way in which oral language is developed. For him, language results from reinforcement of the child's utterances delivered by the verbal community, initially the parents and siblings. Thus, beginning with rather crude forms of babbling in infancy, the child's verbal behavior is gradually shaped until it comes to resemble the language of adults. Skinner's *Verbal Behavior* (1957) provides a more detailed explanation of how the "rules of language" are learned by the same operant principles as any other behavior. As might be expected, others have challenged Skinner's contention that language is simply the product of verbal utterances being selectively reinforced during the formative years of life. Noam Chomsky (1972), one of Skinner's most severe critics, argues that the tremendous acceleration of verbal skills during early childhood could never be explained in operant conditioning terms. In Chomsky's view, the way in which the brain is structured at birth causes the child to acquire language. In other words, there is an innate capacity to grasp the complex rules of spoken communication.

We have now completed our coverage of Skinner's learning-behavioristic perspective. As we have seen, Skinner considered it unnecessary to posit internal forces or motivational states within a person as causal factors of behavior. Rather, he concentrated on the relationship between identifiable environmental events and overt behavior. In turn, Skinner maintained that personality is nothing more than stable behavior patterns that have been learned through the principles of operant conditioning. Whether or not these principles add up to a coherent theory of personality, Skinner has had a profound impact on the way we think about the larger issues of the human condition. The philosophical assumptions underlying Skinner's view of the person clearly set him apart from most of the personologists we have considered thus far. It is these assumptions that we next consider.

SKINNER'S BASIC ASSUMPTIONS CONCERNING HUMAN NATURE

Because he rejected intrapsychic explanations of behavior, Skinner's conception of human beings is radically different from that of most personologists. Moreover, his basic assumptions about human nature tend to be both strong and explicit. Skinner's positions on these assumptions are depicted in Figure 7-3.

Freedom–Determinism For Skinner, we humans are completely determined by our conditioning history. More specifically, our behavior is a product of prior

	Strong	Moderate	Slight	Midrange	Slight	Moderate	Strong	
Freedom							■	Determinism
Rationality				Not applicable				Irrationality
Holism							■	Elementalism
Constitutionalism							■	Environmentalism
Changeability	■							Unchangeability
Subjectivity							■	Objectivity
Proactivity							■	Reactivity
Homeostasis				Not applicable				Heterostasis
Knowability	■							Unknowability

FIGURE 7-3   Skinner's position on the nine basic assumptions concerning human nature.

reinforcements; we do what we have been reinforced to do. Individual differences in behavior result exclusively from variable reinforcement histories, since freedom is not even acknowledged in the experimental analysis of behavior. In fact, Skinner argued that the deterministic assumption is an absolute necessity for a science of human behavior: "If we are to use the methods of science in the field of human affairs, we must assume that behavior is lawful and determined" (Skinner, 1953, p. 6).

In Skinner's system an infant has an infinite number of possibilities for behavior acquisition. It is the parents first who reinforce and thus shape development in specific directions; in turn, the infant will behave contingent upon their rewards. Behavior consistently followed by nonreinforcement will not be strengthened. Gradually, as development proceeds, the child's behavior is "shaped" into patterns as a direct function of ongoing conditioning experiences. In more traditional, "non-Skinnerian" terms, the child's "personality" is emerging.

As the child's social world expands, other reinforcement sources assume importance in affecting behavioral development. School, athletic, and peer-group experiences are especially powerful and common sources of reinforcement. The principle of behavior determination by reinforcement remains the same—it is only the kinds and sources of reinforcement that change. Sexual and career types of reinforcement occur later. By the time adulthood is reached, the person behaves in a characteristic fashion because of his or her unique conditioning history; the person's behavior can be expected to change only as a consequence of the contemporary reinforcement contingencies to which she or he is exposed. Throughout the entire developmental process, previously reinforced behaviors drop out of the person's repertoire as a result of either nonreinforcement or punishment from the current social environment. In short, no one has the freedom to choose how to behave; rather, behavior is molded exclusively by external reinforcements.

Rationality–Irrationality   Skinner viewed the human organism as an "unopened box." That the box may eventually prove to contain rational and/or irrational processes may be an interesting speculation—but neither possibility has anything to do with explaining human behavior. Instead, behavior is a function only of its consequences or of lawful stimulus-response relationships. What goes into the box, what comes out of the box, and what follows therefrom are the only relevant variables needed in analyzing behavior—not what may or may not occur inside. The principles of behavior, uncovered by means of this functional approach, apply equally to rats, pigeons, and human beings; the latter's presumably more highly developed rational processes are simply not relevant in behavior causation. Because both extremes of the rationality–irrationality dimension refer to hypothetical internal processes that underlie behavior, this assumption plays no important role in Skinner's thinking. It is simply not applicable to his position.

Holism–Elementalism Skinner regarded "personality" as nothing more than a collection of behavior patterns that are characteristic of a given person. These behavior patterns can be further reduced to specific responses—all of which have been acquired through learning. An individual's personality, then, is composed of relatively complex but nonetheless independently acquired responses. To understand behavior, we need only understand the person's conditioning history. Most clearly, in Skinner's system behavior is composed of specific elements (operant responses).

Skinner's basic elementalism is also revealed in his approach to the study of behavior. He methodically examined the conditions under which single responses are acquired and modified (e.g., rats pressing bars, pigeons pecking disks). The unit of analysis in Skinner's experimental work was focused on single response acquisition. Such an approach demands a commitment to the underlying elementalist assumption that behavior can be understood only by detailed analysis of its constituent parts.

In Skinner's view, individual *personality differences* are nothing more than what meets the eye—individual differences in behavior. Each personality is constructed over time—element by element—and people differ only because their individual conditioning histories differ. This elementalistic view is in sharp contrast to holistic conceptions that portray individual uniqueness in terms of some single, unifying, and idiosyncratic factor underlying the person's behavior. In opposition to gestalt psychology, then, Skinner believed that the whole is the sum of its parts.

Constitutionalism–Environmentalism The fact that Skinner devoted his professional life to studying how behavior is modified by environmental effects clearly reveals a wholehearted commitment to environmentalism. While he recognized that constitutional factors limit a person, these factors are largely ignored in accounting for the person's behavior. Instead, Skinner portrayed the person as supremely subject to environmental whim; characteristic ways in which he or she learns to behave (personality) result exclusively from situationally based reinforcement contingencies (conditioning). Skinner's emphasis on environmentalism is undeniable.

In explaining how people differ from one another, Skinner bypassed the role of constitutional variation. Following the lead of earlier behaviorists (e.g., Watson), he envisioned environmental variation as the basic cause of individual differences. Baldly, he asserted: "The variables of which human behavior is a function lie in the environment" (Skinner, 1977, p. 1). Thus, Janice and Susan differ from one another not primarily because of their unique genetic endowments but because of the different environments to which they have been exposed. If their environments had been interchanged at birth, their personalities at age 20 would also have been interchanged.

Changeability–Unchangeability There is no ambiguity about where Skinner stood on this issue: he was strongly committed to the view that human behavior is changeable throughout life. Yet, he disagreed with most developmental psychologists about what conditions and factors instigate behavioral change. "Psychological growth is not a naturally occurring process that emerges from the individual" (*APA Monitor*, 1977, p. 6). For Skinner, changes in people's behavior over the life span are due to variations in their environments—as the environment varies in terms of its reinforcing properties, so also does the behavior under its direct control. Unlike developmental stage theorists such as Erikson, then, Skinner would explain life crises in terms of the environment changing but leaving the individual behind—left with a repertoire of behaviors inadequate to obtain reinforcement in the new situation. From this perspective, developmental changes reflect alterations in the contingencies of reinforcement throughout the life cycle.

Despite his differences with developmental stage theorists, Skinner shared their general emphasis on behavioral change. But consistent with the rest of his position, he viewed changes in behavior as resulting from environmental changes. As we have repeatedly noted, the central focus of behavioristic-learning theory is the study of those forces that produce changes in behavior. Thus, Skinner's commitment to the changeability assumption appears quite strong and seems to underlie the entire thrust of his scientific work in psychology.

Subjectivity–Objectivity Skinner's view of the organism as an unopened box suggests an unequivocal commitment to the objectivity assumption. We do not need to look into the box to explain overt behavior. Consistent with much of behaviorism, Skinner argued that human activities can be explained solely in terms of objective stimulus–response relationships. Input occurs, output results—that which follows output (reinforcement) determines the likelihood that it will again follow similar inputs in the future. What the person may presumably think or feel about incoming stimuli or outgoing responses is irrelevant when explaining his or her behavior. As Skinner wrote, "Cognitive processes are behavioral processes; they are things people do" (1989, p. 17).

Subjective experience is not totally irrelevant in Skinner's system, but references to it are held to be the main source of confusion about the cause of our actions. He believed that the hypothetical constructs used by all other personologists in this text (e.g., Freud's "ego," Jung's "archetype," Erikson's "identity crisis'') simply obscure the issue of behavior explanation. These mentalistic concepts are *explanatory fictions* superimposed upon the real external causes of human actions. And the most significant of these fictitious internal agents is the concept of personality itself! While his system allows for the description and explanation of both the similarities and differences among persons (just as does any other personality theory), Skinner accomplished these objectives without any reference to "personality." Objectivity is an all-important assumption underlying this system; Skinner took Watson's earlier rejection of "mind" to its logical and extreme conclusion.

Proactivity–Reactivity   Skinner's account of human behavior in stimulus-response-reinforcement terms emphasizes an underlying commitment to the reactivity assumption. Such reactivity is most evident in classical conditioning, where responses are automatically elicited by stimuli immediately preceding them in time. Pavlov's *dogs react* (salivate) to the sound of a bell; *humans react* in much the same way to the sight and smell of turkey on Thanksgiving.

But even in operant conditioning there is clear evidence of reactivity. While the organism's responses appear to be "freely" emitted, it cannot be assumed that they are proactively based. Certainly the rat bar pressing in a Skinner box is not internally generating its behavior in a future-oriented fashion. Rather, operant responses seem to suggest the "active" more than the "proactive" nature of the organism. All the individual's actions are triggered by some stimulus events, however subtle or elusive, with the majority of these initiating stimuli being external. Close scrutiny indicates that people are totally reactive in Skinner's system.

Homeostasis–Heterostasis   Both extremes of this dimension refer to the nature and properties of internal motivational states that presumably cause behavior. A person acts to reduce internal tensions or to seek growth and self-actualization. For Skinner, there was no need to speculate about the properties of such hypothetical inner states because they are irrelevant to the explanation of behavior. Only external factors are needed to account for behavior. Wondering about the nature of motives is like wondering what kind of spirit within a tree causes its branches to bend in the wind. Skinner took no position on either side of this dimension—both homeostasis and heterostasis are *irrelevant* assumptions in his system.

How then did Skinner account for motivated behavior? What causes a person's behavior to change while the environment remains relatively constant? To answer these questions, Skinner would ask that you examine your own behavior. For the sake of an example, suppose that you volunteer for a nutrition study in which you are deprived of food for 48 hours. If you are like most people, you will rush home after the study and eat whatever is available. A "mentalistic" theorist would no doubt attribute your eating behavior to a hunger motive. To Skinner, however, the term "hunger" has no meaning or status apart from the fact that it designates a relationship between groups of external stimuli and observable responses. Hunger is simply a convenient word to describe the relation of certain objective operations (being deprived of food) to the occurrence of certain responses (increased consumption of food). Hunger as a presumed internal motivational state does not cause behavior; the environmental operations actually produce the behavior. Consistent with his overall position, Skinner did not rely on inner motives to explain behavior. He assumed nothing about the particular properties (homeostatic versus heterostatic) of such motives.

Knowability–Unknowability Skinner's strong stands on the assumptions of determinism and objectivity logically require an equally strong commitment to the knowability assumption. He insisted that behavior is determined by external, objective factors; these factors can be elucidated by means of rigorous scientific investigation; therefore, all of human behavior (nature) is ultimately knowable in scientific terms.

While studying behavior is difficult, Skinner argued that science can do so only when its practitioners rid themselves of the mythological notion that people are free and responsible agents who internally initiate their own actions. In effect, scientists' basic assumptions about human nature hinder them in studying behavior. To apply scientific methodology profitably to human nature, it is necessary to view people as *objectively determined*. Stated another way, Skinner believed that a true science of behavior will be achieved only when other psychologists adopt his particular basic assumptions about human nature!

Let us now consider some illustrative research generated by this highly stimulating and provocative position.

EMPIRICAL VALIDATION OF OPERANT CONDITIONING CONCEPTS

It would be a monumental task simply to highlight the thousands of animal and human studies that empirically validate the behavioristic principles of operant conditioning. More than any other contemporary psychologist, Skinner has provided and stimulated massive amounts of experimental data to support his conceptual ideas. Furthermore, he attracted a large group of adherents who have carried on and extended his efforts to develop a scientifically based approach to behavior. There is no question that Skinner's behavioristic-learning position has had widespread impact in both basic and applied fields of American psychology. The following discussion examines the methodological features of Skinner's approach to behavioral research and concludes with an illustration of how his principles have been validated in the context of clinical treatment. Students who wish to explore these aspects of Skinner's position in more detail are directed to the following texts: *International Handbook of Behavior Modification and Behavior Therapy* (Bellack et al., 1982); *Dictionary of Behavior Therapy Techniques* (Bellack & Hersen, 1985); *Behavior Therapy: Techniques and Empirical Findings*

(Rimm & Masters, 1979). *The Journal of the Experimental Analysis of Behavior*, *The Journal of Applied Behavior Analysis*, and *Behavior Research and Therapy* also publish reports of experimental research relevant to the empirical verification and behavioral application of Skinnerian concepts.

Skinner's methodological strategy was quite unconventional. First, as previously noted, his experimental analysis of behavior concentrated on the *single subject* as opposed to the more prevalent method of selecting a group of subjects as the focus of study. This reliance on a single-subject research design reveals Skinner's belief that psychological science should ultimately lead to precise and quantifiable laws which are applicable to actual individual behavior.

A second feature of Skinner's methodological orientation was his automated experimental apparatus and well-defined control over the conditions under which behavior is assessed. In the typical experimental setting, an investigator would proceed through the following steps: (1) initially establish a baseline measure of stable response rates (e.g., a cumulative record of a rat's spontaneous rate of pressing a lever); (2) introduce a treatment or controlling variable (e.g., a fixed-interval reinforcement schedule); and (3) withdraw that variable after some level of performance has been attained in order to measure and determine its effect upon the behavior under investigation. Any changes in operant behavior that occur as a result of introducing and then withdrawing the treatment variable can thus be reliably attributed to that variable.

Finally, it should be stressed that Skinner's research exclusively focused on variables amenable to change or modification through manipulation of environmental stimuli. Accordingly, much of the recent research emanating from Skinner's system is pertinent to our understanding of personality development.

The Token Economy: A Research Illustration

Although he was not a clinical psychologist, Skinner held views concerning operant conditioning which have had considerable impact on modifying the behavior of severely disturbed individuals (e.g., Kazdin, 1977; Lazarus & Fay, 1984). In fact, his approach to behavior change or modification has been instrumental in establishing a new breed of behavior therapists in this country.

Behavior therapy is anchored in experimental principles and methods derived from behavioristic-learning theory. The details of this form of psychological treatment are beyond the scope of this book (see Bellack et al.'s *International Handbook of Behavior Modification and Behavior Therapy*, 1982, for a comprehensive account). However, the underlying premise upon which this therapy is practiced is relatively simple—psychological disorders have been learned through some faulty history of conditioning. No matter how self-defeating or pathological a person's behavior might be, the behavior therapist believes that it is the result of environmental contingencies that reinforce and sustain it. Accordingly, the task facing the behavior therapist is to pinpoint those of the person's maladaptive behaviors ("symptoms") that are to be eliminated, specify the desired new behaviors, and determine the reinforcement schedules that are required to shape the desired behaviors. These objectives are accomplished by creating an environment in which the person's attainment of the "good things in life" are made contingent on performing adaptive or socially desirable behaviors. Thus, behavior therapy is a logical extension of the principles of classical and operant conditioning through which many maladaptive behaviors may be effectively eliminated.

The development of what is called a *token economy* illustrates one procedural application of behavior therapy. In a token economy, people, usually hospitalized adults manifesting severe behavioral disturbances, are rewarded with tokens (i.e., symbolic or secondary reinforcers) for engaging in various activities that are deemed desirable. The token is simply a stimulus, like a plastic chip or a numerical rating, which represents something for which certain desired items or activities may be exchanged. Thus, individuals might be rewarded for engaging in such positive activities as cleaning their rooms, feeding themselves, completing a work assignment, or initiating conversations with other patients or staff members. The tokens they receive for participating in such activities are then exchanged at a later date for a variety of desired incentives (e.g., candy, cigarettes, magazines, movie tickets, and passes to leave the hospital). In some programs, patients may also lose tokens for negative behaviors, like picking fights, acting bizarre, or shirking assigned duties.

How effective is a token economy in abolishing maladaptive behavior and establishing healthy, responsible behavior in people? A study conducted by Atthowe and Krasner (1968) suggests a most encouraging answer. These two clinicians made the first attempt to institute a token reinforcement program in a psychiatric ward of a Veterans Hospital. Its purpose "was to change the chronic patients' aberrant behavior, especially that behavior judged to be apathetic, overly dependent, detrimental, or annoying to others" (Atthowe and Krasner, 1968, p. 37). The individuals (N = 60) selected had a median age of 57 and had been hospitalized for a median number of 22 years. Most had been previously diagnosed as chronic schizophrenics; the remainder were classified as brain-damaged.

The study extended across 20 months and consisted of three distinct phases. The first 6 months served as a baseline or operant period during which the investigators recorded daily the frequency of target behaviors that were to be subsequently extinguished. This was followed by a 3-month shaping period during which the patients were instructed about the types of activities they must perform in order to receive and exchange tokens for items in the hospital canteen. Finally, during the experimental period, which continued for 11 months, patients received tokens for performing specified desirable behaviors involving self-care, attendance at activities, interaction with others, or demonstration of responsibility. Whenever possible, each person was given a token immediately after completing the desired activity, accompanied by an expression of social approval from a hospital attendant (e.g., the words "fine job" or a smile).

The results indicated a significant increase in reinforced "desirable" behaviors

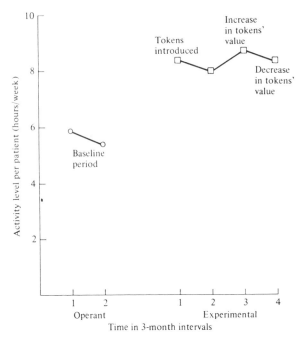

FIGURE 7-4   Attendance at group activities as a function of tokens given for the activity. (*Source: Adapted from Atthowe & Krasner, 1968, p. 39.*)

and general improvement in patient initiative, activity, responsibility, and social interaction. Figure 7-4 shows, for instance, how attendance at group activities increased and decreased as a function of token reinforcement level. During the operant baseline period, the average attendance rate per week was 5.8 hours per patient. With the introduction of the token economy, this rate increased to 8.4 hours for the first month and averaged 8.5 hours throughout the experimental period. Moreover, the rate increased to 9.2 hours during a 3-month span within the experimental period when the reinforcing value of the tokens was raised from one to two tokens per hour of attendance.

A second set of findings reported by Atthowe and Krasner focuses on the number of infractions committed by patients. Ordinarily many hospitalized patients refuse to get out of bed in the morning, take care of personal hygiene, or leave the bedroom area by a specified time, thus necessitating the help of extra personnel. Immediately prior to the onset of the token economy, the number of infractions in these three areas was recorded for a one-week period. This yielded an average of 75 infractions (or a little more than 1 per patient) per week. A token was then given daily, contingent upon not having a recorded infraction in any of these areas. As shown in Figure 7-5, the number of infractions dropped following the establishment of the contingency program. The unexpected rise in infractions during the fourth week of the token program (increased to 39) was not explained

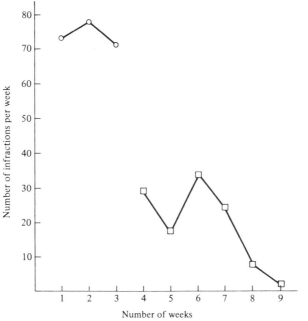

FIGURE 7-5   Number of infractions in performing morning routines. (*Source: Adapted from Atthowe & Krasner, 1968, p. 41.*)

by the investigators. During the last 6 months of the experimental period, the frequency of infractions averaged 9 per week (not indicated in Figure 7-5).

Despite the impressive results found in this clinical research program, it is not altogether clear whether the changes in behavior were a function of the specific reinforcement procedures used. For example, the possibility exists that patients who participate in a token economy are merely responding to the enthusiasm, attention, and hopeful expectancies of the hospital staff. Advocates of behavior therapy strongly insist that this type of interpretation is not valid, and that the changes in patient behavior are a direct result of the shaping and contingency methods they employ. One study that clearly supports this contention is that of Ayllon and Azrin (1965). They found that performance of desired behaviors directly fluctuated as a function of the presence or absence of token reinforcements. Based on six specific experiments of the token economy, they concluded that desired performance was maintained "at a high level for as long as the reinforcement procedure was in effect" (Ayllon & Azrin, 1965, p. 381).

Thus, it seems safe to conclude that a token economy can be used to penetrate patients' apathy while strengthening their normal adaptive behavior. Studies also indicate that token economies can lead to more rapid discharge of patients and lower readmission rates than traditional hospital environments (Curran et al., 1982; Paul & Lentz, 1977). It should be further noted that token economies have been used extensively in classroom situations with "normal" children, delinquent youngsters, people with drug-abuse problems, and mentally retarded people (Kazdin & Bootzin, 1972; O'Leary & Drabman, 1971). Finally, token economies have been used to eliminate fear, hyperactivity, and aggressive behavior in children and to decrease marital discord (Kazdin, 1977; Stuart, 1969).

APPLICATION: TREATMENTS BASED ON OPERANT CONDITIONING

The number of potential and actual applications of Skinner's operant conditioning concepts is enormous. Major areas of application include (1) psychopharmacology, or the study of the effects of drugs on behavior; (2) educational technology, including programmed instruction devices and classroom management systems; (3) psycholinguistics and the acquisition of verbal behavior; (4) industrial management, including employee morale and job satisfaction; and (5) therapeutic treatment of psychological problems (e.g., alcoholism, drug addiction, mental retardation, childhood autism, phobias, and eating disorders). In this section we will limit ourselves to two treatments that depend primarily on operant principles: social skills training and biofeedback.

Social Skills Training

Many people who display abnormal behavior have either failed to learn the skills needed to cope with the problems of everyday living or have acquired faulty skills and coping patterns that are being maintained by some kind of reinforcement. Behavior therapists reason, for instance, that some people do not learn how to be friendly, how to make conversation, how to express anger appropriately, how to turn away unreasonable requests, and so forth. Such social ineptitude may lead not only to increased social isolation but also to depression, anxiety, a tendency to seek attention by destructive or disruptive actions, and a failure to learn more advanced social skills (Craighead et al., 1981; Mattson & Ollendick, 1988). It is evident from these problems that social skills are likely to affect a very broad range of psychological response patterns. Indeed, persons who evince these problems may become unproductive members of society and, as such, become a drain on the resources of society. The cost in psychological and physical suffering as well as the overall negative financial and social cost can be considerable for those persons affected.

Social skills training is designed to improve interpersonal skills in dealing with a variety of real-world interactions. The particular skills that are taught vary widely depending on the kind of problems experienced by the individual. For example, assume that a woman responds to unreasonable demands from her boss by giving the kind of submissive responses that she learned as a child. The therapist would not only seek to extinguish these self-defeating responses but also try to train her to refuse to comply with such demands in a way that is straightforward and forceful. Alternatively, an extremely shy college student who is distressed because he lacks meaningful friendships would be taught communication skills required to develop new friendships and future intimate relationships.

Social skills training, like other treatment approaches, is tailored to specific persons who function in particular settings with particular problems. There is no "one way" to do social skills training. Two general problem areas that have received special attention are heterosexual interactions, such as dating and marital communication, and assertive behavior. We shall focus on assertiveness training.

Assertiveness Training   Behavior therapists (Hersen & Bellack, 1985; Kazdin, 1984) believe that assertive skills lie on a continuum. At one end of the continuum the person is nonassertive. This person has difficulty expressing positive emotions toward others, greeting strangers, asking others for information or advice, refusing unreasonable requests, and so on. Furthermore, this person has difficulty knowing how to begin or end conversations, making responses that will be socially effective, and expressing annoyance and resentment under appropriate circumstances. At the other end of the continuum is the aggressive person whose sole concern is for him- or herself. This person is frequently perceived as being uncaring about the rights and privileges of others and as being very self-centered in his or her behavior. Between these two extremes is the assertive (socially skilled) person. This person clearly and directly expresses both positive and negative feelings without violating the rights and privileges of others. The assertive person sticks up for his or her legitimate rights, actively seeks to construct new relationships with others, and is generally effective in handling complicated and delicate social situations. The questionnaire presented in Table 7-1 will afford you insight into how assertive you are in various situations.

Assertiveness training builds social skills through techniques such as behavioral rehearsal and self-monitoring. In *behavioral rehearsal*, the client practices interpersonal skills in structured role-playing exercises. Becker et al., (1987) recommend that each role-play exercise be designed according to the following guidelines:

   1 Give the client explicit instructions about the role he or she is to rehearse.
   2 Demonstrate the desired performance to the client and follow this demonstration with questions, to make certain that the client has attended to the salient aspects of performance that are being trained.
   3 Ask the client to enact the role play he or she just observed. The role can be enacted overtly (actually in action) or covertly (mentally rehearsing the action).
   4 Provide corrective feedback to the client about various aspects of the performance and give new instructions and demonstrations for skills that need to be improved.
   5 Give approval for following instructions and trying to enact the role play and encouragement to continue with the next role play. (pp. 42–43)

Eventually, of course, the client will test out the newly acquired skills in the natural world. For example, a client who feels afraid or silly about asking for a

TABLE 7-1 THE FOLLOWING TEN ITEMS ARE HELPFUL IN ASSESSING YOUR ASSERTIVENESS

All you have to do is circle the number that best describes you. For some items, the assertive end of the scale is at 0; for others, at 4.

Code:	0 = no or never
	1 = somewhat or sometimes
	2 = average
	3 = usually or a good deal
	4 = practically always or entirely

1 When a person is highly unfair, do you call it to his or her attention?	0	1	2	3	4
2 Do you speak out in protest when somebody takes your place in line?	0	1	2	3	4
3 Do you often avoid people or situations for fear of embarrassment?	0	1	2	3	4
4 When a salesman makes an effort, do you find it hard to say "No" even though the merchandise is not really what you want?	0	1	2	3	4
5 If a person has borrowed money (or a book, a garment, a thing of value) and is overdue in returning it, do you mention it?	0	1	2	3	4
6 If someone keeps kicking or bumping your chair in a movie or a lecture, do you ask the person to stop?	0	1	2	3	4
7 When you discover merchandise is faulty, do you return it for an adjustment?	0	1	2	3	4
8 When you differ with a person you respect, are you able to speak up for your own viewpoint?	0	1	2	3	4
9 If you are disturbed by someone smoking near you, can you say so?	0	1	2	3	4
10 When you meet a stranger, are you the first to introduce yourself and begin a conversation?	0	1	2	3	4

Source: Adapted from Alberti & Emmons, 1990.

raise might rehearse the skills needed by repeatedly role-playing the situation with the therapist or other members of a therapy group. Similarly, if the client has difficulties in job interviews and will soon be seeking a job, the therapist might role-play hypothetical job interviews. Later each client will be given "homework assignments" in order to apply the newly learned assertive skills to actual real-life situations. Completed assignments are then reviewed at subsequent treatment sessions, usually via a role play, and the therapist insures that the client understands what is expected of him or her.

In *self-monitoring*, the client keeps a record of discrete social events as they occur. Such a record enables the client to pinpoint instances of social avoidance, clumsiness, and feelings of anxiety or frustration. The most commonly used self-monitoring strategy is some kind of homework log sheet that the client fills out on a daily basis. Homework sheets are important because they can be used both as a guide for new behavioral goals and as a tool for assessing the client's progress in assertiveness training.

Research suggests that social skills training is very useful in helping people to overcome their shyness and assert themselves more effectively when they feel they should (Pilkonis & Zimbardo, 1979; Twentyman & McFall, 1975). Furthermore, such training has been shown to be effective in helping people who are unable to express or control anger (Novaco, 1977). It should be apparent, then, that training in social skills has many positive effects on anyone who wishes to be more effective in dealing with other people, whether roommates, boss, spouse, or parent. Such training boosts feelings of self-esteem and gives the person increased confidence to pursue social and material rewards leading to greater satisfaction with life.

Biofeedback

Biofeedback (short for "biological feedback") represents another way in which operant conditioning concepts are used in therapeutic behavior change. This application of operant principles involves learning how to gain control over normally involuntary bodily functions (such as heart rate, blood pressure, and muscle tension). Specifically, biofeedback training is based on the notion that when people are given precise information (feedback) about unobservable internal physiological processes, they can learn to exert some conscious control over those processes.

For many years psychologists believed that operant conditioning was effective only with voluntary responses. The focus of behavior modification was on such voluntary behaviors as shyness, aggression, and achievement. Therapeutic efforts enabled individuals to be more assertive and outgoing, to reduce their aggression, and to acquire better study habits. Internal behaviors such as pulse rate, glandular secretions, brain waves, or skin temperature were thought to be outside the boundaries of volitional control because they are governed by the autonomic or involuntary nervous system. In the late 1960s, however, it was discovered (Miller, 1969, 1974; Kamiya, 1969) that people could learn to control these internal processes through operant conditioning procedures.

To see how biofeedback works, let us look at *electromyograph (EMG) feedback* intended to enhance deep muscle relaxation. An EMG is an instrument used to measure skeletal-muscular tension in the body. In a typical biofeedback session, a client is hooked up to an EMG via electrodes and instructed to try and reduce the level of tension in the frontalis muscle in the forehead. It should be noted that the client is not told how to do this, just that he or she is to try to do it. While doing so, electrical activity detected by the electrodes is transformed into an auditory signal, such as a tone that increases or decreases in volume through a loudspeaker. The therapist explains to the client that as muscle tension increases,

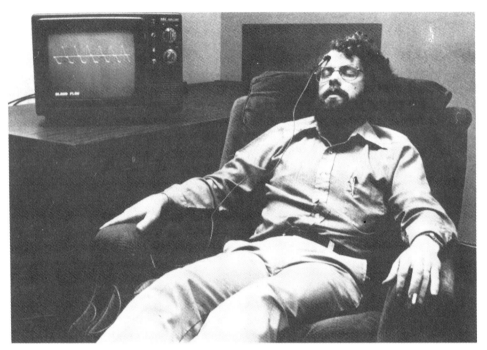

This man uses biofeedback to reduce the level of tension in certain facial muscles. (*Ken Robert Buck and University Hospital, Boston/The Picture Cube*)

the tone will become louder; as it drops, the tone will become softer. The raising or lowering of the tone (the "biofeedback") thus serves as a reinforcer since it feeds back information on the success of the client's efforts to control muscle tension. Once control is well-established, the feedback from the tone is gradually phased out by omitting it on an increasing number of trials. This procedure enables the client to transfer his or her control from the laboratory to everyday life. Presumably once the control over subtle internal processes is well-learned, it will continue to occur even without the biofeedback.

   Although people often have difficulty describing how they do it, most can learn to exert better control over their level of muscular tension. In fact, EMG feedback has been used in the treatment of a variety of physical problems that seem to involve subtle muscular activity. For instance, encouraging results have been obtained with EMG feedback in the treatment of chronic anxiety (Raskin et al., 1981), migraine headaches (Blanchard & Andrasik, 1982; Elmore & Tursky, 1981), and hypertension (Lustman & Sowa, 1983). It has even been suggested that biofeedback provides a way to help people regain use of muscles after spinal cord injuries or strokes (Runck, 1980). The idea is that feedback from recordings of muscle activity can be used to regain mastery over a little bit of muscle that remains under functional control of intact nerves. Even though there is a theoretical reason why this might be possible, the promise has remained unfulfilled despite continuing research.

The means by which biofeedback produces control over bodily responses remain uncertain (Miller, 1974, 1985; Norris, 1987). Early proponents of biofeedback may have also made exaggerated claims about its success and potential for treating stress-related problems (Roberts, 1985). As more carefully designed studies have been conducted, the enthusiastic claims have given way to a more conscientious understanding of the complexities of biofeedback. In any case, biofeedback appears clinically useful when used as part of a larger treatment strategy (Budzynski & Stoyva, 1984).

SUMMARY

The learning-behavioral approach to personality as espoused by B. F. Skinner is concerned with the overt actions of people as determined by their life experiences. Skinner contended that behavior is lawfully determined, predictable, and environmentally controlled. He firmly rejected the notion of an inner ''autonomous'' agent as the cause of human actions and disregarded physiological-genetic explanations of behavior.

Skinner recognized two major kinds of behavior: respondent behavior, which is elicited by a known stimulus, and operant behavior, which is emitted and controlled by the consequence that follows it. Skinner's work focused almost entirely on operant behavior. In operant conditioning, the organism operates on its environment, producing consequences that influence the likelihood that some behavior will be repeated. An operant response followed by a positive outcome tends to be repeated, whereas an operant response followed by a negative outcome tends not to be repeated. For Skinner, behavior is best understood in terms of responses to the environment.

Reinforcement is a key concept in Skinner's system. Four different schedules of reinforcement that result in different patterns of responding were described: fixed-ratio, fixed-interval, variable ratio, and variable interval. Primary or unlearned and secondary or learned reinforcers were also noted. For Skinner, secondary or conditioned reinforcers (money, attention, approval) exert a strong influence on human behavior. He also stressed how behavior is controlled by aversive stimuli such as punishment and negative reinforcement. Positive punishment occurs when a response is followed by an unpleasant stimulus and negative punishment occurs when a response is followed by removal of a pleasant stimulus. In contrast, negative reinforcement occurs when an aversive stimulus is terminated or avoided by the organism. Skinner opposed the use of aversive methods (especially punishment) in the control of behavior and emphasized control through positive reinforcement.

In operant conditioning, stimulus generalization occurs when a response reinforced in the presence of one stimulus also occurs in the presence of other, similar stimuli. Stimulus discrimination, on the other hand, is responding differently to various environmental stimuli. Both are seen by Skinner as essential for effective functioning in life. The method of successive approximations or shaping involves reinforcing the organism only as its behavior comes to resemble the desired behavior. Skinner claimed that verbal behavior or language is acquired through the process of shaping.

Skinner's basic assumptions about human nature are strong and explicit. His system reflects a strong commitment to determinism, elementalism, environmentalism, changeability, objectivity, reactivity, and knowability. The basic assumptions of rationality–irrationality and homeostasis–heterostasis are not applicable to Skinner's position since he rejected all internal sources of behavior.

Operant conditioning concepts have been subjected to extensive experimental testing. Both the amount and diversity of this research is enormous. Skinner's own approach to behavioral research is characterized by study of single subjects, use of automated equipment, and well-defined control over experimental conditions. The efficacy of a token economy system in bringing about improved behavior patterns in a group of hospitalized mental patients was presented as an illustration of research.

Current applications of operant conditioning principles are widespread. Two key areas of such application are social skills training and biofeedback. Evidence suggests that assertiveness training, based on behavioral rehearsal and self-monitoring techniques, is quite useful in helping people deal more effectively with various social interactions. Similarly, biofeedback training has been found to be effective in treating anxiety, migraine headaches, muscle tension, and hypertension. It remains unclear, however, how biofeedback actually produces control over involuntary bodily functions.

BIBLIOGRAPHY

Alberti, R. E., & Emmons, M. L. (1990). *Your perfect right: A guide to assertive living.* (6th ed.). San Luis Obispo, CA: Impact.

American Psychological Association (1977). A chat with Skinner. *APA Monitor,* **8,** 6.

American Psychologist, January 1972, **27,** 72.

Atthowe, J., & Krasner, L. (1968). Preliminary report on the application of contingent reinforcement procedures (token economy) on a "chronic" psychiatric ward. *Journal of Abnormal Psychology,* **73,** 37–42.

Ayllon, T., & Azrin, N. (1965). The measurement and reinforcement of behavior of psychotics. *Journal of the Experimental Analysis of Behavior,* **8,** 357–384.

Becker, R. E., Heimberg, R. G., & Bellack, A. S. (1987). *Social skills training treatment for depression.* New York: Pergamon Press.

Bellack, A. S., Hersen, M., & Kazdin, A. E. (Eds.). (1982). *International handbook of behavior modification and behavior therapy.* New York: Plenum.

Bellack, A. S., & Hersen, M. (Eds.). (1985). *Dictionary of behavior therapy techniques.* New York: Pergamon Press.

Blanchard, E. B., & Andrasik, F. (1982). Psychological assessment and treatment of the headache: Recent developments and emerging issues. *Journal of Consulting and Clinical Psychology,* **50,** 859–879.

Budzynski, T. H., & Stoyva, J. M. (1984). Biofeedback methods in the treatment of anxiety and stress. In R. L. Woolfolk & P. M. Lehrer (Eds.), *Principles and practice of stress management*. New York: Guilford Press.

Chomsky, N. (1972). *Language and mind* (2nd ed.). New York: Harcourt Brace Jovanovich.

Craighead, W. E., Kazdin, A. E., & Mahoney, M. J. (1981). *Behavior modification: Principles, issues, and applications*. Boston: Houghton Mifflin.

Curran, J. P., Monti, P. M., & Corriveau, D. P. (1982). Treatment of schizophrenia. In A. S. Bellack, M. Hersen, & A. E. Kazdin (Eds.), *International handbook of behavior modification and behavior therapy*. New York: Plenum.

Davis, S., Thomas, R., & Weaver, M. (1982). Psychology's contemporary and all-time notables: Student, faculty, chairperson viewpoints. *Bulletin of the Psychonomic Society*, **20**, 3–6.

Dews, P. (Ed.). (1970). *Festschrift for B. F. Skinner*. New York: Appleton-Century-Crofts.

Elmore, A. M., & Tursky, B. (1981). A comparison of two approaches to the treatment of migraine. *Headache*, **21**, 93–101.

Evans, R. B. (1968). *B. F. Skinner: The man and his ideas*. New York: Dutton.

Hersen, M. & Bellack, A. S. (Eds.). (1985). *Handbook of clinical behavior therapy with adults* (pp. 201–226). New York: Plenum.

Kamiya, J. (1969). Operant control of the EEG and some of its reported effects on consciousness. In C. T. Tart (Ed.), *Altered states of consciousness*. New York: Wiley.

Kazdin, A. E. (1977). *The token economy: A review and evaluation*. New York: Plenum.

Kazdin, A. E. (1984). *Behavior modification in applied settings*. Homewood, IL: Dorsey Press.

Kazdin, A. E., & Bootzin, R. (1972). The token economy: An evaluative review. *Journal of Applied Behavior Analysis*, **5**, 343–372.

Lazarus, A. A., & Fay, A. (1984). Behavior therapy. In T. B. Karasu (Ed.), *The psychiatric therapies*. Washington, DC: American Psychiatric Association.

Lustman, P. J., & Sowa, C. J. (1983). Comparative efficacy of biofeedback and stress inoculation for stress reduction. *Journal of Clinical Psychology*, **31**, 191–197.

Mattson, J. L., & Ollendick, T. H. (1988). *Enhancing children's social skills: Assessment and training*. New York: Pergamon Press.

Miller, N. E. (1969). Learning of visceral and glandular responses. *Science*, **163**, 434–445.

Miller, N. E. (1974). Applications of learning and biofeedback to psychiatry and medicine. In A. M. Freedman, H. I. Kaplan, & B. J. Sadock (Eds.), *Comprehensive textbook of psychiatry* (2nd ed.). Baltimore: William & Wilkins.

Miller, N. E. (1985). Rx: Biofeedback. *Psychology Today*, February, 54–59.

Norris, P. (1987). Biofeedback, voluntary control, and human potential. *Journal of Biofeedback and Self-Regulation*, **11**, 1–20.

Novaco, R. W. (1977). Stress inoculation: A cognitive therapy for anger and its application to a case of depression. *Journal of Consulting and Clinical Psychology*, **45**, 600–608.

O'Leary, K., & Drabman, R. (1971). Token reinforcement programs in the classroom. *Psychological Bulletin*, **75**, 379–398.

Paul, G. L., & Lentz, R. J. (1977). *Psychosocial treatment of chronic mental patients: Milieu versus social-learning programs*. Cambridge, MA: Harvard University Press.

Pilkonis, P. A., & Zimbardo, P. G. (1979). The personal and social dynamics of shyness. In C. E. Izard (Ed.), *Emotions in personality and psychopathology*. New York: Plenum.

Raskin, R., Bali, L. R., & Peeke, H. V. (1981). Muscle biofeedback and meditation: A controlled evaluation of efficacy in the treatment of chronic anxiety. In D. Shapiro, Jr.,

J. Stoyva, J. Kamiya, T. X. Barber, N. E. Miller, & G. E. Schwartz (Eds.), *Biofeedback and behavioral medicine 1979/80: Therapeutic applications and experimental foundations*. Chicago: Aldine.

Rimm, D., & Masters, J. (1979). *Behavior therapy: Techniques and empirical findings* (2nd ed.). New York: Academic Press.

Roberts, A. A. (1985). Biofeedback: Research, training, and clinical roles. *American Psychologist*, **40**, 938–941.

Runck, B. (1980). *Biofeedback—Issues in treatment assessment*. Rockville, MD: National Institute of Mental Health.

Skinner, B. F. (1938). *The behavior of organisms: An experimental analysis*. New York: Appleton-Century-Crofts.

Skinner, B. F. (1948). *Walden two*. New York: Macmillan.

Skinner, B. F. (1953). *Science and human behavior*. New York: Macmillan.

Skinner, B. F. (1956). A case history in scientific method. *American Psychologist*, **11**, 221–233.

Skinner, B. F. (1957). *Verbal behavior*. New York: Appleton-Century-Crofts.

Skinner, B. F. (1961). *Cumulative record*. New York: Appleton-Century-Crofts.

Skinner, B. F. (1967). Autobiography of B. F. Skinner. In E. Boring & G. Lindzey (Eds.), *History of psychology in autobiography* (Vol. 5, pp. 387–413). New York: Appleton-Century-Crofts.

Skinner, B. F. (1968). *The technology of teaching*. New York: Appleton-Century-Crofts.

Skinner, B. F. (1969). *Contingencies of reinforcement: A theoretical analysis*. New York: Appleton-Century-Crofts.

Skinner, B. F. (1971). *Beyond freedom and dignity*. New York: Knopf.

Skinner, B. F. (1974). *About behaviorism*. New York: Knopf.

Skinner, B. F. (1976). *Particulars of my life*. New York: Knopf.

Skinner, B. F. (1977). Why I am not a cognitive psychologist. *Behaviorism*, **5**, 1–10.

Skinner, B. F. (1978). *Reflections on behaviorism and society*. Englewood Cliffs, NJ: Prentice-Hall.

Skinner, B. F. (1979). *The shaping of a behaviorist*. New York: Knopf.

Skinner, B. F. (1983). *A matter of consequences*. New York: Knopf.

Skinner, B. F. (1987). *Upon further reflection*. Englewood Cliffs, NJ: Prentice-Hall.

Skinner, B. F. (1989). The origins of cognitive thought. *American Psychologist*, **44**, 13–18.

Skinner, B. F., & Ferster, C. B. (1957). *Schedules of reinforcement*. New York: Appleton-Century-Crofts.

Skinner, B. F., & Vaughan, M. E. (1983). *Enjoy old age*. New York: Norton.

Stuart, R. (1969). Operant-interpersonal treatment for marital discord. *Journal of Consulting and Clinical Psychology*, **33**, 675–682.

Twentyman, C. T., & McFall, R. M. (1975). Behavioral training of social skills in shy males. *Journal of Consulting and Clinical Psychology* **43**, 384–395.

Watson, J., & Rayner, R. (1920). Conditioned emotional reactions. *Journal of Experimental Psychology*, **3**, 1–14.

Williams, C. (1959). The elimination of tantrum behavior by extinction procedures. *Journal of Abnormal and Social Psychology*, **59**, 269.

SUGGESTED READINGS

Axelrod, S., & Apsche, J. (1983). *The effects of punishment on human behavior*. New York: Academic Press.

Domjan, M., & Burkhard, B. (1986). *The principles of learning and behavior*. Pacific Grove, CA: Brooks/Cole.

Skinner, B. F. (1982). *Notebooks*. Englewood Cliffs, NJ: Prentice-Hall.

Skinner, B. F. (1987). Whatever happened to psychology as the science of behavior. *American Psychologist,* **42,** 780–786.

Watson, D. L., & Tharp, R. G. (1989). *Self-directed behavior: Self-modification for personal adjustment*. Pacific Grove, CA: Brooks/Cole.

DISCUSSION QUESTIONS

1 Based on what you know about Skinner's early life, can you see any factors that might have led him in the direction of developing the kind of theory of human behavior that he did? Indeed, can Skinner's own theory-construction behavior be explained in reinforcement terms? How?

2 What are some of the basic differences between respondent and operant behavior? What does Skinner mean by the term *operant* in his account of learning?

3 Now that you have read about schedules of reinforcement, can you detect how these different schedules operate in your own life? Give one example of how each reinforcement schedule—fixed-ratio, fixed-interval, variable-ratio, and variable-interval—operates to maintain different aspects of your behavior.

4 Cite examples illustrating how positive and negative punishment differ. Why did Skinner oppose the use of punishment as a means of eliminating undesirable behavior? Can you think of any circumstances in which punishment might be effective in getting a person to stop behaving in maladaptive ways?

5 How did Skinner explain the process of learning to speak one's own native tongue?

6 To what degree do you agree with Skinner's basic assumptions about human nature—his basic image of the human being? If you agree to a large extent, what are some of the important implications for what you fundamentally are as a person and how you should live your life?

7 What are some of the techniques used in social skills training? How does social skills training employ operant conditioning principles in helping individuals to function more effectively in social settings?

8 Describe the biofeedback approach to the treatment of hypertension. In what ways does biofeedback reflect operant conditioning principles?

9 How does Skinner's view of the human condition differ from other perspectives previously described in this book?

GLOSSARY

Assertiveness training A behavior therapy procedure used to help a client become more effective in dealing with interpersonal situations.

Behavioral rehearsal An assertiveness training technique in which the client practices interpersonal skills in structured role-playing exercises.

Behavior therapy A collection of therapeutic techniques that seek to change maladaptive or unhealthy behaviors through application of operant conditioning principles.

Biofeedback A type of behavior therapy in which the client learns to control some aspect of physiological functioning (e.g., blood pressure) by means of special equipment which provides information about internal bodily processes.

Classical conditioning A type of learning, first described by Pavlov, in which a previously neutral stimulus is paired with a stimulus that naturally elicits a response so that the neutral stimulus comes to elicit the same response. For example, a child hears an angry voice paired with a spanking and subsequently responds to an angry voice in fear.

Conditioned response   A learned response similar to an unconditioned response which is elicited by a previously neutral stimulus.

Conditioned stimulus   A previously neutral stimulus that acquires the capacity to elicit particular responses through repeated pairing with another stimulus capable of eliciting such responses.

Continuous reinforcement   A reinforcement schedule in which every instance of a desired or correct response is reinforced.

Discriminative stimulus   A stimulus (cue) whose presence indicates that some particular form of behavior will or will not be rewarded.

Electromyograph   A special instrument that measures muscular activity and tension (used in biofeedback).

Extinction   The process whereby conditioned responses are weakened and eventually eliminated when no longer reinforced.

Fixed-interval schedule   Reinforcement schedule in which the first response that occurs after an absolute amount of time has elapsed is reinforced.

Fixed-ratio schedule   Reinforcement schedule in which the first response following an absolute number of responses is reinforced.

Functional analysis   The establishment of specifiable relationships between the organism's behavior and the environmental conditions that control it.

Intermittent reinforcement   Reinforcement schedule in which reinforcers are applied to given responses occasionally or intermittently.

Negative punishment   The condition that occurs when a response is followed by the removal of a pleasant stimulus.

Negative reinforcement   Reinforcement that occurs when a response is strengthened because it is followed by the removal of an unpleasant stimulus.

Operant behavior   Responses freely emitted by an organism, the frequency of which is strongly affected by the application of various reinforcement schedules.

Operant conditioning   A form of learning in which a correct response or change of behavior is reinforced and becomes more likely to occur; also called *instrumental conditioning*.

Positive punishment   The condition that occurs when a response is followed by the presentation of an unpleasant stimulus.

Positive reinforcement   Reinforcement that occurs when a response is strengthened because it is followed by the arrival of a pleasant stimulus.

Primary reinforcement   Any event or object that possesses inherent reinforcing properties; also referred to as *unconditioned reinforcement*.

Punishment   Presentation of aversive stimuli following a behavior considered undesirable, which results in a decrease in the performance of that behavior.

Reinforcement   In classical conditioning, the association formed through repeated pairing of the conditioned stimulus and the unconditioned stimulus; in operant conditioning, the association that is formed when an operant response is followed by a reinforcing stimulus.

Respondent behavior   A specific response that is elicited by a known stimulus, the latter always preceding the former in time.

Schedule of reinforcement   Rule stating the contingencies under which reinforcements will be delivered.

Secondary reinforcement   Any stimulus that acquires reinforcing properties through close association with a primary reinforcement in the past conditioning history of the organism; also known as *conditioned reinforcement*.

Self-monitoring   Method of assertiveness training in which the client keeps a daily log of social events as they occur.

Shaping   In operant conditioning, the reinforcement of closer and closer approximations of the desired response.

Single-subject experimental design   Attempt to establish basic laws of behavior by studying the influence of one or more controlled variables upon a specific component of a single organism's behavior in a controlled environment.

Skinner box   A small experimental chamber that Skinner invented in order to study principles of operant conditioning.

Social skills training   A behavior therapy procedure designed to improve a client's interpersonal skills in dealing with real-world interactions.

Unconditioned response   An unlearned response that is automatically elicited by an unconditioned stimulus.

Variable-interval schedule   Reinforcement schedule in which the reinforcement is given after a variable amount of time has elapsed.

Variable-ratio schedule   Reinforcement schedule in which responses are reinforced an average number of times but on an unpredictable basis.

CHAPTER 8

THE SOCIAL COGNITIVE PERSPECTIVE IN PERSONALITY THEORY: ALBERT BANDURA AND JULIAN ROTTER

It is difficult to overstate the tremendous impact that basic principles of learning have had on psychology and the field of personality. The concepts of classical and operant conditioning described in Chapter 7 provide powerful tools for explaining how behavior patterns are acquired, maintained, and modified as a result of the person's learning history. In recent decades, however, personologists have begun to theorize that human behavior is governed by complex interactions between internal events (including beliefs, expectations, and self-perceptions) and environmental forces. Such theorizing, expanding on the classic behaviorist position in many ways, has culminated in what may be called a *social cognitive perspective*. The emergence of this perspective is most clearly represented in the works of two prominent personologists, Albert Bandura and Julian Rotter. Their respective theories represent a significant departure from Skinner's radical behaviorism but retain the rigorous methodology and scientific procedures that characterize the behaviorist approach.

Bandura believes that psychological functioning is best understood in terms of a continuous reciprocal interplay among behavioral, cognitive, and environmental influences. This means that behavior, personal factors, and social forces all operate as interlocking determinants of one another—that behavior is influenced by the environment but that people also play an active role in creating the social milieu and other circumstances that arise in their daily transactions. This view is strikingly different from Skinner's approach, which limits explanations of human behavior to a two-factor, one-way model, in which external events cause behavior. Moreover, unlike Skinner, who was almost entirely concerned with learning by direct experience, Bandura places primary emphasis on the role of *observa-*

tional learning in behavioral acquisition. Indeed, the most distinctive feature of Bandura's social cognitive theory is the belief that most human behavior is learned through observation or by example.

> Humans have evolved an advanced capacity for observational learning that enables them to expand their knowledge and skills on the basis of information conveyed by modeling influences. Indeed, virtually all learning phenomena resulting from direct experience can occur vicariously by observing people's behavior and its consequences for them. (Bandura, 1989a, pp. 14–15)

Bandura also emphasizes the importance of self-generated influences as a causal factor in all aspects of human functioning—motivation, emotion, and action. This is nowhere more evident than in his concept of self-efficacy or the belief that one can exercise control over events that affect one's life. A major portion of this chapter is devoted to Bandura's social cognitive perspective.

Julian Rotter is another personologist who stresses the role of social and cognitive variables in understanding personality. Like Bandura, he believes that people are active agents in influencing events in their lives. A particular aspect of Rotter's work that warrants special attention is the concept of locus of control. Other major concepts of his social learning theory (e.g., behavior potential, expectancy, reinforcement value, and psychological situation) will be briefly discussed later in the chapter. A biographical sketch of Bandura follows.

ALBERT BANDURA: A Social Cognitive Theory of Personality

BIOGRAPHICAL SKETCH

Albert Bandura was born in a small town in Alberta, Canada, in 1925. The son of wheat farmers of Polish heritage, he attended a combined elementary and high school that had only 20 students and 2 teachers. Largely obliged to educate himself, as were his classmates, Bandura recalls that virtually every graduate went on to a successful professional career. Summer jobs included patching highways in the forbidding Yukon. Little other published information is available on his childhood.

After high school, Bandura attended the University of British Columbia in Vancouver, where he received his B.A. degree in 1949. He then enrolled in graduate study at the University of Iowa, where he received his M.A. in 1951 and his Ph.D. in 1952. He next served a year's clinical internship at the Wichita Kansas Guidance Center, following which he accepted a position in the psychology department at Stanford University, where he has remained ever since.

Throughout his career, Bandura has been actively engaged in the development of a social cognitive learning approach to the study and understanding of personality. He has also maintained an impressive record of scholarship, publishing several books and countless research articles. His early books, *Adolescent Aggression* (1959) and *Social Learning and Personality Development* (1963), were written in collaboration with Richard H. Walters, his first Ph.D. student. Then he

Albert Bandura. (*Courtesy of Albert Bandura*)

published *Principles of Behavior Modification* (1969), an extensive review of the psychosocial principles that govern behavior. In 1969, Bandura was named a Fellow of the Center for Advanced Study in the Behavioral Sciences at Stanford University. He used that year both to write his book *Aggression: A Social-Learning Analysis* (1973) and, by his own admission, to study the subculture of the daily volleyball games played by the highly competitive fellows at the center. He has also published a module entitled *Social-Learning Theory* (1971), an abbreviated treatment of key concepts that help to explain behavior. In two of his recent books, *Social Learning Theory* (1977b) and *Social Foundations of Thought and Action* (1986), Bandura presents an overview of current theoretical and experimental advances relating to a social cognitive model of personality.

Bandura has been frequently recognized for his contributions to psychology. He was elected president of the American Psychological Association in 1973. In 1980 he received the American Psychological Association's award for Distinguished Scientific Contributions and was cited for "innovative experiments on a host of topics including moral development, observational learning, fear acquisition, treatment strategies, self-control. . . . self-referent processes, and cognitive regulation of behavior. . . . His vigor, warmth, and humane example have inspired his many students' own self-efficacy'' (*American Psychologist*, 1981, p. 27).

After nearly 40 years of teaching and research, Bandura now occupies an endowed chair at Stanford. He and his wife, Virginia, delight in the opera and symphony, with their favorite Friday diversion being a visit to one of San Francisco's fine restaurants. Bandura also enjoys hiking in the Sierra Mountains.

Today Bandura is acknowledged as the premier figure of social cognitive theory, one of the pioneers of behavior modification, and a renowned scholar in theories of aggression and sex-role development. His views have had a widespread impact on contemporary psychology, especially in the clinical and developmental areas, and thus merit our special attention.

BASIC TENETS OF SOCIAL COGNITIVE THEORY

We begin our study of Bandura's social cognitive theory with an overview of his assessment of how other theories have sought to explain the causes of human behavior. In this way we can contrast his view of the person with others presently available.

Out with Inner Forces

Bandura (1989b) notes that until recently the most common view, popularized by various psychodynamic doctrines, depicted people's behavior as emerging from an assortment of inner processes (e.g., drives, impulses, needs) often operating below the threshold of awareness. Although this view gained widespread professional and popular acceptance, it is open to question on both conceptual and empirical grounds. Bandura describes the conceptual limitations of such theories this way:

> The inner determinants often were inferred from the behavior they supposedly caused, resulting in description in the guise of explanation. A hostile impulse, for example, was derived from a person's irascible behavior, which was then attributed to the action of an underlying hostile impulse. Similarly, the existence of achievement motives were deduced from achievement behavior; dependency motives from dependent behavior; curiosity motives from inquisitive behavior; power motives from domineering behavior; and so on. There is no limit to the number of motives one can find by inferring them from the kinds of behavior they supposedly produce. (1977b, p. 2)

In addition, psychodynamic theories disregard both the enormous complexity and diversity of human responses. In Bandura's view, internal entities such as drives and motivations cannot possibly account for the marked variation in the frequency and strength of a given behavior in different situations, toward different persons, and in different social roles. How a mother reacts to a child at home one day compared to the next, how she reacts to her daughter as opposed to her son in a comparable situation, and how she reacts when her husband is present rather than when she is alone with a child is a case in point. The empirical adequacy of psychodynamic formulations has also been questioned. At the risk of oversimplification, experimental personologists contend that while drives and motives may offer ready interpretations of events that have already occurred, they lack the power to predict how people will behave in a given situation (Mischel & Peake, 1982). For these reasons, it eventually became evident that if we were ever to improve our understanding of human behavior, we have to improve our explanatory systems (theories) along both conceptual and empirical lines.

Behaviorism from the Inside

Advancements in learning theory shifted the focus of causal analysis from hypothetical inner forces to environmental influences (e.g., Skinner's operant conditioning perspective). In this view, human behavior was explained in terms of the social stimuli that evoke it and the reinforcing consequences that maintain it. But to Bandura (1989b), such a drastic explanatory shift was something like throwing the baby out with the bath water. The internal "baby" that should have been retained and emphasized was, for Bandura, people's self-generated cognitive processes; in other words, radical behaviorism neglected determinants of people's behavior arising from their cognitively generated processes. For Bandura, persons are neither autonomous agents nor simply mechanical conveyers of animating environmental influences. Rather, they possess superior capabilities that enable them to predict the occurrence of events and to create the means for exercising control over those that affect their daily lives. To the extent that traditional behavior theories could be faulted, it was for providing an incomplete rather than an inaccurate account of human behavior.

From Bandura's perspective, people are neither driven by intrapsychic forces nor buffeted by environmental ones. Instead, the causes of human functioning are to be understood in terms of the continuous reciprocal interaction of behavioral, cognitive, and environmental influences. In this approach to analyzing the causes of behavior, which Bandura has termed *reciprocal determinism*, dispositional and situational factors are considered to be interdependent causes of behavior (see Figure 8-1). Put more simply, internal determinants of behavior, such as beliefs and expectations, and external determinants, such as rewards and punishments, are part of a system of interacting influences that affect not only behavior but also the various parts of the system.

Bandura's triadic model of reciprocal determinism indicates that while behavior is influenced by the environment, the environment is also partly a product of a person's own making, so that people can exercise some influence over their own behavior. For example, a rude person's behavior at a party can lead those around him to create an environment with punishments and few rewards. By contrast, a friendly person at the same party might create an environment of many rewards and few punishments. In either case, the behavior has changed the environment. Bandura also argues that because of their extraordinary capacity to use symbols, human beings are able to think, create, and plan—cognitive processes that are constantly revealed through overt actions.

Notice that the arrows in Figure 8-1 point in both directions, indicating that each of the three variables in the reciprocal determinism model is capable of influencing each of the other variables. But how can we predict which of the three parts in the model is going to influence which other part? This mainly depends on the strength of each of the variables. At times environmental forces are most powerful; at other times, internal forces dominate. Still at other times, expectations, beliefs, goals, and intentions give shape and direction to behavior. In the final analysis, however, Bandura believes that because of the bidirectionality of influence between overt behavior and environmental circumstances, people are both products and producers of their environment. Thus, social cognitive theory subscribes to a model of reciprocal causation in which cognitive, affective, and other personal factors, and environmental events all operate as interacting determinants.

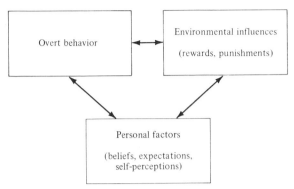

FIGURE 8-1 Schematic representation of Bandura's reciprocal determinism model. Human functioning is seen as a product of the interaction of behavior, personal factors, and environmental influences. (*Source: Adapted from Bandura, 1989a.*)

Beyond Reinforcement

What factors allow people to learn? Traditional learning theorists stressed reinforcement as a necessary condition for the acquisition, maintenance, and modification of behavior. Skinner, for instance, maintained that external reinforcement is necessary for learning to occur. While Bandura accepts the importance of external reinforcement, he does not regard it as the only way in which our behavior is acquired, maintained, or altered. People can also learn by observing or reading or hearing about other people's behavior. As a result of prior experiences, people come to expect that certain kinds of behavior will have the effects they value, others will produce undesired outcomes, and still others will have little appreciable impact. Our behavior is therefore regulated to a large extent by *anticipated consequences* (Bandura, 1989a). For instance, as homeowners we do not wait until we experience the trauma of a burning house to buy fire insurance. Instead, we rely on information gained from others about the potentially devastating consequences of lacking fire insurance in making our decision to purchase it. Similarly, we do not wait until caught in a blinding snowstorm or a torrential rainstorm to decide what to wear on a venture into the wilderness. In each instance, we can imagine the consequences of being inadequately prepared and take precautionary steps. Through our capacity to represent actual outcomes symbolically, future consequences can be translated into current motivators that influence behavior in much the same way as potential consequences. Our higher mental processes thus provide us with the capability for both insight and foresight (Bandura, 1989c).

At the heart of social cognitive theory is the notion that new patterns of behavior can be acquired *in the absence of external reinforcement*. Bandura notes that much of the behavior we eventually display is acquired through the influence of example: we simply attend to what others do and then repeat their actions. This emphasis on *learning by observation* or example, rather than by direct reinforcement, is the most distinctive feature of Bandura's theory.

Self-Regulation and Cognition in Behavior

Another salient feature of social cognitive theory is the prominent role it assigns to the unique human capacity for *self-regulation*. By arranging their immediate environment, by creating cognitive supports, and by producing consequences for their own actions, people are able to exercise some influence over their behavior. To be sure, self-regulative functions are created and not infrequently supported by environmental influences. Having external origins, however, does not diminish the fact that, once established, self-generated influences partly govern which actions the person performs. Furthermore, Bandura maintains that our superior intellectual capacity to engage in symbolic thought provides us with a powerful means of dealing with our environment. Through *verbal* and *imaginal representations* we process and preserve experiences in ways that serve as guides for future behavior. Our ability to form images of desirable future outcomes fosters behavioral strategies designed to lead us toward long-range goals. On the strength of our symbolizing powers, we can solve problems without having to resort to actual, overt trial-and-error behavior, and we can thus foresee the probable consequences of different actions and modify our behavior accordingly. To illustrate, a child anticipates that if he breaks his younger sister's favorite toy, she will cry, bring out their mother to investigate the commotion, blame the toy breaker, and mete out some form of punishment. Realizing the probable consequences, the child would probably choose to play with his own toys, thus avoiding parental wrath and keeping intact positively reinforcing maternal approval. In short, the child's ability to foresee the consequences of different actions enables him to behave appropriately.

Let us next examine the kind of observational learning that Bandura believes to be so central to these facets of human behavior.

LEARNING THROUGH MODELING

Learning would be quite laborious, not to mention inefficient and potentially dangerous, if we had to depend exclusively on the outcome of our own actions to guide us. For instance, suppose a motorist had to rely solely on immediate consequences (e.g., being hit by another vehicle, running over a child) in order to learn not to go through an intersection against a red light at the peak of rush-hour traffic. Fortunately, verbal transmission of information and observation of competent models (i.e., other people) provide the basis for the acquisition of most complex human behaviors. Indeed, Bandura (1986) maintains that virtually all learning phenomena resulting from direct experience can occur on a vicarious basis by observing other people's behavior and its consequences for them. We do not need to experience terminal cancer, for example, to appreciate the emotional upheaval it causes, since we have seen others stricken by the disease, have read accounts of those dying, and have witnessed dramas about the struggles. Thus, to ignore the role of observational learning in the acquisition of new behavior patterns is to ignore a uniquely human capacity.

Each of us has had the experience of struggling with a problem only to find that it is ridiculously easy after seeing someone else solve it. The observation factor is the key. Children learn by watching, whether it is to enjoy studying, to do household chores, or to play certain games. They may also learn through observation to be aggressive, altruistic, cooperative, or even obnoxious. In many instances, the behavior modeled must be learned in essentially the same way it is performed. Riding bicycles, skateboarding, typing, and dental surgery, for example, permit little, if any, departure from essential practices. However, in addition to transmitting specific response patterns, modeling influences can create innovative behavior. Should a child learn to share jelly beans with her dolly, it is but a short leap for her to share toys with peers, attention with her baby brother, chores with her mother, and later in life, to share time with her church and money with less fortunate people she has never met. Through the modeling process, observers extract common features from seemingly diverse responses and formulate rules of behavior that enable them to go beyond what they have seen or heard. Indeed, learning through observation may lead to styles of behavior quite different from those that have actually been observed.

In Bandura's view, people form a cognitive image of how certain behaviors are performed through the observation of a model, and on subsequent occasions this coded information (stored in long-term memory) serves as a guide for their actions. Furthermore, he believes that because people can learn what to do from example, at least in approximate form, they are spared the burden of needless mistakes and time-consuming performance of inappropriate responses. Thus, for example, someone who has watched an expert tennis player will have a mental representation of the expert's serve. When she practices the serve, she will match her attempted serve against her mental image of the expert's prototypical serve.

Basic Processes of Observational Learning

Social cognitive theory proposes that modeling influences generate learning chiefly through their informative function (Bandura, 1986). That is, during exposure, observers (learners) acquire mainly symbolic representations of the modeled activities which serve as prototypes for both appropriate and inappropriate behavior. According to this formulation, summarized schematically in Figure 8-2,

FIGURE 8-2 Component processes governing observational learning. *(Source: Adapted from Bandura, 1989a.)*

Attentional processes	Retention processes	Motor reproduction processes	Motivational processes
Person attends to and accurately perceives the model's behavior.	Person remembers (long-term retention) the model's behavior previously observed.	Person translates symbolically coded memories of the model's behavior into new response patterns.	If positive reinforcement (external, vicarious, or self-reinforcement) is potentially present, person enacts modeled behavior.

observational learning is governed by four interrelated components or processes: *attentional*, *retention*, *motor reproduction*, and *motivational*. Viewed from this perspective, learning by observation emerges as an active judgmental and constructive process. The four processes outlined by Bandura (1986, 1989a) are considered next.

Attentional Processes: Perceiving the Model A person cannot learn much by observation unless she or he attends to, or accurately perceives, the salient cues and distinctive features of the model's behavior. In other words, it is not sufficient for a person merely to see the model and what it is doing; rather, the individual must attend to the model with enough perceptual accuracy to extract the relevant information to use in imitating the model. Attentional processes thus influence what is selectively perceived in the model to which the person is exposed and what is acquired from such exposure. Any professor can verify that the presence of a student in class in no way guarantees that student's assimilation of the presented material. Spring fever, a nasty cold, the room temperature, a late night preceding the class, daydreaming, or a myriad of other possibilities may cause the student to ''lose'' the train of thought (or never even get on the train), thereby vitiating the learning process.

Several factors, some involving the observer, others involving the modeled activities, and still others involving the structural arrangement of human interactions, can greatly influence the likelihood that a bit of exemplary behavior will be attended to by the observer well enough to be encoded. Bandura (1989a) indicates that among the attentional determinants influencing modeling, *associational patterns* are of utmost importance. The people with whom we regularly interact restrict the types of behavior that will be observed and hence learned most thoroughly. Opportunities for learning altruistic behavior, for instance, differ markedly for members of street gangs or religious groups. Similarly, within any

Modeling is the core of observational learning. Young children often imitate adults, especially their parents and others they like and respect. (*Suzanne Szaszs/ Photo Researchers*)

social group some people are likely to command greater attention than others by virtue of their power, status, and assigned roles. The functional value accompanying the behaviors displayed by different models (i.e., who metes out rewards and punishments) is therefore highly influential in determining which models people will observe and thus emulate and which they will ignore. Attention to models is also governed by their interpersonal attractiveness. Models who personify charismatic qualities are generally sought out, while those who demonstrate displeasing qualities are usually ignored or rejected. The fact that many black and Hispanic adolescents sneer at the values of the white middle class illustrates this truth.

Models who appear high in competence, who are alleged experts, or who are celebrities or superstars are likely to command greater attention than models who lack these attributes. Advertisers of everything from footwear to feminine products capitalize on this idea, utilizing television personalities, athletic superstars, and financial wizards to hawk their products. Other variables that are especially important at this stage are the observer's own, preexisting capabilities and motives. For instance, if a male observer is paying attention to the physical charms of a female model, he may overlook what she is doing altogether. Essentially, any set of characteristics that causes a model to be perceived as intrinsically rewarding for prolonged periods of time increases the probability of more careful attention to the model, and, consequently, the probability of modeling.

Retention Processes: Remembering the Model A second set of processes involved in observational learning concerns the long-term mental representation of what was observed at one time or another (Zimmerman & Rosenthal, 1974). Simply put, a person cannot be affected much by observation of a model's behavior if he or she has no memory of it. Indeed, without the capacity to recall what the model did, the observer is unlikely to demonstrate any enduring behavioral change.

Bandura proposes two main internal representational systems by which the model's behavior is retained and converted into later action. The first is *imaginal coding*. As the person is observing modeling stimuli, a process of sensory conditioning produces relatively enduring and easily retrievable images of what has been seen. The mental images are formed so that any reference to events previously observed immediately calls forth a vivid image or picture of the physical stimuli involved. Bandura suggests that this is an everyday phenomenon and accounts for the person's ability to "see" an image of a friend he or she had lunch with last week or an image of the activities (cycling, golfing, sailing) he or she engaged in last summer. In passing, it should be noted that visual imagery plays a crucial role in observational learning during early developmental stages when linguistic skills are lacking, as well as in learning behavior patterns that do not lend themselves readily to verbal coding.

The second representational system involves the *verbal coding* of previously witnessed events. While observing the model, a person might recite to himself or herself what the model is doing. These subvocal descriptions (codes) can later be rehearsed internally, without an overt enactment of the behavior; for example, a person might silently "talk through" the steps involved in mastering a complicated motor skill (e.g., downhill skiing). In effect, the person is silently rehearsing a sequence of modeled activities to be performed at a later time, and, when she or he wishes to perform the skill, the verbal code will provide the relevant cues. Bandura maintains that observational learning is greatly facilitated by such verbal codes because they carry considerable information in an easily stored form.

Motor Reproduction Processes: Translating Memories into Behavior The third component involved in observational learning consists of translating the *symbolically coded memories* into appropriate action. Despite the fact that a person may have carefully formed and retained mental images of a model's behavior and rehearsed that behavior numerous times, he or she may still be unable to enact the behavior correctly. This is especially true for highly skilled motor acts that require the execution of many individual responses for their skillful performance (e.g., performing gymnastics, playing an instrument, or piloting a plane). The fine or delicately balanced movements involved may be learned by watching someone else (perhaps with the aid of slow-motion audiovisual reproduction), and the symbolic representation of the model's behavior may be repeated silently a number of times, but the translation into actual behavior will likely be clumsy and uncoordinated at first. Mere observation in such instances is not sufficient to ensure a smooth and coordinated performance of the act. Persistent practice in performing the motor movements (and self-corrective adjustment on the basis of informative feedback) is essential if the observer is to perfect the modeled behavior. Of course, observing and intentionally rehearsing certain behaviors may facilitate learning, for one is at least able to begin to perform the necessary movements based on what had been earlier observed. This silent rehearsal is helpful with skills such as driving but may not be as useful with more complicated skills, such as diving from a 10-meter springboard.

Motivational Processes: From Observation to Action The fourth and final component involved in modeling concerns *reinforcement* variables. These variables influence observational learning by exerting selective control over the types of modeling cues to which a person is most likely to attend, and they also affect the degree to which a person tries to translate such learning into overt performance.

Bandura points out that no matter how well people attend to and retain the modeled behavior or how much ability they possess to perform the behavior, they will not perform it without sufficient incentive to do so. In other words, a person can acquire, retain, and possess the capabilities for skillful execution of modeled behavior, but the learning may seldomly be converted into overt performance if it is negatively sanctioned or otherwise unfavorably received. A woman who views herself as "queen of the kitchen" may exclude her husband from all cooking duties despite the fact that he talks to her nightly while she prepares dinner. His reliance on her culinary skills is total until she becomes ill. Prompted by the motivation of an empty stomach and whining children, he may execute the modeled behavior of fixing dinner. His attentional and retentional behavior will no doubt increase in the future as his mind stumbles to recall where the peanut butter or sauerkraut is kept.

Generally speaking, if reinforcements are presented, modeling or observational learning is promptly translated into action. Also, not only does positive reinforcement enhance the likelihood of overt expression or actual performance of the behavior in question, but also it influences the person's attentional and retentional processes. In everyday life, we rarely pay attention to something or somebody if no incentive impels us to—and when little attention has been paid, there is virtually nothing to retain! We may often ride with the same friend to a specific destination, yet become confused or even lost when we are required to drive the route ourselves. We have not paid attention to the route previously traveled because we have not had to—someone else was driving the car. Once we come to depend on ourselves to reach the place we want, we retain the directions.

One way in which a person's desire to attend to, retain, and perform a modeled behavior may be enhanced is through the anticipation of reinforcement or punishment for so doing. The observation that another's behavior brings about positive reward, or prevents some aversive condition, can be a compelling incentive to attend to, retain, and later (in a comparable situation) perform that behavior. In this case, the reinforcement is experienced vicariously, after which the person can anticipate that enactment of the same behavior will lead to similar consequences. A child may spontaneously sweep the porch, vacuum his or her room, or set the table, thereby anticipating grateful smiles and appreciative words for his or her considerate actions. As this example suggests, the child's vicarious anticipation of reinforcement was effective in initiating the helping behavior.

REINFORCEMENT IN OBSERVATIONAL LEARNING

Bandura believes that while reinforcement often serves to facilitate learning, it is not necessary in order for learning to occur. There are many other factors, he notes, other than reinforcing consequences of behavior that can influence what people will or will not attend to. We do not have to be reinforced, for example, to attend to fire sirens, flashes of lightning, putrid smells, and novel stimuli. In fact, when our attention to modeled activities is gained through the sheer impact of physical stimuli, the addition of positive incentives does not enhance observational learning. This fact is supported by research showing that children who watched a model on television in a room darkened to minimize distractions later displayed the same amount of imitative learning regardless of whether they were told in advance that such imitations would be rewarded or were given no prior incentives to learn the modeled performances. In short, direct reinforcement can aid modeling, but it is not vital to it (Bandura, 1986).

Bandura considers the notion of human behavior as *exclusively controlled* by its external consequences to be too restrictive: ''If actions were determined solely by external rewards and punishments, people would behave like weather vanes, constantly shifting in radically different directions to conform to the whims of others'' (1971, p. 27). Thus, while social cognitive learning theory does acknowledge the powerful role played by extrinsic reinforcement, it posits a broader range of reinforcement influences. People are not only influenced by the experiences produced by their actions but also regulate their behavior on the basis of anticipated consequences as well as those they create for themselves. These two forms of reinforcement—*vicarious* and *self-reinforcement*—will be discussed shortly.

Bandura's analysis of the role of reinforcement in observational learning reveals his cognitive orientation. Unlike Skinner, he argues that external reinforcement seldom operates as the automatic determiner of behavior. More often, it serves two other functions, as *information* and as *incentive*. Reinforcement following a given response indicates, or at least enables the person to form hypotheses about, what the correct response is. This informative, or feedback, function can operate whether the reinforcement is experienced directly or vicariously. To take one example, witnessing someone else punished for a certain deed is as informative as being punished oneself. In addition, reinforcement informs us what to expect as a result of making the correct or incorrect response. The student who aspires to become a physician during high school and then discovers that she can earn excellent grades (reinforcement) in her college pre-med courses is a case in point. This kind of information—usually called *incentive*—is essential if we are to correctly anticipate the probable consequences of our actions and to regulate our behavior accordingly. Indeed, without the capacity to anticipate likely outcomes of prospective actions, people would likely act in ways that might prove highly unproductive, if not perilous.

Vicarious Reinforcement

It is evident from the preceding discussion that people can profit immensely from the observed successes and failures of others, as well as from their own direct experiences. Indeed, as social beings, we repeatedly attend to the actions of others and the situations in which they are rewarded, ignored, or punished. Consider, for instance, a child who observes a classmate reprimanded for interrupting the teacher. This experience will likely inhibit interrupting, unless, of course, the observing child expects that the consequences in his or her case will be different. Or, consider the waitress or waiter who sees fellow workers generously tipped for a friendly smile and cheerful chatter with the patrons. This experience will no doubt enhance her or his tendency to smile and chatter with subsequent customers as well. As these two examples illustrate, the observed or vicarious consequences (punishments and rewards) accruing to the actions of others often play an influential role in regulating our behavior. It means that a good deal of the trial and error of operant conditioning can take place secondhand. Taking advantage of this principle not only saves energy but also allows us the opportunity to learn from other people's mistakes, as well as from their successes.

Vicarious reinforcement is operative whenever an observer witnesses an action of a model who experiences some tangible outcome which the observer perceives to be contingent on the model's earlier action. *Vicarious positive reinforcement* is said to occur when observers increase behavior for which they have seen others reinforced, whereas *vicarious punishment* occurs when observed aversive consequences reduce people's tendency to behave in similar or related ways. In each instance, the information conveyed by observed consequences enables the observer to determine whether a particular externally administered reinforcer will serve as a reward or a punishment. Thus, if you see someone else rewarded for doing something, you are likely to conclude that you will receive the same kind of reinforcer for acting that way. Alternatively, if you see someone else punished after doing something, you are likely to conclude that the same thing would happen to you if you acted that way.

Self-Reinforcement

Thus far we have considered how people regulate their behavior on the basis of external consequences that they either observe or experience firsthand. From the perspective of social cognitive theory, however, many of our actions are governed by self-imposed reinforcement. Indeed, Bandura (1988) argues that most human behavior is regulated through self-generated reinforcement.

Self-reinforcement is evident whenever people set standards of performance for achievement and proceed to reward or punish themselves for attaining, exceeding, or falling short of their own expectations. In preparing a book or writing a journal article for publication, for example, authors do not require the presence of someone looking over their shoulders and reinforcing each sentence until a satisfactory manuscript is produced. Rather, they possess an internalized standard of what constitutes an acceptable end product and engage in continuous self-corrective editing that often exceeds accepted standards. In many other areas of functioning, people similarly evaluate their own behavior and reward and punish themselves. They congratulate themselves for their own characteristics and actions; they praise or debunk their own accomplishments; and they self-administer social and material rewards and punishments from the enormous array available to them. Bandura's emphasis on self-reinforcement greatly enhances the explanatory power of reinforcement principles as they apply to human behavior.

How Self-Regulation Occurs

As we have seen, self-reinforcement is the process whereby people give themselves rewards over which they have control whenever they attain certain self-imposed standards of performance. Since both negative and positive self-reactions are possible, Bandura (1989b) uses the more inclusive term *self-regulation* to encompass both the enhancing and reducing effects of self-evaluative influences.

In Bandura's view, self-regulated incentives increase performance mainly through their motivational function. That is, by making self-gratification or tangible rewards conditional upon realizing certain accomplishments, people motivate themselves to expend the effort needed to attain the desired performance. The person's level of self-induced motivation aroused by this means usually varies according to the type and value of the incentives and the nature of the performance standards. According to Bandura, there are three component processes involved in the self-regulation of behavior by self-produced consequences: self-observation, judgmental, and self-response processes.

Human behavior typically varies along a number of *self-observation* dimensions (e.g., the quality or rate of a person's responses). The functional significance of these dimensions depends on the type of activity in question. For example, track and field performances are judged in terms of time and distance. Artistic endeavors, on the other hand, are generally judged on the basis of aesthetic value and originality. Social behavior, by contrast, is commonly judged in terms of dimensions such as sincerity, deviance, ethicalness, and a host of other evaluative qualities.

The second component involved in the self-regulation of behavior is the *judgmental* process. It is often the case that whether a given performance will be regarded as commendable and hence rewardable or unsatisfactory and punishable depends upon the personal standards against which it is evaluated. In general, those actions that measure up to internal standards are judged positively, whereas those that fall short of the mark are judged negatively. Of course, absolute measures of the adequacy of our performance are often lacking. The time in which the 100-meter freestyle is swum, the number of points earned on a biology exam, or the amount given to a charitable organization may not convey sufficient information for self-appraisals even when compared against an internal standard. In these and many other instances, the adequacy of performance must be defined relationally (i.e., by comparing them with those of others). To illustrate, consider the student who scores 85 points on a biology test and who strives to be in the upper 5 percent of her class. Clearly, her score would provide no basis for making either a positive or a negative self-assessment unless she knew the scores of her classmates. In the case of still other activities and tasks, the adequacy of our performance may be defined in terms of standard norms or accomplishments of reference groups.

The person's previous behavior also provides a standard against which the adequacy of ongoing performance may be assessed. Here it is self-comparison that supplies the benchmark of adequacy or inadequacy. Bandura suggests that past performance influences self-appraisal principally through its impact on goal setting: "After a given level of performance is attained, it is no longer challenging, and new self-satisfactions are sought through progressive improvement. People tend to raise their performance standards after success and to lower them to more realistic levels after repeated failure" (1977b, p. 132).

Evaluation of activities is another key factor in the judgmental component of self-regulation of behavior. It is obvious, for instance, that people expend little or no effort in activities that have no personal relevance for them. Rather, it is in those areas of life affecting their sense of well-being and self-esteem that self-appraisal activates persistent effort and commitment. Additionally, the way people perceive the causes of their behavior strongly influences self-appraisal. Most people feel a sense of pride and pleasure for the accomplishments which they attribute to their own ability and effort. Conversely, they seldom derive much satisfaction when they attribute their success to external factors such as luck or chance. The same holds true for judgments of failure and blameworthy conduct. People tend to respond self-critically to poor performances for which they view themselves responsible but not to failures which they perceive to be due to mitigating circumstances or insufficient abilities. Performances that are deemed to have no relevance to self do not usually elicit any reactions one way or another. For example, should a person achieve first-chair trumpet, he would likely believe that practice and musical aptitude brought him the reward. However, the same person would take little pride in the accomplishment if he felt his conductor-father awarded him the position based on something other than ability. Should he be denied the honor, he might justify his poor performance with the idea that he was experiencing the flu during the tryouts. The drummer viewing all this from afar has no more than a passing interest in the whole affair.

Bandura (1977b, 1982) maintains that a wide spectrum of human behavior is regulated through self-evaluative consequences as expressed in the form of self-satisfaction, self-pride, self-dissatisfaction, and self-criticism. Thus, the third and final component involved in behavioral self-regulation concerns *self-response* processes, particularly self-evaluative reactions. Other things being equal, positive self-appraisals of performance give rise to rewarding self-reactions, whereas negative appraisals inspire punishing self-responses. Furthermore, "self-evaluative reactions acquire and retain their rewarding and punishing value through correlation with tangible consequences. That is, people usually engage in self-gratifications after achieving a sense of self-pride, whereas they treat themselves badly when they judge themselves self-critically" (Bandura, 1977b, p. 133).

Bandura recognizes that an adequate account of behavior must also deal with such puzzling questions as why people deny themselves rewards, why they demand of themselves high levels of performance when no one compels them to do so, and why they inflict punishment upon themselves. Clearly, these are challenging questions, and Bandura (1977b, 1986) readily admits that they have by no means been sufficiently studied. What follows are a set of tentative interpretations offered by Bandura.

Why We Punish Ourselves   In the social cognitive view, people tend to engage in self-deprecatory and other distressing thoughts when they function inadequately or violate their own internal standards of conduct. This tendency is repeatedly experienced throughout the course of socialization and involves the following sequence of events: *transgression–internal distress–punishment–relief*. In this process, transgressive behavior arouses anticipatory fear and self-condemnation that often persist until the person is reprimanded. Punishment, in turn, not only terminates anguish over the transgression and possible social repercussions, it also tends to restore the approval of others. Accordingly, self-administered punishment can provide relief from thought-produced distress and apprehension which may last longer and be more punishable than the actual reprimand itself.

Self-punishing responses persist because they alleviate thought-created anguish and attenuate external punishment. By criticizing and debunking themselves for reprehensible moral actions, people stop tormenting themselves about their past behavior. Similarly, self-criticism may reduce disconcerting thoughts about faulty or disappointing performance. Still another reason for self-punitive behavior is that it often serves as an effective means of downplaying negative reactions from others. In other words, when certain actions are likely to evoke disciplinary measures, self-punishment may be the "lesser of two evils." Finally, verbal self-punishment can be used to encourage compliments from others. By criticizing and belittling themselves, individuals can get others to articulate their positive qualities and abilities, and to offer reassuring statements that sustained effort will produce future successes.

Although self-punishment can serve to end or at least reduce thought-produced distress, it can also intensify personal distress. In fact, excessive or prolonged self-punishment based on inordinately severe standards of self-evaluation may give rise to chronic depression, feelings of apathy and worthlessness, and lack of purpose. This is tragically evident in persons who suffer considerable self-devaluation as a result of a loss in ability due to aging or some physical handicap but who continue to adhere to their original standards of performance. They may belittle themselves and their achievements so severely that they eventually become apathetic and abandon activities that formerly brought them great personal fulfillment. Behavior that is the source of self-produced distress may also facilitate the development of various forms of psychopathology. To illustrate, some people whose efforts generate a continuing sense of inadequacy and failure may resort to alcoholism or drug addiction as a way of coping with their environment. Others may protect themselves from feelings of self-contempt by escaping into a world of grandiose thinking, where they attain in delusional fantasy what is unattainable in reality. Bandura (1988), in fact, believes that most maladaptive behavior is the result of stringent internal standards of self-evaluation.

Self-Efficacy: Avenue to Attainment of Competent Behavior

In recent years, Bandura (1977a, 1989b, 1989c) has extended his position by postulating a cognitive mechanism of *self-efficacy* to account for personality functioning and change. The concept of self-efficacy relates to judgments people make concerning their ability to execute behaviors relevant to a specific task or situation. In Bandura's view, self-efficacy, or the perceived ability to cope with specific situations, influences several aspects of psychosocial functioning. Specifically, self-percepts of efficacy can enhance or impair people's choices of which activities to engage in, how much effort they will expend in the face of obstacles and frustrations, how long they will persist in the face of difficult circumstances, and their emotional reactions while anticipating a task or while involved in it. In short, self-judged efficacy influences behavior patterns, motivation, performance, and emotional arousal.

According to Bandura, people who have a strong sense of perceived self-efficacy exert greater effort to master challenging tasks than do people who entertain serious self-doubts about their capabilities. In turn, high self-efficacy, entailing expectations of success, usually leads to a successful outcome and thus bolsters self-esteem. Low self-efficacy, by contrast, entailing expectations of failure, usually leads to an unsuccessful outcome and thus lowers self-esteem. Seen from this perspective, people who judge themselves ineffectual in coping with challenging or threatening situations are likely to become excessively preoccupied with their personal deficiencies and persistently engage in debilitating self-criticism about their incompetence. Bandura says that those who judge themselves "as inefficacious are more inclined to visualize failure scenarios and to dwell on how things will go wrong. Such inefficacious thinking weakens motivation and undermines performance" (1989c, p. 729). People who believe strongly in their problem-solving capabilities, by contrast, are likely to persist in the pursuit of their goals despite the presence of obstacles and to engage in a minimum of debilitating self-criticism. As Bandura notes, "Those who have a high sense of efficacy visualize success scenarios that provide positive guides for performance and they cognitively rehearse good solutions to potential problems" (1989c, p. 729).

Bandura (1989b, 1989c) suggests that self-efficacy is acquired through any one or a combination of four sources: performance accomplishments, vicarious experiences, verbal persuasion, and states of bodily (emotional) arousal. Each of the four now will be described.

1 Performance Accomplishments Bandura argues that the most important source of efficacy is past experiences of success and failure in attempts to achieve desired outcomes. Simply put, personal mastery experiences tend to create high expectations, whereas prior failure experiences tend to generate low expectations. Entertainers suddenly struck with fear before a performance may tell themselves that they have performed many times before without incident and therefore they can do it again. On the other hand, people who are beset by self-doubts about their ability to speak in front of an audience due to a history of failure to do so will probably conclude that they cannot perform this behavior. Of course, if a person with low self-efficacy can somehow be induced to perform the feared behavior, self-efficacy will be bolstered.

2 Vicarious Experiences Although not as influential as actual past performances, vicarious experiences can also serve as a source of efficacy expectations. That is, seeing other people successfully perform a behavior can instill strong perceptions of self-efficacy in observers that they, too, are able to master comparable activities. Students who are afraid of asking questions in a large class may, for instance, change their efficacy expectation from "I can't do that" to "maybe I can" after observing fellow classmates ask questions without disastrous results. By the same token, watching others of similar competence repeatedly fail despite sustained efforts would likely lower observers' judgments of their own capabilities to perform comparable actions.

Bandura believes that enactive attainment or performance is the most potent source of self-efficacy. (*Robert Holmgren/Jeroboam*)

3   Verbal Persuasion   Efficacy expectations may also be acquired and or modified through convincing people that they possess the capabilities needed to accomplish their goals. Consider the parent who encourages her daughter to believe that she has the ability to master a difficult subject in school. To the extent that such verbal encouragement persuades the daughter to accept the belief "I can do it," it may promote development of study skills and effort leading to eventual success. Of course, such confidence may be easily eliminated if the actual performance in the difficult subject is not matched by the expected result. Furthermore, efforts to verbally persuade a child to try to accomplish goals must be kept within the realistic boundaries of aptitude or talent. If not, such efforts are likely to lessen the credibility of the parent and to leave the child with lower efficacy expectations. Bandura hypothesizes that the power of verbal persuasion is limited by the perceived status and authority of the persuader. A therapist might convince an overweight client to eat less and exercise more; but the same therapist is not likely to convince the client that he or she has the ability to climb Mount Everest.

4   Emotional Arousal   Finally, since people monitor their level of efficacy by reference to their level of emotional arousal in the face of stressful or threatening situations, any method that lowers arousal will increase efficacy expectations. A man who lacks confidence in approaching women may find his heart begins beating rapidly and his palms start perspiring as he begins to make a phone call to a woman for a date. If he attributes these physiological responses to anxiety, he may promptly decide he is too nervous to go through with it. If, however, he notices how calm and relaxed he is just before dialing, he may decide he is more efficacious than he realized. As this example suggests, people are far more likely to expect to succeed when they are not tense and emotionally aroused.

BANDURA'S BASIC ASSUMPTIONS CONCERNING HUMAN NATURE

In terms of the basic theoretical positions that can be taken within psychology, Bandura is often portrayed as a "moderate behaviorist." Yet his social cognitive theory suggests a different image of the person from that espoused by Skinner (1989). One indication of this difference is the strong emphasis that Bandura places on the mutual interaction of environmental events, behavior, and personal factors, especially cognitive processes. But Bandura's most essential differences from other brands of behavioristic theory (especially Skinner's) can best be appreciated by considering his positions on the basic assumptions about human nature (see Figure 8-3).

Freedom–Determinism Bandura's position on this dimension can be conceptualized as falling midway between the extremes of freedom and determinism. The key to understanding his position lies in the concept of *reciprocal determinism*, the continuous interplay of behavior, the person, and the environment in all human activity: "Because people's conceptions, their behavior, and their environments are reciprocal determinants of each other, individuals are neither powerless objects controlled by environmental forces nor entirely free agents who can do whatever they choose" (Bandura, 1978, pp. 356–357).

From the perspective of social cognitive theory, then, people are somewhat free to control their own behavior. Bandura's emphasis on self-regulation of behavior also supports this conclusion. Nonetheless, the environment affects people as much as people affect the environment. As noted earlier, for instance, self-reinforcement standards and self-efficacy are partially determined by environmental influences. Therefore, the relationship between person and environment is truly *bidirectional*: people shape environments while environments simultaneously shape people. This continuous interplay of forces allows for both a measure of freedom and determinism in Bandura's conception of humanity.

Rationality–Irrationality Bandura's distinctiveness from traditional behaviorism in general, and from Skinner in particular, can be traced to his strong commitment to the rationality assumption. The cognitive thrust of many of his theoretical concepts indicates a highly rational view of the person. There is no doubt that Bandura stresses conscious thought over unconscious determinants of behavior. To him, people make rational decisions about how their actions will affect their own circumstances.

	Strong	Moderate	Slight	Midrange	Slight	Moderate	Strong	
Freedom				■				Determinism
Rationality	■							Irrationality
Holism						■		Elementalism
Constitutionalism							■	Environmentalism
Changeability	■							Unchangeability
Subjectivity				■				Objectivity
Proactivity				■				Reactivity
Homeostasis			Not applicable					Heterostasis
Knowability	■							Unknowability

FIGURE 8-3 Bandura's position on the nine basic assumptions concerning human nature.

Rationality is especially evident in Bandura's emphasis on modeling or observational learning. Without the ability to form and store in memory cognitive images of observed behaviors, modeling would be impossible. Moreover, Bandura's treatment of reinforcement emphasizes its informative and incentive functions, as opposed to construing external reinforcement as an automatic determiner of behavior. Stated simply, reinforcement in Bandura's view (whether direct or vicarious) gives a person something to think about in generating future behavior—again, a cognitive concept quite foreign to Skinnerian theory. Thus, the central place and pervasiveness of cognition in social cognitive theory reveals the rationality assumption as its base.

Holism–Elementalism Much more in line with traditional behaviorism is Bandura's moderate commitment to the elementalism assumption. Nowhere in Bandura's theory, for instance, is there a global construct absolutely vital to the explanation of behavior (such as the construct of "self" or "self-concept" in phenomenological theory). Indeed, when Bandura speaks of self-evaluation, he consistently argues against a global approach to its conceptualization and measurement. But even more revealing is the fact that modeling can be understood only in terms of its component subfunctions: "Understanding how people learn to imitate becomes a matter of understanding how the requisite subfunctions develop and operate" (Bandura, 1974, p. 864). However, the requisite subfunctions—discriminative observation, memory encoding, coordinating ideomotor and sensorimotor systems, judging probable consequences for matching behavior (Bandura, 1974)—are themselves reasonably broad and complex concepts. Thus, while Bandura appears to believe that behavior is best understood through its constituent parts, the constituents are not particularly molecular. For this reason, his commitment to elementalism might best be judged as moderate.

Constitutionalism–Environmentalism Bandura's work is mainly concerned with the social setting and the learning processes through which environmental factors have an impact on behavior. When placed on the constitution-alism–environmentalism scale, then, Bandura's theory leans heavily toward environmentalism. Yet, in social cognitive terms, the environment lacks the awesome and automatic control over behavior that it possesses in Skinner's theory. Rather, in accordance with Bandura's (1989b) doctrine of reciprocal determinism, people affect their environments as much as their environments affect them. Through self-regulation and cognition, the direct effects of the environment are considerably modified, since there is a constant interaction among behavioral, cognitive, and environmental factors. At the same time, Bandura clearly invests the environment with considerable potency in the production and modification of human behavior, although it is not seen as the sole or automatic cause of that behavior. In opposition to the relative absence of constitutionalism in Bandura's thinking, however, environmentalism clearly is the more dominant assumption underscoring social cognitive theory. Futhermore, the particular interplay of rationality and environmentalism at the root of Bandura's position seems in large measure responsible for the unique cognitive orientation of social cognitive theory against the historical backdrop of the behavioristic tradition in psychology.

Changeability–Unchangeability A personologist whose major theoretical concept is that of modeling would necessarily seem strongly committed to the changeability assumption. After all, the entire thrust of modeling deals with how people learn and how they acquire and change their behavior. And in Bandura's system, as people mature, they gain progressively greater control over the direction that such behavior changes take with the aid of self-reinforcement and environment arrangement to yield more positive reinforcement. Thus, people arrange the external inducements for desired behavior, they evaluate their performances, and they serve as their own reinforcing agents (Bandura, 1989b).

Instead of focusing on internal variables that persist and characterize an individual's behavior over time, Bandura attends closely to the processes governing behavioral change. A strong commitment to the assumption of changeability is thus implied, one which Bandura shares with other theorists who emphasize learning, be they of the behavioristic persuasion or not.

Subjectivity–Objectivity The continuous interplay between person and environment as it is emphasized in Bandura's concept of reciprocal determinism reflects a blending of the subjectivity and objectivity assumptions. On the subjectivity side, people do not indiscriminately absorb objective influences impinging upon them. Rather, these influences are processed through private and presumably subjective, internal factors (i.e., cognitive structures) before they affect behavior. Further suggestions of subjectivity are found in Bandura's concept of self-evaluative standards; because of differences in such standards among people, objectively identical situations may be perceived and responded to differently by any two people. Thus, Bandura acknowledges the role of private experience in human activity.

But Bandura by no means ventures into the subjective world of the person with the abandon of a phenomenologist; he treads cautiously, like a reformed behaviorist peering into the depths of an unexplored and possibly scientifically unacceptable jungle of subjective experience. Whenever possible, he makes a concerted effort to anchor all internal constructs to objective, observable factors. And while people do influence the environment in social cognitive theory, it cannot be overlooked that the environment (objective factors) also influences people's behavior. Thus there appears to be equal room for both subjectivity and objectivity in the household of social cognitive theory.

Proactivity–Reactivity   The person in social cognitive theory continually reacts to external influences, but *reacts proactively!* To understand this apparent paradox, consider the following statement made by Bandura:

> Theories that seek to explain human behavior solely as the product of external influences or the remnants of past stimulus inputs present a truncated image of human nature. This is because people possess self-directive capabilities that enable them to exercise some control over their thoughts, feelings, and actions by the consequences they produce for themselves. Psychosocial functioning is, therefore, regulated by an interplay of self-produced and external sources of influence. (1989b, p. 1179)

In essence, this statement reflects Bandura's doctrine of reciprocal determinism, a doctrine encompassing equal parts of both the proactivity and reactivity assumptions.

In Bandura's view, people react to external influences by observing and then processing these influences through their cognitive structures. People observe, think, plan, and anticipate the probable external consequences of their actions. Indeed, in social cognitive theory, it is fair to say that people's behavior is governed more by their reactions to *anticipated consequences* than by their reactions to past or present external consequences. A person generates behavior in a future-oriented fashion (proactivity), but primarily as a reaction to the anticipated outcomes of his or her actions (reactivity). At bottom, the basic assumptions of proactivity and reactivity blend together in social cognitive theory.

Homeostasis–Heterostasis   The issue involved in this assumption is the nature and properties of the motives presumed to underlie behavior. Do people act to reduce tensions and maintain internal equilibrium, or is human behavior functionally directed toward personal growth and self-actualization? In Bandura's theory, there is an apparent lack of speculation about these questions, and in no case does the issue discernibly affect the nature of his theoretical constructs. In other words, people can model many kinds of behaviors regardless of the nature of the possible motives underlying those behaviors.

This is not to suggest that Bandura rejects the concept of motivated behavior. He does not; he simply conceptualizes motivation in a fashion that does not readily lend itself to a homeostasis–heterostasis type of analysis. More specifically, rather than dwelling on the properties of presumed inner motives, Bandura

(1986) instead analyzes motivation in terms of antecedent, incentive, and cognitive inducements, all potentially verifiable by experimentation. Motivation is definitely present in social cognitive theory, but it is couched largely in terms of cognitive structures and various types of reinforcement (e.g., external, vicarious, and self-reinforcement). Thus, unless we are willing to stretch things unduly, the homeostasis–heterostasis assumption is not directly applicable to Bandura's position.

Knowabiiity–Unknowability Bandura clearly endorses the view that human nature is knowable. This is evidenced by the respect he shows for empirical data, by his attempts to establish theoretical concepts open to empirical test, and by his many contributions to personality research. To provide but one illustration, while Bandura employs internal cognitive structures in explaining human behavior, he believes that such internal processes must eventually be tied to observable actions in a complete account of human behavior (Bandura, 1974, 1986). For Bandura, there are no allusions to mysterious variables beyond scientific comprehension and no real attempt to transcend the realm of what many consider to be proper psychological science. Thus, like the broad behavioristic tradition from which social cognitive theory has in part emerged, Bandura is strongly committed to the assumption that human nature is ultimately knowable through science.

Social cognitive theory is well-grounded in empirical research, and it is to a discussion of that research that we turn next.

EMPIRICAL VALIDATION OF SOCIAL COGNITIVE THEORY CONCEPTS

Bandura's social cognitive position has generated an impressive amount of evidence in support of its basic concepts and principles. This research has greatly enhanced our knowledge of how parental modeling practices influence children's social development, how language and thought processes are acquired, and how self-reinforcement can be used in the treatment of a variety of psychological problems. Additionally, Bandura himself has conducted numerous studies concerning the importance of observational learning in the acquisition and modification of aggressive behavior (Bandura, 1973). These contributions coupled with countless empirical findings in related areas of personality functioning (e.g., sex-role development, helping behavior, social skills, self-efficacy) are already an integral part of contemporary psychology. In general, then, Bandura's theory has a high degree of empirical support and there is every reason to expect a continued growth of interest in it for years to come.

In this chapter section we shall consider illustrative studies pertaining to (1) the effects of observing televised violence on children's aggressive behavior and (2) the importance of self-perceptions of efficacy in relation to coping with specific fears. These are but two of the many areas in which Bandura's theory has been the focus of and impetus for vigorous scientific inquiry.

Violence on Television: Aggressive Models in Every Living Room

Obviously not all observational learning leads to socially acceptable outcomes. Indeed, people can learn undesirable and antisocial forms of behavior through the same processes that foster the development of cooperation, sharing, altruism, and effective problem-solving skills. Violence as portrayed in the mass media, especially on television, has long been suspected of having such a negative impact on those who consume it.

Beginning with a series of laboratory studies by Bandura and his colleagues in the 1960s (Bandura, 1965; Bandura et al., 1963), a considerable body of evidence has been gathered about the effects of televised violence on social behavior. This literature, reviewed several times (Bandura, 1979; Eron & Huesmann, 1985; Geen & Thomas, 1986), indicates that prolonged exposure to televised violence tends to (1) increase aggressive styles of conduct, (2) lower restraints on aggressive behavior, (3) desensitize viewers to violence, and (4) shape their images of social reality upon which they base many of their actions. Let us look at each of these effects more closely.

Most of the evidence indicating that exposure to filmed violence increases aggressive behavior comes from controlled laboratory research. Typically, subjects view a segment from either a violent or an arousing but nonviolent program. Then they are given the opportunity to aggress against another person, usually by administering electric shocks they believe are hurting another subject. Though there are occasional exceptions (see Freedman, 1986, for a cautionary note on this finding), researchers typically find that subjects who viewed the violent program act more aggressively than those who watched the nonviolent program (Friedrich-Cofer & Huston, 1986; Geen, 1983; Geen & Thomas, 1986; Husemann & Malamuth, 1986). As impressive as this research evidence is, it contains some serious limitations. The effects persist over only a brief time span, and the opportunity to hurt another person provided by the experimenter is remote from real life (e.g., pushing a shock button). Accordingly, it is reasonable to ask how much these studies tell us about the impact of television mayhem and aggressive movies in everyday life.

In response to this problem, several investigators have conducted field studies to gauge the impact of exposure to violent fare over various periods of time outside the confines of the laboratory setting (Eron, 1987; Hicks, 1968; Leyens et al., 1975; Singer & Singer, 1981). The most notable of these long-term correlational studies have been conducted by Eron and his colleagues (Eron, 1980; Eron et al., 1972, 1987). In 1960 they began with the entire third-grade population of a semirural town in upstate New York, 875 boys and girls. They examined several behavioral and personal characteristics of these children, and also collected data on their parents and the home environments from which they came. A major finding of this initial study was that children who preferred violent television programs at age 8 were among the most aggressive in school. Ten years later the researchers restudied 427 of their original sample in order to examine the relationship between the amount and kind of television they had watched at age 8 and how aggressive they now were. They found that the viewing of violence at age 8 modestly predicted aggressiveness at age 18. Also, the children who had been rated as aggressive by their 8-year-old peers tended to be rated as aggressive by the young adults who knew them at age 18, indicating stability in aggressive behavior over 10 years. What is even more striking, however, was the finding that the children who had been rated aggressive at age 8 were three times more likely to have generated a police record within the next 10 years than those who had been rated as unaggressive (Lefkowitz et al., 1977). In fact, the single best predictor of the males' aggression at 18, even after controlling for a host of other factors, was the degree of violence in the television programs they had preferred to watch at age 8 (Eron, 1980).

More recently, Eron and his colleagues (Eron et al., 1987) have reported on a second follow-up of over 400 of the original subjects, now approximately age 30. Consistent with earlier findings, aggressive behavior was very stable over the years of the study, with the most aggressive third graders not only getting into more trouble with the law, but also being more severe and punitive with their spouses and children 22 years later. What is more, the researchers found a significant relationship between the amount of violent television the subjects had watched at age 8 and the likelihood they would have been convicted of a serious crime at age 30 (see Figure 8-4). In short, the seriousness of the criminal offense committed at age 30 was directly related to the amount of violent television watched at age 8. Eron (1987) admits, however, that the correlational nature of his research prevents drawing any definite cause-and-effect conclusions.

Research likewise indicates that viewing violence can diminish one's own restraints about acting aggressively. For example, Berkowitz (1964) found that after college males view someone getting a well-deserved beating, they are less

FIGURE 8-4 Seriousness of criminal act at age 30 as a function of frequency of television viewing at age 8. (*Source: Adapted from Eron & Huesmann, 1985.*)

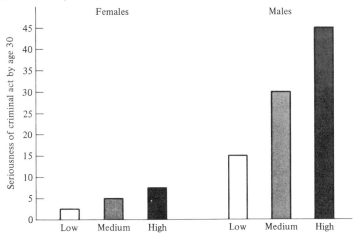

inhibited about shocking someone who is similar to the film's victim. To account for this finding, Berkowitz (1984) suggests that violence viewing primes the viewer for aggressive behavior by activating violence-related ideas, feelings, and memories. In support of this line of reasoning, Anderson and Ford (1986) found that playing an aggression-oriented video game increased feelings of hostility and anxiety in a group of college students.

Experimental evidence that repeated exposure to violence "desensitizes" observers to the occurrence of subsequently encountered violence comes from several sources (Cline et al., 1973; Geen, 1981; Thomas et al., 1977). In the study by Thomas et al. (1977), subjects were attached to a machine that measured their emotional reactions in terms of arousal in their galvanic skin response records. They first viewed a videotape of either a violent TV program or an exciting volleyball championship. Both tapes were found to be equally arousing. Later, during follow-up sessions, subjects encountered what they thought was a real confrontation resulting in physical violence and property damage. As the researchers had predicted, those who had watched the violent TV program reacted less emotionally to this aggression than did the other group. Apparently, watching the TV violence desensitized these subjects to the occurrence of the later "real life" violence.

Does viewing television's fictional world also influence our perceptions of social reality? Gerbner and his associates (1976, 1986) contend that this is television's most potent effect. Their surveys of both adolescents and adults reveal that heavy viewers (4 hours a day or more) are more likely than light viewers (2 hours or less) to feel vulnerable to the aggression of others and to see the world as a dangerous place. However, it should be noted that the context of reported violence has an important influence on people's fears. Heath (1984) classified newspaper reports of violent crime in terms of randomness (lack of a clear-cut motive), sensationalism (bizarre and gruesome elements), and proximity (near to home or far away). Newspaper readers were then surveyed about their fear of crime. When people read about local crimes, they tended to be more fearful if the motive was described as random and the sensationalistic elements were highlighted than if neither of these factors was stressed in the newspaper account. In contrast, when people read about crimes in other localities, they were less fearful if the motive was random and the presentation was sensationalized. Thus, it appears that people can protect themselves against at least some of the onslaught of media violence. By using geographical distance to create a sense of psychological security, they can deny their own vulnerability to being victimized.

The potential long-term consequences of viewing heavy doses of media violence are distressing to contemplate. Consider these few facts about watching television alone. Recent research indicates that the average 10-year-old in this country spends more time in front of a television than in a classroom (Tangney & Feshbach, 1988), a pattern that has not changed in more than 20 years (Liebert & Sprafkin, 1988). In fact, it is estimated that the average American child watches about 30 hours of TV each week. Given this enormous diet of television viewing, what social behaviors are being modeled? Since 1967, Gerbner and his associates

(1980, 1986) have sampled network prime-time and Saturday morning children's entertainment programs in the United States. Their findings reveal that viewers are fed a steady diet of violent images. Specifically, prime-time programs have averaged 5 violent acts per hour; Saturday morning children's programs, about 20 per hour. A follow-up report from the National Institute of Mental Health (1982) estimates that by age 16, the average television viewer is likely to have witnessed about 13,000 killings and numerous other acts of violence. Given these statistics, we may safely infer that observing violence on TV does promote, at least indirectly, aggression as an appropriate way to deal with interpersonal problems. Moreover, correlational and experimental studies (cited previously) converge on the conclusion that viewing TV violence desensitizes viewers to aggression, lowers their restraints on acting aggressively, and alters their perceptions of reality.

If we accept the possibility that watching media violence can increase the likelihood of acting aggressively, especially among young viewers, what steps can we take to counteract the depiction of aggressive behavior? Bandura (1973) has put forth many recommendations. He suggests, for example, that on a personal level parents model nonaggressive forms of behavior for their children and reward nonviolent behavior. This idea has considerable merit insofar as Bandura (1979) believes that in everyday life aggressive models are found most often in the family setting. In addition, he urges parents to try to curtail their children's exposure to violence in the media by monitoring the content of such programs in advance. Bandura further recommends that parents can watch television alongside their children and comment on it, thereby resensitizing rather than desensitizing their children to the harm and suffering that violent acts can cause. At the same time, Bandura does not naively assume that his recommendations would automatically eliminate the problem: "Like so many other problems confronting man, there is no single grand design for lowering the level of destructiveness within a society. It requires both individual corrective effort and group action aimed at changing the practices of social systems" (1973, p. 323).

Self-Efficacy: Learning How to Overcome Your Fears

Bandura (1986) has increasingly directed his efforts toward developing methods of therapeutic behavior change and toward establishing a unifying theory of behavioral change. In fact, he now argues that "the value of a theory is ultimately judged by its usefulness as evidenced by the power of the methods it yields to effect psychological changes" (1986, p. 4). Although Bandura emphasizes the development of behavior change techniques, he firmly believes that their clinical application should follow an understanding of the basic principles involved and suitable tests of the effects of the techniques.

How is the therapeutic change process conceptualized from the social cognitive viewpoint? It should come as no surprise that changes in the self-perceived ability to confront and cope with threatening or aversive situations play an important role in the therapy techniques identified with this perspective. Specifically, B

(1982, 1986) hypothesizes that when therapy is effective (through whatever psychological procedure used), it is effective primarily because it strengthens a client's *perceived self-efficacy*. He further contends that the amount of effort and persistence a client expends in the face of obstacles and setbacks is governed by efficacy expectations. Enhanced expectations of personal efficacy enable the client to undertake various tasks that have important implications for improved psychosocial functioning.

The emphasis placed on change in perception of self-efficacy as the cognitive mechanism underlying therapeutic change has particular application to fear and anxiety-related behavior problems. Dozens of studies have been conducted in which clients with phobias (i.e., specific and irrational fears) have received treatment aimed at increasing their level of perceived self-efficacy (Bandura & Adams, 1977; Bandura et al., 1977; Bandura & Schunk, 1981; Bandura et al., 1982; DiClemente, 1981; Gauthier & Ladouceur, 1981). As an illustration, consider an experiment by Bandura et al. (1982), in which subjects who were recruited through a newspaper advertisement for severe spider phobias were assigned to either a low- or medium-efficacy condition. The 14 subjects, all female, sought help because they were tormented and incapacitated in every imaginable way by their fear. In some cases, for example, if they noticed a spider in their residence they fled until a neighbor destroyed it with insect spray. Others, upon noticing a spider inside the auto they were driving, would leap from the car. Still others were unable to enter places where they had previously seen a spider or even imagined spiders might inhabit.

Subjects first were administered a *behavioral avoidance test*. The test consisted of 18 performance tasks (see Table 8-1) requiring progressively more threatening interactions with a large wolf spider. This species was used because pilot testing showed it to be especially frightening to people with spider phobias. The series of performance tasks ranged from remote (approaching the spider in a plastic bowl) to intimate (allowing the spider to crawl in their lap). During the behavioral avoidance test, subjects rated orally, using a 10-point scale, the inten-

TABLE 8-1   EXAMPLES OF TEST ITEMS ON BANDURA ET AL.'S BEHAVIORAL AVOIDANCE TEST

Approach a plastic bowl containing a wolf spider.

   Look down at the spider.

   Place bare hands inside the bowl.

Allow spider to crawl freely in a chair placed immediately in front of them.

Allow spider to crawl over gloved hands.

Allow spider to crawl over bare hands.

Allow spider to crawl over forearm.

Handle spider with bare hands.

Allow spider to crawl on lap.

Source: Bandura, Reese, & Adams, 1982, p. 13.

sity of their fear both in anticipation of each task and while they performed the relevant activity. In addition, subjects were presented a list of each of the 18 behavioral tasks and were asked to rate on a 100-point scale the degree to which they felt confident that they could perform the behavior. A "1" indicated no efficacy for a given behavior, whereas a "100" indicated complete mastery of the behavior in question. A subject's efficacy score was the number of performance tasks for which the efficacy rating was 20 or above on the 100-point scale.

Next, subjects were matched in avoidance behavior and assigned randomly from matched pairs to a low- or medium-efficacy condition. The treatment to induce either a low or a medium level of efficacy was conducted by a female experimenter using a large wolf spider, noticeably different in shape and color patterns from the one used in the initial behavioral avoidance test. Treated one at a time, subjects first were asked to look at a spider placed in a glass vial until they felt familiar with its appearance and movements. The experimenter then modeled several threatening activities as subjects watched—first at a considerable distance, and later from close by (e.g., the experimenter placed the spider in a plastic bowl and poked it with her finger as it scooted about). Next she removed the spider from the container and modeled how to handle it as it scurried over her hands, arms, and upper body. Finally, she modeled additional strategies for controlling a freely moving spider by placing it on a towel draped over a chair and herding it about on a piece of furniture.

To expand further on personal control of spiders, the experimenter next released the spider on the floor and allowed it to dash about in search of a safe hiding place. She pursued the insect and captured it by placing a cup over it and sliding a thin card underneath the container—thereby showing how easy it was to trap and transport the creature to more hospitable outside environs. These treatment episodes were capped by escorting the subject to a nearby lobby where a wolf spider's web was located. Here, the experimenter modeled inquisitiveness about the spider's habitat.

At periodic intervals during the modeling sequence, each subject recorded on the 18-item efficacy scale the tasks she felt she could perform and the strength of her efficacy. These self-efficacy probes were repeated until each subject reached the preselected level of efficacy to which she had been assigned (low or medium level). *Low-efficacy* subjects were treated until they were able to allow the spider to crawl freely on a chair placed nearby and place their bare hands inside the bowl containing the spider. *Medium-efficacy* subjects, by contrast, were treated until they could engage in physical contact with the spider by holding it in a gloved or bare hand. After subjects had reached the assigned level of efficacy, the previously completed behavioral and fear-arousal tests were repeated. Following this post-treatment assessment, subjects in the low-efficacy condition were raised to the medium level by further modeling, and their behavior and fear were again measured. Finally, at the conclusion of the experiment, all subjects received supplementary participant modeling until they achieved maximum efficacy.

As shown in Figure 8-5, subjects assigned to the low-efficacy condition achieved low performance on the behavior test after treatment, while those in the

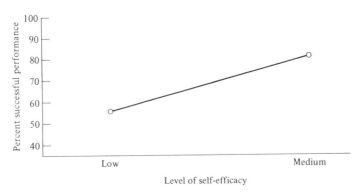

FIGURE 8-5 Mean performance scores on the behavioral avoidance test by subjects assigned to low and medium levels of perceived self-efficacy following an efficacy induction treatment procedure. (*Source: Adapted from Bandura, Reese, & Adams, 1982, p. 14. Copyright 1982 by the American Psychological Association. Reprinted by permission.*)

medium-efficacy condition achieved medium behavioral performance after treatment. Further, all subjects' behavioral performance was assessed when they were at low efficacy and again when they were at medium efficacy (recall, the low group was raised to medium efficacy at the end of the main part of the experiment). As Figure 8-6 reveals, there was a direct relationship between performance attainments when subjects were at low efficacy and when the same subjects were at medium levels of efficacy. Bandura et al. (1982) also found an almost perfect correspondence between subjects' efficacy judgments and their level of performance. If a subject indicated that she felt she could at most look down at the spider inside the plastic bowl, she rarely tended to be able to go beyond that performance. Finally, the level of fear arousal (accompanying performance on the threatening tasks) reported by subjects corresponded almost perfectly with level of self-efficacy. If a subject judged herself to be highly efficacious on a particular task, she experienced little or no apprehension about the prospect of performing it and felt less fear while actually doing it. If, however, a subject judged herself to be highly inefficacious on a particular task, she experienced considerable apprehension about the idea of performing it and felt more fear when actually doing it.

The generality of efficacy perceptions has been documented across a wide variety of domains, including fears aroused by snakes (Bandura et al., 1977), the fearfulness aroused by injections, surgery, and dental work (Melamed & Siegel, 1975; Melamed et al., 1975), and the fears aroused by taking exams (Cooley & Spiegler, 1980; Sarason, 1975). Similarly, in the area of health-related behavior, cognitive strategies focused on increasing self-efficacy have proved useful in helping people to (1) stop smoking (Becona et al., 1988; Wojcik, 1988); (2) lose weight (Weinberg et al., 1984); (3) increase pain tolerance (Barrios, 1985); and (4) comply with medical regimens, such as rehabilitative exercise (Kaplan et al., 1984). Bandura (1986) views such documentation as support for his more general claim that changes in efficacy expectancies mediate life-style changes.

FIGURE 8-6   Mean performance scores on the behavioral avoidance test by subjects when at the low-efficacy level and when at the medium-efficacy level. (*Source: Adapted from Bandura, Reese, & Adams, 1982, p. 14. Copyright 1982 by the American Psychological Association. Reprinted by permission.*)

Let us now turn to an important application of social cognitive theory: self-management strategies for modifying problem behaviors.

APPLICATION: "POWER TO THE PERSON"—SELF-DIRECTED CHANGE

People have always shown an interest in managing their own lives. Unfortunately, however, far too many people seem to lack adequate self-management skills and thus are not living as effectively as they might. To illustrate, some people eat too much, others smoke or drink too much, others fail to exercise regularly, and still others have poor study skills. Most, if not all, of these people would like to change their unwanted behavior, but they simply do not know how. Some rely on "willpower," while others seek professional help, frequently to no avail. Implicit in social cognitive theory, however, is the promise of *self-control*, an empirically based means of systematically achieving more desirable patterns of behavior— what otherwise might be called "power to the person." Looking ahead, it is entirely possible that self-control may prove to be the most far-reaching practical application of Bandura's theory.

Self-Control of Behavior

Self-control is said to occur whenever "a person engages in a behavior whose previous probability has been less than that of alternatively available responses" (Mahoney & Thoresen, 1974, p. 22). For instance, self-control is exhibited if you formerly smoked cigarettes and no longer do so, or if you ate excessively in the past and now maintain a more modest and reasonable diet. In self-control, then, the desired response (not smoking, eating moderately) often involves immediately pleasant but ultimately desired consequences, while alternative responses (smok-

Development of a self-control program enables people to improve their physical fitness. (*Margaret Thompson/The Picture Cube*)

ing, eating excessively) involve immediately pleasant but ultimately aversive results.

From a social cognitive view, self-control does not reside exclusively within the province of either internal forces (e.g., willpower) or outer forces (e.g., external reinforcement in the Skinnerian sense). Rather, it is embedded in a person's reciprocal interaction with the environment in a carefully planned fashion. To see how this process works, let us examine five basic steps that can be particularly helpful in the effort to improve self-control.

Basic Steps Involved in Self-Control

Watson and Tharp (1989) suggest that the process of behavioral self-control involves five basic steps. They include specifying the target behavior to be changed, gathering baseline data, designing a program to increase or to decrease the frequency of a target behavior, executing and evaluating the program, and bringing the program to an end.

1   Specifying the Target Behavior   The initial step to take in self-control is to identify the exact target behavior to be changed in some way. Unfortunately, this crucial step can be more complicated than it sounds. Many of us tend to describe our problems in terms of vague negative personality traits and can be hard-pressed to give clear descriptions of the specific overt behaviors that lead us to think we have those traits. Asked what behaviors she would like to change, a woman might say, "I'm too sarcastic." That may well be true, but it does not help much in creating a self-modification program. To design an effective approach, we need to translate vague statements about traits into precise descriptions of the specific responses that lead to the trait description. Thus, the woman who views herself as "too sarcastic" might identify two specific examples of overly frequent responses that illustrate her sarcasm, such as belittling her husband in public and criticizing her children. These constitute specific target behaviors for which she could design a self-control program.

2 Gathering Baseline Data   The second step taken in behavioral self-control is to gather baseline information about the factors that influence the target behavior we intend to change. In effect, we must become a sort of personal scientist, not only monitoring our responses but also recording their frequency of occurrence for the purposes of feedback and evaluation. Thus, a person who is attempting to curtail smoking systematically would count the number of cigarettes smoked per day or during a specified time span. Similarly, a person who is attempting to lose weight systematically would keep a daily weight chart over several months. As these examples suggest, in social cognitive theory gathering accurate data of target behavior (using whatever appropriate unit of measurement) is quite unlike the kind of global self-understanding emphasized in other therapeutic procedures. These would include Freud's emphasis on insight into unconscious processes and the importance in yoga and Zen of focusing attention on inner experience. The rationale underlying this step of self-control is that a person must first get a clear fix on the frequency of a target behavior (including its eliciting cues and consequences) before he or she can effectively change it.

3 Designing a Self-Control Program   The next step in a self-modification effort is to design a program that will effectively change the frequency of a specified target behavior. According to Bandura, the goal of modifying the frequency of a targeted response can be accomplished in a number of ways. The principal options include self-reinforcements, self-punishments, and environmental planning.

a Self-Reinforcements   Bandura believes that if people want to shape their own behavior in desired directions, they must consistently reward themselves for behaving appropriately. Although the basic strategy is quite simple, there are a number of considerations in designing an effective self-reinforcement program. First, since behavior is controlled by its consequences, it behooves the person to arrange these consequences beforehand to effect desired behavior change. Second, if self-reinforcement is the preferred strategy of a self-control program, it is necessary to select a reinforcer that is both realistic and available to the person. In a program designed to increase study behavior, for instance, a student might make listening to her stereo each night contingent upon studying 4 hours each day. And who knows? Her grades may also improve as a result—more overt positive reward! Likewise, in a program aimed at increasing physical exercise, the person might make spending $20 on clothes (the self-administered reinforcer) contingent upon walking 10 miles during the week (the target behavior).

b Self-Punishments The strategy of self-imposed punishment in order to decrease the frequency of an unwanted behavior is also an obvious option. However, a major drawback of punishment is that many people find it difficult to follow through and consistently punish themselves in the event they fail to meet their behavioral goals. For best results, Watson and Tharp (1989) recommend that two guidelines be kept in mind. First, whether the target behavior is study habits, smoking, overeating, drinking, shyness, or whatever, it is preferable to use punishment in conjunction with positive self-reinforcement. A combination of aversive and pleasant self-administered consequences is more likely to ensure compliance with a self-modification program. Second, it is generally better to use a relatively mild punishment in order to enhance the likelihood that it will actually be self-administered.

c Environmental Planning This strategy for decreasing the occurrence of an undesirable response involves changing the environment so that either the stimuli preceding the response or the consequences following it are changed. Instead of facing temptation, then, the person is able to avoid the tempting situation in the first place or, perhaps, to be punished for yielding to it.

The all-too-common situation of obese people attempting to reduce their overeating serves as an excellent example. Viewed in terms of social cognitive theory, overeating is nothing more than a bad habit; it is eating without physiological hunger in response to environmental cues, and it is sustained by immediate pleasant consequences. Through careful self-monitoring, however, it is possible to identify the antecedent cues for overeating (e.g., guzzling beer and munching pretzels while watching television or eating excessively in response to emotional upset). Once these cues are accurately identified, it becomes possible to dissociate the eating response from them. Thus, the person might drink diet soda or consume nothing while watching television, or develop alternative responses to emotional tension (e.g., muscle relaxation, meditation).

4 Executing and Evaluating a Self-Control Program Once a self-modification program has been designed, the next logical step is to put it into action and make whatever adjustments that seem necessary. Watson and Tharp (1989) caution that a successful behavioral program requires constant vigilance during the intervention period in order to avoid slipping back to old self-defeating patterns of behavior. An excellent vehicle toward this end is the *self-contract*, a written agreement outlining a promise to adhere to the specified target behaviors and response consequences (rewards and punishments) of a self-control program.

Terms for such contracts should be clear, consistent, positive, and fair. There should also be a periodic review of the contract terms to be sure that they are reasonable; many people initially set unrealistically high goals, which often lead to unnecessary discouragement and abandonment of the self-control program. Also, to maximize effectiveness, at least one other person (spouse, friend) should participate. This seems to make people take their program more seriously. Likewise, the consequences in self-contracts should be individualized in terms of rewards and punishments. Finally, the rewards and punishments should be immediate, frequent, and attend actual performance—not verbal promises or stated intentions.

Watson and Tharp (1989) note that several flaws are especially common in executing self-control programs. Among those that the person should be aware of are (a) trying to accomplish too much too quickly by setting unrealistic goals, (b) allowing lengthy delays to occur between appropriate behavior and delivery of rewards, and (c) depending on weak rewards. Accordingly, the person should be prepared to make minor adjustments in a program once it is set into motion.

5   Terminating a Self-Control Program   The final step in the process of designing a self-control program is to specify the conditions under which it will end. In other words, the person should spell out terminal goals, such as exercising with a certain regularity, reaching a certain weight, or going without cigarettes for a prescribed length of time. Generally speaking, it is a good idea to phase out a self-control program by gradually reducing the frequency of rewards for appropriate behavior.

A successful program may simply fade away spontaneously or with minimal conscious effort on the person's part. Or, the person may deliberately decide when and how to end it. Ultimately, however, the goal is to acquire new, improved patterns of behavior that are self-perpetuating—responses such as studying diligently, smoking no cigarettes whatsoever, exercising regularly, and eating right. Of course, the person should always be prepared to reinstate the strategies of self-control if maladaptive responses reappear.

In conclusion, it seems clear that Bandura's theory offers rich and exciting possibilities for scientifically based self-control, possibilities which, at this point, may have only begun to be realized. Attention is now shifted to Julian Rotter and his social learning theory of personality.

JULIAN ROTTER: A Social Learning Theory of Personality

During the time Julian Rotter's theory began to take formal shape in the late 1940s and early 1950s, the most influential personality theories were either psychoanalytic or phenomenological. For Rotter, both of these approaches contained concepts that seemed vaguely defined, and so he resolved to establish a terminology that would be clear and precise. In doing this, he sought to develop a conceptual framework that included well-defined terms and hypotheses that were capable of being tested. He also set out to construct a theory that would emphasize the role of motivational and cognitive factors in human learning. Finally, Rotter intended to build a theory that stressed the understanding of behavior in the context of social situations. His *social learning theory* is, then, an attempt to explain how behavior is learned through interactions with people and other elements of the environment. In Rotter's own words, "It is a social learning theory because it stresses the fact that the major or basic modes of behaving are learned in social situations and are inextricably fused with needs requiring for their satisfaction the mediation of other persons" (1954, p. 84).

In addition to focusing attention on how behavior is learned in a social context, Rotter believes that most of our behavior is determined by our unique capacity to think and to anticipate. He argues that to predict what people will do in a certain situation we have to take into account such cognitive variables as perceptions, expectancies, and values. In Rotter's (1982) position there is also the assumption that human behavior is *goal-directed*—i.e., people strive to move in the direction of anticipated goals. For Rotter, the person's behavior is determined by expectations that a given action will, in fact, bring about future rewards. The integration of expectancy and reinforcement concepts within the same theory is thus a unique feature of Rotter's superstructure. Like Bandura, Rotter has evolved a theory of human functioning that stands in sharp contrast to the radical behaviorism of Skinner.

BIOGRAPHICAL SKETCH

Julian Rotter was born in Brooklyn, New York, in 1916, the third son of Jewish immigrant parents. Noting the obligation to acknowledge the "teacher who most contributed to my intellect," Rotter (1982) credits the Avenue J library in Brooklyn, where he spent a great deal of his grade school and high school years. He was an avid reader. One day, searching the stacks for something new to read, he stumbled onto books by Adler and Freud. His appetite for psychology thus stimulated, Rotter pursued psychology while an undergraduate at Brooklyn College, but only as an elective. He majored in chemistry because "there was no profession of psychology that I knew of" (1982, p. 343). It was during his junior year of college that Rotter discovered that Alfred Adler was teaching at the Long Island School of Medicine. Soon he began attending Adler's lectures, and eventually Adler invited Rotter to attend monthly meetings of the Society of Individual Psychology held in Adler's home.

Following his undergraduate work in 1937, Rotter entered the University of Iowa to pursue graduate work in psychology. He received his M.A. from Iowa in 1938 and his Ph.D. in clinical psychology from the University of Indiana in 1941. During World War II, Rotter worked as a psychologist in the U.S. Army. In 1946 he accepted a position at Ohio State University, where he eventually succeeded George Kelly as director of the clinical psychology program. During his tenure at Ohio State, Rotter published his best-known work, *Social Learning and Clinical Psychology* (1954).

In 1963, Rotter accepted a position as a full professor at the University of Connecticut. During his stay at Connecticut he also served as director of the Clinical Psychology Training Program and became a diplomate in clinical psychology of the American Board of Examiners in Professional Psychology. Throughout his career, Rotter authored numerous papers, chapters, books, and test manuals. In 1972, with the collaboration of June Chance and Jerry Phares, he published *Applications of a Social Learning Theory of Personality*. He also coauthored the text *Personality* (1975) with Dorothy Hochreich. A chapter entitled "Social Learning Theory" may be found in a book edited by N. T. Feather, *Expectations and Actions: Expectancy-Value Models in Psychology* (1981), and provides an excellent overview of his theoretical position. The most recent statement of his

Julian Rotter. (*Courtesy of Julian Rotter*)

ideas appears in a book entitled *The Development and Applications of Social Learning Theory* (1982). Although Rotter retired in 1987, he continues to write and supervise graduate student research projects. He and his wife currently reside in Storrs, Connecticut.

SOCIAL LEARNING THEORY: BASIC CONCEPTS AND PRINCIPLES

The main focus of Rotter's social learning theory is the prediction of human behavior in relatively specific situations. In order to accurately predict how a person will behave, Rotter believes that four variables and their interaction must be carefully analyzed. These variables include behavior potential, expectancy, reinforcement value, and the psychological situation.

Behavior Potential

Rotter contends that the key to predicting what a person will do in a given situation lies in understanding the *behavior potential*. This is the likelihood of a given behavior "occurring in any situation or situations as calculated in relation to any single reinforcement or reinforcements" (Rotter et al., 1972, p. 12). Imagine, for example, that someone insults you at a party. How do you respond? In Rotter's view, several response options are available from which to choose. You might remark that the insult was out of line and demand an apology. You could ignore the insult and shift the conversation to your latest personal accomplishment. You could punch the person in the face or simply leave the scene. Each of these responses to the insult has a different behavior potential. If you decide to ignore the insulter, it means the potential for that response was stronger than for any of the other possible responses. Obviously, the potential for a particular behavior to occur may be strong in one situation and weak in another. Screaming and yelling may be high in potential at a boxing match but very weak when attending a funeral (at least in American culture).

Rotter's concept of behavior includes virtually anything that a person may do in response to a stimulus situation, provided that it can somehow be detected and measured. Swearing, pouting, crying, laughing, and fighting are included. Planning, analyzing, studying, rationalizing, and procrastinating also qualify. In short, behavior consists "of actual motor acts, cognitions, verbal behavior, nonverbal expressive behavior, emotional reactions, and so on" (Rotter & Hochreich, 1975, p. 96).

Expectancy

For Rotter, *expectancy* refers to the subjectively held probability that a certain reinforcement will occur as a result of a specific behavior. For example, before you decide whether or not to attend a party, you probably try to figure out the probability that you will have a good time. Similarly, when deciding whether to study all weekend for an exam, you probably ask yourself what the likelihood is that the weekend of concentrated study will enable you to do better on the test. In Rotter's view, such expectancies can vary in magnitude between zero and 100 (from 0 percent to 100 percent) and are based largely on previous experiences in the same or a similar situation. Thus, if you never seem to enjoy yourself at a party, the expectancy of being rewarded for attending a party is slim. Likewise, if you always do well after studying all weekend, you probably will have a high expectancy of receiving the reward of a high grade again.

Rotter's concept of expectancy clearly indicates that people are more likely to engage in a behavior when it has been consistently reinforced in the past. For instance, if you always have a great time at parties, you are likely to accept an invitation to attend a party this weekend. But how can expectancies explain behavior in situations we encounter for the first time? According to Rotter, in this instance expectancy is based on our experiences in a comparable situation. The recent graduate who was rewarded for spending weekends writing term papers in college probably expects that devoting a weekend to completing a report for the boss will lead to similar rewards. This example illustrates how expectancies may result in consistent behavior patterns over time and across situations. Rotter, in fact, theorizes that stable expectancies generalized from past experiences do account for stability and unity of personality. It should be noted, however, that expectancies do not necessarily correspond to reality. Some people, for instance, may hold unrealistically high expectancies for their success regardless of the situation at hand. Conversely, other people may be so lacking in confidence as to consistently underestimate the chances of their own success in a given situation. In either case, Rotter maintains if we are to predict behavior accurately, we must consider the person's subjective estimates of success or failure, and not those that someone else believes are realistic.

Rotter (1966) further distinguishes between expectancies that are specific to one situation and those that are more general or apply to a number of situations. The former, called *specific expectancies,* reflect experience in one particular situation and are not especially relevant to the prediction of behavior. The latter, called *generalized expectancies,* reflect experiences accumulated over a variety of related situations and are highly relevant to the study of personality in Rotter's view. Later in this section, we will examine an important generalized expectancy called *internal-external* locus of control.

Reinforcement Value

Rotter defines *reinforcement value* as the degree to which we prefer one reinforcement over another if the likelihood of obtaining each were equal. By the use of this concept, he is stating that people differ in the importance they attach to different activities and the reinforcements they bring. Some of us, given the option, may attach more importance to watching a game of basketball on TV than on playing bridge with friends. Likewise, some of us like to take long walks; others do not.

Like expectancies, the values associated with different reinforcements are based on our prior experiences. Furthermore, the reinforcement value we assign to a certain activity can vary from situation to situation and across time. For example, social contact would likely hold a higher value when we are lonely as opposed to when we are not. Nonetheless, Rotter maintains that there are relatively stable individual differences in degree of preference we have for one reinforcement over another. Some people always take free movie tickets over free opera tickets. Accordingly, enduring behavior patterns also can be traced to relatively stable emotions and cognitions about what constitutes an inherently rewarding activity in life.

It should be emphasized that reinforcement value is independent of expectancy in Rotter's theory. In other words, knowing the value a person places on a particular reinforcement in no way indicates that person's expectancy of obtaining that reinforcement. A student, for example, may place high value on academic achievement and yet have a low expectancy of obtaining high grades due to a lack of initiative or ability. Reinforcement value reflects Rotter's motivational emphasis, whereas expectancy reflects his cognitive emphasis.

The Psychological Situation

The fourth and final variable employed by Rotter to predict behavior is the *psychological situation* as it is viewed from the perspective of the individual. Rotter maintains that social situations are in the "eye of the beholder." In this sense, his approach bears striking resemblance to Rogers' phenomenological view of the person, discussed in Chapter 11. Like Rogers, Rotter feels that if a given environmental circumstance is perceived in a certain way by a particular person, that is the way it is for him or her, no matter how bizarre the perception might seem to others.

Rotter emphasizes the influential role of situational contexts and their powerful impact on human behavior. Specifically, he theorizes that the array of cues in a given social situation evoke in the person expectancies for behavior-reinforcement outcomes. Thus, a student about to deliver a speech to her social psychology

People differ in the reinforcement value they associate with different activities. Given a choice, some prefer to watch a football game; others prefer to visit an art museum. (*Top, Jock Pottle/ Design Conceptions; bottom, Kent Reno/Jeroboam*)

class might anticipate that she will do poorly and thereby receive a low grade from her instructor and ridicule from her classmates. As a result, we might predict that she will drop the course or pursue some other action designed to prevent the expected unpleasant outcome.

The interaction of the person with his or her meaningful environment is a theme deeply embedded in Rotter's perspective on personality. As an *interactionist*, he argues that the psychological situation must be considered along with expectancies and reinforcement value in predicting the potential for any behavior to occur. He concurs with Bandura that personal factors and environmental events in interaction provide the best predictor of human behavior.

A Basic Formula for Predicting Behavior

In order to predict the potential for a given behavior to occur in a specific situation, Rotter (1967) proposed the following formula:

$$\text{Behavior Potential} = \text{Expectancy} + \text{Reinforcement Value}$$

This equation tells us that two variables need to be considered when predicting the likelihood of a given behavior in a particular situation: expectancy and reinforcement value. Consider the following example. You are faced with a choice between going to the computer center on a Sunday afternoon or staying in your dorm to watch an NFL football game on TV. We could probably predict which of the two behavioral choices would occur if (1) we knew the value of the reinforcements associated with each choice and (2) the corresponding expectancies that each choice would lead to the reinforcements involved. However, it should be noted that Rotter's basic formula represents a hypothetical rather than a pragmatic means of predicting behavior. In fact, he suggests that the four variables we have just considered (behavior potential, expectancy, reinforcement, psychological situation) are useful only in predicting behavior in a highly controlled setting such as a psychological experiment. As we shall see later, Rotter uses a more general formula for the prediction of goal-oriented behavior in the various situations that people encounter on a daily basis.

Needs

You will recall that Rotter views people as goal-oriented. He believes that people strive to maximize rewards and to minimize or avoid punishments. Furthermore, he argues that goals determine the direction of the person's behavior in the quest to satisfy basic needs. Therefore, in Rotter's judgment, knowing a person's goals and needs allows for more generalized predictions than that permitted by the four variables cited above.

Rotter proposes that specific goals commonly cluster into broader categories that are conceptualized as needs. The concept of *need* can be described as a set of behaviors that are similar in that they are concerned with the acquisition of the same or similar sets of reinforcement. The following six categories of needs are viewed by Rotter as being especially relevant in predicting the person's behavior.

Recognition-Status   This concerns our need to feel competent in a wide variety of behavioral areas such as school, work, athletics, or socially related activities. The need to be recognized by others as intellectually talented is an example of a need subsumed under this category.

Protection-Dependency   This involves the need to have others protect us against harm and to help us achieve valued goals. Asking a family member to take care of us when we are ill would be an example of this need category.

Dominance   This involves the need to exercise power and influence over the lives of others and to be able to establish consequences on the basis of such control. Persuading friends and neighbors to contribute to our favorite charity illustrates the need for dominance.

Independence   This concerns our need to make our own decisions and to achieve goals without being dependent on others. The high school senior who refuses to accept a guidance counselor's help in selecting a college is expressing the need for independence. Any behavior suggesting the desire to be self-reliant reflects this need category.

Love and Affection   This involves the need to be accepted and liked by other persons. A specific example here would be a young woman who devotes considerable time and effort to caring for her boyfriend, hoping that he will tell her that he loves her.

Physical Comfort   This final category involves satisfactions associated with physical security, good health, and freedom from pain. Rotter indicates that all other needs are learned as a result of their association with the basic needs for physical well-being and pleasure. Behavior leading to sexual gratification illustrates the need for physical comfort.

Need Components

Rotter suggests that each category of needs is comprised of three essential components: need potential, need value, and freedom of movement (including minimal goal). These three components are analogous to the more specific concepts of behavior potential, reinforcement value, and expectancy. When combined, they also provide the basis for Rotter's general prediction formula (discussed on page 380).

Need Potential   A *need potential* refers to the likelihood that a behavior will be enacted that leads to satisfaction of a certain need category, such as love and affection. For instance, a person's need potential for love and affection could be described as the behavior potential that he has for bringing his wife candy to receive a hug or calling his mother to wish her well in return for her affection. Each of these behaviors is functionally related in the sense that it is focused on receiving love and affection from significant others.

Need Value   The concept of *need value* is defined by Rotter as the average value of a set of reinforcements. It will be recalled that reinforcement value refers to the relative desirability of a certain reinforcement, given that all reinforcements possible under the circumstances are equally likely to occur. Need value broadens this notion to include the relative desirability of different reinforcers associated with the six categories of needs previously described. Consider, for example, a student who graduates from high school and has to decide whether to attend college, seek employment, join the military, or tour the country for a year. If the student's most valued reinforcers include status and comments by others confirming his competence, it could be said that his need value was highest for recognition-related reinforcements. Rotter believes that most people display reasonable levels of consistency in their preferences for reinforcements related to the six need categories. Thus, for one person the most preferred category is the need to gain love and affection; for another, it may be the need to be free of the control of others; and for another, it may be the need to exert power over others.

Freedom of Movement and Minimal Goal   Rotter's concept of *freedom of movement* refers to the degree of expectancy that a person has that a set of related behaviors will lead to reinforcements connected with one of the six need categories. It reflects the subjectively held probability that satisfying reinforcements will occur as a result of performing a set of behaviors. As an example, if a man believed that there was a low probability that his wife would hug him for bringing candy and his mother would react negatively to a phone call, it would be said that he had low freedom of movement at that time in relation to love and affection. In Rotter's view, low freedom of movement coupled with high need value results in a very frustrated individual who feels ineffective in achieving important goals. In a more general sense, Rotter maintains that maladjustment results when the person places a high value on the satisfaction of a particular need yet has very low freedom of movement (expectancies) for the success of behaviors that could lead to the satisfaction of that need.

·   *Minimal goal level* refers to the lowest point at which a reinforcement continues to be perceived positively by the person. In other words, a minimal goal establishes the dividing line between those rewards that are positively reinforcing and those that are punishing on some dimension. Thus, for some students a course grade of C may be viewed as reinforcing—their minimal goals are low in the academic need area. In contrast, other students may only find a course grade of A as reinforcing—they would be said to have a higher minimal goal than the former students. According to Rotter, in the absence of competency or skill, extremely high minimal goal levels enhance the possibilities of experiencing failure and discouragement. In a related way, extremely low minimal goal levels reduce the likelihood of engaging in behaviors that would establish competency or skill. In other instances, Rotter notes that the value of a need becomes so high that it dominates the person's life to the exclusion of all else. This may lead to either distortions of reality or the inability to discriminate among situations. For instance, a person may have such a compelling need to be liked that he or she indiscriminately gives expensive gifts to passing acquaintances. Undoubtedly, such behavior would be seen by others as quite bizarre.

It is important to reiterate Rotter's conception of maladaptive behavior. For him, the combination of high need value and low freedom of movement is a common cause of maladjustment. The tendency to set overly high goals contributes to high need value and leads to inevitable frustration and failure. Maladaptive people also have low freedom of movement because they wrongly assume that they lack the skills or information needed to attain their goals. Rotter believes that maladjusted individuals often seek to achieve goals through fantasy or in ways that avoid or defend against the risk of failure.

General Prediction Formula

As noted previously, Rotter considers his basic formula as limited to predicting specific behaviors in controlled settings where reinforcements and expectancies are relatively uncomplicated. The prediction of behavior in actual day-to-day situations, in his view, requires a more generalized formula. Therefore, Rotter (1982) offers the following prediction model:

$$\text{Need Potential} = (\text{Freedom of Movement} + \text{Need Value})$$

This equation indicates that two separate factors determine the potential for the occurrence of a set of related behaviors directed toward the satisfaction of a certain need. The first factor is the person's freedom of movement or overall expectancy that these behaviors will result in the need being satisfied. The second factor is the value the person places on the need associated with whatever goal is being contemplated or pursued. In simpler terms, Rotter's general prediction formula means that a person is most likely to act to obtain goals for which he or she expects to be reinforced and the expected reinforcements are highly valued. Provided that we know these facts, Rotter believes that an accurate prediction concerning which one of several behaviors the person is likely to enact should be possible.

The general prediction formula also emphasizes the impact of a person's generalized expectancy that reinforcement will occur as a result of behaving in certain ways across different situations. Rotter has identified two such generalized expectancies: locus of control and interpersonal trust. Locus of control, discussed next, is the basis for Rotter's Internal-External (I-E) Scale, one of the most widely used self-report measures in personality research.

Internal versus External Locus of Control

The bulk of research that has been conducted relative to Rotter's theory has focused on a personality variable called *locus of control* (Rotter, 1966, 1975). As a core construct in social learning theory, locus of control represents a generalized expectancy about the degree to which people control reinforcements in their lives. Persons with an *external* locus of control believe that their successes and failures are governed by external factors such as fate, luck, chance, powerful others, and unpredictable environmental forces. "Externals" believe that they are pawns of fate. In contrast, persons with an *internal* locus of control believe that their successes and failures are determined by their actions and abilities (internal or personal factors). "Internals" thus feel that they have more influence over their reinforcements than people with an external locus of control orientation.

Although belief in external or internal control might be viewed as a trait, in the sense of individual differences, Rotter (1982) clearly indicates that externals and internals are not "types," each sharing characteristics with others in their category and few with everyone else. Instead, the construct should be thought of as a continuum bounded on one end by external and on the other by internal, with people's beliefs located at all points in-between, mostly in the middle. In other words, a few people are very external, a few people are very internal, and most people fall in-between the extremes. With this perspective in mind, we can turn attention to the measurement of locus of control and some of the major psychosocial characteristics associated with individual differences along this important dimension.

Measuring Locus of Control Although there are several measures of control orientation for use with children and adults, the *I-E Scale* constructed by Rotter (1966) has been used most often by researchers in the area. It consists of 23 forced-choice items, along with 6 filler items added to help disguise the purposes of the test. Some sample items are presented in Table 8-2. Scores are computed by assigning 1 point for each external alternative selected by the subject and summing across all 23 items. Scores can thus range from 0 to 23, with higher scores reflecting greater externality. Researchers using the I-E Scale usually identify subjects who fall at either extreme of the particular distribution of sample scores (e.g., above the seventy-fifth and below the twenty-fifth percentiles). If subjects are classified as either externals or internals in this manner, those who score between the extremes are therefore excluded from further study. Researchers then proceed to look for differences between the two extreme groups in reference to other self-report personality measures and/or behavioral measures.

Characteristics of Externals and Internals Research based on Rotter's I-E Scale

TABLE 8-2 SAMPLE ITEMS FROM ROTTER'S INTERNAL-EXTERNAL SCALE

1 **a** I have often found that what is going to happen will happen (E)
  b Trusting to fate has never turned out as well for me as making a decision to take a definite course of action (I)

2 **a** No matter how hard you try some people just don't like you (E)
  b People who can't get others to like them just don't understand how to get along with others (I)

3 **a** In the long run, people get the respect they deserve in this world (I)
  b Unfortunately, an individual's worth often passes unrecognized no matter how hard he tries (E)

Source: Rotter, 1966, p. 11.

indicates that externals and internals differ in several ways other than their respective beliefs about where the sources of control of their behavior lies (Strickland, 1989). One key difference distinguishing externals from internals centers around the ways they seek information about their environment. Several studies reveal that internals are more likely than externals to actively seek information about possible health problems (Strickland, 1979; Wallston & Wallston, 1981). Internals also have a greater tendency than externals to take preventive steps to maintain or improve their health, such as giving up smoking, embarking on an exercise program, and getting regular medical checkups (Strickland, 1978; Wallston & Wallston, 1982). One explanation for this consistent finding is based on the early family experiences of internals and externals. Specifically, Lau (1982) has found that internals more than externals were encouraged by their parents when they were children to practice a variety of health habits, such as following a good diet, brushing their teeth properly, and getting regular dental and medical checkups. As a result of these early experiences, internals are more likely than externals to know about the conditions that cause poor health and to be more likely to show enhanced efforts to maximize their health and well-being.

Research also indicates that people with an external locus of control develop psychological disorders more often than people characterized by an internal locus of control (Lefcourt, 1982, 1984; Phares, 1978). For instance, Phares (1976, 1978) reports that externals are higher in anxiety and depression and lower in self-esteem that internals. Internals are also less likely to be classified with psychiatric labels than are externals. Research (Boor, 1976) has even shown that suicide rates correlate positively ($r = .68$) with the average level of externality among people in a country. Why is externality associated with poor adjustment? We can only speculate that people tend to function more effectively in their lives when they believe that their own destiny is under personal control. In turn, this would lead to better adjustment on the part of internals noted in so many studies (Parkes, 1984).

Finally, numerous studies indicate that externals are much more compliant and susceptible to social influence attempts than are internals (Phares, 1978; Strickland, 1977). Indeed, Phares (1965) found that internals not only resist influence attempts by others but also, when given an opportunity, make more efforts to control the behavior of others. Internals also tend to like people they can readily manipulate and dislike those they cannot influence (Silverman & Shrauger, 1970). In short, internals seem to have greater confidence in their own problem-solving ability than externals and thus tend to make judgments independently of the demands of others.

Concluding Comments

Rotter's emphasis on the importance of social and cognitive factors in accounting for human learning has clearly widened the scope of traditional behaviorism. His theory is predicated on the assumption that the most significant aspects of personality are learned within a social context. Rotter's theory also complements Bandura's in that it stresses the reciprocal interaction of the person with his or her environment. Both theorists strongly reject the Skinnerian view that people passively respond to external reinforcement. As we have seen, Rotter argues that people are capable of knowing that they will probably be rewarded for certain behaviors in certain situations but not in others. In addition, he views people as cognitive creatures who actively construct their own goals and strategies of behavior throughout life. Finally, Rotter's theory offers a parsimonious and internally consistent framework for organizing what is known about human behavior. By concentrating on a limited number of well-defined concepts and principles of personality functioning, his ideas will likely contribute to personology indefinitely. On the down side, however, aside from locus of control, Rotter's theory has not generated the needed research it so richly deserves.

SUMMARY

The social cognitive perspective in personality is represented by two personologists, Albert Bandura and Julian Rotter. Bandura depicts psychological functioning in terms of the continuous reciprocal interaction of behavioral, cognitive, and environmental influences. This conception of human behavior casts people into a role of neither pawns controlled by external forces nor free agents able to become whatever they choose; rather, the reciprocal interplay of behavioral and environmental forces is highlighted, a fluid, dynamic process in which cognitive factors play a central role in the organization and regulation of human activity.

Bandura's major theoretical concept is that of modeling or learning through observation. A key assumption here is that modeling influences generate learning chiefly through their informative function, an account of learning which clearly reflects the cognitive orientation of Bandura's thinking. Furthermore, observational learning is governed by four interrelated factors—attentional, retention, motor reproduction, and motivational processes.

Bandura's treatment of reinforcement in observational learning also reflects his cognitive orientation. In social cognitive theory, external reinforcement often serves two functions—information and incentive—for the person. Further, Bandura emphasizes the role of vicarious reinforcement, the observation of others being reinforced, and self-reinforcement, in which people reinforce their own behavior.

Self-regulation, or how people regulate their behavior, is also an important feature of social cognitive theory. In self-regulation, the major processes of self-observation, judgment, and self-evaluation are highlighted. Bandura also considers the issue of why people punish themselves.

In recent years, Bandura has extended his social cognitive view to include the cognitive mechanism of self-efficacy to account for several aspects of psychosocial functioning. The concept of self-efficacy refers to the person's perceived ability to execute behaviors relative to a specific task or situation and is acquired from four main sources: performance accomplishments, vicarious experiences, verbal persuasion, and emotional arousal.

While Bandura is often characterized as a moderate behaviorist, his basic assumptions suggest a different view of the person from that espoused by traditional behaviorists, especially Skinner. Social cognitive theory reflects (1) a strong commitment to the assumptions of rationality, environmentalism, changeability, and knowability; (2) a moderate commitment to the elementalism assumption; and (3) a midrange position on the freedom–determinism, subjectivity–objectivity, and proactivity–reactivity dimensions. The homeostasis–heterostasis assumption does not apply to Bandura's position, since he conceptualizes motivation in a fashion that does not readily lend itself to this type of analysis.

Bandura's theory has been well-researched and there is ample empirical support for it. In this chapter, research dealing with both the short- and long-term effects of observing televised violence on the viewer's aggressiveness was presented. Studies concerned with therapeutic instigated changes in self-efficacy as a strategy for reducing fear and anxiety-related behavior problems were also discussed.

In the application section of the chapter, social cognitive concepts were applied to the phenomenon of self-control. Five basic steps involved in behavioral self-control were described—specifying the target behavior, gathering baseline data, designing a self-control program, executing and evaluating a self-control program, and terminating a self-control program—along with illustrations designed to demonstrate how self-control could be implemented in a person's life.

Julian Rotter's social learning theory of personality emphasizes the role of motivational and cognitive factors in explaining behavior in the context of social situations. In particular, Rotter stresses four major variables: behavior potential, expectancy, reinforcement value, and the psychological situation. Rotter combines these variables into a basic prediction formula. The formula predicts that the potential for a given behavior to occur in a specific situation is a function of the person's expectancy that a reinforcement will follow the behavior plus the value of the anticipated reinforcement.

Rotter uses a more general formula to predict behavior in the day-to-day situations that people encounter. This formula indicates that need potential is a function of freedom of movement and need value. The concepts of need, need potential, need value, freedom of movement (including minimal goal) are viewed by Rotter as allowing for more precise predictions of real-life behavior than does the basic formula.

A core construct in Rotter's social learning theory is locus of control or the generalized expectancy about the degree to which people control reinforcements in their lives. The measurement of locus of control was discussed in terms of Rotter's Internal-External Scale, and certain behavioral characteristics associated with individual differences using this scale were noted.

BIBLIOGRAPHY

Anderson, C. A., & Ford, C. M. (1986). Affect of the game player: short-term effects of highly and mildly aggressive video games. *Personality and Social Psychology Bulletin*, **12**, 390–402.

Awards for Distinguished Scientific Contributions: 1980—Albert Bandura. (1981). *American Psychologist*, **36**, 27–34.

Bandura, A. (1965). Influence of models' reinforcement contingencies on the acquisition of imitative responses. *Journal of Personality and Social Psychology*, **1**, 589–595.

Bandura, A. (1969). *Principles of behavior modification*. New York: Holt, Rinehart and Winston.

Bandura, A. (1971). *Social-learning theory*. New York: General Learning Press, pp. 1–46.

Bandura, A. (1973). *Aggression: A social-learning analysis*. Englewood Cliffs, NJ: Prentice-Hall.

Bandura, A. (1974). Behavior theory and the models of man. *American Psychologist*, **29**, 859–869.

Bandura, A. (1977a). Self-efficacy: Toward a unifying theory of behavior change. *Psychological Review*, **84**, 191–215.

Bandura, A. (1977b). *Social-learning theory*. Engelwood Cliffs, NJ: Prentice-Hall.

Bandura, A. (1978). The self system in reciprocal determinism. *American Psychologist*, **3**, 344–358.

Bandura, A. (1979). Psychological mechanisms of aggression. In M. Von Cranach, K. Foppa, W. LePenies, & D. Ploog (Eds.), *Human ethology: Claims and limits of a new discipline*. Cambridge, MA: Cambridge University Press.

Bandura, A. (1982). Self-efficacy mechanism in human agency. *American Psychologist*, **37**, 122–147.

Bandura, A. (1986). *Social foundations of thought and action: A social cognitive theory*. Englewood Cliffs, NJ: Prentice-Hall.

Bandura, A. (1988). Self-regulation of motivation and action through goal systems. In L. A. Pervin (Ed.), *Goal concepts in personality and social psychology*. Hillsdale, NJ: Erlbaum.

Bandura, A. (1989a). Social cognitive theory. In R. Vasta (Ed.), *Annals of child development* (Vol. 6, pp. 1–60). Greenwich, CT: JAI Press.

Bandura, A. (1989b). Human agency in social cognitive theory. *American Psychologist*, **44**, 1175–1184.

Bandura, A. (1989c). Regulation of cognitive processes through perceived self-efficacy. *Developmental Psychology*, **25**, 729–735.

Bandura, A., & Adams, N. E. (1977). Analysis of self-efficacy theory of behavioral change. *Cognitive Therapy and Research*, **1**, 287–310.

Bandura, A., Adams, N. E., & Beyer, J. (1977). Cognitive processes mediating behavioral change. *Journal of Personality and Social Psychology*, **35**, 125–139.

Bandura, A., Reese, L., & Adams, N. E. (1982). Microanalysis of action and fear arousal as a function of differential levels of perceived self-efficacy. *Journal of Personality and Social Psychology*, **43**, 5–21.

Bandura, A., Ross, D., & Ross, S. (1963). Imitation of film-mediated aggressive models. *Journal of Abnormal and Social Psychology*, **66**, 3–11.

Bandura, A., & Schunk, D. H. (1981). Cultivating competence, self-efficacy, and intrinsic interest. *Journal of Personality and Social Psychology*, **41**, 586–598.

Bandura, A., & Walters, R. (1959). *Adolescent aggression*. New York: Ronald.

Bandura, A., & Walters, R. (1963). *Social learning and personality development*. New York: Holt, Rinehart and Winston.

Barrios, F. X. (1985). A comparison of global and specific estimates of self-control. *Cognitive Therapy and Research*, **9**, 455–469.

Becona, E., Frojan, M. J., & Lista, M. J. (1988). Comparison between two self-efficacy scales in maintenance of smoking cessation. *Psychological Reports*, **62**, 359–362.

Berkowitz, L. (1964). The effects of observing violence. *Scientific American*, February, 35–41.

Berkowitz, L. (1984). Some effects of thoughts on anti- and prosocial influences of media events: A cognitive-neoassociation analysis. *Psychological Bulletin*, **95**, 140–427.

Boor, M. (1976). Relationship of internal-external control and national suicide rates. *Journal of Social Psychology*, **100**, 143–144.

Cline, V. B., Croft, R. G., & Courrier, S. (1973). Desensitization of children to television violence. *Journal of Personality and Social Psychology*, **27**, 360–365.

Cooley, E. J., & Spiegler, M. D. (1980). Cognitive versus emotional coping responses as alternatives to test anxiety. *Cognitive Therapy and Research*, **4**, 159–166.

DiClemente, C. C. (1981). Self-efficacy and smoking cessation. *Cognitive Therapy and Research*, **5**, 175–187.

Eron, L. D. (1980). Prescription for reduction of aggression. *American Psychologist*, **35**, 244–252.

Eron, L. D. (1987). The development of aggressive behavior from the perspective of a developing behaviorism. *American Psychologist*, **42**, 425–442.

Eron, L. D., & Huesmann, L. R. (1985). The role of television in the development of prosocial and antisocial behavior. In D. Olweus, M. Radke-Yarrow, and J. Block (Eds.), *Development of antisocial and prosocial behavior*. Orlando, FL: Academic Press.

Eron, L. D., Huesmann, L. R., Debow, E., Romanoff, R., & Yarmel, P. (1987). Aggression and its correlates over 22 years. In D. Crowell, I. Evans, and C. O'Donnell (Eds.), *Childhood aggression and violence: Sources of influence, prevention and control*. New York: Plenum.

Eron, L. D., Huesmann, L. R., Lefkowitz, M. M., & Walder, L. O. (1972). Does television cause aggression? *American Psychologist*, **27**, 253–263.

Feather, N. T. (Ed.) (1981). *Expectations and actions: Expectancy-value models in psychology*. Hillsdale, NJ: Erlbaum.

Freedman, J. L. (1986). Television violence and aggression: A rejoinder. *Psychological Bulletin*, **100**, 372–378.

Friedrich-Cofer, L., & Huston, A. C. (1986). Television violence and aggression: The debate continues. *Psychological Bulletin*, **100**, 364–371.

Gauthier, J., & Ladouceur, R. (1981). The influence of self-efficacy reports on performance. *Behavior Therapy*, **12**, 436–439.

Geen, R. G. (1981). Behavioral and physiological reactions to observed violence: Effects of
prior exposure to aggressive stimuli. *Journal of Personality and Social Psychology*, **40**,
868–875.

Geen, R. G. (1983). Aggression and television violence. In R. G. Geen and E. I. Donnerstein (Eds.), *Aggression: Theoretical and empirical reviews: Vol. 2. Issues in research.*
New York: Academic Press.

Geen, R. G., & Thomas, S. L. (1986). The immediate effects of media violence on
behavior. *Journal of Social Issues*, **42**, 7–28.

Gerbner, G., & Gross, L. (1976). The scary world of TV's heavy viewer. *Psychology
Today*, April, 41–44, 89.

Gerbner, G., Gross, L., Morgan, M., & Signorielli, N. (1980). The "mainstreaming" of
American Violence: Profile no. 11. *Journal of Communications*, **30**(3), 10–29.

Gerbner, G., Gross, L., Morgan, M., & Signorielli, N. (1986). Living with television: The
dynamics of the cultivation process. In J. Bryant and D. Zillman (Eds.), *Perspectives on
media effects* (pp. 17–40). Hillsdale, NJ: Erlbaum.

Heath, L. (1984). Impact of newspaper crime reports on fear of crime: Multi-meth-
odological investigation. *Journal of Personality and Social Psychology*, **47**, 263–276.

Hicks, D. (1968). Effects of co-observer's sanctions and adult presence on imitative
aggression. *Child Development*, **39**, 303–309.

Huesmann, L. R., & Malamuth, N. M. (1986). Media violence and antisocial behavior: An
overview. *Journal of Social Issues*, **42**, 1–6.

Kaplan, R. M., Atkins, C. J., & Reinsch, S. (1984). Specific efficacy expectations mediate
exercise compliance in patients with CAPD. *Health Psychology*, **3**, 223–242.

Lau, R. A. (1982). Origins of health locus of control beliefs. *Journal of Personality and
Social Psychology*, **42**, 322–334.

Lefcourt, H. M. (1982). *Locus of control: Current theory and research* (2nd ed.). Hillsdale,
NJ: Erlbaum.

Lefcourt, H. M. (Ed.) (1984). *Research with the locus of control construct: Extensions and
limitations* (Vol. 3). New York: Academic Press.

Lefkowitz, M. M., Eron, L. D., Walder, L. O., & Huesmann, L. R. (1977). *Growing up to
be violent.* New York: Pergamon Press.

Leyens, J., Camino, L., Parke, R., & Berkowitz, L. (1975). Effects of movie violence on
aggression in a field setting as a function of group dominance and cohesion. *Journal of
Personality and Social Psychology*, **32**, 346–360.

Liebert, R. M., & Sprafkin, J. (1988). *The early window* (3rd ed.). Elmsford, NY: Pergamon Press.

Mahoney, M., & Thoresen, C. (1974). *Self-control: Power to the person.* Monterey, CA:
Brooks/Cole.

Melamed, B. G., & Siegel, L. J. (1975). Reduction of anxiety in children facing hospitaliza-
tion and surgery by use of filmed modeling. *Journal of Consulting and Clinical Psychology*, **43**, 511–521.

Melamed, B. G., Weinstein, D., Hawes, R., & Katin-Borland, M. (1975). Reduction of
fear-related dental management problems using filmed modeling. *Journal of American
Dental Association*, **90**, 822–826.

Mischel, W., & Peake, P. K. (1982). Beyond déjà vu in the search for cross-situational
consistency. *Psychological Review*, **89**, 730–755.

National Institute of Mental Health (1982). *Television and behavior: Ten years of scientific progress and implications for the eighties* (Vol. 1). Washington, DC: U.S. Department of Health and Human Services.

Nurnberger, J. I., & Zimmerman, J. (1970). Applied analysis of human behavior: An alternative to conventional motivational inferences and unconscious determination in therapeutic programming. *Behavior Therapy*, **1**, 59–69.

Parkes, K. R. (1984). Locus of control, cognitive appraisal, and coping in stressful episodes. *Journal of Personality and Social Psychology*, **46**, 655–668.

Phares, E. J. (1965). Internal-external control as a determinant of amount of social influence exerted. *Journal of Personality and Social Psychology*, **2**, 642–647.

Phares, E. J. (1976). Locus of control in personality. Morristown, NJ: General Learning Press.

Phares, E. J. (1978). Locus of control. In H. London and J. E. Exner, Jr. (Eds.), *Dimensions of personality* (pp. 263–304). New York: Wiley.

Rotter, J. B. (1954). *Social learning and clinical psychology*. Englewood Cliffs, NJ: Prentice-Hall.

Rotter, J. B. (1966). Generalized expectancies for internal versus external control of reinforcement. *Psychological Monographs*, **80** (entire No. 609).

Rotter, J. B. (1967). A new scale for the measurement of interpersonal trust. *Journal of Personality*, **35**, 651–665.

Rotter, J. (1975). Some problems and misconceptions related to the construct of internal versus external control of reinforcement. *Journal of Consulting and Clinical Psychology*, **43**, 56–67.

Rotter, J. B. (1981). Social learning therapy. In N. T. Feather (Ed.), *Expectations and actions: Expectancy-value models in psychology*. Hillsdale, NJ: Erlbaum.

Rotter, J. B. (1982). *The development and applications of social learning theory: Selected papers*. New York: Praeger.

Rotter, J. B., Chance, J. E., & Phares, E. J. (1972). *Applications of social learning theory of personality*. New York: Holt, Rinehart and Winston.

Rotter, J. B., & Hochreich, D. J. (1975). *Personality*. Glenview, IL: Scott, Foresman.

Sarason, I. G. (1975). Test anxiety and the self-disclosing coping method. *Journal of Consulting and Clinical Psychology*, **43**, 148–153.

Silverman, R. E., & Shrauger, J. S. (1970). Locus of control and correlates of attraction toward others. Paper presented at the annual meeting of the Eastern Psychological Association, Atlantic City, NJ.

Singer, J. L., & Singer, D. G. (1981). *Television, imagination, and aggression: A study of preschoolers*. Hillsdale, NJ: Erlbaum.

Skinner, B. F. (1989). The origins of cognitive thought. *American Psychologist*, **44**, 13–18.

Strickland, B. R. (1977). Internal-external control of reinforcement. In T. Bass (Ed.), *Personality variables in social behavior*. Hillsdale, NJ: Erlbaum.

Strickland, B. R. (1978). Internal-external expectancies and health-related behaviors. *Journal of Consulting and Clinical Psychology*, **46**, 1192–1211.

Strickland, B. R. (1979). Internal-external expectancies and cardiovascular functioning. In L. C. Perlmutter and R. A. Monty (Eds.), *Choice of perceived control*. Hillsdale, NJ: Erlbaum.

Strickland, B. R. (1989). Internal-external control expectancies: From contingency to creativity. *American Psychologist*, **44**, 1–12.

Tangney, J. P., & Feshbach, S. (1988). Children's television viewing frequency: Individual differences and demographic correlates. *Personality and Social Psychology Bulletin*, **14**, 145–158.

Thomas, M. H., Horton, R. W., Lippincott, E. C., & Drabman, R. S. (1977). Desensitization to portrayals of real-life aggression as a function of exposure to television violence. *Journal of Personality and Social Psychology*, **35**, 450–458.

Wallston, K. A., & Wallston, B. S. (1981). Health locus of control scales. In H. F. Lefcourt (Ed.), *Research with the locus of control construct* (Vol. 1, pp. 189–243). New York: Academic Press.

Wallston, K. A., & Wallston, B. S. (1982). Who is responsible for your health?: The construct of health locus of control. In G. Sanders and J. Suls (Eds.), *Social psychology of health and illness*. Hillsdale, NJ: Erlbaum.

Watson, D. L., & Tharp, R. G. (1989). *Self-directed behavior: Self-modification for personal adjustment*. Pacific Grove, CA: Brooks/Cole.

Weinberg, R. S., Hughes, H. H., Critelli, J. W., England, R., & Jackson, A. (1984). Effects of preexisting and manipulated self-efficacy on weight loss in a self-control group. *Journal of Personality Research*, **18**, 352–358.

Wojcik, J. (1988). Social learning predictors of the avoidance of smoking relapse. *Addictive Behaviors*, **13**, 177–180.

Zimmerman, B. J., & Rosenthal, J. T. (1974). Observational learning of rule governed behavior by children. *Psychological Bulletin*, **81**, 29–42.

SUGGESTED READINGS

Bandura, A. (1984). Recycling misconceptions of perceived self-efficacy. *Cognitive Therapy and Research*, **8**, 231–255.

Bandura, A. (1986). *Social foundations of thought and action*. Englewood Cliffs, NJ: Prentice-Hall.

Bandura, A., & Wood, R. E. (1989). Effect of perceived controllability and performance standards on self-regulation of complex decision-making. *Journal of Personality and Social Psychology*, **56,** 805–814.

Evans, R. I. (1989). *Albert Bandura: The man and his ideas*. Westport, CT: Greenwood Press.

Kavanagh, D. J., & Bower, G. H. (1985). Mood and self-efficacy: Impact of joy and sadness on perceived capabilities. *Behavior Therapy and Research*, **9**, 507–525.

Rotter, J. B. (1981). The psychological situation in social learning theory. In D. Magnusson (Ed.), *Toward a psychology of situations: An interactional perspective*. Hillsdale, NJ: Erlbaum.

Scheier, M. F., & Carver, C. S. (1988). A model of behavioral self-regulation: Translating intention into action. In L. Berkowitz (Ed.), *Advances in experimental social psychology* (Vol. 21). San Diego, CA: Academic Press.

DISCUSSION QUESTIONS

1 Now that you have studied and thought about his theory, do you believe that Bandura is truly a behaviorist? In considering this question, compare and contrast Bandura's social cognitive view of the person with the views expressed by Skinner.

2 Think of a particular skill that you have learned through modeling. Can you see how each of the four component processes—attentional, retention, motor reproduction, and motivational—played an important role in this observational-learning process? Be specific—give an example of each. Now repeat this exercise by citing a particular personality characteristic that you have; can it, too, be understood in terms of observational learning?

3 Take the same skill that you cited for the above question and show how vicarious reinforcement played a part in its acquisition. Do the same with the personality characteristic that you also cited.

4 What are the main sources of self-efficacy in Bandura's theory? Does Bandura account for individual differences in perceived self-efficacy in terms of his observational learning concepts? If yes, explain.

5 What are some important implications of the studies and surveys of violence on television presented in this chapter? Do you believe that watching television over the years has affected you in any way? What would you recommend to parents regarding their child's watching violence on television?

6 Cite and discuss illustrative research showing that changes in perceived self-efficacy are essential if a client is to overcome his or her fear in a therapy setting. Does available research support Bandura's claim that enhanced self-efficacy mediates various life-style changes?

7 Pick a specific aspect of your behavior that you would like to change—something that you are not doing now that you would like to do (e.g., ''I'd like to exercise more often'') or a current behavior that you would like to curtail (''I overeat, and I wish I didn't''). Based upon the application section on self-directed behavior change, describe how you might employ the five basic steps involved in self-control to bring about the desired change in your behavior. Be specific—give concrete examples of each step.

8 Describe the four major concepts of Rotter's social learning theory of personality. Provide some examples of how the concepts could be integrated to predict the behavior of a close acquaintance.

9 Based on research cited in the chapter, what are some key ways in which ''internals'' and ''externals'' differ from each other? How do researchers assess an individual's locus of control orientation?

10 Which concepts in Rotter's theory bear resemblance to those emphasized by Bandura? Why do you think that both theorists are discussed together as representing a social cognitive view of personality?

GLOSSARY

Anticipated consequence   The expectancy, based on prior experience, that performance of a certain behavior will lead to a specific outcome.

Attentional processes   The salient cues of a model's behavior that govern which aspects of the model an observer will attend to and thus what will be acquired by the observer.

Behavior potential   In Rotter's theory, the likelihood that a given behavior will be performed as a function of the person's expectancy and the reinforcement value associated with the behavior in a given situation.

Cognitive processes   Those mental processes that provide us with the capability for both insight and foresight.

Environmental planning A type of self-control strategy whereby the person alters the environment so that either the stimuli preceding an unwanted response or the consequences following it are changed.

Expectancy In Rotter's theory, the belief held by the person that a particular reinforcement will occur as a function of a specific behavior in a specific situation.

External reinforcement A reinforcing environmental stimulus that immediately follows the occurrence of a particular behavior (e.g., social approval, attention, money).

Freedom of movement In Rotter's theory, high freedom of movement reflects a person's expectancy that various behaviors will lead to success, while a low freedom of movement reflects a person's expectancy that various behaviors will be unsuccessful.

Generalized expectancy An expectancy that goes beyond a specific situation as is illustrated by Rotter's locus of control construct.

Imaginal representation Mental image a person has formed from a previously observed event or modeled activity. For Bandura, imagery enables the observer to retain the model's behavior and convert it into subsequent action (e.g., the person can "see" the image of his or her tennis teacher demonstrating how to serve a month ago.).

Internal-external control of reinforcement Term used by Rotter to represent people's beliefs that their behavior is determined by their own efforts and skills (internal control) or by outside forces such as fate, change, and luck (external control).

Locus of control Term used by Rotter to refer to whether people believe that reinforcements are dependent on their own behavior or are controlled by forces outside of themselves.

Minimal goal The dividing line between those reinforcements that generate feelings of satisfaction and those that generate dissatisfaction.

Modeling Form of learning in which a person learns by watching someone (the model) perform the desired or correct response (see also *observational learning*).

Motivational processes A component of observational learning having to do with reinforcement variables which exert selective control over the types of modeling cues to which a person is likely to attend; such variables influence the degree to which a person tries to enact behaviors based on observational learning.

Motor reproduction processes A component involved in observational learning which consists of translating symbolically coded memories of modeled behavior into appropriate action. For Bandura, "silent rehearsal" of the model's behavior is of definite help in perfecting motor skills such as driving a car.

Need In Rotter's theory, a set of behaviors that are similar insofar as they are concerned with the acquisition of similar reinforcements (e.g., recognition, love and affection).

Need potential In Rotter's theory, the likelihood that a behavior enacted will lead to satisfaction of a certain need such as independence.

Need value In Rotter's theory, the relative desirability of different reinforcements associated with different categories of needs.

Observational learning The process through which the behavior of one person, an observer, changes as a function of being exposed to the behavior of another, the model (also called *imitative learning*).

Psychological situation In Rotter's theory, the subjective perception of an environmental setting by a particular person.

Reciprocal determinism In Bandura's theory, the regulation of human behavior through the continuous reciprocal interaction of behavioral, cognitive, and environmental factors.

Reinforcement value Term used by Rotter to reflect the degree to which a person prefers one reinforcement over another if the likelihood of obtaining each were equal.

Retention processes A component of observational learning involving long-term memory of what a model did. Bandura maintains that a person cannot be much affected by observational learning without a stored memory of the modeled behavior.

Self-contract A written agreement specifying target behaviors and response consequences in a self-control program.

Self-efficacy In social cognitive theory, judgments people make concerning their ability to execute behaviors relevant to a specific task or situation.

Self-regulation Term used by Bandura to represent the person's capacity to exert influence over his or her own behavior.

Self-reinforcement The process whereby people improve and maintain their own behavior by giving themselves rewards over which they have some control.

Social cognitive learning theory A personality perspective represented by Bandura and Rotter that emphasizes the view that behavior occurs as a result of a complex interplay between cognitive processes and environmental influences.

Verbal coding An internal representational process whereby a person silently rehearses a sequence of modeled activities to be performed at a later time.

Vicarious reinforcement Any change in a person's behavior due to observing a model being reinforced or punished for the same behavior. For instance, a child refrains from crying as a result of seeing his sister scolded by his mother for crying.

THE COGNITIVE PERSPECTIVE IN PERSONALITY THEORY: GEORGE KELLY

It is a fundamental fact of life that human beings are thinking organisms. Indeed, intellectual processes are so self-evident that virtually all personality psychologists today in some way acknowledge their effects on human behavior (Fiske & Taylor, 1991; Wyer & Srull, 1984). George Kelly, a practicing clinical psychologist, was one of the first personologists to emphasize cognitive processes as the dominant feature of personality functioning (Jankowitz, 1987). According to his theoretical system, the *psychology of personal constructs*, a person is basically a scientist, striving to understand, interpret, anticipate, and control the personal world of experience for the purpose of dealing effectively with it. This view of the person as a scientist underlies much of Kelly's theorizing as well as the current cognitivist orientation in personality psychology.

Kelly urged his fellow psychologists not to proceed as if their subjects were passive "reactors" to external stimuli. He reminded them that their subjects also behave like scientists, inferring on the basis of the past and hypothesizing about the future. His own theory, highly original and different from the dominant forms of psychological thought prevalent in America in his day, has greatly contributed to the recent surge of interest in the study of how people perceive and process information about their worlds. Walter Mischel, a prominent cognitive psychologist, has given Kelly much of the credit for launching the cognitive perspective in personality. "What has surprised me . . . [is] the accuracy with which he anticipated the directions into which psychology would move two decades later. Virtually every point of George Kelly's theorizing in the 1950s . . . has proved to be a prophetic preface for the psychology of the 1970s and . . . for many years to come'' (Mischel, 1980, pp. 85–86). Accordingly, in this chapter we will highlight Kelly's personal construct theory as illustrative of a cognitive approach to personality. Let us begin with a biographical sketch of George Kelly.

GEORGE KELLY: A Cognitive Theory of Personality

BIOGRAPHICAL SKETCH

George Alexander Kelly was born in a farming community near Wichita, Kansas, in 1905. His early education was limited to a one-room country school. His parents later sent him to Wichita, where in the course of 4 years he attended four different high schools. Kelly's parents were religiously devout, hardworking, and firmly opposed to the evils of drinking, card playing, and dancing. His family was imbued with traditional Midwestern values and aspirations, and Kelly himself was afforded considerable attention as an only child.

Kelly attended Friends University for 3 years, followed by 1 year at Park College, where he received his B.A. degree in physics and mathematics in 1926. Originally he had sought a career in mechanical engineering but, partly because of his experience in intercollegiate debates, he shifted his interests to social problems. Kelly described his first psychology course as boring and unconvincing. The instructor devoted considerable time to discussing learning theories, but Kelly was unimpressed.

Following college, Kelly attended the University of Kansas to study educational sociology and labor relations. He wrote a thesis based on a study of the distribution of leisure-time activities of workers in Kansas City and was awarded a M.A. degree in 1928. He then moved to Minneapolis, where he taught speech classes for the American Bankers Association and an Americanization class for prospective citizens. Thereafter, he joined the faculty at a junior college in Sheldon, Iowa, where he met his future wife, Gladys Thompson, a teacher at the same school. They were married in 1931.

In 1929 Kelly was awarded a fellowship to study at the University of Edinburgh in Scotland. There, in 1930, he earned the B.Ed. degree after only 9 months in residence. Under the direction of Sir Godfrey Thomson, a prominent statistician and educator, his thesis dealt with the prediction of teaching success. That same year he returned to the United States to enroll as a psychology doctoral candidate at Iowa State University. In 1931 Kelly received his Ph.D. His dissertation dealt with common factors in speech and reading disabilities.

Kelly began his academic career teaching physiological psychology at Fort Hays Kansas State College. There, in the midst of the Great Depression, he soon decided that he should "pursue something more than teaching physiological psychology" (1969, p. 48). Consequently, he switched his interests to clinical psychology, even though he lacked formal training in treating emotional problems. During his 13-year stay at Fort Hays (1931–1943), Kelly developed a program of traveling psychological clinics in Kansas. He and his students traveled widely, providing needed psychological services in the state's public school

George A. Kelly. (*Courtesy of Brandeis University, Photography Department*)

system. This experience stimulated numerous ideas that were later incorporated into his formulations of personality and therapy. During this period Kelly abandoned the Freudian approach to treatment which he had been using. His clinical experiences taught him that people in the Midwest were more victimized by prolonged drought, dust storms, and economic setbacks than by libidinal forces.

During World War II, as a naval aviation psychologist, Kelly headed a training program for local civilian pilots. His interest in aviation continued at the Bureau of Medicine and Surgery of the Navy, where he remained in the Aviation Branch until 1945. That year he was appointed associate professor at the University of Maryland.

The war's end created considerable demand for clinical psychologists because large numbers of American military personnel were returning home plagued with a variety of personal problems. Indeed, World War II was the single most important factor contributing to the development of clinical psychology as an integral part of the health sciences. Kelly became a prominent figure in this evolution. In 1946 he attained national status when he became professor and director of clinical psychology at Ohio State University. In his 20 years there, Kelly completed and published his theory of personality. He also piloted the clinical psychology program to the forefront of graduate training in the United States.

In 1965 Kelly departed for Brandeis University, where he was appointed to the Riklis Chair of Behavioral Science. This position, a professor's dream come true, would have given him great freedom to pursue his own scholarly interests. However, he died in 1967 at the age of 62. At the time of his death, Kelly was assembling a volume composed of the numerous papers he had delivered in the previous decade. Under the editorship of Brendan Maher, a revised version of this work appeared posthumously in 1969.

In addition to his distinguished career as a teacher, scientist, and theorist, Kelly held many positions of leadership among American psychologists. He served as president of both the Clinical and the Counseling Divisions of the American Psychological Association. He also lectured extensively in the United States and abroad. During the concluding years of his life, Kelly devoted much of his time to suggesting how his personal construct theory could be applied to help resolve various international problems.

Kelly's best-known scholarly contribution is a two-volume work entitled *The Psychology of Personal Constructs* (1955). These volumes describe his theoretical formulations of personality and their clinical ramifications. Students who wish to pursue other aspects of Kelly's works are advised to consider the following books: *New Perspectives in Personal Construct Theory* (edited by Bannister, 1977); *Personal Construct Psychology* (edited by Landfield & Leitner, 1980); and *The Development of Personal Construct Psychology* (Neimeyer, 1985).

CORNERSTONES OF COGNITIVE THEORY

A major theme of this text is that all theories of personality have their origin in certain philosophical assumptions about human nature. That is, the way in which a personologist views the essence of human existence profoundly influences his or her model of the person. Unlike many personologists, George Kelly explicitly acknowledged that all conceptions of human nature, including his own, are predicated on basic assumptions. He developed his own personality theory on the basis of a single philosophical position—constructive alternativism.

Constructive Alternativism

Now that people of all ages are exploring alternative life-styles and ways of understanding things, George Kelly's vintage-1955 theory appears to have been curiously ahead of its time. Kelly's underlying philosophy, *constructive alternativism,* furnishes a dazzling array of options for people seeking alternatives to the commonplace. In fact, the philosophy practically demands that people do so.

As a doctrine, constructive alternativism asserts "that all of our present interpretations of the universe are subject to revision or replacement" (Kelly, 1955, p. 15). Nothing is sacred nor etched in stone. There are no politics, religions, economic principles, social mores, or even foreign policies toward Third World countries that are absolutely and unalterably "right." All would be changed if people simply viewed things from different perspectives. Kelly argued that there is no such thing as an "interpretation-free" view of the world. A person's perception of reality is always subject to interpretation; in Kelly's judgment, objective reality does exist but different people perceive it in different ways. Therefore, nothing is fixed or final. Truth, like beauty, exists only in the mind of the beholder.

Since facts and events (anything in a person's experience) exist in the human mind alone, it follows that there are various ways to construe them. To illustrate, consider the event of a girl taking money from her mother's purse. What does it signify? The event is simple: money has been removed from the purse. However, if we ask a child therapist to interpret the event, she or he may give an elaborate account of the girl's feelings of rejection by the mother—rejection itself the result, perhaps, of the mother's frustration at having to stay home and raise a daughter instead of pursuing her own career goals. If we ask the mother, she may say that her daughter is "bad" and untrustworthy. The girl's father may suggest that she is "undisciplined." Grandfather may consider the event a childish prank. The girl herself may regard it as reflecting her parents' unwillingness to provide her with a sufficient allowance. While the event itself obviously cannot be undone—the money was taken—its meaning is open to alternative interpretations. Any event, then, can be viewed from several different perspectives. Persons have a dazzling choice of options available when interpreting the inner world of experience or the outer world of practical affairs. Kelly summarized his commitment to constructive alternativism in the following way: ". . . whatever nature may be, or howsoever the quest for truth will turn out in the end, the events we face today are subject to as great a variety of constructions as our wits will enable us to contrive" (1970, p. 1).

The intriguing nature of constructive alternativism can be appreciated more clearly if it is contrasted with one of Aristotle's philosophic principles. Aristotle first put forth the principle of identity: *A* is *A*. A thing, in and of itself, is experienced and interpreted the same way by everyone. For example, a car parked across the street is the same physical object no matter who looks at it. It follows, then, that the events of social reality are the same for all. By contrast, Kelly believed that *A is whatever the individual construes as A!* Reality is what we construe reality to be; events can always be viewed from a variety of diverse perspectives. In this scheme of things, then, there is no one true or valid way of interpreting a person's behavior. Whether we are attempting to understand another person's behavior, our own behavior, or the nature of the universe itself, there are always "constructive alternatives" open for our consideration. Furthermore, the concept of constructive alternativism implies that our behavior is never totally determined. We are always free to some extent to revise or replace our interpretation of events. Yet, Kelly also believed that some of our thoughts and behavior are determined by antecedent events. For, as will become increasingly evident, cognitive theory is constructed on a joint freedom–determinism base. In Kelly's words: "Determinism and freedom are inseparable, for that which determines another is, by the same token, free of the other" (1955, p. 21).

People as Scientists

As already mentioned, Kelly emphasized the manner in which people perceive and interpret their life experiences. Construct theory thus focuses on the processes that enable people to understand the psychological terrain of their lives. This brings us to Kelly's model of personality based on the analogy of a *person as a scientist*. Specifically, he theorized that, like the scientist who studies her or him, the human subject also generates working hypotheses about reality with which she or he tries to anticipate and control the events of life. To be sure, Kelly did not assume that every person is literally a scientist who attends to some limited aspect of the world and employs sophisticated methods to gather and assess data. That analogy would have been foreign to his outlook. But he did suggest that all persons are scientists in that they formulate hypotheses and follow the same psychological processes to validate or invalidate them as those involved in a scientific enterprise (Kelly, 1963). Thus, the basic premise underlying personal construct theory is that science constitutes a refinement of the aims and procedures by which each of us generates new ideas about what the world is like. The aims of science are to predict, to modify, and to understand events (i.e., the scientist's main goal is to reduce uncertainty). Not only the scientist, but also all people share these same aims. We are all motivated to anticipate the future and make plans based on expected outcomes.

To illustrate this model of the human being, consider a college student who encounters a new professor at the beginning of a semester (assuming that she has no prior knowledge of the professor's "reputation"). Based on limited observation (perhaps 50 minutes of class time), the student may perceive and interpret the professor to be "fair." Kelly's word for this process is *construe*; the student "construes" (or sees) fairness in the professor. Essentially, what is happening is that the student is generating a hypothesis about the professor that will help her anticipate and control events involving that course. In the event that the student's hypothesis proves "valid," the professor can be expected to assign a reasonable amount of reading, give decent tests, and grade fairly. However, should the professor's subsequent behavior differ markedly, the student would then need an alternative hypothesis (e.g., the prof is unfair, the prof is a nerd, or whatever). The point is that the student (like all of us) needs a useful and consistent means of anticipating events affecting her life if she is to function effectively.

In developing his unique conception of humanity based on the analogy of the person as a scientist, Kelly was amazed to discover the contrast between views the psychologist uses to explain his or her own behavior and those used to explain the behavior of research subjects. He described this discrepancy as follows:

> It is as though the psychologist were saying to himself, "I, being a psychologist, and therefore a scientist, am performing this experiment in order to improve the prediction and control of certain human phenomena; but my subject, being merely a human organism, is obviously propelled by inexorable drives welling up within him, or else he is in gluttonous pursuit of sustenance and shelter." (1955, p. 5)

Kelly rejected the tunnel-vision notion that only the psychological scientist wearing a lab coat and behaving like a scientist is concerned with predicting and controlling the course of events in life. Rather than viewing the human organism as some kind of unwilling and unthinking blob of protoplasm, he credited the human subject with the same aspirations as the so-called scientific psychologist. This notion, namely, that the psychologist is no different from the subject she or he studies, epitomizes Kelly's cognitive theory of personality. It reveals Kelly's belief that all people operate as scientists in everyday life. For him, the distinction between the scientist and the nonscientist was not a valid one.

At the beginning of a semester, students develop hypotheses concerning their course work based on limited observation of their professor's behavior. (*Ulrike Welsch*)

To view all persons as if they were scientists leads to a number of important consequences for Kelly's theory. Foremost, it suggests that people are fundamentally oriented toward future rather than past or present events in their lives. In fact, Kelly (1963) maintained that all behavior can be understood as anticipatory in nature. He also noted that a person's outlook on life is transitory, insofar as it is rarely the same as it was yesterday or will be tomorrow. In attempting to anticipate and control future events, the person's view of reality is constantly being tested: "Anticipation is not merely carried on for its own sake; it is carried on so that future reality may be better represented. It is the future which tantalizes man, not the past. Always he reaches out to the future through the window of the present" (Kelly, 1955, p. 49).

A second consequence following from the analogy of people as scientists is that people have the capacity to actively represent their environment rather than merely passively respond to it. Just as the psychologist rationally formulates and revises theoretical notions about phenomena, so can a layperson interpret and reinterpret, construe and reconstrue, his or her environment. For Kelly, then, life is characterized by the continuous struggle to make sense of the tangible world of experience; it is this quality of life that enables persons to shape their own destiny. People need not be enslaved victims of their past history or present situation— unless they decide to construe themselves in such ways. In short, a person is not controlled by present events (as Skinner suggests) or past ones (as Freud proposed) but rather *controls events* depending on the questions raised and the answers found.

PERSONAL CONSTRUCT THEORY: BASIC CONCEPTS AND PRINCIPLES

The heart of Kelly's cognitive theory lies in the manner in which individuals perceive and interpret things (or people) in their environments. Labeling his approach *personal construct theory,* Kelly focused on the psychological processes that enable people to organize and understand the events happening in their lives.

Personal Constructs: Templates for Reality

Scientists formulate theoretical constructs to describe and explain the events with which they are concerned. In Kelly's system, the key theoretical construct is the term *construct* itself:

> Man looks at his world through transparent patterns or templates which he creates and then attempts to fit over the realities of which the world is composed. The fit is not always very good. Yet without such patterns the world appears to be such an undifferentiated homogeneity that man is unable to make any sense out of it. (Kelly, 1955, pp. 8–9)

It is these "transparent patterns or templates" which Kelly designated *personal constructs.* Stated otherwise, a personal construct is an idea or thought that a person uses to construe or interpret, explain, or predict his or her experiences. It represents a consistent way for the person to make sense of some aspect of reality in terms of similarities and contrasts. Examples of personal constructs include "excitable versus calm," "intelligent versus stupid," "masculine versus feminine," "religious versus nonreligious," "good versus bad," and "friendly versus hostile." These are but a few of the countless constructs people use to give meaning to events in their daily lives.

As an illustration of constructs in action, let us examine how different people might construe the same event. The event in question involves a recent college graduate, who, instead of pursuing his earlier plans to attend graduate school, collects his personal belongings and goes off with his companion and lover to live in a remote commune. The young man's father might construe this event as "distressing" or "embarrassing," while his mother might construe him to be "living in sin" ("sinful"). His college counselor, well-versed in Eriksonian theory, may think that he is "searching for his identity," and his sociology professor may believe that he is simply "rejecting the norms of a Yuppie-oriented society." The young man himself may regard the event as "natural," as "the right thing for me to do at this time." Which interpretation is correct? In Kelly's theory, there is no way to tell. Kelly's point is simply that, for each of us, reality is filtered through different templates or constructs—that we need in order to understand the world in a consistent fashion.

In line with his model of humans as scientists, Kelly maintained that once a person hypothesizes that a given construct will adequately anticipate and predict some event in his or her environment, he or she will then test that hypothesis against events that have not yet occurred. If the construct leads to an accurate prediction of the event, the person is likely to retain the construct. Conversely, if a prediction is disconfirmed, the construct from which it was derived is likely to undergo some revision or may even be eliminated altogether (recall our earlier example of the professor initially construed as ''fair''). The validity of a construct, then, is tested in terms of its *predictive efficiency,* of which there are varying degrees.

Kelly assumed that all personal constructs are *bipolar* and *dichotomous* in nature—that the essence of human thought is to perceive life's experiences in black versus white terms, not shades of gray. More specifically, in experiencing events, a person observes that certain events seem similar to each other (they share common properties) and different from other events. A person may notice, for instance, that some people are fat and some are skinny, some are black and some are white, some are affluent and some are poor, some things are dangerous to touch and some are not. It is this cognitive process of observing similarities and differences that leads to the formation of personal constructs. Thus, at least three elements (events or things) are needed to form a construct: two of the construct elements must be perceived as similar to each other, while the third element must be perceived as different from these two. A construct would be formed if we see that Jean and Lois are honest and Martha is not, or if we view Jean and Lois as attractive and Martha as unattractive. Both the comparison and contrast must occur within the same context.

Like a magnet, all constructs have two opposite poles. The way in which two elements are construed to be similar or alike is called the *emergent* or *similarity* pole of the construct dimension; the way in which they are contrasted with the third element is called the *implicit* or *contrast* pole of the construct dimension. Every construct thus has an emergent and an implicit pole. The thrust of personal construct theory is to discover how people interpret and anticipate their experiences in terms of similarities and contrasts.

Unfortunately, Kelly neglected to elaborate on the processes by which the person comes to construe his or her experiences along particular lines. He simply did not consider the issue of individual differences vis-à-vis the origin and development of personal constructs. This is understandable insofar as Kelly's theory is *ahistorical,* placing no special emphasis on the person's early experiences. However, constructs must come from somewhere, and it seems most reasonable to assume that they are products of the person's past history. It is likely that differential histories of life experiences account for the variability among individual construct systems.

Formal Properties of Constructs

Kelly proposed that certain formal properties characterize all constructs. First, a construct resembles a theory in that it encompasses a particular domain of events. This *range of convenience* includes all of the events to which the construct is relevant or applicable. The construct dimension, ''scholarly versus not scholarly,'' for instance, is quite applicable to understanding a vast array of intellectual and scientific accomplishments but is hardly appropriate for construing the relative merits of being married or single. Kelly noted that the predictive efficiency of a construct is seriously jeopardized whenever it is generalized beyond the range of events for which it was intended. Thus, all constructs have a limited range of convenience, though the scope of the range may vary widely from construct to construct. The construct "good versus bad" has a wide range of convenience since it applies to most situations requiring personal evaluation. In contrast, the construct "virginity versus prostitution" is substantially narrower in scope.

Second, each construct has a *focus of convenience*. This refers to events within the range of convenience to which a construct is most readily applied. For instance, one person's construct of "honest versus dishonest" might have as its focus of convenience keeping his or her hands off other people's money and property. Another person may apply the same construct to political events. Hence, a construct's focus of convenience is always specific to the person employing the construct.

Permeability–impermeability is another dimension along which constructs vary. A permeable construct admits to its range of convenience elements not yet construed within its boundaries. It is open to construing new events. On the other hand, an impermeable construct, while embracing events that made up its original formulation, remains closed to the interpretation of new experiences. There are relative degrees of permeability and impermeability. One person's construct of "competent versus incompetent" physicians might be sufficiently permeable to account for any new doctor he encounters. That is, after interacting with any new doctor for some time, the person could construe him or her as either competent or incompetent; the construct is completely permeable. But another person may use the same construct in a totally impermeable way, insisting that competent physicians no longer exist—that the last competent one was her pediatrician, who is now dead. Thus, the distinction between competent and incompetent doctors is no longer relevant for her. All doctors are incompetent! Note that permeability is applicable only to a given construct's range of convenience; a construct is impermeable by definition to any experience beyond its range of convenience. Thus, "competent versus incompetent" has no meaning when judging the taste of seafood.

Types of Constructs Kelly also suggested that personal constructs can be classified according to the nature of the control they implicitly exercise over their elements. A construct that freezes ("preempts") its elements for membership exclusively in its own realm Kelly termed a *preemptive construct*. This is a type of pigeonhole construct; what has been placed in one pigeonhole is excluded from any other. Preemptive construing may be likened to the "nothing but" kind of thinking characteristic of a rigid person. Ethnic labels illustrate the use of preemptive constructs. For instance, if a person is identified as Hispanic, then she or he may be thought of by some as nothing but a Hispanic. Or, to a lesser degree, once a professor has been labeled as "hard-nosed," some students may disregard the possibility of thinking of him or her in other ways (such as having tender feelings for his or her children or being concerned about social reform issues). Preemptive thought represents a kind of denial of the right of both others and ourselves to re-view, reinterpret, and see in a fresh light some part of the world around us (Bannister, 1985).

A *constellatory construct* permits its elements to belong to other realms concurrently but fixes their realm membership. That is, once an event is subsumed under one construct, its other characteristics are fixed. Stereotyped thinking illustrates this type of construct. For example, constellatory thinking accepts "if this man is a car salesman, he must be dishonest, conniving, and manipulative." In this instance there is no latitude as to what else he may be considered to be. By definition, constellatory constructs restrict our chances of adopting alternative views; once we assign a person to a given category, we then attribute a cluster or constellation of other characteristics to him or her.

A construct that leaves its elements open to alternative constructions is called a *propositional construct*. This type of construct directly contradicts preemptive or constellatory constructs since it allows the person to be open to new experiences and to adopt alternative views of the world. In this case, construing someone as a car salesman is propositional to the extent that other personal attributes do not

A car salesman who is stereotyped as always being dishonest reveals the nature of constellatory thinking. (*Ray Solomon/Monkmeyer*)

necessarily follow. Accordingly, propositional thinking is flexible thinking. The person is open to new experience and is capable of modifying existing constructs. While it is tempting to "construe" preemptive and constellatory constructs as undesirable and propositional constructs as desirable, Kelly clearly stated that such is not necessarily true. If we used only propositional constructs, we would have an extremely difficult time getting along in the world since we could not reach pressing decisions.

As an illustration, consider a baseball game in which the ball is speedily coming in the direction of your head. You could begin to construe the ball propositionally, considering and reconsidering it from all perceptual angles. As it smacked you in the face, you might then see that it would have been far better in this circumstance to construe the ball preemptively (i.e., this event is a baseball coming at my head and nothing else). However, Kelly believed that to avoid intellectual rigor mortis, we must be able to engage in propositional thinking. Without it, we would be doomed to a sterile, unchanging, and stereotyped mode of perceiving reality. Thus, preemptive, constellatory, and propositional forms of thinking are all necessary to construe events, things, and people in life. Propositional thinking is simply a contrast to preemptive and constellatory ways of making sense of reality.

There are several ways in which personal constructs can be categorized or typed. For example, there are *comprehensive constructs,* which subsume a relatively wide spectrum of events, and *incidental constructs,* which subsume a small range of events (i.e., have a much narrower range of convenience). There are *core constructs* that govern a person's basic functioning and *peripheral constructs* that may be altered without serious modification of the core structure. Finally, some constructs are *tight* insofar as they lead to unvarying predictions, whereas others are *loose* in that they lead a person to arrive at different predictions under similar conditions.

Personality: The Personologist's Construct

Kelly never offered an explicit definition of the term "personality." However, he discussed the concept in general terms in one paper, stating that personality is "our abstraction of the activity of a person and our subsequent generalization of this abstraction to all matters of his relationship to other persons, known and unknown, as well as to anything else that may seem particularly valuable" (1961, pp. 220–221). Kelly thus believed that personality is an abstraction made by personologists of the psychological processes they observe and/or infer in others. It is not a separate entity to be discovered by them. Furthermore, he argued that personality is by its very nature embedded in a person's interpersonal relationships. Meshing these two ideas and adding one of our own, a more focused definition of personality within Kelly's system is possible; specifically, an individual's personality consists of an organized system of more or less important constructs. The person uses personal constructs to interpret the world of experience and to anticipate future events; indeed, for Kelly, personality is equivalent to the constructs used by the individual to anticipate the future. To understand another person involves knowing something about the constructs he or she employs, the events subsumed under these constructs, and the way in which they are related to each other in an organized and coherent fashion. In short, to know someone's personality is to know how she or he construes personal experience.

Motivation: Who Needs It

Psychologists have traditionally used the concept of motivation to explain two aspects of behavior: (a) why people are active (behave) at all and (b) why their activity takes one direction rather than another. In Kelly's view, the term "motivation" assumes that humans are by nature static beings and act only when some special enlivening force prods them. In contrast, he rejected the notion that *humans are inactive or reactive* by nature and behave only when pushed into action by some internal or external force. For Kelly (1958), people are motivated for no other reason than that they are alive. In fact, the essence of life itself is seen as a form of process or movement; human beings represent one species of such all-pervasive movement. Following from this reasoning, no special concepts (e.g., drives, needs, instincts, rewards, motives) are required to explain what produces or motivates human behavior.

Kelly's objection to the need for motivational concepts to explain behavior came from his experience as a practicing therapist. He found that it makes virtually no difference, in terms of helping clients, whether or not one attributes a set of motives to them. Motivational concepts are interpretations that therapists impose on their clients' behavior. They may be useful for predicting someone's behavior (e.g., Pam is lazy and, therefore, probably won't complete her graduate school applications on time), but they are useless for understanding and helping a person because they reflect the way the *therapist,* rather than the client, thinks about the world. Kelly further noted that motivational statements usually reveal more about the speaker than about the person whose motives are in question: "When we find a person who is concerned about motives, he usually turns out to be the one who is threatened by his fellowmen and wants to put them in their place" (1969, p. 77).

Kelly characterized the state of modern motivation theories and contrasted them with his own position in the following way:

> Motivational theories can be divided into two types, push theories and pull theories. Under push theories we find such terms as drive, motive, or even stimulus. Pull theories use such constructs as purpose, value, or need. In terms of a well known metaphor, there are pitchfork theories on the one hand and the carrot theories on the other. But our theory is neither of these. Since we prefer to look to the nature of the animal himself, ours is probably best called a jackass theory. (1958, p. 50)

Personal construct theory construes the human being to be an active and thinking organism simply by virtue of being alive. Therefore, "motivation" is a redundant construct.

Since Kelly outrightly rejected motivation to account for human activity, how did he explain its direction? The source of explanation is presented in his fundamental postulate, discussed in the next section.

THE FUNDAMENTAL POSTULATE AND SOME COROLLARIES

The formal structure of personal construct theory is both economical and parsimonious in that Kelly advanced his central tenets by using one fundamental postulate followed by 11 corollaries that elaborated on the postulate. After we describe his basic postulate, we will discuss those corollaries that most appear to add to our account of Kelly's cognitive position presented to this point.

Fundamental Postulate

Each personologist seems to have a language of his or her own when portraying human behavior. Kelly is no exception, as can be seen in his *fundamental postulate:* "A person's processes are psychologically channelized by the ways in which he anticipates events" (1955, p. 46). This postulate forms the cornerstone for Kelly's theory because it reveals the basic force behind personality and behavior in a way quite different from other major perspectives. Let us, therefore, break it down for better understanding since it is central to his formal system.

The fundamental postulate stipulates that how people predict future events determines their behavior. In other words, all human behavior (thoughts and actions) is aimed at predicting events. The postulate also means that Kelly is primarily interested in the whole person rather than any single part of him or her (e.g., intergroup relations). The phrase "person's processes" suggests that human beings are dynamic organisms, not inert substances pushed by unconscious impulses or pricked into action by environmental stimuli (recall Kelly's "jackass" view of human motivation). In Kelly's man-as-scientist analogy, people are guided by their future-oriented constructs.

Kelly's fundamental postulate also reveals that his system is psychological in scope, that its range of convenience is limited to understanding human behavior. The term "channelized" means that behavior is relatively stable across time and situations. Kelly (1955) believed that people operate through a network of pathways or channels as opposed to fluttering about in an unpredictable void. In other words, people channelize or direct their processes toward anticipating the future.

The word "ways" is synonymous with *constructs,* while the pronoun "he" highlights the individuality of construing events. Concerning this latter point, Kelly (1955) noted that each person erects and characteristically uses different ways (constructs), and it is the way the person chooses that channelizes his or her processes. Finally, the phrase "anticipates events" conveys the predictive and motivational features intrinsic to cognitive theory. Like a scientist, a person seeks to predict reality to facilitate the anticipation of events affecting his or her life. This notion is what accounts for the directionality of human activities in Kelly's scheme. In this system, people look at the present so that they may anticipate the future through the unique template of their personal constructs.

Major Corollaries

Eleven corollaries, all of which can be inferred from the fundamental postulate, serve to elaborate Kelly's personal construct theory. We will discuss the major ones next.

Individuality and Organization The *individuality corollary* is especially helpful in understanding the uniqueness of personality: "Persons differ from each other in their construction of events" (Kelly, 1955, p. 55). For Kelly, no two people, be they identical twins or supposedly similar in outlook, approach and interpret the same event in exactly the same way. Each person construes reality through his or her unique personal construct "goggles." Thus, differences between people are rooted in their construing events from different perspectives.

Examples abound of the idea that each person's construct system is unique. Consider the traditional differences of opinion between political liberals and conservatives on such issues as welfare, military intervention in foreign lands, abortion, taxation, forced racial integration, pornography, and capital punishment. Or reflect on why students may disagree with professors, professors with department chairpersons, department chairpersons with deans, and everybody with college presidents. Or what is popularly called the "generation gap"—the fundamental differences of viewpoint between parents and their offspring—a situation which, in Kelly's theory, might more properly be labeled a "personal construct gap." In all these instances, persons are in disagreement because each is operating from a different construct system. No wonder there is such a lack of accord among people—from Kelly's vantage point, they are not even talking about the same things!

In addition to the idiosyncrasy of personal constructs, Kelly also maintained that constructs are organized within persons in different ways. This is clearly stated in his *organization corollary*: "Each person characteristically evolves, for his convenience in anticipating events, a construction system embracing ordinal relationships between constructs" (1955, p. 56). This corollary indicates that persons organize their personal constructs hierarchically to minimize incompatibilities and inconsistencies. Perhaps even more important, it implies that people differ not only in the number and kinds of constructs they use to view the world but also in the ways in which they organize their constructs. In short, it would be a mistake to think of constructs as rattling around loose in the person's mind, to be applied piecemeal.

For Kelly, the organization of personal constructs is essentially a logical one: constructs are ordered in a pyramidal structure so that some constructs are either superordinate or subordinate in relation to other parts of the system. (Of course, a construct may be quite independent of all others in the person's repertoire.) A *superordinate* construct subsumes other constructs, whereas a *subordinate* construct is one that is included in another (superordinate) construct. The construct "good versus bad," for instance, may subsume within its two poles the construct "sexy versus nonsexy." In this instance, the former construct is superordinate to the latter. To illustrate, consider a male-chauvinist type in the process of construing the playmate of the month in *Playboy* magazine. He would probably construe her as "sexy" and hence, superordinately speaking, "good." But even in the most blatant male chauvinist's construct system, "good" usually incorporates more than "sexy." For example, he may also construe the interview of the month in the same magazine as "good" because, to him, it is "insightful." In this case, then, the constructs "sexy versus nonsexy" and "insightful versus noninsightful" are both subordinate to the "good versus bad" superordinate construct. The basic point is that people create different hierarchies of personal constructs. What is a superordinate–subordinate construct relationship in one person's system is not necessarily the same in another's system. Kelly suggested that only by knowing a person's mode of organizing constructs can we make meaningful statements about his or her behavior.

The hierarchical arrangements among constructs are not, however, assumed by Kelly to be permanently fixed. The organization among constructs is retained in relation to events only if it has predictive efficiency—just as is true of the constructs themselves. Indeed, Kelly believed that it is possible for two constructs to reverse their placement in the hierarchy, so that the formerly subordinate construct becomes superordinate and vice versa. For example, consider the person who once felt that "loving versus unloving" subsumed "accepting versus rejecting" (among other constructs). As a result of ensuing experience, however, the person may come to a different conclusion: namely, that the sense of "accepting" is far more fundamental and broader of the two characteristics and that "loving" is subordinate to that. Accordingly, the hierarchical arrangement of constructs should not be thought of as stagnant or perfect.

To Construe or Not to Construe: That Is the Question From Kelly's perspective, people have several constructs by which to construe events in their lives. In addition, they must choose which construct and which pole of the construct to use in making predictions about events every day. Kelly's *choice corollary* describes how a person makes these selections: "A person chooses for himself that alternative in a dichotomized construct through which he anticipates the greater possibility for extension and definition of his system" (1955, p. 64). Thus, for Kelly, if we are confronted with a choice (i.e., a situation in which we must use our constructs in one way or another), we will opt for the alternative that is most likely to either enhance our understanding of the world or clarify our present construct system. In other words, we will choose the construct pole that renders that event most understandable—the one that will contribute most to the predictive efficiency of our construct system. Kelly called this the *elaborative choice*.

The choice corollary also suggests that our construct system is elaborated in the direction of either *definition* or *extension*. Definition involves choosing the alternative with the greater probability of validating aspects of experience that have already been fairly accurately construed. That is, the person wagers a relatively safe bet as to how things will turn out, based on previous experience, and then observes the evidence. If the anticipated event does occur and the construct system is confirmed, then the construct becomes consolidated and clear-cut by virtue of its having led to a correct prediction. Therefore, definition can be thought of as using a construct in a familiar way, applying it to an event that is very likely to fit. The other kind of elaboration, extension, involves choosing that alternative which has the greater likelihood of broadening our understanding of events (increasing the construct's range of convenience) in new and different ways. If the prediction is correct, then the construct is validated and becomes, at least temporarily, more comprehensive. Of course, extension also has a greater potential for predictive error than does definition, given the fact that it involves using the construct to predict an event for which it has not been used before. But it also provides more information than does definition.

Kelly characterized the difference between definition and extension as one of *security* or *adventure*. Persons must continuously decide which of these two modes will further articulate their personal constructs. College students, for example, must often choose between courses similar to ones they have previously taken—courses in which acceptable grades are somewhat assured—and unfamiliar courses where failure is a risk but which offer possibilities of broadening their knowledge and understanding. A ''gut'' course in a familiar subject represents ''security,'' while organic chemistry, for most students, is an ''adventure.'' In this instance, if a student chooses the alternative that minimizes risk, then the construct system (if validated) is further consolidated and defined. However, if a student opts for the alternative that will extend her or his system, this invites greater risk: she or he may not be able to correctly anticipate events (e.g., passing exams). Of course, the likelihood of acquiring additional information which will serve in future predictions is increased.

Although Kelly detailed the basis for recognizing whether a person defines or extends his or her construct system, there is scant empirical evidence or theoretical rationale as to why or when one kind of choice will be favored over another. Nonetheless, it seems likely that if people feel secure and confident in predicting events correctly and can even risk being wrong, they will more likely choose to extend their construct system. Conversely, persons who feel insecure and inadequate in correctly predicting events will be more likely to choose definition. Momentary situational factors probably also influence the preference for extension or definition. For instance, being bored may lead to a desire for extension, whereas being upset may lead to definition. Which of these two processes will occur at any given time may ultimately require knowing whether the person is currently motivated toward security or adventure.

C-P-C Cycle Kelly presented various models to illustrate the actions of a person faced with a novel or ambiguous situation. One of key importance is called the *circumspection-preemption-control (C-P-C) cycle,* which involves a sequential progression from pondering several possible constructs to deciding which construct seems best for construing the situation.

In the *circumspection* phase, a person considers several constructs that could be used to interpret a particular situation—that is, she tentatively contemplates the various possibilities facing her in a propositional fashion. This is analogous to looking at all sides of the question. The *preemption* phase follows when the person reduces the number of alternative constructs (hypotheses) to ones most appropriate to the situation at hand. Here she decides which of the preemptive alternatives is most relevant to use. Finally, during the *control* phase of the cycle, she decides on a course of action and its accompanying behavior. The choice is made, in other words, based on an estimate of which alternative construct is most likely to lead to extension and definition of the system.

Kelly noted that a person may go through a number of C-P-C cycles before deciding which construct should be used to construe the situation. He cites Hamlet as the classic example of a person who, after preemption ("To be, or not to be; that is the question. . . ."), could not decide on the final choice and instead returned to the circumspection phase of the cycle. The notion of the C-P-C cycle is consistent with Kelly's belief that we are continually considering the alternatives in given situations, reducing the options to those that will work, and acting in accordance with our choices. Thus, if we could only change our constructs, we could literally change our lives; the options in Kelly's system are dazzling. Kelly also contended, however, that since the world is multidimensional and a person possesses a number of different dimensions in his or her construct system, the dimensions must be sorted, until there is a single dichotomous choice to be made before the person can act. In Kelly's view, only when a person says "this and this only is the important dimension" is she or he ready to implement a strategy for dealing with life's experiences. Ultimately, then, we must construe in order to function intelligently.

Change in a Construct System A construct system enables a person to anticipate future events as accurately as possible. It follows, then, that a construct system changes in relation to its inability to correctly anticipate the unfolding sequence of events. In this regard, Kelly postulated that a change in our construct system occurs most often when we are exposed to novel or unfamiliar events which do not conform to our preexisting system of constructs. Accordingly, the *experience corollary* states: "A person's construct system varies as he successively construes the replication of events" (1955, p. 72).

Also called the *learning corollary,* it suggests that a personal construct system is a set of hypotheses about our ever-changing world that are perpetually being tested by experience. The feedback on how well these hypotheses have aided us to predict the future leads to a modification of constructs which, in turn, are used as new hypotheses to progressively change the system. Those constructs found to be useful are retained, whereas those that are not are revised or discarded. Thus, for Kelly, a construct system undergoes successive revision with the ebb and flow of its validational fortunes.

For Kelly, a person's *experience* is the reconstruction of his or her life based upon revisions of his or her constructs as they are affected by events in time. This means that a person gains little or no experience if after having observed a succession of events he or she still construes the events in the same way. If, for example, a professor has been teaching for 10 years and is still presenting the same lectures in the same way that she did in her first year, Kelly would question whether she has really had 10 years of teaching experience. On the other hand, if what she taught during her first year led her to alter and improve her teaching in her second year and successively through the tenth year, she could legitimately claim to have had a decade of teaching experience.

Kelly's *modulation corollary* specifies the conditions under which the person's construct system changes: "The variation in a person's construction system is limited by the permeability of the constructs within whose range of convenience the variants lie" (1955, p. 77). As discussed previously, "permeability" refers to the degree to which a construct can assimilate novel experiences and events within its range of convenience. Thus, this corollary implies that the more permeable (open) a person's superordinate constructs, the greater the possible variation (systematic change) within the substructures they subsume. If the person has no superordinate constructs for construing change, then change cannot occur within the person's system. By implication, the person is psychologically rigid. Consequently, a person must be capable not only of construing new events or reconstruing old ones, but also of construing change itself. In other words, since modification of a construct or a set of constructs is an event in itself, the person must have some conceptual framework in order to interpret the changes in his or her construct system. Otherwise, change cannot take place, although chaos might.

By way of illustration, consider a 21-year-old male who construes his relationship to his mother in such a way that he still reacts to her as "Mommy's little boy," i.e., overdependently. Obviously, he is going to encounter a great deal of distress in life unless he can change this construction of the relationship. The young man is in luck if he happens to have a permeable superordinate construct like "mature versus immature" which he can apply to this situation. If he does, he can begin to construe himself as "mature" and thus begin to respond differently to his mother, i.e., less dependently. In essence, he reconstrues his relationship to his mother in terms of his application of the construct "mature" to himself.

Changes in relationships with significant others are not the only circumstances that initiate changes in our constructs. Sometimes even very useful constructs that have been used for a long time simply fail to accurately predict events later in time. Indeed, Kelly held that in such cases the comfortable, familiar construct will be modified, even if only subtly. This presumably occurs almost constantly among frequently used constructs because our prediction of events is almost never perfect. However, changes made in this way do not constitute a drastic reorganization in the construct system. They are simply minor adjustments in how people understand events.

Social Relationships and Personal Constructs   If, as Kelly asserted in his individuality corollary, people differ as a result of the way they interpret situations, then it follows that they may be similar to others to the extent that they construe experiences in similar ways. Birds of a feather construe together. This idea is explicitly stated in Kelly's *commonality corollary*: "To the extent that one person employs a construction of experience which is similar to that employed by another, his psychological processes are similar to those of the other person" (1955, p. 90). Thus, if two people share similar views of the world (i.e., are similar in their constructions of personal experiences), they are likely to behave in a similar way (i.e., have similar personalities). The essential point to note is that people are not similar neither because they have experienced the same set of life events nor because they manifest similar behavior: they are similar because events have approximately the same psychological meaning for them. In line with his cognitive orientation, Kelly's emphasis is upon construing rather than relying on past experience or observable behavior.

Interestingly, the commonality corollary implies that the similarities evident among members of a particular culture are not behavioral similarities alone. More fundamentally, Kelly (1962) believed that people from a given culture typically construe their experiences in much the same way. To him, the "culture shock" often experienced when encountering people from a different culture is the result of basic differences in the way people from different cultures construe events. In support of this view, recent research indicates that cultural differences are rooted in variations in the constructs that people use (Triandis et al., 1984).

Another important aspect of Kelly's theory of personal constructs deals with relationships between people and their construct system. This is formally defined in the *sociality corollary* which specifies the conditions necessary for an effective interpersonal relationship: "To the extent that one person construes the construction processes of another, he may play a role in a social process involving the other person" (1955, p. 95). With this corollary Kelly emphasized that social interaction consists primarily of one person trying to understand how another person perceives his or her reality. In other words, to interact meaningfully with someone else requires that a person try to construe some part of the construct system that is held by the other. This differs from the assumption that people can interact only when they have similar construct systems or are in some sense similar people. For Kelly, harmonious social interaction requires that one person psychologically place himself or herself in the shoes of another so that he or she is better able to understand and predict the other's present and subsequent behavior. To "role-play" your father, for instance, it would be necessary to understand how he views things (including yourself) through his constructs and to structure your actions appropriately.

Playing a role in relation to another person does not necessarily mean agreeing with him or her, as parent–child and teacher–student relationships readily attest. As indicated by the commonality corollary, it is far easier to understand how another person thinks if we share similar outlooks, but it is not essential for effective role-playing. What is critical in interpersonal relations is that at least one person attempt to understand how the other person views the role being played.

Kelly's use of "role" should not be confused with usage of the term in sociological role theory. For the sociologist, a role is a unit of the social structure to which people are recruited (e.g., airline attendant, union president, postal clerk). A role in Kelly's system, however, is defined as a "pattern of behavior that follows from a person's understanding of how the others who are associated with him in his task think'' (1955, pp. 97–98). This definition suggests that significant social interaction does not automatically exist because two or more people are communicating with one another or are involved in a common task. Role taking requires that at least one of the interacting individuals have some perception of the other person's ways of seeing things. Further, Kelly held that roles need not be reciprocal—i.e., the person enacting the role need not be construed by the person or persons toward whom the role is directed—in order for a person to become involved in a social relationship. The other person need not enter into a role relationship with the construing individual. Indeed, our society is dominated by one-sided role relationships (e.g., doctor–patient, lawyer–client, employer–employee). In this regard, Kelly noted that an optimal relationship involves mutual understanding of one another's views of life, as is the case of a healthy relationship between wife and husband.

Kelly believed that his theory could be applied to help resolve international problems. He suggested that a peaceful world depends on the ability of people representing various governments to accurately understand one another's constructs. (*Owen Franken/Stock, Boston*)

Kelly believed that it is intrinsically satisfying to have our social predictions about other people confirmed. We have certain ideas about what others expect of us. When we act in accordance with these ideas and discover that we have correctly predicted the expectations of others, we are strongly encouraged toward further socialized behavior.

Kelly's sociality corollary has profound relevance for the field of human relations. In particular, it offers a potentially unifying link between individual and social psychology (Jankowicz, 1987). The implicit notion that a lasting and genuine human relationship cannot develop until at least one person attempts to see the other through the other's glasses may explain those problems people have in communicating with each other in situations ranging from everyday discourse (parents, relatives, friends, neighbors) to international affairs. A peaceful world may ultimately depend upon the capacity of human beings (particularly heads of state) to construe sensitively and accurately one another's construction processes.

Let us now consider the basic assumptions about human nature underlying personal construct theory.

KELLY'S BASIC ASSUMPTIONS CONCERNING HUMAN NATURE

As already mentioned, the philosophy of constructive alternativism assumes that the universe is real, but that different people construe it in different ways. This means that our interpretations of events have more influence on our behavior than the events themselves. Kelly's doctrine likewise means that differences among personality theorists concerning human nature are reflections of their unique construct systems. Kelly himself was no exception to this principle. Like all other theorists discussed in this text, Kelly presents an image of human nature based on his own interpretations of psychological reality. His philosophical assumptions, discussed below, are depicted in Figure 9-1.

Freedom–Determinism   In personal construct theory, people are depicted as *freely determining* their own behavior. As Kelly neatly puts it:

> This personal construct system provides him with both freedom of decision and limitation of action—freedom, because it permits him to deal with the meaning of events rather than forces him to be helplessly pushed about by them, and limitation, because he can never make choices outside the world of alternatives he has erected for himself. (1958, p. 58)

Thus, for Kelly, human beings have an enormous range of constructs from which to choose in construing events, but, once selected, their constructs determine their behavior. Humans operate only within the boundaries of the constructs they have acquired. A person facing an unfamiliar event, for example, is free to use or not use the construct "good-bad" in construing it. Should she decide to employ it, she will likely choose that pole of the construct that offers greater opportunity for further elaboration of her anticipatory system (*choice corollary*). However, once she has made her choice, she is no longer free until she decides to construe the

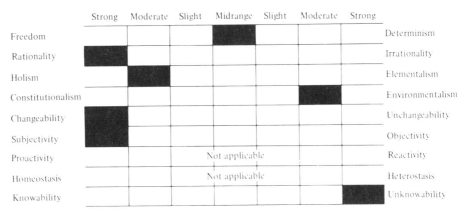

	Strong	Moderate	Slight	Midrange	Slight	Moderate	Strong	
Freedom				■				Determinism
Rationality	■							Irrationality
Holism		■						Elementalism
Constitutionalism						■		Environmentalism
Changeability	■							Unchangeability
Subjectivity	■							Objectivity
Proactivity				Not applicable				Reactivity
Homeostasis				Not applicable				Heterostasis
Knowability							■	Unknowability

FIGURE 9-1   Kelly's position on the nine basic assumptions concerning human nature.

unfamiliar event in other terms, thereby establishing different self-imposed boundaries and related interpretations. Of course, a person may construe and reconstrue the same event throughout her lifetime, thus allowing the freedom–determinism cycle underlying her behavior to manifest itself again and again. Freedom and determinism are inextricably interwoven in Kelly's theory.

Rationality–Irrationality   Kelly's strong commitment to the rationality assumption pervades every aspect of his theory. Indeed, rationality plays a more central part in Kelly's system than in any other perspective presented in this text. He viewed people as constantly engaged in the intellectual quest to understand the world around them. For Kelly to construe individuals in this fashion clearly reveals the basic assumption of rationality. In fact, Kelly's cognitive theory could not exist as a viable "constructive alternative" without a rational position as its base.

Holism–Elementalism   Kelly is moderately committed to a holistic view of human nature. While his unit of analysis, the personal construct, appears at first glance to reflect an elementalist approach to the study of persons, Kelly did not suggest that personality can be understood "one construct at a time." Instead, he emphasized the manner in which constructs are related to one another in an organized manner. Therefore, to understand the person, it is necessary to understand his or her entire construct system.

Student A's construct of "good," for example, as applied to his or her drama professor, might merely be subordinate to his or her construct of "entertaining." In contrast, the "good" construct of student B in this same situation may be subordinate to "intellectually stimulating." For Kelly, it would be virtually impossible to appreciate this difference simply by studying in isolation the "good" constructs of A and B. The myriad of additional construct interrelationships within a system would also be missed in an element-by-element approach. Nevertheless, constructs can be assessed individually; in this sense, Kelly adopts a less than complete commitment to the holistic assumption.

Constitutionalism–Environmentalism   Kelly is noticeably inclined toward the environmentalism pole of this dimension. While he never addressed himself directly to the constitutional versus environmental origins of personal constructs, there is simply no acknowledgment of heredity in Kelly's theory. On the other hand, the environment is theoretically ubiquitous; for Kelly, people are construing and reconstruing events taking place in the environment all the time. Personal constructs are presumably abstracted from experience, employed to anticipate future events, and modified or discarded if they do not help to predict these events. Thus, the ultimate function of the person's construct system is to interpret the surrounding world.

Yet in Kelly's theory, the environment is not invested with the awesome determinative power that it is in Skinner's system. The cognitive person actively interprets, evaluates, construes, and reconstrues the environment, rather than just being molded by its effects. Unlike Skinner's radical behaviorism, Kelly's system regards the person as fundamentally cognitive and rational. The environment is there in Kelly's system, but never to the point of overwhelming the person. His commitment to environmentalism is thus best described as moderate.

Changeability–Unchangeability   Kelly's theory is permeated by dynamic change. Life is seen as constant movement, with all events subject to reinterpretation in light of different constructs. This kinetic awareness reflects Kelly's belief that people change their outlook and form new constructs throughout life. Such a view indicates a strong commitment to changeability.

The changeability assumption is clearly evidenced by the fact that Kelly found it necessary to explain the circumstances under which change occurs in a construct system. Specifically, people change their construct systems as they successively construe the replication of events (*experience corollary*). Viewed in terms of the basic assumptions model, this means than an individual's personality can change over time as a function of experience. And Kelly's *modulation* corollary partly explains how: a person's construct system can change to the degree that his or her constructs are permeable. The more permeable the constructs, the more events they can subsume within their range of convenience and the greater the latitude for change in the overall system. However, Kelly acknowledged that not all people are capable of change to the same degree. For example, a person who does not revise his or her constructs in light of ongoing experiences, because his or her constructs lack permeability, is not going to change very much over time. Such a person will go through life construing and behaving in a rigid fashion regardless of the ongoing flow of events. But a person with permeable constructs can truly profit from experience—such a person is capable of constructive change throughout life. Insofar as Kelly clearly recognized the possibility of such change and attempted to explain how it occurs, he must be judged as strongly committed to the assumption of changeability.

Subjectivity–Objectivity   Kelly contended that human beings live in a highly subjective world of personal constructs. People may construe and reconstrue external events however they wish, but they, nonetheless, remain encapsulated within their subjective constructive systems. Each individual views reality through a template of personal constructs, and the templates are unique to each person.

Objective external factors have no uniform or standardized effects on the person because they are always construed by him or her in idiosyncratic ways. What is a "worthwhile" experience to one person is "anxiety-provoking" to another; what is "relevant" for one person may be simply "superficial" in another's construct system. Objective reality is always filtered through a person's constructive apparatus—*reality is what each of us subjectively construes it to be.* Thus, for Kelly, each person lives in a unique constructive world of his or her own making. To be sure, that world can change, but only to the extent that we are willing to reconstrue it in new and different ways. Kelly is firmly committed to the subjectivity assumption. In fact, the particular blend of the rationality and subjectivity assumptions contributes markedly to the unique character of his theory.

Proactivity–Reactivity   The proactivity–reactivity assumption is directly concerned with the issue of *motivation*: Do human beings internally generate their own behavior or is their behavior a reaction to external stimuli? Since Kelly regards motivation as a redundant construct, he makes no assumption about its proactive versus reactive nature. Simply stated, for Kelly humans are neither proactive nor reactive—they are just alive! To be alive is to be active; life is a form of movement. Thus, Kelly finds it quite unnecessary to consider the issue of what motivates behavior since, by simply being alive, the person is already engaged in behavioral activity. Given Kelly's unorthodox position on motivation, then, the proactivity–reactivity assumption is not applicable to his theoretical system.

Homeostatis–Heterostasis   This assumption also reflects a basic motivational question: Do people behave to reduce drives and maintain internal harmony or is their behavior directed toward growth and self-actualization? For Kelly, neither category applies. Instead, he believed that people seek to acquire and organize coherent construct systems so that they can accurately anticipate future events. In so doing, they engage in *elaborative choice*—that is, they choose that alternative that leads to greater extension and definition of their construct systems (*choice corollary*). To the heterostatically oriented, this may sound suspiciously like growth and self-actualization. On the other hand, advocates of homeostasis might argue with equal cogency that persons choose in this manner because they are attempting to reduce inner uncertainties about the world. Kelly himself, however, took no position on this key motivational issue. Motivation is a nonessential concept in his view. As a basic assumption about human nature, then, the homeostasis–heterostasis issue is not applicable to Kelly's cognitive system.

Knowability–Unknowability   Kelly did not regard human nature as knowable in terms of traditional modes of scientific inquiry. He rejected the philosophical position of *realism,* which asserts that objective reality can be understood independently of our perceptions of it. Objecting to realism, Kelly advanced his own epistemological doctrine of constructive alternativism which holds that only individual events have reality. Objective reality has no existence apart from our personal constructions of it. Launched from this basic premise, human nature can never really be known but only alternatively construed.

The obvious question, then, becomes: Why bother with science? Kelly's answer is that scientific theories serve as differentially useful construct systems in the process of explaining events. Some are more useful than others in this regard—only future events will tell—but the more durable theories have served well as constructive alternatives. Consider a few select personality theories as an example. Freud construed human beings in terms of unconscious motivation; Adler discerned a style of life; Erikson discovered psychosocial stages of ego development; Cattell sensed source traits underlying behavior; Skinner observed instrumentally conditioned responses; and Bandura saw observational learning as a key aspect of human behavior. And Kelly? Kelly stressed the person's subjective interpretation of the world.

By implication, Kelly's personological theory carries within it the seeds of its own demise. Since reality remains open to multiple interpretations, there will come a day when the events presently construed by Kelly's theory will be better anticipated by some other personological construct system. He recognized this and, with disarming candor, admitted it. In discussing the various ways in which personal construct theory has been categorized by responsible scholars, he concluded: "It has also been classified as nonsense, which indeed, by its own admission, it will likely some day turn out to be" (1970, p. 10). By virtue of his philosophical position, then, Kelly assumed that human behavior is unknowable through empirical investigation.

EMPIRICAL VALIDATION OF COGNITIVE THEORY CONCEPTS

To what extent has personal construct theory generated evidence supporting the empirical validity of its major concepts? This question was the focus of a literature survey conducted over 25 years ago by Bonarius (1965) who, on the basis of evaluating nearly 100 published studies stimulated by Kelly's ideas or directly related to them, concluded that it would be premature to assume that Kelly's theory had been validated at that point. However, more recent sources indicate that experimental evidence does support certain aspects of Kelly's theory (e.g., Duck & Craig, 1978; Higgins et al., 1982; Lord, 1982; Tobacyk & Downs, 1986). Close scrutiny reveals that much of this research is based on a test that Kelly developed to assess the personal constructs that people use to construe events in their lives (called the Role Construct Repertory Test). As we will see, this test has provided some support for Kelly's seminal ideas about thought disorder in schizophrenia (Fransella & Bannister, 1977; Neimeyer & Neimeyer, 1981). An account of its rather interesting nature thus seems warranted before considering any investigations prompted by Kelly's cognitive theory.

Role Construct Repertory Test

Kelly (1955) developed the *Role Construct Repertory Test* (*Rep Test* for short) to assess the important constructs a person uses to construe significant people in his or her life. Specifically, the Rep Test was originally devised as a diagnostic instrument to assist the therapist in understanding a client's personal construct system and the way the client uses it to structure his or her personal and material environment. Unfortunately, the format of the Rep Test does not readily lend itself to traditional psychometric assessment; no data for its reliability, validity, or standardization are in a form that permits a potential user to apply the test routinely. But then, there was very little that was traditional about Kelly. Thus, although the Rep Test was developed within the framework of Kelly's theory, studies pertaining to its clinical and research applications are not necessarily indicative of the underlying validity of the theory itself. With this cautionary note in mind, let us consider how this assessment device is used to measure a person's construct system.

Many forms of the Rep Test, individual and group, exist, but one procedure is common to all of them. The subject is presented a *Role Title List* of 20 to 30 different role definitions of persons assumed to be of special importance to the test taker (e.g., a teacher she or he liked). For each role, the subject is asked to write the name of a person known personally who best fits the role description. Some of the roles that typically appear on a role title list are shown in Table 9-1.

The names assigned to these designated roles are called *figures*. After the role title list has been completed, the subject is presented with three of the names of figures from the list and asked to state "in what important way are two alike but different from the third." A subject might be asked, for example, to compare and contrast the persons he or she named for sister, brother, and mother. In considering this triad, the subject might say that brother and sister are similar in that they are "calm" but different from mother, who is "hyperactive." In Kelly's terms, the construct dimension elicited from this "sort" is that of "calm versus hyperactive." This procedure is repeated with several other triads (Kelly recommends about 20 to 30 such trials or "sorts") to determine how the subject categorizes and differentiates these persons. All the roles are used approximately equally in triads, so that the sampling of the subject's principal constructs is not biased. Based on the verbal content of the elicited constructs, the psychologist can then formulate hypotheses about the way the subject perceives and copes with significant persons in life. This form of the Rep Test is called the *Listform* and is administered individually.

Kelly also devised a *Gridform* of the Rep Test (illustrated in Figure 9-2). The procedure for administering this version of the test consists of presenting the subject with a specially prepared grid or matrix in which the significant figures in his or her life are listed on one axis and the various sorts he or she is required to make are listed on the other axis. The subject inserts the names of persons who fit each role in the space on the form corresponding to those illustrated at the top of Figure 9-2 (i.e., after reading the brief role definition of each). Next, the subject is instructed to enter the first row of the matrix to the columns where three people

TABLE 9-1 ROLE TITLE LIST DEFINITIONS FOR THE GRIDFORM OF THE REP TEST

Role titles	Definitions
1 Self	Yourself
2 Mother	Your mother or the person who has played the part of a mother in your life
3 Father	Your father or the person who has played the part of a father in your life
4 Brother	Your brother who is nearest your own age or, if you have no brother, a boy near your own age who was most like a brother to you during your early teens
5 Sister	Your sister who is nearest your own age or, if you have no sister, a girl near your own age who was most like a sister to you during your early teens
6 Spouse	Your wife (or husband) or, if you are not married, your closest present friend of the opposite sex
7 Accepted teacher	The teacher who influenced you most when you were in your teens
8 Rejected teacher	The teacher whose point of view you found most objectionable when you were in your teens
9 Boss	An employer, supervisor, or officer under whom you worked during a period of great stress
10 Doctor	Your physician
11 Pitied person	The person whom you would most like to help or for whom you feel most sorry
12 Rejecting person	A person with whom you have been associated, who, for some unexplained reason, appeared to dislike you
13 Happy person	The happiest person whom you know personally
14 Ethical person	The person who appears to meet the highest ethical standards whom you know personally
15 Intelligent person	The most intelligent person whom you know personally

Source: Adapted from Kelly, 1955, p. 227.

designated by circles are located. These circles designate the three figures whom the subject is to consider in the first sort. In Figure 9-2, for instance, row 1 of the matrix contains circles in the squares under columns 9, 10, and 12 (i.e., "Boss," "Doctor," and "Rejecting Person"). The subject is instructed to think of an important characteristic that makes two of these three people similar to each other and makes them different from the third person. Having decided how two of the figures are alike but different from the third, the subject then inserts an "X" in the two circles which correspond to the two persons who are similar. The third circle is left blank. Next, the subject writes a word or brief phrase that indicates how these two figures are alike in the column marked "Construct pole." In the column marked "Contrast pole" he or she writes a word or brief phrase that tells how the third figure is different from the other two. As shown in Figure 9-2, boss and doctor are seen as alike in terms of being "authorities," whereas rejecting person is seen as being a "nonauthority." Finally, the subject examines the remaining figures in the first row (those not considered in the sort which elicited the

Self	Mother	Father	Brother	Sister	Spouse	Accepted teacher	Rejected teacher	Boss	Doctor	Pitied person	Rejecting person	Happy person	Ethical person	Intelligent person	Sort No.	Construct pole	Contrast pole
1	2	3	4	5	6	7	8	9	10	11	12	13	14	15	Sort No.	Construct pole	Contrast pole
							✓	⊗	⊗		○			✓	1	Authorities	Nonauthority
○	○	○													2		
	○						○					○			3		
				○								○	○		4		
			○				○						○		5		
○					○	○									6		
	○	○								○					7		
○		○	○												8		
										○		○	○		9		
				○		○					○				10		
						○			○			○			11		
										○	○	○			12		
	○		○											○	13		
				○		○		○							14		
○		○							○						15		

FIGURE 9-2   Illustration of grid form of the Rep Test.
(*Source: Adapted from Kelly, 1955, p. 270.*)

construct dimension) and puts a check mark in the square of each if the construct pole characteristic can be used to construe that figure. This process is continued until the subject has completed each of the remaining rows. The end result is a grid with the figures at the top, the various constructs in the right-hand columns, and a pattern of voids and check marks inside the rectangle. The reader may find it an intellectually stimulating and self-revealing exercise to complete Figure 9-2 with his or her own social constructs.

How to Construe Rep Test Results   The end product of the Rep Test is a sample of the constructs that a person uses to construe his or her social reality. Results of the Listform are generally subjected to a clinical analysis in which the examiner considers (1) the number and variety of constructs elicited, (2) the substance and tone of the constructs, (3) the way in which various figures are related to the constructs and to one another, and (4) additional characteristics of the subject's constructs such as their permeability, looseness or tightness, and communicability. This is a subjective interpretation of Rep Test results. Kelly (1961) devised a mathematical scheme for analyzing the Gridform so that it is less susceptible to interpretive error or bias. In brief, this type of statistical analysis reduces the grid to a few basic construct dimensions which capture most succinctly the dominant world views of subjects.

Another way of analyzing Rep Test results has been proposed by Bieri (1955,

1961). This investigator suggests that by inspecting the pattern of checks across the various rows of the Gridform one can determine the relative *cognitive complexity-simplicity* of an individual's construct system. A pattern of similar check marks signifies a small number of constructs and thus an undifferentiated view of others (cognitive simplicity). On the other hand, a pattern of dissimilar check marks indicates a large number of constructs and thus a highly differentiated construction system (cognitive complexity). According to Bieri, cognitively simple persons are likely to ignore information that denies or contradicts the impression they have of others. They oversimplify and show a lack of versatility in their interpersonal relationships. Furthermore, they have difficulty seeing differences between themselves and others (they tend to assume that others resemble themselves). By contrast, cognitively complex persons are likely to code the full range of nuances and subtleties in another's personality, including their inevitable contradictions. They are also better able to predict the behavior of others than those who are cognitively simple. Table 9-2 summarizes the key characteristics of cognitively simple and cognitively complex people.

Assumptions Underlying the Rep Test   Kelly (1955) acknowledged that researchers and therapists alike must make several assumptions when using the Rep Test to measure personal constructs. One such assumption is that the constructs elicited by the test are not limited to people on the role title list, that they will apply to new people in new situations. If a respondent used the constructs elicited by the test only for people on the list, this would undermine the value of results for an investigator seeking to understand how the person views the social world in general. A related assumption is that the people on the test are representative of people that subjects are likely to interact with in their daily lives. A sample of constructs used only for unique people that subjects rarely encounter are of little value in understanding how subjects construe the majority of people with whom they regularly interact.

Kelly's most "tenuous assumption" is that people are able to accurately describe (provide labels for) the constructs they use to construe what makes others similar or different. However, the inherent limits of our language suggest

TABLE 9-2   THE COGNITIVE COMPLEXITY–SIMPLICITY DIMENSION

Cognitively complex person	Cognitively simple person
Has a construction system containing constructs that are clearly differentiated.	Has a construction system in which the distinction among constructs is blurred.
Can draw sharp distinctions between self and others.	Has difficulty seeing distinctions between self and others.
Has skill in predicting the behavior of others.	Lacks skill in predicting the behavior of others.
Views others in terms of many different categories.	Views others in terms of few categories.

that people's constructs cannot always be adequately verbalized. Kelly recognized that words do not necessarily come to mind when people are asked to describe their construct systems. In fact, he believed that sometimes people formulate "preverbal constructs" prior to learning to speak. Nevertheless, even when subjects do supply words that come close to what they mean, investigators may interpret those words differently. Thus, the words that subjects choose to describe constructs may be interpreted so differently by an investigator that the latter will end up with false impressions of how the former view the world.

Given the fact that the Rep Test has important limitations (Bonarius et al., 1980), the best advice seems to be, as with most self-report assessment procedures, to regard it as but one of several sources of information about how people construe their world. Specifically, if researchers and therapists are cognizant of the several assumptions built into the procedure, the Rep Test may be a useful tool in learning about subjects' construct systems.

Schizophrenic Thought Disorder: A "Destructive" Alternative

Much of the research utilizing Kelly's Rep Test has focused on psychiatric patients who have been diagnosed as schizophrenic. Clinical descriptions of schizophrenia generally stress that it is marked by language and thought disturbances (Epting, 1984; Gottesman & Shields, 1982). Confusion and vagueness of ideas, heavy use of new words with idiosyncratic meanings (*neologisms*), unusual shifts in the direction of thought, and fragmented communication patterns are quite commonly observed (Singer et al., 1978). In construct theory terms, schizophrenics are employing an overly loose and inconsistent construct system for construing their experiences. Their ideas about people are both poorly integrated and unstable in that they suffer from a relative lack of structure and consistency. In short, their worldview literally makes no sense. Since the Rep Test provides a method of assessing degree of cognitive structure and organization in construing other people, it offers a promising approach for understanding the disordered thinking processes characteristic of schizophrenia.

Bannister and Fransella (1966) attempted to assess the validity of the assertion that schizophrenics use overloose and highly inconsistent constructs. They also sought to establish an economical and standardized grid test for detecting the presence of schizophrenic thought disorder. The subjects for this study consisted of six different groups: (1) thought-disordered schizophrenics, (2) non-thought-disordered schizophrenics, (3) normals, (4) neurotics, (5) organics (i.e., mild forms of brain damage), and (6) depressives. A variant of the Rep Test was used to measure disordered thinking. Precisely, each subject was presented with an array of eight passport-type photos of strangers and instructed to rank-order them on six construct dimensions that normal people usually consider highly interrelated. Subjects were first asked to rank all eight photos from the *most kind* to the *least kind*. Then the eight photos were reshuffled and each subject was asked to rank-order them again along a dimension of *stupidity*. This procedure was then repeated with the same photos (reshuffled each time) using the construct dimensions of *selfishness, sincerity, meanness,* and *honesty.* Immediately after the subjects completed this task (administration 1), they were asked to repeat the entire procedure again (administration 2), using the same photos and rank-ordering them for the same construct dimensions. They were also told that this was not to test their memory but that they should undertake the second test as if they were doing it for the first time.

Bannister and Fransella computed two statistical measures from each subject's test protocol—one for *intensity* and one for *consistency.* The intensity score reveals how closely the subject ranked the photos on one construct relative to his or her rankings on the other constructs. A high intensity score indicates that the subject has rank-ordered as if the judged constructs are related, whereas a low intensity score indicates that he or she has treated them as relatively independent characteristics. The consistency score reflects the degree to which the subject has maintained the pattern of relationships between his or her constructs from administration 1 to administration 2 of the grid test. In effect, it is a test-retest correlation indicating the degree to which the subject on retest uses the constructs in the same way he or she did on the original test. Thus, for example, a consistent score would reflect rating a given photo as most kind the first time and as most kind the second time. By contrast, an inconsistent score would reflect rating a particular photo as highly sincere the first time and highly insincere the second time.

It was predicted that thought-disordered schizophrenics would have lower intensity and consistency scores than subjects in the other five groups. The results provided substantial support for these predictions. Table 9-3 presents the means and standard deviations for intensity and consistency for the six groups. This table shows that the constructs of the thought-disordered schizophrenics were considerably less highly interrelated (i.e., lower intensity) than were those of the other groups, and that their immediate test-retest reliability (i.e., consistency) was also significantly lower.

A second experiment conducted by Bannister and Salmon (1966) examined the question of whether schizophrenics are disordered across their entire construct system (i.e., are equally perplexed by every aspect of the world in which they live) or whether they are disordered in a more focal sense (i.e., are perplexed by some aspects of life more than others). This question was investigated by administering two grid forms of the Rep Test to thought-disordered schizophrenics and normal controls. The first, a "people" form, used passport-type photos of strangers and, as in the preceding study, subjects ranked the photos on each of six psychological constructs. The second form of the test, an "object" form, required subjects to rank a set of 15 objects (e.g., English bowler hat, loaf of bread) on six constructs (e.g., curved-straight, heavy-light). Subjects completed both forms of the test in the same experimental session so that both the degree of structure and stability of the pattern of construct interrelationships across elements could be assessed.

Bannister and Salmon reported that while schizophrenics did not differ from normal controls in their construing of objects, they were vastly less stable and consistent in their construing of people. This finding suggests that schizophrenic thought disorder may not be diffuse but, rather, may be particularly related to

TABLE 9-3   MEANS AND STANDARD DEVIATIONS OF INTENSITY AND CONSISTENCY SCORES FOR SIX GROUPS OF SUBJECTS

	Thought-disordered schizohprenics	Normals	Non-thought-disordered schizophrenics	Depressives	Neurotics	Organics
Intensity mean	728	1,253	1,183	1,115	1,383	933
Standard deviation	369	339	390	456	517	524
Consistency mean	0.18	0.80	0.73	0.75	0.74	0.73
Standard deviation	0.39	0.34	0.34	0.41	0.45	0.47

Source: Adapted from Bannister and Fransella, 1966, p. 98.

illogical connections between interpersonal constructs. That is, it is the highly fluid nature of interpersonal construing that is the essence of schizophrenia. Contemplating results such as those considered in these two experiments, Bannister (1985) proposed a theory of schizophrenic thought disorder based on a *serial invalidation hypothesis*. In brief, this theory states that schizophrenics live in a world that continually invalidates their constructs such that a gross loosening of their construct systems is the ultimate form of psychological adjustment. In support of his theory of schizophrenic thought disorder, Bannister asked normal individuals to make predictions about hypothetical people. Subjects were then informed that their predictions were consistently wrong. This process was repeated numerous times. As predicted, Bannister found that serial invalidation does indeed lead subjects to make inconsistent predictions. Subjects were found to flip-flop between opposite poles of an invalidated construct, sometimes choosing one and sometimes another, suggesting the failure to predict accurately of actual schizophrenic patients. Bannister and others (1975) report evidence that it is possible to reverse the kaleidoscopic process of cognition in schizophrenics by providing them with new experiences that strengthen their capacity to accurately predict the behavior of others.

Construct Similarity and Friendship Formation

A final example of research aimed at validating Kelly's personal construct theory is concerned with understanding why friendships develop and why they sometimes dissolve. This area of research grew out of two of Kelly's corollaries. First, the commonality corollary states that people construe the world in a similar manner to the extent that they use systems of constructs that are similar. Second, the sociality corollary asserts that meaningful social interaction with someone else requires us to understand how that person perceives reality.

Applying these two corollaries to the development of intimate and rewarding friendships is illustrated in research conducted by Duck (1973, 1977, 1979). In line with Kelly, Duck contends that people who share a perception of what the world is like are more likely to be attracted to one another and eventually become friends than are those who perceive the world differently. To test this notion that

Research suggests that similarity of personal constructs plays a key role in the development of close relationships. (*Mark Antman/The Image Works*)

construct similarity plays a role in friendship formation, Duck and Craig (1978) gave incoming college students assigned to the same residence hall several personality tests one month after their arrival on campus. Included were measures of various personality traits and a Rep Test profile. The subjects also indicated the strength of their friendships with each of the other participants in the study. The researchers subsequently returned twice during the year, 3 months and 8 months following the initial testing session, to measure friendship patterns. Results indicated that similarity of scores on the various personality trait measures were minimally useful in predicting the formation of friendships, and that this was limited to early in the academic year. Similarity of personal constructs as assessed by the Rep Test, however, proved to be the only significant predictor of who would become friends at the end of the academic year. Surprisingly, construct similarity did not predict friendship formation at the initial testing session or at the 3-month follow-up. Duck and Craig suggest that choice of friends at the onset of the academic year may have been based on perceived similarity of superficial personality traits, and that these obvious similarities exert less influence in choosing friends as students learn more about each other's "deeper level" constructs. In other words, the effect of construct similarity on the process of friendship formation is greatest only after a student has had sufficient time to discover which of the other subjects shared his or her perceptions of the world at a more personal level.

If Kelly is correct in assuming that construct similarity predicts friendship formation, then it logically follows that friendship bonds will tend to weaken if two people discover that they have dissimilar views about important issues. A study by Duck and Allison (1978) provides support for this view of the breaking-up process. They recruited subjects at a university that required on-campus residency during freshman year but encouraged living off-campus their sophomore year. This arrangement enabled these researchers to determine which students would choose to remain together and which would break up during their second year of college. The Rep Test was used to measure each subject's personal constructs. As predicted, those subjects who remained roommates showed higher construct similarity than those who chose to live apart. Friendship breakups following the freshman year were especially evident among subjects who had highly dissimilar Rep Test profiles.

As noted previously, the effect of construct similarity on friendship formation may not surface until two people have had ample opportunity to get to know each other quite well. That is, differences in construct structure may not become apparent until people have had reasonable time to really learn how the other person sees the world. This possibility may explain why some romantic relationships endure while others do not. A study by Neimeyer (1984), for example, revealed that married couples who shared similar constructs reported significantly higher levels of marital satisfaction than did couples who did not share similar constructs. By implication, it seems that long-term happiness in a marriage may largely depend on two people's construing the world in the same general way.

Recently the Rep Test has been applied to the area of industrial/organizational psychology. For instance, one study used the test in market research to determine how consumers evaluate and compare various products they are considering purchasing (Stewart & Stewart, 1982). Jankowicz (1987) cites numerous other examples of how Kelly's test is used by management psychologists in the business world. Although such applications of the Rep Test appear to be growing rapidly, it should be emphasized that little research is presently being conducted on specific hypotheses drawn from Kelly's personal construct theory. This is surprising given the fact that the theory is clearly stated and offers a straightforward account of human behavior.

APPLICATION: EMOTIONAL STATES, PSYCHOLOGICAL DISORDERS, AND FIXED-ROLE THERAPY

Kelly's theory represents a cognitive approach to personality. He proposed that the best way to understand human behavior is to think of people as scientists. Like scientists, other people have a need to predict and control events that occur in their environment with some degree of regularity. Yet this personological system emerged, in the main, from *clinical psychology,* a professional discipline devoted to the understanding and treatment of psychological disturbances. Kelly's ultimate goal was to create a more empirical approach to the challenging work of clinical psychology. In fact, Volume 2 of *The Psychology of Personal Constructs* (1955) is subtitled "Clinical Diagnosis and Psychotherapy," while an entire chapter in Volume 1 describes Kelly's own particular psychotherapeutic approach, fixed-role therapy. How, then, does a *cognitive, intellectually oriented* theory of personality apply to issues that directly affect people's lives? Kelly felt that his theory offered useful applications to the understanding of emotional states, psychological health and disorder, and the practice of therapy.

Emotional States

Kelly retained but reconceived several traditional psychological concepts of emotion in accordance with his personal construct theory. Here we will consider four emotional states as viewed from Kelly's perspective: anxiety, guilt, threat, and hostility.

Anxiety   Kelly defined *anxiety* as "the recognition that the events with which one is confronted lie outside the range of convenience of one's construct system" (1955, p. 495). Thus, the vague feeling of uncertainty and helplessness commonly labeled as "anxiety" is, for Kelly, a result of being aware that our available constructs are not applicable to anticipating the events we encounter. Kelly emphasized that it is not the fact that our construct system is not functioning that is anxiety-provoking; we are not anxious merely because our anticipations are inaccurate. Anxiety is created (experienced) only when we realize that we have no adequate constructs with which to interpret the events of our lives. Kelly often facetiously referred to a person in this state as being "caught with his constructs down." Under such circumstances a person cannot predict, hence, cannot fully comprehend, what is happening or cannot solve the problem. Consider, for example, two people who find themselves caught up in the midst of a divorce. Suddenly they are faced with an event unlike anything they have ever experienced before. Part of the difficulty involved in going through a divorce (or anything for the very first time) is the lack of constructs by which to understand and anticipate its consequences and implications.

This view of anxiety is far different from the Freudian conception of the neurotically anxious individual as a victim of unconscious conflicts and dammed-up instinctual energy. Rather than being threatened by the breakthrough of sexual and aggressive impulses into consciousness, the anxious person is really overwhelmed by events which she or he can neither understand nor anticipate. Viewed in this manner, psychotherapy assists a client either in acquiring new constructs, which will enable him or her to better predict the distressing events, or in making his or her existing constructs more permeable, so they admit new experiences to their range of convenience.

Guilt   Kelly's sociality corollary assumes that we all have a core construct system. Certain aspects of this core structure, which he termed *core roles,* are a major determinant of our sense of identity. Examples of such core roles are occupational or professional roles, the roles of parent and child, close friend, student, and so on. Because core roles are so central to our lives, failing to perform them adequately can have unpleasant consequences. According to Kelly, failure to enact a core role as that role is construed by another person results in *guilt:* "Guilt arises when the individual becomes aware that he is alienated from the roles by which he maintains his most important relationships to other persons" (1963, p. 228). The guilty person is aware of having acted in ways that are inconsistent with his or her self-image. For example, a college student who construes himself as a scholar will feel guilty if he spends too much time at the local campus pub with his roommates, thus violating the most basic aspects of his core role as a scholar, namely, studying. Presumably a student who construes himself as a playboy would not experience such guilt. Kelly's concept of guilt is somewhat similar to Freud's concept of moral anxiety. In Kelly's view, we experience guilt whenever we behave in ways that depart from our sense of who we are. In Freud's view, we experience moral anxiety whenever we act in ways that violate our sense of what is right and wrong (conscience). For both theorists, we experience discomfort when we behave in ways inconsistent with either what is expected from us or what we expect of ourselves: guilt for Kelly, moral anxiety for Freud.

Threat   Still another familiar emotional experience, *threat,* is viewed by Kelly as the awareness that our construct system is about to be drastically altered by what has been discovered. The experience of threat occurs when a major shake-up in our personal constructs is imminent. For example, we may feel threatened if our beliefs about the honesty and integrity of high-ranking political and business leaders seem no longer to be validated by experience. Kelly believed that threat does psychological violence to the person. The thought of our own death is perhaps the most formidable type of threat, unless we construe it as basic to the meaning of our lives.

Hostility   As defined by Kelly, *hostility* is the "continued effort to extort validational evidence in favor of a type of social prediction which has already proved itself a failure" (1955, p. 510). Traditionally considered a disposition to behave vindictively toward or to inflict harm upon others, hostility in Kelly's theory is merely an attempt to hold onto an invalid construct in the face of contradictory (invalidating) evidence. The hostile person, rather than resign himself to the fact that his expectations about other people are unrealistic and therefore in need of revision, tries to make others behave in ways that fit his preconceived notions. Consider, for instance, the reaction of a father who discovers that his college-aged daughter is living the life of a "sexually liberated" woman. No matter how compelling the contrary evidence, the hostile father persists in his belief that she is his "little girl." Changing our constructs is difficult, threatening, and sometimes even impossible. How much better it would be if we could change the world, rather than our way of viewing it, so that it would conform to our preconceptions! Hostility represents just such an attempt. This is not unlike the Greek mythological figure Procrustes who would stretch or amputate the legs of his victims to adapt them to the length of his bed!

Psychological Health and Disorder

Each day clinical psychologists deal with the realities of psychological health and disorder. How are these concepts to be understood within the context of personal construct theory? Turning first to health, four distinct characteristics define the well-functioning person from Kelly's perspective. First, healthy persons are willing to evaluate their constructs and to test the validity of their perceptions of other people. In other words, such people assess the predictive efficiency of their personal constructions of social experiences. Second, healthy persons are able to discard their constructs and reorient their core role systems whenever they appear to be invalid. In Kelly's terminology, their constructs are permeable, meaning not only that they can admit when they are wrong, but also that they can update their constructs when their life experiences so dictate. The third characteristic of personal soundness is a desire to extend the range, scope, and coverage of one's construct system. In Kelly's view, healthy people remain open to new possibilities for personal growth and development. The fourth and final characteristic of psychological health is a well-developed repertoire of roles. Kelly suggested that a person is healthy to the extent that he or she can effectively enact a variety of social roles and comprehend the perspectives of others involved in the process of social interaction.

Kelly also took a unique stance in relation to psychological disorders, reconstruing them in terms of a personal construct orientation. For him, a *psychological disorder* is "any personal construction which is used repeatedly in spite of consistent invalidation" (1955, p. 831). Psychological disturbances thus represent the apparent failure of a person's construct system to achieve its purpose. Or, more to the point, psychological disorders involve anxiety and the person's repeated efforts to regain the sense of being able to predict events. Caught up in a lack of capacity to predict, the disturbed person searches frantically for new ways of construing the events of his world. Or he or she may swing in the opposite direction and rigidly adhere to the same predictions, thereby keeping his or her defective personal construct system intact in the face of repeated failure. In either case, the maladjusted person cannot predict events with much accuracy and hence fails to learn about or cope with the world. The dissatisfaction that accompanies such ineffective prediction of events is what leads the person to seek therapeutic help.

Kelly had little interest in formulating complex diagnostic schemes for classifying psychological disorders. Instead, he interpreted psychological problems in accordance with his own unique set of diagnostic constructs. *Dilation* serves as a good example of one such construct for viewing psychological disorders. In Kelly's theory of psychopathology, dilation occurs when a person has no superordinate constructs by which to impose organization on the perceptual field of experience. Having abandoned or lost governing constructs, the person then attempts to broaden (dilate) and reorganize the personal constructs at a more bizarre and comprehensive level of plausibility. What happens? Kelly suggested that the disorders traditionally labeled "mania" and "depression" result.

Historically, *mania* has been viewed as a disturbed state in which the person's thinking is overinclusive (the person is unable to preserve conceptual boundaries, and so thought becomes less accurate, more vague, and overly general). Affect often appears quite euphoric. Manic persons are forever frantically beginning a variety of projects and activities that they likely will never finish, talking feverishly about their plans in grandiose terms all the while. They jump from topic to topic and make sweeping generalizations with few substantive ideas. Kelly suggested that the manic person's exploration has simply exceeded the capacity of the construct system to function effectively. The result is that the person is left with "loose constructions" of reality. The expressed excitement represents a kind of frenzied attempt to cope with a rapidly dilating perceptual field.

Another pathological response to a faulty construct system is *depression*. Kelly believed that depression tends to occur in people who have *constricted* their perceptual field (i.e., narrowed their interests to a smaller and smaller area). The depressed person has considerable difficulty in making even the simplest everyday decisions. The extremely depressed person often contemplates suicide—the ultimate act of constriction. In short, depression represents a psychological disorder in which people attempt to construe their experiences from the opposite side of the dilation construct: constriction.

To summarize Kelly's view of psychopathology, we return to the analogy of persons as scientists. Scientists seek to predict and control events through the use of hypotheses. When scientists generate poor hypotheses about what the world is like, when they account for things that fall outside the range of convenience of their hypotheses, and when they cling tenaciously to their hypotheses in the face of contradictory evidence, we say they are bad scientists. Similarly, when people attempt to construe important events that lie outside the range of convenience of their personal constructs and thus become confused, disoriented, and anxious, we refer to them as sick people. In effect, people suffer from psychological problems because of defects in their construct systems.

Fixed-Role Therapy

While many of the therapeutic procedures described by Kelly (1955) are similar to those used by other therapists, there are two distinguishing features of his approach: first, his conception of what the goal of psychotherapy should be and, second, the development and practice of fixed-role therapy.

Kelly viewed the goal of the therapy process in terms of assisting people to alter their construct system in ways that improve its predictive efficiency (Epting, 1980). Since disorders involve using constructs in the face of consistent invalidation, psychotherapy is directed toward the psychological reconstruction of the client's construct system so that it is more workable. But more than this, it is an exciting process of scientific experimentation. The therapy setting is a laboratory in which the therapist encourages the client to develop and test new hypotheses, both within and outside the clinical situation. The therapist is highly active—constantly prodding, pushing, and stimulating the client to construe events in ways that differ from those used previously. If the new constructs fit, the client can use them in the future; if not, other hypotheses are generated and tested. Science is thus the model clients use in reconstructing their lives. Along with this, it is the therapist's task to make validating data (information feedback) available, against which the client can check his or her own hypotheses. By providing these data in the form of responses to a wide variety of the client's constructions, the clinician gives the client an opportunity to reorganize and validate his or her construct system, an opportunity that is not normally available to him. The result, according to Kelly, is that the client has a framework with greater predictive efficiency than the preexisting framework.

Kelly went beyond this unique interpretation of psychotherapy to develop his own specific brand, *fixed-role therapy*. This therapy process maintains that human beings are not only what they construe themselves to be but also what they do. To be even more concrete, Kelly believed that the therapist's role is one of encouraging and helping the client to change his or her overt behavior. This change, in turn, will enable the client to perceive and construe himself or herself in new ways, thereby becoming a new, more effective person. It is important to keep in mind that Kelly did not believe that fixed-role therapy works for everyone. Indeed, he cautioned that therapists should be creative in using whatever techniques are needed "to get the human process going again so that life may go on" (1969, p. 223).

How does fixed-role therapy actually work? The process begins with assessment in which the client writes a *self-characterization sketch* in the third person. The self-sketch has no detailed outline, and the client is given only the following instructions:

> I want you to write a character sketch of Harry Brown, just as if he were the principal character in a play. Write it as it might be written by a friend who knows him very intimately and very sympathetically, perhaps better than anyone even really could know him. Be sure to write it in the third person. For example, start out by saying, Harry Brown is . . . (Kelly, 1955, p. 323)

Careful study of Harry Brown's self-characterization will uncover many of the constructs he habitually uses in construing himself and his relationships to significant others. What is then needed is a tailor-made means of helping Harry to revise his personal construct system in a way that will be functional from his personal viewpoint. The vehicle for accomplishing this objective is called the *fixed-role sketch*. Based on the information provided by the self-characterization, it is essentially a personality role description of a fictional individual, preferably compiled by a team of experienced therapists. The fictional person is given a name other than the client's and furnished with a construct system that, it is judged, would be therapeutically beneficial for Harry to act out. The sketch is not intended to "remake" Harry but, rather, to invite him to explore, to experiment, and—more to the point—to reconstrue himself and his life situation. In short, the fixed-role sketch is designed to provide an imaginary person for the client to role-play. Its purpose is to stimulate the client to reconstrue his life experiences so that he will become better able to deal with them effectively.

In the next phase of fixed-role therapy, the therapist presents the fixed-role sketch to the client, making an *acceptance check* to determine if the client understands and accepts it as representing a person he or she would like to be. The client is then instructed to enact the role sketch for a period of time. This instruction makes it clear to the client that he or she must read the sketch at least three times a day and to try to think, act, talk, and be like the fictional character portrayed in the sketch. If, for instance, the character is Tom Cruise, then the client is told the following: "For a few weeks you are to try to forget who you are or who you ever were. You are Tom Cruise. You behave like him. You think and feel like him. You do the things you think he would do." While the idea of behaving like Tom Cruise may seem a bit alien if not downright ridiculous to the reader, the point is that the client is asked to temporarily suspend being himself so that he can discover new aspects of himself. Furthermore, it often happens that the client stops thinking of the role as a role and starts to regard it as a natural part of himself.

During this phase of the therapy process, therapist and client meet often to discuss the latter's problems in enacting the role sketch. There may also be some rehearsing of the sketch during therapy sessions so that therapist and client are able to explore the new construct system firsthand. Through techniques such as role-playing, the client is encouraged to test out the sketch character's constructs in the context of social relationships, work setting, family life, and other key areas of life. Throughout this period, the therapist responds to the client as if he or she were actually the character in the sketch.

How effective is fixed-role therapy in facilitating the reconstruction of the client's construct system? As is the case with most forms of psychotherapy, the results are mixed. While some clients respond positively to Kelly's unorthodox approach, others do not (Epting, 1984). Furthermore, evidence suggests that superordinate constructs are far more difficult to change than subordinate constructs, presumably because they involve more threat of potential disruption of the construct system. It also appears that resistance to change through the loosening of the client's constructs must be overcome before change in behavior can occur. Although the process of therapy is very complex, Kelly remained optimistic that a more functional construct system would emerge from the application of the principles of his personal construct theory of change.

In conclusion, the psychology of personal constructs is applicable to aspects of human experience far removed from those traditionally considered to be cognitive. In particular, emotional states, psychological health and disorder, and psychotherapy can all be construed from Kelly's novel perspective. If George Kelly's purpose in developing his cognitive theory was, as he sometimes noted, to stimulate, challenge, and to open our minds to the incredible spectrum of life's possibilities, he has indeed succeeded.

SUMMARY

The cognitive perspective on personality emphasizes the impact of intellectual or thinking processes on human behavior. George Kelly was an early pioneer of this approach with his personal construct theory. He based his approach on the philosophical position of constructive alternativism, which holds that any event for any person is open to multiple interpretations. Kelly compared people to scientists, constantly generating and testing hypotheses about the nature of things so that adequate predictions of future events can be made.

Kelly believed that persons comprehend their worlds through transparent patterns or templates called constructs. Each person has a unique construct system (personality) which he or she uses to construe or interpret experience. Kelly theorized that all constructs possess certain formal properties: range of convenience, focus of convenience, and permeability–impermeability. Kelly also described various types of personal constructs: preemptive, constellatory, propositional, comprehensive, incidental, core, peripheral, tight, and loose.

Kelly maintained that personality is equivalent to the personal constructs used by the person to predict the future. He further proposed that no special concepts (drives, rewards, needs) are needed to explain human motivation. Instead, he suggested that people are motivated simply by virtue of the fact that they are alive and seek to predict the events that they experience.

Kelly's theory is formally stated in terms of one fundamental postulate and 11 elaborative corollaries. The former stipulates that a person's processes are psychologically channelized by the ways in which he or she anticipates events, while the corollaries explain how a construct system functions, changes, and influences social interaction. In particular, Kelly viewed constructs as bipolar and dichotomous. He also characterized the organization of constructs in terms of a hierarchical system such that some constructs are either superordinate or subordinate in relation to other parts of the system. This organization is not permanently fixed, however, just as the constructs themselves are not permanent. Numerous other facets and implications of the personal construct perspective were also discussed.

Kelly was much more cognizant of and explicit about the philosophical underpinnings of personality theory than most personologists. His position is nonetheless founded upon basic assumptions concerning human nature. Personal construct theory reflects (1) a strong commitment to the assumptions of rationality, changeability, subjectivity, and unknowability; (2) a moderate commitment to the assumptions of holism and environmentalism; and (3) a midrange position on the freedom–determinism dimension. The proactivity–reactivity and homeostasis–heterostasis assumptions do not apply to Kelly's position since he regarded motivation as a redundant construct.

Although Kelly's theoretical concepts have directly stimulated only modest research to date, he devised a personality assessment instrument, the Rep Test, which has been widely employed in a variety of studies. The Rep Test assesses the personal constructs that people use in construing their role relations and other aspects of their experience. Its use was illustrated in investigations of schizophrenic thought disorder and the formation of friendships.

Kelly's personal construct theory is applicable to behavioral domains far beyond those traditionally defined as cognitive. In the application section of the chapter, Kelly's theory was extended to the practical concerns of the clinical psychologist—emotional states, psychological health and disorder, and psychotherapy.

BIBLIOGRAPHY

Bannister, D. (Ed.). (1977). *New perspectives in personal construct theory*. New York: Academic Press.

Bannister, D. (1985). *Issues and approaches in personal construct theory*. London: Academic Press.

Bannister, D., Adams-Weber, J. R., Penn, W. L., & Radley, A. R. (1975). Reversing the process of thought-disorder: A serial validation experiment. *British Journal of Social and Clinical Psychology*, **14**, 169–180.

Bannister, D., & Fransella, F. (1966). A grid test of schizophrenic thought disorder. *British Journal of Social and Clinical Psychology*, **5**, 95–102.

Bannister, D., & Salmon, P. (1966). Schizophrenic thought disorder: Specific or diffuse? *British Journal of Medical Psychology*, **39**, 215–219.

Bieri, J. (1955). Cognitive complexity-simplicity and predictive behavior. *Journal of Abnormal and Social Psychology*, **51**, 263–268.

Bieri, J. (1961). Complexity-simplicity as a personality variable in cognitive and preferential behavior. In D. Fiske & S. Maddi (Eds.), *Functions of varied experience*. Homewood, IL: Dorsey Press.

Bonarius, J. (1965). Research in the personal construct theory of George A. Kelly: Role construct repertory test and basic theory. In B. Maher (Ed.), *Progress in experimental personality research* (pp. 1–46). New York: Academic Press.

Bonarius, J., Holland, R., & Rosenberg, S. (Eds.) (1980). *Personal construct theory: Recent advances in theory and practice*. London: Macmillan.

Duck, S. W. (1973). *Personal relationships and personal constructs: A study of friendship formation*. London: Wiley.

Duck, S. W. (1977). *Theory and practice in interpersonal attraction*. London: Academic Press.

Duck, S. W. (1979). The personal and interpersonal in construct theory: Social and individual aspects of relationships. In P. Stringer & D. Bannister (Eds.), *Constructs of sociality and individuality* (pp. 279–297). London: Academic Press.

Duck, S. W., & Allison, D. (1978). I liked you but I can't live with you: A study of lapsed friendships. *Social Behavior and Personality*, **6**, 43–47.

Duck, S. W., & Craig, G. (1978). Personality similarity and the development of friendship: A longitudinal study. *British Journal of Social and Clinical Psychology*, **17**, 237–242.

Epting, F. R. (1980). *Personal construct theory psychotherapy*. New York: Wiley.

Epting, F. R. (1984). *Personal construct counseling and psychotherapy*. Chichester, Eng.: Wiley.

Fiske, S. T., & Taylor, S. E. (1991). *Social cognition*. New York: McGraw-Hill.

Fransella, F., & Bannister, D. (1977). *A manual for repertory grid technique*. New York: Academic Press.

Gottesman, I. I., & Shields, J. (1982). *Schizophrenia: The epigenetic puzzle*. Cambridge, MA: Cambridge University Press.

Higgins, E. T., King, G. A., & Mavin, G. H. (1982). Individual construct accessibility and subjective impressions and recall. *Journal of Personality and Social Psychology*, **43**, 35–47.

Jankowitz, A. D. (1987). Whatever became of George Kelly? Applications and implications. *American Psychologist*, **42**, 481–487.

Kelly, G. (1955). *The psychology of personal constructs* (Vols. 1 and 2). New York: Norton.

Kelly, G. (1958). Man's construction of his alternatives. In G. Lindzey (Ed.), *Assessment of human motives* (pp. 33–64). Orlando, FL: Harcourt Brace Jovanovich, Inc.

Kelly, G. (1961). A nonparametric method of factor analysis for dealing with theoretical issues. Unpublished manuscript. Mimeograph, Ohio State University.

Kelly, G. (1962). Europe's matrix of decisions. In M. R. Jones (Ed.), *Nebraska symposium on motivation* (Vol. 10). Lincoln: University of Nebraska Press.

Kelly, G. (1963). *A theory of personality: The psychology of personal constructs*. New York: Norton.

Kelly, G. (1969). Clinical psychology and personality. In B. Maher (Ed.), *Clinical psychology and personality: The selected papers of George Kelly*. New York: Wiley.

Kelly, G. (1970). A brief introduction to personal construct theory. In D. Bannister (Ed.), *Perspectives in personal construct theory* (pp. 1–29). New York: Academic Press.

Landfield, A. W., & Leitner, L. M. (Eds.). (1980). *Personal construct psychology*. New York: Wiley.

Lord, C. G. (1982). Predicting behavioral consistency from an individual's perception of situational similarities. *Journal of Personality and Social Psychology*, **42**, 1076–1088.

Mischel, W. (1980). George Kelly's anticipation of psychology: A personal tribute. In M. J. Mahoney (Ed.), *Psychotherapy process*. New York: Plenum.

Neimeyer, G. J. (1984). Cognitive complexity and marital satisfaction. *Journal of Social and Clinical Psychology*, **2**, 258–263.

Neimeyer, R. A. (1985). *The development of personal construct psychology*. Lincoln: University of Nebraska Press.

Neimeyer, G. J., & Neimeyer, R. A. (1981). Personal construct perspectives on cognitive assessment. In T. V. Merluzzi, C. R. Glass, & M. Genest (Eds.), *Cognitive assessment* (pp. 188–232). New York: Guilford Press.

Singer, M. T., Wynne, L. C., & Toohey, M. L. (1978). Communication disorders and the families of schizophrenics. In L. C. Wynne, R. L. Cromwell, & S. Matthysse (Eds.), *The nature of schizophrenia: New approaches to research and treatment*. New York: Wiley Medical.

Stewart, V., & Stewart, A. (1982). *Business applications of repertory grid*. London: McGraw-Hill.

Tobacyk, J. J., & Downs, A. (1986). Personal construct threat and irrational beliefs as cognitive predictors of increases in musical performance anxiety. *Journal of Personality and Social Psychology*, **51**, 779–782.

Triandis, H. C., Hui, H., Albert, R. D., Leung, S., Lisansky, J., Diaz-Loving, R., Plascencia, L., Marin, G., Betancourt, H., & Loyola-Cintron, L. (1984). Individual models of social behavior. *Journal of Personality and Social Psychology*, **46**, 1389–1404.

Wyer, R. S., Jr., & Srull, T. K. (Eds.). (1984). *Handbook of social cognition* (Vols. 1–3). Hillsdale, NJ: Erlbaum.

SUGGESTED READINGS

Adams-Weber, J. (1979). *Personal construct theory: Concepts and applications.* New York: Wiley-Interscience.

Baldwin, A. C., Critelli, J. W., Stevens, L. C., & Russell, S. (1986). Androgyny and sex role measurement: A personal construct approach. *Journal of Personality and Social Psychology*, **51**, 1081–1088.

Epting, F. R., & Neimeyer, R. A. (Eds.). (1984). *Personal meanings of death: Applications of personal construct theory to clinical practice.* New York: Hemisphere/McGraw-Hill.

Landfield, A. W., & Epting, F. R. (1987). *Personal construct psychology: Clinical and personality assessment.* New York: Human Sciences Press.

Neimeyer, R. A., & Neimeyer, G. J. (Eds.). (1987). *Personal construct therapy casebook.* New York: Springer.

Thompson, G. G. (1968). George Alexander Kelly: 1905–1967. *Journal of General Psychology*, **79**, 19–24.

DISCUSSION QUESTIONS

1 Describe Kelly's philosophy of constructive alternativism. What implications does this philosophy have for your life? For example, are your "anxieties and concerns" largely of your own making (because of the way in which you construe events)? Viewed in this fashion, can you reconstrue events to lighten the unnecessary psychological burdens that you now carry? How?

2 A difficult exercise. If you had only one word to describe your feelings about your entire life to this point, what would that word be? Write it down. Now write down its opposite. Can you see how this construct dimension plays a part in the way you construe events in various areas of your life (e.g., personal relationships, school, work)?

3 What does Kelly mean when he says that all people are scientists?

4 Why does Kelly object to traditional concepts of motivation to explain human behavior?

5 Explain the meaning of Kelly's fundamental postulate. What are some of the major corollaries that serve to elaborate it?

6 Do you believe that "personality" is the personologist's construct? If so, might this explain why we have so many different theories of personality? What, then, is the relationship between personologists' constructs and their basic assumptions concerning human nature?

7 Complete the Gridform of the Rep Test in Figure 9-2 with your own constructs. Does this exercise help you to understand your own constructs as well as what is meant precisely by the term "construct"? How?

8 What does research using the Rep Test reveal about the formation and breakup of friendships? Do you think it is possible for two people to maintain a friendship even though they do not share similar constructs?

9 How does Kelly reinterpret the emotional states of anxiety and guilt in line with his personal construct theory of personality?

10 What is fixed-role therapy? Do you believe that certain kinds of clients would respond to this form of therapy better than others? What kinds of clients and why?

GLOSSARY

Anxiety The feeling of dread and apprehension that results from one's being aware of not having constructs by which to interpret an event.

Choice corollary The proposition that, when confronted with a choice, people will opt for the alternative that is most likely either to enhance their understanding of reality or to clarify their present construct system.

Circumspection-preemption-control cycle The process by which a person considers several constructs before deciding how to construe a novel or uncertain event.

Cognitive complexity-simplicity The extent to which a person's personal construct system is elaborate or simple; usually refers to the number of constructs that someone displays when taking the Rep Test.

Commonality corollary The proposition that people are similar to one another to the extent that they interpret experiences in similar ways.

Cognitive theory Any theory of personality that emphasizes the importance of cognitive processes (e.g., thinking, perceiving, judging) in understanding human behavior.

Constellatory construct Type of construct that permits its elements to belong to other realms concurrently; however, once the elements are identified in a particular way, they are fixed. Stereotyped thinking illustrates this type of construct.

Construct *See* personal construct.

Constructive alternativism Kelly's philosophical assumption that human beings are capable of revising or changing their interpretation of events. Also, objective reality can be looked at from a number of different perspectives.

Experience corollary The proposition that a person's construct system changes in relation to its inability to correctly predict the unfolding sequence of events; those constructs found to be useful are retained, whereas those that are not are revised or discarded.

Fixed-role sketch Description of the personality of a fictional individual designed to help a client construe himself or herself in a different way so that he or she will be better able to deal with various life situations.

Fixed-role therapy A psychotherapy procedure developed by Kelly and aimed at helping clients to reconstrue themselves and their life situations. Clients are encouraged to develop and act out new roles, both within and outside the therapeutic setting.

Focus of convenience A point or area within a construct's range of convenience at which it is maximally useful in construing certain events; it is always specific to the person employing the construct.

Fundamental postulate A term that reflects Kelly's belief that a person's behavior is determined by the personal constructs used to predict future events.

Guilt The person's awareness of having deviated from the important roles by which he or she maintains relationships to others.

Hostility The attempt to hold onto an invalid construct in the face of contradictory evidence. A hostile person attempts to make others behave in ways that fit his or her unrealistic expectations.

Individuality corollary The proposition that differences between people are rooted in their construing events from different perspectives.

Modulation corollary The proposition that a person's construct system will change to the extent that he or she is capable of construing new events or reconstruing old events.

Organization corollary The proposition that a person's constructs are arranged hierarchically so as to minimize incompatibilities and inconsistencies.

Permeability–impermeability Dimension concerned with the issue of whether new elements will or will not be admitted within the boundaries of a construct. A permeable construct allows new information into its context; an impermeable one cannot.

Personal construct   A category of thought by which the person interprets or construes his or her life experiences. At least three elements are needed to form a construct; two of the elements must be perceived as similar to each other, while the third element must be perceived as different from these two.

Personality   For Kelly, the term personality refers to the personal constructs used by a person to anticipate future events.

Predictive efficiency   The extent to which a construct is useful in enabling a person to correctly predict and anticipate some event in his or her environment.

Preemptive construct   Type of construct that freezes (''preempts'') its elements for membership exclusively in its own realm; e.g., use of ethnic labels.

Propositional construct   Type of construct that allows a person to be open to new experiences and to adopt alternative views of the world.

Range of convenience   The scope of events for which a particular construct may be relevant or applicable.

Role Construct Repertory Test   Test devised by Kelly to assess the individual's personal construct system; also known as the *Rep Test*.

Serial invalidation hypothesis   Bannister's theory that schizophrenia results from repeated contradiction of interpersonal constructs.

Sociality corollary   The proposition that harmonious interpersonal relationships depend on the participants' mutual understanding of each other's construct system.

Subordinate construct   Personal construct that is subsumed under a more general construct.

Superordinate construct   Personal construct that controls and subsumes many different constructs.

Threat   The person's awareness that his or her construct system is about to be drastically changed.

CHAPTER 10

THE HUMANISTIC PERSPECTIVE IN PERSONALITY THEORY: ABRAHAM MASLOW

Theoretical perspectives on personality are often classified in terms of three major categories. The first, that of *psychoanalysis,* presents an image of humans as creatures of instinct and intrapsychic conflict. This bleak conception of humanity emerged from Freud's study of mentally disturbed persons and emphasized unconscious and irrational forces as the controlling factors in behavior. The second perspective in personality psychology, that of *behaviorism,* views humans as little more than malleable and passive victims of forces in the environment. As exemplified by B. F. Skinner, behaviorists stress learning and experience as the basic building blocks of the qualities we think of as personality. *Humanistic* psychology, the third and most recent perspective on personality, offers a radically different picture of our species. Personologists who align themselves with this orientation (also referred to as the "third force" or "human potential movement") proclaim that human beings are intrinsically good and self-perfecting. According to this view, it is human nature to move consistently in the direction of personal growth, creativity, and self-sufficiency, unless there are extremely strong environmental conditions to the contrary. Proponents of humanistic psychology also maintain that people are largely conscious and rational beings who are not dominated by unconscious needs and conflicts. In general, humanistic personologists view people as active shapers of their own lives, with freedom to choose and develop a life-style limited only by physical or social constraints.

Several personality theorists share significant humanistic emphases (for instance, Fromm, Allport, Kelly, and Rogers). However, Abraham Maslow is generally acknowledged as the foremost spokesperson for humanistic personality theory. His self-actualization theory of personality, based on the study of healthy and mature people, clearly illustrates the themes and assumptions that characterize the humanistic perspective:

> Human life will never be understood unless its highest aspirations are taken into account. Growth, self-actualization, the striving toward health, the quest for identity and autonomy, the yearning for excellence (and other ways of phrasing the striving "upward") must now be accepted beyond question as a widespread and perhaps universal tendency. (Maslow, 1987, p. xx)

Maslow's theory—emphasizing as it does the uniqueness of the person and the potential for self-direction and enhanced functioning—has tremendous appeal for those who share his optimistic view of humanity. His contributions to the study and understanding of personality are the focus of this chapter.

ABRAHAM MASLOW: A Humanistic Theory of Personality

BIOGRAPHICAL SKETCH

Abraham Harold Maslow was born in Brooklyn, New York, in 1908, the son of uneducated Jewish parents who had emigrated from Russia. The eldest of seven children, Maslow was encouraged by his parents to be academically successful, yet by his own admission he experienced considerable loneliness and suffering during most of his childhood years: "With my childhood, it's a wonder I'm not psychotic. I was a little Jewish boy in the non-Jewish neighborhood. It was a little like being the first Negro enrolled in the all-white school. I was isolated and unhappy. I grew up in libraries and among books, without friends" (Hall, 1968, p. 37). Later he experienced the practical side of life, working many summers for his family's barrel manufacturing company.

Maslow's relationship with his mother was marked by bitterness and animosity. A recent biographer (Hoffman, 1988) describes how Maslow's intense hatred toward his mother persisted until the day she died. She was a very religious woman who often threatened her son that God would punish him for the slightest misdeed. As a result, Maslow learned to despise and mistrust religion.

> He even refused to attend her funeral. He characterized Rose Maslow as a cruel, ignorant, and hostile figure, one so unloving as to nearly induce madness in her children. In all of Maslow's references to his mother—some uttered publicly while she was still alive—there is not one that expresses any warmth or affection. (Hoffman, 1988, p. 7)

Maslow recalled his father as a man who "loved whiskey and women and fighting" (Wilson, 1972, p. 131). Furthermore, his father instilled in him the feeling of being ugly and stupid. Later in life, Maslow made peace with his father and often spoke of him affectionately. However, he never forgave his mother for the way she treated him during his childhood and adolescence.

Maslow began his college education by studying law in an effort to please his father. Two weeks of study at City College of New York convinced him that he

Abraham H. Maslow. (*Courtesy of Abraham Maslow*)

could not become a lawyer, so he undertook a more eclectic course of study at Cornell University. In his junior year Maslow transferred to the University of Wisconsin, where he subsequently received all his formal academic training in psychology, obtaining his B.A. degree in 1930, his M.A. in 1931, and his Ph.D. in 1934. During his graduate years at Wisconsin, he worked with Harry Harlow, a well-known psychologist who was in the process of developing a primate laboratory to study the behavior of rhesus monkeys. Maslow's own doctoral study focused on the sexual and dominance characteristics in a colony of monkeys!

Shortly before he moved to Wisconsin, Maslow married Bertha Goodman, his high school sweetheart. His parents strongly protested the marriage since the couple were first cousins and it was feared they might produce children with genetic defects. Nonetheless, his marriage to Bertha and his academic experiences at Wisconsin were extremely important events in Maslow's life. He once stated that "Life didn't really start for me until I got married and went to Wisconsin" (Hall, 1968, p. 37).

After receiving his Ph.D., Maslow returned to New York to work with the famous learning theorist E. L. Thorndike at Columbia University. He then moved to Brooklyn College, where he remained for the next 14 years. Maslow described New York City during this period, particularly the late 1930s and early 1940s, as the center of the psychological universe. It was here that he personally encountered the cream of European intellectuals who were forced to flee from Hitler. Erich Fromm, Alfred Adler, Karen Horney, Ruth Benedict, and Max Wertheimer were a few of those whom Maslow sought out to enhance his understanding of human behavior. The informal conversations and challenging experiences afforded by such distinguished scholars helped shape the intellectual foundations for Maslow's later humanistic views. He was also psychoanalyzed during this time.

In 1951 Maslow was appointed chairperson of the Psychology Department at

Brandeis University and held that position until 1961, after which he continued as professor of psychology. In 1969 he took a leave of absence from Brandeis to become a resident fellow at the W. P. Laughlin Charitable Foundation in Menlo Park, California. This nonacademic post would have allowed him complete freedom to pursue his interests in the philosophy of democratic politics, economics, and ethics. But in 1970, at the age of 62, Maslow died of a heart attack, after a chronic history of heart disease.

Maslow was affiliated with a number of professional and honorary societies. As a member of the American Psychological Association he was president of the Division of Personality and Social Psychology as well as of the Division of Esthetics and was elected president of the entire association for 1967–1968. He was also a founding editor of both the *Journal of Humanistic Psychology* and the *Journal of Transpersonal Psychology* and served as consulting editor of numerous other scholarly periodicals. Maslow was vitally interested in growth psychology and, toward the end of his life, he supported the Esalen Institute in California and other groups involved in the human potential movement.

The majority of Maslow's books were written within the last 10 years of his life and include: *Toward a Psychology of Being* (1968); *Religions, Values, and Peak Experiences* (1964); *Eupsychian Management: A Journal* (1965); *The Psychology of Science: A Reconnaissance* (1966); *Motivation and Personality* (1987, 3rd edition); and *The Farther Reaches of Human Nature* (1971, a collection of articles previously published by Maslow in various psychological journals). A volume compiled with the assistance of his wife and entitled *Abraham H. Maslow: A Memorial Volume* was published posthumously in 1972.

BASIC TENETS OF HUMANISTIC PSYCHOLOGY

The term *humanistic psychology* was coined by a group of personologists who, in the early 1960s under the leadership of Maslow, joined to establish a viable theoretical alternative to the two most influential intellectual currents in mainstream psychology—psychoanalysis and behaviorism. Unlike the others, humanistic psychology is not a single organized theory or system; it might better be viewed as a movement (i.e., a diverse group of theoretical approaches to personality and clinical psychology). Maslow called it *third force psychology*. Although proponents of this movement represent a wide spectrum of views, they do share certain fundamental conceptions of human nature. Practically all these shared concepts have deep roots in the history of Western philosophical thinking (Durant, 1977). More specifically, humanistic psychology is heavily steeped in existential philosophy as developed by such European thinkers and writers as Soren Kierkegaard (1813–1855), Karl Jaspers (1883–1969), Martin Heidegger (1889–1976), and Jean-Paul Sartre (1905–1980). Several prominent psychologists have also been influential in promoting a humanistic approach to personality. The best known among these include Erich Fromm, Gordon Allport, Carl Rogers, Victor Frankl, and Rollo May.

An *existentialist* perspective on the person begins with the concrete and specific consciousness of a single human being existing at a particular moment in time and space. Existentialists suggest that each of us exists as a "being-in-the-world," consciously and painfully aware of our existence and eventual nonexistence (death). We have no existence apart from the world and the world has no meaning for us apart from the people who are in it. Rejecting the notion that a person is either a product of hereditary (genetic) factors or environmental influences (especially early ones), existentialists stress the idea that ultimately each of us is responsible for who we are and what we become. As Sartre put it, "Man is nothing else but what he makes of himself. Such is the first principle of existentialism" (1957, p. 15). Thus, existentialists believe that each of us is challenged to make something meaningful out of our lives in a world that appears absurd. In a profound sense, then, "life is what we make of it." The uniquely human experiences of freedom and responsibility for creating meaning are not to be taken lightly. At times, they can be burdensome and even frightening. As the existentialists see it, as people realize that they are in charge of their own destiny, they experience the pain of despair, loneliness, and anxiety.

Human beings, thrown into the world at a given moment in time and space, are solely responsible for the choices they make. This does not mean that given freedom of choice, people will necessarily act in their own best interests. Having the freedom to choose does not ensure that all the choices will be good or wise ones. If this were so, people would not be afflicted with despair, alienation, anxiety, boredom, guilt, and a host of other self-imposed ailments. For the existentialists, the question is whether or not the person can live an authentic (honest and genuine) existence in the wake of life's perceived randomness and ambiguity. Because existential philosophy believes each person is responsible for his or her actions, it appeals to humanistic psychology; humanistic theorists also stress that each person is the chief architect of his or her behavior and experience. The human being is a conscious agent—experiencing, deciding, and freely choosing his or her actions. Humanistic psychology, then, takes as its basic model the responsible human being freely making choices among the possibilities that are open. As Sartre noted: "I *am* my choices."

The most important concept that humanistic psychologists have extracted from existentialism is that of *becoming*. A person is never static; she is always in the process of becoming a new person. A college senior is decidedly different from the clothes-swapping, giggling teenager of 4 years ago. And 4 years from now she may be radically different as a result of pursuing new and different avenues of fulfillment in life, such as becoming a parent or advancing in a career. Accordingly, it is the person's responsibility as a free agent to realize as many of his or her potentialities as possible; only by actualizing these can the person live a truly authentic life. Thus, in the existential-humanistic view, the quest for an authentic existence requires more than the fulfillment of biological needs and of sexual and aggressive urges. Conversely, people who refuse to become have refused to grow; they have denied themselves the full possibilities of human existence. Humanistically speaking, this is a tragedy and a distortion of what human beings can be since it limits life's possibilities. In simple terms, it is wrong for people to refuse making the most of every moment of their existence, and for fulfilling that existence to the best of their ability. Men and women who refuse to accept the challenge of creating a meaningful and authentic life reflect what the existentialists call bad faith. Those who live in bad faith fail to grapple with the ultimate issues concerning their existence. Who am I? Is my life meaningful or absurd? How can I realize my humanity, even though I am forever alone in the world? Instead, they affirm the meaning of their lives through blind conformity to society's expectations and are said to be living an inauthentic life.

Despite the high value placed on becoming, humanistic psychologists recognize that the quest for a meaningful and fulfilling life is not an easy one. This is especially true in an age of profound cultural change and conflict, where traditional beliefs and values no longer provide adequate guidelines for the good life or for finding meaning in human existence. In a bureaucratic society the individual tends to be depersonalized and submerged in the group. Thus, some people become alienated and estranged—strangers to themselves and to other men and women. Other people lack "the courage to be"—to break away from old patterns, to stand on their own, and to seek new and more fulfilling pathways to greater self-actualization. They prefer to rely on what is sanctioned or valued by friends, family, teachers, religion, social customs, or society at large. But the freedom to shape their existence can be a blessing as well as a curse: humanistic psychologists maintain that this predicament can challenge people to make something worthwhile of their lives. They must all accept responsibility for making choices and directing their own destiny. For whether any of them asked to be born or not, here they are in the world and they are responsible for one human life—their own. To flee from their freedom and responsibility is to be inauthentic, to show bad faith, and ultimately to live in despair.

Finally, existentialists assert that the only "reality" anyone ever knows is subjective or personal, not objective. This outlook may be designated in a shorthand way as the *phenomenological* or "here-and-now" perspective. Existentialists and humanists alike emphasize subjective experience as the primary phenomenon in the study and understanding of humanity. Both theoretical explanations and overt behavior are secondary to immediate experience and its unique meaning to the experiencer. As Maslow reminded us: "There is no substitute for experience, none at all" (1966, p. 45).

Scattered throughout his various theoretical writings Maslow set forth his version of what constitutes a humanistic personality theory. As will become increasingly evident, his personological perspective sharply contradicts theories dominant for the past half century, especially psychoanalysis and behaviorism. But before exploring in more depth what this approach to personality is all about, let us examine the key elements of Maslow's humanistic perspective.

The Individual as an Integrated Whole   One of the most fundamental themes underlying Maslow's humanistic stance is that each person must be studied as an integrated, unique, organized whole. He felt that for too long psychologists had focused on minute analyses of separate events, neglecting what they were trying to understand, namely, the whole person. In a commonplace metaphor, psychologists studied the trees, not the forest. In fact, Maslow's theory was primarily developed as a revolt against those theories (especially behaviorism) that dealt in bits and pieces of behavior while ignoring the person as a unified whole. For Maslow, the human organism always behaves as a *unified* whole, not as a series of differentiated parts, and what happens in any part affects the entire organism. This holistic view, captured in the often quoted Gestalt phrase, "The whole is greater than and different from the sum of its parts" is unmistakably evident in all of Maslow's theoretical writings.

In Maslow's theory, motivation affects the person as a whole rather than just in part:

> In good theory there is no such entity as a need of the stomach or mouth, or a genital need. There is only a need of the individual. It is John Smith who wants food, not John Smith's stomach. Furthermore, satisfaction comes to the whole individual and not just to a part of him. Food satisfies John Smith's hunger and not his stomach's hunger. . . . when John Smith is hungry, he is hungry all over. (1987, p. 3)

For Maslow, then, the central characteristic of personality is its essential unity and totality.

Irrelevance of Animal Research   Proponents of humanistic psychology recognize a profound difference between human and animal behavior. For them, human beings are more than just animals; they are special kinds of animals. This is in sharp contrast to radical behaviorism, which relies heavily on infrahuman research (e.g., rats and pigeons) in developing explanations of human behavior. Unlike the behaviorists, who emphasize humanity's continuity with the animal world, Maslow regarded the human being as different from all other animals. He believed that behaviorism and its accompanying philosophies have "dehumanized" the person, leaving little more than a machine composed of chains of conditioned and unconditioned reflexes. Thus, animal research is irrelevant to the understanding of human behavior because it ignores those characteristics that are uniquely human (e.g., ideals, values, courage, love, humor, jealousy, guilt) and, equally important, what it takes to produce poetry, music, science, and other works of the mind.

Humanity's Inner Nature   Freud's theory explicitly assumed that human beings are at the mercy of unconscious and irrational forces. Furthermore, Freud argued that unless instinctive impulses are controlled, destruction of others or the self will result. Whether or not this view is accurate, Freud placed little faith in human virtue and speculated pessimistically on the course of human destiny. Those who endorse a humanistic view maintain that *human nature is essentially good*—or, at the very least, neutral. You might not be able to accept this view while being mugged during a stroll in the park at night. However, from Maslow's perspective, the evil, destructive, and violent forces in people result from the frustration or thwarting of basic needs rather than from any inherent wickedness on their part. He believed that human nature has a built-in structure comprised of potentialities for positive growth and improvement that are common to all people. It was this optimistic and uplifting portrayal of humanity that Maslow promoted during his lifetime.

Human Creative Potential   The primacy of human creativity is perhaps the most significant concept of humanistic psychology. Maslow (1950) merits the distinction of being the first to point out that creativeness is the most universal characteristic of the people he studied or observed. Describing it as an attribute common to human nature, Maslow (1987) viewed creativity as potentially present in all people at birth. It is natural—trees sprout leaves, birds fly, humans create. However, he also recognized that most human beings lose it as they become "enculturated" (formal education stamps out a lot of it). Fortunately, a few individuals hold onto this fresh, naive, and direct way of looking at things or, if they number among the majority who lose it, are able to recover it later in life. Maslow theorized that since creativity is potential in anyone, it requires no special talents or capacities. We need not write books, compose music, or produce art objects to be creative. Comparatively few people do. Creativity is a universal human function and leads to all forms of self-expression. Thus, for example, there can be creative disc jockeys, computer programmers, business executives, sales clerks, and even college professors!

Emphasis on Psychological Health   Maslow argued that none of the available psychological approaches to the study of behavior does justice to the healthy human being's functioning, mode of living, or life goals. In particular, he strongly criticized Freud's preoccupation with the study of sickness, pathology, and maladjustment. Quite simply, Maslow considered psychoanalytic theory to be one-sided and lacking in comprehensiveness since it was grounded in the abnormal or "sick" part of human nature (i.e., its frailties and shortcomings), ignoring humanity's strengths and virtues.

To correct this deficiency, Maslow focused attention on the psychologically *healthy person* and the understanding of such a person in terms other than comparison with the mentally ill. It was his belief that we cannot understand mental illness until we first understand mental health. Stated more baldly, Maslow (1987) argued that the study of crippled, immature, and unhealthy specimens can yield only a "crippled" psychology. He strongly urged the study of self-actualizing, psychologically healthy persons as the basis for a more universal science of psychology. Accordingly, humanistic psychology considers self-fulfillment to be the main theme in human life—a theme never revealed by studying disturbed individuals alone.

Maslow's humanistic writings on personality found a receptive audience among psychologists in the 1960s and 1970s. For many, his approach, emphasizing the study of joy, love, creativity, choice, and self-realization, offered an optimistic alternative to what they considered as mechanistic and dehumanizing models of human behavior. Although the popularity of the humanistic perspective has faded somewhat since then, its impact on mainstream psychology and personality theory is still quite evident. The fields of counseling, social work, education, nursing, business management, and marketing have also been influenced by Maslow's ideas (Leonard, 1983).

MOTIVATION: THE HIERARCHY OF NEEDS

The question of motivation may be the most fundamental issue in all of personality psychology. Maslow (1968, 1987) believed that people are motivated to seek personal goals that make their lives rewarding and meaningful. In fact, *motivational processes* lie at the very core of his personality theory. Maslow depicted the human being as a "wanting organism" who rarely reaches a state of complete and total satisfaction. The absence of wanting or needing something, if and when it exists, is short-lived at best. As one general type of need is satisfied, another surfaces and commands the person's attention and efforts. When a person satisfies this one, still another clamors for satisfaction. It is characteristic of human life that people are almost always desiring something.

Maslow proposed that all human needs are *innate* or *instinctoid* and that they are systematically arranged in an ascending hierarchy of priority or prepotency. Figure 10-1 is a schematic representation of this need-hierarchy conception of human motivation. The needs are, in order of their priority: (1) physiological needs; (2) safety and security needs; (3) belongingness and love needs; (4) self-

FIGURE 10-1   A schematic representation of Maslow's hierarchy of needs.

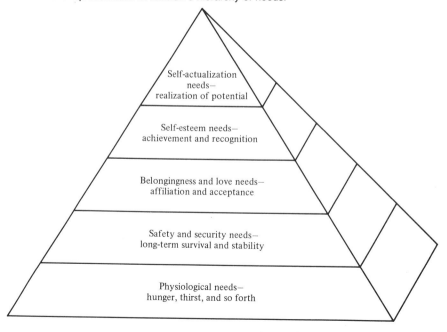

Self-actualization needs— realization of potential

Self-esteem needs— achievement and recognition

Belongingness and love needs— affiliation and acceptance

Safety and security needs— long-term survival and stability

Physiological needs— hunger, thirst, and so forth

esteem needs; and (5) self-actualization needs, or the need for personal fulfillment. Underlying this scheme is the assumption that lower-order, prepotent needs must be relatively satisfied before the person can become aware of or motivated by higher-order needs. That is, one general type of need must be satisfied fairly well before another higher-order need emerges and becomes operative. Gratification of needs lower in the hierarchy allows for awareness of and motivation by needs higher in the hierarchy. Thus, physiological needs must be reasonably met before safety needs become salient; both physiological and safety-security needs must be satisfied to some degree before the needs for belongingness and love emerge and press for satisfaction, and so forth. For Maslow, this sequential arrangement of basic needs in a nested hierarchy of lesser or greater potency is the chief principle or organization underlying human motivation. He posited that the hierarchy of needs is species-wide and that the farther up the hierarchy the person is able to go, the more individuality, humanness, and psychological health he or she will demonstrate.

Maslow acknowledged that there may be exceptions to this hierarchical arrangement of motives. He recognized that some creative people have pursued the development and expression of their special talents despite serious hardships and social ridicule. There are also people whose values and ideals are so strong that they are willing to suffer hunger or thirst or even die rather than renounce them. For example, social and political activists in South Africa, the Baltic states, and eastern European countries have continued their struggles despite harrassment, jail sentences, physical deprivation, and, often, certain death. The staged hunger strikes by hundreds of Chinese students in Tiananmen Square is still another example. Finally, Maslow speculated that some people might get their hierarchies scrambled due to unusual factors in their personal history. For instance, people may place a higher priority on their esteem needs than on their love and belongingness needs. Such people are more concerned about their prestige and career advancement than they are about their intimate relationships or family. In general, however, the lower the need in the hierarchy, the greater its strength or priority tends to be.

A key notion in Maslow's need hierarchy is that needs are not gratified in an all-or-none manner. Instead, needs overlap and a person may be motivated by two or more need levels at any one time. Maslow (1970) speculated that the average person has his or her needs met to these levels: 85 percent physiological, 70 percent safety and security, 50 percent love and belongingness, 40 percent self-esteem, and 10 percent self-actualization. Furthermore, the needs appearing in the hierarchy emerge gradually. People do not simply move in lock-step fashion from one need level to the next, but are both partially satisfied and not satisfied in their needs at the same time. It should also be noted that no matter how far up the need hierarchy a person has advanced, if a lower level need is frustrated the person will return to the unsatisfied level and remain there until that need is reasonably satisfied.

Let us now examine each of Maslow's need categories and see what each involves.

Physiological Needs

The most basic, powerful, and urgent of all human needs are those that are essential to physical survival. Included in this group are the needs for food, drink, oxygen, exercise, sleep, protection from extreme temperatures, and sensory stimulation. These *physiological needs* are directly concerned with the biological maintenance of the person and must be gratified at some minimal level before the next higher order need attains importance. Put another way, a person who fails to satisfy this basic level of needs will not be around long enough to become concerned about needs at higher levels in the hierarchy.

Admittedly, the social and physical environment in American culture provides for the satisfaction of primary needs for most persons. However, if one of these needs remains unsatisfied, the individual rapidly becomes dominated by it, so that all other needs quickly vanish or become secondary. The chronically hungry person is not likely to strive to compose music, pursue a career, or build a brave new world. Such a person is too preoccupied with getting something to eat.

Life-sustaining needs are crucial to the understanding of human behavior. The devastating effects on behavior produced by the lack of food or water have been chronicled in numerous experiments and autobiographies. One example of how human behavior can be dominated by hunger is provided by a study of men who were excused from required military duty during World War II because they were conscientious objectors. They agreed to go on a semi-starvation diet to investigate the effects of food deprivation (Keys et al., 1950). As the study progressed and the men began to lose substantial body weight, they became apathetic about nearly everything but eating. They talked about food constantly, and cookbooks became their favorite reading material. Many of the men even lost interest in their girlfriends! This and many other recorded incidents illustrate how attention usually shifts from higher needs to the lower needs that are being thwarted.

Safety and Security Needs

Once the physiological needs are fairly well satisfied, the person becomes concerned with a new set, often called the *safety and security needs*. Included here are the needs for structure, stability, law and order, predictability, and freedom from such threatening forces as illness, fear, and chaos. Thus, these needs reflect concern about long-term survival.

Maslow suggested that the safety and security needs are most readily observed in infants and young children because of their relative helplessness and dependence on adults. Infants, for instance, respond fearfully if they are suddenly dropped or startled by loud noises or flashing lights. The urgency of safety needs is also evident when a child becomes ill. A child with a broken leg may temporarily experience fears, have nightmares, and manifest a need for protection and reassurance not evident before the accident.

Another indication of the need for safety is the child's preference for some kind of dependable, undisrupted routine. According to Maslow, young children function most effectively in a family setting that has at least a certain degree of structured routine and discipline. If such elements are absent in the environment, a child will feel insecure, anxious, mistrustful, and seek out more stable areas of life. Maslow further noted that parents who apply only unrestricted, permissive child-rearing practices do not satisfy a child's safety and security needs. Not to require a child to go to bed at a certain time or to eat at somewhat regular intervals will only cause confusion or fright. The child then has nothing stable in the environment upon which to depend. Maslow cited parental quarreling, physical assault, separation, divorce, and death within the family as particularly harmful to a child's sense of well-being. In effect, these factors render the child's environment unstable, unpredictable, and, hence, unsafe.

Safety and security needs also exert an active influence beyond childhood. The preference for a job with tenure and financial protection, the establishment of savings accounts, and the acquisition of insurance (e.g., medical, unemployment) may be regarded as partly motivated by safety seeking. In part, religious and philosophical belief systems may help a person to organize his or her world and the people in it into a coherent and meaningful whole, thus making the person feel ''safe.'' Other expressions of the needs for safety and security occur when people are confronted with real emergencies (such as war, floods, earthquakes, riots, societal disorganizations, and similar conditions).

Maslow further suggested that certain types of neurotic adults (especially obsessive-compulsive types) are predominantly motivated by the search for safety. Some neurotics behave as if a great catastrophe were imminent, frantically attempting to stabilize their world in a neat, disciplined, orderly fashion so that new contingencies may not appear. The neurotic's safety needs ''often find specific expression in a search for a protector, or a stronger person or system, on whom he may depend'' (Maslow, 1987, p. 19).

Belongingness and Love Needs

The third tier in Maslow's pyramid is comprised of *belongingness and love needs*. These needs become prominent when the physiological and safety/security needs have been met. The person operating at this level longs for affectionate relationships with others, for a place in his or her family and/or reference groups. Group affiliation becomes a dominant goal for the person. Accordingly, a person will feel keenly the pangs of loneliness, social ostracism, friendlessness, and rejection, especially when induced by the absence of friends and loved ones. Students who attend college far from home fall prey to the effects of belongingness needs, striving to be recognized and accepted within a peer group.

Love and belongingness needs play a significant role throughout our lives. The child longs for a loving and caring atmosphere, one in which all his or her needs are provided for, coupled with a great deal of physical affection. The adolescent, seeking love in the form of respect and acknowledgment of his or her independence as a self-governing person, gravitates toward membership in religious, musical, athletic, academic, or other closely knit groups. The young adult wants love in the form of sexual intimacy, that is, to experience romantic involvement

The child's belongingness and love needs can be satisfied through an affectionate relationship with a parent. (*Joel Gordon*)

with a member of the opposite sex. The lyrics of popular songs give ample testimony to the powerful hold that love and belongingness needs have at this stage of life.

Maslow (1968) identified two kinds of adult love: *Deficiency* or *D-love* and *Being* or *B-love*. The former (D-love) is based on a deficit need—it is love out of a need for something we lack, such as self-esteem, sex, or someone to keep us from being lonely. For instance, a relationship may satisfy our need for comfort and security—whether it be going steady, living with another, or marriage. Thus, it is a selfish love, concerned with taking, not giving. The latter (B-love), by contrast, is based on valuing the other person as a person, as an end in himself or herself, without any desire to change or to use that individual in any way. Maslow expressed this as loving the "being" of the other despite his or her imperfections. It is nonpossessive, nonintrusive, and concerned primarily with fostering in the other person a positive self-image, self-acceptance, a feeling of love-worthiness, all of which permit the individual to grow. Furthermore, Maslow rejected the Freudian notion that love and affection are derived from sublimated sexual instincts; to Maslow, love is not synonymous with sex. Rather, he contended that mature love involves a healthy, loving relationship between two people, which includes mutual respect, admiration, and trust. Being loved and accepted is instrumental to healthy feelings of worth. Not being loved generates futility, emptiness, and hostility.

Despite the scarcity of empirical data concerning the belongingness and love needs, Maslow insisted that their behavioral effects are potentially disruptive in a fluid and mobile society such as the United States. America has become a land of nomads (census experts estimate that approximately one-fifth of the population change their addresses at least once a year), a nation of people who are rootless, alienated, indifferent to community and home problems, and afflicted with shallowness in personal relationships. Despite the fact that people live in densely populated settings, they often do not interact. Many people barely recognize the names and faces of the people next door, let alone socialize with them. In brief, there is no escaping the conclusion that the search for intimate relationships ranks as one of the most widespread social needs across humanity.

It was Maslow's contention that the belongingness and love needs are often frustrated in American society, resulting in maladjustment and pathology. Many people are reluctant to disclose themselves in intimate relationships, since they fear rejection. Maslow concluded that there is mounting evidence to prove a substantial correlation between affectionate childhood experiences and a healthy adulthood. Such data, in his view, support the generalization that love is a basic prerequisite of healthy development of the human being.

Self-Esteem Needs

When our needs for being loved and for loving others have been reasonably gratified, their motivating force diminishes, paving the way for *self-esteem needs*. Maslow divided these into two basic types: self-respect and respect from others. The former includes such concerns as desire for competence, confidence, achievement, independence, and freedom. A person needs to know that he or she is worthwhile—capable of mastering tasks and challenges in life. Respect from others entails such concerns as desire for prestige, recognition, reputation, status, appreciation, and acceptance. In this case the person needs to know that what he or she can do is recognized and valued by significant others.

Satisfaction of the self-esteem needs generates feelings and attitudes of self-confidence, self-worth, capability, and the sense of being useful and necessary in the world. In contrast, the frustration of these needs leads to feelings and attitudes of inferiority, ineptness, weakness, passivity, and dependency. These negative self-perceptions, in turn, may give rise to basic discouragement, a sense of futility and hopelessness in dealing with life's demands, and a low evaluation of self vis-à-vis others. Children who are denied their need for respect and recognition are particularly prone to acquiring a poor self-image (Coopersmith, 1967).

Maslow emphasized that healthy self-esteem is based on earned respect from others rather than on fame, social status, or adulation. Accordingly, there is a real psychological danger in basing our esteem needs on the opinions of others rather than on demonstrated ability, achievement, and adequacy. Once we come to rely exclusively upon the opinions of others for our self-esteem, we are in psychological jeopardy. To be solid, self-esteem must be founded on our *actual* worth, not on external factors outside our control.

It is evident that esteem needs vary widely in expression and intensity throughout the life cycle. Peer approval, the very essence of esteem for a teenager, may be defined as being popular and being invited to parties, whereas for the adult, esteem typically derives from being a parent, having a well-paying job, and contributing to civic organizations in the community. Maslow (1987) suggested

Satisfaction of the need for self-esteem allows a child to feel confident in the presence of peers. (*Elizabeth Hamlin/Stock, Boston*)

that esteem needs tend to reach a plateau in adulthood and then diminish in intensity during the middle years. The reasons for this are twofold. First, adults usually acquire a more realistic appraisal of their true worth and value, so that the esteem needs no longer continue as significant forces in their lives. Second, most adults have already experienced an adequate amount of esteem gratification, thus enabling them to move onto higher and more satisfying levels of growth motivation. These reasons may account in part for Maslow's claim that true self-actualization occurs only in the years following middle age.

Self-Actualization Needs

Finally, if all the foregoing needs are sufficiently satisfied, the need for self-actualization comes to the fore. Maslow (1987) characterized *self-actualization* as the person's desire to become everything that he or she is capable of becoming. The person who has achieved this highest level presses toward the full use and exploitation of his or her talents, capacities, and potentialities. In short, to self-actualize is to become the kind of person we are capable of becoming—to reach the peak of our potential. In Maslow's words, "Musicians must make music, artists must paint, poets must write if they are to be ultimately at peace with themselves. What humans can be, they must be. They must be true to their own nature" (1987, p. 22).

Self-actualization need not take the form of creative and artistic endeavors. A parent, an athlete, a student or teacher, or an ardent laborer may all be actualizing their potentials in doing well what each does best; specific forms of self-actualization vary greatly from person to person. It is at this uppermost level of Maslow's need hierarchy that individual differences are the greatest.

As an illustration of self-actualization in action, suppose that Nancy is taking a personality course as part of a long-term plan to become a clinical psychologist. Other theorists could probably explain why she selected this career alternative. Freud might say it is related to her deeply repressed childhood curiosity about sex, while Adler might see it as an attempt to compensate for some childhood inferiority. Skinner, on the other hand, might say it is a product of her conditioning history, while Bandura could relate it to social cognitive variables. Maslow, however, would argue that Nancy might be moving toward becoming the kind of person that she really wants to become—that she is pulled toward this career goal by the need for self-actualization.

Now, suppose further that Nancy has passed the numerous psychology graduate courses, completed the required 2000-hour internship, conducted a doctoral dissertation, and finally obtained a Ph.D. in clinical psychology. Then somebody offers her a job as a drug enforcement officer in Miami. The job pays extremely well, provides excellent perks, and guarantees steady employment and challenging experiences. Would these benefits lead her to accept the position? If her answer is yes, go back three spaces to level two (safety needs)—psychologically, that is where she is. If she would not take it, why not? Certainly not because the job lacks social value: Miami certainly would not be as safe a place in which to live without drug enforcement officers than without psychologists. From Maslow's perspective, the key issue is that what Nancy can be, she must be. Given her talents and aspirations, she would simply have less chance for self-actualization if she decided to pursue a career in drug enforcement because of the pay, job security, perks, and so on. She would probably hold out instead for a job as a clinical psychologist so that she could develop her capacities, become the kind of person that she really wants to become, and, in brief, self-actualize. Maslow's concept of self-actualization is exciting and refreshing because it makes a person look up to what he or she can be—and thus live with zest and purpose.

Why Self-Actualization Is Rarely Achieved

Maslow theorized that most, if not all, of humanity needs and seeks inner fulfillment. His own research led him to conclude that the impulse toward realizing our potentialities is both natural and necessary. Yet only a few—usually the gifted—ever achieve it (less than 1 percent of the entire population, Maslow estimated). In part, he believed that this extremely unfortunate state of affairs exists because many people are simply blind to their potential; they neither know that it exists nor understand the rewards of self-enhancement. Rather, they tend to doubt and even fear their own abilities, thereby diminishing their chances of becoming self-actualized. Maslow referred to this as the *Jonah complex*. It is characterized by a fear of success that prevents a person from aspiring to greatness and self-fulfillment.

In addition, the social and cultural environment often stifles the tendency toward actualization by imposing certain norms on segments of the population. One example is the cultural stereotype of what is masculine and what is not. Such human qualities as sympathy, kindness, gentleness, and tenderness are often discouraged among males because of the cultural tendency to consider such characteristics "unmasculine." Or consider the stifling effects that the traditional female role has upon the psychosocial development of women (Eagly, 1987; Tavris & Wade, 1984). Following from such considerations, actualization of the highest potentials—on a mass basis—is possible only under "good conditions." Or, more directly, people will generally need a "facilitative" society in which to maximize their human potentials to the fullest. At this point in human history, no society fully facilitates the self-actualization of all its members, although, admittedly, some are far superior to others in terms of providing opportunities for individual self-fulfillment.

A final obstacle to self-actualization mentioned by Maslow is the strong negative influence exerted by safety needs. The growth process demands a constant willingness to take risks, to make mistakes, to break old habits. This requires courage. It follows that anything that increases the person's fear and anxiety also increases the tendency to regress toward safety and security. It is also evident that most people display strong tendencies to continue specific habits—to persist in past behavior. Realization of our need for self-actualization, by contrast, requires an openness to novel ideas and experiences. Maslow maintained that children reared in a secure, friendly, caring atmosphere are more apt to acquire a healthy taste for the growth process. In short, under healthy conditions (where the person's basic need satisfactions are not endangered), growth is rewarding and the person will strive to become the best that he or she is able to become. By contrast, people who fail to develop their true potential—to become what they as individuals could become—are reacting to the deprivation of their basic needs. If more people are to attain self-actualization, then, the world needs to be changed to permit more widespread opportunities for people to satisfy their lower-level needs. Obviously, this task would necessitate a major reorganization of many of our social institutions and political structures.

DEFICIT MOTIVATION VERSUS GROWTH MOTIVATION

In addition to his hierarchical conception of motivation, Maslow (1987) distinguished two broad categories of human motives: *deficit* motives and *growth* motives. The former (also designated *deficiency* or *D-motives* by Maslow) entail little more than the lower needs in Maslow's motivational hierarchy, especially those concerned with our physiological and safety requirements. The exclusive aim of deprivation motivation is to fend off organismic tension arising from deficit states (e.g., hunger, cold, insecurity). In this sense, D-motives are urgent determiners of behavior. According to Maslow (1968, 1987), deficit motives share five criteria: (1) their absence produces illness (using hunger as an example, a person who does not eat will eventually get sick); (2) their presence prevents illness (the person who eats sensibly will not get sick); (3) their restoration cures illness (there is no cure for starvation like food); (4) under certain complex, free-choice conditions, they are preferred by the deprived person over other gratifications (the starving person will choose food over affection from family or friends); and (5) they are found to be inactive or functionally absent in a healthy person (healthy people are fortunate enough that their behavior is not constantly dominated by a quest for food). Thus, deficiency motivation aims at changing existing conditions because they are felt as unpleasant, frustrating, or tension-arousing.

Unlike D-type motives, *growth motives* (also designated *metaneeds* and *being* or *B-motives*) are distant goals associated with the urge to actualize our potentials. The objective of growth motives, or metaneeds (*meta* means "beyond" or "after") is to enrich and enlarge the experience of living, to increase tension through new, challenging, and diverse experiences. Growth motivation does not involve the repairing of deficit states (i.e., tension reduction) as much as the expansion of horizons (i.e., tension increase). The student who elects to take a course in organic chemistry, for example, simply because she wants to know more about it is more reflective of B- than D-type motivation. Such a student would certainly not be interested in taking organic chemistry if she were starving to death. Thus, growth or B-type motives come into play chiefly after the D-motives have been gratified adequately.

Maslow (1968, 1987) identified a number of metaneeds or being values to describe the motivations of self-actualizing people (see Table 10-1). In considering these growth needs, bear in mind that although they are presented in a highly abstract form, in actual life situations they are quite concrete and specifiable. Further, all of the metaneeds or metavalues are closely enmeshed with the overriding need for self-actualization. A lawyer, for instance, may seek justice (fairness, orderliness, lawfulness) through her law activities. Her quest for justice is an ultimate value for her; she loves justice, not for prestige, or power, or wealth, but simply because she loves the pursuit of the unattainable goal. Another person might find truth a dominant value; he might derive considerable fulfillment from learning how microorganisms invade and attack the body's biological defenses. His success in finding a cure for AIDS might be an unexpected by-product of the inner sense of accomplishment which the pursuit of truth alone affords.

Maslow theorized that metaneeds, unlike deficiency needs, are equally potent and are not arranged in an ascending order of priority. Consequently, one metaneed can be easily substituted for another when a person's life circumstances so dictate. The metamotivated artist, for instance, may strive for beauty through her artistic activities. Later, as a metamotivated parent, she may derive joy and pleasure from being a contributing agent to her child's growth and development. Both equally involve the "metalife," but clearly differ in their expression of it.

Maslow (1967) advanced the thought-provoking hypothesis that metaneeds are as instinctive or biologically rooted in people as are the deficiency needs. There-

TABLE 10-1   MASLOW'S LIST OF METANEEDS OR B-VALUES

Metaneeds	Characteristics
1 Wholeness	Unity, integration, tendency to oneness, interconnectedness, simplicity, organization, structure, dichotomy transcendence, order
2 Perfection	Necessity, just-rightness, just-so-ness, inevitability, suitability, justice, completeness, oughtness
3 Completion	Ending, finality, justice, "it's finished," fulfillment, destiny, fate
4 Justice	Fairness, orderliness, lawfulness, oughtness
5 Aliveness	Process, non-deadness, spontaneity, self-regulation, full-functioning
6 Richness	Differentiation, complexity, intricacy
7 Simplicity	Honesty, nakedness, essentiality, abstractness, skeletal structure
8 Beauty	Rightness, form, aliveness, simplicity, richness, wholeness, perfection, completion, uniqueness, honesty
9 Goodness	Rightness, desirability, oughtness, justice, benevolence, honesty
10 Uniqueness	Idiosyncrasy, individuality, non-comparability, novelty
11 Effortlessness	Ease; lack of strain, striving, or difficulty; grace, perfect functioning
12 Playfulness	Fun, joy, amusement, gaiety, humor, exuberance, effortlessness
13 Truth, Honesty, Reality	Nakedness, simplicity, richness, oughtness, pure and unadulterated beauty, completeness, essentiality
14 Self-Sufficiency	Autonomy, independence, not-needing-other-than-itself-in-order-to-be-it-self, self-determining, environment transcendence, separateness, living by its own laws

Source: Adapted from *Toward a Psychology of Being* by A. Maslow, 1968.

fore, they, too, must be satisfied if psychological health is to be maintained and the fullest growth achieved. What, then, prevents most people from functioning at the metaneed level? Maslow believed that most people do not become metamotivated because they neglect their deficiency needs. In so doing, their metaneeds are frustrated. Furthermore, the deprivation of metaneeds, unlike the deprivation of deficiency needs, is not usually experienced as a conscious desire. There is no conscious lack when metaneeds are ignored as is the case with deficiency needs. In fact, metaneeds, when satisfied, often lead to an increase in tension, whereas deficiency needs, when satisfied, always lead to a decrease in tension. Yet, whether or not the person directly experiences his or her metaneeds does not alter the fact that their frustration stifles healthy personality growth and functioning.

Metapathologies

As mentioned earlier, metamotivation is not possible until the person has adequately satisfied lower-order deficiency needs. Rarely, if ever, do metaneeds become dominant forces in the person's life unless his or her lower needs are at least comfortably gratified. Nonetheless, the deprivation and frustration of metaneeds may cause the person to become psychologically sick. Maslow (1971) characterized illnesses resulting from failure to satisfy the metaneeds as *meta-pathologies*. Such psychological states as apathy, alienation, depression, and cynicism are examples of what Maslow meant by this higher level of psychic disturbance. In humanistic psychology, not only is the person more highly regarded than in psychoanalysis or behaviorism, but also he or she is even endowed with psychological disorders of a distinctly higher class! Table 10-2 presents additional examples of specific metapathologies that result from metaneed frustration.

Maslow suggested that numerous symptoms associated with an affluent and consumption-oriented but unfulfilled life-style are indicative of metapathologies. Such symptoms include the inability to love anyone deeply, living for today only, perceiving nothing in life as precious or virtuous, not being able to see the value in perseverance at a task and personal accomplishment, and behaving unethically. The person who suffers from metapathologies is often blind to their presence. He or she may vaguely sense that something is missing in life, but not know what. Maslow even proposed that disturbances in cognitive functioning may be understood in terms of metaneed deprivation (i.e., as an expression of metapathologies). Being denied the truth (a metaneed), for instance, tends to make a person suspicious and fearful of others. Clinical psychologists have traditionally labeled such a person as *paranoid*. A healthy sense of curiosity may likewise be deadened if a person's cognitive metaneeds are deprived or denied. Some people are disinterested in everything that is transpiring in the world about them—e.g., foreign affairs, scientific discoveries, new styles in artistic or musical expression, and the meteorologist's prediction for tomorrow. Even the great mysteries of life may be ignored or taken for granted. Metamotivated people, on the other hand, are intensely interested in what is happening in the world about them and are constantly dazzled by new discoveries. They do not take the mysteries of life for granted.

TABLE 10-2   EXAMPLES OF MASLOW'S METAPATHOLOGIES

Mistrust, cynicism, skepticism

Hatred, repulsion, disgust, reliance only upon self and for self

Vulgarity, restlessness, loss of taste, bleakness

Disintegration

Loss of feeling of self and individuality, feeling oneself to be interchange-
   able or anonymous

Hopelessness, nothing to work for

Anger, cynicism, lawlessness, total selfishness

Grimness, depression, cheerlessness, loss of zest in life, paranoid humor-
   lessness

Responsibility given to others

Meaninglessness, despair, senselessness of life

Source: Adapted from *The Farther Reaches of Human Nature* by A. Maslow, 1971.

Finally, Maslow speculated that metapathologies may be responsible for a distortion in value development. He felt that many people are confused about what is right and wrong (e.g., drinking, drugs, war) because their metaneeds for perfection, goodness, honesty, and justice have been deprived. All too often, he added, this culminates in a lack of social feeling, disrespect for the rights of others, and disregard of such ethical values as generosity and compassion.

Deficit Living versus Metaliving: The Way to Fulfillment

You might wonder what it would be like to live within the realm of metaneeds, the metalife, or the life of being. Fortunately, Maslow (1968, 1987) has offered us a coherent picture of his vision of the highest reaches of human experience by contrasting the deficit life (D-life) with the being or metalife (B-life).

The D-life is principally one of striving to meet deficits in ourselves or demands from the environment. It is a style of living centered on tension reduction, homeostasis, and impulse gratification. "Live for today because tomorrow may not come" symbolizes the general outlook of the D-oriented person. Maslow noted that the D-life transforms the person into a responder, ". . . simply reacting to stimuli, to rewards and punishments, to emergencies, to pains and fears, to demands of other people, to superficialities" (1968, p. 61). To this we might add that the D-life is characterized by routine and drabness, by the refusal to treat anything with real seriousness and concern, and by the urge to have things uncomplicated but pleasant. Consider, for example, the events that transpire in the lives of many working adults today. They perform a monotonous job from 8 to 5, come home to their families, eat dinner, put the children to bed, and watch television for the evening. Maslow would claim that people who live in this manner are bored, empty, and only half alive because their lives are focused on maintaining the status quo. Nothing inspires them. Happiness for them consists in being secure and satisfied. They prefer the security of average and undemanding achievements—just getting by—as opposed to truly ambitious goals that would require them to extend themselves fully. In effect, they have failed to cross over the threshold to self-actualization.

Maslow believed that a totally different life-style accompanies metaliving or the B-life. The B-life may be defined as an episode or a spurt during which the person uses all his or her capacities effectively and effortlessly. Maslow (1968) noted that during these episodes of metaliving the person is more integrated, spontaneous, creative, and open to experience. Thus, B-living represents the person's happiest and most thrilling moments, but also moments of greatest maturity, individuation, and fulfillment. Needless to say, such moments are rare in the average person's life and are therefore not easily recognized for what they are. And so, for most of us, they fade into the stream of memory as unimportant items in that huge accumulation of past events to which we hardly pay heed.

Maslow observed that living in the B-realm is often accompanied by a quality of non-striving, non-needing, or non-wishing; it is as if the person has transcended the ordinary needs and drives of life. In other words, B-living, as contrasted with

D-living, may be characterized as unmotivated, purposeless, effortless, as a state of completion and goal attainment. The person no longer acts to avoid pain or discomfort, nor to pursue a future goal. "He just is. Joy has been attained which means a temporary end to striving for joy" (Maslow, 1968, p. 103).

Maslow's concept of *peak experiences* is also germane to the lives of metamotivated people. Generally, peak experiences are moments during which the person feels great ecstasy, awe, and rapture. These experiences tend to be reported by self-actualizing persons and are often pivotal in bringing about major changes in their lives. In a very real sense, peak experiences reflect the embracing of B-values insofar as the person feels strengthened and transformed in his or her daily life by such experiences. Maslow insisted that peak experiences are part of our human makeup. However, only metamotivated people are likely to appreciate and benefit from these experiences because they are not threatened by them in any way.

Now let us next examine Maslow's assumptions regarding human nature.

MASLOW'S BASIC ASSUMPTIONS CONCERNING HUMAN NATURE

As was noted earlier, humanistic psychology evolved largely out of protest against the images of humanity prevalent in the psychoanalytic and behavioristic traditions. The key differences separating these other "forces" from humanistic theory are most evident when considering the basic assumptions espoused by each. Careful scrutiny of Maslow's basic assumptions (depicted in Figure 10-2), particularly when contrasted with those of Freud and Skinner, should prove illuminating in this respect.

Freedom–Determinism Although hesitant to endorse the idea of total freedom espoused by many prominent existentialists, Maslow certainly approximates their belief. For him, the human being is fundamentally free and responsible in deciding the kind of life to lead. This personal freedom is especially manifest in terms of what a person decides his or her potentialities are and how he or she will strive to actualize them.

In Maslow's view, the older a person becomes and the higher he or she climbs on the need ladder, the more freedom that person has. For example, infants are not really "free" because they are dominated by physiological needs; they do not actually "decide" when to eat, sleep, or eliminate. But their potential is already present in their nature. As people mature, they move up the need hierarchy and progressively create their own individuality. In effect, they begin to carve out the kind of person they wish to become from a host of possibilities. The higher they progress on the need ladder, the more free they are of pressing D-type motivation and hence the more free they are to create their own destinies. Maslow's commitment to the freedom assumption is really very strong indeed.

Rationality–Irrationality When considering Maslow's position on the rationality–irrationality dimension, it is important to remember that he regarded

	Strong	Moderate	Slight	Midrange	Slight	Moderate	Strong	
Freedom	■							Determinism
Rationality	■							Irrationality
Holism	■							Elementalism
Constitutionalism		■						Environmentalism
Changeability	■	■						Unchangeability
Subjectivity	■							Objectivity
Proactivity				■				Reactivity
Homeostasis							■	Heterostasis
Knowability							■	Unknowability

FIGURE 10-2   Maslow's position on the nine basic assumptions concerning human nature.

animal research as largely irrelevant for human psychology. One major reason for this rejection is that an animal that is lower on the phylogenetic scale does not consciously review past experiences, think about present circumstances, consider future possibilities, and then cognitively decide on a course of action. Human beings, on the other hand, engage in these activities daily. Therefore, from Maslow's perspective, rationality is a central feature of the human being.

While Maslow allows for irrationality—seen in conflict among needs, compulsions, and inconsistencies in behavior—human behavior, to him, is largely governed by rational forces. As one instance of this conviction, Maslow (1966) regarded a person's conscious self-report of his or her own subjective experience as valid data for personality study. No personologist supports an "introspective method of inquiry" unless he or she thinks that the person giving it is sufficiently rational and self-aware to understand and reveal the reasons for his or her behavior. At the same time, however, Maslow (1970) accepted data from projective techniques (e.g., Thematic Apperception Test and Rorschach) which are designed to tap unconscious, irrational aspects of personality. But irrational processes do not dominate most people's lives. The basic thrust of Maslow's humanistic theory presents a picture of human beings who *rationally* make decisions and strive to actualize their potentials. His commitment to rationality is unmistakably strong.

Holism–Elementalism   It is difficult to imagine a personality theorist more committed to the holism assumption than Abraham Maslow. As noted earlier, one of the basic tenets of humanistic psychology is of "the individual as an integrated whole." Even among fellow humanistic psychologists, he stands out in terms of the extent to which holism characterizes his theory (Maddi & Costa, 1972).

Earlier, Maslow was quoted in this respect, observing that "it is John Smith who wants food, not John Smith's stomach" (1987, p. 3). But it is also John Smith who wants safety, self-esteem, and, above all, self-actualization. All aspects of personality are intertwined and fused in Maslow's account of the human condition. The individual as a totality is the only valid target for psychological study. His position on the holism assumption is indeed extreme.

Constitutionalism–Environmentalism The emphasis on freedom evident throughout Maslow's theory would seem to diminish the relevance of the issue raised by this assumption. If people are largely free to shape themselves and to creatively determine their own destinies, then neither constitution nor environment plays a significant role in molding human behavior. Of the two, however, Maslow is inclined to give constitution more weight. Physiological needs, obviously constitutional in origin, are the basis for his entire need-hierarchy model of human motivation. Yet, he seems to use this concept more to recognize the biological communality of humanity than to explain individual differences in personality.

Maslow proposed that all human needs are instinctoid or innately determined. He used the term *instinctoid* to emphasize the biological and genetic basis of needs common to all members of the species. At the same time, he contended that humans do not possess instincts like lower animals do. "Humans no longer have instincts in the animal sense, powerful, unmistakable inner voices which tell them unequivocally what to do, when, where, how and with whom. All that we have left are instinct-remnants" (Maslow, 1968, p. 191). He further suggested that higher level needs are weak and easily inhibited or altered by fear, adverse cultural conditions, and faulty learning. In other words, even though instinctoid needs are intrinsic to the human being, they can be changed or even overwhelmed by powerful environmental forces. Nevertheless, human nature is inborn, not made, in Maslow's view.

Further traces of constitutionalism are found in Maslow's concepts of meta-need and self-actualization. In discussing these earlier in the chapter, terms like "inborn urge," "instinctive," and "inherent in humanity" were used. Indeed, Maslow regarded the urge to actualize potentials as an inherent aspect of what a person is, rather than what he or she learns. This urge is inborn. Maslow did recognize the influence of early environment on personality development, but seemed to give weight to this factor only when it was a devastatingly destructive force contributing to a later emotional disturbance. On balance, although Maslow did not deny that personality is affected by environmental forces, he placed more emphasis on biological needs common to the entire species. In our view, Maslow's system reflects a moderate commitment to constitutionalism.

Changeability–Unchangeability An understanding of the relationship between freedom and growth motivation is essential to appreciating Maslow's position on this assumption. You will recall that Maslow believed that people are capable of fashioning their own lives. Also central to his theory is the notion that individuals are forever striving for personal growth—with the concept of self-actualization as the pinnacle of the need-hierarchy pyramid. Freedom and growth motivation interact in humanistic theory, and change occurs in the individual's personality makeup over time. That is, as the person continues to ascend the need hierarchy, he or she becomes progressively freer to chart the directions of his or her personal growth. As these directions are charted and pursued, the person necessarily undergoes change. Thus, in Maslow's theory, people have the capacity to decide what kind of persons they wish to become; as they continue to grow in various directions, personality changes necessarily take place.

In humanistic theory, personality change might best be regarded as movement toward the actualization of one's potentials. Even though some of these potentials may be innate, the degree to which the person actualizes them, as well as how he or she decides to do so, is almost entirely a matter of personal choice. So in the constant process of moving from D- to B-type motives, people are continually making choices about the direction of their lives and are thereby changing in the process. Viewed in this light, Maslow's commitment to the changeability assumption is indeed strong.

Subjectivity–Objectivity The existential, phenomenological, "here-and-now" perspective in Maslow's theory reveals a strong allegiance to the subjectivity assumption. While not elevating it to the apex of importance that his fellow humanistically inclined colleague Carl Rogers does (see Chapter 11), Maslow definitely believed that human subjective experience constitutes the cardinal data of psychological science. People cannot be understood without reference to their private world; subjective experience is more important than observable behavior for personology.

While he posited a hierarchical set of needs common to humanity, Maslow (1964) argued that how these needs are expressed is unique to each person. For example, while both Ruth and Betty have a need for self-esteem, each will subjectively experience and seek to satisfy this need in different ways. One may enhance her position as a mother so that others will recognize her outstanding parenthood, while the other may derive self-esteem from a career outside the home. Finally, it should be noted that the word "self" in Maslow's key phrase "self-actualization" is firmly rooted in the subjectivity assumption. Humanistic psychology favors the idea that each person is constantly striving toward the actualization of a unique self which only he or she can subjectively experience and appreciate.

Proactivity–Reactivity Although Maslow believed that human needs are innate, he also recognized the role of situational variables. Specifically, he pointed out that human behavior is influenced by both motivation (the innate needs that drive us) and the social and physical environment. "Sound motivation theory," Maslow wrote, "must then take account of the situation" (1987, p. 11). However, he also cautioned against "too great a preoccupation with the exterior, the culture, the environment, or the situation" (Maslow, 1987, p. 10). Maslow's view that behavior results from an interaction between needs and the environment indicates that he is midrange on the proactivity–reactivity assumption.

Homeostasis–Heterostasis   Maslow is strongly inclined toward the heterostatic assumption: the image of the person pushing on to greater and greater heights of personal growth is an integral part of his theory. Yet Maslow recognized two broad categories of human motivation: D- and B-type motives. Examination of these clearly indicates that D (deficit) motives are homeostatically based. Thus a human being does not strive for growth all the time—part of human life necessarily involves tension reduction.

But Maslow did not achieve prominence in psychology because of his account of D-motives. Others, particularly animal psychologists, had already studied these thoroughly. Instead, Maslow seems to treat D-motives as almost a necessary theoretical evil. They are something to be recognized, worked through, and dealt with successfully on the way to becoming fully human. This is done by rising above D-level functioning and working toward growth and self-realization. In Maslow's view, human beings are focused on becoming whatever they have the potential to become. The entire thrust of his theory points to the person rising above those motives that form a link with the rest of the animal kingdom and seeking personal fulfillment. Such a conception of personality could not exist without a solid foundation in the heterostasis assumption.

Knowability–Unknowability   Implicit in Maslow's writings is an image of people that cannot be fully captured by traditional modes of scientifc inquiry. Persons are unknowable in this sense. Thus, to approach a more comprehensive understanding of human nature, we will either have to look beyond the conventional arena of science or restructure psychological science to incorporate subjective, intuitive concepts befitting the nature of the subject. Like Allport, Maslow felt that the study of personality should stress idiographic methods as opposed to nomothetic ones. People should be allowed to reveal their subjective experiences in a holistic manner instead of the more orthodox approach that studies people in bits and pieces.

Maslow was quite critical of scientists who adopt a value-free and sterile approach to the study of human behavior. In particular, he chastised psychology and its graduate training for studying "Dry bones. Techniques. Precision. Huge mountains of itty-bitty facts, having little to do with the interests that brought the students into psychology" (Maslow, 1956, p. 229). As the "spiritual father" of the humanistic movement, Maslow sought a drastically redefined psychology—one that would address itself squarely to his image of humanity. We are forced to conclude that this is because the Maslowian person is simply unknowable within the traditional domain of psychological science. Thus, the third force movement emerged.

EMPIRICAL VALIDATION OF HUMANISTIC THEORY CONCEPTS

Not surprisingly, efforts aimed at verifying Maslow's humanistic perspective on personality have focused almost exclusively on the concept of self-actualization. Though Maslow developed a broad and engaging picture of human motives, it was self-actualization that captured his real interest and imagination. He devoted a good deal of effort to describing the process of self-actualization, in large part because self-actualization is such a difficult concept to grasp completely. By attempting to give an accurate description of those people who appeared to manifest its properties to a high degree, Maslow hoped to be able to help people to recognize self-actualization in their own lives.

Regrettably, other aspects of Maslow's theory have not generated a great deal of empirical research. This is largely due to the fact that the theory is not very precise and, as a result, tests of its validity are difficult to conduct. For example, there is lack of precision concerning the exact amount of gratification the person must experience before the next higher need will emerge. In addition, Maslow allows for so many exceptions to his hierarchical scheme of human motivation (e.g., the possible emergence of a higher need despite the deprivation of a lower one) that his theory appears marked by deficiencies. It should also be noted that there is no firm evidence to substantiate the claim that the various metaneeds emerge or become dominant once the basic needs have been gratified.

Despite the lack of research support for Maslow's theoretical contentions, his humanistic views have had a decided impact on scholars in a variety of disciplines (Lester et al., 1983). Not only has he encouraged personological theorists and researchers to consider the positive aspects of human nature, but also he has forced some of them to reconsider their own myopic view of the scientific enterprise and its limitations for understanding human behavior. Specifically, Maslow admonished his fellow psychologists for inevitably stressing "elegance, polish, technique, and apparatus [that] has, as a frequent consequence [led to] a playing down of meaningfulness, vitality, and significance of a problem and of creativeness in general" (1987, p. 188). As a result, he has helped some researchers to think of science as an enterprise in which appropriate techniques are used to tackle significant questions rather than as a method in which sophisticated techniques are used to study trivial problems.

Self-Actualization: An Informal Study of Healthy People

The view of human nature espoused by Maslow and other humanistic psychologists is an optimistic one. Not only do they emphasize humanity's innate potential for positive and constructive growth, but also they are highly confident about the realization of these human potentials given favorable environmental circumstances. Allied to this image is the belief that most people are imprisoned by different layers of circumstances which do not always allow them to attain full humanness. Thus, if self-actualization is to be achieved, people must transcend the restraints of society and their deficit needs and assume responsibility for becoming whatever they are capable of becoming. Empirical validation for this conception of human nature is tenuous at best, and what little does exist comes from Maslow's (1950, 1987) own study of self-actualizing people.

In a modestly conducted informal study, Maslow sketched a compelling portrait of people whom he considered to be self-actualized. The people studied were selected from his personal friends and acquaintances, from public figures living and dead, and from college students. These were people who by all conventional standards appeared to have achieved genuine maturity. Notably, they showed no tendencies toward neurotic, psychotic, or other gross psychological disorders. At the same time, there was considerable evidence of self-actualization—loosely defined by Maslow as evidence that the person appeared to be fulfilling himself or herself and to be doing the best that he or she was capable of doing. Maslow justified his lack of methodological rigor in selecting subjects this way:

> If we want to know how fast a human being can run, then it is no use to average out the speed of a "good sample" of the population; it is better to collect Olympic gold medal winners and see how well they can do. If we want to know the possibilities for spiritual growth, value growth, or moral development in human beings, then I maintain that we can learn most by studying our most moral, ethical, or saintly people. (1969, p. 726)

Abiding by this rationale, Maslow made extensive use of biographical information gathered from interviews with living subjects and from written accounts of historical figures. Thus, his research strategy relied heavily upon observation rather than hypothesis testing. Further, by focusing on a relatively small and select group of subjects (48 in all), he deviated markedly from sampling theory, the orthodox conception of statistics. Nonetheless, his assessment of self-actualized people and the kinds of qualities that characterize them has captured the imagination of personologists and laypersons alike (Leonard, 1983).

Maslow divided his self-actualizing subjects into three categories. Examples of the first category, "fairly certain cases," included Thomas Jefferson, Abraham Lincoln (in his later years), William James, Jane Addams, Albert Einstein, and

Albert Einstein was one of several people included in Maslow's study of self-actualization. (*Karsh/Woodfin Camp & Associates*)

Eleanor Roosevelt. Category two of "highly probable cases" consisted entirely of contemporary individuals who fell short somewhat of self-actualization but still could be used for study. Ethical considerations prevented giving their names. Finally, a "potential or possible cases" category included people who appeared to be striving toward self-actualization but who never quite attained it. This category included Benjamin Franklin, Pablo Casals, George Washington Carver, Thomas Eakins, Walt Whitman, and Aldous Huxley, among others. Maslow regarded all these individuals as rare specimens of psychological health who could be used as touchstones to explore the farther reaches of human nature.

The data accumulated on these prominent persons did not consist of the usual gathering of discrete facts. Rather, it involved the gradual development of *global* or *holistic impressions* of the sort that one forms of new friends and acquaintances. Specifically, Maslow compiled biographical material relevant to each subject (much like a case history) and, whenever possible, he questioned friends and relatives. In many cases it was impossible for him to question or test his older subjects, although such measures (including free association, the Rorschach inkblot test, and the Thematic Apperception Test) were administered to the younger ones. Hence, quantitative analysis of the data was impossible. This procedure yielded a list of 15 key characteristics or traits of self-actualizing people which will be discussed in the next section of this chapter. Despite its inadequacies and technical flaws (which will be discussed next), this study serves as the foundation for Maslow's portrait of the self-actualizing person as a model of optimal psychological health.

A major criticism of Maslow's study concerns the criteria he used to select his sample of self-actualizers. In effect, he chose people for whom he personally had the highest admiration as human specimens. His operational definition of self-actualization thus rests solely on his own implicit and highly subjective values. We may well question whether these characteristics pertain to a psychological process called self-actualization or are merely reflections of Maslow's particular value system (Daniels, 1988). The array of characteristics that he reports must, then, be considered not as a factual description of self-actualizing people but rather as a reflection of Maslow's personalized conception of ideal human values.

Other problems also make it difficult to evaluate Maslow's claim that his self-actualizing subjects represent the best possible specimens of the human race. Foremost is the fact that he did not address the issue of how self-actualizing characteristics are developed. Are they inherited or acquired as a result of life experiences? Is it possible that some factor such as intelligence, talent, or privileged background may have made them unrepresentative of the general populace and, therefore, a *biased* sample from which to generalize about the species? Unfortunately, basic questions such as these cannot be answered from the available data.

The issue of replication is another source of criticism leveled against Maslow's study. Critics claim that Maslow was vague about the criteria he used to select self-actualizers and employed unreliable research procedures. To these critics, it would be difficult to replicate Maslow's original study and be certain that the same characteristics of self-actualization had been identified. In addition, Maslow has been accused of failing to compare his group of self-actualizers with an appropriate control group of non-self-actualizers (Daniels, 1982).

In light of these problems, it is easy to see why Maslow's account of the metapsychology of the self-actualizing person has been soundly criticized (Daniels, 1988). To his credit, Maslow admitted that his study left much to be desired in the way of complying with the requirements for strict empirical research. "By ordinary standards of laboratory research, i.e., of rigorous and controlled research, this simply was not research at all" (Maslow, 1971, p. 42). He also noted that the alternative would have been to not study self-actualization at all, or to wait until appropriate scientific procedures were developed. Finally, he regarded his study as pilot work, which, however inadequate in terms of scientific rigor, would one day be confirmed by others.

Assessing Self-Actualization

Lack of an adequate assessment instrument to measure self-actualization originally blocked any attempts to validate Maslow's major assertions. However, development of the *Personal Orientation Inventory (POI:* Shostrom, 1964, 1974) has made it possible for researchers to measure values and behaviors related to self-actualization (Knapp, 1976; Kelly & Choran, 1985). The POI is a self-report questionnaire designed to assess various dimensions of self-actualization in accordance with Maslow's thinking. It consists of 150 forced-choice items. For each pair of items, respondents are asked to choose the alternative that is most descriptive of them. Sample items from the test are shown in Table 10-3.

The POI is scored for 2 major scales and 10 subscales. The first major scale measures the extent to which a person is characteristically *inner-directed* as compared to *other-directed* in the search for values and meaning in life. Inner-directed people tend to depend on internalized principles and motives as the basis for determining their judgments and actions. Their lives are marked by autonomy,

TABLE 10-3   SAMPLE ITEMS FROM THE PERSONAL ORIENTATION INVENTORY
Respondents read each pair of statements and then select the item in each pair that is more descriptive of them.

1 a I live by the rules and standards of society.
   b I do not always need to live by the rules and standards of society.

2 a I do what others expect of me.
   b I feel free to not do what others expect of me.

3 a People should always control their anger.
   b People should express honestly felt anger.

4 a It is important to me how I live in the here and now.
   b It is of little importance to me how I live in the here and now.

5 a I feel guilty when I am selfish.
   b I don't feel guilty when I am selfish.

Source: Shostrom, 1964, pp. 207–218.

self-support, and freedom. Other-directed people, by contrast, tend to depend on others and social norms as the basis for determining their judgments and actions. Their lives are marked by dependence, conformity, and need for approval and acceptance. Obviously, no one could function effectively in a society without a sense of other-directedness. Self-actualizers, however, as would be expected, tend to be more inner-directed than are people who are less self-actualizing.

The second major scale is called *time competence*. It measures the extent to which a person is living in the present, as opposed to being focused on the past or the future. Time-competent people are considered to be able to reflect on the past as it relates to the present and to realistically connect long-range aspirations to current goals. They have a sense of continuity among these three aspects of time. In contrast, time-incompetent people have split off their past and future from their present. Their current lives are based on regrets and resentments about their past and idealized goals or fears about their future. They also have difficulty linking their past accomplishments and future aspirations with each other. Self-actualizers are primarily time-competent.

In addition to the 2 major POI scales, there are 10 complementary subscales designed to measure conceptually important elements of self-actualization. The subscales include *self-actualizing values, existentiality, feeling reactivity, spontaneity, self-regard, self-acceptance, nature of man, synergy, acceptance of aggression,* and *capacity for intimate contact.* Interpretation of the POI involves examining the pattern of scores obtained on the 2 major scales and the 10 subscales. It should also be noted that the POI has a built-in lie-detection scale to assess whether or not respondents fake their responses.

The POI is the most frequently used instrument for research on self-actualization. The test shows good test-retest reliability for various samples, although the coefficients for certain subscales are low to moderate in certain studies (Ilardi & May, 1968). As for validity, a number of studies indicate that the test does differentiate between groups of individuals nominated by personologists as representing different categories of self-actualization and non-self-actualization. A study by McClain (1970) illustrates how the POI has been validated as a measure of a person's level of positive mental health. He examined the personalities of 30 guidance counselors who were attending a summer counseling institute. Their scores on the POI, administered during the first week of the institute, indicated that they were a psychologically healthy group. A composite self-actualization score for each counselor was then derived from the evaluations of the three staff members who knew him or her most intimately. One of these was a practicum supervisor who supervised only six counselors. He reviewed the taped counseling sessions with his counselors and thus was able to become acquainted with each one in terms of his or her personality dynamics and ways of behaving in personal confrontations. Second was a group process leader who also had six counselors in his group. The group sessions focused on sensitivity training, enabling the staff leader to know the counselors in his group in depth. Third was a clinical psychologist who studied each of the 30 counselors by means of self-report and projective personality instruments.

At the end of the 9-week session, these staff members reviewed a long list of characteristics of self-actualizers summarized from Maslow's various writings. Based on these characteristics, each staff member rated each counselor in his charge along a six-point scale for overall self-actualization. The three staff ratings for each counselor were summed for a composite rating which was then correlated with the POI scales. The correlations between the POI scores and the composite behavioral ratings for self-actualization by staff members are given in Table 10-4. Of a total of 12 correlations, 9 were statistically significant in the predicted direction. These data are offered as evidence that the POI does measure self-actualization among normal adults.

Several studies indicate that the POI can be used to distinguish between normal and abnormal groups. Fox et al. (1968), for example, found that groups of psychiatric patients scored lower (were less self-actualized) on virtually all the POI scales than groups of people judged by experienced clinical psychologists to be self-actualized. Other studies report negative correlations between high self-actualization scores on the POI and alcoholism (Zaccaria & Weir, 1967), depression and hypochondriasis (Shostrom & Knapp, 1966), and neuroticism (Knapp, 1965). Additional research has shown that people's POI scores improve after they participated in a series of group therapy sessions (Dosamantes-Alperson & Merrill, 1980).

The POI has also been studied in relationship to several other standardized measures of behavior or personality. For instance, the majority of the POI scales are positively correlated with self-report measures of autonomy (Grossack et al., 1966), creativity (Braun & Asta, 1968), and emotional adjustment (Mattocks & Jew, 1974). Furthermore, POI scales are positively correlated with academic achievement among college students (LeMay & Damm, 1968; Stewart, 1968). These and other studies suggest that the POI has adequate validity (Maddi, 1988).

TABLE 10-4   PRODUCT-MOMENT CORRELATIONS BETWEEN COUNSELOR PERSONAL ORIENTATION SCORES AND COMPOSITE RATINGS FOR SELF-ACTUALIZATION

POI scale	r	p
Time competence	.40	.05
Inner-support	.69	.01
Self-actualizing value	.41	.05
Existentiality	.43	.05
Feeling reactivity	.45	.05
Spontaneity	.53	.01
Self-regard	.36	ns
Self-acceptance	.56	.01
Nature of man constructive	.23	ns
Synergy	.32	ns
Acceptance of aggression	.42	.05
Capacity for intimate contact	.42	.05

Source: Adapted from McClain, 1970, p. 22.

Although the POI appears to have adequate psychometric properties, Shostrom has attempted to improve the test by extending and refining the concepts of actualizing measured by it. This effort has led to the creation of an instrument called the *Personal Orientation Dimensions (POD:* Shostrom, 1975, 1977). The POD consists of 260 forced-choice items which are scored for two major scales, time orientation and core centeredness. A few empirical studies indicate that the POD has acceptable reliability and validity (Jansen et al., 1979; Knapp & Knapp, 1978). However, it is likely that researchers will continue to use the POI until they are convinced that the POD has superior psychometric properties.

A Short Form of the Personal Orientation Inventory

One practical limitation in using the 150-item POI for research purposes is its length. Accordingly, Jones and Crandall (1986) developed a short index of self-actualization. Their 15-item scale is reproduced in Table 10-5. In a study of several hundred college students, Jones and Crandall found that scores on this short scale correlated positively with overall scores from the much-longer POI (r = +.67) and with measures of self-esteem and "rational behaviors and beliefs." The scale has acceptable test-retest reliability and does not seem to be susceptible to the "social desirability" response set. Also, it has been shown that college students who participated in assertiveness training displayed significant increases in self-actualization as measured by this scale (Crandall et al., 1988). The increased scores were maintained for more than one year.

Research on Peak Experiences

Maslow claimed that self-actualizing people frequently experience moments of intense awe, wonder, and ecstasy. During such moments of very intense self-actualization, which he called *peak experiences,* people tend to become so totally immersed in some activity that their sense of time and place is transcended. Maslow further observed that people having peak experiences often believe that something very significant and valuable has occurred.

A few empirical studies have supported Maslow's concept of peak experience. For example, Ravizza (1977) interviewed athletes in 12 different sports who reported expanded views of themselves during moments of outstanding performance. Their "greatest moments" as athletes closely resembled Maslow's description of the peak experience. Based on a sample of 20 athletes, 100 percent reported loss of fear, 95 percent reported full attention or immersion, perfect experience, God-like feeling of control, and self-validation, and 90 percent reported their exceptional performance as effortless. Contrary to Maslow's description, however, the athletes' experiences were more limited in importance to immediate circumstances than instrumental in bringing about major changes in their lives.

TABLE 10-5   A SHORT SCALE MEASURING SELF-ACTUALIZATION

_____	**1** I do not feel ashamed of any of my emotions.
_____	**2** I feel I must do what others expect of me. (N)
_____	**3** I believe that people are essentially good and can be trusted.
_____	**4** I feel free to be angry at those I love.
_____	**5** It is always necessary that others approve of what I do. (N)
_____	**6** I don't accept my own weaknesses. (N)
_____	**7** I can like people without having to approve of them.
_____	**8** I fear failure. (N)
_____	**9** I avoid attempts to analyze and simplify complex domains. (N)
_____	**10** It is better to be yourself than to be popular.
_____	**11** I have no mission in life to which I feel especially dedicated. (N)
_____	**12** I can express my feelings even when they may result in undesirable consequences.
_____	**13** I do not feel responsible to help anybody. (N)
_____	**14** I am bothered by fears of being inadequate. (N)
_____	**15** I am loved because I give love.

Note: Respondents answer each statement using a 4-point scale: 1 = disagree, 2 = disagree somewhat, 3 = agree somewhat, and 4 = agree. Items followed by an "N" are scored in the reverse direction when calculating the total score (e.g., 1 = 4, 2 = 3, 3 = 2, 4 = 1). The higher the toal score, the more self-actualized the respondent is assumed to be.
Source: Jones & Crandall, 1986, p. 67.

The instrument that is most often used to measure peak experience tendencies is the Peak Scale (Mathes et al., 1982). Research using this 70-item test has provided some data supporting Maslow's theorizing. For instance, individuals who scored high on the scale evidenced experiences of a transcendent and mystical nature and feelings of intense happiness. High scorers also reported living their lives in terms of "being" values such as truth, beauty, and justice (Mathes et al., 1982).

In conclusion, as research interest in Maslow's humanistic theory continues to grow, we should expect progressively more empirical light to be cast on his central theoretical constructs (Haymas & Green, 1982). In the meantime, a definitive assessment of the theory's empirical status lies well ahead of us.

APPLICATION: CHARACTERISTICS OF SELF-ACTUALIZING PERSONS

For anyone attracted to humanistic psychology, the attainment of self-actualization epitomizes the ideal life-style. This section discusses a number of the common characteristics Maslow (1950, 1987) found among people who seemed to be functioning at full capacity, doing the best that they were capable of doing. For Maslow, these people represented the "very best" personalities humankind has to offer. He also regarded them as having attained a level of human development that is potentially present in all of us. It is in this spirit that this final chapter section is offered—tentative ideas about what it means to be a healthy, fully functioning human being as seen by a humanistic personologist. Of course, as is the case with any caricature of ideal psychological development, self-actualization cannot be achieved simply by following pat prescriptions propounded by "experts." Rather, it is a slow and painful process that is best understood as a continuing quest, not a fixed endpoint. Also, every person strives to realize his or her inner potentialities in a somewhat different way. Therefore, any attempt to apply Maslow's criteria for self-actualization should be tempered by the fact that each person must consciously choose how best to fulfill his or her own potential for becoming everything he or she can in life.

From his informal study described earlier, Maslow concluded that self-actualizing people manifest the following characteristics.

1 *More efficient perception of reality.* Self-actualizers are able to perceive the world around them, including other people, correctly and efficiently. They see reality exactly as it is, not as they might want or need it to be. They are less emotional and more objective about their perceptions; they do not allow their hopes and fears to distort their perceptions. Because of their superior perception, self-actualizers can more easily detect phoniness and dishonesty in others. Maslow discovered that this ability to see more efficiently extended to many other areas of life, including art, music, science, politics, and philosophy.

The self-actualized person's perception is also less distorted by expectations, anxieties, stereotypes, false optimism, or pessimism. Maslow called this non-biased kind of perception "being or B-cognition." Related to this highly objective perception is the finding that self-actualizing people have a greater tolerance of ambiguity and uncertainty than do most people. They feel comfortable with problems and puzzles that have no definite right or wrong solutions. They welcome doubt, indefiniteness, and uncharted paths.

2 *Acceptance of self, others, and nature.* Self-actualizers can accept themselves the way they are. They are not overly critical of their own shortcomings, frailties, and weaknesses. They are not burdened by undue guilt, shame, and anxiety—emotional states which are so prevalent in the general population.

Self-acceptance is also vividly expressed at the physiological level. Self-actualizers accept their own animal nature with a kind of gusto or *joie de vivre.* They have hearty appetites, sleep well, and enjoy their sex lives without unnecessary inhibition. Basic biological processes (e.g., urination, pregnancy, menstruation, growing old) are considered part of human nature and are graciously accepted.

In similar fashion, they are accepting of others and of humankind in general. They have no compelling need to instruct, inform, or control. They can tolerate weaknesses in others and are not threatened by their strengths. They realize that people suffer, grow old, and eventually die.

3 *Spontaneity, simplicity, and naturalness.* The behavior of self-actualizing people is marked by spontaneity and simplicity, by an absence of artificiality or straining for effect. This does not imply consistently unconventional behavior. It is their inner life (thoughts and emotions) that is unconventional, natural, and spontaneous. Their unconventionality is not intended to impress others and may even be suppressed in order not to distress others, so that they may even abide by ceremonies and rituals. Thus, they may conform if it means protecting themselves or others from pain or injustice. For this reason, if it suits their purposes, self-actualizers may, in fact, tolerate practices within educational institutions that they regard as foolish, repetitive, or mind-debilitating. However, when the situation warrants it, they can be uncompromising even at the price of ostracism and censure. In short, they do not hesitate to defy social rules when it is deemed necessary to do so.

4 *Problem-centered.* Without exception, Maslow found his subjects to be committed to some task, duty, vocation, or beloved job which they regard as important. That is, they are not ego-centered but rather oriented toward problems beyond their immediate needs, problems to which they are dedicated like a mission in life. In this sense, they live to work rather than work to live; their work is subjectively experienced as a defining characteristic of themselves. Maslow portrayed the self-actualizer's commitment to and absorption in work as analogous to a love affair: the job and person seem "meant for each other. . . . the person and [the] job fit together and belong together perfectly like a key and a lock" (1971, pp. 301–302).

Self-actualizers are also deeply concerned with philosophical and ethical issues. Accordingly, they live and work within the widest frame of reference, tending to devote themselves to nonpersonal "missions" or tasks. Such a lifestyle denotes a lack of concern for the trivial and petty, thus enabling them to clearly distinguish between the important and the unimportant issues in the world.

5 *Detachment: need for privacy.* Self-actualizing persons are described by Maslow as having an intense need for privacy and solitude. Because they do not have a clinging relationship with others, they can enjoy the richness and fulness of others' friendship.

Unfortunately, this quality of detachment is not always understood or accepted by others. In social encounters they are often viewed by "normal" people as aloof, reserved, snobbish, and cold. This is particularly the case for those people who have not had their love and belongingness needs adequately satisfied. But in self-actualizing people, these deficiency needs have been met, and, thus, they do not need other people in the usual sense of friendship. As a result, there is a need for another level of encounter—with the self. As one of Maslow's subjects put it, "When I'm alone, I'm with my best friend." This comment could be construed as the height of narcissism. Maslow's point is simply that self-actualizers can be alone without being lonely.

The need for privacy and self-reliance encompasses other aspects of behavior as well. For instance, they remain calm and serene during periods of personal misfortune or setback. Maslow explained that this comes in part from the self-actualizer's tendency to stand by his or her own interpretation of situations instead of relying upon what other people think or feel about matters. In effect, they are self-movers, resisting society's attempts to make them adhere to social convention.

6 *Autonomy: independence of culture and environment.* As characteristics already discussed would suggest, self-actualizers are free to act independently of their physical and social environment. This autonomy enables them to rely on their own potentialities and latent resources for growth and development. Thus, for example, truly self-actualizing college students do not really need the "right" academic atmosphere on campus to learn. They can learn anywhere because they have themselves. In this sense, they are a "self-contained" entity.

Healthy people also have a high degree of self-direction and "free will." They regard themselves as self-governed, active, responsible, and self-disciplined agents in determining their own destinies. They are strong enough to be oblivious to others' opinions and affection; thus, they shun honors, status, prestige, and popularity. Such extrinsic satisfactions are perceived as less significant than self-development and inner growth. Of course, attaining this point of relative independence depends upon having received love and security from others in the past.

7 *Continued freshness of appreciation.* Self-actualizing people possess the capacity to appreciate even the most ordinary events in their lives with a sense of newness, awe, pleasure, and even ecstasy. Thus, for instance, the hundredth rainbow is as lovely and majestic as the first; a ride through the woods never ceases to be a joyful experience; watching a child at play uplifts the spirit. Unlike others who take their blessings for granted, self-actualizers have an appreciation of their good fortune, health, friends, and political freedom. They seldomly complain about a boring, uninteresting experience.

Childbirth often produces a peak experience. (*Suzanne Arms/ Jeroboam*)

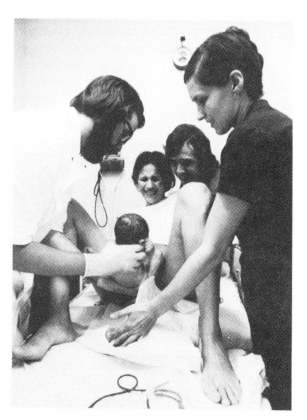

A key aspect of this quality of open responsiveness to new experiences is that self-actualizers avoid lumping experiences into categories and then dismissing them. Rather, their subjective experience is very rich, and the day-to-day business of living and working remains thrilling and exciting to them.

8 *Peak or mystic experiences.* As Maslow's study of the process of self-actualization continued, he made the unexpected discovery that many of his subjects commonly had what he called *peak experiences.* These are moments of intense excitement and high tension as well as those of relaxation, peacefulness, blissfulness, and stillness. Representing the most ecstatic moments of life, such occurrences usually come from love and sexual climax, bursts of creativity, insight, discovery, and fusion with nature. These people can "turn on" without artificial stimulants. Just being alive turns them on.

For Maslow, peak or mystic experiences are not theological or supernatural in nature, though they are religious at their core. He found that "peakers" feel more in harmony with the world, lose their self-awareness or transcend it, feel simultaneously more powerful and more helpless than before, and become less conscious of time and space. According to Maslow, the peak experiences that really change a person come about when they are earned: "The person comes to some glorious insight as the result of a year of sweating on a psychoanalytic couch; or a philosopher who has been working for fifteen years at some problem comes to an illumination" (Hardeman, 1979, p. 24).

9 *Social interest.* Even though self-actualizers are sometimes troubled, saddened, and even enraged by the shortcomings of the human race, they nevertheless possess a deep feeling of kinship for humanity. Consequently, they have a genuine desire to help improve the lot of their fellow mortals. This nurturant attitude is evidenced by a feeling of compassion, sympathy, and affection for all humanity. Oftentimes this is a special kind of brotherhood, like the attitude of an older brother or sister toward younger siblings.

10 *Profound interpersonal relations.* Self-actualizing people tend to form deeper and closer personal relationships than those of the "average" adult. For the most part, those with whom they associate are likely to be healthier and closer to self-actualization than the average person. That is, self-actualizers are more inclined to associate intimately with others of similar character, talent, and capacity ("birds of a feather"), though their social interest allows them to have a special feeling of empathy for less healthy people. Usually their circle of intimate friends is small, since befriending in the self-actualizing style demands a great deal of time and effort. They also have especially tender feelings for children and are easily touched by them.

11 *Democratic character structure.* Maslow described self-actualizers as being "democratic" in the deepest sense. Since they are free of prejudice, they show respect for other people regardless of their class, race, religion, sex, age, occupation, or other group membership traits. Moreover, they are willing to learn from anybody without adopting a superior or authoritarian attitude. The self-actualizing musician, for example, is genuinely respectful toward the skilled mechanic because the mechanic possesses skills and knowledge that the musician does not possess. At the same time, Maslow discovered that self-actualizers do not indiscriminately equalize all human beings: "These individuals, themselves elite, select for their friends elite, but this is an elite of character, capacity, and talent, rather than of birth, race, blood, name, family, age, youth, fame, or power" (1987, p. 139).

12 *Discrimination between means and ends.* In their day-to-day living, self-actualizing people show less confusion, inconsistency, and conflict than the average person about what is right or wrong, good or bad. They have definite moral and ethical standards, although very few of them are religious in the orthodox sense of the term. Maslow's subjects also showed an unusually keen ability to discriminate between ends (goals) and the means for accomplishing those ends. On the other hand, they often enjoy the means, or instrumental behavior leading to a goal, which more impatient persons would dislike. That is, they are more likely to appreciate doing something for its own sake (e.g., exercising) and not just because it is a means to some other end (e.g., fitness).

13 *Philosophical sense of humor.* Another distinguishing characteristic of self-actualizing people is their distinct preference for philosophical, nonhostile humor. Whereas the average person may enjoy humor that pokes fun at another's inferiority, that hurts or degrades someone, or that is "off-color," the healthy person typically finds humor expressing the foolishness of humanity in general most appealing. Abraham Lincoln's humor serves as a relevant example. His jokes always had something to convey, a purpose beyond just producing a laugh. They often dealt with a parable or fable. Maslow noted that philosophical humor usually elicits a smile rather than a laugh. This attitude toward humor often makes the self-actualizer appear rather sober and serious.

14 *Creativeness.* Maslow found that, without exception, self-actualizing people were creative in some sense of the word. However, the creativeness manifested by his subjects was different from unusual talent or genius as reflected in poetry, art, music, or science. Maslow likened it to the natural and spontaneous creativeness found in unspoiled children. This kind of self-actualizing creativity appears in everyday life as an expression of a personality that is perceptive, innovative, and refreshingly simple.

The self-actualizing person need not write books, compose music, or produce art objects to be creative. In speaking of his mother-in-law, whom he regarded as self-actualizing, Maslow vividly emphasized this fact. He said that while his mother-in-law had no special talents as a writer or artist, she was highly creative in preparing home-made soup. Maslow remarked that first-rate soup was more creative than second-rate poetry any day!

15 *Resistance to enculturation.* Finally, self-actualizers are in harmony with their culture and yet maintain a certain inner detachment from it. Being essentially autonomous and self-reliant, they are free to resist social and cultural pressures to think and behave along certain lines. This resistance to enculturation does not mean that self-actualizers are unconventional or antisocial in all realms of behavior. For instance, they remain well within the limits of conformity concerning choice of clothes, speech, food, and the manner of doing things, which are not really important enough to prompt objection. Similarly, they do not waste energy fighting against insignificant social rituals and regulations of society. However, they can become extremely independent and unconventional when they feel basic issues are involved. For this reason, they are sometimes considered as rebellious and eccentric by those who do not take the time to know and appreciate them. Self-actualizers also manifest a calm, long-term commitment to cultural improvement. Although cognizant of society's imperfections, they accept the fact that social change can be slow and painstaking but is best achieved by working within the system.

Self-Actualizers Are Not Angels

The preceding discussion may have invited the illusion that self-actualizers are a select group of superstars in the art of living who stand apart and above the rest of humanity as to approach perfection. Maslow clearly refuted this. As *imperfect* human beings, self-actualizers are just as susceptible to silly, nonconstructive, and wasteful habits as the rest of us mortals. They can be obstinate, irritable, boring, petulant, selfish, or depressed, and they are by no means immune from superficial vanity, undue pride, and partiality to their own friends, family, and children. Temper outbursts are not unusual. Maslow also found his subjects capable of displaying a certain "surgical coldness" when confronted with interpersonal conflicts. One of his subjects, for instance, once she realized that she no longer loved her spouse, and then decided on divorce, did it with a decisiveness that touched upon ruthlessness. Other subjects were found to recover from the death of people close to them so easily as to seem heartless.

Furthermore, self-actualizers are not free from guilt, anxiety, sadness, and self-doubt. Their intense concentration may produce a lack of tolerance for idle gossip and light conversation. In fact, they may use language or engage in behavior that is distressing, shocking, or insulting to others. Finally, their kindness toward others may leave them vulnerable to exploitative relationships (such as becoming deeply involved with boring or unhappy people). Despite such imperfections in their makeup, self-actualizers were regarded by Maslow as excellent specimens of psychological health. At the very least, they remind us that humanity's potential for psychological growth is far greater than has yet been attained.

Psychological Utopia: Eupsychia

No account of Maslow's contributions to personology would be complete without attention directed toward what he felt were necessary changes to bring about self-actualization on a broad scale. He maintained that environmental circumstances have the power to either facilitate or debilitate the pursuit of the metalife. The Good Person and The Good Society are one and the same in Maslow's view. To him, our current cultural practices and institutions are based on a hedonistically distorted conception of human nature. Specifically, he believed that the prevailing assumption underlying child-rearing practices, formal education, employer–

employee relations, and even our major religions, is that the human being is no more than a narcissistic beast. To control such a creature, only strict discipline and the continual threat of punishment can prevent these tendencies from being expressed. Much energy is spent on keeping down the devil in us. By contrast, Maslow felt that self-actualization is most likely to occur when the environment is conducive to the satisfaction of human needs: "Under such conditions, the deepest layers of human nature could show themselves with greater ease" (1987, p. 122).

Maslow (1971, 1987) speculated about the kind of utopia that would be developed if one thousand healthy families migrated to a deserted island where they could determine their own destiny. He called this potential utopia *Eupsychia* (pronounced Yew-sigh-key-a). Its philosophical base would be anarchistic, meaning there would be no governmental imposition on individual liberty. Basic needs and metaneeds would be respected much more than they are in our society. People would be allowed to make free choices wherever possible. In Eupsychia there would be complete synergy or working together. Such a society would also be Taoistic in its philosophy, valuing what is simple and unselfish. In a word, the inhabitants of Eupsychia would be honest with each other and far less controlling, violent, and contemptuous than we are.

Maslow's real value as a psychological theorist lies in his concern for the areas of human functioning that most other theorists have almost totally ignored. He is one of the few personologists who seriously investigated the positive dimensions of human experience and, notably, took the time to articulate his ideas to the lay public as well as to his fellow erudite psychologists. He envisioned a society that would allow us to elevate ourselves and our treatment of one another to a truly humanistic level based on knowledge gained from psychology. Indeed, for Maslow, this is the ultimate value of psychology: "If we die in another war or if we continue being tense and neurotic and anxious in an extended cold war, then this is due to the fact that we don't understand ourselves and we don't understand each other. Improve human nature and you improve all. . . . We need psychology. . . ." (1956, p. 227). These words, written some 35 years ago, have equal relevance today as we approach a new century filled with renewed promise for the human condition.

SUMMARY

Humanistic psychology, or the third force movement, has given rise to an image of humanity in psychology radically different from that of either psychoanalysis or behaviorism. Heavily influenced by existential philosophy, humanistic psychology has as its basic tenets the individual as an integrated whole, the irrelevance of animal research, the perception of the person as a basically good, creative being, and an emphasis on the study of psychological health.

One major statement of humanistic psychology, the theory of Abraham Maslow, depicts human motivation in terms of a hierarchy of ascending priorities. Lower (more basic) needs in the hierarchy must be reasonably satisfied before higher-level needs emerge as dominant energizing forces in the person's behavior. In order of prepotency or urgency, Maslow's hierarchy of human needs is: (1) physiological; (2) safety and security; (3) belongingness and love; (4) self-esteem; and (5) self-actualization. The humanistic nature of Maslow's theory is epitomized in the self-actualization level, the highest fulfillment of self.

Maslow also distinguished two broad categories of human motives: deficit motives and growth motives. Deficiency motivation is aimed at reducing tension whereas growth motivation (also called metamotivation) is aimed at increasing tension through seeking new and challenging experiences. Maslow proposed several metaneeds (e.g., truth, beauty, and justice) by which to describe self-actualizers and theorized that such needs are as biologically rooted in people as are the deficiency needs. Frustration of the metaneeds produces metapathologies. Apathy, cynicism, and alienation are a few of the many symptoms indicative of metapathologies as evidenced by people who have failed to satisfy their meta-needs.

Maslow's basic assumptions concerning human nature are explicitly stated. His humanistic theory reflects (1) a strong commitment to the assumptions of freedom, rationality, holism, changeability, subjectivity, heterostasis, and un-knowability; (2) a midrange position on the proactivity–reactivity assumption; and (3) a slight commitment to the constitutionalism assumption.

Empirical research generated by Maslow's theory has focused primarily on the concept of self-actualization. Maslow's own study of a select group of self-actualizing persons based on biographical material was discussed in the chapter. Maslow has been criticized for using subjective criteria in selecting his subjects. The Personal Orientation Inventory is a self-report test designed to measure self-actualization as conceptualized in Maslow's theory. Numerous studies indicate that the POI has adequate reliability and validity and distinguishes normal from abnormal groups in the predicted direction. A short index of self-actualization is also available for research purposes. Finally, studies based on the Peak Scale have supported Maslow's concept of peak experiences.

In the concluding chapter section, some ideas stemming from Maslow's study of healthy people were offered to further detail his self-actualization concept. Fifteen notable characteristics of self-actualizing persons were listed and discussed. In addition, Maslow's vision of psychological utopia, called Eupsychia, a society in which basic needs and metaneeds would be satisfied, was briefly described.

BIBLIOGRAPHY

Abraham H. Maslow: A memorial volume. (1972). Monterey, CA: Brooks/Cole.

Braun, J., & Asta, P. (1968). Intercorrelations between the Personal Orientation Inventory and the Gordon Personal Inventory scores. *Psychological Reports*, **23**, 1197–1198.

Coopersmith, S. (1967). *The antecedents of self-esteem.* New York: Freeman.

Crandall, R., McGown, D. A., & Robb, Z. (1988). The effects of assertiveness training on self-actualization. *Small Group Behavior*, **19**, 134–145.

Daniels, M. (1982). The development of the concept of self-actualization in the writings of Abraham Maslow. *Current Psychological Review*, **2**, 61–76.

Daniels, M. (1988). The myth of self-actualization. *Journal of Humanistic Psychology*, **28**, 7–38.

Dosamantes-Alperson, E., & Merrill, N. (1980). Growth effects of experiential movement psychotherapy. *Psychotherapy: Theory, Research, and Practice*, **17**, 63–68.

Durant, W. (1977). Humanism in historical perspective. *The Humanist*, January/February. **37**, 24–26.

Eagly, A. H. (1987). *Sex difference in social behavior: A social-role interpretation.* Hillsdale, NJ: Erlbaum.

Fox, J., Knapp, R., & Michael, W. (1968). Assessment of self-actualization of psychiatric patients: Validity of the Personal Orientation Inventory. *Educational and Psychological Measurement*, **28**, 565–569.

Grossack, M., Armstrong, T., & Lussiev, G. (1966). Correlates of self-actualization. *Journal of Humanistic Psychology*, **6**, 87.

Hall, M. H. (1968). A Conversation with Abraham H. Maslow. *Psychology Today*, **2**, 35–37, 54–57.

Hardeman, M. (1979). A dialogue with Abraham Maslow. *Journal of Humanistic Psychology*, **19**, 23–28.

Haymas, M., & Green, L. (1982). The assessment of motivation within Maslow's framework. *Journal of Research in Personality*, **16**, 179–192.

Hoffman, E. (1988). *The right to be human: A biography of Abraham Maslow.* Los Angeles: Jeremy P. Tarcher.

Ilardi, R. L., & May, W. T. (1968). A reliability study of Shostrom's Personal Orientation Inventory. *Journal of Humanistic Psychology*, **8**, 68–72.

Jansen, D. G., Knapp, R. R., & Michael, W. B. (1979). Construct validation of concepts of actualizing measured by the Personal Orientation Dimensions. *Educational and Psychological Measurement*, **39**, 505–509.

Jones, A., & Crandall, R. (1986). Validation of a short index of self-actualization. *Personality and Social Psychology Bulletin*, **12**, 63–73.

Kelly, R. B., & Choran, V. (1985). Yet another empirical test of the relationship between self-actualization and moral judgment. *Psychological Reports*, **56**, 201–202.

Keys, A., Brozek, J., Henschel, A., & Mickelson, H. (1950). *The biology of human starvation.* Minneapolis: University of Minnesota Press.

Knapp, R. R. (1965). Relationship of a measure of self-actualization to neuroticism and extraversion. *Journal of Consulting Psychology*, **29**, 168–172.

Knapp, R. R. (1976). *Handbook for the Personal Orientation Inventory.* San Diego, CA: EdITS Publishers.

Knapp, R. R., & Knapp, L. (1978). Conceptual and statistical refinement and extension of the measurement of actualizing concurrent validity of the Personal Orientation Dimensions (POD). *Educational and Psychological Measurement*, **38**, 523–526.

Leonard, G. (1983). Abraham Maslow and the new self. *Esquire,* December, 326–336.

LeMay, M., & Damm, V. (1968). The Personal Orientation Inventory as a measure of self-actualization of underachievers. *Measurement and Evaluation in Guidance*, 110–114.

Lester, D., Hvezda, J., Sullivan, S., & Plourde, R. (1983). Maslow's hierarchy of needs and psychological health. *The Journal of General Psychology*, **109**, 83–85.

Maddi, S. R. (1988). *Personality theories: A comparative analysis* (5th ed.). Chicago: Dorsey Press.

Maddi, S. R., & Costa, P. (1972). *Humanism in personology: Allport, Maslow, and Murray*. Chicago: Aldine-Atherton.

Maslow, A. H. (1950). *Self-actualizing people: A study of psychological health. Personality symposia: Symposium #1 on values* (pp. 11–34). New York: Grune & Stratton.

Maslow, A. H. (1956). A philosophy of psychology. In J. Fairchild (Ed.), *Personal problems and psychological frontiers*. New York: Sheridan House.

Maslow, A. H. (1964). *Religions, values and peak experiences*. New York: Viking.

Maslow, A. H. (1965). *Eupsychian management: A journal*. Homewood, IL: Irwin-Dorsey.

Maslow, A. H. (1966). *The psychology of science: A reconnaissance*. New York: Harper and Row.

Maslow, A. H. (1967). A theory of metamotivation: The biological rooting of the value-life. *Journal of Humanistic Psychology*, 7, 93–127.

Maslow, A. H. (1968). *Toward a psychology of being* (2nd ed.). New York: Van Nostrand.

Maslow, A. H. (1969). Toward a humanistic biology. *American Psychologist*, 24, 724–735.

Maslow, A. H. (1970). *Motivation and personality* (2nd ed.). New York: Harper and Row.

Maslow, A. H. (1971). *The farther reaches of human nature*. New York: Viking Press.

Maslow, A. H. (1987). *Motivation and personality* (3rd ed.). New York: Harper and Row.

Mathes, E. W., Zevon, M. A., Roter, P. M., & Joerger, S. M. (1982). Peak experience tendencies: Scale development and theory testing. *Journal of Humanistic Psychology*, 22, 92–108.

Mattocks, A. L., & Jew, C. (1974). Comparison of self-actualization levels and adjustment scores of incarcerated male felons. *Journal of Educational and Psychological Measurement*, 34, 69–74.

McClain, E. (1970). Further validation of the Personal Orientation Inventory: Assessment of self-actualization of school counselors. *Journal of Consulting and Clinical Psychology*, 35, 21–22.

Ravizza, K. (1977). Peak experiences in sport. *Journal of Humanistic Psychology*, 17, 35–40.

Sartre, J. P. (1957). *Existentialism and human emotions*. New York: Wisdom Library.

Shostrom, E. L. (1964). An inventory for the measurement of self-actualization. *Educational and Psychological Measurement*, 24, 207–218.

Shostrom, E. L. (1974). *Manual for the Personal Orientation Inventory*. San Diego, CA: EdITS Publishers.

Shostrom, E. L. (1975). *Personal Orientation Dimensions*. San Diego, CA: EdITS Publishers.

Shostrom, E. L. (1977). *Manual for the Personal Orientation Dimensions*. San Diego, CA: EdITS Publishers.

Shostrom, E. L., & Knapp, R. R. (1966). The relationship of a measure of self-actualization (POI) to a measure of pathology (MMPI) and to therapeutic growth. *American Journal of Psychotherapy*, 20, 193–202.

Stewart, R. A. (1968). Academic performance and components of self-actualization. *Perceptual and Motor Skills*, 26, 918.

Tavris, C., & Wade, C. (1984). *The longest war: Sex differences in perspective*. New York: Harcourt Brace Jovanovich.

Wilson, C. (1972). *New pathways in psychology:* Maslow and the post-Freudian revolution. New York: Taplinger Publishing.

Zaccaria, J. S., & Weir, R. W. (1967). A comparison of alcoholics and selected samples of non-alcoholics in terms of a positive concept of mental health. *Journal of Social Psychology*, **71**, 151–157.

SUGGESTED READINGS

Csikszentmihalyi, M. (1982). Toward a psychology of optimal experience. In L. Wheeler (Ed.), *Review of personality and social psychology* (Vol. 3, pp. 13–36). Beverly Hills, CA: Sage.

Deci, E. L., & Rayn, R. M. (1985). *Intrinsic motivation and self-determination in human behavior.* New York: Plenum.

Goble, F. (1970). *The third force: The psychology of Abraham Maslow.* New York: Pocket Books.

Royce, J. R., & Mos, L. P. (1981). *Humanistic psychology: Concepts and criticisms.* New York: Plenum.

Valle, R. S., Kennedy, J. F., & Halling, S. (Eds.). (1989). *Existential-phenomenological perspectives in psychology: Exploring the breadth of human experience.* New York: Plenum.

Walsh, R., & Shapiro, D. (Eds.). (1983). *Beyond health and normality: Explorations of exceptional psychological well-being.* New York: Van Nostrand Reinhold.

Williams, D. E., & Page, M. M. (1989). A multidimensional measure of Maslow's hierarchy of needs. *Journal of Research in Personality*, **23**, 192–213.

Yankelovich, D. (1981). *New rules: Searching for self-fulfillment in a world turned upside down.* New York: Random House.

DISCUSSION QUESTIONS

1 Of the three dominant movements in twentieth-century psychology—psychoanalysis, behaviorism, and humanistic psychology—which most closely resembles your own view of personality and human behavior? Why? Can you see any relationship between your theoretical preference and your own basic assumptions concerning human nature? Explain.

2 One of the key tenets of humanistic psychology is the irrelevance of animal research for understanding people. Do you agree with this idea? Why? If not, specify exactly what we have learned about human behavior from the study of lower organisms.

3 How would you evaluate Maslow's hierarchical theory of motivation? Does his view of human motivation make sense in terms of understanding your own behavior and that of others? Give some examples.

4 In Maslow's account of self-esteem needs, there are two subsidiary sets: self-respect and respect from other people. If you had to make a choice, which of these two need sets would you consider to be most important in maintaining your own psychological health? Explain.

5 What are some of the major reasons why so few people attain self-actualization as envisioned by Maslow? What, according to Maslow, is the consequence of a person's failure to satisfy his or her metaneeds?

6 Discuss differences in life-style associated with deficit living versus growth living.

7 How does Maslow's view of human nature differ from that of Freud's? Cite specific basic assumptions to support your answer.

8 How would you assess the empirical status of Maslow's humanistic theory? Is there any research evidence that supports key concepts and/or principles found in Maslow's work? How do investigators usually measure individual differences in self-actualization?

9 What are some of the major behavioral characteristics found in self-actualizing people? How did Maslow discover these characteristics? Has his research been found to be lacking by others in terms of methodological rigor? Explain.

10 Briefly describe Maslow's psychological utopia—i.e., the kind of society that would be most conducive to the attainment of self-actualization for the greatest number of people. Do you consider this utopia to be at all practical or feasible in the context of our rapidly changing world or simply an exercise in armchair philosophizing? Explain your views.

GLOSSARY

B-love   Being love, a type of love in which the person values another as an end in himself or herself, without any desire to change or use that other in any way.

Becoming   Developmental process whereby an individual assumes responsibility as a free agent to realize as many of his or her potentials as possible.

Belongingness need   Basic need that motivates a person toward affectionate relationships with others. Gratification of this need is found through friends, family life, and membership in groups and organizations.

D-love   Deficiency love, a selfish type of love in which the person is concerned more with receiving love than with giving love to another.

Deficiency motives (D-motives)   Basic needs aimed at eliminating organismic tension, especially those needs arising from physiological and safety demands. For Maslow, deficiency needs must be satisfied before a person can progress toward self-actualization.

Eupsychia   Maslow's humanistic utopia characterized by free choice, social harmony, and psychological health.

Existential philosophy   Philosophical view that each person is ultimately responsible for his or her own life. Emphasis is also placed on the person as a "being-in-the-world."

Growth motive   Higher level needs (metaneeds) associated with the inborn urge to actualize one's potentials. Growth motives emerge only if basic needs have been satisfied. They increase the joy of being alive. Also known as *being* or *B-motives*.

Hierarchy of needs   The arrangement of human needs from lowest to highest in terms of their prepotency or urgency.

Humanistic psychology   Type of psychology primarily focused on the study of healthy and creative individuals. Humanistic psychologists emphasize the uniqueness of the individual, the quest for values and meaning, and the freedom inherent in self-direction and self-fulfillment (also called *third force psychology*).

Inner-directed   A major scale on the Personal Orientation Inventory which assesses an individual's tendency to depend on internalized principles and motives as the basis for determining judgments and actions.

Instinctoid   A term used by Maslow to describe the innate basis of human needs.

Jonah complex   The doubt and fear of one's own abilities to achieve self-actualization.

Metapathology   Term used by Maslow to indicate psychological disorders (e.g., apathy, depression, cynicism) resulting from failure to satisfy one's metaneeds.

Meta value   Those higher aspects of life pursued by self-actualizing individuals. Included are such values as truth, goodness, beauty, justice, and perfection. Also called *meta-needs*.

Other-directed   A major scale on the Personal Orientation Inventory which assesses an individual's tendency to depend on others and social norms as the basis for determining judgments and actions.

Peak experience   State in which a person feels intense excitement and/or relaxation. Such a state is often accompanied by a feeling of power and confidence, a profound sense that there is nothing one could not accomplish or become.

Peak scale   A self-report scale used to measure the tendency to have peak experiences.

Personal Orientation Dimensions (POD)   A new test to measure self-actualization.

Personal Orientation Inventory (POI)   A self-report personality questionnaire designed to measure an individual's degree of self-actualization.

Phenomenological   The viewpoint that the only reality anyone ever knows is subjective or personal, not objective.

Physiological need   Most basic and powerful of all human needs, it includes the need for water, food, oxygen, sleep, etc.

Safety-security need   Basic need that motivates a person to establish a reasonble amount of order, structure, and predictability in his or her environment.

Self-actualizers   People who have satisfied their deficiency needs and developed their potentials to the extent that they can be considered supremely healthy human beings.

Self-actualization   Process postulated by Maslow as involving the healthy development of the abilities of people so that they can become all that they are capable of becoming and thus live a meaningful and fulfilling life.

Self-esteem need   Basic need that motivates a person to gain recognition and esteem from others.

Time competence   A major scale on the Personal Orientation Inventory which assesses a person's tendency to live in the present, as opposed to being focused on the past or the future.

Third force psychology   An approach to psychology that Maslow and others viewed as a viable alternative to psychoanalysis and behaviorism (also called *humanistic psychology*). An emphasis on the human capacity for personal growth is the defining feature of third force psychology.

1.

THE PHENOMENOLOGICAL PERSPECTIVE IN PERSONALITY THEORY: CARL ROGERS

The *phenomenological* perspective on personality emphasizes the idea that a person's behavior can be understood only in terms of his or her subjective perceptions and cognitions of reality. Phenomenologists believe that it is the person's internal frame of reference—or subjective apprehension of reality—that plays the key role in determining the person's overt behavior. Pressed to its logical extreme, this perspective rejects the notion that the surrounding environment is something that really exists "out there" as a fixed reality shared by others. Instead, it is claimed that material or objective reality is reality as it is consciously perceived and interpreted by the person at a particular point in time. This assumption is a cornerstone of the phenomenological approach to personality (Watzlawick, 1984).

Another major theme characterizing the phenomenological perspective is the idea that people have the capacity to determine their own destinies. In effect, phenomenologists believe that people are free to decide what their lives are to be like within the context of inborn capabilities and limitations. The view that self-determination is an essential part of human nature leads, in turn, to the belief that people are ultimately responsible for what they make of themselves. Unfortunately, some people tend to function in such a way as to suggest that they do not perceive themselves as the main controlling agents in their own lives. Like expendable pawns on a chessboard, these people experience life as if they are "moved around" by larger forces over which they have very little control. According to the phenomenological position, if this happens it is only because these people have lost sight of the freedom of self-determination that is theirs by nature.

A final theme characterizing the phenomenological approach to personality is that human beings are inherently good and self-perfecting. In particular, this viewpoint assumes that it is natural and inevitable for people to progress in the direction of greater differentiation, autonomy, and maturity. This growth process—focused on realizing inner possibilities and potentials over the life span—clearly reflects a positive and optimistic view of humanity.

Traces of the three basic themes associated with a phenomenological perspective on personality are evidenced in the theories of Maslow and Kelly, presented in the two preceding chapters. Nonetheless, it is generally acknowledged that the concepts and emphases accompanying the phenomenological approach to personality are expressed most directly in the work of Carl Rogers. His theoretical position is presented in this chapter because it represents a focused effort to understand how the person perceives the world in a unique way. Rogers' theory also is presented because it gives attention to the concept of *self* and experiences related to the self, and because it emphasizes the importance of growth-promoting tendencies inherent in all people. The impact of Rogers' writings is widespread and is by no means limited to personological theorizing. He played a key role in the development of encounter groups as a means of helping people from all segments of society to improve and enrich their interpersonal relationships. Additionally, his ideas have had a monumental impact on such disciplines as social work, nursing, pastoral and marital counseling, group dynamics, and education. It is difficult to overestimate Rogers' profound influence on therapeutic and educational approaches used by helping professionals today.

CARL ROGERS: A Phenomenological Theory of Personality

BIOGRAPHICAL SKETCH

Carl Ransom Rogers was born in Oak Park (a Chicago suburb), Illinois, in 1902. He was the fourth of six children, five of whom were boys. His father was a civil engineer and contractor who achieved financial success in his profession, so the family was economically secure throughout Rogers' early life. When he was 12 years old, Rogers' parents moved to a farm west of Chicago, and it was in this rural setting that he spent his adolescence. The family members were self-reliant yet inwardly dependent upon one another, and there is no impression of actual joy or contentment among its members. Rogers (1973) recalled his boyhood years as structured by a strict and uncompromising religious and ethical atmosphere. He described his parents as sensitive and loving, but nonetheless devoutly and dogmatically committed to fundamentalist religious views.

Having no close friends outside his family, Rogers spent much time in solitary pursuits, especially reading adventure books. In fact, he read any book he could find, including the dictionary and encyclopedia. The pattern of social isolation and loneliness continued throughout Rogers' high school years. He attended three different high schools, none for more than two years, commuting long distances

Carl R. Rogers. (*Courtesy Carl Rogers Memorial Library*).

by train to each one, so that he was never able to participate in extracurricular activities with other students. However, Rogers was an excellent student. He received straight "A" grades in almost all his courses and did his best work in English and science. Summer vacations were consumed by long hours of tiring work on the farm:

> I rode a cultivator all day long, usually being assigned to the cornfield at the far end of the farm which was full of quack grass. It was a lesson in independence to be on my own, far away from anyone else. . . . It was a type of responsibility experienced by few young people today. (Rogers, 1967, p. 347)

During his adolescence, Rogers developed a passionate interest in nature and adopted a scientific attitude toward farming, taking detailed notes of his observations of both plants and animals. He collected, bred, and raised a certain species of moth and read everything he could find about moths. He likewise read the books that his father brought home about agriculture and how scientific methods could be applied to farming.

Upon graduation from high school Rogers intended to become a farmer. He entered the University of Wisconsin in 1919, a family alma mater, and chose scientific agriculture as his field of study. During his sophomore year, however, he became deeply involved with religious activities on campus and attended a student religious conference which had as its slogan "Evangelize the world in our generation." This experience encouraged him to prepare for the ministry. The following year, in 1922, an event occurred that changed the direction of his life. He was selected as one of 10 United States college students to attend the World Student Christian Federation Conference in Peking, China. Abroad for more than six months, he observed a range of religious and cultural attitudes far different from his own. The experiences in the Orient not only liberalized Rogers' outlook on life but also caused him to question the divinity of Jesus. This trip also marked Rogers' declaration of independence from the intellectual and religious ties with his parents. Following his sojourn in the Orient, Rogers returned to Wisconsin and completed his B.A. degree in history in 1924. At this point he had had only one psychology course—by correspondence!

Following graduation, Rogers married Helen Elliott, a Wisconsin classmate whom he had known since childhood. That summer the newlyweds set out in a Model-T Ford for the liberal Union Theological Seminary in New York City. Rogers found life in New York stimulating and exciting: "I made friends, found new ideas, and fell thoroughly in love with the whole experience" (1967, p. 353). While at Union Seminary, Rogers first realized that the goal of helping distressed persons was one that the ministry and mental health professions shared. Gradually, however, he became disenchanted with the academic courses in religion—a disenchantment augmented by his growing skepticism about doctrinaire attitudes of religious work. Finally, at the end of his second year he transferred from the seminary to Columbia University Teachers College to pursue graduate study in clinical and educational psychology. Rogers obtained his M.A. in 1928 and his Ph.D. in clinical psychology in 1931.

In 1931 Rogers accepted a position as staff psychologist at the Child Study Department of the Society for the Prevention of Cruelty to Children in Rochester, New York. For the next decade Rogers was very active in applied psychological service for delinquent and underprivileged children. He was also instrumental in forming the Rochester Guidance Center, of which he emerged as director despite strong feelings that the office should be held by a psychiatrist. As a result of publishing a highly successful volume entitled *The Clinical Treatment of the Problem Child* in 1939, Rogers was offered a faculty appointment with the rank of full professor in the psychology department at Ohio State University. In 1940 Rogers moved to Columbus to begin a new career. The move into academia brought Rogers wide recognition in the burgeoning field of clinical psychology. He attracted many talented graduate students and began to publish numerous articles detailing his views of psychotherapy and how it might be empirically investigated. These ideas were put forth in his book *Counseling and Psychotherapy*, published in 1942.

In 1945 Rogers took a position at the University of Chicago, where he was professor of psychology and director of the university counseling center. This position enabled him to establish a counseling center for undergraduates where professional staff and graduate students worked as equals. The years 1945 to 1957 at Chicago were among the most productive and creative of his career. During this period he completed his major work, *Client-Centered Therapy: Its Current Practice, Implications, and Theory* (1951), a book detailing the theory underlying his approach to interpersonal relations and personality change. He also conducted several investigations on the process and outcome of psychotherapy. It was also a period of personal setbacks. While counseling an extremely disturbed client, Rogers became engulfed in her pathology. Close to breakdown himself, he literally fled the counseling center, took a three-month vacation, and returned to enter therapy with one of his former students. In later years he reflected: "I have often been grateful that by the time I was in dire need of personal help, I had trained therapists who were persons in their own right, not dependent upon me, yet able to offer me the kind of help I needed" (1967, p. 367).

In 1957 Rogers returned to the University of Wisconsin, where he held joint appointments in the departments of psychology and psychiatry. He subsequently initiated an intensive research program utilizing psychotherapy with schizophrenic patients in a state mental hospital. Unfortunately, this research program encountered several problems and proved to be far less successful than Rogers had anticipated. Several staff members were opposed to Rogers' therapeutic approach, data mysteriously disappeared, and findings indicated that schizophrenics in the program showed little improvement when compared with patients exposed to routine hospital activities.

Rogers resigned from his academic post in 1964 to become a fellow at the Western Behavioral Sciences Institute (WBSI) in LaJolla, California, a nonprofit organization devoted to humanistically oriented research in interpersonal relationships. Four years later he left WBSI to take a position with the Center for the Studies of the Person, also situated in LaJolla. There he remained active until he died of a heart attack following surgery for a broken hip in 1987. In his final years, Rogers conducted workshops around the globe in which he demonstrated to psychologists and other mental health workers, educators, and politicians how concepts derived from his person-centered philosophy could be used to ease world tensions and promote peace. "The problem of preventing a nuclear holocaust has top priority in my mind, my heart, and my work" (Rogers, 1984, p. 15).

Rogers received many awards for his contributions to psychology and was active in numerous scholarly societies. He was elected as president of the American Psychological Association in 1946–1947 and was awarded the APA's first Distinguished Scientific Contribution Award in 1956. He was also a recipient of the APA Distinguished Professional Contribution Award in 1972. In an address presented to the 1972 APA convention, he summed up his contributions to psychology in the following way: "I expressed an idea whose time had come, as though a pebble was dropped in water and spread ripples. The idea was that the individual has vast resources within himself for altering his life and these resources can be mobilized given the proper climate" (1973, p. 4). If a theory is judged solely on the basis of its influence on professional psychology, then the theory of Carl Rogers must be ranked very high indeed. No one since Freud has had more impact on the practice of counseling and therapy than Rogers.

Rogers authored several readable books on counseling and personality, including *Psychotherapy and Personality Change* (with R. Dymond, 1954); *On Becoming a Person: A Therapist's View of Psychotherapy* (1961); *Person to Person: The Problem of Being Human* (with B. Stevens, 1967); *Freedom to Learn: A View of What Education Might Become* (1969); *Carl Rogers on Encounter Groups* (1970); *Becoming Partners: Marriage and Its Alternatives* (1972); *Carl Rogers on Per-*

sonal Power (1977); *A Way of Being* (1980); and finally, *Freedom to Learn for the 80s* (1983). His autobiography appears in *A History of Psychology in Autobiography* (Volume 5, 1967, pp. 341–384).

ROGERS' VIEW OF HUMAN NATURE

Rogers' view of human nature, like Freud's, grew out of his personal experiences in working with emotionally disturbed people. He acknowledged that the major impetus to his ideas was his concern for people in need of professional help: "From these hours, and from my relationships with these people, I have drawn most of whatever insight I possess into the meaning of therapy, the dynamics of interpersonal relationships, and the structure and functioning of personality" (1959, p. 188).

As a result of his clinical experiences, Rogers concluded that the innermost core of human nature is essentially purposive, forward-moving, constructive, realistic, and quite trustworthy. He regarded the person as an active force of energy oriented toward future goals and self-directed purposes, rather than as a creature pushed and pulled by forces beyond his or her control. Such a viewpoint clearly implies the faith of a Rousseau in the inherent goodness of human nature—a belief that if the innate potential of this nature is allowed to unfold and blossom, optimal personal development and effectiveness will result.

Rogers contended that Christianity nourished the belief that human beings are innately evil and sinful. He also argued that this negative view of humanity was reinforced by Freud, who presented a portrait of the person with an id and an unconscious which would, if permitted expression, manifest itself in incest, homicide, thievery, rape, and other horrendous acts. According to this view, humanity is fundamentally irrational, unsocialized, selfish, and destructive of self and others. Rogers (1980) conceded that people occasionally express bitter and murderous feelings, abnormal impulses, and bizarre and antisocial actions, but he insisted that at such times they are not behaving in concert with their true inner nature. Thus, when people are *functioning fully*, when they are free to experience and to satisfy their inner natures, they show themselves to be positive and rational creatures who can be trusted to live in harmony with themselves and others. Aware that his view of human nature may be considered to be nothing more than naive optimism, Rogers noted that his conclusions were based on almost 30 years of psychotherapeutic experience. He declared:

> I do not have a Pollyanna view of human nature. I am quite aware that out of defensiveness and inner fear individuals can and do behave in ways which are incredibly cruel, horribly destructive, immature, regressive, anti-social, and harmful. Yet one of the most refreshing and invigorating parts of my experience is to work with such individuals and to discover the strongly positive directional tendencies which exist in them, as in all of us, at the deepest levels. (1961, p. 27)

In stark contrast to the Freudian tradition, Rogers accented the natural development of human beings toward the "constructive fulfillment" of their inherent possibilities. "So when a Freudian such as Karl Menninger tells me (as he has, in a discussion of this issue) that he perceives man as 'innately evil' or more precisely, 'innately destructive,' I can only shake my head in wonderment" (quoted in Kirschenbaum, 1979, p. 250). In conclusion, Rogers had a profound (almost religious) sense of respect for human nature. He affirmed that all of humanity has a natural tendency to move in the direction of independence, social responsibility, creativity, and maturity. It should be noted that such assumptions about human nature appear throughout Rogerian theory and are closely identified with the humanistic perspective in personology.

Although Rogers and Maslow shared the belief that human beings have virtually unlimited potential to develop in self-fulfilling ways, three key differences in their respective theories can be observed. First and foremost, Rogers believed that personality and behavior are largely a function of the person's unique perception of the environment. Maslow, on the other hand, took the view that the person's behavior and experience are guided by a hierarchy of needs. Unlike Rogers, Maslow did not stress the phenomenology of the person. Secondly, Rogers' theory evolved mainly from his work with people suffering psychological pain. Indeed, Rogers focused his attention on the therapeutic conditions that facilitate the person's growth toward self-actualization and expanded what he learned from therapy into a general theory of personality. Maslow, by contrast, never practiced therapy and urged psychology to turn its attention from the study of abnormality to the study of psychologically healthy people. Finally, Rogers identified certain developmental patterns as promoting the person's propensity toward fulfillment of innate potential. In Maslow's theory, however, the developmental processes governing the person's course of movement toward full actualization of inner potential are virtually ignored. In fact, Maslow wrote almost entirely on adulthood, though he did acknowledge that people are vulnerable to the lack of need satisfaction at certain "critical stages" in the life cycle. Despite these noted theoretical differences, both Rogers and Maslow believed that people are essentially forward-moving and, under the proper conditions, will realize their full potential for psychological health.

LIFE'S MASTER MOTIVE: THE ACTUALIZING TENDENCY

In line with his positive view of human nature, Rogers hypothesized that all behavior is energized and guided by a single, unitary motive which he called the *actualizing tendency*. This represents "the inherent tendency of the organism to develop all its capacities in ways which serve to maintain or enhance the person" (Rogers, 1959, p. 196). Thus, the primary motive in people's lives is to actualize, maintain, or enhance themselves—to become the best self that their inherited natures will allow them to be. This basic actualizing tendency is the *only* motivational construct postulated by Rogers. Indeed, Rogers (1980) felt that there was nothing to be gained from postulating specific motives—such as hunger, sex, and security—and using these hypothetical motives to explain the why of behavior. Take hunger as an illustration. Traditionally, psychology has regarded it as a separate drive or motive, a thing unto itself. In Rogers' system, hunger is just one specific expression of the master motive underlying human existence; specifically, it serves to "maintain" the person. If you don't believe this, stop eating. You will come to believe it in less than a week—or die trying. Or consider sex as a motive. Sex serves to "enhance" the person. This requires no elaboration. Or the need for achievement—the desire to excel and strive to accomplish difficult tasks. In Rogers' view, such a need can easily be construed as one expression of the actualizing tendency. A person seeks achievement as a way of fulfilling his or her inner potential as a human being.

Rogers believed that the actualizing tendency will naturally express itself through a wide range of behaviors provided there are no strong external constraints or opposing influences. Furthermore, certain definitive characteristics mark the actualizing tendency as the "one central source of energy in the human organism" (Rogers, 1980, p. 123). First, it is rooted in the physiological processes of the entire body (i.e., it is a *biological fact*, not a psychological tendency). At an organic level this inborn predisposition involves not only the maintenance of the organism by meeting deficiency needs (air, food, water) but also the enhancement of the organism by providing for development and differentiation of the body's organs and functions, its growth and continual regeneration. Of even greater significance is the motivating force which the actualizing tendency exerts on psychological processes pertaining to the self. The actualizing tendency is an active process and accounts for the organism's always being up to something, whether initiating, exploring, producing change in the environment, playing, or even creating. It moves the person in the direction of enhanced autonomy and self-sufficiency.

Secondly, the actualizing tendency does not merely aim at tension reduction (the preservation of life processes and the pursuit of comfort and quiescence). It also involves *tension increase*. Instead of seeing all behavior as having the discharge of tension as its ultimate goal, Rogers viewed behavior as motivated by the person's need to develop and improve. A person is governed by a growth process in which potentialities and capacities are brought to realization. Additionally, Rogers maintained that this constructive biological tendency is common to all forms of life—it is characteristic not only of human beings, or only of animals, but also of all living beings. It is the essence of life.

Rogers neglected to give many concrete behavioral examples of the actualizing tendency, but it might be characterized in terms of wanting to achieve or accomplish something that makes the person's life more enriching and satisfying (e.g., getting good grades, obtaining a job promotion, striving to be independent, helping people with AIDS). Numerous other examples also illustrate the operation of Rogers' actualizing principle. For example, a young child learning to walk is impressive by virtue of her tenacity—she really "hangs in there" and actualizes. She falls backward, buckles at the knees, bumps her head, and smashes her nose. Yet, eventually, she walks. Similarly, tennis players strive to perfect their forehand and backhand, golfers their putting and driving, college professors their publication records, and adolescents their identities. This movement toward self-

A young child taking his first steps demonstrates the actualizing tendency seen not only in humans, but in all living things. *(Ray Ellis/Photo Researchers)*

development is often accompanied by struggle and pain, but because the urge is compelling, the person perseveres despite the pain and setback she may have to endure. In short, Rogers assumed that virtually everything that humans do is aimed at increasing their competence, or actualizing themselves.

For Rogers, all life experiences are evaluated in terms of how well they serve the actualizing tendency. This assumption is reflected in another term he used in connection with the tendency: the *organismic valuing process.* This phrase reflects the idea that those experiences that people perceive to be promoting or enhancing of the self are sought after and assigned a positive value. People derive a feeling of satisfaction from such positive experiences. Conversely, those experiences perceived as negating or hindering actualization of the self are avoided and valued negatively. The organismic valuing process enables people to evaluate experiences in light of whether they facilitate or impede their actualizing tendency. Accordingly, the natural tendency is to approach actualizing experiences and avoid those perceived to be otherwise. Rogers suggested that even infants, if given the opportunity, will act according to the organismic valuing process: "The simplest example is the infant who at one moment values food, and when satiated, is disgusted with it; at one moment values stimulation and soon after, values only rest; who finds satisfying the diet which in the long run most enhances his development" (1959, p. 210).

The most critical aspect of the actualizing tendency from the standpoint of personality is the person's drive toward self-actualization. In the context of

Rogerian theory, the *self-actualizing tendency* is a person's lifelong process of realizing his or her potentialities to become a fully functioning person. In so doing, the person lives a life filled with meaning, challenge, and personal excitement. Additionally, the self-actualizing person lives existentially, flowing spontaneously with each moment of life and participating fully in it. For Rogers, no special motivational constructs (i.e., specific drives) are required to understand why a human being is active; every person is inherently motivated simply by being alive. Motives and drives do not account for the activity and goal-directedness of the organism. Humanity is basically active and self-actualizing by virtue of its nature.

It must be emphasized that self-actualization is not a final state of perfection. Indeed, Rogers believed that no person ever becomes self-actualized enough to abandon the motive altogether. There are always more talents to develop, more skills to enhance, more efficient and pleasurable ways to satisfy biological urges. It is possible, however, to speak of some people as engaging in the self-actualizing process to a greater degree than others; they have moved further toward a way of functioning that is self-fulfilling, creative, and autonomous. We will say more about the self-actualizing tendency when we describe the fully functioning person in a later section of this chapter.

ROGERS' PHENOMENOLOGICAL POSITION

As we have seen, Rogers' theory is illustrative of the phenomenological approach to personality. A *phenomenological* perspective holds that what is real to an individual (i.e., what reality is thought, understood, or felt to be) is that which exists within that person's *internal frame of reference*, or subjective world, including everything in his awareness at any point in time. It follows that subjective perceptions and experiences not only constitute the person's private reality but also form the basis for his actions. Phenomenologically, each of us responds to events in accordance with how we subjectively perceive them. For example, a thirsty man stranded in the desert will run as eagerly to a pool of water that is a mirage as to a real pool. Similarly, two people observing an identical set of circumstances may later recall two very different outcomes, which is often the case with "eyewitness" accounts of unidentified flying objects, traffic accidents, and other unexpected events.

Phenomenological psychology asserts as its basic doctrine that the psychological reality of phenomena is exclusively a function of the way in which they are perceived. A person's senses do not directly mirror the world of reality; instead, effective reality is reality as it is observed and interpreted by the reacting organism. Each person, then, according to Rogers (1959), construes reality in accordance with his private world of experience, and this experiential world can be completely known only to the person. A final point here is that Rogers (1961), unlike Kelly, avoided making any assertions about the nature of "objective" reality. He concerned himself only with *psychological reality* (i.e., how the person perceives and interprets whatever information is received through the senses), leaving objective reality to the philosophers.

One important implication of a phenomenological perspective for a theory of personality is that understanding of a person's behavior depends on study of his or her subjective personal experiences of reality. If we wish to explain why a person thinks, feels, and behaves in a given way, we need to get inside his personal world of meaning. Subjective experience is thus the key to understanding behavior. This means that the most important aspect of psychological inquiry is a person's subjective experiences, because these experiences alone are ultimately responsible for guiding behavior. It is this phenomenological reality that the personologist, according to Rogers, must attempt to analyze and understand.

The Supremacy of Subjective Experience

The relationship between experience and behavior is an essential theme in Rogers' phenomenological theory. He insisted that a person's behavior cannot be understood without reference to the person's subjective interpretation of events. In terms of predicting behavior, Rogers maintained that a person acts in accordance with his impression of what is happening at the moment. He thus advocated abandoning Skinner's notion that the regularities of behavior can be explained in terms of a person's response to the objective stimulus situation—rather, it is *the interpretation* of the stimulus situation and of its personal meaning that governs his or her behavior. What is critical in life is the perception of things; it is what eggnog tastes like to me, what love and anger feel like to me, what a particular person means to me. It follows that no one can legitimately claim that his sense of reality is necessarily better or more correct than that of anyone else; no one has the right to impose his reality upon others.

For the most part, Rogers rejected Freud's position that historical aspects or derivatives of behavior are the primary factors underlying personality. Behavior is not determined by something that occurred in the past. Instead, Rogers emphasized the need to understand the person's relationship to the environment as he now exists and perceives it. It is our present interpretation of past experiences rather than their factual existence that influences our current behavior. If Rogers were asked, for instance, "What causes that person to act in such a hostile way?" he would respond, "He views the world as a dangerous place and considers himself unloved and unlovable." Rogers would not respond, "He was deprived and abused when he was a child."

The significance of this *ahistorical* view is that it is unnecessary to retrace a distant past in order to discover why a person is behaving as she is today. To be sure, Rogers recognized that past experiences exert an influence on the meaning of present experiences. However, he insisted that current behavior is always affected by present perception and interpretation. Moreover, Rogers believed that ongoing behavior is strongly affected by how people foresee their future (note the similarity to Kelly's personal construct system here). For instance, if a young woman regards herself as a socially unskilled person who has experienced difficulty with men, her present dilemma is not so much due to past failures as it is to her perceived anticipation of future failures. She is governed by a self-fulfilling prophecy, namely, that she will be unable to interest men because of her lack of social charm. Changing her negative self-image would presumably result in more rewarding heterosexual experiences in the future. Thus, Rogers favored the idea that personality should be studied within a "present-future" framework.

Finally, Rogers stressed that the complexity of behavior can only be understood by reference to the entire person. In other words, he espoused a *holistic* view of personality, the view that a person behaves as an integrated organism and that his or her unity cannot be derived by attempting to reduce it to its component parts. Rogers' commitment to a holistic perspective is manifest in practically every facet of his theoretical system.

CONCEPT OF SELF: WHO AM I ANYWAY?

It should be clear from the preceding discussion that the concept of self is crucial to the approach taken by Rogers. In fact, the construct of self is such an indispensable part of Rogerian theory that some psychologists have designated it "self theory" (Patterson, 1973). Surprisingly, however, Rogers did not begin his theorizing by assuming the importance of the self in human experience. Rather, he started with a notion of the self as "a vague, ambiguous, scientifically meaningless term" no longer in vogue among respected psychologists (1959, p. 200). However, his therapy clients persisted in expressing their problems and attitudes in terms of the self, and gradually he realized that self was a significant element in human experience and that the client's goal was to become her or his "real self." The *self* or *self-concept* (Rogers used the terms interchangeably) is defined as:

> the organized, consistent conceptual gestalt composed of perceptions of the characteristics of the "I" or "me" and the perceptions of the relationships of the "I" or "me" to others and to various aspects of life, together with the values attached to these perceptions. It is a gestalt which is available to awareness though not necessarily in awareness. (Rogers, 1959, p. 200)

Thus, the self is a differentiated portion of the person's *phenomenal* or *perceptual field* (defined as the totality of experience) and consists of the conscious perceptions and values of the "I" or "me." The self-concept denotes the person's conception of the kind of person he or she is. The self-concept reflects those characteristics that the person perceives as being part of himself or herself. To illustrate, a person may have the self-perceptions "I am intelligent, loving, honest, considerate, and attractive." From Rogers' perspective, the self-concept often reflects how we view ourselves in relation to the various roles we play in life. Such role images are formed as a result of increasingly complex transactions with other people. A person's self-concept may thus include a conglomeration of self-images such as parent, spouse, student, employee, supervisor, athlete, musician, and artist. It is easy to see how a person's self may be comprised of different sets of perceptions reflecting many specific "roles" in each of various life contexts (Markus & Nurius, 1986).

The self-concept includes not only our perceptions of what we are like but also what we think we ought to be and would like to be. This latter component of the self is called the *ideal self*. For Rogers, the ideal self reflects those attributes that the person would like to possess but currently does not. It is the self a person most values and aspires to be.

Rogers' notion of the self may be further understood in terms of its various properties and functions. To begin, Rogers posited that a person's self-conception follows the general laws and principles of perception established in scientific psychology (see Epstein, 1973, for additional discussion). This means that the self-structure functions in terms of such perceptual processes as figure-ground, closure, and similarity. Second, Rogers viewed the self-concept as being configurational in nature, meaning that it represents an organized, coherent, and integrated pattern of self-related perceptions. Thus, for example, although the person's self is fluid and constantly evolving as a result of new experiences, it always retains a patterned, gestalt-like quality. No matter how much people change over time, they always retain a firm internal sense that they are still the same person at any moment in time. Rogers further suggested that the self-concept is not a homunculus, or "little man in the head" who controls a person's actions. The self does not regulate behavior; instead, it symbolizes the individual's existing body of conscious experience. Finally, the panorama of experience and perception known as the self is, in general, conscious and admissible to awareness. Rogers believed that a concept of the self that incorporates unconscious mentation could not yield an operational definition and would therefore not be amenable to research, a necessity in his system.

Development of the Self-Concept

Unlike theorists such as Freud, Adler, and Erikson, Rogers did not formulate a specific timetable of critical stages through which people pass in acquiring a self-concept. Instead, he concentrated on the ways in which evaluations of a person by others, particularly during infancy and early childhood, tend to promote the development of a positive or negative self-image.

At first, the neonate perceives all experiences as unitary, whether produced by bodily sensations or by external stimuli such as the movement of a mobile in the crib. The infant is not aware of himself or herself as a separate being, as an "I"; therefore he or she makes no distinction between what is "me" and what is "not me." Hence, early in life self is a nonentity (does not exist); only the unitary, all-encompassing, and undifferentiated phenomenal field is present. However, out of the general tendency toward differentiation which is a part of the actualizing process, a child gradually begins to distinguish herself or himself from the rest of the world. It is this process of differentiating the phenomenal field into that which is recognized and felt as a distinct object of which one is aware that accounts for the emergence of the person's self-concept in Rogers' theory.

Rogers theorized that when the self is first formed, it is governed by the organismic valuing process alone. In other words, the infant or child evaluates each new experience in terms of whether it facilitates or impedes his or her innate actualizing tendency. For instance, hunger, thirst, cold, pain, and sudden loud noises are negatively valued, since they interfere with the maintenance of biological integrity. Food, water, security, and love are positively valued because they are seen as favoring the enhancement of the organismic tendency. In a sense, the organismic valuing process is a monitoring system that keeps the human infant on the proper course of need satisfaction. Infants evaluate their experiences according to whether or not they like them, whether they are pleasing or displeasing, and so on. Such evaluations result from their spontaneous responses to direct experiences, be they sensory, visceral, or emotional.

The structure of self is subsequently shaped through interaction with the environment, particularly the environment composed of significant others (e.g., parents, siblings, relatives). In other words, as the child becomes socially sensitive and as his or her cognitive and perceptual abilities mature, his or her self-conception becomes increasingly differentiated and complex. To a large extent, then, the content of a person's self-concept is a product of the socialization process. Elements important in self-concept development follow.

Need for Positive Regard Rogers contended that all persons have a strong desire to be loved and accepted by others that matter to them. This *need for positive regard,* which Rogers believed was universal, develops as the awareness of self emerges, and it is pervasive and persistent. It is first seen in the infant's need to be loved and cared for, and is subsequently reflected in the person's satisfaction when approved by others and frustration when disapproved. Rogers indicated that positive regard may be either learned or innately given to all persons, and although he preferred the former explanation (i.e., it is a secondary, learned motive), its origin is unimportant to his theory. An intriguing aspect of positive regard is its reciprocal nature; that is, when a person views himself or herself as satisfying another's need for positive regard, he or she necessarily experiences satisfaction of his or her own need.

In Rogers' view, the child will do almost anything, even sacrifice his organismic valuing process, to satisfy the need to be held in positive regard by others. For example, if a parent insists that a child behave like a "nice little boy" in order to receive love and affection, the child will begin to value experiences in terms of the parental image of "niceness" rather than in terms of his own organismic reaction to them. Instead of being free to discover how it would feel to say a "naughty" word, put a frog in his sister's bed, or steal a toy from a friend, he prejudges these experiences as "bad" and condemns them. Thus, the child's behavior comes to be guided not by the degree to which experiences maintain or enhance his self-concept but instead by the likelihood of receiving positive regard from the relevant people in his life. Rogers considered this state of incongruity between self and experience as the most serious obstacle in the path of development toward psychological maturity.

Rogers also proposed that people have a need to view themselves positively. The need for *positive self-regard* is a learned need that develops out of the association of self-experiences with the satisfaction or frustration of the need for

The self-concept is shaped through interaction with significant others. *(Spencer Grant/Photo Researchers)*

positive regard. To put it differently, positive self-regard refers to the satisfaction at approving and dissatisfaction at disapproving ourselves. It is as if the self-structure had become its own "significant social other." The development of positive self-regard assures that the person will strive to act in ways that are viewed favorably both by others and by himself or herself. Consequently, the person is unlikely to behave in ways that are inconsistent with his or her self-concept because this would frustrate the need for positive self-regard.

Conditions of Worth   Given the fact that children have a compelling need for positive regard, it is not surprising that they become increasingly sensitive to, or influenced by, the attitudes and expectations toward them of relevant people in their lives. To put it more bluntly, as a typical part of the socialization process, children learn that there are things they can do and things they cannot do. Most often parents will make positive regard contingent on desirable behavior by the children. That is, if the children do certain things, they will experience positive regard, if they do other things, they will not. This creates what Rogers called *conditional positive regard* or *conditions of worth*, which specify the circumstances under which children will experience positive regard. The conditions may vary widely from case to case, but the principle remains the same: I will love, respect, and accept you only if you are the kind of person I expect you to be. Conditional positive regard means that children receive praise, attention, approval, and other forms of reward for behaving in accordance with the expectations imposed by significant others, especially parents. In effect, children learn from years of experience that if they act in certain ways, ways that are valued by their parents, then they will be prized and loved. By contrast, if they act in ways that are considered as wrong or unacceptable by their parents, then they will not be valued and loved.

For example, such is the case when a father tells his son that bringing home a straight "A" report card will not only earn him an increase in his weekly allowance but also excuse him from having to wash the family car and mow the grass. Conditional positive regard is also manifest in many other types of human relationships involving the giving or withholding of approval and support. Elementary school teachers frequently award a gold star (pasted to the classroom bulletin board for all to see) to the student who is most attentive or cooperative in class. The college president awards or denies promotions to faculty members on the basis of their excellence in teaching or research activities. In each instance, the person's view of his or her self-importance (self-esteem) is dependent upon fulfilling the demands or standards imposed by others. Such conditional positive regard from others leads the person to feel prized in some respects, but not in others.

Rogers emphatically stated that conditions of worth imposed on a child are *detrimental* to his or her becoming a fully functioning person. This is because the child tries to attain standards set by others rather than to identify and attain what she or he is or wants to be. Under this circumstance, the child comes to evaluate himself and his worth as an individual (what is valuable and what is not valuable about himself) in terms of only those of his actions, thoughts, and feelings that received approval and support. The child will feel that in some respects he or she is valued and in others not. This process results in a self-concept that is out of kilter with organismic experience and hence does not serve as a solid foundation for healthy personality development.

According to Rogers, conditions of worth act like blinders on a horse, cutting off a portion of available experience. Persons with conditions of worth must restrict their behavior and distort reality because even becoming aware of forbidden behaviors and thoughts can be as threatening as displaying them. As a result of this defensiveness, such persons cannot interact fully and openly with their environment. For instance, a young child who, on an organismic level, is afraid of the diving board, may hear his peers say, "Don't be a sissy. Go ahead and jump in." The child may then distort or deny his fear in order to receive praise from his peers.

Unconditional Positive Regard   While it is obvious that no person is completely devoid of conditions of worth, Rogers felt that it is possible to give or receive positive regard irrespective of the worth placed on specific aspects of a person's behavior. This means that a person is accepted and respected for what he or she is—without any ifs, ands, or buts. Such *unconditional positive regard* is strikingly evident when a mother bestows her respect and affection on her son, not because he has fulfilled any specific condition or lived up to any specific expectation, but simply because he is her child. No matter how objectionable or repugnant the behavior and feelings of her child may be, she still prizes and values him as a worthy and lovable individual.

For Rogers, the only way not to interfere with a c
to give him or her unconditional positive regard. This n
and accepted by others in an uncritical and nonconting
that if the child should experience only unconditional po

> then no conditions of worth would develop, self-regard would
> needs for positive regard and self-regard would never be at varia
> evaluation, and the individual would continue to be psychologically a
> be fully functioning. (1959, p. 224)

In Rogers' view, nothing in a child's behavior is so objectionable
parent a reason to say, "If you do this, or if you feel this way, than I ca
value and love you." Admittedly, for the average parent, this is a
principle to remember while a 3-year-old is systematically kicking in the f
new color TV screen. However, it is important to understand that uncondit
positive regard does not literally mean that significant others must condone
approve everything the child does or says. Nor does it mean that the child shou
be permitted to do whatever he or she wants to do without being disciplined or
reprimanded. If this were the case, few children would survive childhood since
they would not be protected from real dangers. What it does mean is creating a
family environment in which the child is prized and acknowledged for exactly
what he or she is—a growing individual who can be a real pain at times but who is
nonetheless lovable. Following this line of reasoning, it would be permissible for
parents to express disapproval with certain of their child's actions—e.g., throwing food at the dinner table, hitting a younger sibling, smearing paint on dad's
newly decorated wall, pulling the dog's tail—provided that they make it known to
the child that they accept the fact that he or she wants to do these things. In other
words, Rogers felt that the best parental strategy for dealing with a misbehaving

Children who receive unconditional positive regard from others
come to view themselves favorably and to feel accepted.
*(Spencer Grant/The Picture
Cube)*

...age: "We love you deeply as you are but what you are
...efore we would be happier if you would stop." The
...and respected, but some of his or her behaviors may

...gers' emphasis on unconditional positive regard as
...ng does not imply an absence of discipline, social
...havioral control. What it does mean is providing
...valued and loved for exactly what he or she is—
...dren perceive themselves in such a way that no
...hy of positive regard than any other, they are
...*self-regard.* This, in turn, allows them to
...ctions in accord with their real experiences,
...others. Although they will be aware of expecta-
...should" do, they will trust themselves and their judgments
...ng governed by conditions existing outside themselves. In short,
...believed that treating children with unconditional positive regard provides
the foundation for their becoming fully functioning adults. Unconditional positive
self-regard unlocks the natural self-actualizing tendency present in all persons.

Experience of Threat and the Process of Defense

Rogers argued that most ways of behaving that a person adopts are consistent
with the structure of his or her self-concept. In other words, the person seeks to
maintain a state of consistency among self-perceptions and experience. It logically
follows that experiences that are in accord with the person's self-concept and its
conditions of worth are permitted entry to awareness and are perceived accurately. Conversely, incoming experiences that conflict with the self and its conditions of worth constitute a threat to the self-concept; they are prevented from
entering awareness and being accurately perceived. It should be noted here that
the person's conception of himself or herself is the criterion against which experiences are compared and either symbolized in awareness or denied symbolization.

Suppose a young man has been taught by his parents to believe that it is a sin to
engage in premarital intercourse. However, while attending college he is exposed
to attitudes and values that give unqualified support to sexual relations, especially
when one feels genuine love for another person. Although he continues to accept
his earlier introjected values, the young man is about to marry a woman who feels
that making love presents no moral dilemma since she and the young man are
deeply committed to each other. He complies but on an emotional level finds the
experience to be quite distressing. For Rogers, this experience is in direct vio-
lation of his self-image; he regards this behavior as immoral and definitely out of
line with who he really is. Consequently, engaging in sexual behavior in these
circumstances is threatening to him. It simply does not fit his self-concept.

In Rogers' theory, *threat* exists when people recognize an incongruity between
their self-concept (and its incorporated conditions of worth) and some aspect of
their actual experience. Experiences incongruent with the self-concept are per-

ceived as threatening; they are kept from entering aware.
ual's personality is no longer a holistic, unified whole. 1
herself as an honest person but finds herself doing somethii.
a state of threat. Or, as in the earlier example, the young ma
premarital sex is wrong and yet experiences it is threatened.
sponse to such a state of incongruence is usually one of tension
guilt.

Incongruency between self and experience need not be perceiv
scious level. In fact, Rogers postulated that it is quite possible for a pe
threatened without being aware of it. Consequently, whenever incc
between the self-concept and experience exists and the person is unawa
she is potentially vulnerable to anxiety and personality disorganization. A
is thus an emotional response to threat which signals that the organized
structure is in danger of becoming disorganized if the discrepancy between it a
the threatening experience reaches awareness. The anxiety-ridden person is on
who dimly perceives that the recognition or symbolization of certain experiences
would force a drastic change in her current self-image. Thus, awareness of deep
feelings of aggression and hostility would demand a major reorganization in the
self-concept of a person who conceives of herself exclusively as a loving person.
This person will experience anxiety whenever she feels and acknowledges anger
and hostility.

For Rogers, as long as a person is in no way threatened, she is open to experience and does not need to exhibit defensiveness. When, however, an experience
is perceived or *subceived* (detected before it enters full awareness) to be incongruent or inconsistent with the self-concept, threat exists, which, in turn, is
followed by a defensive response. Rogers (1959) defined the process of *defense* as
the behavioral response of the organism to threat; the goal of defense is the
maintenance of the wholeness or integrity of the self-structure: "This goal is
achieved by the perceptual distortion of the experience in awareness, in such a
way as to reduce the incongruity between the experience and the structure of the
self, or by the denial of any experience, thus denying any threat to the self" (1959,
pp. 204–205). Another way to put it is that defenses protect and enhance the
person's self-esteem from the impending danger of threatening experiences.

Defense Mechanisms Rogers proposed only two mechanisms of defense used
to minimize awareness of incongruities within the self or between the self and
experience: *perceptual distortion* and *denial*. It should be noted that a threatening
experience, according to Rogers, is not denied symbolization because it is "sinful" or contrary to moral standards, as Freud proposed. It is denied symbolization
in awareness because it is incompatible with the self-structure. Thus, a person
behaves in a defensive manner to protect the current structure of self and avoid
the loss of self-esteem.

Perceptual distortion is operative whenever an incongruent experience is allowed into awareness but only in a form that makes it consistent with some aspect
of the person's self-image. For instance, suppose that a college student perceives

herself as bright but receives an unexpected and yet fully justified grade of "F" on an examination. She can maintain her self-concept intact by distorting the symbolized conceptualization of this failure by saying, "The professor has unfair grading practices" or "I just had bad luck." Rogers occasionally referred to such selective perceptions or distortions as *rationalizations*. As this example suggests, the experience is perceived in awareness, but its true meaning is not understood. In the case of denial, a far less common defensive response, the person preserves the integrity of his or her self-structure by completely avoiding any conscious recognition of threatening experiences. In effect, denial is evidenced whenever a person refuses to admit to himself or herself that an experience took place or that something is the way it is. An example of denial familiar to many professors is that of a student who repeatedly fails unit exams in a course and then appears on the morning of the final examination to ask what he or she needs on the final to pass the course. Because it is incompatible with his or her self-concept, the student has denied the mounting evidence that it would be mathematically impossible to pass. Obviously, when denial is carried to an extreme, it can have psychological consequences far graver than flunking a course. Rogers indicated that denial can lead to paranoia, delusions, and a multitude of other debilitating psychological problems.

Personality Disorganization and Psychopathology

Thus far in our coverage of Rogers' theory of personality we have described events that apply to everyone to a greater or lesser degree. Even the most psychologically healthy individual is periodically confronted by an experience that threatens his or her self-concept and that forces him or her to distort or deny the experience. Correspondingly, most people possess adequate defenses for dealing with moderate levels of anxiety and will act in ways that will minimize or reduce them. When, however, experiences become more than moderately inconsistent with the self-structure or when incongruent experiences occur frequently, then the person experiences a level of anxiety that is distinctly offensive and may seriously disrupt the daily routine. A person in such an incongruent state is typically labeled "neurotic" (although not by Rogers himself, since he avoided the use of such diagnostic labels). In such instances, a person's inner discomfort level is such that he or she is likely to seek the help of a psychotherapist as a means of alleviating anxiety. Nonetheless, the neurotic's defenses are still partially effective in preventing threatening experiences from being accurately symbolized in awareness. The result is that the neurotic's self-structure is allowed to remain in a whole, if somewhat tenuous, state. Such a person may not, however, consciously appreciate the tenuousness of the position; he or she is really quite vulnerable in a psychological sense.

According to Rogers, if there is a significant degree of incongruency between the self and ongoing experiences, then the person's defenses may become inoperable. In such a "defenseless" state, with incongruent experiences accurately symbolized in awareness, the self-concept becomes shattered. Thus, personality disorganization and psychopathology occur when the self is unable to defend itself against the onslaught of threatening experiences. Persons undergoing such disorganization are commonly tagged "psychotic." They manifest behaviors that are to an objective observer bizarre, irrational, or "crazy." Rogers posited that psychotic behavior is often congruent with the denied aspects of experience, rather than with the self-concept. For example, a person who has kept his aggressive impulses under rigid control, denying that they were a part of his self-image, may make obvious threatening gestures toward those whom he encounters during his psychotic break with reality. Many irrational and self-defeating behaviors associated with psychosis are of this nature.

Rogers suggested that personality disorganization can occur either suddenly or gradually over an extended period of time. In either case, whenever a large degree of incongruence between the self and experience exists, the person's defenses no longer operate adequately, and the previously unified self-structure becomes broken. When this happens, the person's vulnerability to anxiety and threat is increased and he or she behaves in ways that are incomprehensible not only to others but also to himself or herself. In effect, Rogers viewed disorganized behaviors as resulting from incongruence between the self and experience. The magnitude of discrepancy between the perceived self and experience determines the resulting severity of psychological maladjustment.

THE FULLY FUNCTIONING PERSON

Like most other therapy-oriented personologists, Rogers (1980) offered certain ideas as to what constitutes the "good life" in terms of concrete personality characteristics. Such views were largely based on his experiences with troubled people who struggled to live in accordance with their organismic valuing process rather than conditions of worth.

The Rogerian view of the good life begins with an assessment of what it is not. Specifically, the good life is neither a fixed state of being (i.e., it is not a state of virtue, contentment, happiness) nor a condition in which the person is adjusted, fulfilled, or actualized. Nor is it, to use psychological terms, a state of drive reduction, tension reduction, or homeostasis. The good life is not a destination but a direction in which the person is participating fully according to his or her true nature.

"Fully functioning" is a term used by Rogers to designate individuals who are using their capacities and talents, realizing their potentials, and moving toward complete knowledge of themselves and their full range of experiences. Rogers (1961) specified five major personality characteristics common to people who are fully functioning. They are enumerated and briefly discussed below.

1 The first and foremost characteristic of the fully functioning person is *openness to experience*. To be open to experience is the polar opposite of defensiveness. People who are completely open to experience are able to listen to themselves, to intensely experience the full range of visceral, sensory, emotional, and cognitive experiences within themselves without feeling threatened. They are acutely aware of their own deepest thoughts and feelings (but not self-consciously); they do not try to suppress them; they often act upon them; and even if they do not act upon them, they are able to admit them to awareness. In fact, all experiences, whether they originate internally or externally, are accurately symbolized in awareness rather than being distorted or denied.

For example, the fully functioning person may suddenly, while listening to a boring lecture, strongly experience the feeling that he would like to publicly reprimand the professor for being so dull. If he has any sense, he will not follow through with this impulse—it would disrupt the class and not, in the long run, facilitate his actualizing tendency. But the point is that he would not be threatened by the feeling itself—there are no internal barriers or inhibitions preventing conscious awareness of his feeling states. The fully functioning person is sufficiently rational to recognize his or her feelings and is able to make judgments about the prudence of acting on them at any given time. Feeling something does not automatically mean that the person acts upon that feeling. Thus, the person in this instance would probably recognize and accept the hostile impulse for what it is, realize that it would be damaging to himself and others (particularly the professor who is unknowingly its "object"), and thus put it aside and turn his attention to other matters. For the fully functioning person, then, no internal experience or emotion is threatening in its own right—she or he is truly *open* to all possibilities.

2 The second characteristic of the optimally functioning person noted by Rogers is *existential living*. This is the tendency to live fully and richly in each moment of existence as it comes. By doing so, each experience in the person's life is perceived as fresh and unique—different from all that existed before. Thus, as Rogers (1961) described it, what a person is or will be in the next moment grows out of that moment without the prejudice of prior expectations. A related aspect of existential living is that the person's self and personality emerge from experience, rather than experience being translated or twisted to fit some preconceived or rigid self-structure. Hence, people living the good life are flexible, adaptable, tolerant, and spontaneous. They discover the structure of their experiences in the process of living them.

3 A third attribute of a fully functioning person is what Rogers called *organismic trusting*. This quality of the good life is best illustrated in the context of decision making. Specifically, in choosing the course of action to take in any situation, many people rely upon a code of social norms laid down by some group or institution (e.g., the church), upon the judgments of others (from spouse and friend to Ann Landers), or upon the ways they have behaved in other similar situations. In short, their decision-making capacities are strongly, if not totally, dominated by external sources of influence. Conversely, fully functioning persons depend on their organismic experiences as the valid sources of information for deciding what they should or should not do. Or, as Rogers wrote, "Doing what 'feels right' proves to be a competent and trustworthy guide to behavior which is truly satisfying" (1961, p. 190). Organismic trusting thus signifies the person's ability to consult and abide by his or her inner feelings as the major basis for making choices.

4 A fourth characteristic of the fully functioning person noted by Rogers is *experiential freedom*. This facet of the good life involves the person's sense that he or she is free to live in any way so desired with a lack of constraint or inhibition. It is subjective freedom, a sense of personal power that he or she has the capacity to choose and to become self-directed. At the same time, Rogers did not deny that a person's behavior is influenced by his or her genetic endowment, social forces, and past experiences, which, in fact, determine the choices that are made. Indeed, Rogers firmly held that there can be no absolute freedom in accounting for the possibilities of human choice. Yet, he also believed that fully functioning people operate as free choice agents, so that whatever happens to them depends on themselves exclusively. Experiential freedom thus refers to the inner feeling that "I am solely responsible for my own actions and their consequences." Because of this feeling of freedom and power, the fully functioning person sees a great many options in life and feels capable of doing practically anything he or she might want to do!

5 The final characteristic associated with optimal psychological maturity is *creativity*. For Rogers, the person who is involved in the good life would be the type from whom creative products (ideas, projects, actions) and creative living would emerge. Creative people also tend to live constructively and adaptively in their culture while at the same time satisfying their own deepest needs. They would be able, creatively, to flexibly adapt to changing environmental conditions. However, Rogers added that such people are not necessarily fully adjusted to their culture and are almost certainly not conformists. Their relation to the society around them might best be put this way—they are in and of the society of which they are members, but they are not its prisoners.

Rogers attempted to weld these qualities of the *fully functioning person* into a composite picture when he wrote:

> the good life involves a wider range, a greater richness, than the constricted living in which most of us find ourselves. To be a part of this process means that one is involved in the frequently frightening and frequently satisfying experience of a more sensitive living, with greater range, greater variety, greater richness.
>
> I believe it will have become evident why, for me, adjectives such as happy, contented, blissful, enjoyable, do not seem quite appropriate to any general description of this process I have called the good life, even though the person in this process would experience each one of these feelings at appropriate times. But the adjectives which seem more generally fitting are adjectives such as enriching, exciting, rewarding, challenging, meaningful. This process of the good life is not, I am convinced, a life for the faint-hearted. It involves the stretching and growing of becoming more and more of one's potentialities. It involves the courage to be. It means launching oneself into the stream of life. (1961, pp. 195–196)

It is evident that Rogers, like Maslow and to some extent Allport before him, wanted the person to look up to what she or he *can be*. For Rogers, this meant being fully alive, fully aware, fully involved in what it means to be a human being—in brief, "fully functioning." Rogers was confident that fully functioning individuals of the future will prevail and illuminate the inherent goodness of human nature that is so essential to our survival.

We now turn our attention to the basic assumptions concerning human nature that underlie Rogers' positive and optimistic view of humanity.

ROGERS' BASIC ASSUMPTIONS CONCERNING HUMAN NATURE

Without question, Skinner and Carl Rogers are considered to be among the most influential American psychologists of our time. Inasmuch as all psychologists have been exposed to the thinking of each, they have both attracted numerous followers. Symbolic figureheads of the deep split in contemporary American psychology between behaviorism and phenomenology, Skinner and Rogers differ from one another on many important issues, but nowhere do they differ more profoundly than in their respective images of humanity. And this difference is most apparent in the basic assumptions that each makes concerning the nature of human beings. Examination of Rogers' assumptions (depicted in Figure 11-1) makes this profound philosophical difference evident. In fact, on practically every assumption on which Skinner and Rogers can legitimately be compared, the reader will find that they are virtually *polar opposites*.

Freedom–Determinism In discussing his differences with behavioristic psychology in general and Skinner in particular, Rogers (1974) noted that his clinical experience made it impossible for him to deny the reality and significance of human choice. For years, he observed all sorts of persons in both individual therapy and encounter group situations struggling to grow, facing difficult life

FIGURE 11-1 Rogers' position on the nine basic assumptions concerning human nature.

	Strong	Moderate	Slight	Midrange	Slight	Moderate	Strong	
Freedom	■							Determinism
Rationality	■							Irrationality
Holism	■							Elementalism
Constitutionalism		■						Environmentalism
Changeability	■							Unchangeability
Subjectivity	■							Objectivity
Proactivity	■							Reactivity
Homeostasis							■	Heterostasis
Knowability							■	Unknowability

decisions, and ultimately making those decisions. The choices that an individual makes, much as in existential philosophy, help to create in turn the kind of person he or she becomes. For Rogers, then, it is not an illusion that people are able to make free choices and to play an active role in shaping their lives.

In Rogers' theory, freedom is viewed as an integral part of the actualizing tendency. The natural course of that tendency is away from control by reinforcement contingencies in the environment toward progressively greater internal and autonomous behavioral directions (1980). That is, the more the actualizing tendency can operate, (1) the more people can overcome the "conditions of worth" placed upon them in early life, (2) the more aware and open they are to inner and outer experiences, and (3) the more free they will be in creating themselves and charting the courses of their lives. The actualizing tendency is maximally operative in "fully functioning persons" who, as has already been noted, can be described in terms of experiential freedom, organismic trusting, and existential living. Here, the existence of human freedom reaches its peak; these individuals know they are free, look to themselves as the fountainhead of that freedom, and really "live" it every moment. Rogers' overall commitment to the freedom assumption at the individual level is indeed strong. He acknowledged that science must assume determinism, but insisted that the existence of responsible choice cannot be denied.

Rationality–Irrationality   A key premise of Rogers' theory is that people are rational. The irrationalities in human affairs so apparent in everyday life (e.g., murder, rape, child abuse, war) result from humanity's being "out of tune" with its true inner nature. Again, as in the case of human freedom, humanity's true rationality will come to express itself when the actualizing tendency, which is the driving force in everyone's life, is allowed to become operative. When social conditions permit people to behave in accordance with their true nature, rationality will guide their conduct.

As Rogers clarified in a published interview with Willard Frick (Frick, 1971), freedom, rationality, and the actualizing tendency are all inextricably interwoven in his basic image of humanity. When the operation of the actualizing tendency is facilitated, a person becomes progressively more free and aware in directing his or her behavior. In the ideal situation, human behavior "is exquisitely rational, moving with subtle and ordered complexity toward the goals the organism is endeavoring to achieve" (Rogers, 1961, p. 195). Such a conception of human beings would not be possible without the rationality assumption firmly implanted at its base.

Holism–Elementalism   Rogers was quite committed to understanding and studying the person as a gestalt, or unified whole. Indeed, a holistic emphasis is evident throughout his theorizing. But it is perhaps most evident in his central theoretical construct of self. For a theorist to posit such a global, all-inclusive, and unitary construct to explain behavior requires as a precursor the holistic assumption.

Moreover, in Rogers' system, the self is constantly moving in the direction of greater wholeness. This view is a salient feature of Rogers' (1963) account of human development, which begins with the infant's undifferentiated phenomenological field, continues unabated as that field becomes differentiated into self and environment (as the self-concept emerges), and culminates in the organism's continuing efforts to achieve a unity of self and self-consistency. Developmentally speaking, then, if a person is healthy, she is always moving toward progressively greater wholeness and unification. Holism is a basic theme commonly found among humanistically oriented personologists; Rogers' theory clearly epitomizes this principle.

Constitutionalism–Environmentalism   Rogers' theory reveals a moderate commitment to constitutionalism in its very broadest sense. That is, in scrutinizing his various theoretical writings, one is struck by the relative frequency of his use of such phrases as "human nature," "man's true self," "man's innate potential," all of which imply a biological base of human development and personality. This constitutional leaning is perhaps most evident in Rogers' concept of the actualizing tendency. It cannot be forgotten that *life's master motive* is inherent, rooted in the physiological processes of the body, and a biological fact of life. To describe the unitary motive underlying all human activity in such terms clearly reflects the constitutionalism assumption.

But that is not the whole story. As the self emerges early in life, it is significantly influenced by environmental variables. "Unconditional positive regard" from others who count in the environment facilitates healthy self-development; the imposition of "conditions of worth" impedes it. Thus, the person's emergent self-concept is laden with environmental influences. Rogers' theory is therefore by no means devoid of the environmentalism assumption.

Yet, to place Rogers' position on the constitutionalism–environmentalism assumption in proper perspective, it is necessary to see its relationship to his position on the freedom and rationality assumptions. As indicated in Chapter 1, the nine basic assumptions are not entirely independent of one another; the same most certainly holds true for the position of any given theorist on them. In this instance, Rogers felt that human beings are the only animals who really can be aware of both their past and present life circumstances, thus making it possible for them to make choices about their futures (Frick, 1971). Insofar as people are by nature rational and free, they are therefore somewhat able to rise above the constitutional and, particularly, the environmental influences impinging upon their development. In brief, Rogers' belief that human beings shape their own destinies moderates the potency of his position on the constitutionalism–environmentalism issue.

Changeability–Unchangeability   One clear indication of a personologist's commitment to changeability is a theoretical emphasis on continuous personal growth. Rogers' theory reveals just such an emphasis in the concept of an actualizing tendency. For through the actualizing tendency, all humans, as well as all other

living organisms, are depicted as forever growing, unfolding their innate
tialities, and changing in the process. Viewed in this light, personality change
integral part of what it means to be a human being in Rogers' system.

The possibilities for personality change become even more evident when
again consider the interaction of the actualizing tendency with freedom an
rationality in phenomenological theory. According to Rogers, as a person ma-
tures, he or she becomes progressively freer and more rational in directing the
course of that personal maturity. Thus, to a large extent, the individual can decide
what kind of person he or she intends to become in the future. All of this clearly
suggests that people can change significantly in their lifetimes. Therefore, Rogers'
commitment to the changeability assumption is indeed undeniably strong.

Subjectivity–Objectivity Subjectivity is the key assumption in Rogers' personological system. The entire structure of phenomenological theory is based
squarely upon it. For Rogers, each person lives entirely in a rich, ever-changing,
private, subjective world of experience of which he or she is the center. Each
person perceives the world in subjective terms and responds to it accordingly.
And at the very core of each person's perceptual system is the self-concept. In
Rogers' theory, then, human behavior is forever unintelligible without reference
to the private world of experience. In direct opposition to Skinner and much of
contemporary behaviorism, Rogers insisted that we can never adequately understand human actions simply by examining objective, environmental conditions
alone. Instead, we must *always look within the person* and attempt to see the
world from his or her perspective in order to achieve an understanding of behavior. Subjectivity is the essence of the phenomenological position and Rogers'
commitment to it could not be stronger.

Proactivity–Reactivity Rogers firmly held that the person is purposive, forward-moving, and oriented toward the future. As a being who internally generates
his or her own behavior, this person is eminently proactive. A person's proactivity, in Rogers' system, becomes even more apparent when we consider the
energy source of all human behavior—the actualizing tendency. Because of this
master motive inherent in all life, humanity is forever moving forward, growing, in
brief, "proacting."

While Rogers recognized that a certain amount of external stimulation is
necessary for self-actualization to unfold, outer stimuli appear to be things that the
innate actualizing tendency feeds upon rather than reacts to. In a very real sense,
the person psychologically consumes external stimuli rather than simply reacting
to them. A classroom learning environment is a good example of this distinction.
In Rogers' (1969) view, a person does not learn simply as a direct function of being
"taught" (i.e., reacting to external stimuli). But people can profit from classroom
learning; they have an innate tendency to grow and expand their horizons (the
actualizing tendency), and the right classroom can facilitate this growth by
prompting them to move in directions that they might otherwise not consider.
Thus, in Rogers' system, a person feeds upon external stimuli—they nourish his

'rowth. But the sole moving force of human behavior is the actualizing
a person is not prodded into activity by external stimulation. This view
, Rogers' strong commitment to the proactivity assumption.

Homeostasis–Heterostasis Since this assumption deals with a motivational
question, we need only turn again to Rogers' sole dynamic construct to determine
his position on it. Specifically, the actualizing tendency is a heterostatic concept.

As is by now clear, Rogers' actualizing tendency is always moving in the
direction of growth, enhancement, and self-realization of the person. Drives that
other theorists regard as homeostatic (e.g., hunger, sex, and competence), are
subsumed by the heterostatic master motive in Rogers' system. Furthermore, the
actualizing tendency thrives on *tension increase, not tension reduction.* Humans
naturally seek stimulation, challenge, and novel possibilities for personal growth.
All this culminates in Rogers' view of the good life. Recall that it was described as
a direction rather than a destination. Thus, Rogers' fully functioning person is
always striving, always stretching, always seeking actualization of his or her
potentialities. Rogers' endorsement of the heterostatic assumption could not be
stronger.

Knowability–Unknowability Rogers' phenomenological position clearly implies that the human organism is unknowable in traditional scientific terms. More
specifically, as already noted, the subjectivity assumption is the philosophic
essence of the phenomenological position. And subjectivity means that each
person lives in a private world of experience which he alone has the potential to
comprehend. According to this view, it is misleading to think that psychological
science will some day completely understand the subject it investigates, namely,
the human being.

Rogers (1959) clearly addressed himself to this point in what is probably the
most rigorous presentation of his theory. While he admitted that there may be
such a thing as "objective" truth or reality, he also insisted that no person will
ever arrive at it because each of us lives in a private world of subjective experience. As Rogers put it: "Thus there is no such thing as Scientific Knowledge,
there are only individual perceptions of what appears to each person to be such
knowledge" (1959, p. 192). If there is no such thing as scientific knowledge, it is a
sure bet that human nature is never going to be understood by it.

What, then, from Rogers' perspective, is the purpose of psychological inquiry?
Perhaps his answer here explains why he has been dubbed a "respected gadfly"
of psychology by a scientific awards committee of the American Psychological
Association and why he accepted this label so readily. Throughout his career,
Rogers opposed the traditional strongholds of scientific psychology (e.g., the
structure and inhumane nature of graduate education in the field); pioneered
scientific research in areas pertaining to subjective experience (e.g., psychotherapy research); and, in general, did everything that he could to broaden the
scope of scientific concepts and methodology to incorporate as much human
subjectivity as possible. While he undoubtedly profited much from his scientific

endeavors, however, we must conclude from reading him that he learned far more about *human experience* and behavior from his many clients than he did from reading the literature of psychology or doing empirical research. Generally, he wrote, "I never learned anything from research. . . . I'm not really a scientist. Most of my research has been to confirm what I already felt to be true" (Bergin & Strupp, 1972, p. 314).

The following section presents illustrative research findings generated by Rogers' phenomenological theory of personality.

EMPIRICAL VALIDATION OF PHENOMENOLOGICAL THEORY CONCEPTS

Rogers' theory pertains not only to personality but also to psychotherapy and the process of change in human behavior. Practically all the empirical studies he conducted were aimed at elucidating and understanding the nature of the therapeutic process, the conditions which facilitate personality growth, and the effectiveness of therapy in bringing about permanent behavioral change. The emphasis on psychotherapy research has indirectly produced considerable data concerning the self-concept and its impact on the person's psychological adjustment. This is understandable insofar as the concept of self is pivotal in Rogers' theory. It is to Rogers' credit that he opened up psychotherapy and the nature of self as meaningful areas of research. Largely through his efforts, personologists now recognize the self as a useful explanatory construct in accounting for human behavior (Markus, 1983; Markus & Nurius, 1986). More importantly, Rogers' formulation of a phenomenological theory has made the self an object of respectable empirical investigation (Suls & Greenwald, 1983). No one in contemporary psychology has been more influential than Rogers in providing an intellectual climate in which research on the self-structure has flourished.

In this section we will consider two research areas bearing upon the scientific validity of Rogerian concepts. First, however, it is necessary that we become acquainted with Rogers' view of psychological science and research, the method by which he measured the self-concept, and the research strategy he employed to study the changes in self-concept during the course of therapy.

Rogers' View of Science and Research

Rogers was committed to phenomenology as the basis for developing a science of persons and as a method of examining the empirical validity of theoretical concepts. The focus of the phenomenological method emphasizes the data, or phenomena, of consciousness with the ultimate goal of comprehending the essence of things appearing in the person's subjective world of conscious experience. Rogers believed that such a method provided the best vantage point for understanding the complexity of processes underlying human behavior.

Relevant to the research enterprise, Rogers considered clinical observations, as obtained during psychotherapy, to be a valid source of phenomenological data.

These clinical observations, usually based on selected excerpts from tape-recorded interviews in client-centered therapy and sometimes filming them as well, enabled researchers for the first time to investigate the client/therapist interaction. It should be noted that Rogers always obtained prior permission of a client to tape or film, and he found that it did not seem to impede the course of therapy. At the same time, he stressed that the process of scientific inquiry is never divorced from the framework of human values and purposes. "Science exists only in people. Each scientific project has its creative inception, its process, and its tentative conclusion in a person or persons. Knowledge—even scientific knowledge—is that which is subjectively acceptable" (Rogers, 1955, p. 274). Rogers applied similar logic to the utilization of science. He believed that since science itself is neutral, it will never depersonalize, manipulate, or control individuals. It is only people who can and will do that. Consequently, the way research findings in personology are utilized will depend on *value choices* made by human beings.

Rogers' notions of science are diametrically opposed to those espoused by Skinner and others representing the behavioristic approach to psychology. The views of these two eminent psychologists concerning the scientific control of human behavior were dramatized in a debate held before the 1956 convention of the American Psychological Association. In this debate, Rogers (1956) noted that both he and Skinner were committed to a science of human behavior. Moreover, both agreed that psychological science has made substantial progress in explaining behavior and developing the capacity to predict and control it. However, Rogers also felt Skinner vastly underestimated the seriousness of the problems associated with behavioral control. To Rogers, the possibility that behavioral principles could be used in designing a culture that was more efficient in satisfying human needs raised several important questions. Who will control whom? Who will control the controllers? By what means will behavioral control be exercised? And what forms of behavior will be deemed desirable in a Skinnerian-designed culture? The fact that values and subjective choice are implicitly involved in dealing with these kinds of questions is what made Rogers reluctant to give unlimited power to the behavioral scientist. Ironically, Rogers had great faith in humanity, whereas he lacked Skinner's confidence in the scientist. Rogers proposed that science be used to create an open society (as opposed to Skinner's closed one) in which people are afforded the opportunity to develop the values of responsibility, happiness, security, productivity, and creativity. He maintained that personological research must ultimately be addressed to questions concerning the good life and how it may best be achieved by the greatest number.

Measuring the Self-Concept: The Q-Sort Technique

In the early 1950s William Stephenson (1953), then a colleague of Rogers' at the University of Chicago, developed a general methodology, called the *Q-sort technique,* for investigating a person's self-concept. Rogers soon recognized the potential value of Stephenson's work for his own studies on changes in the perceived self during the course of psychotherapy. Accordingly, he adopted the Q-sort as one of his basic research tools in gathering data about therapeutic improvement.

What is the Q-sort? Although it has myriad possibilities, essentially it is a method of empirically defining the person's image or picture of himself or herself. The procedure followed in administering the Q-sort is quite simple. The subject is given a deck of cards, each containing a printed statement or adjective concerning some personality characteristic. The cards may contain such self-referent statements as "I am emotionally mature," "I often feel humiliated," "I am intelligent," "I enjoy being alone," and "I despise myself." Or the items might be "methodical," "aggressive," "quick-witted," and "sincere." The subject's task is to sort the cards into a series of categories (usually seven in number), each corresponding to a point along a continuum ranging from those attributes that are *most like* to those that are *least like* him or her. The chief feature of the method is that the subject must sort the cards according to some prearranged or forced distribution. That is, he or she is required to place a specific number of cards in each of a specific number of categories. Although the number of categories varies from one study to another in accordance with the number of Q cards, the forced distribution is usually approximately normal. For example, in the Q-sort distribution illustrated in Figure 11-2, the subject is first required to select the 2 statements she believes to be most descriptive of the way she is and place them in category seven. Then she chooses 4 statements that are more self-descriptive than the remaining 36 (and less self-descriptive than those in category seven) and places them in category six. The subject continues in this manner until she places the remaining 2 least self-descriptive statements in category one. As the example indicates, the number of cards to be placed under each category fan out symmetrically from the center pile (number four), resulting in a normal distribution.

Two additional facts regarding the Q-sort should be noted. First, statements or adjectives may be culled from numerous sources—there is no fixed set of standardized Q-sort items. They may stem from a particular personality theory, from recorded therapeutic interviews, or from personality questionnaires. Second, the forced normal distribution allows for easy computation of statistical results since

FIGURE 11-2   A forced Q-sort distribution for self-descriptive statements.

	Least characteristic			Neutral			Most characteristic
Number of statements	2	4	8	12	8	4	2
Category number	1	2	3	4	5	6	7

the mean and variance are held constant across subjects. The forced distribution also helps to control for response sets, since tendencies to give "average" or "extreme" ratings do exist. Conversely, the Q-sort has been criticized for forcing subjects to sort statements in ways which may not accurately reflect their self-conceptions. For instance, a subject might feel that the majority of statements do not apply at all, yet he or she is required by the directions to sort them into the prescribed categories. Another subject might feel that most of the statements are highly self-descriptive and do not belong in the middle category, yet he or she is also forced to abide by the instructions.

Research-oriented Rogerians generally have their subjects Q-sort the statements twice: once for *self-description* and once for *ideal self-description*. For the perceived self-sort, subjects are instructed to sort the cards to describe themselves as they see themselves at the present time. This *self-sort* depicts the picture the subject has of himself or herself. Following completion of the self-sort, subjects are then instructed to use the same cards to describe the kind of person they would most like to be. This second sort is called the *ideal-sort*.

Q-sort data can be analyzed in several ways. However, the product-moment correlation coefficient is the most commonly used statistic for indicating how closely a subject's self-image or perceived self corresponds to his or her ideal self. Employing this method, each Q-sort statement is assigned two numbers, the first number representing the category number for the self-sort and the second the category number for the ideal-sort. It is these two numbers that are correlated. The magnitude of the correlation coefficient thus becomes an index of the degree of congruence or incongruence between the perceived self and the ideal self. A positive correlation reveals a state of congruence—whereas a negative correlation reveals incongruence—between the perceived self and the ideal self. Correlation coefficients not significantly different from zero indicate that there is no relationship (similarity) between the way a person sees herself and the way she should like to be.

The research strategy employed by Rogers and his associates for investigating psychotherapeutic personality change (i.e., changes in a client's self-image) is quite simple. Clients repeatedly perform self and ideal Q-sorts during therapy, at the end of therapy, and in some instances during post-therapy intervals. Each time, the correlation between the two sorts is computed. It thus becomes possible to chart a progressive pattern of change in the relationship between the client's perceived self and ideal self over the course of therapy by comparing the correlations between the two sorts. Rogers' research methodology also includes a control group to ensure that any detectable changes are due to therapy rather than the mere passage of time, familiarity with the Q-sort, or other extraneous influences. Control subjects are matched with client subjects on such demographic variables as age, sex, education, and socioeconomic status. They complete self and ideal Q-sorts at the same time intervals as the client group. The only difference between the two groups is that the client group is subjected to the independent treatment variable, person-centered (Rogerian) therapy, while the control group is not. This procedure enabled Rogers to validate many of his theoretical notions concerning personality growth and change and the therapeutic conditions that bring them about (Carkhuff, 1969).

Self-Perception and Psychological Adjustment

As explained earlier, Rogers believed that psychological maladjustment results from incongruence between the self-structure and experience. In other words, a psychologically disturbed person perceives himself and his relation to people and things in his environment in ways that fit some preconceived self-structure. He is therefore prone to deny or distort any experience that conflicts with his current self-image because awareness of it would leave him vulnerable to anxiety, threat, and disorganization. In contrast, a psychologically healthy person tends to perceive himself and his interaction with others in a realistic manner (i.e., as detached observers would see them). Furthermore, the healthy person is open to experience (i.e., is nondefensive), accepts responsibility for his own behavior, and evaluates experience in terms of the evidence of his own senses.

An example of how some of these theoretical assertions have been empirically tested is provided by the case of Mrs. Oak. Prior to the start of therapy, Mrs. Oak (a fictitious name) was a housewife in her late thirties who had been experiencing difficulties in relationships with her husband and her adolescent daughter. Rogers (1954) conducted numerous therapy sessions with this client over the course of 5 months. Thereafter ensued 7 months of no therapeutic contact, following which she resumed therapy with Rogers for an additional period of 2 months. At several points before, during, and after therapy, Mrs. Oak completed Q-sorts of her real and ideal self.

Findings based on the Q-sort data indicated considerable change in Mrs. Oak's self-concept as therapy progressed. Specifically, descriptions of her ideal self at the beginning and end of therapy were more highly correlated ($r = +.72$) than her descriptions of her real self at the same two points in time ($r = +.30$). To Rogers, this suggested that her real self underwent greater change as a consequence of therapy than did her ideal self. Moreover, the correlation between her descriptions of her real and ideal self were much higher at the end of therapy ($r = +.79$) than at the beginning ($r = +.21$). This indicated that her real self corresponded to her ideal self more closely at the conclusion of therapy than at the beginning. Finally, as expected, the correspondence between her perceived self and ideal self became closer as therapy continued, indexed by correlations of increasing magnitude over time: $r = +.21, +.47, +.69, +.71,$ and $+.79$. Rogers took this to mean that Mrs. Oak had become more like the person she had described as ideal.

Marked changes in the placement of specific Q-sort items also indicated that Mrs. Oak had restructured her self-concept as a result of therapy. Prior to therapy, she perceived herself as quite insecure, disorganized, self-centered, and responsible for her problems. Twelve months later, following therapy, she perceived herself as far more self-reliant, emotionally mature, expressive, and secure. Q-sort descriptions of Mrs. Oak completed by Rogers himself also confirmed these changes in her perceived self. It should further be noted that by the time therapy was over, Mrs. Oak had divorced her husband, improved her relationship with her daughter, and taken a job.

Several other studies likewise support Rogers' proposal that discrepancy between the perceived self and ideal self is indicative of poor psychological adjustment. In general, the higher the incongruence or discrepancy, the higher the degree of anxiety, insecurity, social immaturity, and emotional disorder (Achenbach & Zigler, 1963; Higgins, 1987; Turner & Vanderlippe, 1958). Furthermore, persons with a great discrepancy between the real and ideal selves are lower in self-actualization than are those with little or no discrepancy (Mahoney & Hartnett, 1973).

Self-Acceptance and Acceptance of Others

A final group of studies stemming from Rogers' theoretical position concerns the proposition that the more a person accepts himself or herself, the more likely he or she is to accept others. Such a relationship between self-acceptance and acceptance of others is based on Rogers' observation that when clients enter therapy they typically have negative self-concepts; they are unable to accept themselves. However, once such clients become more accepting of themselves, they become more accepting of others. In other words, Rogers proposed that if self-acceptance occurs (i.e., if the real and ideal self discrepancy is small), then acceptance, respect, and valuing of others follows. Other theorists have also suggested that attitudes toward the self are reflected in attitudes toward others. Erich Fromm (1956), for example, maintained that self-love and love of others go hand in hand. He further noted that a failure to love the self is accompanied by a basic hostility toward others.

While several studies have supported the relationship between self-acceptance and acceptance of others, a majority of these have used as subjects college students or individuals receiving therapy (e.g., Berger, 1955; Suinn, 1961). With regard to Rogerian theory specifically, however, evidence indicates that self-acceptance and acceptance of others characterizes parent–child relationships. Coopersmith (1967), for instance, investigated the developmental antecedents of general self-esteem in 10–12-year-old boys. He found that parents of boys with high self-esteem were more affectionate and loving and used noncoercive types of discipline such as denial of privileges and isolation in guiding their son's behavior. Further, the parents were democratic in the sense that they considered the child's opinions and viewpoints in making family decisions. By contrast, parents of low-esteem boys were found to be more aloof, less accepting, and more likely to use physical punishment in controlling their son's behavior. Hales (1979) has obtained a similar pattern of findings with parents of daughters. Another study tested the hypothesis that there is a significant positive relationship between self-acceptance and child acceptance in a group of mothers of young children (Medinnus & Curtis, 1963).

TABLE 11-1   CORRELATIONS BETWEEN MATERNAL SELF-ACCEPTANCE AND
CHILD-ACCEPTANCE MEASURES

Measures	Bills self-acceptance	Semantic differential child-acceptance
Semantic differential self-acceptance	− .57 +	.33*
Bills self-acceptance		− .48 +

Source: Adapted from Medinnus & Curtis, 1963, p. 543.
*<.05
+<.01
Note: The negative correlations are due to the method of scoring the tests. On the Bills self-acceptance measure, the higher scores indicate greater self-acceptance while the semantic differential self-acceptance and child-acceptance scores are discrepancy scores with the higher scores denoting less favorable attitudes.

Subjects were 56 mothers of children enrolled in a cooperative nursery school. Two measures of maternal self-acceptance were obtained. The first consisted of mothers' responses to the Bills Index of Adjustment and Values, a self-report questionnaire yielding a measure of the degree to which self and ideal are different. A semantic differential scale of 20 bipolar adjectives in which the difference between the mothers' ratings of ''Me (as I am)'' and ''Me (as I would most like to be)'' was defined operationally as the second measure of maternal self-acceptance. The measure of child acceptance was derived from the same set of bipolar adjectives. Specifically, the distance between the mothers' ratings of ''My child (as he is)'' and ''My child (as I would most like him to be)'' was defined as the extent of the mother's acceptance of her child.

The intercorrelations between the two maternal self-acceptance scores and the child acceptance measure are shown in Table 11-1. As can be seen, each of the three correlation coefficients is statistically significant in the predicted direction. These results support the Rogerian notion that mothers who are self-accepting (i.e., who possess positive self-regard) are far more likely to accept their children as they are than are nonself-accepting mothers. Additionally, the findings suggest that the extent to which a child develops a positive self-image depends crucially upon the extent to which his or her parents are able to accept themselves.

APPLICATION: PERSON-CENTERED THERAPY

The variety of past and present types of psychotherapy available to troubled individuals is enough to boggle the imagination. Psychologists and psychiatrists have asked people to lie down on black leather couches and free associate, tried to teach them appropriate social skills, encouraged them to go into empty rooms to let out primal screams, and told them to sit around nude in swimming pools and ''encounter'' one another. Yet, in spite of earlier evidence that various forms of insight therapy did not work (Eysenck, 1952, 1966), more recent and thorough evidence indicates that many types of therapy are effective in helping people cope with problems that affect their lives (Bergin, 1979; Landman & Dawes, 1982;

Smith et al., 1980). How can so many different methods of therapy serve to help distressed people as opposed to no therapy at all?

Rogers' answer to this question is that all effective forms of psychotherapy have one element in common—a *relationship between persons*. Specifically, he maintained that the quality of the relationship between the therapist and the client is the single most important factor responsible for successful therapeutic outcomes. Specific therapeutic techniques are secondary to the therapist–client relationship and the emotional climate in which the therapy takes place. This currently widespread approach to psychotherapy instituted by Rogers is known as *person-centered therapy* (Rogers, 1986).

Evolution of Rogerian Therapy: From Techniques to Relationships

Rogers' approach to psychotherapy, which bears only slight resemblance to psychoanalysis and behavior modification, evolved over several years. While his basic assumptions have remained stable, his means of implementing them, like the Rogerian person that he depicted, have continually developed. Rogers' approach was initially called *nondirective therapy* (some still refer to it that way today). This term reflected Rogers' main concern at the time with techniques by which behavioral change might be achieved. Because the client was assumed to have the capacity for self-directed personality change, Rogers pioneered techniques that enabled the therapist to be much less directive in the relationship than was the case with other forms of therapy. For instance, nondirective therapists of old never gave advice, nor answered questions, nor probed by asking their own questions. Instead, they attempted to reflect back to the client what he or she said and to clarify his or her feelings in the process (*reflection* and *clarification*). In effect, the therapist acted as a kind of mirror exactly the opposite of the type found in amusement parks. Amusement-park mirrors distort the person's body image in various ways. Conversely, in nondirective therapy, it is the client's self-image that is distorted so that the therapist's essential task, as a "mirror," was to reflect back to the client more accurately what he or she was really saying and feeling. These techniques, while still employed today, are somewhat limiting if they constitute the only function that the therapist provides in the relationship.

Later, Rogers shifted his emphasis on techniques to the therapist's need to be aware of what it is like to be the client at any moment in the therapeutic setting. He rechristened his approach as "client-centered" in order to emphasize his belief that the therapist's task is to understand the client's self-perceptions. In the final stage of Rogers' thinking, however, his approach to therapy evolved to still another level. Starting in the early 1960s, he became more concerned with the issue of precisely what therapeutic conditions must be met before the client can begin to resolve his or her interpersonal problems. As stated earlier, he regarded the relationship between therapist and client as the single most important factor facilitating personality change. At present, the "label" that best captures the emphasis on the therapist–client relationship as the key to promoting personality change is "person-centered therapy" (Rogers, 1977). This term best reflects the evolution of Rogers' thought—from techniques to relationships:

> The shift in emphasis to person-centered points out more than the widespread applicability of the theory. It attempts to emphasize that it is as person, as I am, as being, and not just in terms of some role identity as client, student, teacher, or therapist that the individual is the unit of all interactions. (Holdstock & Rogers, 1977, p. 129)

Therapeutic Conditions For Personality Change

Rogers (1959) suggested that *six therapeutic conditions* are essential and must be present if constructive personality changes are to occur. These conditions, when taken together, provide the framework for understanding what actually happens during the course of person-centered therapy.

1 *Two persons are in psychological contact.* Really more of a precondition than a condition, Rogers' first assertion simply means that some relationship or psychological contact between two people must exist. A therapist, no matter how skillful she or he is, cannot aid a client if that client does not know the therapist. Perhaps even more important, Rogers postulated that no significant positive personality change can occur outside a relationship.

2 *The first, whom we shall term the client, is in a state of incongruence, being vulnerable or anxious.* As described earlier, Rogers construed personality disorganization and psychopathology in terms of a significant discrepancy between the actual experience of a person and the person's self-concept with regard to that experience. To illustrate this perspective, Rogers (1957) cited an example of a

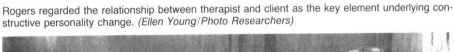

Rogers regarded the relationship between therapist and client as the key element underlying constructive personality change. *(Ellen Young/Photo Researchers)*

college student who, at a total or organismic level, experienced a fear of the university and of examinations given on the third floor of a certain building, since these demonstrated a fundamental inadequacy in himself. He was dreadfully afraid of his academic inadequacy and it was decidedly at odds with his self-conception. Consequently, he distorted the organismic experience in his awareness by representing it instead as an unreasonable (phobic) fear of climbing stairs in the building (or any building) and by an equally intense fear of crossing the open campus.

From Rogers' perspective, this student was out of touch with the wellsprings of his conscious experience, his total organismic experience; in a very real sense, he was a stranger within himself. Such an existential situation necessarily left him highly vulnerable since, at any unexpected moment, the world could thrust the truth upon him. Furthermore, to the degree that he dimly perceived this deep incongruence within himself, he necessarily experienced tension or anxiety. His total position resembled the unfortunate existential condition of Chicken Little who, as the childhood tale would have it, was constantly awaiting and expecting the sky to fall. Given such an uncomfortable subjective state, it is easy to understand why the student sought out the college counseling center for help.

3 *The second person, whom we shall term the therapist, is congruent or integrated in the relationship.* When the student arrives at the counseling center, Rogers' third condition specifies that he should meet a person who is congruent, integrated and genuine in the relationship. That is, in the particular therapeutic relationship itself, the therapist needs to accurately represent his or her organismic experience in awareness and genuinely be himself or herself without any knowing or unknowing facade. For Rogers, the therapist must be whole and real (completely and fully himself or herself), and the client must have the distinct and accurate feeling that he is baring his soul to a genuine person in that relationship.

Rogers did not believe that the therapist needs to be open to all life experiences. Outside the therapeutic relationship, for example, the therapist may occasionally experience anxiety, depression, hostility, or any other mood state that might suggest that she or he may not be fully integrated in all aspects of life. But in the therapeutic relationship, for that one or two hours per week, it is imperative that he or she be congruent. This means that the therapist may occasionally experience feelings not traditionally considered ideal for psychotherapy, e.g., "Although I really like this client, I just don't feel like listening to him today—I wish I were playing tennis." Of course, since therapy is focused on the client's feelings rather than the therapist's, the therapist need not verbalize this feeling as long as she or he is consciously aware of it. Sometimes, however, the therapist's feelings become so intense that he or she may need to express them directly to the client or to a colleague, e.g., "This client constantly reveals what I regard as racist attitudes, and I'm having great difficulty accepting him because of this."

4 *The therapist experiences unconditional positive regard for the client.* The phrase "unconditional positive regard" essentially means that the therapist warmly accepts the client, prizes him as a person in the process of becoming, and passes no judgments on his feelings or experiences. In short, the therapist imposes no "conditions of worth" upon the client, but rather fully accepts him as he is without approval or disapproval. So when the student begins to describe his fear of climbing stairs and walking across campus, the therapist unconditionally accepts these feelings as part of the student's world of subjective experience. He does not make judgments on the student's feelings, e.g., "Look, son, I was in the marines and the only way you're going to become a man is to forget these stupid feelings and get out there right now and climb those stairs and walk head held high across that open campus."

Person-centered therapy thus proceeds in a nonthreatening atmosphere in which the client feels understood and accepted as a whole person. Such a therapeutic climate permits the client to get back in touch with his or her organismic level of experiencing, allowing him or her to represent that experience in conscious awareness without feeling threatened. The client is likely to conclude: "If this therapist, who is genuine and truly likes me, can unflinchingly accept these feelings as a legitimate part of who I am, why can't I?" Thus the therapeutic setting allows the client to delve ever more deeply into himself, express his true feelings without fear of reproach, and ultimately integrate these feelings with a necessarily changed self-concept. Unconditional positive regard, to the degree that it can be achieved in any therapeutic relationship, enables the client to examine those experiences which have been inconsistent with his self-concept and of which he was previously unaware because they were anxiety provoking.

5 *The therapist experiences an empathic understanding of the client's internal frame of reference and endeavors to communicate this experience to the client.* The person-centered therapist has accurate empathy for the client. As Rogers (1959) described it, empathy indicates that the therapist senses the client's private world of experience as if it were her or his own—but without ever losing that "as if" quality. In brief, the therapist *understands*. She or he is able to move about freely in the client's subjective world, perceiving as he perceives, feeling as he feels, experiencing as he experiences.

According to Rogers (1959), the client often experiences the therapist's empathy as akin to a sudden burst of sunlight through a dense tangle of foliage in a forest. As the client struggles with his confused and distorted representations of experience, the therapist, precisely because she or he has entered fully into the client's subjective world, is able to make empathic statements that shed considerable insight upon it. The therapist accepts and understands the client and, in the therapeutic relationship, both are led to progressively greater heights of mutual acceptance and understanding.

6 *The communication to the client of the therapist's empathic understanding and unconditional positive regard is to a minimal degree achieved.* Careful attention to this condition should erase the stereotype of the now defunct nondirective therapist who did nothing but sit around, occasionally grunting warmly at the client and saying "Um-hum." Nor are contemporary person-centered therapists limited to simple restatement and/or clarification of what the client says (e.g., "I've just cut myself and if you don't give me that Band-Aid, I'm going to bleed to death."— "You feel you're bleeding to death."), which, when carried off improperly in the past, probably led many a client to want to ask, "Polly wants a cracker?"

While examination of taped interviews of today's person-centered therapists indicates that they still engage in the use of warm responding—saying "Um-hum" or "I see," reflecting and clarifying feelings—they do this to make every effort to *communicate* their empathy and positive regard for the client: It is worthless for the therapist to experience these attitudes unless the client knows it. So the therapist must communicate these attitudes through his or her every word and action, and the client must perceive these as reflecting the therapist's acceptance and understanding of him. To the degree that the client does feel accepted, condition six is met and positive personality change in the client should be observed.

Rogers insisted that it is the client, not the therapist, who is responsible for whatever personal growth occurs during the course of therapy. The therapist does, in fact, establish the necessary conditions for change, but it is the client who is the real agent of change itself.

Rogers' approach to therapy makes perfect sense to anyone who shares his optimistic philosophy of the human condition. Believing that people will naturally move toward growth, actualization, and health if the conditions are right, in person-centered therapy Rogers is simply creating the right conditions. The client's own organismic valuing process can be relied upon to do the rest. In this sense, a Rogerian therapist is more a "facilitator of growth" than a "curer of ills" (as in psychoanalysis) or "modifier of behavior" (as in behavior therapy). Person-centered therapy is designed to eliminate incongruity between experience and the self. When the person is acting in accordance with his or her organismic valuing process, rather than with conditions of worth, the defenses of denial and distortion are no longer needed and the individual is said to be a fully functioning person. The fully functioning person's mandate in life is to become all that he or she can become over the lifespan.

No one since Freud has had more impact on the practice of psychotherapy than Rogers. His person-centered approach to counseling and therapy has been fruitfully applied to such diverse areas as education, race relations, family relationships, politics, and organizational development (Levant & Schlien, 1984). His affirmation of the integrity and uniqueness of the person coupled with his emphasis on the importance of the self-concept have likewise had a tremendous influence on contemporary theorizing and research in personology. We can conclude that the impact of Rogers' theory of the person will be felt in the realm of personology for a long time to come.

SUMMARY

The phenomenological perspective on personality emphasizes the view that a person's behavior can be understood only in terms of his or her subjective experiences of reality. The phenomenological approach also holds that people have the capacity to shape their own destinies and that the innermost core of human nature is purposive, trustworthy, and self-perfecting. Carl Rogers is widely acknowledged as having formulated a personality theory in which the themes associated with phenomenology are emphasized along with special attention devoted to the self.

In Rogers' system, all human motives are subsumed under a single master motive—the actualizing tendency—the innate tendency of the person to actualize, maintain, and enhance himself or herself. This tendency drives all people toward greater complexity, autonomy, and fulfillment of potentials. Somewhat more specific is the organismic valuing process, which indicates whether or not experiences are in tune with the actualizing tendency. According to Rogers, those experiences perceived to be self-enhancing are sought, whereas those experiences perceived to be self-negating are avoided.

As illustrative of the phenomenological perspective, Rogers held that the only reality, from the person's perceptual vantage point, is subjective reality—the person's private world of experience. And central to that subjective world is the concept of self, Rogers' most important personological construct. In his system, elements important in self-concept development are the need for positive regard, conditions of worth, and unconditional positive regard. Rogers stressed that children must be given unconditional positive regard if they are to develop a positive self-concept and thereby become fully functioning persons. By contrast, conditions of worth cause children to live in accordance with introjected values rather than their own organismic valuing processes.

Rogers argued that most ways of behaving that a person adopts are consistent with his or her self-concept. Threat exists when a person senses incongruency between the self-concept and total organismic experience; he or she then attempts to protect self-integrity by means of perceptual distortion and denial. When the incongruence between self-concept and actual experience becomes too great, personality disorganization and psychopathology result. In sharp contrast, persons who are open to their experience, fully trust it, and are freely moving in the direction of actualizing themselves are termed ''fully functioning'' in Rogers' system.

Rogers' basic assumptions concerning human nature are generally strong, explicit, and reflective of the fundamental cleavage between phenomenology and behaviorism in American psychology. Rogers' phenomenological theory reflects (1) a strong commitment to the assumptions of freedom, rationality, holism, changeability, subjectivity, proactivity, heterostasis, and unknowability and (2) a moderate commitment to the constitutionalism assumption.

Rogers' phenomenological approach to personality, particularly in terms of its psychotherapeutic aspects, has stimulated a substantial amount of research. In this chapter, a primary method of studying the self-concept, the Q-sort, was discussed along with illustrative research bearing upon aspects of the self-concept. Brief attention was also given to Rogers' view of science as it relates to the study of persons.

In the concluding chapter section, Rogers' unique and widely employed approach to psychotherapy, person-centered therapy, was described as it has evolved over the years. Emphasizing the critical importance of the therapist–client relationship, Rogers' six conditions for positive personality change were identified and discussed. For Rogers, the goal of therapy is to eliminate incongruity between experience and the self, thereby allowing the person to live a richer, fuller life.

BIBLIOGRAPHY

Achenbach, T., & Zigler, E. (1963). Social competence and self-image disparity in psychiatric and nonpsychiatric patients. *Journal of Abnormal and Social Psychology,* **67,** 197–205.

Berger, E. (1955). Relationships among acceptance of self, acceptance of others and MMPI scares. *Journal of Counseling Psychology,* **2,** 279–284.

Bergin, A. E. (1979). The evaluation of therapeutic outcomes. In A. Bergin & S. Garfield (Eds.), *Handbook of psychotherapy and behavior change* (2nd ed.). New York: Wiley.

Bergin, A. E., & Strupp, H. H. (1972). *Changing frontiers in the science of psychotherapy.* New York: Aldine-Atherton.

Carkhuff, R. (1969). *Helping and human relations* (Vols. 1 and 2). New York: Holt, Rinehart and Winston.

Coopersmith, S. (1967). *The antecedents of self-esteem.* New York: Freeman.

Epstein, S. (1973). The self-concept revisited: Or a theory of a theory. *American Psychologist,* **28,** 404–416.

Eysenck, H. J. (1952). The effects of psychotherapy: An evaluation. *Journal of Consulting Psychology,* **16,** 319–324.

Eysenck, H. J. (1966). *The effects of psychotherapy.* New York: International Science Press.

Frick, W. (1971). *Humanistic psychology: Interviews with Maslow, Murphy, and Rogers.* Columbus, OH: Merrill.

Fromm, E. (1956). *The art of loving.* New York: Harper and Row.

Hales, S. (1979). Developmental processes of self-esteem. Paper presented at the Society for Research in Child Development, San Francisco.

Higgins, E. T. (1987). Self-discrepancy: A theory relating self and affect. *Psychological Review,* **94,** 319–340.

Holdstock, T. L., & Rogers, C. R. (1977). Person-centered therapy. In R. J. Corsini (Ed.), *Current personality theories.* Itasca, IL: Peacock Publishers.

Kirschenbaum, H. (1979). *On becoming Carl Rogers.* New York: Delacorte Press.

Landman, J. T. & Dawes, R. M. (1982). Psychotherapy outcomes. *American Psychologist,* **37,** 504–516.

Levant, R. F., & Schlien, J. M. (Eds.). (1984) *Client-centered therapy and the person-centered approach: New directions in theory, research, and practice.* New York: Praeger.

Mahoney, J., & Hartnett, J. (1973). Self-actualization and self-ideal discrepancy. *Journal of Psychology,* **85,** 37–42.

Markus, H. (1983). Self-knowledge: An expanded view. *Journal of Personality,* **51,** 543–565.

Markus, H., & Nurius, P. (1986). Possible selves. *American Psychologist,* **41,** 954–969.

Medinnus, G., & Curtis, F. (1963). The relation between maternal self-acceptance and child acceptance. *Journal of Counseling Psychology,* **27**, 542–544.

Patterson, C. (1973). *Theories of counseling and psychotherapy* (2nd ed.). New York: Harper and Row.

Rogers, C. R. (1939). *The clinical treatment of the problem child.* Boston: Houghton Mifflin.

Rogers, C. R. (1942). *Counseling and psychotherapy: New concepts in practice.* Boston: Houghton Mifflin.

Rogers, C. R. (1951). *Client-centered therapy: Its current practice, implications, and theory.* Boston: Houghton Mifflin.

Rogers, C. R. (1954). The Case of Mrs. Oaks: A research analysis. In C. R. Rogers & R. F. Dymond (Eds.), *Psychotherapy and personality change: Co-ordinated research studies in the client-centered approach.* Chicago: University of Chicago Press.

Rogers, C. R. (1955). Persons or science? A philosophical question. *American Psychologist,* **10**, 267–278.

Rogers, C. R. (1956). Some issues concerning the control of human behavior (symposium with B. F. Skinner). *Science,* **124**, 1057–1066.

Rogers, C. R. (1957). The necessary and sufficient conditions of therapeutic personality change. *Journal of Consulting Psychology,* **21**, 95–103.

Rogers, C. R. (1959). A theory of therapy, personality, and interpersonal relationships, as developed in the client-centered framework. In S. Koch (Ed.), *Psychology: A study of a science* (Vol. 3, pp. 184–256). New York: McGraw-Hill.

Rogers, C. R. (1961). *On becoming a person: A therapist's view of psychotherapy.* Boston: Houghton Mifflin.

Rogers, C. R. (1963). The actualizing tendency in relation to "motives"; and to consciousness. In M. Jones (Ed.), *Nebraska symposium on motivation* (Vol. 2, pp. 1–24). Lincoln: University of Nebraska Press.

Rogers, C. R. (1967). Autobiography. In E. Boring & G. Lindzey (Eds.), *A history of psychology in autobiography* (Vol. 5, pp. 341–384). New York: Appleton-Century-Crofts.

Rogers, C. R. (1969). *Freedom to learn: A view of what education might become.* Columbus, OH: Merrill.

Rogers, C. R. (1970). *Carl Rogers on encounter groups.* New York: Harper and Row.

Rogers, C. R. (1972). *Becoming partners: Marriage and its alternatives.* New York: Delacorte Press.

Rogers, C. R. (1973). My philosophy of interpersonal relationships and how it grew. *Journal of Humanistic Psychology,* **13**, 3–15.

Rogers, C. R. (1974). In retrospect: Forty-six years. *American Psychologist,* **29,** 115–123.

Rogers, C. R. (1977). *Carl Rogers on personal power.* New York: Delacorte Press.

Rogers, C. R. (1980). *A way of being.* Boston: Houghton Mifflin.

Rogers, C. R. (1983). *Freedom to learn for the 80s.* Columbus, OH: Merrill.

Rogers, C. R. (1984). Rogers calls peace results "surprising." *APA Monitor,* November.

Rogers, C. R. (1986). Client-centered therapy. In I. L. Kutush & A. Wolf (Eds.), *Psychotherapist's casebook.* San Francisco: Jossey-Bass.

Rogers, C. R., & Dymond R. (Eds.). (1954). *Psychotherapy and personality change.* Chicago: University of Chicago Press.

Rogers, C. R., & Stevens, B. (1967). *Person to person: The problem of being human.* New York: Simon and Schuster.

Smith, M. L., Glass, G. V., & Miller, R. L. (1980). *The benefits of psychology*. Baltimore: Johns Hopkins University Press.

Stephenson, W. (1953). *The study of behavior: Q-technique and its methodology*. Chicago: University of Chicago Press.

Suinn, R. (1961). The relationship between self-acceptance and acceptance of others: A learning-theory analysis. *Journal of Abnormal and Social Psychology, 63*, 37–42.

Suls, J., & Greenwald, A. G. (Eds.). (1983). *Psychological perspectives on the self* (Vol. 2). Hillsdale, NJ: Erlbaum.

Turner, R. H., & Vanderlippe, R. H. (1958). Self-ideal congruence as an index of adjustment. *Journal of Abnormal and Social Psychology, 57*, 202–206.

Watzlawick, P. (Ed.). (1984). *The invented reality*. New York: Norton.

SUGGESTED READINGS

Evans, R. I. (1975). *Carl Rogers: The man and his ideas*. New York: Dutton.

Gendlin, E. T. (1988). Carl Rogers (1902–1987). *American Psychologist, 43*, 127–128.

Harrington, D. M., Block, J. H., & Block, J. (1987). Testing aspects of Carl Rogers' theory of creative environments: Child-rearing antecedents of creative potential in young adolescents. *Journal of Personality and Social Psychology, 52*, 851–856.

Lietaer, G. (1984). Unconditional positive regard: A controversial basic attitude in client-centered therapy. In R. F. Levant & J. M. Schlien (Eds.), *Client-centered therapy and the person-centered approach: New directions in theory, research, and practice*. New York: Prager.

Ogilvie, D. M. (1987). The undesired self: A neglected variable in personality research. *Journal of Personality and Social Psychology, 52*, 379–385.

Wexler, D., & Rice, L. (1974). *Innovations in client-centered therapy*. New York: Wiley.

DISCUSSION QUESTIONS

1 How would you evaluate Rogers' concept of the actualizing tendency? More specifically, do you believe that all human motives can be subsumed under one master motive such as this one? Defend your position, pro or con.

2 How well does Rogers' phenomenological position fit your own experience? Specifically, do you feel that you live in a private world of experience of which you are the center—and does reference to this subjective experiential world within serve to explain your behavior better than any account of your actions based only on objective environmental factors outside yourself?

3 Explain Rogers' concept of organismic valuing process and how it is related to the need to self-actualize. Give specific examples.

4 Discuss the terms "need for positive regard," "need for positive self-regard," and "conditions of worth" as they apply to the process of self-concept development.

5 Compare Rogers' concept of the fully functioning person to your own idea of what constitutes mental health. Would you aspire to become a fully functioning person in your own life? Why or why not?

6 Skinner and Rogers seem to differ sharply on virtually all major issues in personology. Which of the two positions do you prefer? Can you see any relationship between your preference and your own basic assumptions concerning human nature?

7 How does the Q-sort technique measure the self-concept?

8 What does research indicate about the discrepancy between the perceived self and ideal self and its relationship to psychological adjustment?

9 Do you believe that the six conditions for therapeutic personality change described in relation to person-centered therapy are applicable to other significant human relationships? That is, do these six conditions seem to apply to the positive personality growth that takes place in love relationships, marriage, friendships, and child rearing? Try to give examples for each.

10 How does Rogers explain personality disorganization and psychopathology? Also, indicate how Rogers' phenomenological approach to disordered behavior differs from Freud's psychoanalytic approach.

GLOSSARY

Actualizing tendency In Rogerian theory, the primary motive in people's lives to maintain and enhance themselves—to become the best that their inherited natures will allow them to be.

Anxiety An emotional response that results when a person perceives an experience as being inconsistent or discrepant with his or her self-structure and its introjected conditions of worth.

Conditional positive regard The situation in which a person receives praise, attention, and approval for behaving in accordance with others' expectations. In other words, positive regard is contingent on certain acts or thoughts.

Congruence A state of harmony that occurs when there is no discrepancy between a person's experience and his or her self-concept.

Creativity A characteristic of the fully functioning person that leads to unique ideas, products, and solutions to problems.

Defense The person's attempt to change or modify a threatening experience through denial or distortion.

Denial Defense mechanism with which we protect ourselves from unpleasant aspects of reality by refusing to allow them to enter awareness.

Existential living The quality of living in the "here and now" so that each moment of one's life is new and different from all that existed before.

Experiential freedom The subjective feeling that one is free to live one's life in any way one chooses, e.g., "I am solely responsible for my own actions and their consequences."

Fully functioning person Term used by Rogers to designate a person who functions according to his or her own organismic valuing process rather than internalized conditions of worth.

Ideal self The person an individual thinks he or she could and should be or become (includes aspirations, moral ideals, and values).

Ideal-sort The statements a subject sorts when describing the person he or she would like to be.

Incongruence State of disharmony that occurs when there is a discrepancy between a person's experience and his or her self-concept.

Internal frame of reference The subjective experience of reality according to which a person lives his or her life.

Need for positive regard Learned or innate tendency on the part of individuals to seek acceptance, respect, and love from significant people in their lives.

Need for positive self-regard   Learned need which develops out of the association of self-experiences with the satisfaction or frustration of the need for positive regard. It refers to the individual's satisfaction at approving and dissatisfaction at disapproving of himself or herself.

Openness to experience   The ability to experience what is going on within ourselves without being threatened; the opposite of defensiveness.

Organismic trusting   The ability to consult and rely on our inner experiences and feelings as the basis for making important decisions.

Organismic valuing process   The Rogerian principle that experiences which are perceived as maintaining or enhancing the person are sought after and valued positively, whereas experiences which are perceived as negating or opposing the person's maintenance or enhancement are valued negatively and avoided.

Perceptual distortion   Type of defense mechanism used to transform threatening experiences into a form consistent or congruent with the person's current self-image.

Person-centered therapy   A form of psychotherapy developed by Rogers based on acceptance and unconditional regard for the client. Special emphasis is placed on the relationship between therapist and client as the vehicle for personality change.

Phenomenal field   The totality of a person's experience (also designated *perceptual field*).

Phenomenology   An approach to personology that emphasizes the importance of understanding the person's subjective experiences, feelings, and private concepts as well as his or her personal views of the world and the self.

Q-sort technique   A self-report assessment procedure used to measure the degree to which a person's actual and ideal self-concepts are congruent or incongruent.

Self-actualizing tendency   The person's tendency to develop in the direction of increased complexity, self-sufficiency, maturity, and competence.

Self-concept   The overall pattern or configuration of self-perceptions as viewed by the person himself or herself. Specifically, the person's conception of the kind of person she or he is.

Self-sort   The statements a subject sorts when describing the person he or she actually is at the present time.

Threat   Any experience that is perceived to be inconsistent with the person's self-structure.

Unconditional positive regard   Rogers' term for respect and acceptance given to another whether or not that person behaves in accordance with the accepting person's expectations. In other words, positive regard is not contingent on certain acts or thoughts.

Unconditional positive self-regard   Term used to designate a person who perceives himself or herself in such a way that no self-experience is more or less worthy of positive regard than any other. For Rogers, unconditional positive self-regard enables a person to progress toward becoming fully functioning.

CHAPTER 12

PERSONALITY PSYCHOLOGY: NEW DIRECTIONS IN THE DISCIPLINE

We have now reached the end of a long and sometimes arduous journey through a series of different theoretical perspectives on the nature of human personality. The reader who has completed the journey will probably agree that the study of personality is at once the most exciting and yet most baffling and frustrating area in psychology. We hope that the subject matter has proved interesting and enlightening.

The course we have traveled has revealed a wealth of unique concepts and formulations by which personologists have attempted to explain the complexity of human behavior, both normal and psychopathological. Each theoretical perspective presented in this text, while containing elements to admire or approve, does not overwhelm the others. All the perspectives, in fact, seem to have something of value to offer toward the goal of piecing together a "more well rounded" picture of what personality is really like. Nonetheless, the reader may feel that it is imperative that new conceptual approaches be developed if our understanding of people's actions is to be advanced. If so, this text has succeeded in conveying a sense of the field as it exists today. Considered together, past and present theories provide the foundation for understanding the causes of people's behavior. Nevertheless, we recognize that future progress depends on the ability of the current generation of personologists to create more adequate theoretical frameworks for understanding the enormous complexities of human existence.

What remains to be done in this concluding chapter is to take stock of what we have studied and to identify some of the issues, trends, and problems that are likely to influence future developments in personological theory and research. It is important to have a sense of emerging trends and critical issues in order to know the directions in which personality psychology is headed in the future. Before proceeding, however, one word of caution: our perspective is not to be construed as the "final word" in the field; indeed, one of the few things that may be assumed with certainty is that new and challenging issues will continue to appear as the field of personology evolves and changes. Accordingly, our efforts to identify emerging trends and critical problems is intended only to offer a tentative look at what may lie ahead. We also need to consider the degree to which the various perspectives discussed in this volume are likely to continue to exert an influence on present and future developments in personality theory and research.

First, however, a few final thoughts are warranted on the approach taken in this text to the study and comparison of personality perspectives. It is our conviction that philosophical assumptions about human nature offer a compelling and useful model for appreciating the broad spectrum of viewpoints and theoretical orientations which exist in current personology. In fact, these assumptions represent the conceptual pillars of personality psychology; they provide a framework for understanding how psychologists have sought to develop valid accounts of the behaviors, thoughts, and feelings of people.

BASIC ASSUMPTIONS IN RETROSPECT

The central, unifying theme of this text is that basic assumptions about human nature provide the framework within which various perspectives on personality are formulated and, ultimately, tested. They also highlight the fundamental issues and concerns about which personality theorists find themselves in agreement or disagreement. (For an overview of where the theorists accorded major attention in this text stand on each of these philosophical issues, see Figure 12-1.) In this concluding chapter, then, it is only fitting that we raise a few new questions and offer some speculative thoughts on the nature of these basic assumptions and their role in present and future theorizing in personality psychology.

The first question to consider is the origin of the various assumptions, one which we have already addressed in Chapter 1. It is worth reiterating briefly here. Your authors believe that root assumptions about humanity partially reflect a *theorist's own personal experiences*. To understand a theorist's underlying assumptions (i.e., where he is "coming from"), it is to some extent necessary to understand his religious and socioeconomic background, family size and birth order, relationship with parents, education, and professional experiences. We trust that our biographical sketches in each chapter helped the reader to appreciate how the individual life circumstances of theorists influenced their assumptions and theories of human nature.

In addition, we believe that the time and place in which personality theorists lived is an important source of influence on their basic assumptions and related concepts of humanity. For instance, Freud's views concerning human nature were formulated during what historians have termed the Victorian Age in Europe. Victorian society was characterized by a highly rational and moralistic view of the person. It was also a society that regarded sexuality as a frightening and obscene aspect of human nature. Freud shocked and offended many Victorians by claiming that people, even in infancy, are motivated by unconscious sexual and ag-

FIGURE 12–1 An overview of the positions of major personality theorists on the basic assumptions concerning human nature.

	STRONG	MODERATE	SLIGHT	MIDRANGE	SLIGHT	MODERATE	STRONG	
Freedom	Adler Maslow Rogers		Allport	Bandura Kelly		Erikson	Freud Skinner	Determinism
Rationality	Allport Bandura Kelly Maslow Rogers	Adler Erikson					Freud	Irrationality
Holism	Adler Erikson Maslow Rogers	Freud Allport Kelly				Bandura	Skinner	Elementalism
Constitutionalism		Freud Kelly Maslow Rogers		Adler Allport			Bandura Erikson Skinner	Environmentalism
Changeability	Erikson Skinner Bandura Maslow Rogers			Allport		Kelly	Freud Adler	Unchangeability
Subjectivity	Adler Kelly Maslow Rogers		Freud Allport	Bandura		Erikson	Skinner	Objectivity
Proactivity	Adler Allport Maslow Rogers	Freud Erikson		Bandura			Skinner	Reactivity
Homeostasis	Freud					Erikson	Adler Allport Maslow Rogers	Heterostasis
Knowability	Freud Skinner Bandura	Erikson Allport					Adler Maslow Rogers	Unknowability

gressive urges. Like Freud, other intellectuals of the day, such as Schopenhauer and Nietzsche, also argued that human behavior is governed by powerful unconscious and irrational forces. In sharp contrast with Freud, Maslow developed his personality concepts and assumptions during the 1950s and 1960s, a period during which the existentialist and phenomenological perspectives captured the attention of many American psychologists. Maslow's views of human nature were also influenced by his earlier contacts with eminent personologists who had immigrated to the United States to escape the darkening political situation in Europe. Adler, Fromm, and Horney were among those who had a lasting effect on Maslow's thinking by virtue of their emphasis on human consciousness, values, and becoming. If Freud, Maslow, or any other theorist had lived in a different social, cultural, or historical setting, his or her assumptions concerning the human condition may well have been different.

A second question pertains to the role of basic assumptions in the construction of theoretical frameworks. Precisely what effects do they have upon a person-ologist in the initial stages of theory construction? In our view, whether they are consciously acknowledged or not at the outset, *a theorist's philosophical assumptions about human nature simultaneously broaden and narrow his or her perspective on personality*. As an illustration, consider the freedom–determinism assumption. Any theorist who assumes the freedom position will, by definition, explore and emphasize those aspects of human functioning that suggest that people are able to control their own behavior. Further, this freedom assumption coupled with the sheer creativity of a theorist is apt to lead him or her in several new directions as he or she seeks to explain the essence of human nature.

Thus, a theorist's perspective on personality has been significantly broadened by the assumption of freedom. The theorist has been prompted to explore in detail explicit areas of human functioning and to invent theoretical concepts to describe and explain them. At the same time, however, the immense complexity of human behavior and experience suggests that his or her perspective has also been narrowed. The theorist has ignored or minimized those aspects of human behavior that are more readily explicable in deterministic terms. A theorist who stresses the idea that human beings have unlimited freedom, for example, will undoubtedly deemphasize or dismiss the importance of physiological, genetic, and situational determinants of behavior. Insofar as these are also valid aspects of human behavior to be explained, the theorist has ignored some considerations or at least downplayed their relevance. The freedom assumption, then, has guided the personologist down certain theoretical paths, opening his or her eyes to some aspects of human behavior that might otherwise not have been seen, while, at the same time, producing theoretical "gaps" about possible significant areas of human psychological makeup.

Of course, this is also true of a theorist who assumes a *deterministic* position. This assumption will take him or her down other theoretical pathways, focusing on those aspects of behavior that appear to be deterministically based and ignoring or deemphasizing human actions that might reflect free choice. Nevertheless, the complexity of human beings is such that it makes sense to acknowledge that freedom is also a salient feature of the human condition. If a theorist takes a narrow view and assumes only determinism, the result is a rather lopsided picture of people. It should be apparent that whether a theorist is a staunch determinist or a firm believer in free choice, the position taken on this assumption limits his or her account of the human mosaic to some extent.

The freedom–determinism assumption is only one of nine discussed in this book. It is our contention that the other eight basic assumptions function in precisely the same way in the construction and refinement of personological theories. While each may be more or less potent in a given theorist's thinking (e.g., subjectivity–objectivity is central in the theories of Rogers and Skinner and peripheral in the positions of Allport and Bandura), all nine assumptions influence the way in which a personologist builds a theory. No theorist conceptualizes within a vacuum, but gathers data and makes speculations within a preexisting framework of philosophical assumptions concerning the nature of humanity.

Given the fact that such assumptions reflect differences among the theorists in their perception of human behavior, it follows that there are several ways of looking at personalilty.

Still a third issue is whether or not these assumptions about human nature are the sole influences upon theory building in personality. Simply put, of course not. A personologist's overall philosophical stance constantly interacts with a host of other influences while a theory is constructed or revised. Factors other than basic assumptions which can influence a theorist's thinking include the historical period in which he or she lives, what is known in psychology and other disciplines at the time, what he or she actually knows about psychology and other disciplines at the time, degree of academic training and other exposure to the world of ideas, interactions with his or her colleagues (and, in some instances, clients or patients), and, more generally, the theorist's total life experiences. In brief, it cannot be forgotten that personality theorists are human beings engaged in the task of theorizing about human beings. Like the rest of us, what makes sense to them is influenced by numerous life experiences occurring over time and in a social context. Thus, we should realize that each personality theory reflects the biography as well as the basic assumptions of its creator.

As an illustration of this *interactive effect*, again consider the freedom–determinism assumption. Both Freud and Skinner were staunch determinists; they agreed completely that all human actions are utterly and totally determined, with no such possibility as free choice. But on the question of precisely what determines human behavior, these two theorists differed sharply, because the deterministic assumption interacted with other sources of influence in each man's life. Freud, for example, was trained as a physician, lived in a time and a society that rendered sexuality a virtual taboo, and treated patients for a living. Thus, he was led to look *within* people for behavioral determinants, to a biological kind of theoretical construct, to some locus of causality which his patients were unaware of in themselves, to that which was bound up with the sexuality that his patients could not express in their daily lives and that troubled them so. The *id*, in all its unconscious, irrational, and sexual power and glory, was the end result of Freud's search for the behavioral determinant.

In striking contrast, Skinner, who showed a preference for ''gadgets'' even in his younger days, was academically nurtured on the brass instrumentation, rigor, animal interests, preoccupation with the learning process, and wholehearted environmentalism of American behaviorism. Skinner earned his living as an academic psychologist in laboratories, working with animal and human subjects, inventing and building ingenious experimental devices, designing and carrying out experiments on the learning process, and, in general, manipulating environmental variables. Quite naturally, then, it is not surprising that Skinner looked *outside* the person for behavioral determinants. Obviously he succeeded admirably in finding them in the environment in terms of his central and well-articulated concept of *reinforcement*.

In summary, when we envision the position of a given theorist on all nine basic assumptions as they continually interact with the theorist's unique life experiences, we begin to grasp what really goes into the formal construction of a personality theory. This view in no way diminishes the important role of basic assumptions about human nature in theory building; it merely places these assumptions in proper perspective. As noted earlier, the very act of theorizing about humanity rests on certain philosophical assumptions. But differences in concepts and points of view articulated by theorists are also shaped by their personal backgrounds.

One final question remains: what will be the role of these assumptions in the personality psychology of the future? Our somewhat cautious answer is that because they deal with the fundamental issue of what humanity is, their role will remain unchanged. Basic assumptions about the nature of human beings will remain the foundation of all future theories of personality, regardless of their specific content or form. What will change, though, are the theories, hypotheses, methodologies, and research findings that make up the discipline of personality psychology. New theorists will emerge, bringing their unique personalities and experiences to bear on these assumptions. Most certainly, they will glean new knowledge about human behavior from psychology and other relevant disciplines. At the same time, we can expect that changed world conditions will have an impact on personality theorizing simply because they have done so in the past. All of the theorists covered in this text were influenced to some extent by social and cultural events that occurred during the time they lived. The effect of World War I on Freud's theorizing about human aggression is but one example. Nevertheless, we believe that philosophical assumptions will continue to serve as the framework for creating personality theories in the foreseeable future.

Let us now consider theoretical perspectives on personality from yet another vantage point.

EVALUATION OF PERSONALITY THEORIES

In Chapter 1 we offered six major criteria for evaluating theories of personality. Now that we have completed our study of the several theories presented in this volume, it seems only fitting that we consider how the approaches offered by Freud, Adler, Erikson, Bandura, Kelly, Rogers, and others have fared with respect to these criteria. No attempt at exhaustive analysis will be made here. Instead, the focus will center upon a brief comparison of the major perspectives on each criterion. In this way, the reader should be able to compare and contrast the current status of leading theories previously studied. For our purposes, three broad categories can be used to evaluate each personality perspective in terms of the six criteria. The *high* category indicates that a theory meets the criterion in question quite well; the *moderate* category means that the theory meets the criterion to some acceptable degree; and the *low* category suggests that the theory fails to meet the criterion. A summary of category ratings for each theory accorded major attention in this text is provided in Figure 12-2. Needless to say, the ratings are approximate and reflect your authors' subjective but, hopefully, informed judgment.

	LOW	MODERATE		HIGH	
Verifiability	Freud Allport Adler Kelly Erikson	Maslow		Skinner Bandura Rogers	
Heuristic value	Allport Kelly	Adler Maslow Erikson		Freud Skinner	Bandura Rogers
Internal consistency		Freud Allport		Adler Erikson Skinner	Bandura Kelly Maslow Rogers
Parsimony		Freud		Adler Erikson Skinner Bandura	Allport Kelly Maslow Rogers
Comprehensiveness		Erikson Allport Skinner Kelly Bandura Maslow		Freud Adler Rogers	
Functional significance	Allport Kelly	Adler Erikson Bandura		Freud Skinner	Maslow Rogers

FIGURE 12-2   The positions of personality theorists on the six major criteria for evaluating theories of personality. (The categories of high, moderate, and low indicate the extent to which a theory meets the criterion in question.)

Verifiability

The criterion of verifiability requires that a theory contain concepts that are clearly and explicitly defined, logically related to one another, and amenable to empirical validation. The basic question here is: Are the theory's concepts capable of being empirically investigated? While personality theories generally do not fare very well in this regard, there are reasonably distinct differences among them.

Given our overall evaluative framework, the positions of Skinner, Bandura, and Rogers can be rated as high on verifiability. Skinner is particularly impressive here, as his concepts and their relationships to one another are precisely defined. His position has sparked a wealth of experimental data. Likewise, Bandura's social cognitive theory has generated a substantial amount of empirical evidence in support of its major concepts and principles of psychological functioning. His rigorously constructed formulations will no doubt yield numerous testable hypotheses in years to come. Finally, Rogers has formulated theoretical concepts designed to explain a complex set of phenomena (e.g., self, personality growth, how psychotherapy affects change in people), concepts which have clearly led to much empirical testing and support. Although Rogers' theory lends itself to the formation of testable hypotheses, some of his concepts such as "actualizing tendency," "fully functioning," and "organismic experiencing" are too nebulous to verify empirically.

Satisfying the verifiability criterion to a moderate degree is Maslow's humanistic theory. Fundamental concepts in his theory that have been the target of study include the hierarchy of needs, peak experiences, and self-actualization. The theory has also stimulated efforts to establish an adequate self-report measure of actualization. Unfortunately, Maslow's position is characterized by the presence of several ambiguous terms. As a result, empirical evidence in support of certain aspects of his theory is not very strong.

The positions of Freud, Adler, Erikson, Allport, and Kelly must be judged low on the verifiability criterion. Enlightening as these theories may seem, each is composed of global constructs (e.g., Freud's structural concepts, Adler's creative self, Erikson's epigenetic principle, Allport's proprium, Kelly's basic postulate and supporting corollaries) lacking operational specificity, so empirical testing is currently difficult if not impossible. In defense of these theorists, it should be recognized that they did offer original perspectives from which to interpret both the stable and the dynamic qualities of human behavior. Nonetheless, at this juncture, their basic concepts are such that we cannot empirically evaluate their overall merits.

Heuristic Value

The criterion of heuristic value refers to the degree to which a theory has directly stimulated research. We do not, then, use this criterion in a global sense to address the question of how well a theory has captured the public's attention; rather, it is confined to whether or not hypotheses derived from a theory have, in fact, generated research. In other words, a theory's heuristic value is its ability to stimulate research activity within the general field of personality. In contrast, the criterion of verifiability reflects the extent to which hypotheses can be derived from a theory and, if tested through empirical research, support the theory's major claims.

The theories of Freud, Skinner, Bandura, and Rogers fare quite well on the criterion of heuristic value. Although many studies relating to Freud's psychodynamic theory may not offer strong support for his concepts (due to the low verifiability of the theory), he has served as an inspiration to many scholars by showing them the kinds of contributions that can be made to our knowledge of behavior through painstaking and courageous investigation. Literally thousands of studies have been prompted by Freud's theoretical assertions. Skinner's operant conditioning concepts, as noted earlier, are precisely defined and quite testable. He has had a tremendous impact on the research activities of investigators in many disciplines. Likewise, Bandura's theory has had considerable impact on the work of psychologists in a variety of areas (e.g., sex-role development, helping behavior, self-efficacy), employing subjects in widely different age groups. We are likely to see an increase in its heuristic value for professionals in other disciplines

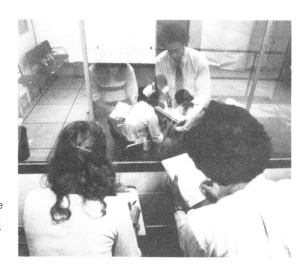

The criterion of heuristic value reflects the degree to which a theory generates empirical research. *(Bohdan Hrynewych/ Stock, Boston)*

in the future. Similarly, Rogers' theorizing has generated much research activity, especially in the realm of psychotherapy, with Rogers himself pioneering empirical work in this domain. His thinking has also led to an abundance of research on the linkages between self-discrepancies and negative emotional experiences.

The theories of Adler, Erikson, and Maslow can be judged as moderate on this criterion. Adler's theorizing has sparked a healthy upsurge of interest recently in testing ideas about the role of birth order in personality development as well as efforts to construct a reliable and valid measure of social interest. Adler has also directly or indirectly influenced such prominent personologists as Rogers, Maslow, and Rotter. Nonetheless, much of his theory remains untested, and empirical support generally is not very strong at present. In turn, Erikson's theorizing related to the stages of ego development, especially those of identity and intimacy, has inspired some empirical research. Erikson's use of psychohistory to study the lives of political, religious, and literary figures has also influenced the thinking of others, both within and outside psychology. However, many of Erikson's concepts are highly abstract so that it is difficult to convert them into testable hypotheses. Finally, Maslow's theorizing has been a prime stimulus for research on self-esteem, peak performance, and self-actualization. In addition to its impact on investigators in the personality area, Maslow's theory has been influential in the areas of education, organizational management, and health care. While we can admire the heuristic value of Maslow's work, the fact remains that many of his concepts are poorly defined and thus difficult to test properly.

The theories of Allport and Kelly fare poorly when measured by the yardstick of heuristic value. This is not to say that these theories have not stimulated people's thinking, for they most certainly have. For instance, it is difficult to read Allport without reflecting on how we describe others (traits) or Kelly without thinking about our own thinking (constructs). Moreover, Allport's emphasis on the idiographic approach to the study of personality and Kelly's development of the REP test to assess personal constructs have had some influence on the work of others within the field of personology. Nevertheless, neither of these perspectives has stimulated much of the current empirical research within the scope of personality. Regardless of their other considerable merits, the theories of Allport and Kelly reflect relatively low heuristic value at the present time.

Internal Consistency

Internal consistency means that a personality theory should account for whatever phenomena it encompasses in a logical and coherent fashion. In addition, separate components of a theory should be compatible with one another. As we noted in Chapter 1, most theories of personality generally do well on this criterion.

The theories of Adler, Erikson, Skinner, Bandura, Kelly, Maslow, and Rogers can be judged as high in terms of internal consistency. Each of these theorists' positions is based on a particular set of assumptions about human nature, leading to a network of theoretical concepts which account for human behavior in a sensible manner. We may disagree with the explanation of behavior provided by any of these theories, while acknowledging that the explanation is nonetheless consistent with other concepts embedded within the system.

Of the various theoretical perspectives presented in this book, Freud's and Allport's seem to fall a bit short on this criterion; their positions are best judged as moderate on internal consistency. In the case of Freud, it is widely recognized that the postdictive nature of the theory allows for essentially opposite behaviors to be accounted for by the same concept or the same behavior to be explained by different concepts. For example, is always showing up on time for your analyst's appointment a sign of good motivation for therapeutic progress or an indication of compulsiveness rooted in the anal stage of development? Such explanatory problems suggest less than ideal internal consistency. In Allport's case, the emphasis on the idiographic approach suggests that a set of common traits to account for people's behavior has yet to be specified. This problem, coupled with the ambiguous relationship between traits and the proprium in the theory, renders it difficult to determine just how consistently human behavior can be accounted for from Allport's perspective. But neither of these theories could be said to be seriously deficient in this area, and indeed none of the perspectives presented in this text can be judged as low on internal consistency.

Parsimony

The criterion of parsimony highlights the notion that the preferred theoretical account of psychological phenomena is the one requiring the fewest number of concepts—the fewer the concepts, the more parsimonious or economical the theory. The idea of parsimony also includes simplicity—the simpler the theoretical account, the more parsimonious the theory. A parsimonious theory, then, is lean in both the number and the unnecessary complexity of concepts required to explain human behavior. Given the nature and utter complexity of the phenomena with which our many theorists are attempting to grapple, their theories come off rather well on this criterion.

The positions of Adler, Erikson, Skinner, Bandura, Allport, Kelly, Maslow, and Rogers can be rated as high on the parsimony criterion. Adler's theory is extremely parsimonious in the sense that a limited number of core concepts support the entire theoretical system. Likewise with Erikson: personality is depicted in terms of psychosocial crises and eight major stages of ego development. Skinner, too, has a modest number of concepts, with a particular strength resulting from the fact that they all are anchored firmly to observable behavior. In Bandura's system, there are again comparatively few concepts, and these for the most part appear well-related to the cognitive social learning phenomena that he is attempting to explain. And in Allport's theory, there are a relatively few, mostly straightforward, concepts which, with the possible exception of the proprium, do not seem unnecessarily complex for describing personality functioning. Kelly's theory, too, ranks high on parsimony, with his basic notion of constructs elegantly fitting the cognitive realm he addresses. Likewise with Maslow: his motivational hierarchy concepts, while limited in number, seem to fit the complexities of human motivation without being too abstract. Finally, Rogers' theory seems almost too parsimonious, subsuming all motives under one master motive (the actualizing tendency) and all possible defensive strategies under two basic defenses (perceptual distortion and denial); nonetheless, his phenomenological perspective satisfies the parsimony criterion.

Freud's theory ranks moderate on parsimony. There is little problem with the number of concepts he advances, with some indeed being especially economical and potent for understanding personality dynamics. For instance, many aspects of human conflict can be accounted for in terms of id-ego-superego interactions. Yet in the current psychological Zeitgeist, Freud's system seems overly complicated in nature in that it purports to offer explanations for virtually all of human personality. In addition, the theory is conspicuous by its heavy emphasis on sex and aggression as the sole motivators of behavior. For these reasons, it is a theory that falls short on parsimony. This is a small criticism, however, in comparison with the incredible impact on human thought that Freud has had.

Comprehensiveness

Comprehensiveness refers to the range and diversity of phenomena encompassed by a theory. In essence, the more comprehensive a personality theory, the more behavioral ground it covers. Of course, to be selected for major coverage in this text, a theory had to be at least reasonably comprehensive. And yet, for the most part, we do not presently have personality theories that squarely address all significant aspects of human functioning. One reason for this state of affairs is the basic modus operandi of the theorists: a theorist's assumptions about human nature partially lead him to focus on certain aspects of human behavior while downplaying or even neglecting others. The net result is that most personality theories have a "focus of convenience" (Kelly's term), a domain of human behavior which they account for very well. A related effect is that most theories lack comprehensiveness, since they do not adequately describe and interpret areas of behavior removed from their focus of convenience.

Nonetheless, the perspectives of Freud, Adler, and Rogers can be rated high on the criterion of comprehensiveness. Freud developed a system of thought that is indeed extraordinary in this respect, covering as it does an enormous range and diversity of behavioral phenomena. Psychological disorders, dreams, humor, unconscious motivation, death, creativity, slips of the tongue and pen, forgetfulness, marriage, incest, myths and fairy tales, war, and social taboos can all be explained within the psychoanalytic framework. Without question, his theory constitutes the most comprehensive conceptual system ever formulated by a personologist. Adler's theory practically rivals Freud's in this respect, encompassing a broad range of phenomena such as the etiology of psychological disorders, nuclear family relationships, mental health, and numerous ways in which political, educational, and religious institutions affect personality development. Like Freud's theory, however, Adler's perspective is somewhat limited in terms of its motivational base. Finally, much that is currently known about human personality can be explained within a Rogerian framework. Rogers' primary source of data was his experiences as a psychotherapist. As such, he offered a viable perspective from which to understand the origins of pathological behavior and the means of treating it in therapy. In addition, his theory is useful in explaining how the self-concept and the inner world of subjective experience influence behavior, the conditions that allow people to reach their full potential, the way in which education might be improved at all levels, and even ways to reduce global strife and achieve world peace. However, the theory's comprehensiveness is limited by its lack of a detailed account of how cultural factors have an impact on both abnormal and normal personality development.

Ranking moderate on the comprehensiveness criterion are the remaining six major theoretical views of personality discussed throughout this text. To illustrate, although Erikson's position addresses itself to a wide variety of phenomena, both normal and abnormal, his focus on the eight stages of ego development necessarily limits the range of his theory. Skinner deliberately emphasized the simple elements of behavior, and at first his position, grounded as it was in animal experimentation, was severely limited in scope. Over the years, however, Skinner's concepts have been developed and applied to wider areas of human behavior, including behavior disorders, education, industry, and penal reform. As a consequence, his theory is now much more comprehensive than it was originally. Bandura's position provides a relatively thorough analysis of the social-cognitive variables responsible for the acquisition, maintenance, and modification of aggressive behavior. Furthermore, his observational learning concepts have increased our knowledge of the ways in which disordered behaviors are acquired, how language development comes about, and how self-reinforcement can be successfully utilized in the modification of behavior. Other topics of vital importance in today's world that have been extensively studied by Bandura include moral behavior, delay of gratification, and perceived self-efficacy. However, Bandura's is a theory that is still in the process of being developed, and we may reasonably expect increasing comprehensiveness in the future.

Allport's theory focuses on healthy functioning to the relative exclusion of psychopathology, and his account of the various developmental stages of the proprium is articulated in quite general terms. In addition, the theory is restricted in the sense that it recognizes the impact of environmental influences in the development of personality but does not specify the ways in which the environment operates to affect functioning. His theoretical perspective thus falls somewhat short on the comprehensiveness criterion. The thrust of Kelly's theory, in turn, is primarily cognitive, resulting in a rather one-sided intellectualized account of personality which highlights human rationality while downplaying the irrational thoughts and desires that sometimes control human functioning. Moreover, Kelly's perspective tends to neglect the role the situation plays in determining behavior. Personal construct theory is not very comprehensive, although it has the potential to incorporate far more phenomena than it does currently. Maslow's theory addresses itself to the issue of personal growth and development in human beings. While such an emphasis is sorely needed in contemporary psychology, the theory unfortunately does not spell out precisely the variables that control the expression and modification of self-actualization phenomena. Nor does the theory provide an explanatory system to account for a diversity of abnormal phenomena. Accordingly, Maslow's perspective can be judged as somewhat limited in both the range and the variety of psychological processes encompassed by its humanistic framework.

Functional Significance

To people outside the mainstream of academic psychology, there is probably no more relevant way to judge a personality perspective than by the degree to which it helps us to understand ourselves and others. The criterion of functional significance addresses exactly this issue (i.e., how useful or pragmatic a theory is in enabling people to understand everyday human behavior). And there seems to be a kind of circular relationship between functional significance and the "visibility" of a theory to laypersons. If a theory seems particularly germane to helping people either understand or overcome their problems, it tends to become widely known and accepted by laypersons; in turn, as it becomes more widely known and endorsed (regardless of its other scientific strengths or weaknesses), its functional significance both within and outside psychology seems to increase as well.

The positions of Freud, Skinner, Maslow, and Rogers rank exceptionally high in terms of applied value. Freud's theory is remarkable in this respect. Psychodynamic concepts (e.g, repression, ego, Oedipus and Electra conflicts) have become part of the vocabulary of educated laypersons, countless individuals have been affected by some form of psychoanalytically based therapy, Freudian theory has been applied to human behavior in many different disciplines (e.g., anthropology, history, economics, literature), and psychoanalysis has reshaped our image of human nature in the twentieth century. In short, psychodynamic theory has had considerable functional significance. Likewise, Skinner's concepts have been applied to a number of significant problems faced by human beings, with the prospect of affecting all of society. The theory's functional significance at present is most clearly evident in the areas of psychopathology and education. In fact, there are few areas of psychotherapy or teaching where Skinnerian theory cannot be applied. Maslow's humanistic formulations have had a decided impact on the enormous interest in personal growth and creativity evidenced today. His ideas and their applications have become especially widespread in contemporary pastoral and educational counseling programs as well as in various business-management programs. Rogers' theory is equally strong in the sense of applied value. Aspects of it have been applied to such diverse areas as classroom learning, administration, race relations, family relationships, and politics. Rogers' views on therapy have likewise had a decisive impact on the counseling and community mental health movement.

Ranking moderate on functional significance are the positions of Adler, Erikson, and Bandura. Adler constructed a very practical theory of personality—yet, especially when compared with Freud's position, his concepts have not had great impact outside the realms of psychotherapy, education, and parent–child relationships. Erikson's ideas cut across many disciplines, but his theory of psychosocial stages and the crises inherent in them has not enjoyed enormous practical influence, except within developmental psychology, vocational counseling, and social work. Bandura's work has generated some useful applications in our understanding of human aggression in general, and the influence of models (e.g., parents, television, and films) on aggressiveness in particular. For many, his theory has important implications for the control of crime. Bandura's extensive research on self-efficacy has also significantly contributed to the treatment of a variety of behavioral disorders. Nonetheless, his social cognitive perspective is still expanding and has yet to reach its full potential in terms of applied value.

The positions of Allport and Kelly must be judged low on the criterion of functional significance. While some of Allport's concepts seem enormously practical (e.g., traits and self-development), they have actually had little applied impact on disciplines outside psychology. Similarly, Kelly's ideas, intriguing and novel as they are, have had no appreciable impact on disciplines outside psychology and have not contributed much to the solution of social problems. One has the haunting feeling in the case of Kelly, however, that his concepts and measurement techniques (i.e., REP test) could have much more positive impact if only more people within psychology were made keenly aware of them.

Let us next consider where personality psychology will go in the future, what empirical issues will likely command serious attention, and what research strategies will be developed for the study of persons.

COMING OF AGE IN PERSONOLOGY

The development of personology as a bona fide scientific discipline is the product of the twentieth century (the origins of the discipline are much older, of course).

Consider Figure 12-3. With the exception of Freudian, Adlerian, and a few notable psychodynamic-derivative theories (e.g., Jungian and Frommian), all of which blossomed during the first third of this century, it is only within the last 50 or so years that major theoretical models of personality functioning have emerged. It should also be noted that some of the theorists discussed in this book (e.g., Bandura, Cattell, Erikson, and Eysenck) are still actively engaged in the study of human behavior. It is obvious, then, that personality psychology is a very young field of inquiry. But with age, it is hoped, comes wisdom. In less than five decades, personology has "come of age" by establishing itself as a viable and vigorous area of study. No doubt the flourishing activity in personology points toward a growing awareness that humanity's most pressing problems are within; they concern the person's life and his real relationships with specific others. Indeed, understanding the way in which human beings function—the mysteries about sexuality, aggression, conflict, interpersonal relationships and the like—has become a precondition for the survival of our species. Gardner Murphy eloquently expressed the real significance of the study of personality for our lives when he wrote:

> Lack of knowledge about human beings is not a trivial, but a major threat to life. Lack of knowledge about personality is perhaps the central core of the issue that is most relevant for us today; the issue of understanding what human beings can become under a new set of social arrangements. (1968, p. 38)

This statement, written more than two decades ago, seems more applicable than ever. Without such knowledge firmly anchored in empirical research, the human species may not survive.

FIGURE 12-3   Historical period during which personality theories were constructed.

Personality theorist		1890	1930	1940	1950	1960	1970	1980	1990	
Freud	(1856–1939)	[1890 – 1939]								Psychodynamic Theory
Adler	(1870–1937)	[1907 – 1937]								Individual Psychology Theory
Jung	(1875–1961)	[1913 – 1961]								Analytical Psychology Theory
Erikson	(1902–)				[1950 – 1975]					Psychosocial Theory
Fromm	(1900–1980)			[1941 – 1965]						Humanistic Psychoanalytic Theory
Horney	(1885–1952)			[1937 – 1973]						Sociocultural Psychoanalytic Theory
Allport	(1897–1967)			[1937 – 1961]						Trait Theory
Cattell	(1905–)			[1946 – 1990]						Structured-Based Systems Theory
Eysenck	(1916–)			[1947 – 1990]						Trait-Type Theory
Skinner	(1904–1990)			[1938 – 1985]						Behavioristic-Learning Theory
Bandura	(1925–)				[1959 – 1990]					Social Cognitive Learning Theory
Rotter	(1916–)			[1947 – 1982]						Social Learning Theory
Kelly	(1905–1966)				[1955–1965]					Cognitive Theory
Maslow	(1908–1970)				[1950 – 1970]					Humanistic Theory
Rogers	(1902–1987)				[1951 – 1975]					Phenomenological Theory

The Value of Alternative Perspectives

Broadly speaking, whatever the formal shortcomings and deficiencies of the various theoretical perspectives presented in this text, we believe that the themes, insights, and research findings embedded within them will have a decisive impact upon conceptions of human behavior in the foreseeable future. Put another way, *theoretical and empirical progress in the realm of personality will be based squarely on the contributions of past and present personologists.* This does not mean we should make light of criticism of existing approaches, hypotheses, methodologies, and research findings that make up the discipline. Nor does it mean that future frameworks and emphases will be carbon copies of existing ones. On the contrary, as the short history of personology has disclosed, there is virtually no limit to the diversity of theoretical models of humanity that personologists can invent! There are as many alternative conceptions of human nature as there are minds to conceive them. In turn, new concepts and perspectives are likely to rise to the fore. However, while personality theories, like fads, may come and go, the issues and problems with which our theorists have struggled will continue to attract serious attention in years to come.

The question that one is apt to ask next is, What are the critical and persisting issues in personality psychology? Basically, they can be enumerated in terms of eight global questions: (1) How does the human personality *develop*? (2) What *motivates human behavior*? (3) How does a person come to *think* and *know* about the self and the environment? (4) What is the nature of human *social* life? (5) What accounts for individual *uniqueness*? (6) What are the principal determinants of personality *disturbance*? (7) What are the defining characteristics of the psychologically *healthy* adult? (8) Why the direction of *competence* and *maturity* for some people and incompetence and immaturity for others? These are enormously complex questions and their answers may never be known with certainty. Yet the necessity to investigate and understand more about each will be highly relevant to charting the future course of personality theorizing. This, then, returns us to our original premise, namely, that creative theorists of the future will be guided by the rich intellectual heritage of their predecessors. It is this belief that makes the open-minded study of Freud, Jung, Erikson, Horney, Cattell, Eysenck, Bandura, Maslow, Rogers, and other theorists presented in this text worthwhile. Each in his or her own way has contributed something of enduring value to the understanding of human experience and behavior.

Of course, no one theory can adequately account for everything known about personality. The realm of human behavior is far too complex and elusive to be explained in terms of a particular theory or perspective. Therefore, your authors believe that it is presumptuous to assume that one can understand personality with only one theory. Instead, we believe that different theories may be useful for different problems or issues. This position, known as *eclecticism,* means that we should remain open to diverse points of view. An eclectic orientation also means that we should consider assumptions, concepts, and methods from various sources rather than being committed to a single theory. Most, if not all, of the existing theories of personality will undoubtedly be revised as more empirical studies are conducted. Future efforts aimed at integrating theories and research findings—creating a more comprehensive picture of the breadth and complexity of phenomena falling under the umbrella of personality—can also be expected. In the meantime, however, we should seek to explore ways in which concepts from all the various perspectives, even ideas that seem contradictory, enable us to better understand what it means to be human.

The Foundation of Empirical Research

Throughout this text we have presented studies bearing upon the empirical validity of various perspectives on personality. Our objective was to convince students taking a course in personality psychology that in the final analysis a theory's most important scientific function is to stimulate or generate new research. To perform this function successfully, a theory not only must be capable of aiding us in the comprehension of existing knowledge but also must be a fertile source of hypotheses that will lead to the discovery of new knowledge. Thus, if different theoretical approaches to personality are to be more than fanciful or wild speculations about human behavior, we must be able to convert them into testable form and study them empirically. This is what constitutes the essence of the scientific enterprise, differentiating it from common sense or the simple assertion of opinions or beliefs. It is also what in our judgment will determine the *ultimate scientific significance* of current approaches to the person offered by personality psychology. In short, critical scrutiny is not just a technical amenity—it is crucially important to establishing the validity of alternative theoretical viewpoints of human nature and individuality.

This brings us to another point. Any theory of personality functioning and behavior is merely a tentative statement that needs constant revision based on evidence gained from the testing of its offspring hypotheses. It must be so formulated that it can accommodate and incorporate new empirical data. Accordingly, there may come a time in the life of any personality theory when it loses elasticity and becomes obsolete. When our shoes no longer perform their function, we discard them for a new pair. Or if we gain weight, we buy a new belt. In the same way, a theoretical perspective must be considered ultimately expendable, to be cast aside when it ceases to perform its function of incorporating new discoveries about human behavior. Therefore, personality theories must be self-corrective in the light of new evidence.

Despite the importance of understanding existing theories, we can hope that personality psychology will eventually develop a set of theoretical constructs grand enough to encompass the whole person in a way satisfying to a majority of the scientific community. Personology has come a long way since Freud, Adler, Jung, and others, but no one can rightfully claim that human behavior is knowable or that fruitful lines of thought and inquiry have been exhausted. The following section outlines some tentative notions on the creative impetus for personality theorizing and research in the near future.

NEW FRONTIERS IN PERSONALITY THEORIZING AND RESEARCH

What sorts of problems and issues are likely to capture the attention of future personological investigators? Without appearing too prophetic, we predict that the agenda of future work will demand a high priority of serious inquiry into five general problem areas. Each area, from our admittedly subjective viewpoint, will require imaginative and critical study if our understanding of the person is to be enriched.

1 Study of Cognitive Processes and Their Relationship to Other Aspects of Psychological Functioning

With the exceptions of Kelly, Bandura, and Rotter, the personality theorists discussed in this text have either overlooked or minimized the role of cognitive processes in understanding human functioning. Freud asserted that all human behavior could be explained in terms of instinctual needs, early childhood experiences, and unconscious motivation. Skinner, on the other hand, believed that personality is observable behavior, learned through experiences with the environment. Rogers admittedly devoted some attention to the cognitive dimensions of human experience, but he placed more emphasis on feelings or emotions than on the intellect. Although Adler, Jung, Erikson, Fromm, Horney, Allport, Cattell, Eysenck, and Maslow all recognized the importance of internal mental processes, none directly addressed a basic question about human life: How do people assimilate information from the external environment, process and store that information in memory, and later retrieve what they have stored in order to use that information in an adaptive way? As psychology has developed, however, it has become apparent to students of personality that cognitive processes (e.g., perception, memory, attention, and problem solving) are absolutely central to an understanding of everything about human functioning. Accordingly, recent years have seen extensive and significant developments in cognitive personality theory and research (Cantor & Kihlstrom, 1985; Markus, 1983; Mischel, 1976). In fact, it could be said that the study of *cognitive processes* (of how people process information available to them and create mental representations of their realities) virtually dominates the discipline today—not just personology, but all psychology. And, by all signs, investigations of cognitive processes and the provocative results this research has yielded will gain ascendancy in the coming years.

George Kelly has played a key role in the advancement of a cognitive perspective in contemporary personology. He deserves special credit for urging psychologists to study the rational and intellectual aspects of psychological functioning. Granting the importance of Kelly's contributions, Albert Bandura's cognitive social learning theory has proven itself to be an even more important catalyst for the emergence and current popularity of the cognitive approach to understanding personality. Inspired by his success in demonstrating that the key to observational learning is the human capacity to represent observed behavior symbolically, personologists are now beginning to explore the person's vast storehouse of information, how it is organized, and how it is utilized in daily information processing. Not surprisingly, approaches to personality that emphasize the person's cognitive activity have had a marked impact on clinical psychology, where "cognitive therapies" are rapidly becoming among the most popular (Beck, 1976; Beck et al., 1979).

A central focus of current personality research in relation to cognitive processes has to do with the different ways in which individuals process social information and the relationship between such processes and other aspects of psychological functioning. Of particular interest to personality researchers has been the concept of schema. A *schema* is an organized structure of knowledge about a particular object, concept, or sequence of events (Fiske & Taylor, 1991). Stated differently, schemas are hypothetical cognitive structures that we use to perceive, organize, process, and utilize information about the world. Much like Kelly's concept of "personal constructs," schemas are useful because they simplify the flow of incoming information and make our complex social environments more manageable. Additionally, schemas allow us to form expectations about people and events, to focus our attention on relevant information while ignoring or downplaying the rest, and to interpret ambiguous information into preexisting frameworks (Fiske & Linville, 1980; Taylor & Crocker, 1981).

The cognitive approaches to personality contend that every person employs a vast and complex set of schemas to make sense of the world. Furthermore, recent advances in the study of social cognition suggest that schemas provide an overall framework by which to process and organize self-relevant information. *Self*-schemas are "cognitive generalizations about the self, derived from past experience, that organize and guide the processing of self-related information" (Markus, 1977, p. 64). A self-schema consists of those self-defining properties that we view as most representative of who we are. This includes such personally significant information about ourselves as our name, representative aspects of our physical appearance, representative features of our relationships with significant people, and perceived traits, motives, values, and goals that we regard as comprising our overall self-concept. It should be recognized that self-schemas may also undergo change as we redefine both who we are and who we might become in a new situation.

A body of research evidence indicates that people process information that is relevant to their self-schemas in highly efficient ways (Lewicki, 1984; Markus, 1983; Markus & Smith, 1981). In one study, for example, Markus (1977) investigated the dimension of "independence–dependence" in self-schemas. Based on this initial phase of the study (i.e., self-reports on several personality questionnaires), female subjects were classified as having a strong independence schema, a strong dependence schema, or as aschematic (those with neither schema). Three to four weeks later, these subjects participated in an experiment in which a list of personality trait adjectives were presented on a screen one at a time. The adjectives were either schema-relevant (synonyms of independence such as assertive and individualistic or synonyms of dependence such as timid and conforming) or schema-irrelevant (a set of trait adjectives related to the dimension of "creativity"). The subject's task was to press one of two buttons, labeled either

ME or NOT ME, to indicate whether the adjective was self-descriptive. A clock connected to the buttons recorded how quickly subjects in each of the three groups responded to each type of word.

Markus found that subjects with strong independence schemas pressed the ME button quickly in response to independence-related adjectives but took longer to respond to dependence-related adjectives and schema-irrelevant adjectives. An opposite pattern of results was found for subjects with strong dependence schemas, with faster reaction times to the dependent adjectives that characterized them. The aschematic subjects, on the other hand, showed no difference in their processing times for any of the types of words. These results clearly support the existence of self-schemas, since they demonstrate that people process information more rapidly when they have a strong cognitive structure related to that information. This support for the self-schema concept, in turn, supports the schema theory of personality, which explains relatively stable individual differences in behavior in terms of differences in cognitive structures.

Studies similar to Markus' have shown that when processing information, people (1) make rapid judgments and decisions about themselves on matters pertinent to their self-schemas, (2) are quick to retrieve or reconstruct episodes from their past that fit their self-schemas, (3) often perceive others through the lenses of their own schemas, and (4) reject information that is inconsistent with their self-schemas (Cantor & Kihlstrom, 1987). Together, these findings are of particular importance because they support the basic claim of the cognitive paradigm that the processing of self-relevant information exerts control over the causes and consequences of overt behavior. It is also possible to interpret these overall results as supporting Rogers' idea that experiences incompatible with the existing self-structure are distorted or denied symbolization into awareness.

The last decade has witnessed a significant increase in the acceptance of cognitive approaches to personality theory and research (Lazarus, 1984). Furthermore, one of the most striking aspects of the cognitive "revolution" has been its pervasiveness. Virtually no area of human behavior has escaped the speculation of possible cognitive influence. Cognitive processes have been implicated in such diverse areas as anxiety, depression, obesity, speech disorders, sexuality, art, and athletic performance. Recent research even suggests that cognition plays an important role in affecting an individual's physical well-being (Peterson et al., 1988; Suls & Mullen, 1981). As we see it, the cognitive perspective offers an image of the person that promises to stimulate a wealth of conceptual and research possibilities in the near future.

2 Study of the Interaction of Situational Factors and Personality Variables and Their Relative Contribution to Behavior

Although their descriptions and explanations vary a great deal, most personality theorists assume that internal dispositions (or what are otherwise called *person variables*) are responsible for and can adequately explain an individual's behavior. Put another way, a major theme of personality psychology is that overt behavior reflects the operation of underlying causal factors that are relatively stable over time and across situations. Freud's psychodynamic theory is the very embodiment of this *person-oriented view*. More than any other theoretical viewpoint presented in this book, the psychodynamic perspective carries the assumption that the person's behavior is dictated by stable personality characteristics that derive from childhood crises. The dispositional perspective on personality as exemplified by three of the most prominent trait theorists, Allport, Cattell, and Eysenck, also emphasizes that behavior is determined by factors that reside within the person. These three theorists, despite their disagreement concerning the source and number of dispositional qualities, share the important assumption that such characteristics exert a causal influence on the person's behavior across many situations. In fairness to Cattell, it must be noted that he does not ignore the influence of specific environmental situations on behavior. As you may recall, Cattell believes that each one of a person's traits must be weighted in terms of its relevance to a certain situation. Nonetheless, the concept of source trait constitutes the most important construct in his theory.

To a lesser extent, the importance of intrapsychic structures and processes is also evident in post-Freudian theories such as Jung's (psychological types), Adler's (inferiority feelings), and Horney's (basic anxiety). These theorists, despite the dissimilarity among their approaches, concur that personality dispositions do have an enduring impact on the person's life experiences. Kelly's cognitive perspective focuses almost exclusively on person variables, since he is most concerned with understanding how a person's unique construct system influences overt behavior. Similarly, the phenomenological viewpoint espoused by Rogers favors person variables (drive for self-actualization, self-concept) as the primary source of the individual's behavior. The common assumption shared by all of these theorists is that personality is composed of broad and stable dispositions which shape and give expression to behavior in a variety of situations.

Relatedly, the assumption shared by these different theorists is that situational influences play a secondary role in the acquisition and modification of behavior. Yet we know that people change their behavior in response to changing environmental conditions throughout their lives. A person who marries changes in several ways as a result of the new status; so does a person who divorces. Entrance into an occupation and the playing of new roles—for example, student, parent, athlete, and employee—also bring changes in behavior. We are changed by educational experiences, deaths of loved ones, and advancements in technology and science. On a broader scale, it is obvious that at least some portion of our behavior is governed by the sociocultural context in which we live (e.g., living in a sparsely populated setting versus living in a crowded, drug-infested ghetto). Fromm's emphasis on social, political, and economic factors as major sources of influence on the development of character types illustrates this line of thinking. Erikson's theory, too, is concerned with the interconnectedness of self and environmental contexts, but his primary focus is within the person. Skinner's position is exclusively environmental in emphasis, to the point of recognizing no organismic or intrapsychic variables with which situational factors can interact! Finally, Bandura's position, while considerably less extreme than the radical behaviorist assumption of environmentalism, also acknowledges the impact of situational variables upon behavior.

Although the *situation-oriented view* just cited may seem reasonable, perhaps even compelling, most personologists have traditionally downplayed the situational components of behavior in their theories and studies (Gergen, 1982; Veroff, 1983). We should note, however, that the idea that situational variables are more important than personality variables in determining people's actions has always seemed to be a sensible position to social psychologists. That fact notwithstanding, recent developments in personology suggest a changing perspective. Specifically, a growing number of personologists are beginning to acknowledge that the impact of different aspects of the environment on behavior must be understood (Blass, 1984; Bronfenbrenner, 1979; Schutte et al., 1985). For example, one approach to the understanding of situations that has attracted attention among personologists is provided by Moos (1973, 1976). Moos proposed that six general dimensions of human environments play an influential role in shaping the behavior of people. These dimensions include (1) physical ecology, (2) behavior settings, (3) organizational structure, (4) characteristics of persons in the situation, (5)

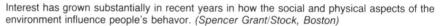

Interest has grown substantially in recent years in how the social and physical aspects of the environment influence people's behavior. *(Spencer Grant/Stock, Boston)*

perceived social climate, and (6) functional and reinforcement qualities. Obviously, many different taxonomies are possible by which to study human behavior in relation to the social and physical environment. Nevertheless, the personologist's interest in how environments influence people's actions has grown substantially in recent years (Cantor et al., 1982). As a result, we know a good deal more than we once did about the pervasive and powerful influence that environments have on people who inhabit and behave in them.

Although any viable approach to studying the person must consider the impact of situations coexisting simultaneously outside the person, it must also be recognized that dispositional qualities likewise have a place in a comprehensive account of the person's behavior. Another way of saying this is that behavior is determined by both person and situation variables and their reciprocal influence on each other. This idea that behavior is a function of the interaction of person and environment is an ascending theme in personality psychology today (Houts et al., 1986; Pervin, 1978; Snyder & Ickes, 1985). Commonly described as the *interactionist approach,* it is no more evident than in Bandura's concept of reciprocal determinism. According to Bandura's version of interactionism, person, situation, and behavior are parts of an interdependent and dynamic system of causes and effects. Rotter's social learning theory also holds that the explanation of human behavior requires an understanding of the interaction of people with their meaningful environments.

Within an interactionist framework, personality is construed as a hypothetical construct that "refers to the distinctive patterns of behavior (including cognitions and emotions) that characterize each individual's adaptation to the situations of his or her life" (Mischel, 1976, p. 2). More precisely, person variables represent the totality of past experiences encoded in the central nervous system which help the individual to cope effectively with the demands of his or her current life circumstances. Situational variables, on the other hand, represent the environmental conditions within which the person's behavior is embedded and that affect her or him in some appreciable way. The ensuing reaction may range from a thought or affective response to an overt action of some kind. From an interactionist perspective, then, people are viewed as having the capacity to exercise considerable choice over what environments they enter and what behaviors they display. This dynamic approach to understanding how the person and the environment continually and reciprocally influence each other provides a very different account of the complexities in behavior from what is offered by person-oriented or situation-oriented theories.

There are many different versions of interactionism (Ozer, 1986). Nonetheless, an increasing number of theorists and researchers agree that an interactional model of personality provides the best framework for generating an adequate account of human behavior (Emmons et al., 1986; Endler, 1981). In particular, such an approach should prove useful in determining to what extent complex behavior is regulated by interactions that depend intimately on situational variables, as well as on dispositions. At the very least, an interactional model is a much needed corrective for an area of psychology that has heretofore focused on the individual as a unit, often ignoring the mutual links between a person and the constantly changing conditions of his or her life. Furthermore, an interactionist approach should enhance our understanding of the circumstances where dispositional differences matter a lot and circumstances where they do not matter at all. Finally, an interactionist perspective should foster the development of theoretical constructs that will more adequately characterize a person's total ecological situation, so that it may be taken into account in the explanation and prediction of behavior (Bronfenbrenner, 1979; Gergen, 1982). Recently, for instance, terms such as "role dispositions," "interpersonal reaction systems," "situational prototypes," and "behavioral settings" have crept into the personologist's vocabulary.

What we envision for the future, then, are psychological studies that consider the person and the environment "coming to terms" with each other via dynamic transactions. For example, Mary Jones will be studied not only in terms of her self-concept structure and dynamics, as she traditionally has been studied in the past but also as chairperson of a conference, consumer of goods, vacationer, school administrator, and churchgoer. Rather than being depicted as one person with a variety of occupational and social roles, she will be studied at home, at the office, at the camp grounds, at the supermarket, and in church. In short, the attempt to understand Mary Jones will reflect the recognition that many important aspects of her behavior not only fluctuate as her life situation changes but also depend crucially on the reciprocal relationship, or interaction, between her unique trait structure and the situation. To be sure, the question of how person variables and situational factors interact in producing behavior is a challenging one requiring new research strategies. It is an urgent empirical issue that will in all likelihood receive substantial attention in the years ahead.

3 Study of the Neurophysiological, Biochemical, and Genetic Bases of Personality

In all likelihood, the contemporary scientific era will be recorded as the age of biology—and as a period in which advances in behavioral genetics, biochemistry, and neurophysiology produced remarkable and decisive changes in the constructs and methods that guide inquiry in psychology in general. Yet, with the exceptions of Freud, Cattell, Eysenck, Maslow, and Rogers (the only five theorists in this text who truly acknowledge and stress the biological underpinnings of behavior), personologists have traditionally paid only lip service to the study of neurophysiological, biochemical, and genetic components of human behavior. Fortunately, most personologists today recognize that individual differences are partly rooted in underlying biological processes and genetic predispositions (Rowe, 1989). In the wake of the upsurge of our knowledge of the biological basis of behavior and mental processes, combined with the development of sophisticated research designs, resistance to understanding personality in terms of biology and genetics appears to be breaking down.

Consistent with the trend just noted, a growing body of evidence suggests that genetic factors can explain a substantial part of the individual differences in personality. This can be seen in the recent proliferation of studies focused on the heritability of personality traits (Loehlin et al., 1987; Plomin, 1989; Rushton et al., 1986; Tellegen et al., 1988). Much of this research supports the idea that individual differences in traits (e.g., emotionality, sociability, activity, and impulsivity) have a substantial level of genetic influence. Efforts to frame new theories that incorporate the biological bases of social behavior are also becoming more prominent with each passing year. A notable example is the *socioanalytic theory* of psychologist Robert Hogan (1982). Bringing together strands of sociobiology, psychoanalytic theory, and symbolic interactionism, he argues that there are two striking features of human evolution. First, human beings have always lived in social groups. Second, these groups have always been organized in terms of status hierarchies. Furthermore, Hogan proposes that people are genetically predisposed to live together and to achieve and maintain a status hierarchy. Hogan's socioanalytic theory is but one example of the creative advances being made in personality psychology couched in terms of biology.

Research-oriented personologists of the future can ill afford to ignore the current surge of knowledge suggesting that many manifestations of personality are mediated by biological and genetic factors. It is our belief that those studies that seek to link personality dimensions with the functioning of the nervous system (made possible by powerful electrophysiological and other techniques) will highlight future progress in the discipline. In particular, studies concerned with how biochemical and neurophysiological processes are related to psychological functioning (cognition, affect, sensation) will clearly merit attention. Additionally, investigators will need to provide a coherent account of the meaning of biological mechanisms in terms of the development, behavior, and experience of the individual (Buss, 1984; Wilson, 1978). Such accounts will inevitably lead to innovative constructs in personality theorizing. Progress in personality research will thus be made on two fronts: (1) empirical study of the biochemical and genetic underpinnings of behavior and (2) development of conceptual schemes that will more adequately explain the individual's biological heritage and how it affects various forms of behavior commonly associated with the domain of personality (e.g., aggression, attachment, altruism, temperament, and intelligence). To be sure, some progress in this direction has already been achieved as a result of Eysenck's effort to link personality dimensions with specific structures or functions of the brain. His account of the biological basis of personality illustrates the larger effort under way to understand the role of biochemistry and genetics in human behavior.

4 Study of Personality Development in Middle and Old Age

About one-quarter of our lives is spent growing up and three-quarters growing old. It is ironic, therefore, that personologists have devoted so much of their attention to the study of childhood and adolescence (Sarbin, 1986). Two major assumptions underlie and partially explain this one-sided emphasis on the study of child and adolescent development: (1) adult behavior patterns are firmly established at an early age and (2) parental treatment during the initial years of life is a significant determinant of personality formation. The enduring impact of Freudian psycho-sexual theory is clearly evident in both these assumptions. There are a number of other personality perspectives which also emphasize that the basic foundation of an adult's life-style is formed during childhood based on the nature of parent–child interactions. Adler, Horney, Fromm, and Rogers all endorse this view to some extent. It is further evident that children and adolescents are more readily avail-able and cooperative subjects for study than are older individuals; for example, college freshmen are easier to recruit and test than are 45-year-old business executives. Nevertheless, several prominent personologists, most notably Erik-son, Allport, and Maslow, have convincingly argued that children and adolescents are "unfinished" personalities. Erikson merits special credit for making us aware of the fact that the hurdles of personality development continue in some ways until death completes the life cycle. His formulation of a series of interlocking developmental crises encompassing the individual's entire life span has inspired psychologists to reexamine traditional beliefs concerning personality growth and change in adult life.

The past two decades have witnessed a dramatic upsurge of interest in the study of developmental changes brought about by the aging process (Perlmutter & Hall, 1985; Schaie, 1985). In particular, research on age-related physical, sensory, hormonal, and cognitive changes has blossomed (Birren & Schaie, 1985; Schaie, 1988). Similarly, increasing numbers of psychologists have addressed the issue of developmental transformations centered around marital and family roles, work values, and friendship patterns as adults grow into and through middle age (Gould, 1980; Levinson, 1986; Vaillant, 1977). Continued study of adult developmental processes is likely for both practical and theoretical reasons. For one thing, the percentage of the population in the United States over age 65 is increasing at a steady rate and is projected to continue to increase. People older than 65 now compose approximately 12 percent of the population, and it is expected to ap-proach 20 percent by the year 2020 (U.S. Bureau of the Census, 1989). Further-more, for babies born in the United States today, life expectancy is an un-precedented 71.1 years for a boy and 78.3 years for a girl. Clearly, one impetus for the continued study of adult development is the increasing proportion of middle-aged and older people in the population. Society has also assumed a more sensitive posture in relation to the care of senior citizens (e.g., nursing homes and retirement villages), which makes these people more accessible to the scientist. Finally, adults will command greater study for no other reason than to achieve a full narrative account of how the "story of human development ends." The final chapter in the story of a person's life confronts us with a great many psychosocial issues that we do not yet clearly understand.

Future basic research in personality will surely broaden its base of inquiry to include large-scale *life-history study* of individuals representing various na-tionalities, ethnic groups, social classes, and occupations (Bertaux, 1981; Craik, 1986). Such research, largely autobiographical in nature and supplemented by other personal documents, will better inform us of the complex interaction of

Future research in personality will include people representing a greater diversity of nationalities, ethnic groups, and social-economic classes. *(Joel Gordon)*

social systems and persons played out against a larger background of historical themes. It would also seem reasonable to expect that the formulation of ever more complex and comprehensive conceptions of human development (especially in relation to the middle and late years of life) will be a consuming task for future theorists (Woodruff-Pak, 1988). This effort, in our view, will eventually open up opportunities for thoughtful integrations of developmental trends across the expanse of adulthood.

5 Study of Problems Relevant to the Practical World of Human Affairs

For all practical purposes, the formal study of personality had its beginnings in Freud's concern with the causes and treatment of pathological behavior. The history of personological inquiry, therefore, reflects a strong emphasis on behavioral phenomena observed most readily in psychotherapeutic situations. This orientation especially characterizes the approach of Adler, Horney, Jung, and to some extent, Erikson. Concern for pathological and defensive aspects of human functioning is also evident in the theories of Fromm, Kelly, Rogers, Bandura, and Rotter. But times are changing, and so are the themes and emphases in personality psychology. One notable example of such inevitable change is that personologists appear to be more willing and able now than they were 20 years ago to study real-world social problems. The thrust of efforts in this area predict an important and exciting future.

Many events occurring within recent years have produced an accelerating demand for the personological study of significant *social problems* that threaten our human future. The nuclear arms race, ecological violations, global energy crises, expanding birthrates in impoverished countries, exploitation and persecution of minority groups, and exploration of unknown areas of land, sea, and space have caused us to reexamine our relationships to ourselves, to each other, and to our environment. Wherever we look, we see the world changing with incredible rapidity—and established customs, traditions, and values changing with it. Indeed, one of today's major problems is the uncertainty of what to believe and how to live as an adult. Young people are especially overwhelmed by a smorgasbord of values, ideologies, and life-styles in their search for an overall approach to life that seems to "fit." It is not surprising, then, that psychological investigators have become increasingly concerned about the social relevance of their work and the contributions they might ultimately make toward solving the problems and challenges of the contemporary world. This trend toward a socially relevant psychology will undoubtedly have a profound impact on the study of personality. Personality researchers of the future will need to broaden the scope of their activities considerably if they are to maintain a respectable and influential position in the behavioral sciences. Similarly, areas of application will need to become more diverse.

Contemplating this situation against the background of events in the world as a whole, it seems safe to predict that attention will be focused on the following areas: poverty, racial and sexual discrimination, population control, alienation, suicide, divorce, child abuse, drug addiction (including alcoholism), and crime. Clearly, the list could go on, and the problems span the length and breadth of human existence itself. Psychology obviously has a crucial role to play in helping people to achieve meaningful and productive lives. Some time ago, Bandura expressed the matter this way: "As a science concerned with the social consequences of its applications, psychology must promote understanding of psychological issues that bear on social policies to ensure that its findings are used in the service of human betterment" (1977, p. 213).

The consequence of this projected trend toward greater involvement in the concrete world of human affairs may be that personality concepts and perspectives will become considerably more complex and eclectic than those we know today (Buss, 1984; Lamiell, 1987). Another likely outcome is that personologists will become more involved with the work of social psychologists, sociologists, anthropologists, and ethologists. It follows that the field of personality will adopt a more *interdisciplinary approach* in dealing with research issues. In turn, greater emphasis will be placed on naturalistic modes of inquiry (i.e., observation and study of persons in settings such as the home, factory, hospital, and courtroom). Field research is, in principle, an ideal setting for investigating human functioning in the personality area; we do wish to understand behavior outside the psychology building! That personology will eventually pervade all sectors of the social world seems inevitable.

Conclusion

The study of personality is very much like the assembly of a complex jigsaw puzzle. The various perspectives considered throughout this text have provided us with many possible pieces of the puzzle. Some pieces will probably be discarded as not fitting the puzzle at all, and many others remain to be discovered. Nonetheless, we suggest that when a more definitive and illuminating picture emerges, several of the component pieces offered by the different perspectives on personality will be included. From this standpoint, it seems reasonable to conclude that the difficult task of fitting all the pieces together into an internally consistent and broader picture will be guided by the many rich and fascinating approaches that exist in the study of persons. Accordingly, we encourage you to learn as much as possible about every perspective on the person offered by personality theorists. Then, after you have studied each perspective in detail, you will be better prepared to develop your own ideas about the nature of human personality. Considered together, the theories of personality presented in this text provide a useful starting point in the quest for how to live a good life and understand people.

SUMMARY

The central theme of this text is that basic assumptions about human nature constitute the bedrock from which perspectives on personality are fashioned and tested. It was further noted that a theorist's assumptions about human nature are acquired and developed in the same way as his or her other basic beliefs about the nature of the world.

Basic assumptions serve to both broaden and narrow a theorist's perspective on personality. For example, a theorist who adopts a free-will position will, by definition, attend to and emphasize those aspects of human functioning that bespeak the capacity to act as a free agent. At the same time, she or he will tend to ignore or downplay aspects of human behavior more readily explicable in deterministic terms.

Basic assumptions constantly interact with a host of other influences in shaping the personologist's theoretical account of behavior. Sources of influence other than basic assumptions which affect a theorist's thinking are the historical period, what is known in psychology and other disciplines at the time, academic training and exposure to the world of ideas, and personal life experiences.

The importance to personology of these assumptions will not diminish in the future, since they deal with the issue of what humanity is. Thus, philosophical assumptions about human nature will remain the foundation of all future approaches to personality. What will change, however, are the theorists, the state of knowledge in psychology and related disciplines, and the world.

In addition to basic assumptions, personality theories can legitimately be compared and contrasted according to other criteria. In this chapter, we evaluated major perspectives on personality in terms of the six key criteria described in

Chapter 1: verifiability, heuristic value, internal consistency, parsimony, comprehensiveness, and functional significance.

Personality psychology is a very young field of inquiry. With comparatively few exceptions, it is only during the past five decades that bold and viable perspectives on the person have emerged. Personology has nevertheless come of age by establishing itself as a fruitful and legitimate area of study. The flourishing activity in personology today is a function of the growing awareness that people's most vital problems concern themselves and their relationships with others.

Future theories will certainly not be carbon copies of existing ones, yet the ideas and insights embedded within the various perspectives presented in this text cannot but have a decisive impact upon future conceptions of personality. This is because past and current theorists have struggled to resolve critical and enduring issues and because they have each contributed something of value to the understanding of the mystery of human nature. Accordingly, creative theorists of the future will be guided by the rich intellectual heritage of their predecessors. Your authors maintain that an eclectic orientation, the sharing of ideas from one perspective to another, will provide the best explanation of personality in the foreseeable future.

The ultimate scientific significance of existing approaches to the person will depend upon the extent to which they generate new research. Furthermore, theories of personality must be self-corrective in the light of new empirical evidence if they are to remain useful to the scientific enterprise.

In the concluding section of this final chapter we suggested that new frontiers in personality theorizing and research will be explored in five general areas: (1) study of cognitive processes and their relationship to other aspects of psychological functioning; (2) study of the interaction of situational factors and personality variables and their relative contribution to behavior; (3) study of the neurophysiological, biochemical, and genetic bases of personality; (4) study of personality development in middle and old age; and (5) study of problems relevant to the practical world of human affairs. Imaginative and critical study in these areas is becoming more prominent with each passing year and promises to deepen and enrich our understanding of the nature of human personality.

BIBLIOGRAPHY

Bandura, A. (1977). *Social learning theory.* Englewood Cliffs, NJ: Prentice-Hall.

Beck, A. T. (1976). *Cognitive therapy and the emotional disorders.* New York: International Universities Press.

Beck, A. T., Rush, A. J., Shaw, B. F., & Emery, G. (1979). *Cognitive therapy of depression.* New York: Basic Books.

Bertaux, D. (Ed.). (1981). *Biography and society: The life history approach in the social sciences.* Beverly Hills, CA: Sage.

Birren, J. E., & Schaie, K. W. (Eds.). (1985). *Handbook of the psychology of aging* (2nd ed.). New York: Van Nostrand Reinhold.

Blass, J. (1984). Social psychology and personality: Toward a convergence. *Journal of Personality and Social Psychology*, **47**, 1013–1027.

Bronfenbrenner, U. (1979). *The ecology of human development*. Cambridge, MA: Harvard University Press.

Buss, D. M. (1984). Evolutionary biology and personality psychology: Toward a conception of human nature and individual differences. *American Psychologist*, **39**, 361–377.

Cantor, N., & Kihlstrom, J. F. (1985). Social intelligence: The cognitive basis of personality. In P. Shaver (Ed.), *Self, situations, and social behavior* (pp. 15–34). Beverly Hills, CA: Sage.

Cantor, N., & Kihlstrom, J. F. (1987). *Personality and social intelligence*. Englewood Cliffs, NJ: Prentice-Hall.

Cantor, N., Mischel, W., & Schwartz, J. C. (1982). A prototype analysis of psychological situations. *Cognitive Psychology*, **14**, 45–77.

Craik, K. H. (1986). Personality research methods: An historical perspective. *Journal of Personality*, **54**, 18–51.

Endler, N. S. (1981). Persons, situations, and their interactions. In A. I. Rabin, J. Aronoff, A. M. Barclay, & R. A. Zucker (Eds.), *Further explorations in personality* (pp. 114–151). New York: Wiley.

Emmons, R. A., Diener, E., & Larsen, R. J. (1986). Choice and avoidance of everyday situations and affect congruence: Two models of reciprocal determinism. *Journal of Personality and Social Psychology*, **51**, 815–826.

Fiske, S. T., & Linville, P. W. (1980). What does the schema concept buy us? *Personality and Social Psychology Bulletin*, **6**, 543–557.

Fiske, S. T., & Taylor, S. E. (1991). *Social cognition*. New York: McGraw-Hill.

Gergen, K. J. (1982). *Toward transformation in social knowledge*. New York: Springer-Verlag.

Gould, R. L. (1980). Transformations during early and middle adult years. In N. J. Smelser & E. H. Erikson (Eds.), *Themes of work and love in adulthood* (pp. 213–237). Cambridge, MA: Harvard University Press.

Hogan, R. (1982). A socioanalytic theory of personality. In M. Page (Ed.), *Nebraska symposium on motivation* (pp. 55–89). Lincoln: University of Nebraska Press.

Houts, A. C., Cook, T. D., & Shadish, W. R. (1986). The person-situation debate: A critical multiplist perspective. *Journal of Personality*, **54**, 52–105.

Lamiell, J. T. (1987) *The psychology of personality: An epistemological inquiry*. New York: Columbia University Press.

Lazarus, R. S. (1984). On the primacy of cognition. *American Psychologist*, **39**, 124–129.

Levinson, D. J. (1986). A conception of adult development. *American Psychologist*, **41**, 3–13.

Lewicki, P. (1984). Self-schemata and social information processing. *Journal of Personality and Social Psychology*, **47**, 1177–1190.

Loehlin, J. C., Willerman, L., & Horn, J. M. (1987). Personality resemblance in adoptive families: A 10-year follow-up. *Journal of Personality and Social Psychology*, **53**, 961–969.

Markus, H. (1977). Self-schemata and processing information about the self. *Journal of Personality and Social Psychology*, **35**, 63–78.

Markus, H. (1983). Self-knowledge: An expanded view. *Journal of Personality*, **51**, 543–565.

Markus, H., & Smith, J. (1981). The influence of self-schema on the perception of others. In N. Cantor & J. F. Kihlstrom (Eds.), *Personality, cognition, and social interaction* (pp. 233–262). Hillsdale, NJ: Erlbaum.

Mischel, W. (1976). *Introduction to personality* (2nd ed.). New York: Holt, Rinehart and Winston.

Moos, R. H. (1973). Conceptualizations of human environments. *American Psychologist*, **28**, 652–665.

Moos, R. H. (1976). *The human context: Environmental determinants of behavior*. New York: Wiley.

Murphy, G. (1968). Psychological views of personality and contributions to its study. In E. Norbeck, D. Price-Williams, & W. McCord (Eds.), *The study of personality: An interdisciplinary appraisal* (pp. 15–40). New York: Holt, Rinehart and Winston.

Ozer, D. J. (1986). *Consistency in personality: A methodological framework*. New York: Springer-Verlag.

Perlmutter, M., & Hall, E. (1985). *Adult development and aging*. New York: Wiley.

Pervin, L. A. (1978). *Current controversies and issues in personality*. New York: Wiley.

Peterson, C., Seligman, M. E., & Vaillant, G. E. (1988). Pessimistic explanatory style is a risk factor for physical illness: A thirty-five-year longitudinal study. *Journal of Personality and Social Psychology*, **55**, 23–27.

Plomin, R. (1989). Environment and genes: Determinants of behavior. *American Psychologist*, **44**, 105–111.

Rowe, D. C. (1989). Personality theory and behavioral genetics: contributions and issues. In D. M. Buss & N. Cantor (Eds.), *Personality Psychology: Recent trends and emerging directions* (pp. 294–307). New York: Springer-Verlag.

Rushton, J. P., Fulker, D. W., Neale, M. C., Nias, D. K., & Eysenck, H. J. (1986). Altruism and aggression: The heritability of individual differences. *Journal of Personality and Social Psychology*, **50**, 1192–1198.

Sarbin, T. R. (Ed.). (1986). *Narrative psychology: The storied nature of human conduct*. New York: Praeger.

Schaie, K. W. (1985). *Longitudinal studies of psychological development*. New York: Guilford Press.

Schaie, K. W. (1988). Ageism in psychological research. *American Psychologist*, **43**, 179–183.

Schutte, N. S., Kenrick, D. T., & Sadalla, E. K. (1985). The search for predictable settings: Situational prototypes, constraint, and behavioral variation. *Journal of Personality and Social Psychology*, **49**, 121–128.

Snyder, M., & Ickes, W. (1985). Personality and social behavior. In G. Lindzey & E. Aronson (Eds.), *Handbook of social psychology* (3rd ed.). Vol. 2: *Special fields and applications*. New York: Random House.

Suls, J., & Mullen, B. (1981). Life events, perceived control, and illness: The role of uncertainty. *Journal of Human Stress*, **7**, 30–34.

Taylor, S. E., & Crocker, J. (1981). Schematic bases of social information processing. In H. T. Higgins, C. P. Herman, & M. P. Zanna (Eds.), *Social cognition: The Ontario symposium* (Vol. 1). Hillsdale, NJ: Erlbaum.

Tellegen, A., Lykken, D. T., Bouchard, T. J., Wilcox, K. J., Segal, N. L., & Rich, S. (1988). Personality similarity in twins reared apart and together. *Journal of Personality and Social Psychology*, **54**, 1031–1039.

Vaillant, G. E. (1977). *Adaptation to life*. Boston: Little, Brown.

Veroff, J. (1983). Contextual determinants of personality. *Personality and Social Psychology Bulletin*, **9**, 331–343.

Wilson, E. O. (1978). *On human nature*. Cambridge, MA: Harvard University Press.

Woodruff-Pak, D. S. (1988). *Psychology and aging*. Englewood Cliffs, NJ: Prentice Hall.

SUGGESTED READINGS

Aronoff, J., & Wilson, J.P. (1985). *Personality in the social process*. Hillsdale, NJ: Erlbaum.

Carlson, R. (1984). What's social about social psychology? Where's the person in personality research? *Journal of Personality and Social Psychology, 47,* 1304–1309.

Conley, J. J. (1985). A personality theory of adulthood and aging. In R. Hogan & W. H. Jones (Eds.), *Perspectives in personality* (Vol. 1, pp. 81–116). Greenwich, CT: JAI Press.

Loevinger, J. (1987). *Paradigms of personality*. New York: Freeman.

Strelau, J., Farley, F. H., & Gale, A. (Eds.). (1985). *The biological bases of personality and behavior: Theories, measurement techniques, and development* (Vol. 1). Washington, DC: Hemisphere.

DISCUSSION QUESTIONS

1 What do you think of the idea that a theorist's basic assumptions about human nature reflect the theorist's own personal life experiences? If you agree, what do you believe the major theorists presented in this text thought of themselves and those around them? Give some possible examples, speculative though they may be.

2 Of the six criteria for evaluating personality theories discussed in this chapter (and in Chapter 1), which one(s) seem most important? Defend your answer.

3 Of the five general problem areas discussed in the "New Frontiers in Personality Theorizing and Research" section of this chapter, which one do you believe holds the most promise for achieving a better understanding of the human personality? Explain your position.

4 In this chapter we maintained that future progress toward a more integrative view of the person will be guided by the diverse approaches offered by past and current theorists. Of all the perspectives presented in this text (psychodynamic, cognitive, phenomenological, behavioral, etc.) which one do you think will have the greatest impact on future theorizing about human personality? Explain and defend your choice.

5 In the "Discussion Questions" section of Chapter 1 you were asked to define personality and to specify your own basic assumptions about human nature. Now that you have read this book, has your earlier definition of personality changed? If so, how and why? Are you now also more aware of your own basic assumptions and how they affect your relationships with others? Think of some examples, if only for yourself.

GLOSSARY

Cognitive process   The way in which we acquire, transform and store information from the environment; that is, the higher mental processes we use to know and interpret the world.

Eclecticism The view that each perspective on personality has something of value to offer in the study and understanding of human behavior.

Interactionist approach An approach to personology stressing the importance of conceptualizing behavior as being jointly determined by personality and situational variables.

Interdisciplinary approach An approach to personology emphasizing the importance of a multidisciplinary approach, i.e., the contributions which sociologists, anthropologists, ethologists, and other behavioral scientists can make to the understanding of human behavior.

Life history An account of a single person's life based on autobiographical information and other personal document data.

Person-oriented view A theoretical and empirical orientation in personology which assumes that the crucial determinants of human behavior reside within the person (e.g., traits, feelings, motives, instincts).

Schema A hypothetical cognitive structure used to perceive, organize, and process information.

Self-schema A schema consisting of those attributes that we perceive as most representative of our self-concept.

Situation-oriented view A theoretical and empirical orientation in personology which assumes that human behavior is almost exclusively determined by environmental or situational factors.

Socioanalytic theory Hogan's personality theory that stresses the evolutionary basis of social patterns of human behavior (e.g., group living and status hierarchies).

ACKNOWLEDGMENTS

We wish to express our gratitude to the following authors and/or publishers who have granted us permission to use and reproduce material from their books and journals. Full citations are provided elsewhere in this text.

Academic Press, Inc.

from Kelly, G. A brief introduction to personal construct theory. In D. Bannister (Ed.), *Perspectives in personal construct theory*.

American Psychological Association

from Allport, G. Traits revisited. *American Psychologist*; from Atthowe, J., and Krasner, L. Preliminary report on the application of contingent reinforcement procedures (token economy) on a "chronic" psychiatric ward. *Journal of Abnormal Psychology*; from Bandura, A. The self system in reciprocal determinism. *American Psychologist*; from Bandura, A. Human agency in social cognitive theory. *American Psychologist*; from Bandura, A., Reese, L., and Adams, M. Microanalysis of action and fear arousal as a function of differential levels of perceived self-efficacy. *Journal of Personality and Social Psychology*; from Buhler, C. Basic theoretical concepts of humanistic psychology. *American Psychologist*; from Davis, P., and Schwartz, G. Repression and the inaccessibility of affective memories. *Journal of Personality and Social Psychology*; from Fenigstein, A., Scheier, M., and Buss, A. Public and private self-consciousness: Assessment and theory. *Journal of Consulting and Clinical Psychology*; from Greever, K., Tseng, M., and Friedland, B. Development of the social interest index. *Journal of Consulting and Clinical Psychology*; from Holmes, D. Investigations of repression: Differential recall of material experimentally or naturally associated with ego threat. *Psychological Bulletin*; from Kahn, S., Zimmerman, G., Csikszentmihalyi, M., and Getzels, J. Relations between identity in young adulthood and intimacy at midlife. *Journal of Personality and Social Psychology*; from Maslow, A. Toward a humanistic psychology. *American Psychologist*; from McClain, E. Further validation of the Personal Orientation Inventory: Assessment of self-actualization of school counselors. *Journal of Consulting and Clinical Psychology*; from Medinnus, G., and Curtis, F. The relation between maternal self-acceptance and child acceptance. *Journal of Counseling Psychology*; from Rotter, J. Generalized expectancies for internal vs. external control of reinforcement. *Psychological Monographs*; from Silverman, L. Psychoanalytic theory: "The reports of my death are greatly exaggerated." *American Psychologist*; from Silverman, L., Ross, D., Adler, J., and Lustig, D. Simple research paradigm for demonstrating subliminal psychodynamic activation: Effects of oedipal stimuli on dart-throwing accuracy in college males. *Journal of Abnormal Psychology*; from Skinner, B. F. The origins of cognitive thought. *American Psychologist*; from Zuckerman, M. Dimensions of sensation seeking. *Journal of Consulting and Clinical Psychology*; Copyright by the American Psychological Association. Reprinted (or adapted) by permission.

Basic Books, Inc.

from Ansbacher, H., and Ansbacher, R. *The individual psychology of Alfred Adler: A systematic presentation in selections from his writings.*

The British Psychological Society

from Bannister, D., and Fransella, F. A grid test of schizophrenic thought disorder. *British Journal of Social and Clinical Psychology.*

Brooks/Cole Publishing Company

from Maslow, A. *Abraham H. Maslow: A memorial volume.*

EDITS Publishers

from Eysenck, H., and Eysenck, S. *Manual of the Eysenck Personality Questionnaire.*

Educational and Psychological Measurement

from Shostrom, E. An inventory for the measurement of self-actualization. *Educational and Psychological Measurement.*

Richard I. Evans

from Evans, R. I. *B. F. Skinner: The man and his ideas.*

Harcourt Brace Jovanovich, Inc.

from Allport, G. (Ed.), *Letters from Jenny.*

HarperCollins Publishers, Inc.

from Evans, R. *Dialogue with Erik Erikson;* from Maslow, A. *Motivation and personality* (3rd ed.).

The Hogarth Press and Random Century Group

from Freud, S. (J. Strachey, trans. and ed.), *The standard edition of the complete psychological works of Sigmund Freud*, Vol. 23.

Henry Holt and Company (Harcourt Brace Jovanovich, Inc.)

from Adler, A. *The pattern of life;* from Allport, G. *Pattern and growth in personality;* from Fromm, E. *Escape from freedom;* from Kelly, G. Man's constructions of his alternatives. In G. Lindzey (Ed.), *Assessment of human motives.*

Houghton Mifflin Company

from Rogers, C. *On becoming a person.*

Impact Publishers, Inc.

from Alberti, R., and Emmons, M. *Your perfect right* (6th ed.).

The Journal of Individual Psychology

from Crandall, J. A scale of social interest; from Maslow, A. Tribute to Alfred Adler.

Irvington Publishers

from Allport, G. Autobiography. In E. Boring and G. Lindzey (Eds.), *A history of psychology in autobiography*, Vol. 5; from Rogers, C. Autobiography. In E. Boring and G. Lindzey (Eds.), *A history of psychology in autobiography*, Vol. 5; from Skinner, B. F. Autobiography. In E. Boring and G. Lindzey (Eds.), *A history of psychology in autobiography*, Vol. 5.

JAI Press, Inc.

from Bandura, A. Social cognitive theory. In R. Vasta (Ed.), *Annals of child development*, Vol. 6.

Alfred A. Knopf, Inc.

from Skinner, B. F. *Beyond freedom and dignity*; from Skinner, B. F. *About behaviorism*.

Little, Brown and Company

from Coles, R. *Erik H. Erikson: The growth of his work*.

Alan Liss, Inc.

from Eron, L., and Huesmann, L. The relation of prosocial behavior to the development of aggressive and psychopathology. *Aggressive Behavior*.

Macmillan Publishing Co., Inc.

from Erikson, E. Life cycle. In D. Sills (Ed.), *International encyclopedia of the social sciences*, Vol. 9; from Skinner, B. F. *Science and human behavior*.

McGraw-Hill, Inc.

from Rogers, C. A theory of therapy, personality, and interpersonal relationships, as developed in the client-centered framework. In S. Koch (Ed.), *Psychology: A study of a science*, Vol. 3.

Merrill Publishing Company

from Rogers, C. *Freedom to learn: A view of what education might become*.

Northwestern University Press

from Ansbacher, H., and Ansbacher, R. (Eds.). *Superiority and social interest: A collection of writings*.

W.W. Norton & Company, Inc.

from Erikson, E. *Childhood and society* (2d ed.); from Erikson, E. *The life cycle completed*; from Horney, K. *The neurotic personality of our time*; from Horney, K. *New ways in psychoanalysis*; from Kelly, G. *The psychology of personal constructs*; from Kelly, G. *A theory of personality*.

F.E. Peacock Publishers, Inc.

from Holdstock, T., and Rogers, C. Person-centered therapy. In R. Corsini (Ed.), *Current personality theories*.

Plenum Publishing Corp.

from Exner, J., and Clark, B. The Rorschach. In B. Wolman (Ed.), *Clinical diagnosis of mental disorders*; from Mischel, W. George Kelly's anticipation of psychology: A personal tribute. In M. Mahoney (Ed.), *Psychotherapy process*.

Praeger Publishing Company

from Eysenck, H. *Personality, genetics, and behavior*; from Rotter, J. *The development and applications of social learning theory: Selected papers.*

Prentice-Hall, Inc.

from Bandura, A. *Social learning theory*; from Cattell, R. Autobiography. In G. Lindzey (Ed.), *A history of psychology in autobiography*, Vol. 6.

Princeton University Press

from Jung, C. The structure of the psyche. In *The Collected Works of C. G. Jung,* Vol. 8.

Psychology Today

from Evans, R. Gordon Allport: A conversation. April 1971. *Psychology Today Magazine.*

Russell Sage Foundation

from Gottesman, I. Beyond the fringe—personality and psychopathology. In D. Glass (Ed.), *Genetics.*

Julian Rotter

from Rotter, J. *Social learning and clinical psychology*; from Rotter, J., and Hochreich, D. *Personality*; from Rotter, J., Chance, J., and Phares, E. *Applications of social learning theory of personality.*

Sage Publications

from Hardeman, M. *A dialogue with Abraham Maslow*; from Rogers, C. My philosophy of interpersonal relationships and how it grew. *Journal of Humanistic Psychology*; from Jones, A., and Crandall, R. Validation of a short index of self-actualization. *Personality and Social Psychology Bulletin.*

Society for the Experimental Analysis of Behavior

from Allyon, T., and Azrin, N. The measurement and reinforcement of behavior of psychotics. *Journal of the Experimental Analysis of Behavior.* Copyright © 1965 by the Society for the Experimental Analysis of Behavior, Inc.

Society of Multivariate Experimental Psychology

from Wiggins, J. Cattell's system from the perspective of mainstream personality psychology. *Multivariate Behavioral Research.*

Jeremy P. Tarcher, Inc.

from Hoffman, E. *The right to be human: A biography of Abraham Maslow.*

Charles C. Thomas, Publisher

from Eysenck, H. *The biological basis of personality.* Courtesy of Charles C. Thomas, Publisher, Springfield, Illinois.

Touchstone Press

from Fromm, E. *Beyond the chains of illusion: My encounter with Marx and Freud.*

Van Nostrand Reinhold

from Maslow, A. *Towards a psychology of being* (2d ed.).

Viking Press
from Maslow, A. *The farther reaches of human nature.*

John Wiley and Sons
from Kelly, G. Clinical psychology and personality. In B. Maher (Ed.), *Clinical psychology and personality: The selected papers of George Kelly*; from Pervin, L. *Current controversies and issues in personality.*

Yale University Press
from Allport, G. *Basic considerations for a psychology of personality.*

Yale University Press
from Allport, G. *Basic considerations for a psychology of personality.*

NAME INDEX

SUBJECT INDEX

Boldface page numbers indicate figures, whereas *italic* page numbers indicate tables.